HITLER,

THE WAR,

AND THE POPE

HITLER,

THE WAR,

AND THE POPE

RONALD J. RYCHLAK

GENESIS PRESS, INC.

Genesis Press, Inc.
315 3rd Ave. N.
Columbus, MS 39701

Hitler, the War, and the Pope

ISBN 1-58571-006-7

Library of Congress Card Number: 00-105755

Manufactured in the United States of America

FIRST EDITION

To Claire...
"Practically perfect in every way"

To this day, Auschwitz does not cease to admonish, reminding us that anti-Semitism is a great sin against humanity, that all racial hatred inevitably leads to the trampling of human dignity.

Pope John-Paul II (1994)

TABLE OF CONTENTS

FOREWORD
BY JOHN CARDINAL O'CONNOR

None of us can look back upon the last century without a sense of remorse. The phenomenon of "man's inhumanity to man" in the twentieth century is unparalleled and unpardonable. Indeed, it was the century in which Adolf Hitler and his minions seduced a nation, brought about a devastating world war, and inflicted that horror, the Holocaust. Millions upon millions perished and the words of the Lord God spoken so long ago in the Book of Genesis echo in our ears: "Your brother's blood cries out to me." I lived through most of that century. I lived through the Second World War. I lived through the Holocaust. And I, like so many others who have crossed the threshold of the twenty-first century and the third millennium, ask myself, "How could this darkness have enveloped us?" I believe that I shall never know the answer this side of heaven. However, I take tremendous consolation in the fact that there were virtuous men and women who were as lights in that darkness, men and women who did all within their power to fight evil and to protect the innocent. In particular, I am consoled by the heroic virtue of Pope Pius XII, upon whom was placed the cross of shepherding the Church in those most difficult of days.

I am indebted to Professor Ronald J. Rychlak for this book, *Hitler, the War, and the Pope.* In his well-crafted pages, he tells us of the story of Eugenio Pacelli, a saintly priest, a skilled diplomat, and a consummate churchman, who was elected pope only months before Hitler's invasion of Poland. The darkness was settling upon Europe, even as the papal tiara was placed upon his head. As the war began and escalated and as Hitler's atrocities against the Jewish people began to be known, Pope Pius XII did all within his power to negotiate peace and to save as many Jewish people as he could. As the war ended, the voices of a free world from the United States to Europe to Israel sang the praises of Pope Pius XII.

Yet, a half-century later, Hitler haunts us still. His so called "final solution" and his ghastly brutality still piques our consciences. Recently, a plethora of books and articles have been published in an effort to cast light on the darkness that was Hitlerism. It comes as no surprise, then, that one whose stature loomed as large as that of Pope Pius XII should come under close scrutiny. Therefore, Professor Rychlak's book comes at a most opportune time.

I am reminded of the words of Thomas Jefferson in his *Notes on Virginia*: "A patient pursuit of facts, and a cautious combination and comparison of them, is the drudgery to which man is subjected by his maker, if he wishes to attain sure knowledge." Professor Rychlak has subjected himself to this drudgery of detail by patiently pursing the facts. With due caution, he has combined and compared them for us so that we might attain knowledge of the part played by Pope Pius XII when darkness fell all around him. The portrait that emerges is one of an extraordinary pastor facing extremely vexing circumstances, of a holy man vying against an evil man, of a human being trying to save the lives of other human beings, of a light shining in the darkness.

John Cardinal O'Connor
Archbishop of New York
February 28, 2000

PREFACE

This project began several years ago when a friend of mine accused Pope Pius XII of having been a Nazi. I had never heard of the controversy surrounding Pius, but a day or two later I went to the public library and found a book about Christian rescuers of Jews in Nazi-occupied Poland. This, I thought, would tell me what had happened and let me discuss the issue with some knowledge. The book raised many questions about Pius XII's actions during World War II and caused me to think that my friend's accusation might be right. I needed to know more.

I went to the library and checked out several biographies on religious leaders of that era, including Pius XII. I also began reading about World War II and the events relating to Hitler's rise to power in Germany. Everything I read raised some new question. To adequately understand Pope Pius XII, it seemed one had to know about Germany following World War I, Hitler's rise to power, international relations throughout the 1920s and the 1930s, the attempts to appease Hitler in the mid-1930s, events in the Soviet Union and other nations prior to World War II, Mussolini's influence in Italy, the military events of World War II, and much more.

As I filled in the missing information and came to a fuller understanding of what actually transpired, I noticed how frequently bits and pieces of the story appeared in the news of the present day. Often these story fragments were misleading. As one example, a *Parade Magazine* article raised the issue of a request for assistance Pius XII received at the beginning of World War II.[1] The article noted that Pius did not meet with the rabbi who made the request, but it failed to point out several other matters of importance. For one thing, the implication in the article was that this dealt in some manner with the persecution that Jewish people were about to face. The request, however, was to discuss "a matter of a religious nature, altogether non-political."[2] Moreover, the article did not mention that the Holy See arranged for the rabbi to have an audience with the Cardinal Secretary of State, that the rabbi's message was forwarded to Pope Pius, that Pius established committees to help Catholic-Jewish refugees and he attempted to organize the emigration of some 3,000 Catholic Jews to Brazil, or that after the war the rabbi wrote to offer thanks for Pius XII's "life-saving efforts on behalf of Jews during the Nazi occupation."[3] To bring up the pre-war request, without mentioning the efforts put forth by Pope Pius, seemed to me extremely unfair.

The controversy over Pius XII even touched Pope John Paul II. An article in the April 7, 1997, *New Yorker* magazine ("The Silence," written by former priest James Carroll), argued that John Paul's "silence"—his unwillingness to condemn Pius XII—has been the great failing of his papacy. Actually, John Paul II has not been silent on the issue. Ten years before the *New Yorker* piece, he said: "I am convinced that history will reveal ever more clearly and convincingly how deeply Pius XII felt the tragedy of the Jewish people, and how hard and effectively he worked to assist them during the Second World War."[4] More recently, he called Pius XII "a great pope."[5]

In 1998, the Vatican released a document entitled *We Remember: A Reflection on the Shoah.* Addressed to all Catholics, and sent to Jewish leaders around the world, it acknowledged that centuries of anti-Jewish attitudes in the Church may have contributed to Christians' lack of resistance to Nazi policies. "We deeply regret the errors and failures of those sons and daughters of the Church. This is an act of repentance, since, as members of the Church, we are linked to the sins as well as the merits of all her children." The fourteen-page text, prepared over an eleven year period by the Pontifical Commission for Religious Relations with the Jews, and at the request of Pope John Paul II, did not acknowledge any culpability on the part of Pius XII. In fact, it said: "During and after the war, Jewish communities and Jewish leaders expressed their thanks for all that had been done for them, including what Pope Pius XII did personally or through his representatives to save hundreds of thousands of Jewish lives."

Reactions to *We Remember: A Reflection on the Shoah* were mixed. While some saw it as a step toward better relations between Jews and Catholics, others saw problems, especially in the section on Pope Pius XII. Abraham Foxman, national director of the Anti-Defamation League, said: "This document rings hollow. It's mostly an apologia, a rationalization for Pope Pius and the church during the Shoah."[6] Phil Baum, executive director of the American Jewish Congress, lamented the Vatican's reluctance to "impose moral culpability on some leading church authorities... who were either indifferent or in some cases actually complicit in the persecution of Jews."[7] Israel's chief rabbi, Meir Lau, a Holocaust survivor, even demanded an "explicit apology for the shameful attitude of the pope at the time."[8]

Many people have tried to evaluate Pope Pius XII's wartime record. Too often, however, the focus has been on individual episodes or limited periods of time. To evaluate properly his performance, one must begin by looking at all of the evidence in context. I did this by taking world events as we know them to have been and looking at Pius XII's actions, inactions, silence, and statements in the context of their time. This required that I lay out a fairly complete discussion of Pius XII's background, the relationship between the Vatican and various world powers, the progress of World War II, and several other issues. This helped bring focus to the picture, but it was only part of the process.

In order to evaluate the Pope's performance, one must take the knowledge gained from looking at his life and times and apply that knowledge to the issues that have arisen concerning his papacy. I have addressed these issues in the final chapter of this book. I did this by answering what I believe are the ten most important questions that surround the leadership of the Catholic Church during World War II.

This approach to the history of Hitler, the war, and the Pope results in a fuller understanding of why things were or were not done. It also offers a view of history from a perspective rarely represented but difficult to ignore. At the very least, having studied these issues it becomes hard to look at World War II without thinking about the difficult, controversial, and often misunderstood role that Pius XII played in it.

I would like to thank those who helped this project come to fruition. The University of Mississippi School of Law, through the Lamar Order, has always been supportive of my work. Among the most important individuals are those I trusted enough to let them read some of the very early (and very rough) drafts. This includes my wife, Claire Rychlak; my parents, Joseph and Lenora Rychlak; my father-in-law, Paul Lindsey; and my friends, John Czarnetzky and Fr. Kevin Slattery. Tim Hall, Samuel DeJohn, Wilbur Colom, James Barnes, Fr. Edmond Bliven, and George Cochran read later versions and provided many useful suggestions. Dimitri Cavalli worked with me for a long time, sending much helpful information, including documents translated especially for this project by Angelo Sedacca and

Rev. Matthew Flood, S.J. Laura Razzolini also translated some Italian documents. Mary Jensen, the librarian at our law school, obtained many out-of-print books and other materials. Fr. Peter Gumpel, S.J., and Fr. Paul Molinari, S.J., both of the Congregation for the Causes of Saints in Vatican City, reviewed a nearly completed draft, providing many important suggestions, and they were of particular help with the epilogue. Dr. Marc Saperstein, Fr. Avery Dulles, S.J., Fr. John Jay Hughes, and Fr. Vincent Lapomarda, S.J., also provided many important comments. Gary Frazier handled the final editing. William Doino, Jr., provided documents, highlighted issues, and was absolutely indispensable to this project.

I am particularly proud that my very good friend Marshall Greene, though suffering from a terminal illness, read and commented on a draft of this book before he passed away. The brave way he faced the inevitable was exceeded only by the proud determination and resilience of his wife, Cathy, as she cared for him and their six young children. They have both been sources of inspiration.

CHAPTER ONE

THE PAPACY AND THE WORLD

The heart of the Roman Catholic Church is at the Vatican, the smallest sovereign state in the world. Vatican City is on the west bank of the Tiber River, lying within the Italian capital city of Rome, and almost completely surrounded by walls which were built in the 16th century. The city covers about 108 acres, but most of the sights can be seen in a comfortable hour-long walk. The Vatican also has extraterritorial jurisdiction over Castel Gandolfo, the papal summer residence near Rome, and thirteen churches and other buildings in Rome.

The Vatican's population consists primarily of employees of the Holy See, the central government of the Roman Catholic Church. The Vatican flies its own flag, mints its own currency, maintains a police force, a court system, two jails, a fire department, and provides mail services. The Vatican also has its own newspaper, railway station, telephone system, five radio stations, and a bank with financial resources in Italy and abroad. At one time, the Vatican had an army of warriors, but Pope Paul disbanded the Noble Guard and the Palatine Guard in 1970 (true military might had disappeared long before that). Today, about ninety members of the Swiss Guard are a largely ceremonial remnant of earlier military prowess.

The leader of the Catholic Church is the Pope, the bishop of Rome. The Catholic Church teaches that Jesus Christ conferred the position of primacy in the Church upon the apostle Peter and on him alone. In defining this doctrine, the First Vatican Council cited three New Testament passages, called the "Petrine" texts:

> **Matthew 16:18-19:** I for my part declare to you, you are "Rock," and on this rock I will build my Church, and the jaws of death shall not prevail against it. I will entrust to you the keys of the Kingdom of heaven. Whatever you declare bound on earth shall be bound in heaven, and whatever you declare loosed on earth shall be loosed in heaven.

> **Luke 22:32:** But I have prayed for you [Peter] that your faith may never fail. You in your turn must strengthen your brothers.

> **John 21:17:** [A] third time Jesus asked him, "Simon, son of John, do you love me?" Peter was hurt because he had asked a third time, "Do you love me?" So he said to him: "Lord, you know everything. You know well that I love you." Jesus said to him, "Feed my sheep."

According to Catholic teaching, these texts signify that Christ himself named Peter as head of the Church, with the authority to pronounce infallibly on matters of faith or morals. The Pope is the successor of Peter, and the powers that were conferred on Peter pass down in perpetuity to his papal successors. The Pope is aided by the cardinals and a bureaucracy known as the Roman Curia. When the cardinals are called together to deal with questions of major importance, they are referred to as the College of Cardinals. Upon the death of the Pope, the cardinals who are under eighty years of age elect his successor.

When elected, each new Pope inherits his many official titles: Bishop of Rome, Vicar of Jesus Christ, Successor of St. Peter, Prince of the Apostles, Supreme Pontiff of the Universal Church, Patriarch of the West, Primate of Italy, Archbishop and Metropolitan of the Roman Province, Sovereign of the State of Vatican City, and Servant of the Servants of God. His ministry is to serve, and his role of authority is to teach and govern in the name of Christ.

In addition to being the head of the Church, the Pope is also a head of state.[1] The Holy See signs treaties and makes international agreements with other countries. Papal nuncios (ambassadors) are sent to most countries, and elsewhere Apostolic Delegates (who do not have formal diplomatic functions) watch over and inform the Pope of the state of the Church in their assigned regions. The Vatican has its own Secretary of State, and though not a permanent member of the United Nations, the Holy See has an observer in this body.

In terms of international relations, most Popes have had similar goals for the Vatican. Perhaps the most controversial Popes of the twentieth century—at least in terms of world politics—were the Nazi-era Popes, Pius XI and Pius XII. Because of the official neutrality of the Vatican during the war, and a clear concern on the part of the Holy See about the spread of Communism across Europe, some historians have argued that Pope Pius XII, in particular, failed to provide the moral guidance that was needed at this time of great crisis. Others have even suggested that he wanted the Germans to win.

Several questions must be addressed in order to evaluate Pius XII's role in World War II. They include: Was he anti-Semitic? Was he blinded by a hatred of Communism? Did he come under the influence of Adolf Hitler? Would a statement by him have diminished Jewish suffering? These are complicated questions which demand careful answers.

The best way to analyze the wartime performance of Pius XII is by viewing the world from the perspective of the Vatican during that era. In particular, one must evaluate the situation in Europe during the 1920s and 1930s; the personal history of the key figures involved; international developments throughout World War II; and the perception of those closest to the situation, especially the Jewish victims of the Nazis. Once these factors have been studied, the picture of the Vatican and its wartime leader becomes much more clear, and the difficult questions concerning the role played by the Pope in World War II can be answered with a fair degree of certainty.

*****

Pope Pius XII, the Church's 262nd Pope, was born in Rome on March 2, 1876, as Eugenio Maria Giuseppe Giovanni Pacelli. Two days after his birth, he was baptized into the Catholic faith by his grand-uncle, Monsignor Giuseppe Pacelli. According to one report, another priest, family friend Monsignor Iacobacci, held the baby in his arms and said: "Sixty-three years from today the people in St. Peter's and all Rome will loudly praise this *bambino*."[2] (Pacelli was elected Pope on his sixty-third birthday.)

The Pacelli family had been supplying the Holy See with lawyers since the early years of the 19th century. Eugenio's grandfather, Marcantonio Pacelli, moved to Rome in 1819 to enter the service of the Holy See. He was promoted by Pius IX to Under Secretary of the Interior in the papal state, and he held that post until 1870. While at the Vatican, Marcantonio helped to establish the Vatican's newspaper, *L'Osservatore Romano*.

Eugenio's father, Filippo Pacelli, was a distinguished Vatican lawyer. He served as a counselor to the Holy See, particularly in financial matters when he headed the Bank of Rome. He was made Dean of the Consistorial College, which was composed of twelve lawyers who contributed outstanding service to the Church. He also belonged to the so-called "Black Nobility." Members of this group stood by the Church and defended the rights and honor of the Pope during the time of the "Roman Question," when the Vatican was in conflict with Italy (1870-1929).[3] Eugenio's brother, Francesco Pacelli, also a lawyer, was right-hand man to the Vatican Secretary of State, Cardinal Pietro Gasparri, during the negotiations with Benito Mussolini that led to the historic Lateran Treaty and the end of the Roman Question.

Eugenio's mother, Virginia Pacelli, was a very religious woman who taught her son the importance of prayer as soon as he could talk. He became a devout child, but not without the typical interests of all children. He learned to play the violin and continued to love music throughout his life. He also enjoyed having stories told to him. Many of the stories, of course, were religiously oriented. One day, his uncle told him the story of a missionary priest who was persecuted and ultimately crucified by his tormentors. Eugenio told his uncle that he too would like to be a martyr, "but—without the nails."[4]

It was thought that Eugenio might follow family tradition and become a lawyer, but his religious influence was stronger. At the age of eighteen, he attended a four-day Church retreat. When he came home, his mind was made up. Eugenio Pacelli would be a priest.

Eugenio was accepted into a prestigious seminary near the Pantheon in Rome, the *Capranica*. Within a very short time, he distinguished himself as one of the best students in his class. He particularly excelled in languages, eventually becoming fluent in Latin, Greek, English, French, German, Spanish, Portuguese, Hebrew, and Aramaic. Eugenio took additional courses at another great seminary, the *Gregoriana* or Gregorian University. This intense program of studies, the dankness of the old buildings, his meager diet, and the demanding schedule caused Eugenio's health to suffer seriously. He developed a hacking cough, and the family doctor warned that he was on the brink of tuberculosis.

These health problems nearly ended Eugenio's study and his religious career, but he had been noticed by Pope Leo XIII who permitted young Pacelli to live at home while completing his courses. This was a rare, if not unprecedented, dispensation. Frail health, however, still plagued Eugenio and prevented his participation in the school's graduation ceremony. Instead, he was ordained on Easter Sunday, April 2, 1899, by Francesco Paola Cassetta, auxiliary bishop of Rome, in the bishop's private chapel.

The new, twenty-three-year-old priest celebrated his first Mass the next day in the Church of St. Mary Major, the largest Marian shrine in the world. Fr. Pacelli was then assigned to the parish of the Chiesa Nuova, where he had previously served as an altar boy.[5] He did not, however, abandon his studies; he followed family tradition and studied law. He already possessed a doctorate in theology, and in 1902 he would be awarded a doctorate in canon and civil law.[6]

Pope Leo XIII had a program for training exceptional young clerics to serve in the Vatican diplomatic service, and two years after Pacelli was ordained, Cardinal Gasparri, Secretary of the Congregation of Extraordinary Ecclesiastical Affairs (and future Vatican Secretary of State), invited Pacelli into this program. Leo died in 1903, but the next year, the new Pope Pius X named Pacelli a monsignor and assigned him to a team which was charged with codifying Church canon law.[7]

For the next decade and a half, Msgr. Pacelli served as a research aide in the office of the Congregation of Ecclesiastical Affairs, helping with the codification project. He also served as the Pope's *Minutante*, editing and correcting the Pope's speeches and minutes, and as a personal envoy from the Pope to the Austrian Emperor. At the same time, he continued to say Mass, hear confessions, and instruct under-privileged children in religious matters.

In 1914, Pope Pius X named Cardinal Gasparri the new Vatican Secretary of State, and Pacelli was promoted to the post Gasparri vacated, Secretary of the Congregation of Ecclesiastical Affairs. Pope Pius X died later this same year and was replaced by Pope Benedict XV. When World War I broke out, the Vatican became a relief station for suffering victims of war. Pacelli and Gasparri were charged with maintaining liaison with the hierarchies on both sides of the conflict, answering appeals for aid from all over Europe, and organizing a war relief program. Together, they helped 30,000 French and German prisoners return to their homes.

In the summer of 1917, the papal nuncio to Bavaria, Archbishop Giuseppe Aversa, passed away. With Germany at the center of a war that affected most of Europe, this post was too important to leave vacant for long. The Pope needed to send a replacement immediately. Pacelli was already well known to both the Secretary of State and the Pope, and he was Benedict's choice to represent the Holy See in Munich.

Before undertaking his new position, Pacelli was consecrated as bishop by Pope Benedict in a special ceremony in the Sistine Chapel.[8] He was at the same time elevated to the rank of Archbishop. He was then sent off to Munich and into a very difficult situation. The British envoy to the Holy See, Sir Henry Howard, wrote in his diary that this move "will be a dreadful loss for our British mission to the Vatican for he is the *one man* who can be trusted implicitly; however, it is also consoling that there should be such an honest man at Munich at present."[9]

As nuncio to Bavaria, Pacelli's job was to try to ease the suffering, stop the fighting, work on a new concordat with the German state of Bavaria, and establish diplomatic relations with the rest of Germany. To these ends, in June 1917, Pacelli went to Berlin to introduce himself to Reich Chancellor Theobald von Bethmann-Hollweg. While there, Pacelli visited many other German officials, including Kaiser Wilhelm II.

Earlier Popes had acted as arbiters in wars, and Benedict XV wanted to do so now. Without taking sides, he put out an appeal to the governments to end the "useless slaughter." He laid out a plan to be presented to German leaders by Pacelli (who had helped draft the plan), but the new nuncio's efforts did not bring an end to the fighting. Kaiser Wilhelm II spent most of the meeting lecturing Pacelli on how the Vatican should deploy its soldiers in the event of an attack.[10] All that Pacelli could accomplish was to convince the Kaiser to end the practice of bringing Belgians to Germany as semi-slave laborers.[11] Pope Benedict's proposal did, however, prepare the way for Woodrow Wilson's settlement plan a year later.[12]

For the remainder of the war, Pacelli concentrated on carrying out Benedict's humanitarian efforts. (He has been credited with helping 65,000 prisoners of war return home.)[13] Pacelli soon became a common sight in the streets of Munich, handing out food to those who were impoverished. Benedict emptied the Vatican treasury as he carried out his efforts to alleviate suffering. He spent so much of the Church's money that at the time of his death in 1922, there was not even enough money to cover the expenses related to his funeral and the ensuing conclave.

War ended only when it became obvious that Germany would have to seek a treaty, and the German people demanded that Kaiser Wilhelm II do so. Inspired by the Communists in Russia, revolutionaries staged uprisings throughout Germany in November 1918. In Pacelli's home region of Bavaria, a short-lived Soviet Socialist Republic was proclaimed. Wilhelm II abdicated and fled to the Netherlands that same month. Germany seemed to be on the verge of a Communist take-over, but the Social Democrats and other more moderate parties were able to establish a parliamentary republic which negotiated an armistice. The terms specified that the German army would immediately evacuate all occupied territory; surrender great quantities of war material, including all submarines; and intern all other surface warships as directed by the Allies.

The Paris Peace Conference was organized by the victors at the end of the war. In attendance were seventy delegates, representing twenty-seven victorious Allied powers. Despite his humanitarian efforts, Pope Benedict was excluded from the post-war Versailles Peace Conference due to the Vatican's official neutrality.[14] Neither Germany nor any other defeated power was permitted to attend. Because the victorious nations often had conflicting proposals, the sessions were tumultuous and the final proposals were controversial. The four major powers, Britain, France, Italy, and the United States, dominated the proceedings.

American President Woodrow Wilson proposed a conciliatory settlement based on fourteen points, many of which had been in Pope Benedict's plan a year earlier. Wilson warned of the consequences of imposing harsh terms on the losing side:

> Victory would mean peace forced upon the loser, a victor's terms imposed upon the vanquished. It would be accepted in humiliation, under duress, at an intolerable sacrifice, and would leave a sting, a resentment, a bitter memory, upon which terms of peace would not rest, not permanently, but only as upon quicksand.[15]

He continued: "Only a peace between equals can last; only a peace the very principle of which is equality and a common participation in a common benefit."[16] Not all of the nations were as willing to permit survival of a strong Germany.

After three and one-half months of argument, the Allied leaders finally reached agreement. The Versailles proposal called for Germany to admit guilt, give up territory,[17] and disarm its military.

Germany's Saar and Rhineland districts were to be placed under Allied occupation for fifteen years, and they were to remain perpetually demilitarized, as was a belt of territory thirty miles deep along the Rhine. All of Germany's overseas possessions were to be occupied by the Allies and organized as "mandates," under the supervision and control of a newly-formed League of Nations. The former emperor and other German war leaders were also to be tried as war criminals (this provision was never enforced).

A number of other provisions were designed to insure the rest of the world against possible future German aggression. The new League of Nations was organized to make the peace secure, administer former colonies of the defeated powers, and foster general disarmament. The German army was limited to 100,000 men and was not to possess any heavy artillery; the general staff was abolished, and the navy was to be reduced. The new Austrian republic was reduced to its essential Germanic core, leaving it only one-quarter of its former size. Germany was prohibited from uniting with Austria, even by means of a customs union. No German air force would be permitted, and the production of military planes was forbidden.

The Germans would also have to pay for the damages caused by the war. In fact, the Allies demanded reparations in excess of what Germany could realistically pay. In addition to providing compensation for all civilian damages caused during the war, Germans had to pay reparations of great quantities of industrial goods, merchant shipping, and raw materials. This burden, it was thought, would prevent Germany from being able to finance any major military buildup. What it actually accomplished was to provide Adolf Hitler with an issue that would unify his supporters throughout the next two decades.[18]

The German delegation denounced the plan, claiming it was in violation of the armistice negotiations and that the economic provisions would be impossible to fulfill. They argued that the Allies had proposed one set of terms to end the fighting, but now a completely different set of demands was being made. Nevertheless, they were over a barrel. The German army was unable to regroup. (Despite Hitler's later claims to the contrary, the German army did not want to continue fighting at this time.) The German delegation took the proposal back to Berlin where it was also denounced by Chancellor Philipp Scheidemann.

The Allies maintained a naval blockade of Germany, and it soon became obvious that Germany would have to sign the treaty. The Socialist Republican leaders resigned rather than sign the treaty. (They had problems at home and had been forced to use the military to maintain order and suppress several revolts.) Shortly thereafter, a freely elected constituent assembly met in Weimar to write a constitution that would give governing power to the German Reichstag.[19] On July 31, 1919, the Weimar Republic was established, and Germany was organized into a federal republic consisting of seventeen separate states.

The new German Chancellor, Gustav Bauer, sent another delegation to Versailles. After informing the Allies that Germany was accepting the treaty only because of the need to alleviate the hardships on its people caused by the "inhuman" blockade, the Germans signed the proposal. Hitler would later argue that this capitulation to foreign demands invalidated the Weimar Republic's claim to represent Germany. When National Socialism swept across Germany, Weimar's leaders (particularly the Social Democrats) came to be called the "November Criminals."[20]

CHAPTER TWO

HITLER AND THE POST-WAR WORLD

Adolf Hitler was born the day before Easter, April 20, 1889, in the small Austrian village of Braunau-on-the-Inn. He was the fourth child of a marriage between Klara Polzl and Alois Hitler (his third marriage).[1] Klara was an affectionate mother, and she nursed sickly Adolf until he was almost five years old. Alois, on the other hand, a retired customs officer, drank heavily and was a strict disciplinarian who regularly beat his sons. Adolf's older brother ran away from home at the age of fourteen, leaving Adolf as the primary target of his father's temper.

Young Adolf was a choirboy who liked to read western novels and play "Cowboys and Indians." He was at the top of his class as a young boy, but he changed as he got older. He became moody and lost most of his friends. His teachers reported that he was lazy and undisciplined. He spent much of his time alone, reading or drawing. Art seemed to provide an outlet from the real world.

When Hitler was thirteen years old, his father died. Five years later, his mother died. This was a devastating loss. For the rest of his life he would keep his mother's picture with him. (Even as a grown man, he kept her picture next to his bed, which caused some of his close associates to speculate that he and his long-time mistress, Eva Braun, did not have a physical relationship.)

At the age of eighteen, Adolf received an allowance from his parents' pension and set off to Austria's largest city, Vienna, to become an artist. Vienna was one of the brightest and most cosmopolitan cities in Europe, but it was not an easy place for an outsider.[2] Adolf sought admission to the Imperial Art Academy, but his application was denied twice. Letters he wrote during this time indicate that he was lonely, ill, and in need of money. When times were particularly rough, he spent nights in the park or sleeping in doorways. At other times he lived in a boarding home and managed to scrape out a living by selling small watercolors and drawings. (Perhaps more important to his standard of living was a loan or gift of money that he received from his aunt, Johanna Polzl). He was described as slight in build, poorly nourished, with hollow cheeks and shabby clothes.[3] He seems to not have had any romantic interest in a city full of romance. In fact, at least one friend considered him an outright misogynist.[4]

Hitler studied and illustrated Austrian architecture, especially the palaces and monuments which had been designed and built in tribute to the 1,000 year Reich of the Holy Roman Empire. He also enjoyed going to Vienna's opera house, which featured music that paid tribute to Germany's noble past. Richard Wagner's operas, in particular, were noted for their portrayals of heroism, despair, hope, treachery, tragedy, and fate.[5] Listening to *Der Ring der Nibelungen* or *Parsifal,* and at the same time studying monuments to Austrian's former glory, Hitler came to believe that Aryans were a superior race of people.[6] He envisioned Germany once again becoming a true empire. This vision led him into local politics, and while still a teenager he began to form the anti-Semitic views that would result in the gas chambers of World War II.

Although Vienna had some serious problems with anti-Semitism,[7] Hitler's anger at this time was not directed toward Jewish people. Rather, "two subjects above all aroused his aggression:" Communists and the Jesuits.[8] His anger toward the Jesuits is thought to have developed through the influence of Georg Ritter von Schonerer, a vehemently anti-Catholic politician who lived in Vienna.[9]

Von Schonerer founded a movement that was known by its slogan: "Away-from-Rome."[10] As it grew in popularity, many Catholic followers converted to Protestantism.[11] Simultaneously, a new faith called *Theosophy* spread across Europe. This was a mixture of various Gnostic, Egyptian, and Hindu beliefs combined with the myth of Aryan superiority.[12] Followers recognized each other by an ancient Eastern symbol of good luck and fertility, the swastika.[13] Schonerer's nationalistic faith combined with *Theosophy,* and the result was an apocalyptic vision promising a new world subject to German domination—an empire inhabited by noblemen and cleansed of all Judeo-Christian influence.[14]

Hitler may have been shaped by the politics in Austria, but he had no intention of serving in the Austrian military, which—he complained—was composed of Czechs, Slovaks, and Croats. He moved to Munich to avoid the draft, but the authorities caught up with him. On January 19, 1914, the day before he was supposed to appear at the Austrian military barracks at Linz, Hitler was served a summons by the Munich police and escorted to the Austrian consulate. If convicted of draft evasion, he could receive a fine, one year of prison, and he would still have to perform his military service. With the help of a lawyer and a self-serving letter of explanation, however, Hitler avoided punishment and was found physically unfit for duty. By 1921, he would rewrite this episode of his life, saying only, "on August 5, 1914, my request to the King having been granted, I reported to the 1st Bavarian Infantry Regiment in order to join the German Army."[15]

For all of his resistance to joining the Austrian army, at the outbreak of war Hitler enlisted in the German army and thrived as a soldier. He was a company runner in the Bavarian infantry, fighting in France and Flanders throughout World War I. He took messages back and forth to headquarters, and was often at the front lines. This was a dangerous assignment, typically given to intelligent, brave, and physically fit young soldiers. Hitler was wounded in 1916 and gassed in 1918. He once even captured four enemy soldiers single-handedly. (It was here, he claimed, that Providence first came to his aid when a voice told him to evacuate a trench just before an explosion killed everyone who remained in it.)

In 1914, Hitler was awarded the Iron Cross, 2nd class. Towards the end of the war, when he was a corporal (his highest rank),[16] he was awarded the high honor of the Iron Cross, 1st Class for volunteering and successfully completing what had appeared to be a suicide mission. As the war closed, Hitler was receiving treatment for temporary blindness caused by a British gas attack.

At the end of the war, Hitler returned from a military hospital to Munich, where he underwent a army-sponsored course of political education for soldiers who were returning home. The program featured Pan-German nationalism, strong anti-Semitism, and a good deal of anti-Socialism. Hitler had been shocked by his country's defeat. He was now convinced that Germany had been betrayed by the Jews and Marxists. His feeling grew into an obsession. Eventually, he would combine these fanatic beliefs with his oratorical skills and nearly achieve world domination.

*****

Pacelli remained in Munich following the war, with the added responsibility of representing the Vatican not only to Bavaria, but also to the

Weimar Republic, which was centered in Berlin. He put together a largely German staff, selected a German nun for his housekeeper (Sister Pascalina Lehnert, who would remain in his service until his death), a German priest as his top aide, and another for his confessor.[17] He also developed a close circle of clerical advisers, mainly Jesuit priests, who were to be collaborators in achieving concordats with the governments of Bavaria (1924), Prussia (1929), and finally with Germany itself (1933). In time he even began preaching and lecturing in German.

Germany's new, democratic government faced serious trouble from the beginning. With six major political parties, and several minor ones, it was hard to form effective coalitions. The German people felt that democracy had been imposed upon them, and the new government's task of paying war reparations to the Allies was highly unpopular. All of this contributed to German resentment, and Hitler was not the only would-be dictator to try to take advantage of the situation. The Communists, monarchists, and nationalists each occasionally resorted to violence in their efforts to overturn the republic.

The Vatican was concerned about the political struggle that was taking place in Germany. The Church had long opposed Communism, and the possibility of a Communist Germany was probably the Holy See's greatest fear at that time. In December 1918, Pacelli mounted the pulpit of the Munich cathedral to speak out in strong language against the post-war menace of Bolshevism.[18] Because of this, he was threatened with physical violence several times. This risk became extraordinarily serious in April 1919, when Communists took over the Bavarian government and declared it a separate Communist state.

With the Communist takeover, almost all diplomats in Munich packed their bags and fled to Berlin. "Only Nuncio Pacelli announced that he was staying at his post."[19] He soon became a target of Communist hostility. One time a car, in true gangland fashion, sped past his house spraying it with machine-gun fire, but Pacelli was not home.[20] Another time, a small group of German Communists broke into the nunciature bent on reprisal. Upon discovering them, the nuncio asked what they were doing. The intruders leveled their revolvers at Pacelli, and demanded his secret stash of money and food. Pacelli replied, "I have neither money nor food. For, as you know, I have given all I had to the poor of the city."[21]

The intruders did not immediately accept Pacelli's claims, and one even threw his gun and struck the nuncio on his chest (bending a jeweled cross),[22] but Pacelli never flinched. He said, "This is a house of peace, not a den of murderers!"[23] After convincing them not to shoot, he proceeded to counsel them in a sympathetic manner. Soon they put their guns away and withdrew. A few days later many of them returned, unarmed, to apologize, ask forgiveness, and return a stolen automobile.[24]

Another attack came when Pacelli was riding home in his car after a meeting with the Archbishop of Munich. An angry mob descended on the car, yelling blasphemies and threatening to turn the car over. Pacelli ordered the driver to open the roof. After initial reluctance, the driver agreed. Pacelli then stood on the back seat to address the astonished crowd. "My mission is peace," he said. "The only weapon I carry is this Holy Cross. I do no harm to you, but only good things. Why should you harm me?" He then raised his hand and blessed the crowed. When he sat back down, the mob moved out of the way and let the car pass.[25]

When word of Pacelli's bravery spread throughout Munich, he was held in even greater awe than before. It was said of him that, "he fears absolutely nothing and no one."[26] When the Communists were ousted from power in May 1919, police began rounding them up. Knowing of the several incidents in which he had been involved, the police asked Pacelli to help identify suspects, but he had no desire for revenge. He always managed to be unavailable when asked to help identify his enemies.[27]

On January 22, 1922, Pope Benedict XV succumbed to influenza. At the ensuing conclave, one of Pacelli's close friends from his days in Rome, Cardinal Ambrogio Damiano Achille Ratti, was elected Pope. He chose the name Pius XI. Cardinal Gasparri, who had brought Pacelli into the Vatican's diplomatic service, was retained as Secretary of State. Two of Pacelli's closest friends and benefactors were now in the top two offices of the Church.

*****

The Catholic Church was strong in Germany, but it had splintered in the mid-1800s. Whereas countries such as Poland (90 percent), Italy (95 percent), Hungary (67 percent), Luxembourg (94 percent), Austria

(85 percent), Belgium (75 percent), and France (93 percent) were largely Catholic, Germany was predominantly Protestant (about 65 percent). The Protestant Reformation, which began under the leadership of Martin Luther, was centered in Germany. When the Catholic Church excommunicated Luther, German noblemen welcomed him. Luther spent much time translating the Bible into German, and his influence in Germany probably exceeded his influence in any other country.[28] As such, in the pre-war years, Protestants outnumbered Catholics by about a 2-1 ratio. Regardless of the denomination, however, the influence of churches in Germany was waning as secular philosophies grew in popularity.[29]

The majority of Christians in Germany considered themselves patriotic, and they would fight for what they saw as their nation's interest. This nationalism caused some religious people to welcome the rise of Nazism. Anti-Semitism was also quite prevalent and would certainly have had an important influence on many people. Hitler knew this, and he considered anti-Semitism "a useful revolutionary expedient."[30] Most Germans rejected the extreme forms of hatred found in Hitler's later actions and statements,[31] but one account of the attitude of a typical German family is as follows:

> Just as the average Protestant was middle class and "national," he was also anti-Semitic. Today you can hardly speak of "harmless" anti-Semitism, but at that time we saw the antipathy toward the Jews as harmless. All of us....I was raised to believe that, until the Jews rejected Jesus, they were a loyal people, a wonderful people. They were farmers and shepherds. Then God rejected them, and since that time they have been merchants, good for nothing, and they infiltrate everything, everywhere they go. And against that you had to defend yourself. In the Nazi party program it said that Jews should not be permitted to be citizens. Most Germans held that to be a matter of consideration.[32]

For those Christians who sympathized with the Nazis, anti-Semitism and nationalism merged to form an Aryan version of Christianity, which Hitler would later exploit to its full advantage.

*****

Germany in the 1920s was ripe for a man with the dynamic oratory skills that Hitler possessed. Physically, it was split in half. Financially, it had not only to rebuild its own economy and industry, but also pay reparations to other nations. In the past, Germany had been able to obtain raw materials from its colonies. These colonies now, however, were supplying France and Britain, while Germany was paying money to those same nations. Berlin was filled with beggars. (Pacelli said that the sight of starving, homeless children in the streets of Germany sent an actual, physical pain through his heart.)[33] Disgruntled Germans were ready to listen to anyone who offered solutions, and Hitler did just that.

Today, many people wonder how a short, dark-haired man could have impressed so many people with the concept of the ideal blond, blue-eyed Aryan. (Indeed, none of the top Nazi officials looked like this ideal.) Although it does not appear so in black and white photographs, Hitler's hair was brown, not black, and his eyes were blue.[34] While the Soviet autopsy of his charred remains showed him to have been 5'5", his followers set forth the claim that he was 5'9". Moreover, when filmed he was always made to appear taller than he really was.

Hitler's publicity machine made him seem bigger than life and a man of tremendous will. He was the first politician to fly from one place to another so that he could appear in several towns in one day. His slogan was "*Führer* over Germany." He did not drink or smoke; he avoided caffeine; he was a vegetarian and ate moderately—though he had an affinity for pastries and cream puffs. He also wrote several plays and the libretto for an opera. In order to maintain the tremendous following he had among German women, his love interests, including Eva Braun, were hidden from the public, and it was suggested that he was celibate.[35] A true politician, Hitler would kiss babies and show friendship to small children. He was an animal-lover who opposed hunting, animal experimentation, and vivisection. (A 1934 postcard showed him feeding two small deer.)[36] Those who knew him personally also reported that he was a good-natured host who enjoyed entertaining people in his country home.[37] It was said that he had a good sense of humor and that he laughed a lot. He also played the piano and had a serious interest in art and classical music.

Hitler's introduction to National Socialism came on September 12, 1919, when he joined the German Workers' Party in Munich. At first, he was a civilian informer for the army, which was very interested in this group. The small party was, like many others in post-war Germany, comprised primarily of unhappy, alienated war veterans who blamed Germany's misfortunes on foreign interests and Jews.

The party was particularly attractive for the marginal groups in Germany: shopkeepers and artisans caught between big labor and big business, small farmers losing out to larger enterprises and middle-men, unemployed university graduates and dropouts who blamed the "system" for their condition, and—of course—numerous former soldiers who were having a hard time adjusting to civilian life.

By February 24, 1920, Hitler was acting as the party's propaganda chief. On the first of April that year, the German Workers' Party changed its name to the National Socialist German Workers' Party (*National-Sozialistische Deutsche Arbeiterpartei*), and this title was abbreviated to the word Nazi. On July 29, 1921, Hitler was named its president. The army then began to supply him with money and members.

The National Socialists had several beliefs and aims. First and foremost was a belief in Aryan German race superiority and a violent hatred of Jews. The Nazis also believed in an extreme nationalism that called for the unification of all German-speaking peoples. (Later, this would lead to the occupation of Austria and Czechoslovakia). They also believed in a form of corporative state socialism and the glorification of strength and discipline. It was similar to Fascism, which had preceded it in Italy.

*****

From the beginning, the Catholic Church had a rocky relationship with the National Socialists. In 1920, Clemens August Graf von Galen (the future Bishop of Münster) declared that Nazism contained ideas "which no Catholic could accept without denying his faith upon cardinal points of belief."[38] On October 1, 1921, the *Bayerischer Kurier* quoted Nuncio Pacelli as saying:

> The Bavarian people are peace-loving. But, just as they were seduced during the revolution by alien elements–above all, Russians–into the extremes of Bolshevism, so now other non-Bavarian elements of entirely opposite persuasion have likewise thought to make Bavaria their base of operation.

This was Pacelli's first published warning to people about Nazism, but it was not his last. Of the forty-four public speeches that Nuncio Pacelli made on German soil between 1917 and 1929, at least forty contained attacks on National Socialism or Hitler's doctrines.[39] Other

Catholic leaders joined with him. German bishops warned against Nazism on five occasions between 1920 and 1927,[40] arguing that National Socialism was totalitarian, racist, pagan, and anti-Christian. Even Pope Pius XI, in 1925, warned not only against Communism, but against "every political conception which makes society or the State an end in itself, from which naturally, fatally indeed, it finishes in absorbing or destroying private rights."[41]

Perhaps in response to these attacks, Hitler tried, with seeming desperation, to base his arguments on Christian principals. In a speech delivered April 12, 1922, he said:

> My feeling as a Christian points me to my Lord and Savior as a fighter. It points me to the man who once in loneliness, surrounded only by a few followers, recognized these Jews for what they were and summoned men to fight against them....
>
> In boundless love as a Christian and as a man I read through the passage which tells us how the Lord at last rose in His might and seized the scourge to drive out of the Temple the brood of vipers and adders. How terrific was his fight against the Jewish poison.
>
> Today, after two thousand years, with deepest emotion I recognize more profoundly than ever before the fact that it was for this that He had to shed his blood upon the Cross.

Many Christians fell for Hitler's professed religious faith, including some church leaders.

Father Rupert Mayer was a highly decorated Catholic military chaplain during the First World War. He later became interested in the Nazi party, and even addressed some crowds along with Hitler. As he came to know the party, however, he had a dramatic change of heart. In 1923, he spoke on the theme "Can a Catholic be a National Socialist?" He proceeded to tell a greatly disillusioned audience that the answer was "no." He was howled down and not allowed to speak further. When the party suffered a major defeat shortly thereafter he was given much of the blame.[42]

Although there was general unrest and concern over the National Socialist movement throughout the nation, Germany gave Pope Pius XI little cause for alarm in the early years of his pontificate. Pacelli reported back to Rome that Hitler was unlikely to achieve any real power. The Nazis were not yet strong enough to be a serious threat, and the Church's interests were safeguarded by a strong Catholic Center Party in the Reichstag and throughout the nation.[43] There was, however, a desire to improve diplomatic relations with the German capital city of Berlin.

Despite years of diplomatic overtures, no nunciature (embassy) had been established in Berlin, primarily because of Protestant opposition and fear of offending Bavaria, which had (and wanted to keep) the Munich nunciature. By 1920, however, things had changed. It was to the advantage of both sides to negotiate a new agreement. In January, Pacelli gave Bavarian Minister Hoffmann a note informing him that the Vatican desired to negotiate a treaty to regulate the relations between Bavaria and the Church. In August 1920, Pacelli met with German President Ebert in Munich. This was the beginning of relations between the Vatican and the government of the Weimar Republic. Within a month, the Republic announced its intention to establish a German embassy at the Vatican. Shortly thereafter, Pacelli traveled to Berlin to meet other German officials. The Germans named an ambassador to the Papal Court, and the Holy See named Pacelli as nuncio to the Republic (in addition to his duties as nuncio to Bavaria.)

Although the Weimar Republic was represented in Rome, so was Bavaria. Thus, there arose a question as to where the Papal nunciature should be maintained. The Bavarians were anxious to keep Pacelli in Munich. They knew that the Vatican wanted to conclude a concordat with the Republic (though this was almost impossible due to the semi-autonomous nature of German states in matters such as this), and they did not wish to see their individual agreement with the Vatican disappear into a treaty dealing with Germany as a whole. The Bavarians argued that Pacelli should remain and first complete the concordat with Bavaria, and that could serve as a model for a later agreement between Berlin and Rome.

Vatican Secretary of State Gasparri announced that Pacelli would remain in Munich for the time being. This pleased Pacelli, who preferred to keep his permanent residence in Munich in order to see the Bavarian concordat through to completion. He also resisted the move (and would continue to do so until 1925) at least in part because Munich was a Catholic city, whereas Berlin was more Protestant, anti-clerical, and the Socialist parties were very strong. Many Protestants, liberals, and Socialists already suspected the Holy See of unfriendliness to Germany and the Republic's secular principles. There was the possibility of an increase in anti-Vatican sentiment if the nuncio's presence in Berlin became too visible. Pacelli retained both posts and regarded the "short distance" between Berlin and Munich as only a minor inconvenience.

*****

Like National Socialism in Germany, the Fascism that took hold in Italy grew from hostility towards that nation's experience in World War I. Following the war, there was disunity throughout Italy. Italy had gained little for its efforts on the victorious side, and internal disorder, labor unrest, and diplomatic frustration created a volatile situation. Had Mussolini (a former Socialist) not captured the imagination of the young war veterans, it is quite possible that a Bolshevik revolution would have taken place in Italy as it had in Russia. In fact, many of Mussolini's followers were former Communists.

On March 23, 1919, Mussolini formed the *Fascio di Combattimento* (Fascist) Party in Milan. The name was taken from the ancient Roman symbol of power, *Fasces*—a bundle of rods bound together with a protruding blade. (An example can be seen on the back of an American Mercury head dime, last minted in 1945.) The symbolism is that there is strength in unity. Strict law and order, as well as glorification of the state, were bedrock principals of the Fascist Party. A number of ex-servicemen joined the party because of its strong nationalistic stance. Some industrialists and landowners also supported the Fascist Party because it stood in opposition to the Communist Party, which had picked up a significant following.

In 1921, just days after Germany unconditionally accepted Allied demands for reparations, Mussolini and thirty-four other Fascists were elected to the Italian Parliament. Later that year, Mussolini renamed the Fascist Party the National Fascist Party and declared himself its leader, or *Il Duce*. For the rest of that year and much of the next, Fascists clashed with various groups, especially Communists and Socialists.

In October 1922, Mussolini rounded up about 4,000 of his followers and led a march on Rome. Mussolini's Fascists wore black shirts and carried bayonets. When they reached Rome, the Blackshirts waited for an order to attack, but it never came. Though he would later claim to have seized power with his might, for the most part Mussolini's men were cheered by the crowds, and King Victor Emmanuel III agreed to Mussolini's demands before the men ever reached Rome. (Mussolini himself traveled to Rome on a train.)

Pius XI had been Pope for less than nine months when Mussolini was named Prime Minister in 1922. Mussolini immediately began directing violence against many institutions, including the Catholic Church. Nevertheless, he was not yet all-powerful. He suppressed the Communists, but the Socialist and Catholic Popular parties together still outnumbered the Fascists in parliament and their combined strength would have been capable of thwarting Mussolini's plans. Such an alliance, however, was not to be.[44]

Pius XI thought that the Church's cause would be better served by a nonpolitical Catholic body with influence in all branches of the national life. Hence, he fostered and expanded Catholic Action, a movement designed to associate the laity more closely with papal aims. Catholic Action soon acquired a very large membership, especially in the professions and the universities. It also ran its own charitable and youth organizations. Catholic Action came to embrace all forms of activity—social, pastoral, and educational. It was not designed to be political, but Pius XI felt that it could accomplish more important social reforms than a political party could.

Not all of Mussolini's political opponents went away overnight, but without an alliance with other parties, Christian political power nearly vanished. Individual parties were unable to counter the growing Fascist movement, especially in light of the violent tactics that Mussolini was using. In fairly short time, serious opposition withered away, and Mussolini was free to impose his dictatorship.

Like Adolf Hitler, Mussolini was acutely aware of the impact of religion on politics. He was an avowed atheist, and early in his political life he expressed extreme contempt for Christianity. In 1908 he described priests as "black microbes who are as fatal to mankind as tuberculosis germs." In 1919 he wrote, "Detesting as we do all forms of Christianity... we feel an immense sympathy with the modern revival of the pagan worship of strength and courage."[45] At one point, the Church banned Mussolini's newspaper, and at another time Pope Benedict XV protested against Mussolini's "terrible blasphemies."[46]

By the early 1920s, Mussolini's view of the Church had changed, likely out of political opportunism. Italy was overwhelmingly Catholic, and he did not want to create a conflict with such a large constituency—or with the Vatican, which (despite the lack of diplomatic relations) was a powerful influence within Italy. In 1923, Mussolini married his common-law wife. He also increased the amount that the government paid to the clergy. Over the next two decades, he would constantly struggle with the Vatican as he acted on his territorial ambitions, but he no longer openly condemned the Church.

*****

About the same time that future Axis nations Germany and Italy were experiencing so much social upheaval, a future Allied nation, the Soviet Union, was having similar problems that would shape world history for decades to come. Moreover, of particular interest to the Vatican, in the Soviet Union religious people in general—and Catholics more often than not—were the subject of state sponsored persecution. As Eugenio Pacelli got more involved in Vatican affairs of state, he came to know of the atrocities that were unknown in the West until decades later.[47]

While Hitler was still a remote threat, Catholics in the Soviet Union were being systematically murdered by the Communists. It is true that the Soviet mass murders were different from the Nazi ones. There was no plan to kill off an entire group of people, but there was an all-out effort to destroy religion.

A Soviet citizen could be religious only if his faith did not hinder him from being, above all, a Soviet patriot. That, as it turns out, was impossible. On January 13, 1918, a decree on the separation of church and state deprived the Church of all its land and legal rights, in effect outlawing it. Religious marriage was abolished. The family was declared obsolete. Over the next five years, thousands of Ukrainian priests, monks, nuns and lay Catholics were sent to prison or to Siberia. Many of these prisoners were shot, and others were allowed to die of starvation, cold, and disease in what the Soviet authorities called "corrective labor camps."[48] Sometimes they were tortured before they died.[49]

Having already confiscated church buildings and land, in February 1922, the government issued a decree that all church valuables, including sacred objects, would be confiscated. Clergy and faithful laypersons fought against this confiscation. In the three months that followed, 1,414 bloody clashes between church people and government troops were recorded. During 1922 alone, a total of 8,100 priests, monks, and nuns were executed.[50]

Needless to say, the Soviet persecution did not go unnoticed in the Vatican; yet the Church had no desire to lose its contacts with Russia.

In fact, the Church sought to improve relations. The Pope asked Pacelli to begin preliminary discussions in Berlin with the Russian ambassador about the possibility of sending an apostolic delegate to Moscow and working toward a concordat between the two nations.[51] Lengthy talks were held throughout the fall of 1924, but nothing came of the initiative.[52]

A renewed persecution of Catholics in the Soviet Union led to another unsuccessful attempt to reach an agreement. The Soviets eventually informed Pacelli that Moscow was not interested in a concordat or any form of bilateral agreement. Pius XI came to believe that with Stalin in power there could be no diplomatic relationship between Moscow and the Vatican.[53] Their relationship was to be one of bitter hostility. Moreover, this hostility was not tied to a particular nation; rather, the basic ideology of Communism was incompatible with Catholicism, if not with organized religion itself.

In 1930, Pius XI personally and openly protested against the anti-religious excesses of the Communist regimes. He also ordered a mass in St. Peter's for all of those who had been killed in the Soviet Union. In 1937, he issued a strong condemnation of Communism in his encyclical *Divini Redemptoris (Of the Divine Redeemer*, commonly called *On Atheistic Communism)*. "Communism is intrinsically wrong," proclaimed the papal document, "and no one who would save Christian civilization may collaborate with it in any field whatsoever."[54] This would create some difficult questions for the next Pope, when the Soviet Union joined the Allies in their war against Hitler's National Socialism.

CHAPTER THREE

THE SPREAD OF NATIONALISM

In October 1922, the same month that Mussolini's Blackshirts marched on Rome, Germany faced a financial crisis. On the 23rd, German Chancellor Joseph Wirth proposed to his cabinet that Germany declare bankruptcy. The mark had been falling so dramatically that prices had risen one hundred percent in the previous month. Public baths in Berlin were closed to save coal. Germans were openly expressing their reluctance to pay war reparations. The government's ability to lead was called into question.

The payment of reparations placed an enormous strain on a country already exhausted by more than four years of war. In early 1923, Germany fell behind in deliveries of coal and timber, prompting French and Belgian forces to move in and occupy the industrial Ruhr province. Germany immediately condemned the occupation as a violation of international law and stopped all reparation payments to those two nations.

Chancellor Wilhelm Cuno urged a program of passive resistance to the occupation. Workers in Ruhr mines and factories went on strike, but this led to greater inflation. In addition, industrial output plummeted, which brought on economic collapse. French and Belgian forces then occupied industrial installations, requisitioned coal, took over the transportation system, confiscated salaries, and did away with the private ownership of some businesses. The resistance continued, however, and in retaliation French forces cut off shipments of coal to other areas of Germany, putting even more pressure on an already distressed economy. More than 150,000 Germans were displaced from the occupied area, primarily due to suspicion of sabotaging the national rail system. This resulted in what was essentially an undeclared state of war between France and the Rhineland.

Pacelli negotiated with the German leaders in Berlin.[1] They had been unwilling to condemn sabotage, even when it resulted in violence. Pacelli argued that condemnation was necessary in order to favorably dispose other nations toward Germany and to help with later reparation negotiations. He explained that the Vatican had often come to the aid of the Weimar Republic when it sought support in international matters, but the German leaders had to condemn the violence if they expected the Vatican to do anything further on Germany's behalf. The Berlin leadership ultimately condemned the violence, but the protests continued.

By June 1923, the German economy was at the breaking point. In just three weeks the German stock market lost about half of its value. Prior to the First World War, a German mark was worth about twenty-five cents. In October 1922, when Germany was already considering bankruptcy, a U.S. dollar bought 4,000 marks. By June 1, 1923, that same dollar could buy 74,500 marks. Two weeks later it would buy 136,000 marks. Many Germans blamed the strain on reparations and the occupation of the Ruhr. Protesting German workers slowed production to such a level that coal, traditionally a major export, had to be imported. Additionally, displaced workers from the Ruhr placed even more strain on the economy. By late June, reserves held by the central bank were depleted.

The financial distress took its toll on the political scene. On October 3, 1923, the Berlin cabinet resigned and Chancellor Stresemann was appointed as the first constitutional dictator of the Weimar Republic (a precedent that would later help Hitler seize total control of the nation). The economy, however, did not improve. The exchange rate hit twelve billion, then (overnight) forty billion marks to the dollar. By the beginning of November, one loaf of bread cost 140 billion marks. By mid-November, a single dollar could buy four trillion marks. Germany was reduced to a nation of scavengers.

The German government tried to counter the problem by issuing a new mark, worth a trillion of the old ones. Unfortunately, this tended to add to the confusion, because there were then three official currencies in circulation, the new one, the old one, and an even older one. To help take care of this problem, the German government instituted even more governmental regulations. Germans were prohibited from buying foreign currency; foreign traders had to accept "blocked marks" which could be spent in Germany only at a discounted rate; and travelers were searched for currency violations at the national border.

Ultimately, currency control would turn Germany into a sort of police-state almost a decade before Hitler became dictator. Letters were opened, accounts were reviewed, and a siege wartime economy took over even though Germany was at peace.[2]   On November 23, 1923, following a "no confidence" vote in the Reichstag, the Stresemann government resigned.   A new government took over power, but it also went through many difficult periods as the German economy continued to stumble.

*****

As Pacelli watched the confusion and disorder that was so devastating to the German people, Adolf Hitler made his move. For several years he had been holding meetings and gathering a following. An early poster advertising one of his rallies read, in part, as follows:

Fellow Citizens:
Come today, Sunday, March 6, 1921, 10 A.M.
to a GIANT PROTEST DEMONSTRATION
at the CIRCUS KRONE

Speaker A. Hitler on:
"LONDON AND US?"

Protest against the Peace Treaty of Versailles which has been foisted upon us by the single guilty party of the war, namely the Jewish-international stock exchange capital. Protest against the latest Paris dictate, and finally protest against the Reich Government, which once again makes the most colossal promises without consulting the German people.

***

Admission 1 Mark. War invalids free.
No Jews admitted.[3]

To his followers, Hitler was seen as a bright new leader who could avenge the defeat of 1918 and lead the Germans to a new era of prosperity by leaving the current government behind. "Democracy," said Hitler, "is a rule by crazy brains. The [Weimar] Republic is a monstrosity."[4]

Bavarian Dictator Gustav Ritter von Kahr was scheduled to appear in a giant Munich beer hall along with most of the other Bavarian leaders on November 8, 1923. While von Kahr was speaking, several hundred storm troopers surrounded the hall and Hitler entered. Protected by a machine-gun crew, Hitler climbed on a table and fired a shot into the ceiling.

Proclaiming that the National Revolution had begun, Hitler forced the Bavarian leaders to join him in a private room. With gun in hand he urged them to turn the Bavarian dictatorship into a national one with a march on Berlin, similar to Mussolini's march on Rome. After a coerced agreement, the group broke up.

Hitler's troopers took over the Munich army headquarters, but soon thereafter von Kahr posted signs explaining that this was a result of extortion and moved his headquarters to a new location. The next morning, Hitler led a column of storm troopers to army headquarters, but they walked into a trap. The police blocked them off in a narrow street. Guns were fired and sixteen of Hitler's men were killed. Many more were wounded. Most of the survivors ran away or were arrested. Hitler was not shot, but his bodyguards threw him to the ground so sharply that he dislocated a shoulder. He was arrested three days later in a villa forty miles outside of Munich, the same day that Albert Einstein fled Berlin to avoid the growing anti-Jewish sentiment.[5]

Adolf Hitler's trial for the failed Beer Hall Putsch began in February and ended on April 1, 1924. He was found guilty of high treason and sentenced to five years in prison. Reporters accurately noted, however, that this was merely a slap on the wrist. He would be eligible for parole in six months. Moreover, at trial Hitler portrayed himself as the spirit of German nationalism and the enemy of Marxism. Newspaper accounts transformed him into a national hero. He vowed not to let prison destroy him. "You may pronounce us guilty a thousand times over," he said, "but the goddess of the eternal court of history will tear to tatters the brief of the state prosecutor and the sentence of this court."[6]

Hitler was very well treated in prison. He had his own room in the fortress at Landsberg, with a magnificent view over the River Lech. He spent much of his time dictating his book *Mein Kampf* (*My Struggle*) to his old friend Rudolf Hess, who was also being held for his participation in the failed coup. (Hess later became deputy leader of the Nazi party and minister without portfolio, and in 1939 he became the third ranking Nazi in Germany.) During this time, the German economy continued to struggle and the national socialist ideas advanced by Hitler became attractive to more and more Germans.

Hitler was released from prison in time for Christmas on December 20, 1924, after only eight months of incarceration. His anti-Semitism was more virulent than ever. The National Socialist Party had been banned after the failed Beer Hall Putsch, but this played right into Hitler's hand by preventing rivals from taking it over. Although he was prohibited from making public speeches, Hitler soon obtained permission from the government to reorganize the Party. He renounced the use of force and promised to gain power only through legal means. He did, however, vow to destroy the Weimar Republic with the weapons of democracy.[7] If out-voting the opposition took longer than out-shooting them, at least the result would be guaranteed by the constitution. Sooner or later he would gain a majority in the Reichstag, and after that, Germany.

*****

For Pacelli, the 1920s brought many international issues affecting both Germany and the Church. The Allies had invaded portions of Germany during the First World War, and some borders were redrawn. Of all the areas in dispute along Germany's eastern borders, the situation in Danzig, Poland was the most controversial. In order to give Poland access to the sea, the Treaty of Versailles gave Poland a narrow corridor through Germany to the port city of Danzig (better known today by its Polish name, Gdansk), which was made a free city under the supervision of the League of Nations.

The population of Danzig spoke German and was overwhelmingly Catholic. Pacelli was well informed about Danzig, which became important when the city government requested incorporation into a Reich diocese. Rather than simply incorporate Danzig, however, the Pope (who was accused of being pro-Polish due to his prior service as a nuncio in Poland) named a German-speaking Irish priest, Eduard O'Rourke, as administrator for Danzig. O'Rourke was given the powers of a diocesan bishop. In this way, German interests in Danzig were maintained without all the difficulties that actual incorporation of the free city into a German diocese would have involved.[8]

Another issue facing Pacelli related to his residence. For several years he had been the Holy See's representative to both Bavaria and to the Weimar Republic. He had offices in both Munich and Berlin, but he maintained his official residence in Munich and returned there as often as possible. The concordat with Bavaria was signed in March

1924, and the more important issues were now centered in Berlin. Despite some Protestant resentment at seeing a representative of the Pope in Berlin, the Weimar Government made clear that it urgently desired his presence on a more full-time basis. Vatican Secretary of State Gasparri agreed, and Pacelli made the move to the German capital on August 18, 1925.[9]

Pacelli had been greatly respected and admired in his more than eight-year stay in Bavaria. The expressions of sorrow at his departure were overwhelming. In addition to banquets in his honor, newspaper editorials praised his achievements. The official farewell party took place on July 14, 1925. Rarely has any town experienced such an outpouring of respect, admiration, and love for a foreign dignitary as took place in the Bavarian capital for Pacelli.[10]

In moving from Munich to Berlin, Pacelli went from an area loyal to Rome to one which was skeptical of Rome's intentions. Nevertheless, the move was necessary so that he could concentrate on the Vatican's long-desired concordat with Germany. Pacelli quickly took an active part in the life of the city and formed acquaintances and friends in all circles. He selected a large home surrounded by park-like grounds so that he could entertain representatives of other nations on a regular basis. Soon, high Germans officials, politicians, aristocrats, students, and workers were regular visitors to the nunciature.[11] With his well-informed opinions, outgoing personality, social grace, and quick wit, Pacelli was very influential throughout Berlin, even in non-Catholic circles. He had the reputation of being "the best informed diplomat in Germany."[12]

*****

In July 1925, Hitler's *Mein Kampf* was released. It was dedicated to his followers who were killed in the street the day after the Beer Hall Putsch. It became "the oft-cited but seldom read bible of the Nazi movement."[13] In it, Hitler called for a national revival and a battle against communism and Jews. It was part personal testament, part manual for the National Socialist Workers' Party, and part demagogic appeal to the German people. Pacelli must have taken special note of Hitler's analysis of religious institutions in general, and the Catholic Church in particular. In *Mein Kampf,* Hitler spent a good deal of time discussing the political use and misuse of religion in times of international conflict. He was unhappy with what he perceived to be a lack of patriotism on the part of German churches during earlier conflicts, while he claimed that opponents used the churches for anti-German reasons. He focused primarily on the Pan-German movement, a late nineteenth century call to unify all German-speaking people and separate them from non-Germans. This "goal had been correct, its will pure," Hitler wrote.[14]

The Pan-Germans fought openly and bitterly with the Catholic Church, as Bismarck struggled to bring Catholic institutions under Prussian state control.[15] Hitler believed that direct confrontation with the Church offended the spiritual nature of the people and caused them to reject the Pan-Germans. He adopted their attitude about the Catholic Church, but he hid his war against it.[16] When others were too strident in their opposition to religion, Hitler distanced himself from their positions.[17] In fact, he found ways to use the Church for his own purposes.

According to Hitler, when others wanted to reshape Austria into a "Slavic state," they used religious institutions "without the slightest qualms," for that purpose.[18]

> Czech pastors were appointed to German communities; slowly but surely they began to set the interests of the Czech people above the interests of the churches, becoming germ-cells of the de-Germanization process.
> The German clergy did practically nothing to counter these methods... [They were] completely useless for carrying on this struggle in a positive resistance to the attacks of the adversary.[19]

Like the Pan-Germans, Hitler was angered that Catholic officials were unwilling to support German causes over Catholic or universal issues. He argued that "the Catholic clergy as such was grossly infringing on German rights."[20]

> Thus the Church did not seem to feel with the German people, but to side unjustly with the enemy. The root of the whole evil lay... in the fact that the directing body of the Catholic Church was not in Germany, and that for this very reason alone it was hostile to the interests of our nationality.[21]

Therefore, Hitler concluded that "Protestantism as such is a better defender of the interests of Germanism."[22] He did, however, note that it would be hard to persuade Protestants to adopt his anti-Semitic position.[23]

Hitler, who once described Christianity as the worst trick the Jews had played on humanity, originally proposed a new German religion, based on the old Germanic gods, to take its place. The existing churches put an end to this part of his plan, at least for the time being, but relations between Germany and the Vatican suffered. Hitler proposed to correct his problem with the Catholic Church's lack of German identity, not by nationalizing the Church, but by cultivating the national identity within the Church. He wrote of the "value of large-scale propaganda."[24]

> Let the German people be raised from childhood up with that exclusive recognition of the rights of their own nationality, and let not the hearts of children be contaminated with the curse of our "objectivity," even in matters regarding the preservation of their own ego. Then in a short time it will be seen that (presupposing, of course, a radically national government) in Germany, as in Ireland, Poland, or France, the Catholic will always be a German.[25]

By carefully crafting a national Catholic Church, Hitler felt that "an astute tactician" would be assured of a strong following.[26]

To do what he proposed, Hitler said it was necessary to understand the current strengths and weaknesses of the existing German churches. His opinion was that German churches were so involved in a Catholic/Protestant dispute that they were blind to the true threat to Germany–the Jews. "[T]he Jew...now again he succeeds in causing the two German denominations to assail one another, while the foundations of both are corroded and undermined by the poison of the international world Jew."[27] Hitler, in fact, argued that Jews deliberately created rifts between the Christian churches in order to take advantage of them. Thus, the "desired goal" of Jews was that "Catholic and Protestants wage a merry war with one another, and the mortal enemy of Aryan humanity and all Christendom laughs up his sleeve."[28] Clearly it was racial purity, not religion, that was most important to Hitler.

Before Hitler came to power, Jews were integrated into the German culture. Under the Weimar Republic, Jews in Germany were treated better than in most other European nations.[29] They had constitutional protections, and many of them married Gentiles. This particularly concerned Hitler.

> This contamination of our blood, blindly ignored by hundreds of thousands of our people, is carried on systematically by the Jew

today. Systematically these black parasites of the nation defile our inexperienced young blonde girls and thereby destroy something which can no longer be replaced in this world. Both, yes, both Christian denominations look on indifferently at this desecration and destruction of a noble and unique living creature, given to the world by God's grace.[30]

The origin of Hitler's extreme hatred of the Jewish race will probably always be a matter of speculation, but whatever it was, he used every means at his disposal to annihilate the Jewish race. To do this, he had to attract a strong following. He looked to practices in the Catholic Church, not as a means of currying favor with the Lord, but as a way to capture devoted adherents.

Hitler once explained, "I have always learned a great deal from my opponents." He then went on to identify Marxists, Freemasons, and the Catholic Church as examples of opponents from whom he had obtained "illumination and ideas."[31] "There has been nothing more impressive in the world than the hierarchal organization of the Catholic Church," he said. "I have taken over many elements of it in the organization of my party."[32]

The first point that Hitler claimed to take from the Catholic religion related to celibacy and personal strength. Priests and nuns, of course, take a vow of celibacy. Hitler thought that this made them stronger. The "very significance of celibacy... is not at all recognized by most people. It is cause of the incredibly vigorous strength which resides in this age-old institution."[33] Hitler's propaganda machine went to great lengths to hide his romances from the public (and some who were fairly close to him thought that he was indeed celibate at least until shortly before his death).

A second point that he claimed to take from the Catholic Church related to maintaining faith in a dogma, regardless of whether the evidence points in different directions.

> Here, too, we can learn by the example of the Catholic Church. Though its doctrinal edifice, and in part quite superfluously, comes into collision with exact science and research, it is none the less unwilling to sacrifice so much as one little syllable of its dogmas. It has recognized quite correctly that its power of resistance does not lie in its lesser or greater adaptation to the scientific findings of the moment, which in reality are always fluctuating, but rather in rigidly holding to dogmas once established, for it is only such dogmas which lend to the whole body the character of a faith. And so it stands more firmly.[34]

Hitler, of course, held to his core beliefs (such as extermination of the Jews), even to the point of damaging his war effort.[35]

Finally, Hitler looked to the Catholic Church for guidance on a matter in which he was to become recognized as a true master: means of persuasion.

> At night, however, [people] succumb more easily to the dominating force of a stronger will.... The same purpose, after all, is served by the artificially made and yet mysterious twilight in Catholic churches, the burning lamps, incense, censers, etc.[36]

Hitler would later perfect the torch-light parades that won him so many followers.[37] Some of these events were so enthralling that anti-Hitler people, even Jews, sometimes found themselves swept up in the emotion of the moment.

This Nazi interest in the Catholic Church as a model for building individual strength continued into the war years. "I have learned above all from the Jesuits," said Hitler.[38] Heinrich Himmler, leader of the German S.S., kept an extensive library about them and dreamed of training his elite *Waffen S.S.* combat troops along Jesuit lines (without, of course, the Christian influence). He even sent his principal officers to the Wewelsburg Castle in Westphalia for a type of "spiritual exercises," based on the new Nordic ideals, the Holy Grail, and the Teutonic Knights of old. He hoped that they would learn the inner subjugation of will and intellect that would make them expert soldiers. Hitler jokingly called Himmler "our very own Ignatius Loyola."[39]

Despite the discussion of religion, *Mein Kampf* was not a holy book;[40] it was a blueprint for Hitler's future action. After being freed from prison in December 1924, he spent the rest of the decade trying to implement these ideas and build his power base. He trained with a professional stage magician to learn gestures and body positions that would help him make better presentations. He also worked on re-building the Nazi Party. An improving economy stalled his efforts, but fortunately for him (and unfortunately for the rest of the world), on October 29, 1929, the Wall Street stock market crashed, leading the world into the Great Depression. Germany, still dependant on outside loans, saw them all dry up. Unemployment soared and the economy tumbled. The unrest led to Communist revolts and fighting in the streets. Hitler knew that all of these matters would work in his favor.[41]

CHAPTER FOUR

THE LATERAN TREATY

Mussolini was called "the most blasphemous journalist in Europe,"[1] but he understood the political importance of religion. Not only in gaining power, but also in running the country, support from the Church was crucial in a country as Catholic as Italy. As he would later (December 1934) write in the French newspaper, *Figaro*:

> History of western civilization from the time of the Roman Empire to our days shows that every time the State clashes with religion, it is always the state which ends defeated. The simple, passive resistance of the clergy and the faithful is sufficient to foil the most violent attacks on the part of the State.[2]

Mussolini was determined not to "clash" with the Church. In the mid-1920s, he increased clerical stipends, reintroduced Catholic teaching into schools, and reformed laws relating to charitable institutions.[3] By far, however, the most important development regarding the relations between Italy and the Vatican was the signing of the Lateran Treaty in 1929.

Benedict XV, Pope from 1914 to 1922, renewed the old practice of making agreements or signing "concordats" with nations, so that the Vatican could safeguard Church interests and better oppose anti-Christian forces. As nuncio, Pacelli had successfully negotiated concordats with two German states, and laid the groundwork for a third with all of Germany. Now, the Holy See needed to strengthen its relations with the Catholic nation of Italy, which surrounded Vatican City on all sides.

The Pope had once been the temporal ruler of the states of the Church, which comprised a considerable portion of central Italy. His last remaining territory was taken away when Italian government troops seized Rome in 1870. The ancient city had been the papal capital; it was now made the capital of the Italian Kingdom.

In order to conciliate the Holy See, in 1871 the Italian government enacted the "Law of Papal Guarantees."[4] Under these provisions, the Pope and his successors were guaranteed possession of St. Peter's, the Vatican and its gardens, the Lateran Palace, and the Villa of Castel Gandolfo. The Pope was also granted sovereign rights within these possessions, including the inviolability of his own person and the authority to receive and send ambassadors. In addition, he was granted free use of the Italian telegraph, railway, and postal systems, and provided with an annual subsidy of approximately $645,000.

The reigning Pope at that time, Pius IX, refused to recognize the Law of Papal Guarantees, because it was a legislative act by the Italian government, not a negotiated treaty or concordat. He and his successors declined the annual subsidy, proclaimed themselves "prisoners of an usurping power," and did not leave Vatican City or even show themselves in public.[5] In October 1926, Mussolini had an intermediary express to Pope Pius XI his strong desire to enter into negotiations for the purpose of eliminating the hostility between the Church and the nation of Italy.[6] These negotiations culminated in 1929 with the signing of the Lateran Treaty.

The Lateran Treaty actually consisted of three documents, which Cardinal Pacelli's brother, Francesco, helped negotiate.[7] In the first document, the Holy See recognized the kingdom of Italy and surrendered territorial claims in exchange for Italy's recognition of a sovereign and independent Vatican City State. A second document provided compensation for Church property that had been seized in 1870. The third document, the true concordat, defined the rights and obligations of both the Church and the State.[8]

Much of the Church's teaching was incorporated into the 1929 concordat, and the Italian government agreed to all of the Church's most important religion-oriented issues:[9] Catholicism was declared the sole and official religion of Italy. All issues involving religion and politics were to be settled according to Church law. Catholic education was made compulsory in all schools, the government recognized Church schools and universities, Church holy days were made State holidays, and the State agreed to pay salaries to priests and bishops. Papal colleges, while not given extra-territorial privileges, were free from taxation and guaranteed against expropriation. Ordained priests, moreover, were exempted from military obligations. Church marriages were given civil effect, and divorce was made subject to the restrictions of canon law.[10] Catholic Action, the Pope's lay organization, was granted freedom for all its activities so long as it conformed to directives from the Holy See. The Church was given autonomous government and legislative power as well as the right to establish its own police force, civil service, postage services, flag, currency, radio station, and a railway station.   Papal churches, palaces, and other buildings outside the Vatican were given the territorial immunities normally reserved for foreign embassies.   The Pope was granted free communication with his bishops throughout the world, and he was free to appoint Italian bishops, subject only to political objections of the State.[11] Italy also provided money to the Vatican.

When Pope Benedict XV died in 1922, the Vatican had to borrow $100,000 to cover the expense of his funeral and the conclave to elect his successor. With the Lateran Treaty, the Church received a cash payment of 750 million lire and one billion lire in State securities.[12] This was intended as compensation for the property seized from the Church in 1871. The approximate value of this settlement was $92.1 million, which did not approach the true value of the seized property, but some commentators have suggested that it saved the Vatican from bankruptcy.[13]   The Vatican's treasurer, Bernardino Nogara, a layman of Jewish ancestry, invested this money wisely, so that the money from the Lateran Treaty became a vast reserve estimated at hundreds of millions by the mid-1930s.

In exchange for Italy's agreement to recognize the Vatican as an independent sovereign state and to guarantee its protection, the Vatican essentially agreed to divorce itself from secular politics.[14] This killed any hope of reviving the Catholic Popular Party, which had once posed a threat to Mussolini, but which had disappeared by 1927.   Pius XI, however, was pleased with the concordat as it was written, and his assessment that "we have given back God to Italy and Italy to God," was widely shared.[15]

On February 11, 1929, Vatican Secretary of State Gasparri and Mussolini met at the Lateran Palace and signed the documents. The Vatican thus officially became the smallest sovereign state, with an area of only slightly more than a hundred acres and less than five hundred citizens, and took its place among the nations of the world. After the signing ceremony, the Pope appeared on the balcony and blessed the crowds in St. Peter's Square. The Italian Chamber of Deputies voted that February 11, the date of the signing of the Lateran Treaty, would replace September 20, the anniversary of the taking of Rome in 1870, as a national holiday.[16]

While there was some expression of disappointment with the Church for having reached an agreement with Mussolini, he was not a completely unpopular world figure. Not only had he "made the trains run on time," Mussolini had accomplished many things for the Italian people.[17] By engaging in big deficit spending (though he had come to power promising a balanced budget), Mussolini built 1,700 sea-side summer camps for children, provided prenatal clinics for expectant mothers, instituted the eight-hour work day, and provided insurance for the elderly, unemployed, and the disadvantaged.[18] From the Church's perspective, it was also important that he had placed crucifixes in every classroom and provided chaplains to Italian soldiers.

In the late 1920s and early 1930s, many people saw Mussolini as a positive influence on Europe. Among his admirers were Albert Einstein (a Jew who fled Germany to escape racism), Mohandas Gandhi (who called Mussolini "a superman"), George Bernard Shaw (a Socialist), the Archbishop of Canterbury (who called Mussolini the "one great figure in Europe"), Winston Churchill (who told Mussolini, "I am sure I would have been with you from the beginning to end" if they had been countrymen), and even Sigmund Freud (a Jew who called Mussolini a "cultural hero").[19] He also attracted the attention of future Fascist leaders, Juan Perón and Adolf Hitler (who adopted the brown shirts for his storm troopers in imitation of Mussolini's black shirts).[20]

Fascists from around the world tended to view the treaty with the Catholic Church as a betrayal by Mussolini.[21] Perhaps regretting that he had gone so far along the path of conciliation, in the month following its signing Mussolini publicly stated: "Within the State, the Church is not sovereign, nor is it even free... because it is subordinate... to the general law of the State. We have not resurrected the Temporal Power of the Popes, we have buried it."[22] In referring to the Christian religion, Mussolini said, "This religion was born in Palestine but became Catholic in Rome. If it had stayed in Palestine, it would very likely have remained one of the many sects that flourished in those perfervid surroundings...and would probably have died out leaving no trace."[23] Pius XI used harsh terms to criticize Mussolini's pronouncements and explained that Catholicism was distinct, separate, and in some ways inconsistent with Fascism.[24]

A decade after the signing of the Lateran Treaty, Pius XII (Pacelli), in *Summi Pontificatus* (*Darkness Over the Earth*), wrote of its importance:

> We can, in this first Encyclical directed to the whole Christian people scattered over the world, rank among such friendly powers Our dear Italy, fruitful garden of the Faith, which was planted by the Princes of the Apostles. For, as a result of the Lateran Pacts, her representative occupies a place of honor among those officially accredited to the Apostolic See. "The Peace of Christ restored to Italy," like a new dawn of brotherly union in religious and in civil intercourse, had its beginning in these Pacts.[25]

Although the Church forged a working agreement with Mussolini, neither Pacelli nor Pius XI sympathized with Fascism. "Where there is a question of saving souls, We feel the courage to treat with the Devil in person," said Pius XI.[26] He was one of the first world leaders to condemn the anti-Christian teachings of Fascism (at a time when other statesmen were still vying for Mussolini's favors). Moreover, as some scholars have concluded, the Church, "by obtaining the freedom of action necessary to exist as a viable spiritual power in Italy, gained more than it lost."[27]

The agreement did not mitigate Pius XI's criticism of Mussolini or Fascism in general.[28] Moreover, Mussolini did not view the treaty with the Holy See as any sign of mutual respect. Before long, he began asserting the right to place his friends in high positions within the Church, and his men openly attacked the lay organization, Catholic Action. Fascists seized the Vatican newspaper, *L'Osservatore Romano*, and suppressed other newspapers.[29] In addition, despite the Lateran Treaty's provision for Catholic religious education in public schools, Mussolini now insisted that public education remain solely the prerogative of the State and that it be kept outside the province of the Holy See. He tried to outlaw all Catholic youth groups, and Italian university professors were forced to swear loyalty to Fascism (only eleven refused).[30] While Mussolini sometimes attended military Masses, he exhibited extreme contempt for the religious services.[31]

By 1931, things had gotten very bad. First, the Fascist newspaper, *Lavoro Fascista*, ran a series of articles attacking Catholic Action as being anti-Fascist and contrary to Italian laws. Then, in May and June, Fascist-inspired anti-papal demonstrations swept across Italy. Catholic buildings were pillaged, Catholic publications were burned, and protestors in the street chanted "Down with the traitor Ratti" and "kill him!"[32] Mussolini himself repeated his famous slogan, "Everything in the State, nothing apart from the State, nothing against the State," but with a foreign journalist he went further, adding: "The child, as soon as he is old enough to learn, belongs entirely to the State, to it alone."[33] Pius XI was compelled to respond, and he did so with the encyclical, *Non Abbiamo Bisogno (We Have No Need)*.

Unlike most encyclicals, which are written in Latin, *Non Abbiamo Bisogno* was written in Italian, to make it more accessible to the Italian people. The Pope signed it on June 29, and Monsignor (later Archbishop) Francis J. Spellman of New York smuggled it out of Italy and released it in Paris, rather than the traditional Vatican release. Pius XI feared that Mussolini (who controlled the press) would prevent its distribution if it were released in Italy.[34] In the encyclical, Pius XI did not expressly condemn the Fascist Party or the régime, but he did warn against "pagan worship of the State."[35] He also disputed Mussolini's charges that groups like Catholic Action were political in nature and that Mussolini's political foes headed the organizations (which would have been a breach of the Lateran Treaty).

There was no doubt about the Pope's meaning. In retaliation, the Fascists forced 50,000 Catholics to either resign from Catholic Action or lose their jobs, effectively bringing that organization to an end.[36] Some in the Vatican feared physical reprisals against the Pope or Secretary of State Pacelli, who was said to be the driving force behind the Pope.[37] Mussolini, however, contented himself with periodic petty insults (once threatening to build a giant mosque and import thousands of Moslems to worship in Rome) and continuing persecution of Catholic institutions.[38]

In reaching an accord with Italy, Pius XI was treating Italy the same way he treated other nations. Even if a state might stand to gain more in the short term than the Church, governments do not last, and eventually the Church would be better positioned if it had a relationship with the people. Thus, the Pontiff was confident that the Church would emerge triumphant in the long run if it had an agreement. In fact, despite the horrid treatment of the Church in Communist nations, the Vatican (through Pacelli) tried to obtain a concordat with the Soviet Union in the mid-1920s,[39] and it did conclude one with the predominantly Socialist government of Prussia in 1929.[40]

Although it was a common provision in the concordats that the Vatican signed with other countries, one provision of the Lateran Treaty was potentially controversial:

> With regard to her sovereignty in the field of international relations, the Holy See declares that she wishes to remain extraneous to all disputes concerning temporal affairs between nations, and to international congresses convened for the purpose of settling such disputes, unless the contending parties call upon her to serve as the mediator of peace. Nevertheless, she reserves the right to exercise her moral and spiritual power in every case. As the result of this declaration, the Vatican State will always be considered neutral and inviolable territory.

A Pope who took this as a literal restriction on his authority might be left in a quandary when thrust into the middle of international conflict.

CHAPTER FIVE

HITLER'S RISE TO POWER AND THE CONCORDAT

Hitler was a mystery to most people in Munich. He gave spine-chilling speeches in the beer halls, but his past was unknown. He was not from Munich, though he spoke like he was. It was rumored that he was from Bohemia, that Hitler was not his real name, that he was Jewish, and that he was being supported by others in the movement, who would one day reveal themselves as the true leaders of National Socialism.[1] This aura of mystery might have contributed to his assent to power, which came as a surprise to many foreign diplomats.

Long after the war, former U.S. Under Secretary of State Robert Murphy was granted an audience with Pope Pius XII. The two men had been in Germany during the mid-1920s, and had come to know one another in the diplomatic circles. As they talked over the old times, Murphy mentioned how they had both underestimated Hitler in the mid-1920s, since they both had reported to their governments that Hitler would never come to power. The Pope smiled and said, "In those days, you see, I wasn't infallible."[2]

Though he was not yet recognized as a threat, in the 1920s Hitler built a power base that was poised to take over Germany in the 1930s. To do this, he relied on a select group of men. Perhaps the most important was his Minister of Propaganda, Joseph Goebbels.

Goebbels' propaganda skills paved the way for the National Socialists to be accepted as a legitimate political party, and he continued shaping public opinion even after the Nazis took control. Goebbels did not simply censor undesirable information or commentary; he exploited the media in a carefully orchestrated campaign. He produced motion pictures focusing on nature and Darwin's "survival of the fittest" theory. Animals who killed their deformed young were said to be practicing proper race theory. Weak and deformed humans were depicted as a drain on the nation. Jewish people were similarly portrayed. Slowly, Goebbels began to shape national opinion.[3]

Unlike the Communists in Russia who promoted class-warfare, Hitler tried to offer something to all Aryan Germans. To the industrialists, he offered protection from nationalization. To the unemployed, he offered massive social programs. To the disgruntled war veterans, he offered scapegoats (the Weimar officials who signed the Treaty of Versailles) and promised to restore Germany's might. He offered solutions to all, primarily by blaming the Jews for the nation's troubles. They, he argued, profiteered from the war while others were dying. This fit well with the party line on race theory.

Despite their propaganda efforts, the Nazis never received an absolute majority of votes in any free election during the Weimar Republic.[4] The first Nazi to win public office in Germany was Wilhelm Frick, who became the Minister of the Interior for Thuringia on January 23, 1930, the month after Pacelli left Germany.[5] In September of that year, the sitting German government suffered a major defeat in the legislative elections. Hitler's National Socialists won 107 seats and became the second most powerful party in Germany.

Rather than concentrating on complex economic questions, Hitler turned Germany's fiscal woes into an issue of national independence. His oft-repeated theme was: "It is not an economic question which now faces the German people; it is a political question—how shall the nation's determination be recovered?"[6] Hitler proclaimed to cheering audiences that he would scrap the Treaty of Versailles if he came to power.

French troops were still in the Rhineland in early 1930. They were scheduled to stay there until 1935 to assure that Germany would abide by its obligations under the Versailles Treaty and not rearm itself. German Foreign Minister Gustav Stresemann, however, negotiated an early pull-out of the French troops in 1930. In exchange, Germany committed not to send any forces to the left bank of the Rhine and to respect a demilitarized zone extending about thirty miles east of the Rhine River. Cardinal Pacelli expressed regret to the French ambassador that France had not more strongly opposed such a violation of international agreements.[7] History may well have been different if the French troops had stayed longer.

*****

As Germany was about to fall into Hitler's control, changes were also taking place in the Vatican. Vatican Secretary of State Gasparri had been in charge of the Holy See's international relations for many years, but at age seventy-seven it was time to turn these tasks over to a younger person. This was a very important position. The Secretary of State counseled the Pope on both foreign and domestic issues. As such, the position has been likened to a combination of prime minister and foreign secretary.[8] Gasparri's personal choice was fifty-three-year-old Eugenio Pacelli.

In 1929, Pacelli was informed of the Pontiff's decision to call him home to Rome, elevate him to the cardinalate, and soon thereafter appoint him as Vatican Secretary of State. Pacelli was not anxious to leave the country where he had served so long. He argued that there were matters dealing with church-state relations in Germany that he had not yet resolved, and he asked that the Pontiff put off the appointment. Pius XI, however, was determined that Pacelli return to Rome.[9]

In Berlin there was a repetition of what had occurred in 1925 when Pacelli left Munich. Testimonial dinners and newspaper editorials expressed sadness in both government circles and in the general public. President Paul von Hindenburg, a Protestant who would play an important role in Hitler's political rise, hosted a farewell luncheon for the departing nuncio. At it, he raised his glass and offered a toast: "I thank you for all you have accomplished during these long years in the cause of peace, inspired as you have been by a high sense of justice and a deep love of humanity; and I can assure you that we shall not forget you and your work here."[10]

Pacelli left Berlin for the last time in December 1929.[11] For his departure, the Weimar government provided him with an open carriage to take him to the train station. Thousands of people lined the road to wish him a fond farewell. They carried candles and called out their best wishes. Pacelli could not hide his emotion. As he gave blessings to the crowd, tears ran down his face. Monsignor Cesare Orsenigo was named as Pacelli's successor in the Berlin nunciature. His role in war-time Germany would prove to be a point of controversy.[12]

In Rome, on December 29, 1929, Pacelli received the red hat of the cardinalate. The aging Gasparri then began to groom Pacelli for the office of Secretary of State, which he would be called upon to fill the next month.

Pacelli was considered "refined, witty, intelligent, and a brilliant conversationalist."[13] He was said to be universally respected, liked by the people, and someone to whom the Italian government would listen. As Secretary of State, Pacelli strove to be of one mind with Pope Pius XI. In fact, the Pontiff said, "Cardinal Pacelli speaks with my voice."[14] This unity of purpose would be crucial in the coming years, as conflicts with the Nazis were already beginning to take place.

In 1930, Cardinal Adolph Bertram of Breslau expressed his opposition to National Socialism and refused a religious funeral for a well-known party official. He had seen the threat growing, as the Nazi vote had risen from one percent to more than twenty-four percent in the preceding two years. In a widely publicized statement, Bertram criticized as a grave error the one-sided glorification of the Nordic race and the contempt for divine revelation which was increasingly taught throughout Germany.[15] He warned against the ambiguity of the concept of "positive Christianity," a highly nationalistic religion that the Nazis were encouraging. Such a religion, he said, "for us Catholics cannot have a satisfactory meaning since everyone interprets it in the way he pleases."[16] Similarly, the bishops of Berlin and Westphalia condemned the Nazis in pastoral letters.[17] In the spring of 1931, the Bavarian bishops also condemned National Socialism and described it as heretical and incompatible with Catholic teaching.[18] Similar statements were made by bishops in Cologne, Paderborn, and the upper Rhine.[19]

In response to Cardinal Bertram, the Nazi press cited some of Pope Leo XIII's pronouncements about the relations of practicing Catholics to political parties to bolster the argument that Catholics could be National Socialists. Pacelli ordered a lengthy article to be published in the Vatican newspaper, *L'Osservatore Romano*. The article defended the Catholic Center Party, corrected the Nazi's distortions of Leo's pronouncements, and said that a Christian should not belong to any political party which works against Christian ideals.[20]

At the local level, the dispute between the Church and National Socialism got very ugly. For instance, one parish priest said of Nazi officials during a Mass one Sunday: "Let those stinking [Nazi] bastards come at me, two thousand of them if you like, and I'll bash in all their skulls so that their brains squirt out. It'll make enough soup for a week."[21] Another priest spoke to school children about the Nazi Brown Shirts: "The Brown Shirt is supposed to be a shirt of honor, isn't it? Yes, Brown's the word. Like something else that's Brown and stinks!"[22]   When Nazi authorities complained, Secretary of State Pacelli confirmed that some priests were making such statements.[23]

Despite the tension between the National Socialists and the Catholic Church, Hitler was moving closer to national prominence. The German constitution provided for an elected president who could appoint a chancellor. These were the two most powerful positions in the government. Paul von Hindenburg, a popular war hero, had been president since the mid-1920s, but Germany experienced an almost constant stream of new chancellors in the late 1920s. The six million jobless men in Germany woke up with little to do each morning, except for the daily routine of street fighting. This, in turn, led to political unrest and a continuing series of elections, and by the early 1930s, even Hindenburg's position was insecure.[24]

In March 1932, Hitler forced a run-off with Hindenburg for the German presidency. Fear of the redistribution that might come with a Communist takeover concerned many German industrialists, and Hitler played on these fears to obtain financial support.[25]   (Hitler's political opponents even made a short animated film suggesting that he was in the industrialists' pocket.)[26]   Hindenburg defeated Hitler, but Hitler drew thirty-seven percent of the vote and called it a victory for National Socialism. The Nazis were clearly a national power. Hitler pledged to cooperate with the government. In return, the government lifted the ban that had been placed on Nazi storm troopers.

In May 1932, Hindenburg withdrew his support from Chancellor Heinrich Brüning and replaced him with the conservative Catholic, Franz von Papen. Papen, however, failed to obtain a popular mandate in two Reichstag elections. Instead, the German political scene became even more difficult as both ends of the spectrum grew in strength and hardened in resolve. Addressing the National Socialist Reichstag members, Hitler said he could no longer tolerate the present government and that a total Nazi victory was just a matter of time.

In June, the German leadership acceded to a long-standing Nazi demand and announced that they would no longer pay war reparations.[27] In July 1932, the Nazis doubled their strength in the German parliament, becoming the biggest party in the Reichstag. With their rise to power, however, came much rioting and fighting between Nazis, Communists, and Socialists. In one seven-week period there were four hundred and sixty-one riots in Prussia alone. Eighty two people were killed and about four hundred were injured.[28]

On August 24th, a Nazi newspaper in Berlin was banned for inciting riots, but only six days later Nazi leader Hermann Goering was elected president of the Reichstag (similar to speaker of the house). The next month, Chancellor von Papen dissolved the Reichstag after a vote of no confidence.[29]

In November 1932, new elections cost the Nazis thirty-five seats in the Reichstag. Communists picked up most of those seats. The strength in Communist ranks deeply concerned those close to President Hindenburg (in his mid-80s and considered senile by some).[30] They determined that obtaining Hitler's support might be one way to shore up the crumbling government. Hindenburg offered Hitler a limited Chancellorship of Germany, but Hitler refused and Kurt von Schleicher was named Chancellor in December. When Schleicher failed to win much support, Hindenburg was forced to return to the one prominent political figure who could unite support behind him.

On January 30, 1933, after a month of secret meetings with Hindenburg and von Papen, Hitler was named chancellor of Germany. Hindenburg had been persuaded that if he appointed Hitler, he could control him, as Hitler had no experience in government and only three National Socialists were members of the new government.[31] This proved to be a serious mistake. With the announcement of Hitler's appointment, Communists rioted, but many more Nazis celebrated. Hitler's storm troopers marched in a torch-light parade. At least a few deaths were reported.

Once in power, Hitler did restore a degree of order to Germany. The street fighting was largely eliminated. Anyone who dared to challenge the government faced immediate imprisonment (or execution) without benefit of trial. It was harsh, but many found the relative peace to be a welcome relief from the constant riots and fighting between opposing political parties that had scarred the Weimar Republic. Moreover, Hitler benefitted from a much improved economy.

Hitler promised that churches would be free, that he would resist bolshevism, and that he was committed to peace. The minutes of a Reich cabinet meeting of March 15, 1933 reveal that the new leadership thought that "the question of coordination of political Catholicism into the new State is of special importance."[32] Eight days later, Hitler said: "The government sees in both Christian confessions the factors most important for the maintenance of our Folkdom.... The Government will devote its care to the sincere living together of Church and State."[33] This tricked some people, but not Pope Pius XI or his Secretary of State.[34] The British Chargé d'Affaires at the Holy See, Ivone Kirkpatrick, in a letter to Sir Robert Vansittart, dated August 19, 1933, explained an encounter he had with Pacelli at this time:

> Cardinal Pacelli... deplored the action of the German Government at home, their persecution of the Jews, their proceedings against political opponents, the reign of terror to which the whole nation was subjected. I said to His Eminence that I had heard the opinion expressed in Italy and elsewhere that these events (persecution of Jews, etc.) were but manifestations of the revolutionary spirit. With the passage of time and the responsibilities of office, Herr Hitler would settle down, temper the zeal of his supporters and revert to more normal methods of government. The Cardinal replied with emphasis that he saw no ground for such easy optimism. It seemed to him that there was no indication of any modification in the internal policy of the German government.[35]

At a party in Rome, one of Pacelli's old friends said that it was good that Germany now had a strong leader to deal with the Communists. Pacelli responded: "Don't talk such nonsense. The Nazis are infinitely worse."[36] (Pacelli was right. Just two weeks after his promise of peace, Hitler said "One is either a German or a Christian. You cannot be both.") [37]

During the spring of 1933, Hitler's representatives met frequently with members of the Church's hierarchy to assure them that Hitler wanted to unite the country and would do nothing to divide it.[38] Hitler supported religious schools. Character, he said, could be built only on the basis of religion, and character would be needed in the German men of the future. Hitler also promised to permit the Catholic organizations to continue in operation as long as they promoted Christian ideals. He stressed the great importance he attached to working closely with the Catholic Church. His anti-Bolshevist stance and his promise to make Christianity the basis of German morality and the family the basic unit for the nation certainly were pleasing to the Catholic hierarchy.

In the first meeting of the new Reichstag, Hitler expressed the government's commitment to Christian principles and said he looked forward to developing amicable relations with the Holy See. He stressed the fundamental agreement between National Socialism and

Catholicism. He said he was convinced that without Christianity one could neither run a personal life nor a state, and that Germany in particular needed the kind of religious and moral foundation only Christianity could provide. Things looked so promising that Protestant churches across Germany formally acknowledged their acceptance of Hitler and his regime on March 26.[39] Two days later, the German bishops lifted the ban on Catholics joining the Nazi party (though they expressly noted that they were not withdrawing their condemnations of Nazism,[40] and their statement "was joined with an uncompromising denial of the core of Nazi ideology.")[41] Secretary of State Pacelli, upon reading the episcopal act of submission, expressed his dismay.[42]

Hermann Goering, a German World War I flying hero, was an early follower of Hitler. He was now Prussian Minister of the Interior, and in that role he made a filmed statement in which he said "I shall sweep clean and remove from office all those Communists and Catholics who are opposing our national endeavors."[43] Soon thereafter, the National Socialists set out to do just that.

*****

On February 1, 1933, Hitler won a dissolution of the Reichstag, with a new election to be held in March. On February 2nd, he put limits on opposition parties. He then ordered Communist houses to be searched without warrants and began censoring the press. He also secured a presidential decree permitting arrest on suspicion and imprisonment without trial. Within the month, twenty-four provincial governors and police chiefs were dismissed and replaced by National Socialists.

At the end of February 1933, less than a week before new Reich elections were scheduled, the Reichstag building was burned to the ground. Though there has always been speculation that the Nazis set the fire to frame their political rivals,[44] a young man named Marinus van der Lubbe, identified as a Communist, was arrested for arson. (He would receive the death sentence in December and be executed a month later.) Hermann Goering had all one hundred Communist members of the Reichstag arrested, preventing them from campaigning in the crucial week before the election. President Hindenburg signed an emergency order suspending the constitutional guarantees of individual freedom, freedom of the press, private property, and the privacy of mail. Hitler's storm troopers, the S.A., served as the police force. They began rounding up Communists and anti-Hitler Catholics.[45] Hundreds of people were incarcerated until the investigation (and election) was over. Communist newspapers and meeting halls were also shut down as Berlin took on the appearance of a police state. Regardless of whether Hitler had anything to do with setting the fire, he certainly took advantage of it. From this point on, there were no real limits on his power.

On March 5, 1933, with many of their opponents in jail or intimidated, the Nazis and their Nationalist allies won a majority in the Reichstag. One week later the flag of the German Republic was lowered and the empire banner was flown alongside the swastika. This month would see the opening of the first concentration camp at Oranienburg, outside of Berlin.[46] Other camps were preparing to open, including one at an old power factory near Dachau. The camps had become necessary due to all of Hitler's political enemies that were being taken into custody and filling the prisons. Hitler was establishing his Third Reich, which he said would follow in the tradition of the Holy Roman Empire and the unified German Empire established by Bismarck and would last for 1,000 years. Its establishment was considered a "major defeat for the powers of Jewry, capital, and the Catholic Church."[47]

On March 23, 1933, the Reichstag adjourned, giving Hitler's cabinet the power to rule by decree. (In 1930 the Reichstag had granted Chancellor Heinrich Brüning's request to govern by means of emergency powers, setting the precedent.) An Enabling Act granted Hitler dictatorial powers for an initial period of four years, making permanent the authority he had already assumed with the emergency order in February.[48] President Hindenburg technically had the authority to dismiss the chancellor, but this was not a realistic possibility.

Hitler had achieved what none before him had dared to try. He did away with the separate powers of the individual states and brought them all under the central authority of the Reich.[49] For the first time in German history the federal character of the nation was destroyed and the Reich was truly unified. In his last address to the disbanding Reichstag, Hitler announced that "treason toward the nation and the people shall in the future be stamped out with ruthless barbarity."[50]

Pope Pius XI proclaimed 1933 to be a holy year.[51] When he inaugurated it on April 2, he held out hopes of peace and prosperity as a result of this observation. Unfortunately, the year was certainly not holy in Germany.

On March 28th, Hitler banned Jews from businesses, professions, and schools. On April 1st, he called for a boycott of Jewish-owned businesses. The National Socialists leadership then proceeded to enact some four hundred anti-Jewish laws.[52] Laws were passed barring "non-Aryans" from the legal profession and parts of the medical professions, establishing a five percent quota of Jewish students in public schools, and prohibiting Jews from voting, serving in the government, appearing in motion pictures and plays, or publishing books.

The 1933 boycott attracted worldwide attention. The idea was that "Jewish businesses" would be identified and Aryans would avoid patronizing them. Those who violated the boycott would at least be publicly humiliated. Jewish and non-Jewish people from around the world led a public outcry denouncing this action and threatening to boycott German goods. The Vatican filed a formal protest. The Nazis, of course, used all of this to their benefit.

Billboards went up around the nation with sayings such as: "Jews the world over are trying to crush the new Germany."[53] Signs were placed in store windows reading, "Germans defend yourselves against Jewish atrocity propaganda, buy only at German Shops!"[54] Joseph Goebbels, the Minister of Popular Enlightenment and Propaganda, said that the boycott would remain in place as long as Jews around the world were boycotting German goods and accusing Germany of atrocities.[55] The Nazis were so effective in turning the international uproar to their favor that German Cardinal Michael von Faulhaber wrote to American Cardinal George William Mundelein of Chicago, urging him to use his influence to stop press reports about German atrocities, lest things be made worse in Germany. Faulhaber also wrote Cardinal Pacelli, telling him that it was impossible to confront the government on the racial issue without persecution of the Jews becoming persecution of the Catholics.[56]

In May, the Nazis broke up all trade unions and began purging the country of non-German books with huge bonfires. German students, from universities that had been regarded as among the finest in the world, gathered to burn books with "unGerman" ideas, including those by Sigmund Freud, Albert Einstein, Jack London, and H.G. Wells.[57] Curricula were revised in the German schools to teach "race science," and other theories related to the superiority of the Aryan race.[58] Many university professors were removed from their positions, including writer Thomas Mann, theologian Paul Tillich, and Nobel Prize winners Gustav Hertz and James Franck.[59] Pope Pius XI responded by assigning many Jewish intellectuals to teach in the colleges over which he had control.[60]

*****

While Hitler was baptized into the Catholic faith, he was not a Christian. His real faith was National Socialism, and the Nazis viewed Christianity as an outmoded superstition that would eventually wither away. "The religions are all alike," Hitler said within a year of coming to power, "no matter what they call themselves. They have no future. Whether it is the Old Testament or the New, or simply the sayings of Jesus...it's all the same old Jewish swindle." Even the Ten Commandments, he said, "have lost their validity."[61]

In 1933-34, Hitler predicted that a "new age of magic interpretation of the world is coming, of interpretation in terms of will and not of intelligence."[62] "Man is becoming God–that is the simple fact. Man is God in the making....National Socialism...is the will to create mankind anew."[63] He saw his job as helping this evolution take place. To accomplish this, he promised that he would not be prevented "from tearing up Christianity root and branch, and annihilating it in Germany."[64]

Regarding the Catholic Church in particular, Hitler was confident that he could bring it down:

> I promise you that, if I wished to, I could destroy the Church in a few years; it is hollow and rotten and false through and through. One push and the whole structure would collapse....I shall give them a few years reprieve. Why should we quarrel? They will swallow anything in order to keep their material advantages... we need only show them once or twice who is the master. Then they will know which way the wind blows. They are no fools. The Church was something really big. Now we are its heirs. We, too, are the Church. Its day has gone.[65]

Hitler knew that there might be resistance among the older Catholics, but he felt that he could accomplish his goals by focusing on youth.

"As long as youth follows me, I don't mind if the old people limp to the confessional."[66] He privately disclosed:

> I shall make them appear ridiculous and contemptible. I shall order films to be made about them. We shall show the history of the monks on the cinema. Let the whole mass of nonsense, selfishness, repression and deceit be revealed: how they drained money out of the country... how they committed incest. We shall make it so thrilling that everyone will want to see it. There will be queues outside the cinemas.[67]

Hitler apparently had no compunction about being duplicitous, because as he saw it, "[c]onscience is a Jewish invention. It is a blemish like circumcision."[68]

Despite his true feelings, Hitler wanted to keep organized religion on his side. He spent these early months trying to build a reputation as a legitimate, moderate statesman. Except for the statements in *Mein Kampf* (which were carefully edited in translated editions) he refused to make negative statements publicly about the Christian churches.[69] When Nazis openly criticized religion, they claimed to be attacking "negative Christianity," which was said to be devouring German moral principles. The Nazi alternative, as set forth in their party platform, was "positive Christianity."[70] In this way, the Christian religion was misused to defend the supremacy of the German people.

Because the Nazis were not open about their view of religion, many German church officials welcomed the morality of the Third Reich. Hitler, they anticipated, would lead a return to piety, virtue, idealism, discipline, morality, and patriotism. He would put an end to vice and licentiousness, to agnosticism and godlessness. Under a Hitler government, they thought, Germany would experience a true rebirth of spirituality. Weimar had become associated with defeat and national humiliation, political violence, severe economic and social dislocation, and a political leadership with no real executive policy-making capabilities. Many religious people saw Weimar as a non-Christian system devised by criminals. The Nazis promised to rectify all of these problems. They were so persuasive that some religious leaders—even those who would later be deported to concentration camps for their anti-Nazi sermons—did not initially take issue with the Nazi regime.[71]

Bishop Theophil Wurm, the Lutheran state bishop of Württemberg, makes a good case study. He would one day be noted as the most outspoken German Protestant opponent of National Socialism. At the beginning, however, like most Protestant Church leaders in Germany, he welcomed the establishment of an authoritarian government. Even before the fall of Weimar, he had argued that Germany's only choice was a dictatorship by Hitler or a dictatorship by Moscow.[72] A few months into Hitler's chancellorship, Wurm proudly noted that National Socialism was living up to its promises. The new regime deserved praise for crushing "at great sacrifice" the "terror" of the far left and for waging a struggle against "the disruptive influences in our cultural life."[73] In April 1933, he wrote a letter to the Lutheran clergy of Württemberg in which he expressed his sense of profound relief at the rise of Nazism. He said that Germany was like a "beleaguered city" in which, after a "very dangerous period of confusion and division," a "united and purposeful leadership" had emerged as a result of the "cooperation of responsible men."[74]

Over the next several years, like many other German churchmen, Wurm began to find fault with Hitler's government. On December 6, 1938, shortly after *Kristallnacht* ("Night of Shattered Glass"), when Nazis went on a violent rampage, Wurm protested in a letter to the Minister of Justice.[75] In 1940, Wurm repeatedly wrote to government officials urging changes in official policies, especially those concerning genocide.[76] In 1943 he began writing officials to protest "the way in which the struggle against other races and nations is being waged."[77] What the Germans were doing, he said, violated God's commandments and shamed a "cultured people." These actions, he warned, "could bring a terrible retribution against our nation."[78]

Finally, in July 1943, Wurm wrote Hitler, protesting against the "Final Solution" of the "Jewish question."[79] He urged Hitler, "in the name of God and for the sake of the German people," to stop "the persecution and annihilation to which many men and women within the German sphere of authority are being condemned without a judicial verdict."[80] "Measures adopted for the extermination of the other non-Aryans," he wrote, "are in clearest violation of God's commandment and undermine the foundation of all Western thought and life, namely, the God-given right to human existence and to human dignity in general."[81] The extermination measures, Wurm also argued, disgraced the German name. The *Führer* did not reply.[82]

None of Wurm's protests ever caused the Nazis to change their behavior. In 1944, he wrote a private letter in which he argued that National Socialism had now become the political embodiment of moral corruption. "A deliverance of the German nation is [impossible], unless its leadership acknowledges its injustice and atones for that injustice."[83] In the meantime, as a man of religion, he could only wait, trust, and pray. Only God could change the system of government established under the Third Reich.[84]

Like the Protestants, Catholic leaders were not completely opposed to Hitler when he first came to power. Catholic doctrine seemed incompatible with National Socialism, but Hitler made many promises that sounded good. Just as important, Catholic leaders were well aware that in the Soviet Union the Communists were waging an inhumane war of annihilation against Christianity. Communists were now trying to spread atheism in Germany. Like others, many Catholics saw Hitler as the best barrier to the spread of Communism. The Nazis had presented themselves as being friendly toward the Christian churches. Moreover, Catholic officials had long condemned Weimar's indifference to Christian values; its attempt to restrict the role of religion in national affairs; its advocacy of secularism and materialism; its tolerance of immorality; and its flirtation with radicalism and Bolshevism.[85] These Church leaders truly believed that Weimar had been established by a wrongful rebellion against legitimate authority, that the Republic placed the interests of the parties above the welfare of the people, and that it acquiesced in the military weakness and humiliation of Germany. These concerns meant that there was little sympathy for Weimar as it was collapsing.

On the other hand, German Catholics were able to identify with the Jews. Both groups were religious minorities, and they both were charged with insufficient patriotism or even disloyalty to the nation due to their allegiance to religious leaders outside of Germany. This caused Jews and Catholics both to be denounced by the Nazis for being "international" or "cosmopolitan" in their allegiance and condemned for serving the interests of alien forces.[86] (The leaders of the Catholic Church also knew that there were several influential groups within the National Socialist party that regarded Catholicism as a sworn enemy.)

This kinship with the Jews, though distant, caused Catholic leaders to be somewhat less than enthusiastic about National Socialism.[87]

On June 8, 1933, a pastoral letter from all the German prelates said: "[W]e believe that a unity of people can be realized not through the identity of blood but rather through the identity of belief, and that the exclusive emphasis on race and blood with regard to membership in a State leads to injustices which burden the Christian conscience...."[88] Once the Third Reich was well established, however, the German Catholic Church sought to get along with the new order.[89] Hitler's government, for its part, tried to reassure Church leaders by proclaiming support for religious ideals and values.

In March 1933, when Hitler received dictatorial powers, he expressed a desire to improve relations with many nations, including the Holy See. A little more than two months later, on June 7, he signed a peace agreement with Italy, France, and the United Kingdom. This agreement, the Four Power Pact, stressed the "entente, collaboration and solidarity" of those nations.[90] Many in the Vatican were hopeful that this signified a period of assured peace.[91] One month later, the Holy See signed an agreement with Germany.

*****

Pius XI believed in establishing diplomatic agreements with many nations. Under his leadership, the Church reached agreement with twenty-one countries, including Czechoslovakia, Austria, Italy, Germany, Poland, Yugoslavia, Latvia, and Lithuania. As nuncio in Germany, Cardinal Pacelli had been largely responsible for negotiating the agreements with Bavaria (1924), Prussia (1929), and Baden (1932). He had also started negotiations with the Weimar Republic for a concordat with the whole of Germany and had attempted to secure an agreement with the Soviet Union.[92] As a lawyer and diplomat, Pacelli agreed with the Pope that this was the best way of preserving the Church's freedom of action.[93]

The Holy See's concordats with individual German states had little meaning now that Hitler had centralized power and control over Germany. The Church had been working toward agreement with Germany long before Hitler rose to power.[94] In fact, Pacelli had worked toward such an agreement ever since he was appointed Papal Nuncio to Bavaria.

Now, however, the Church found itself in a bind. Hitler, who never intended to keep his promises, was happy to accept all of the

Church's long-standing demands. ("I will be one of the few men in history who have deceived the Vatican," he boasted shortly before signing the concordat.)[95]   Moreover, Hitler's negotiator, Former Chancellor Franz von Papen (a Catholic whose primary role in the early years of the Reich was to obtain the support of the Church),[96] made it quite clear that if the Church were to reject the *Führer's* offer, Hitler would simply publish his own terms and blame the Pope for having rejected a very favorable treaty.[97]

In a private conversation with Ivone Kirkpatrick, British Ambassador to the Vatican, Pacelli denied that the treaty constituted an approval of Nazism.   In fact, he expressed "disgust and abhorrence" of Hitler's reign of terror.   "I had to choose between an agreement on their lines," he said on August 11, 1933, "and the virtual elimination of the Catholic Church in the Reich."[98]   Kirkpatrick reported to the British Foreign Office on August 19, 1933:

> These reflections on the iniquity of Germany led the Cardinal to explain apologetically how it was that he had signed a Concordat with such people. A pistol, he said, had been pointed at his head and he had no alternative. The German government had offered him concessions, concessions, it must be admitted, wider than any previous German Government would have agreed to, and he had to choose between an agreement on their lines and the virtual elimination of the Catholic Church in the Reich. Not only that, but he was given no more than one week to make up his mind.... If the German Government violated the Concordat–and they were certain to do that–the Vatican would have at least a treaty on which to base a protest.[99]

Mussolini, who had reached an agreement with the Church four years earlier, supported the treaty because he felt that it would strengthen the German position.[100] He stated that together with the Four Power Pact recently signed by the Reich, Great Britain, France, and Italy, the concordat made Germany's diplomatic position much stronger.   (Hitler also signed a similar agreement with Protestant churches.)[101]   Not all Nazis, however, agreed.   Joseph Goebbels, Reinhart Heydrich, and others in the party objected until the end and may even have tried to sabotage the process by creating violent incidents involving the clergy and Catholic organizations.[102]

The Church had been making agreements with foreign governments for centuries.[103] It did not view them as endorsements of the existing government.[104] In fact, in two separate articles that were published in *L'Osservatore Romano* in early July 1933, Pacelli denied the claim that the concordat was a recognition of the Nazi regime.[105] Pius XI explained his thinking in 1937, in his encyclical, *Mit brennender Sorge* (*With Burning Anxiety*):

> When, in 1933, We consented... to open negotiations for a concordat, We were prompted by the desire... to secure for Germany the freedom of the Church's beneficent mission and the salvation of the souls in her care, as well as by the sincere wish to render the German people a service essential for its peaceful development and prosperity. Hence, despite many and grave misgivings, We then decided not to withhold Our consent for We wished to spare the Faithful of Germany... the trials and difficulties they would have had to face... had the negotiations fallen through. It was by acts that We wished to make it plain, that the pacific and maternal hand of the Church would be extended to anyone who did not actually refuse it.[106]

As others have noted, the concordat was necessary to protect Catholics in Germany from being brutalized.[107]

In addition to being bullied by the Nazis, the Church did feel that there were advantages to the concordat. The modern tradition of the Vatican is that if relations, no matter how strained, are maintained, there is a possibility of influencing the government and of protecting Catholic interests.[108] Without some form of relationship, the Holy See cannot effectively protect and minister to its people. As Pius XI told a meeting of bishops in Rome in May 1933: "If it is a matter of saving a few souls, of averting even graver damage, we have the courage to negotiate even with the devil."[109]

The earlier concordats with the various German states were incorporated into a new concordat covering the whole nation, which was signed on July 20, 1933, following consultation with the German bishops.[110] From the Vatican's perspective, at least on paper the German concordat was surprisingly favorable—one of the best that it had ever signed.[111] The State essentially met all of the demands set forth by the Church, including: independence of Catholic organizations, freedom of the Church, freedom for Catholic schools, free communication with Rome, Church control over religious orders and ecclesiastical property, religious education in public schools (taught by teachers approved by the bishop). Only minimal restrictions were placed on ecclesiastical appointments (bishops were to be appointed by Rome, subject to political objections by the Reich Government; clergy were to be appointed by bishops, the only requirement being that they be German nationals). The Vatican also received the long-sought right to maintain theological faculties at state institutions and to establish seminaries. In short, "the Catholic religion in Germany was placed on an even footing with the Protestant faith and was guaranteed the same rights and privileges as the latter."[112] Thus, more than a decade after Pope Pius XI first made these demands, the Vatican at least got the promise of what it wanted not just in one section of the Reich but throughout the entire country.

A public statement made by Hitler about the rights of the Catholic Church, which was made official policy with the signing of the concordat, was released to the press on July 9, 1933. It read:

> 1. The dissolution of those Catholic organizations which are recognized by the present treaty and which were dissolved without instructions by the government of the Reich, is to be rescinded immediately.
> 2. All coercive measures against priests and other leaders of the Catholic organizations are to be annulled. A repetition of such measures in the future is inadmissible and will be punished in conformity to the existing laws.[113]

The statement ended with an expression of hope that the problems involving the Protestant Churches would also soon be solved. Many people correctly felt, however, that the Germans would never honor the agreement.

Government-sanctioned violence towards the Church in Germany nearly caused negotiations to fail.[114] The French Ambassador at the Vatican, François Charles-Roux, believed that neither Pacelli nor the Pope were under any illusions about Hitler's word, but, as Pacelli stated to him, "I do not regret our concordat with Germany. If we did not have it, we would not have a foundation on which to base our protests."[115] In any event, as Pacelli joked to a British diplomat, the National Socialists "would probably not violate all of the articles of the concordat at the same time."[116]

In addition to a general opposition to racial laws, the Church would not accept that a person who had been duly converted to Catholicism was still a Jew. To the Church, the issue was one of faith, not race. Accordingly, as part of the concordat, German officials agreed to regard baptized Jews as Christians. This would end up being one of the most important agreements between the Vatican and the Third Reich—one that saved the lives of thousands of Jews, officially baptized or not.[117]

The Church, for its part, withdrew priests and bishops from direct participation in party politics.[118] The Center Party had advanced the Church's interests in Germany until Hitler's rise, but by early 1933, he had largely stripped it of power.[119] (In fact, the party had considered forming a coalition with the Nazis in 1932, just for survival.)[120] On July 5, 1933, two weeks before the concordat was signed, it voluntarily dissolved in order to protect its members from greater persecution by the Nazis.[121] Reportedly, when Pacelli heard the news of it being dissolved, he said:

> Too bad that it happened at this moment. Of course the party couldn't have held out much longer. But if it only had put off its dissolution at least until after the conclusion of the concordat, the simple fact of its existence would have still been useful in the negotiations.[122]

Pius XI, like all Popes since at least Pius X (1903-1914), agreed with removing clergy from direct political involvement.[123] (Pope John-Paul II continues with this approach today.)[124] Pius thought that the Church could be more effectively defended by the terms of the concordat than by parliamentary action.[125] Moreover, the Pope was concerned about the legitimacy of direct political activity by the clergy, and he looked with more favor on the lay organization, Catholic Action.[126]

Having signed the four-power pact with Italy, England, and France, Hitler no longer truly needed the recognition a concordat with the Vatican would give him, and within a decade, he would express his intent to "put a swift end" to it.[127] The concordat did at that time, however, reassure German Catholics, and the Nazis fully exploited it for propaganda purposes.[128] According to the minutes from a meeting of the Conference of Ministers on July 14, 1933, Hitler saw "three great advantages" to the concordat:

> 1. That the Vatican had negotiated at all, while they operated, especially in Austria, on the assumption that National Socialism was un-Christian and inimical to the Church;
> 2. That the Vatican could be persuaded to bring about a good relationship with this purely National German State. He, the Reich Chancellor, would not have considered it possible even a short time ago that the Church would be willing to obligate the bishops to this State. The fact that this had now been done was certainly an unreserved recognition of the present regime;

3. That with the concordat, the Church withdrew from activity in associations and parties, *e.g.* abandoned the Christian labor unions. This, too, the Reich Chancellor would not have considered possible even a few months ago. Even the dissolution of the Center Party could be termed final only with the conclusion of the concordat now that the Vatican had ordered the permanent exclusion of the priests from party politics.[129]

Despite Hitler's pleasure at the removal of Catholic clergy from direct participation in the political process, they were not restricted from making statements that went to basic human rights, and many did make such statements about the Nazi government.[130] Moreover, Catholic laypersons were in no way restricted from political activity by the terms of the concordat.[131] The agreement with Germany was very similar in this respect to the Lateran Treaty signed with Italy in 1929 and to instructions given to the French clergy in the mid-1920s.[132] The Church did not in any way agree to restrictions on its right to involve itself in politics whenever "the fundamental rights of man or the salvation of souls requires it."[133] As such, the Catholic clergy was not silenced.[134]

On July 25, just five days after Germany ratified the concordat, the Reich government announced a sterilization law designed to achieve "perfection of the Aryan race."[135] Germans who were less than perfect were to be sterilized for the glory of Reich. Sterilization was, of course, in direct conflict with Catholic teaching about the sanctity of human life, including Pius XI's recent encyclical, *Casti Connubii* (*On Chastity in Marriage,* 1930).[136] Prominent Catholic clergy immediately denounced the program.[137] On July 26 and 27, *L'Osservatore Romano* carried a two-part article by Pacelli in which he vehemently denied any assertion that the concordat indicated approval of National Socialism and instead explained that it was intended to protect the Church's interests in Germany.[138]

The inability of the concordat to protect the German Church quickly became clear. On July 30, the first steps were taken to dissolve the Catholic Youth League.[139] This same month the Nazis began serious enforcement of their racial laws. Jewish people were fired from civil service jobs. Within a month Nazis were arresting large numbers of Jews and political prisoners (primarily Communists and Socialists) and sending them to concentration camps for infractions such as insulting the state, offending storm troopers, or consorting with German girls. Hitler's chief negotiator Vice Chancellor Franz von Papen wrote in 1945: "Hitler sabotaged the Concordat."[140]

On August 28, 1933, the German Catholic bishops issued a joint pastoral letter to be read from the pulpits of all Catholic Churches in the nation. Quoting from the Gospel of Matthew, the letter said that: "the messengers of Christianity are to be the 'salt of the earth,' and 'the light of the world,' and 'should let their light shine before the people.' The Church should be as 'a city on the hill,' visible from afar in the life of the people."[141] Hitler responded on September 11 that he was not against Christianity itself, "but we will fight for the sake of keeping our public life free from those priests who have failed their calling and who should have become politicians rather than clergymen."[142] Four days later, proving that words had no effect on the Nazis, they passed the Nuremberg Laws, which defined German citizenship and paved the way for later anti-Semitic laws.[143]

As the National Socialists became more confident of their control in Germany, persecution of Catholic officials increased. In May and June 1934, S.S. Chief Heinrich Himmler circulated a fifty page memorandum on the religious bodies in the Reich. Under the heading "Hostile Clergy," it reported:

> The most dangerous activity of countless Catholic clergy is the way in which they 'mope about', spreading despondency. Favorite topics are the 'dangers of a new time', 'the present emergency', 'the gloomy future'. Prophecies are made about the speedy downfall of National Socialism or at the very least mention is made of the transience of all political phenomena, compared with the Catholic Church which will outlive them all. National Socialist achievements and successes are passed over in silence.
> There is thus a deliberated undermining of the very basis of the National Socialist programme of reconstruction, the people's trust in the leadership of the state.[144]

Before long Hitler had anti-Nazi Catholic priests imprisoned on immorality charges. Hundreds of priests and Catholic officials were arrested or driven into exile, while others were accused of violating currency regulations or morality rules (including sexual abuse of minors).[145] Erich Klausener, leader of Catholic Action, was murdered in a June 1934 purge. Between April 1, 1933 and June 1936, the Vatican filed more than fifty protests against the Nazis. Even before the concordat was ratified, the Vatican had made many objections to German officials regarding treatment of the Church.[146] (German foreign secretary Joachim von Ribbentrop testified at Nuremberg that he had a "whole deskfull of protests" from Rome.)[147] The first one, dated April 1, 1933, regarding the anti-Jewish boycott, and the ninth one, filed on September 9, 1933, asking for protection of Jews converted to Catholicism, were among the forty-five which Hitler never bothered to answer.[148]

The Vatican issued so many complaints regarding violations of the concordat that by 1938, the Nazis were trying to disavow the concordat. On February 17, 1938, *Das Schwarze Korps*, the official paper of the S.S., contained an article protesting that the concordat presupposed the old Germany resting upon a federation of States, a party system, and a liberal outlook. The argument continued that since this agreement was based largely on the Weimar Constitution of 1918, not the Third Reich of Adolf Hitler, a number of clauses were obsolete. As such, the concordat was out of date, and should be abandoned.[149] The article argued that in 1933 Hitler had expected the moral support of the Church in his work of national reconstruction, but he had not received this support. Instead, pastoral letters, sermons, pamphlets, and encyclicals had insulted the Government. Later, Hitler vowed to end the concordat following the war, saying "it will give me the greatest personal pleasure to point out to the Church all those occasions on which it has broken the terms of it."[150]

*****

In June 1933, shortly after the Vatican signed the concordat with Germany, another religion attempted to forge a working relationship with the new regime. On the 11th of that month, the Nazis put into place a law prohibiting the International Bible Students Union and its subsidiaries because of agitation by the Jehovah's Witnesses against the state.[151] In response, on the 25th, the Jehovah's Witnesses convened a hastily organized convention at the Sporthalle Wilmersdorf in Berlin. Some 5,000 delegates attended.

Like Catholics, the Jehovah's Witnesses were internationalists in a religious sense. They were also generally tolerant of other races, regarded secular authority as evil, and were openly anti-militaristic. They expressed the view that: "Being no part of the world, we take no part in the wars of the nations."[152] All of these factors caused the nationalistic, racist, and militaristic Nazis to despise them. Thus, with Hitler's ascent to power, the government unleashed an immediate wave of persecution against the Jehovah's Witnesses. The 1933 convention was an attempt to bring an end to this persecution so that the Witnesses could go on doing their work.

The Sporthalle was bedecked with Swastika flags for the convention, and the representatives adopted a "Declaration of Facts" (*"Erklärung"*), which attempted to assure the new government that it would receive full cooperation from the Jehovah's Witnesses. Among the most controversial provisions were the following:

> It is falsely charged by our enemies that we have received financial support for our work from the Jews. Nothing is farther from the truth. Up to this hour there has never been the slightest amount of money contributed to our work by Jews. We are faithful followers of Christ Jesus and believe upon Him as the Savior of the world, whereas Jews entirely reject Jesus Christ and emphatically deny that he is the Savior of the world sent of God for man's good. This of itself should be sufficient proof to show that we receive no support from Jews and that therefore the charges against us are maliciously false and could proceed only from Satan, our great enemy.
>
> The greatest and most oppressive empire on earth is the Anglo-American empire. By that is meant the British Empire, of which the United States of America forms a part. It has been the commercial Jews of the British-American empire that have built up and carried on Big Business as a means of exploiting and oppressing the peoples of many nations.
>
> ***
>
> Instead of being against the principles advocated by the government of Germany, we stand squarely for such principles....
>
> ***
>
> The people of Germany have suffered great misery since 1914 and have been the victims of much injustice practiced upon them by others. The nationalists have declared themselves against all such unrighteousness and announced that 'Our relationship to God is high and holy.'
>
> ***
>
> We therefore appeal to the high sense of justice of the government and nation and respectfully ask that the order of prohibition against our work and our literature be set aside, and the opportunity be given us to have a fair hearing before we are judged.

Over 2 million copies of the Declaration were printed, and each delegate was asked to help distribute 250 copies to judges, mayors, and other government officials.

The cover letter mailed to Hitler blamed "clerical, especially Catholic, quarters" for the untrue charges that had been made against the Witnesses, and said that "commercialistic Jews and

Catholics" in the United States were "the most eager persecutors of
our Society's work."[153] The letter expressly rejected "the slanderous
claim that the Bible Students are supported by Jews," and went on to
say that the "Bible Students are fighting for the same high, ethical
goals and ideals" expressed by the National Government. "Respecting
the purely religious and apolitical goals and objectives of the Bible
Students, it can be said that these are in compete harmony with the
similar goals of the National Government of the German Reich." The
letter then delved into politics which might have been attractive to
Hitler. It argued that the "Anglo-American World Empire...—especially England—is to be held responsible for the League of Nations and
the unjustified treaties and burdens placed on Germany."[154]

On June 27, 1933, one day after they began sending copies of the
Declaration by registered mail to German officials, the Prussian state
banned Jehovah's Witnesses, and the police began to carry out widespread raids on their homes and places of business. The next day,
the Society's property was seized and occupied. Their printing plant
was closed on orders of the government. The Jehovah's Witnesses'
property at Magdeburg was confiscated, and the staff of 180 was
forced to leave. Hitler declared: "I dissolve the 'Earnest Bible
Students' in Germany; their property I dedicate to the people's welfare; I will have all their literature confiscated."[155] Between two and
three million marks worth of Watch Tower books, booklets, paintings,
Bibles, and other material was confiscated and destroyed by the
Nazis.[156]

Never again did the Jehovah's Witnesses seek to curry the favor of
the National Socialist regime.[157] The Watch Tower Society henceforth
opposed Nazi policies, refusing to take up arms and remaining strictly *neutral* towards the government.[158] For this, the Witnesses were
required to wear a marker similar to the Star of David worn by the
Jews. Eventually, more than 2,000 Jehovah's Witnesses were sent to
concentration camps.[159] A total of 635 died in prison (203 of these
were actually executed, the rest died due to the harsh conditions).[160]
The 1934 Jehovah's Witness Yearbook reported: "The Papal hierarchy
is really behind of the persecution of God's people in Germany." In
reality, however, the Witnesses were imprisoned for two primary reasons: They refused to take up arms, and they had loyalties to another, higher regime.

*****

The Catholic Church did not normally interfere with what it considered to be the internal matters of another sovereign nation. It was, however, fundamentally opposed to racist theories. In 1928, the Vatican issued a statement declaring that the Church "just as it reproves all rancours in conflicts between peoples, to the maximum extent [*quam maxime*] condemns hatred of the people once chosen by God, the hatred that commonly goes by the name of anti-Semitism."[161] In 1938, Pius XI wrote a letter instructing those in the universities and seminaries to "make use of biology, history, philosophy, apologetics, legal and moral studies as weapons for refuting firmly and completely the... untenable assertions" of race and state put forth by the Nazis.[162] The Pope wanted racial theories to be scientifically refuted so that the clergy would be able to oppose them on rational as well as religious grounds.

German bishops continually complained, either individually or as a collective group, about concordat violations and Nazi policies.[163] Despite assurances to the contrary, Hitler launched a strong campaign to separate churches from schools and youth organizations.[164] He threatened to remove children from parents who refused to follow a Nazi program. "We shall rear them as needful for the Fatherland," he said during one storm trooper review.[165] In 1933, 65 percent of Munich parents sent their children to Catholic schools. By 1937, it was only three percent.[166] Hundreds of Catholic schools were converted to secular institutions. Secretary of State Pacelli, in a formal protest, asserted that "a planned attack is in progress against the Catholic schools."[167]

Once organized religion had served its purpose, Hitler wanted to bring it to an end as quietly as possible. His theory was that religion would simply disappear if he brought young people out from under its influence. Accordingly, in December 1933, he issued an order that all church youth groups be dissolved and that all young people be sent to Nazi party youth organizations (the Hitler Youth for boys; the League of German Maidens for girls).[168] All other youth organizations were forbidden to take part in organized sports, wear uniforms, or march in formation. This legislation led to some violent clashes between the Catholic Boy Scouts and the Hitler Youth.[169]

Weekly meetings of the Hitler Youth were held on Sunday mornings, which prevented children from going to church services. In those cases where churches were permitted to conduct youth activities, Gestapo regulations were often formulated so that actual compliance was impossible. To receive permission to hold outings, for instance, churches had to submit a list of participants, their dates of birth, whether they belonged to the Hitler Youth, how long the activity would last, where it would take place, and a detailed description of what was planned.[170] This application had to be submitted months in advance of the planned outing, and "Hitler Youths" were not permitted to attend unless they had written permission from their Hitler Youth leader. Such rules virtually eliminated church-related youth groups. Cardinal Pacelli, speaking to a representative of the Reich government, said: "We are very much afraid that a German religion could arise."[171]

In October 1933, Hitler pulled Germany out of the League of Nations, withdrew from the disarmament conference, and committed himself to rearming Germany. Hitler justified these moves by claiming that Germany had been treated unfairly under international policies. "The men who today lead Germany have nothing in common with the traitors of 1918 " who signed the Treaty of Versailles, argued Hitler.[172] The next month he offered German voters a referendum, but since all other political parties had been outlawed, no opposition appeared on the ballot and the Nazis captured about 93 percent of the vote.

While Pacelli tried to moderate tensions between the Pope and German officials, his private writings and letters from the mid-1930s reveal the horror he felt toward Nazism. He referred to Nazis as "false prophets with the pride of Lucifer," and "bearers of a new faith and a new gospel."[173] For a religious man and future Pope, there could not be a more damning charge. For their part, the Nazi press published a drawing showing Cardinal Pacelli embracing an unattractive French communist Jewish woman. To the Nazis, there were few allegations that could have been more offensive.

Throughout the rest of 1933, the Nazis concentrated their power. In November they took over the largest press in Germany. In December the storm troopers became an official arm of the Reich. Four hundred thousand "imperfect" Germans were identified for the sterilization program, which was condemned by Pope Pius XI. The year was such that the Nobel Committee decided not to award a Peace Prize.

CHAPTER SIX

WORLD UNREST

In mid-June 1934, Hitler surprised the world by announcing that Germany would not pay its remaining foreign debts. World reaction was restrained, so Hitler was able to help shore up the German economy without creating new international problems. That same month he also acted to secure his political power within Germany.

June 30, 1934 came to be known as the Night of the Long Knives. In one night, Hitler eliminated his rivals with over a hundred summary executions.[1] Hitler's storm troopers, the S.A., had been indispensable to Nazi might, but Hitler feared that they had evolved into a personal army for Captain Ernst Roehm, S.A. Chief of Staff.[2] Roehm was now the greatest threat to Hitler's power. In addition, German military leaders were unwilling to submit to Hitler's rule until he assured them that the army, not the S.A., would be the primary military force in Germany.

Hitler claimed that the storm troopers were poised to stage a revolt and suggested that they might have been working with Russia. (Roehm, according to some accounts, was now demanding a "second revolution" that would make good on Nazi claims to socialist ideals.)[3] Hitler also circulated the rumor that Roehm was plotting his assassination. In retaliation for these offenses—real or imagined—Hitler had Roehm executed.[4] Although Hitler had previously accepted Roehm's homosexual activity,[5] Nazis now circulated the story that he had been found in a compromising position with another man. Karl Ernst, leader of the Berlin storm troopers, was also murdered. Former Chancellor Kurt von Schleicher and his wife were both killed, supposedly because they resisted arrest. More than a hundred other officials and storm troopers were also slain or committed suicide.

Hitler used this opportunity to rid himself of Catholic opposition leaders. Erich Klausener, president of the Berlin Catholic Action and a known opponent of Nazism, was shot and killed. Dr. Edgar Jung, another leader of Catholic Action, was also killed. Adalbert Probst, president of the Sporting Association of German Catholics, was summoned to Berlin under a pretext. His wife received his ashes in the mail a few days later. Michael Gerlich, editor of one of the most widely read Catholic newspapers in Germany, *Der gerade Weg*, was found dead in prison. The bishops' palaces in Würzburg, Rottenburg, and Mainz were sacked, and shortly thereafter more than 500 priests and religious were arrested, many of whom died in jail.[6]

Prior to the Night of the Long Knives, three German bishops (Wilhelm Berning, Conrad Gröber, and Nikolaus Bares) met with Hitler to try to establish a better line of communications between the Church and German leadership.[7] On June 29, the bishops and German negotiators completed a draft agreement which appeared to work out many of the disputes that existed over matters such as the proper role for Catholic youth groups and Catholic lay organizations. Following the bloodshed that came with the Nazi rampage, however, Pope Pius XI vetoed any such accord.[8]

While the S.A. was not disbanded following the Night of the Long Knives, it was relieved of most of its powers. Power had been promised to the military, but Hitler betrayed them and instead gave it to the executive arm of the National Socialists, the black-shirted *Reichsführer S.S.* (*Schützstaffel*) headed by Heinrich Himmler.[9] The S.S. was an elite corps of men who were bound together by their racial and elitist self-understanding. Rather than pledging themselves to the Reich, members of the S.S. were devoted exclusively to Hitler. "Every Catholic in Germany was keenly aware that the elite S.S. would not even admit Catholics—only those who repudiated the Church."[10] These were the men who would later organize the concentration camps and direct the Nazi effort to exterminate the Jews.

Explaining his "blood purge" in a speech shortly thereafter, Hitler said, "Everyone must know for all future time that if he raises his hand to strike the state then certain death is his lot."[11] Any remaining limitation on Hitler's power ended in August with President von Hindenburg's death. Hindenburg had held Hitler in check at least twice in the past. Now there truly were no limits. The role of Kaiser, President, Parliament, and Chancellor were all now filled by one man. With his new powers, Hitler could make war and peace, create and abolish laws, execute suspects and pardon convicts. He was both legislator and executive, and he would reshape the courts in his image as well.[12]

*****

In the Soviet Union too, political upheaval defined the times. After vanquishing first their Trotskyite rivals and then, by 1929, the Bukharinites, Stalin and his followers were ready to put their plans into full swing. On December 27, 1929, Stalin announced the goal of the liquidation of the *kulaks* (wealthier peasants) as a class. It is estimated that about 13 million people were rounded up and shot or deported. "Deportation" meant that those who were considered "class enemies" were packed into cattle cars and shipped to Russia's Arctic wasteland, where almost certain death awaited them.[13]

In the Ukraine, seven million people were starved to death on the Kremlin's orders. Farmers who took grain or vegetables from their own land were shot. Dead bodies littered the streets of Kharkov, the capital. "It was," eyewitnesses later recalled, "as if the Black Death had passed through."[14] Before he was through, Stalin would be responsible for twenty million deaths.[15] According to the head of the parliamentary commission on rehabilitation, "from 1929 to 1953... 21.5 million people were repressed. Of these a third were shot, the rest sentenced to imprisonment where many also died."[16]

While the Soviets were eliminating their "undesirables," they were also waging an all-out battle against the source of most peasants' strength: the Church. In 1929, a law was passed that strengthened the State's control over the parishes.[17] Propagation of religion now became a crime against the state.[18] Priests and their families were deprived of civil rights. As "disenfranchised persons," they did not have the right to ration cards, medical aid, or communal apartments. Many prelates were arrested, tortured, and killed.[19] The children of clergy were not allowed to attend schools or higher educational institutions.[20] Thus, they were forced to renounce their parents in order to obtain an education, if not simply to live.

Hundreds of churches of all denominations were destroyed, including many of historical significance. The churches that survived had their bells removed, so that their ringing would not disturb the workers. Very few Catholic churches in Russia at the time of the revolution survived, and they were maintained mainly to convince foreign visitors that there was still religious freedom in the Soviet Union.[21]

Although Soviet abuses were not widely known until after the war, those in the Vatican had good information. In 1930, Pope Pius XI published an open letter protesting "the horrible and sacrilegious outrages being perpetrated against the Catholic Church in Russia."[22] He specifically noted the murders of priests, the moral blackmail of workers, and the indoctrination of and moral corruption of children. As Vatican Secretary of State, Cardinal Pacelli knew of these Soviet abuses.[23] This knowledge created a problem a few years later when Stalin's Soviet Union joined the Allies in the war against Hitler's Germany, and Pacelli—as Pope Pius XII—had to make difficult decisions concerning the allegiance of his church.

CHAPTER SEVEN

HITLER BATTLES THE CHURCHES

On January 13, 1935, the German inhabitants of the coal-rich Saarland, occupied by the French since the end of the First World War, voted on a return to Germany. There had been some doubt about whether an overwhelmingly Catholic state, comprised mainly of miners and industry workers, would choose to return to a Germany run by a dictator who had crushed trade unions, harassed the Church, and destroyed the democratic republic. The inhabitants, however, resented being held captive by occupying forces even more. With support from local Catholic authorities, they voted 477,000 to 48,000 to return.[1] On March 1, France transferred the Saarland back to Germany in the hopes of appeasing Hitler.

When German troops marched into the Saar, they were enthusiastically greeted, and the feeling was reciprocated. Hitler proudly welcomed the inhabitants of the Saarland back to Germany. In a radio broadcast from Berlin, he promised the world that with the return of the Saar he had no further territorial claims on France.[2] This was important to the French because they thought that it meant he had dropped his claim to Alsace and Lorraine, which had been areas of dispute between the two countries.

Three days after the transfer of the Saarland, citing Germany's aggressive behavior and rearmament, Great Britain announced a new intensified defense policy.[3] This, however, did not slow Hitler down. By mid-month, Germany declared that it was reinstating the military draft. This was a clear breach of the Treaty of Versailles, but the German press hailed the move. Mussolini followed with expanded conscription the next week.

The world situation was in such an unstable state that in October 1934 Pius XI dispatched Pacelli to be his legate to the Eucharistic Congress in Buenos Aires.[4] This broke a tradition that had kept the Vatican Secretary of State close to home for well over a century, but sending the Vatican's most-trusted representative signified the Vatican's deep concern about world events. (Pius XI also told others that he was sending Pacelli around the world because he would one day be Pope.)[5]

It was reported during the war that the Catholic Church severed ties with the Third Reich in 1935.[6] Certainly Pacelli had recognized the evilness of Nazism by this time. In a letter dated March 12, 1935, to Cardinal Carl Joseph Schulte of Cologne, Pacelli referred to the Nazis as "false prophets with the pride of Lucifer," and "bearers of a new Faith and a new Evangile," who were attempting to create a "mendacious antimony between faithfulness to the Church and to the Fatherland."[7] (There are also reports from this time of Pacelli privately referring to the new regime in Germany as "diabolical.")[8] According to one commentator, "the gradual divorce between Church and state was a painful process."[9] The pain seems mainly to have been imposed on the Church. As the Nazis became more certain of their political strength, the persecution of the Church and religious people intensified.

By 1935, Church leaders in Germany were being subjected to physical violence; hundreds of priests and other Church officials were arrested, driven into exile, accused of immorality, or charged with violating currency regulations.[10] In July, Minister of State Adolf Wagner said: "In the days that lie immediately ahead of us the fight will not be against either Communists or Marxists, but against Catholicism. Everyone will find himself faced with the serious question: German or Catholic? This struggle will not be easy."[11]

Catholics were forbidden to hold public meetings, even for purely religious purposes.[12] Convent nuns were declared redundant, and some six hundred teaching nuns were told to seek civilian employment. Church properties were ransacked, Catholic meetings were broken up, and scurrilous stories appeared in the Nazi press. Attempts by the Nazis to remove crucifixes from schools in Bavaria led to such an outcry that several local officials rescinded the orders.[13]

The Nazi press was quite outspoken in its opposition to the Catholic Church. *Deutsche Volkskirche*, a Nazi political magazine, reported on an episcopal conference as a "devilish beginning," to various "treasonable activities" by "these Jewish-Roman Jehovah priests."[14] One passage said: "All accommodation between the Roman Church and National Socialism is impossible; there can only be a struggle for victory or defeat."[15] Another article in *Völkischer Beobachter* reported that the "Catholic Congress" held in Prague on

June 30, 1935, was designed to arrange for closer cooperation between Catholicism and Bolshevism.[16] The following day, the same paper reported that the Vatican was negotiating with the Soviet Union for a concordat.[17] Even the magazine of the Hitler Youth tried to smear the Church by claiming it was closely associated with Communism.[18]

Cardinal Michael von Faulhaber of Munich was an early critic of the Third Reich. He wrote Secretary of State Pacelli, describing the persecution of the Jews as "unjust and painful."[19] He was especially troubled that "also those [Jews] who have been baptized for ten or twenty years and are good Catholics, even those whose parents were already Catholic, are still legally considered to be Jews, and are to lose their positions as physicians or lawyers."[20] Nevertheless, he did not want to engage in direct confrontation with the Nazi authorities. He cautioned Pacelli that for the time being it was impossible to oppose the government on the racial question because of the threat that it would present to his Catholic followers.[21] Such requests for silence, from those Catholic leaders closest to the situation inside Nazi Germany, helped shape Pacelli's thinking on this matter in the future.

*****

As world attention was drawn to the events in Germany, the Nazis promised to stop their campaign of hatred against Jews, Catholics, and "reactionaries."[22] Reports out of Germany, however, were not promising, especially for the Jews. Prior to Hitler's rise to power, Jewish people in Germany were treated as well, if not better, than they were in any other European nation.[23] Things had deteriorated with the early boycott of Jewish businesses and limitations on entry to professions, but the situation was about to get even worse.

A series of laws promulgated at the Nazi party meeting in Nuremberg in September 1935 essentially segregated Jews from the rest of the German people.[24] These "Nuremberg race laws" held that people with one Jewish grandparent were not allowed to call themselves German. Jewish speech, newspapers, and even prayers were censored. Lest the race be further "defiled," marriage between Jews and other Germans was prohibited. Laws were enacted which prohibited Jews from settling in some German towns. Aryan Germans were forbidden from cooperating with Jewish people, and purchasing goods from a Jewish merchant was considered treason. Needless to say, many Jewish businesses were driven into bankruptcy. Vatican Radio condemned the injustice and inhumanity of these new laws.[25]

In September, Hitler announced that Jews were not entitled to vote or participate in German politics. In addition, Jews were prohibited from employing German women under the age of forty-five, raising the German flag, or dating Aryans (arrests of Aryan girls who mixed with Jewish boys resulted in both being sent to concentration camps for the crime of "race defiling.")[26] Plans were even announced to buy out all Jewish businesses, though it seems unlikely that a true purchase was ever seriously contemplated.

One right still allowed to German Jews was emigration, and 150,000 (30 percent of Germany's Jewish population) did so between January 1933 and November 1938.[27] By 1939, eighty percent of Jewish people under the age of forty had left.[28] (Unfortunately, as it turned out, thousands of German Jews fled to Poland.[29]) In 1936, Vatican Secretary of State Pacelli established an organization to help Jewish refugees as they fled from Nazism.[30]

Within Germany, the Catholic Church took a leading role in opposing the racial laws. On February 9, 1936, Bishop Galen of Münster made a speech at Xanten which became very well known. In it, he said:

> There are fresh graves in German soil in which are lying the ashes of those whom the Catholic people regard as martyrs for the Faith, since their lives gave witness to their most dutiful and loyal devotion to God and the Fatherland, to the nation and the Church, while the dark secrecy which surrounds their deaths is most carefully preserved.[31]

The Nazis fought back, protesting that while Catholic priests should thank God that the National Socialists had swept away "the Jewish-Bolshevist underworld," they were instead sheltering "the corrupters of our race."[32]

Catholic leaders outside of Germany also condemned the racial laws. Polish Cardinal Augustyn Hlond spoke of "the very many Jews who are believers, honest, just, kind, and philanthropic... who are ethically outstanding, noble and upright." Cardinal Hlond continued: "I am against that moral stance, imported from abroad, that is basically and ruthlessly anti-Jewish." He then spoke of Catholic teaching on anti-Semitism: "It is contrary to Catholic ethics. One may not hate anyone. It is forbidden to assault, beat up, maim, or slander Jews.

One should honor Jews as human beings and neighbors.... Beware of those who are inciting anti-Jewish violence. They serve an evil cause."[33]

The protests grew so common that the Nazis accused the Catholic Church of acting on behalf of the Jews.[34] Hermann Goering complained that:

> Catholic believers carry away but one impression from attendance at divine services and that is that the Catholic Church rejects the institutions of the Nationalist State. How could it be otherwise when they are continuously engaging in polemics on political questions or events in their sermons... hardly a Sunday passes but that they abuse the so-called religious atmosphere of the divine service in order to read pastoral letters on purely political subjects.[35]

Adolf Wagner, Bavarian Minister of the Interior, said "there will be no peace in Germany until all the political priests are driven out and exterminated."[36]

Many still find it hard to understand how Hitler could have convinced an advanced, industrial nation like Germany to follow his outlandish racial theories, but the same month that he imposed these new racial laws (September 1935), he was also able to announce that the jobless rate had fallen from six million to one million.[37] Strict economic controls caused a short-term expansion in the economy, and living standards improved dramatically. Five years earlier there had been daily rioting in the streets, life savings were wiped out overnight by inflation, and no one had a job. Now unemployment was virtually eliminated; industrial production soared; inflation was under control; and the economy, fueled by expenditures for rearmament and public works, flourished.[38] Hitler had also provided national health and child care, an end to riots, and a strengthened military.[39] Germans, in fact, enjoyed the highest standard of living in all of Europe.[40] (As late as 1951, forty-two percent of adult West Germans and fifty-three percent of those over thirty-five believed that the pre-war years of the Third Reich were the "best" that Germany had experienced in this century.)[41] Even in the British Parliament, National Socialism was hailed as Europe's only protection against the spread of Communism.[42] Such things would never begin to justify Hitler's evil actions, but they might help to explain the difficulty Germans would have had in challenging him. And, of course, those who did challenge

him (including many priests and ministers) were immediately arrested and frequently executed.

*****

As Hitler shaped German minds to his way of thinking, he imposed
his will in many different areas. He made sports compulsory in all
schools. Non-belief in Nazism was made grounds for divorce. Two
great enemies of Nazism were joined together as Germans were called
upon to resist "Jewish Bolshevization."[43] As countries around the
globe pointed fingers at Germany, Hitler condemned the Soviet Union
as an instigator of war. He also tightly controlled the media.

Hitler used the most modern medium, radio, to its fullest advantage. Nazi leadership saw this as the most effective way to influence
the masses. German radio quickly became the voice of the Nazi party,
as the airwaves were flooded with speeches by or about Hitler and
National Socialism. (Jazz music—a free form of expression—was
banned.)[44] To assure wide dissemination of Nazi propaganda, Hitler
ordered the production of small, cheap radios. By the end of the
decade, seventy percent of German families owned radios, the highest
percentage in the world.[45]

In the early 1930s, Hitler's homeland of Austria was experiencing
social upheaval on an only slightly smaller scale than Germany had
in the preceding years. Hundreds of rioting workers in Vienna were
killed when the Austrian army attacked them with machine guns and
howitzers.[46] The Socialist mayor of Vienna was placed under arrest,
as were many other party leaders. As reports began to circulate that
Hitler would annex Austria, leaders in Britain, France, and Italy
issued a joint statement calling for Austrian independence.

Austria was ripe for exploitation, and it came first from within.
Chancellor Engelbert Dollfuss suspended parliamentary government
in March 1933 and put in place a revised constitution largely based
on Mussolini's ideas of a corporate state. In April 1934, perhaps
inspired by Hitler's actions the year before, Dollfuss seized full dictatorial powers. He had the authority to send anyone suspected of
working for an outlawed political party to a concentration camp without a trial.[47] Spies and informers were used to keep tabs on the people. The diminutive chancellor at one point even ordered an end to
jokes about his size.

On July 25, 1934, less than a month after the Night of the Long Knives (and shortly after the Holy See and Austria had signed a concordat),[48] Austrian Nazis took the government by surprise, murdered Dollfuss, and held the Austrian Cabinet hostage.[49] The rebels were soon arrested, however, and the attempted takeover collapsed when Mussolini (a long-time protector of Austria) dispatched troops to the Austrian border. Nevertheless, the Nazis obtained what they sought—increased political power.

In February 1935, Hitler met with Dollfuss' successor, Kurt Schuschnigg, who was bullied into signing a written agreement.[50] A few days later, several Nazis were put in high positions within the Austrian government. Within a week, Hitler demanded self-determination for Germans in Austria and Czechoslovakia. On February 22nd, the Austrian Nazi party chief and seventy-two aides were arrested and charged with conspiracy to overthrow the Austrian government. This set the stage for serious conflicts to come a few years down the line.

Hitler's aggression in Austria did not go unnoticed. Secretary of State Pacelli had predicted the Austria would be the Nazis' first victim.[51] Following Dollfuss' assassination, the Vatican newspaper ran three articles in which National Socialism was equated with national terrorism and said to have come from a gang and not a party.[52]

*****

In February 1936, Hitler presided at the inaugural of the Volkswagen factory at Fallersleben, Saxony.[53] Modeled on Henry Ford's concept of cars for common people, Hitler hoped to emulate Ford's success with this new "people's car." (He had already laid out plans for a 900 mile long, nation-wide highway system.) In addition to providing employment and a consumer product that was popular with the masses, the automotive industry gave Hitler large factories that could be used to build military vehicles. It was almost impossible to determine whether an automotive plant was tooled to produce engines for Volkswagens or to produce airplane engines. When these factories began building planes, they were already equipped to do so; British factories required much more time for retooling.[54]

In early 1936, Nazi Minister of Propaganda Joseph Goebbels declared that "The German people are a truly poor nation. We have no colonies and no raw materials."[55] He warned that Germany would soon need new territories.[56] In March 1936, one year after Hitler re-established obligatory military service in violation of the Treaty of Versailles, the German army entered the Rhineland. His generals argued that the move would be suicidal, but Hitler disagreed. He claimed that the move was necessary due to the recently completed mutual assistance pact between France and the Soviet Union and similar discussions between France and Great Britain. World leaders condemned the move, but Hitler told adoring crowds that Germany needed only to please God and itself.[57]

In retrospect, this might have been a prime opportunity to stop Hitler's expansionist plans. France's Prime Minister and Foreign Minister both urged the Commander of the French Army, General Maurice Gamelin, to eject the Germans.[58] Gamelin, however, overestimated German manpower and was unwilling to take on such a force. British Prime Minister Anthony Eden later said that this was the act of appeasement which he most regretted. (Vatican Secretary of State Pacelli told the French Ambassador that France should have opposed this violation of international agreements.)[59]

*****

From the time he wrote *Mein Kampf*, Hitler regarded organized religion as indispensable to his politics. He needed influence in the churches because he thought it impossible to replace churches with party ideology.[60] He did, however, feel that Christian churches could learn to adapt to the political goals of National Socialism, as they had previously adapted to other political realities. In his March 23, 1933 speech to the Reichstag, Hitler paid tribute to the Christian faiths as "essential elements for safeguarding the soul of the German people," promising to respect the churches' rights, and declaring that his government's "ambition is a peaceful accord between Church and State."[61]

One of Hitler's favorite stories about religion came to him from a delegation of visiting Arabs.[62] They told him that when the Muslims attempted to penetrate beyond France into Central Europe during the eighth century, they were driven back at the Battle of Tours. Had the Arabs won this battle, they said, Germany would be Muslim today. Moreover, much of the world probably would also have been converted, for their religion at that time believed in spreading the faith by the sword and subjugating all nations.

This prospect intrigued Hitler. Such an approach to religion was, he thought, perfectly suited to the Germanic temperament. Hitler felt that the conquering Arabs, because of their racial inferiority, would have been unable to contend with the harsher climate and conditions of Germany. They could not have kept down the more vigorous Aryans, so Islamized Germans would ultimately have led a Muslim German Empire. Hitler often concluded his historical speculation by stating:

> You see, it's been our misfortune to have the wrong religion. Why didn't we have the religion of the Japanese, who regard sacrifice for the Fatherland as the highest good? The Muhammadan religion too would have been much more compatible to us than Christianity. Why did it have to be Christianity with its meekness and flabbiness?[63]

Clearly, the theory of the religion did not much matter, only the possibility of exploiting it. If Christianity was not to his liking, he would change it.

Hitler was born a Catholic, but since Protestants comprised two thirds of the citizens of Germany, he knew that he had to keep them loyal. In 1934 he told a group of Protestant church leaders that inwardly he felt closest to the Evangelical Church.[64] Despite his professed admiration for all Aryans, Hitler had little respect for the German masses. "You can do anything you want to them," he once said about devout Protestants. "They will submit... they are insignificant little people, submissive as dogs, and they sweat with embarrassment when you talk to them."[65] He was also able to tap into certain anti-Semitic teachings of Martin Luther.

Like Hitler, Luther was a ferocious believer in absolute obedience to political authority. (In *Mein Kampf*, Hitler called Luther one of the great heroes of the German people.)[66] Luther wanted to convert Jews to Christianity, but when he failed he developed strong anti-Semitic feelings. He wrote a book entitled *On the Jews and Their Lies,* which was a favorite of the Nazis.[67] In it, he expressed his desire to rid Germany of its Jews, take their wealth, and he further instructed: "that their synagogues or schools be set on fire, that their houses be broken up and destroyed... and they be put under a roof or stable, like the gypsies... in misery and captivity as they incessantly lament and complain to God about us."[68] He wrote that the Jews have been for 1400 years and still remain "our plague, our pestilence, and our misfortune."[69] The Nazis circulated statements like this, as Italian Fascists cited anti-Semitic statements from the Jesuit periodical *La Civiltà Cattolica,*[70] to argue that their political philosophy was not completely inconsistent with Christianity. Besides, that would not have mattered to Hitler anyway. He once said: "The heaviest blow to humanity was the coming of Christianity. Bolshevism is Christianity's illegitimate child. Both are inventions of the Jews."[71]

The Nazis hoped eventually to replace organized religion with their own brand of "Nazi Christianity."[72] The most extreme version of this was set forth in a 1930 book by Alfred Rosenberg called *The Myth of the Twentieth Century.*[73] The book, published by Hocheneichen-Verlag Press (owned by Hitler),[74] was a cross between the Bible and *Mein Kampf.* It was very anti-Semitic, strongly anti-Papal (it was censured by the Vatican),[75] and anti-Christian in spirit. Rosenberg argued that Germany was surrounded by enemies and had been infiltrated by Jews seeking to destroy the Aryan race and by Christians who were draining Germany's national pride. According to Rosenberg, Germany's honor was constantly at odds with the forces of internationalism, including the Christian churches, especially the Catholic Church which had been "judaized and asianized"[76] Rosenberg mocked the Pope as "an infallible God; a medicine man; papacy is servitude," and he argued that "the Christian-Jewish plague must perish."[77]

The Myth of the Twentieth Century sold hundreds of thousands of copies. It was widely regarded as the standard text for party ideology.[78] During the war, Rosenberg drew up a thirty-point program for the National Reich Church. The following selected points were certainly sufficient to put any other churches on notice as to where the Nazis stood:

> 1. The National Reich Church of Germany categorically claims the exclusive right and the exclusive power to control all churches within the borders of the Reich: it declares these to be national churches of the German Reich.
> 5. The National Church is determined to exterminate irrevocably... the strange and foreign Christian faiths imported into Germany in the ill-omened year 800.
> 7. The National Church has no scribes, pastors, chaplains or priests, but National Reich orators are to speak in them.

13. The National Church demands immediate cessation of the publishing and dissemination of the Bible in Germany.

18. The National Church will clear away from its altars all cruci-fixes, Bibles, and pictures of saints.

19. On the altar there must be nothing but *Mein Kampf* (to the German nation and therefore to God the most sacred book) and to the left of the altar a sword.

30. On the day of its foundation, the Christian Cross must be removed from all churches, cathedrals and chapels... and it must be superseded by the only unconquerable symbol, the swastika.[79]

Hitler, while approving of the impact that *Myth of the Twentieth Century* had, privately called it "stuff nobody can understand."[80]

When Hitler came to power, there were at least twenty-nine major Protestant Churches.[81] Hitler, however, wanted to have one single organization, probably because it would be easier to influence. As such it was soon decreed that the diverse churches be united into a single "German Evangelical Church."[82] A constitution for the new church was formally recognized by the Reichstag on July 14, 1933. One of the first issues for the new religion was election of the first "Reich Bishop."

The constitution for the new church provided that it would be led by a Lutheran bishop and that there would be a "spiritual cabinet" made of leaders from other denominations who would advise the bish-op.[83] Representatives of the twenty-nine Protestant denominations originally selected Friedrich von Bodelschwingh, a clergyman widely known for his social welfare work. Bodelschwingh had no real politi-cal ties, and the Protestant leaders hoped that he would be satisfac-tory to Hitler.[84] Unfortunately, Ludwig Mueller, an army chaplain and advisor to Hitler, also wanted the post.

Mueller was a member of the German Christians. This "church" had been founded in 1932, with encouragement from the Nazis.[85] (They called themselves the "storm troops of Jesus Christ.")[86] With support from his church, Mueller was able to force a referendum on the new structure of the German Evangelical Church. On the eve of the election of delegates who would ratify the constitution of the new church and select the bishop, Hitler took to the radio to urge the elec-tion of German Christians who supported Mueller. It worked; the German Christians ended up dominating the new church, and Mueller was made Reich Bishop.[87]

Shortly thereafter the German Christians staged a massive rally in Berlin. The Berlin district leader of the German Christians proposed the abandonment of the Old Testament, "with its tales of cattle merchants and pimps," and the revision of the New Testament with the teaching of Jesus "corresponding entirely with the demands of National Socialism."[88] Resolutions were drawn up demanding "One People, One Reich, One Faith," requiring all pastors to take an oath of fealty to Hitler, and insisting that all churches exclude converted Jews.[89]

This dramatic redefinition of Christianity was far too much for many Protestant leaders and led to the formation of the "Pastors' Emergency League." Headed by The Reverend Martin Niemöller, the League was able to limit some of the German Christians' revisions. In particular, the Pastors' Emergency League was able to eliminate the "Aryan Paragraph" (which would have segregated all Christians with any Jewish blood) from the constitution of the new Protestant Church. Still, the whole issue of making Hitler's dogma part of the foundation of a religion caused a major division in the German Protestant Church.[90]

Niemöller's 1933 autobiography, *From U-Boat to Pulpit*, told the story of how he had gone from U-boat commander in World War I to become a prominent Protestant pastor. Niemöller, like many religious leaders, openly supported the Nazis as they gained power in Germany. He also welcomed Hitler to the chancellorship in 1933. At the close of Niemöller's book he added a note of satisfaction that the Nazi revolution had finally triumphed and that it had brought about the "national revival" for which he had so long fought.[91] The book received high praise in the Nazi press and became a best-seller. Niemöller, however, would see things differently in the years to come.

Niemöller became the leader of the "Confessional Church," which sprang up in 1934 in opposition to the German Christians. The Confessional (or Confessing) Church opposed the Nazification of the Protestant churches, rejected Nazi racial theories, and denounced the anti-Christian doctrines of the Nazi leaders.[92] In 1934, the Confessional Church declared itself to be the legitimate Protestant Church of Germany and set up a provisional Church government.[93] Thus there were then two groups—one associated with Bishop Mueller and the other associated with Niemöller—claiming to constitute the Protestant Church in Germany. Shortly after its founding, the Confessional Church included about a third of all Protestant clergymen in Germany. The Nazi government, of course, suppressed the

Confessional Church (250 members were arrested following one serv-ice),[94] and its numbers dropped dramatically. By the end of 1935, the Gestapo had arrested 700 Confessional Church pastors.[95] In 1937, all five members of the Confessional Church's executive committee were arrested. While some members of this church spoke against Hitler, they had no lasting impact.

Confessional Church realists recognized that "any open profession of political opposition to the Nazi state would be imprudent, if not sui-cidal."[96] Nevertheless, many in the clergy thought that a simple con-fession of faith, which questioned certain Nazi theories, but did not challenge Nazi authority, might be acceptable. Thus, in April 1934, the Confessional Church clergy issued the "Barmen Confession," which served as a declaration of the basic beliefs of the Confessional Church.[97]

Perhaps the most important statement in the Barmen Confession was: "We reject the false doctrine that the state, going beyond its spe-cial mandate, should and could become the sole and entire order of human life and thereby also fulfill the vocation of the church."[98] The Barmen Confession also attacked as heretical the suggestion that God is revealed not only in scripture but also in the German people.

Christians who were sympathetic to the Nazis denounced the Barmen Confession, as in the following German Christian response:

> We as believing Christians thank God our Father that he has given to our people in its time of need the *Führer* as a "pious and faithful sovereign," and that he wants to prepare for us in the National Socialist system of government "good rule," a government with "discipline and honor."
>
> Accordingly, we know that we are responsible before God to assist the work of the *Führer* in our calling and in our station in life.[99]

This mixture of religious and political faith in Hitler would secure his power within Germany for many years to come.

Two years after the Barmen Confession, in May 1936, ten promi-nent members of the Confessional Church, including Niemöller, draft-ed a letter to Hitler criticizing the deification of the *Führer* and the totalitarian structure of the Nazi state. They directed a "simple ques-tion" to the leader of the nation, namely: "whether the attempt to de-Christianize the German people, either with the continuing participa-tion of responsible statesmen or merely with their looking on and

doing nothing, is to become the official course of the government."[100]
The letter went on to state:

> If blood, race, nationality, and honor received here the dignity of eter-
> nal values, then the Protestant Christian is compelled by the First
> Commandment to reject this valuation.... If, within the framework of
> the National Socialist view of the world, an anti-Semitism that
> requires hatred of Jews is forced on a Christian, then the Christian
> commandment to love one's neighbor opposes that within him.[101]

One of the drafters later explained that they thought Hitler simply did
not know about the injustices, and that he might put them to an end
if he were informed.[102]

A copy of this letter was smuggled to Switzerland, where it was
leaked to the press. The Nazis then claimed that those who had composed it were disloyal and unpatriotic, and that they were collaborat-
ing with Germany's enemies.[103] Church leaders—even those who had
been critical of the Nazis—rushed to dissociate themselves from the
letter. Several arrests were made, and other church officials were
removed from office. As a result, the Nazis now had complete administrative control over the Evangelical churches. In the end, the letter
had no effect on the Nazis' treatment of German Jews.

Like the others, Niemöller was arrested and put on trial for "agi-
tory" speech, slander, and opposition to government laws. To
Niemöller is credited the famous verse:

> First they came for the Communists and I did not speak out
>   because I was not a Communist.
>
> Then they came for the Socialists and I did not speak out
>   because I was not a Socialist.
>
> Then they game for the trade unionists and I did not speak out
>   because I was not a trade unionist.
>
> Then they came for the Jews and I did not speak out
>   because I was not a Jew.
>
> Then they came for me and there was no one left
>   to speak out for me.[104]

Although he testified at his trial in February 1938 that he disliked
Jews (having preached in 1937 about their "dark and sinister history" and the curse that was upon them for having "brought the Christ
of God to the cross"), he was convicted.[105] In September 1939 he

wrote to Admiral Erich Raeder from the Sachsenhausen concentration camp asking to be released so that he might return to active duty with the armed forces of the Third Reich. "If there is a war," he later explained, "a German doesn't ask is it just or unjust, but he feels bound to join the ranks."[106]

✠✠✠✠✠

The mid-1930s brought indications of war to come. Italy had unsuccessfully attempted to conquer Ethiopia in 1896. In 1935, Mussolini decided to avenge that defeat. He believed that a victory there would strengthen Italy's position in the Middle East. It would also reveal him as a true military leader.

Ethiopia, also called Abyssinia, lay in Africa adjacent to Italian Somaliland. A dispute arose, perhaps manufactured by Mussolini, regarding the border between these two areas. In October 1935, Mussolini made his move. With mechanized troops facing poorly armed Ethiopians, Mussolini's forces did not take long to finish the job. In spite of appeals for help issued by the Ethiopian Emperor, Italian forces captured the capital in May 1936 and Mussolini claimed victory. Over half a million Ethiopians had been killed. Mussolini was then able to unite Ethiopia with the Italian colonies of Eritrea and Italian Somaliland into one large colony which he named Italian East Africa.

During the Ethiopian war, Mussolini controlled the press and invoked the provisions of the Lateran Treaty that provided for Catholic neutrality, thereby silencing any opposition. After the war, the reaction of other countries was a clear example of appeasement. Although the League of Nations briefly imposed an embargo against Italy, it was of little consequence. "Italy at last has her Empire," Mussolini announced. "It is a Fascist empire because it bears the indestructible sign of the will and power of Rome."[107] Ethiopia was formally annexed, and King Victor Emmanuel III of Italy assumed the title of Emperor. Mussolini announced that Italy was now satisfied and ready for peace.

Prior to the invasion, Pius XI called it a "crime so enormous, a manifestation of such folly, that We hold it to be absolutely impossible that nations could again take up arms against each other... But if anyone should dare to commit this heinous crime, which God forbids, then We could not but turn to Him with bitterness in Our hearts, praying *Scatter the peoples who want war.*"[108]   In September, when receiving Catholic hospital workers, the Pontiff spoke of his "unutterable grief" at this "war that is simply one of conquest."[109] Additionally, when Mussolini ordered Rome illuminated to celebrate Italian victories, Pius kept Vatican City dark, drawing criticism from the Fascist press.[110] Nevertheless, Pius was criticized for his "silence" as he prayed for peace during Italy's war on Ethiopia.[111]   Some charged that his silence was due to the benefit that would come to the Church as Italy expanded its sphere of influence.   There were even reports that Pacelli considered resigning as Secretary of State due to his concerns about the Church's neutrality and apparent willingness to profit from Italy's military.[112]   If Pius XI persuaded Pacelli not to resign, he may also have convinced him of the benefits of neutrality in times of war, for this is the model that Pacelli would follow when he became Pope.

*****

In late October, Hitler began establishing alliances that would be important in the event of war. He sent military aid to Franco's rebels in Spain, and the Reich was the first international power to recognize the Italian conquest of Ethiopia. In November, Hungary and Austria both recognized the Italian Empire, and Italy supported Hungary's right to re-arm. That same month, Rome and Berlin both recognized the Franco government in Spain, while the United States abandoned its embassy in Madrid. (Pius wanted to mediate the situation in Spain, where during the thirty months of war, more than 7,000 priests and religious were slaughtered.)[113] The British government warned Hitler that it would fight to protect Belgium. The most important development of late 1936, however, was the formation of the Axis.

In November 1936, Count Galeazzo Ciano visited Hitler. Ciano was Italy's Foreign Minister, as well as Mussolini's son-in-law (husband to his daughter, Edda). The visit resulted in the announcement on November 25th that Germany, Italy, and Japan had signed an anti-Communist pact, pledging cooperation in defending against the spread of Communism. It was called the "Axis," because Mussolini said Europe would revolve on the axis of Germany and Italy.[114] Mussolini urged France and Britain to join in with them.

Hitler often said that he regretted having allied with the "so-called yellow race" and was sorry about the loss of life sustained by the white race in East Asia, but he respected Japan's military power.[115] Mussolini, who at first objected to inclusion of Japan, would later explain that agreement with Japan was "in perfect line with the Tripartite Pact. The Japanese are a proud, loyal people which would not remain indifferent in the face of American aggression against the Axis powers."[116] In Japan, Prince Fumimaro Konoye explained: "It is natural that Germany and Italy, who were making a new order in Europe, should make common cause with Japan. The division of the world into several spheres of co-existence and mutual prosperity would benefit all nations."[117]

Reactions to the Italian alliance with Hitler were mixed inside the Vatican. It meant that Mussolini might have more influence with Hitler, causing Germany to moderate some of its positions. Pius XI was hopeful of such a result. In fact, about a week after the pact was concluded, Mussolini sent a memorandum to Hitler urging, among other things, a detente between the Third Reich and the Holy See.[118] Ultimately, however, Hitler had more success swaying Mussolini than the other way around.

*****

In March 1937, Pius XI issued three encyclicals concerning international relations. Two of them would prove to be of particular importance. In *Divini Redemptoris* (*Of the Divine Redeemer*, although it is better known by its subtitle, *On Atheistic Communism*) he attacked Communism, which was beginning to spread throughout Europe and other parts of the World. He wrote that:

> This Apostolic See, above all, has not refrained from raising its voice, for it knows that its proper and social mission is to defend truth, justice and all those eternal values which Communism ignores or attacks.... With reference to Communism, Our Venerable Predecessor, Pius IX... as early as 1846 pronounced a solemn condemnation... against "that infamous doctrine of so-called Communism which is absolutely contrary to the natural law itself, and if once adopted would utterly destroy the rights, property and possessions of all men, and even society itself." Later on, another of Our predecessors, the immortal Leo XIII, in his Encyclical *Quod Apostolici Muneris*, defined Communism as "the fatal plague which

insinuates itself into the very marrow of human society only to bring about its ruin."[119]

It was clearly an all-out condemnation of this anti-Christian ideology which had long persecuted the Church.

The Pope wrote that Communism was historically evil, that Communist governments were out to destroy religion, were Godless, were violent, denied the individual and the family, and reigned by terror. He also complained that the world press failed to report Communist atrocities. He concluded that "Communism is intrinsically wrong, and no one who would save Christian civilization may collaborate with it in any undertaking whatsoever."[120]

The other important encyclical of this month dealt with Hitler's National Socialism. German bishops had asked the Pope to prepare an encyclical on the problems that the Church was encountering in Germany as early as August 1936. Since Pacelli was the best informed Vatican official on German matters, Pius XI asked him to draft the document.[121] When the German Catholic hierarchy later thanked Pope XI for the encyclical, he politely declined, pointing to Pacelli and saying: "Thank him; he has done everything. From now on, he will deal with everything."[122]

When Secretary of State Pacelli traveled to the United States in 1936, he was asked about the situation in Germany. He immediately went from a hearty laugh to a gesture of helplessness, and said, "Everything is lost."[123] He expressed similar sentiments in the encyclical that he drafted for Pius XI.[124] *Mit brennender Sorge* was one of the strongest condemnations of any national regime that the Holy See ever published. It condemned not only the persecution of the Church in Germany, but also the neo-paganism of Nazi theories. The encyclical stated in part that:

> Whoever exalts race, or the people, or the State, or a particular form of State, or the depositories of power, or any other fundamental value of the human community–however necessary and honorable be their function in worldly things–whoever raises these notions above their standard value and divinizes them to an idolatrous level, distorts and perverts an order of the world planned and created by God; he is far from the true faith in God and from the concept of life which that faith upholds.[125]

The document took a brazen swipe at Hitler and Nazism, when it said:

None but superficial minds could stumble into concepts of a national God, of a national religion; or attempt to lock within the frontiers of a single people, within the narrow limits of a single race, God, the Creator of the universe, King and Legislator of all nations before whose immensity they are "as a drop of a bucket" (Isaiah XI, 15).[126]

The encyclical also praised leaders in the Church who had stood firm against the Nazis and provided a good example. It concluded that "enemies of the Church, who think that their time has come, will see that their joy was premature."[127]

Unlike most encyclicals, which are written in Latin, *Mit brennender Sorge* was written in German for wider dissemination in that country. (120,000 copies were distributed in the Münster diocese alone.)[128] It was smuggled out of Italy and distributed throughout Germany secretly by an army of motorcyclists, where it was copied and distributed to parish priests to be read from all of the pulpits on Palm Sunday, March 12, 1937.[129] No one who heard the Pontifical document read in church could have any illusion about the gravity of these statements or the significance of its having been written.[130]

The only reason *Mit brennender Sorge* was read to anyone was because the Nazis were caught off guard. It was not published in German newspapers. An internal German memorandum dated March 23, 1937, called the encyclical "almost a call to do battle against the Reich government."[131] All available copies were confiscated (though it continued to be passed from one individual to another).[132] German printers who had made copies were arrested and the presses were seized. Those convicted of distributing the encyclical were arrested, the Church-affiliated publications which ran the encyclical were banned, and payments due to the Church under the terms of the concordat were reduced.[133] In fact, the mere mention of this encyclical was a crime in Nazi Germany.[134]

The day following the release of *Mit brennender Sorge*, the Nazi press struck back. The *Völkischer Beobachter* carried a strong counterattack on the "Jew-God and His deputy in Rome."[135] *Das Schwarze Korps* called it "the most incredible of Pius XI's pastoral letters; every sentence in it was an insult to the new Germany."[136] The German ambassador to the Holy See was instructed not to take part in the solemn Easter ceremonies, and German missions throughout Europe were informed by the Nazi Foreign Office of the "Reich's profound indignation." They were also told that the German government "had to consider the Pope's encyclical as a call to battle... as it calls upon Catholic citizens to rebel against the authority of the Reich."[137]

Hitler verbally attacked the German bishops at a mass rally in the Berlin *Lustgarten*.[138] He warned that the German state would not tolerate any challenge to its authority. When churches "attempt by any other means—writings, encyclicals, etc.—to assume rights which belong solely to the state, we will push them back into their proper spiritual activity."[139] Hitler also dictated a letter to the Pope, complaining that the Vatican had gone to the people instead of coming to him.[140] Pacelli sharply rebuffed German protests, noting that the German government had not been cooperative in the past when the Vatican complained about various matters.[141] The Nazis threatened to cancel the concordat due to *Mit brennender Sorge*, but decided not to do so. Instead, they waged a propaganda campaign against the Church and subjected several priests to currency or morality trials. At Koblenz, 170 Franciscans were prosecuted for corrupting the youth by turning their monastery into a "male brothel," and a Hitler Youth film was circulated that supposedly showed priests dancing in a bordello.[142] In April 1937, Berlin Nazis put 1,000 monks on trial.[143] In May, Hitler was quoted in a Swiss newspaper as saying, "the Third Reich does not desire a *modus vivendi* with the Catholic Church, but rather its destruction with lies and dishonor, in order to make room for a German Church in which the German race will be glorified."[144]

The month after *Mit brennender Sorge* came out,[145] April 1937, Winston Churchill took note of Germany's increased military might and aggressive tendencies. He told the House of Commons: "We seem to be moving, drifting steadily, against our will, against the will of every race and every people and every class, towards some hideous catastrophe." Many times he warned the pacifist-minded government that Britain was not keeping up with Germany's military preparations.[146]

*****

In May 1937, the Archbishop of Chicago, Cardinal Mundelein, lashed out against the barbarity and slavery which were being practiced by "an Austrian paper-hanger—and furthermore, not even a good one—and a few accomplices like Goebbels and Goering."[147] Hitler demanded that the Vatican rebuke Mundelein, and Goebbels even threatened to re-institute morality trials.[148] Pacelli replied: "The German government itself,... bears the responsibility, since State and Party offices... organize and direct this anti-Catholic propaganda campaign."[149] Addressing German Ambassador to the Vatican, Diego von Bergen, Pacelli used some of the insight that he picked up on his visit to the United States in 1936: "We are neither willing, nor are we able to restrict the freedom of speech of an American citizen who wishes to expose the falsities of a foreign government. Freedom of speech is an American birthright."[150] Pacelli's advice to Pius XI was "the Holy See must not... deplore Mundelein's speech. This would be an act to make National Socialism still more arrogant, especially Hitler who thinks in his self-delusion that the entire world should knuckle under to him."[151]

France's Popular Front government, supported by the Communist Party, extended an invitation to the Pontiff to visit France in 1937. The Pope's health prevented him from making the voyage, so he asked Pacelli to go in his place. Pacelli had already made a strong impression in France during an earlier visit to Lourdes when he had protested against the "superstitions of race and blood," that underlie Nazi theology.[152] This time, in a speech at Notre Dame Cathedral in Paris, he spoke of "that noble and powerful nation whom bad shepherds would lead astray into an idolatry of race."[153] He struck out against the "iniquitous violence" and the "vile criminal actions" being perpetrated by German leaders, and he denounced the "pagan cult of race."[154] The Nazis knew what he meant. The Reich and Prussian Minister for Ecclesiastical Affairs wrote to the German Foreign Ministry that Pacelli's "unmistakable allusion to Germany... was very well understood in the France Popular Front and the anti-German world."[155] Other German leaders also complained about the political nature of Pacelli's statement.[156]

Pacelli's appearance was lauded in the French press, and French leaders sought to normalize relations between the Holy See and the French government.[157] His words, however, did not have any positive impact on world events. In August, the Soviets put thirty churchmen on trial for a Fascist plot, and teachers in Berlin were instructed on the need to teach anti-Semitism.

In September 1937, a huge Nazi rally in Nuremberg attracted international attention as Hitler was awarded a prize by the National Socialist Congress for his scientific services to the German People.[158]

The event was the largest display of Nazi power in history, with over 600,000 soldiers on parade. The clear anti-Semitic message did not stop a huge international diplomatic corps from attending, including Mussolini and an American representative.

*****

At the Vatican in late 1937, Pacelli took another step toward his destination. At a consistory on December 16, Pius XI elevated five new cardinals. Pacelli was present, and Pius made an oblique reference and gestured toward Pacelli. While it was unclear to most of those at the consistory, he later explained that he knew his time was running short and it was his desire that Pacelli succeed him.[159]

CHAPTER EIGHT

THE VIOLENCE SPREADS

In early 1938, Hitler's armies had not yet crossed a frontier. The Rhineland province had been remilitarized, and the Saar had been reincorporated into Germany (by an overwhelming vote of the residents), but not a single foreign soldier had been injured by these moves. (Later this year, Gertrude Stein promoted Hitler for the Nobel Peace Prize.)[1]

About 200 Jewish people had been murdered by the Nazis, most in the first fourteen months of Hitler's rule.[2] Jews, however, were permitted to leave Germany, and they did so by the tens of thousands. The number of Jews (and others) in concentration camps was decreasing, but things were soon to become dramatically worse.[3]

In May 1938, Hitler visited Mussolini in Rome and tension between the Vatican and the Nazis reached a new level. Italian officials encouraged Hitler to visit Vatican City as a sign of good will to Catholics.[4] When asked whether he would receive Hitler, Pius XI stipulated that any discussions would have to include persecution of Catholics in Germany.[5] The meeting did not take place. Pius XI, along with Secretary of State Pacelli,[6] left the city for the Pope's summer home three days before Hitler arrived. This was two months before the Pontiff usually left. ("The air here makes me feel sick," he reportedly said to those seeing him off.)[7] He also ordered that all Vatican museums be closed and that no members of the German delegation be admitted into Vatican City. The Vatican's newspaper, L'Osservatore Romano, "studiously ignored" Hitler's visit.[8]

From his summer retreat, Castel Gandolfo, Pius XI held a public audience at which he listed among his sorrows that on the feast of the Holy Cross, people in Rome were hosting "the symbol of another cross which is not that of Christ."[9] Das Schwarze Korps, the official publication of the S.S., published an editorial calling Germany's concordat with the Vatican incompatible with the "modern idea of a totalitarian state's sovereignty."[10] Mussolini, meanwhile, pledged that the Fascist nations would fight together if the Democracies made war.

*****

Italy did not adopt racial laws until July 1938, sixteen years after Fascism came to power. Until then, Italian Jews were as likely to belong to the Fascist Party as were any other Italians.[11] Mussolini put off the imposition of racial laws for as long as possible, perhaps due to the Lateran Treaty and his desire to maintain good relations with the Vatican. Italian Jews were protected by a constitutional provision that was widely praised as a model of Fascist tolerance and enlightenment.[12] The Union of Jewish Communities even struck a special gold medal and presented it to Mussolini.[13] In fact, the "close bond" between Fascist Italy and Jews influenced most Italian Jews to stay in Italy, rather than emigrate, as many German and Eastern European Jews did.[14]

Mussolini's "Aryan Manifesto" was issued on July 14, 1938. It consisted of ten points, the most important of which was the ninth, which stated that "Jews do not belong to the Italian race."[15] The accompanying anti-Semitic laws led to an open, personal feud between Mussolini and Pius XI which continued until the latter's death.

The day after Mussolini announced the new policy, Pius XI used uncompromising terms of condemnation, calling it "nothing but apostasy;" and "the spirit of racist doctrine, contrary to the Faith of Christ."[16] "It is forgotten today that mankind is only one large all-inclusive general race," said the Pope.[17] The German paper, *Voelkischer Beobachter,* responded in its August 2 edition:

> The Vatican has rejected the racial doctrine from the very beginning, partially because it was first proclaimed publicly by German National Socialism and because the latter drew the first practical consequences from this knowledge; for the Vatican adopted a political stance of opposition towards National Socialism. However, the Vatican also had to reject the racial doctrine because it contradicts its dogma of the equality of all men, which is again a consequence of the Catholic claim for universality, which incidentally, it shares with liberals, Jews, and Communists.[18]

This did not stop the Pope from urging his followers to oppose Mussolini's new racial policy. In September, he stated:

Mark well that in the Catholic Mass, Abraham is our Patriarch and forefather. Anti-Semitism is incompatible with the lofty thought which that fact expresses. It is a movement with which we Christians can have nothing to do. No, no, I say to you it is impossible for a Christian to take part in anti-Semitism. It is inadmissible. Through Christ and in Christ we are the spiritual progeny of Abraham. Spiritually, we are all Semites.[19]

Fascists claimed that the racial question was political, not religious, and therefore was outside the Church's legitimate province. The Pope's speeches thereafter were not reprinted in the Fascist press, which regularly distorted his comments. Mussolini warned Jewish people that more severe measures would be adopted unless "the improvised and unexpected friends who are defending them from so many pulpits" cease their campaign.[20]

The Holy See made clear the Pope's opposition to Fascist policy by conducting a vigorous campaign in *L'Osservatore Romano*. Pius XI also sent Mussolini a hand-written letter asking that Jewish Catholics be exempted from the provisions of this new racial law. Thinking that this would "make the law confessional instead of racial," Mussolini left the letter unanswered.[21] Pius also wrote King Victor Emmanuel III, arguing that Mussolini was trying to destroy Italy's concordat with the Holy See.[22]

Perhaps due to the Vatican's influence, most Italian people refused to cooperate with the anti-Jewish laws.[23] Except for one brief period, Jewish relief organizations operated openly during the racial campaign until the German occupation of Italy in September 1943. In fact, the Jewish rescue organization, the Delegation for Assistance to Jewish Emigrants (DELASEM), made many trips into Italian-occupied areas to bring Jews back into Italy, with the full cooperation of the Italian government.[24]

When Mussolini began enforcing the anti-Semitic legislation, Italian Church authorities instructed Catholics to be charitable to the Jews.[25] Many Jewish people were "converted" with falsified baptismal certificates so that they might be protected under the terms of the Lateran Treaty. The Church often focused on legal arguments concerning marriage regulations and how they constituted a breach of the Lateran Treaty. In a Christmas allocution delivered later that year, Pius XI condemned the "inhuman and therefore anti-Christian" racial laws.[26] The Pope also taunted Mussolini, arguing that he changed his attitude about the Jews largely "in imitation of Germany."[27]

While many Catholics were swayed by anti-Semitic laws, some groups and individuals stood out for their opposition. Members of Catholic Action printed fliers and leaflets in a campaign against Fascism. This so angered the Secretary of the Fascist Party that he ordered that the printing presses be broken, leaflets confiscated, and members be beaten and expelled from the party (meaning that many would lose their jobs).[28]

*****

Mussolini had protected Austria in the past, particularly when Hitler threatened it in 1934. When Hitler again presented a threat to Austria, Pius sent the Italian nuncio to ask Mussolini to promise to once again support Austria. Mussolini, however, refused to make any commitments.[29] The Vatican openly scolded Mussolini for this reluctance.[30] Hitler needed no further encouragement.

In March 1938, Hitler moved troops to the Austrian border. Austria was Hitler's native land, and he was quite popular there. Austrian leader Kurt Schuschnigg called for a referendum on the Nazi issue, but that vote never took place (Hitler would win a 99 percent approval in his referendum the next month).[31] On March 12th, German troops moved in. On the 14th, Hitler returned to Vienna and proclaimed a union ("*Anschluss*"). Austria, with its population of 7,008,000 was incorporated into Germany, and its name was officially changed to Ostmark. Schuschnigg and his supporters were all arrested. On March 26, Hermann Goering warned all Jews to leave Austria. Thirty-four thousand arrests were reported by April 2nd.

Austria was at this time between eighty-five and one hundred percent Catholic. It had entered into a well-received concordat with the Vatican in 1933, and the Holy See was strongly opposed to its annexation into Germany. At the direction of Secretary of State Pacelli, *L'Osservatore Romano* published an article in defense of Austrian independence.[32] When the *Anschluss* took place, an undersecretary at the Vatican complained to the British minister that it was "a disaster caused by German vainglory, Italian folly, and Anglo-French weakness."[33]

The Church was clearly correct in fearing the Nazi takeover of Austria.[34]   The Germans introduced their anti-religious laws into Austria and did what they could to suppress the churches.   For example, in Innsbruck and the villages of and North and South Tyrol, from the time that Austria was annexed until April 1940, five churches and twenty-four chapels were closed, three priests were sent to concentration camps, 55 were arrested, 48 were forbidden to visit the schools, 100 were refused permission to teach religion to children, and 93 were deprived of their state subsidy.   Moreover, 52 Catholic schools were closed, as well as 170 other education institutions of various kinds.   Seven convents and other church properties were seized and adapted to non-Catholic uses, and a large number of Catholic associations were disbanded and their buildings seized by the Gestapo.   This was typical of the situation throughout the nation.[35]

Austrian Jews were, of course, subjected to even greater persecution from the Nazis.   In the first few days following the *Anschluss*, all Jewish businesses were branded with large red inscriptions which identified them as being owned by Jews.   Aryans who were caught patronizing such shops were forced to wear a sign around their necks proclaiming "I, Aryan swine, have bought in a Jewish shop."   Jews were deprived of their civil rights, including the right to own property, the right to be employed or to hire others, the right to work in any profession, the right to enter restaurants, cafés, or public parks.[36]   Within a month, more than 500 hundred Jewish people committed suicide in Austria.

Pius XI was particularly troubled by the annexation of Austria because, with the exception of Socialist Vienna, Austria had been on especially good terms with the Church.   For many years, the nation's leader was a priest, Monsignor Ignaz Seipel.   After Seipel's death, Chancellor Engelbert Dollfuss put in place a new constitution based on Pius XI's 1931 encyclical, *Quadragesimo Anno* (*On Reconstruction of the Social Order*).   He also enshrined the terms of the 1933 concordat into law.   After Germany occupied Austria, Hitler refused to respond to Vatican questions concerning the continued validity of the concordat.

Shortly after Austria was annexed, the Archbishop of Vienna, Cardinal Theodor Innitzer, met with Hitler and, based on outward appearances and a German radio broadcast, he welcomed the

Anschluss.[37] Austrian bishops also issued a public statement praising the achievements of Nazism. This was in accord with much of the feeling throughout Austria, where the German troops had been greeted as heroes rather than conquerors. Vatican Radio, however, immediately broadcast a vehement denunciation of these actions, and Pacelli ordered the Archbishop to report to Rome.[38]

Before meeting with the Pope, Innitzer met with Pacelli, who had been outraged by the German cardinal.[39] This has been called one of the "most tempestuous" meetings of the whole pontificate.[40] Pacelli made it clear that Innitzer had to retract his statements.[41] He was made to sign a new statement, issued on behalf of all of the Austrian bishops, which provided: "The solemn declaration of the Austrian bishops on 18 March of this year was clearly not intended to be an approval of something that was not and is not compatible with God's law."[42] The Vatican newspaper also reported that the bishops' earlier statement had been issued without approval from Rome. Before long, Innitzer was recognized as a true enemy of the Nazis.

On Friday, October 7, a group of young Nazis pounded on Innitzer's door and shouted that he should be taken to a concentration camp. The police intervened, and the rioters left. The next night, another hostile demonstration began against the Archbishop's residence. Soon rocks were thrown, and every window in the building was broken. The police were called, but before they could arrive the rioters kicked in the heavy door and entered the palace, smashing everything they found. The invaders beat Archbishop's secretary into unconsciousness, entered the chapel, and smashed a statue. They then broke into the Cardinal's study where they forced open his desk and destroyed a crucifix. The Cardinal's purple robes, pectoral cross, and ring were removed and used for a bonfire. All the furniture was broken, the paintings were torn down, and art objects were ruined. Vienna's newspapers contained not a word about it.[43]

After receiving word of this attack, Pius XI could no longer contain himself. On October 21, in one of his last public appearances, Pius personally attacked Hitler, likening him to Julian the Apostate (Roman Emperor Flavius Claudius Julianus), who attempted to "saddle the Christians with responsibility for the persecution he had unleashed against them."[44]

Shortly after the Pope's pronouncement, on November 9-10, 1938 (the 15th anniversary of Hitler's 1923 putsch), one of the most violent nights in Berlin's history took place. Storm troopers were set loose on the Jewish population. Young Nazis went on a rampage, killing Jews at random, smashing windows, destroying homes and businesses, and burning synagogues. The riot came to be called *Kristallnacht* ("Night of Shattered Glass") because there were so many broken windows. About six hundred synagogues were burned, more than seven thousand Jewish shops were ransacked, and thirty-five thousand Jews were arrested. More than ninety people, most of them Jewish merchants, were killed in the rioting. Most rioters in Berlin wore civilian clothes but drove Nazi party cars and wore the boots of party members.[45]

Kristallnacht has been identified as the beginning of the true war against the Jews.[46]   Soon, Jews in Germany and occupied nations were packed into ghettos, forced to wear the yellow Star of David for identification, and subjected to ever harsher restrictions and persecution. In the following days, thousands of Jews were sent to concentration camps. This led to a mass exodus, as 150,000 Jews emigrated from Germany between *Kristallnacht* and the beginning of World War II.[47]

The morning after the burning of the synagogues, Catholic priest Bernhard Lichtenberg, Provost of Saint Hedwig's Catholic Cathedral in Berlin, spoke out from the pulpit, closing each of his services with a prayer for the Jews:

> What took place yesterday, we know; what will be tomorrow, we do not know; but what happens today, that we have witnessed; outside, the synagogue is burning, and that, also, is a house of God.
> Do not let yourself be led astray by such unChristian thoughts, but act according to the clear command of Christ: "Thou shalt love thy neighbor as thyself."[48]

Because of his outspokenness, Fr. Lichtenberg was sentenced to two years in prison. After that, he was seized by the Gestapo and sent to Dachau. He died on the way there. In 1995, Pope John Paul II announced his beatification (along with that of Fr. Karl Leisner), the first step toward sainthood.[49]

The same month that *Kristallnacht* took place in Germany, racial laws in Italy were tightened with passage of the "law for the defense of the Italian race."[50] This law prohibited interracial marriages involving Italian Aryans, and declared that such marriages would not be recognized. Civil recognition of Church marriages had been one of the most important aspects of the Lateran Treaty, and this seemed a clear breach, despite Mussolini's attempts to argue otherwise. Pius XI was the first official to file a protest, but he had no influence with the Nazis or the Fascists.[51] His protests, however, may have been part of the reason why Italians were never very willing to enforce racial laws.[52] In addition, Vatican leaders set the example of helping Jews. Pursuant to the orders of Cardinal Pacelli and with the agreement of Jewish leaders, the Torah and other Jewish ritual objects were removed from synagogues and transported for safe-keeping by Church officials.[53]

Relations between Italy and the Vatican deteriorated significantly after the racial laws were put in place. On January 2, 1939, Mussolini warned the Holy See that he would not tolerate any opposition to his racial policy. Later that same year Mussolini expressed his displeasure over Pius XI's comments regarding anti-Semitic policies and threatened the security of the Vatican.[54] Police were stationed outside the Vatican City gates, and they reported on all visitors. Lay Vatican employees were recruited to watch the movements of prelates. Mail was opened and telephone conversations were monitored.

As 1938 drew to an end, frantic preparations for war swept across the globe.[55] British leaders drew up a national plan providing instructions for what each person should do in case of war. Germany and France both increased military preparedness. Italy disavowed its 1935 pact with France. In Spain, Franco restored the citizenship of ex-King Alfonso XIII and took final control of the nation. Fascist Baron Kiichiro Hiranuma took over as Japanese Premier. For his part, Hitler demanded the return of colonies to Japan and Italy, warning the United States not to interfere.

CHAPTER NINE

THE PRE-WAR POPE

In 1938 Pius XI was very ill. He spent six months convalescing at his summer retreat, Castel Gandolfo. Cardinal Pacelli repeatedly urged the ailing pontiff to slow down. Pius indignantly replied, "The world would be far better off with a dead pope than with one who cannot work full time."[1]

Pius XI's final public comments on the world situation focused on Hitler's threatened aggression. Though he was nearing death, he could read the writing on the wall. He warned Italian Catholics not to trust Germany.[2] He met with British Prime Minister Chamberlain and Lord Halifax and told them what he thought of the regimes in Italy and Germany, the duties of the democracies, and the urgent need to help the refugees.[3] He also notified American and Canadian bishops of his displeasure at the reluctance of Catholic universities in their countries to hire more European Jewish scholars and scientists and asked them to remedy this situation.[4]

With the tenth anniversary of the signing of the Lateran Treaty at hand, Pius XI summoned the whole Italian episcopate to Rome. He reportedly planned to undertake a major emigration and resettlement project in São Paulo, Brazil, and to make a stinging indictment of Fascism.[5] On January 9, 1939, Secretary of State Pacelli sent out messages to the archbishops of the world, instructing them to petition their governments to open their borders to Jews fleeing persecution in Germany.[6] The following day Pacelli wrote to American Cardinals, asking them to assist exiled Jewish professors and scientists.[7] Unfortunately, Pope Pius XI never made his planned speech. At five in the morning on February 10, 1939, one day before he was scheduled to give his address, Pius XI passed away in his sleep.

On February 13, the *"Alliance Israélite Universelle"* wrote to Rome:

> Never shall we forget the kindness and courage with which the late pope has defended all victims of persecution, irrespective of race and religion, in the name of those eternal principles whose noblest

spokesman he has been on earth.... He has truly earned our eternal gratitude and everlasting admiration.[8]

Bernard Joseph, on behalf of the Executive of the Jewish Agency (the future Government of Israel) published a piece saying:

In common with the whole of civilized humanity, the Jewish people mourn the loss of one of the greatest exponents of the cause of international peace and goodwill.... More than once did we have occasion to be deeply grateful for the attitude which he took up against the persecution of racial minorities and, in particular, for the deep concern which he expressed for the fate of the persecuted Jews of Central Europe. His noble efforts on their behalf will ensure for him for all time a warm place in the memories of the Jewish people wherever they live.[9]

The British representative to Rome reported that the fallen pontiff's courage at the end of his life ensured that he was "one of the outstanding figures of the world."[10]

In Germany, according to the *New York Times*, "the requirements of diplomatic usage were punctiliously fulfilled—but no more."[11] *Das Schwarze Korps* eulogized Pius XI, who the Nazis called "Chief Rabbi of the Christian World,"[12] as "the sworn enemy of National Socialism."[13] Mussolini remarked: "At last that stiff-necked old man is dead."[14]

During the seventeen years of Pius XI's reign, he had tried to protect the spiritual mission of the Church by concluding bilateral concordats with no less than twenty-one countries. However, at the time of his death, the world's stability was in great jeopardy. Aggressive and evil theories were spreading across the globe. The same month that the Pope died, 22,000 Americans attended a pro-Nazi rally in New York City's Madison Square Garden.[15] Pius XI's successor would assume the leadership of the Catholic Church at one of the most difficult periods in history.

*****

On a number of occasions, Pius XI indicated that Cardinal Pacelli would make an ideal Pope, going so far as to say that if he were sure the conclave would elect Pacelli as his successor, he would retire.[16] This made Pacelli a likely candidate, but his election was far from certain.[17] There is an old Vatican saying: He who enters a conclave Pope, will come out of it a cardinal.[18]

Pacelli had a great deal of support due to his experience in dealing with leaders of other nations. He had been a nuncio for thirteen years and Secretary of State for almost ten years. He also had been closely involved in the preparation of several encyclicals and had negotiated many concordats, including one with Germany. Hitler, however, did not want Pacelli to be elected Pope.

Hitler had not gotten along well with Pius XI. He hoped a new Pope would be easier to bully. Pacelli was not his man. Pacelli had been denouncing Nazi breaches of the concordat for several years, and he felt that Nazism posed a threat to Christianity similar to the one posed by Communism. As such, the German government used all possible pressure to bring about the election of a more friendly cardinal.[19]

On February 16, 1939, the German Ambassador to the Holy See, Diego von Bergen, addressed the Sacred College of Cardinals in what was expected to be a customary expression of sympathy over the death of Pius XI. Rather than merely offering condolences, however, the ambassador spoke of an "upbuilding of a new world which struggles to rise on the ruins of the past which in many respects no longer has a *raison d'être*."[20] As the *New York Times* reported, it was a clear request for a Pope more sympathetic to Hitler's expansionist plans.[21] The British Legation to the Holy See reported back to London that it contained a "blackmailing note" and was "a veiled warning against the election of Cardinal Pacelli."[22]

The Germans viewed the election of Pacelli unfavorably because they feared that he would continue the same policy that he had followed as Secretary of State. The French foreign minister expressed his hope that Pacelli would be elected for that very same reason.[23] The British Legation to the Holy See wrote "I should like to back Pacelli if we were in a position to do so, but we are not."[24] The cardinals let everyone know that the choice of a successor to Pius XI rested with God, and not the Rome-Berlin Axis.[25]

On the way into the conclave, Pacelli stumbled and fell to the ground. He was helped to his feet by Jean Cardinal Verdier of Paris who joked in Latin: *"Vicarius Christi in terra!"* ("The Vicar of Christ on earth.")[26] The pun proved prophetic, as Pacelli was elected Pope on the first day of the conclave, March 2, 1939. Although the balloting is officially kept secret, it is now believed that Pacelli was elected on the second ballot with about 48 of the 65 votes cast being in his favor.[27] He did, however, request the confirmation of a third vote, and he was unanimously elected.[28]

In voting, the cardinals, notionally the parish priests of Rome, are electing their bishop. At the time of Pacelli's election, war appeared inevitable. As such, one of the most important considerations was how the new pope would deal with world unrest. Ultimately, the debate over whether they needed a "spiritual" or a "diplomatic" pope was settled in favor of "the most experienced and brilliant diplomat available."[29]

Of all the diplomats in the cardinalate, Pacelli was certainly the most accomplished. He had been groomed for this office almost from the moment his predecessor was elected.[30] Pacelli was know for "cool and critical" thinking, was considered a "modern man," and was seen as "a veritable prince of diplomats."[31] He had traveled widely through the world as Pius XI's Secretary of State and had the overwhelming support of the foreign cardinals.

Following the vote, the traditional signal, white smoke, was seen rising above the Vatican and a huge crowd assembled to await the announcement. *"Nuntio vobis magnum gaudium! Habemus Papam!"* ("I announce to you a great joy! We have a Pope!") The excited crowd raised a long and deafening roar. "The most eminent and reverend Lord Eugenio...." The announcement was drowned out by another explosion form the crowd as the people joyfully finished the name: "Pacelli! Pacelli!"[32]

It was reported at the time that Pius XII was cautious, suave, and tolerant, as opposed to Pius XI who was impulsive, bristling, and authoritarian.[33] Pacelli, it was said "takes a long time to make a decision of importance. Once it is made, however, one may be sure that it is the result of profound analysis and meditation."[34] Pacelli was "ascetic in his personal habits, omniscient in his intellectual aspirations, endowed with the gift of total recall, unswerving in his devotional activities, affable though reticent, thoughtful of subordinates, and eloquent and impenetrable as a personality."[35] Moreover, Pacelli "looked like a casting director's dream of a pope, lean, remote, scrupulously ascetic in gesture and expression."[36]

The choice of Pacelli was welcomed in every country in Europe and in the Western Hemisphere, except for Germany.[37] As reported in the *New York Times*:

The election of Pius XII... brought nearly general applause around the world. Statesmen and the press, laymen and churchmen, hailed him as a man equipped by experience and wide travels to meet the issues of the day and hour. In Washington and London it was held that the new Pope would encourage all forces seeking to lift the threat of war and totalitarianism. In Paris even Socialists and Communists praised Pope Pius XII as a probable barrier to Fascism. The Fascist nations—Italy and Germany—were divided in their opinion. In the Italian press the selection was praised. But the German press, which had opposed Cardinal Pacelli's election, charging that he favored the Western democracies, was at first silent, but later expressed an attitude of watchful waiting.[38]

The lead editorial in *The Canadian Jewish Chronicle* explained that "although the election of two hundred and sixty-one pontiffs has hitherto been a matter of indifference to Jews... the election of the two hundred and sixty-second pope was one which elicited considerable interest."[39] This was so because, regardless of his qualifications:

> The election of Cardinal Pacelli is more than merely a tribute to personal talent. It is the choice of a policy....
> The frantic attempts, therefore, which has [sic] been made by Nazis and Fascists to influence the election, by speech, suggestion, and counsel, in favor of a cardinal friendlier to Hitler and Mussolini... was ultimately foiled. The clumsy advice which... Germany's Ambassador to the Vatican, recently gave to the College of Cardinals... has already received an answer as unequivocal as the advice was arrogant. The plot to pilfer the Ring of the Fisherman has gone up in white smoke.[40]

In Jerusalem, the newspaper reported: "The cordial reception accorded the election, particularly in France, England, and America—and the lukewarm reception in Germany—are not surprising when we remember the large part he [Pacelli] played in the recent papal opposition to pernicious race theories."[41] *The Jewish Chronicle* (London) reported in its March 10 edition, that "among the congratulations received [by the Holy See] are messages from the Anglo-Jewish Community, the Synagogue Council of America, the Canadian Jewish Congress, and the Polish Rabbinical Council."[42] The President of the Rabbinical Council of America heralded the election of Pacelli as "most welcome."[43]

Papers sympathetic to the Nazis bitterly complained about the "prejudiced hostility and incurable lack of comprehension" shown by the Holy See on the racial question.[44] *Das Schwarze Korps*, the official publication of the S.S., wrote:

> We do not know if Pius XII, though young enough to see the developments in Germany, is intelligent enough to sacrifice many old things of his institution. As nuncio and secretary of state, Eugenio Pacelli had little understanding of us; little hope is placed in him. We do not believe that as Pius XII he will follow a different path.[45]

The morning after his election, the Berlin *Morgenpost* reported: "The election of Cardinal Pacelli is not accepted with favor in Germany because he was always opposed to Nazism and practically determined the policies of the Vatican under his predecessor."[46] That same day, the *Frankfurter Zeitung* wrote: "Many of [Pacelli's] speeches have made it clear that he does not fully grasp the political and ideological motives which have begun their victorious march in Germany."[47] *Graz*, an Austrian Nazi paper, said Pacelli was "a servile perpetrator of Pius XI's doomed policy."[48] In an effort to undermine his authority within Germany, the Nazi journal *Das Reich* wrote: "Pius XI was a half-Jew, for his mother was a Dutch Jewess; but Cardinal Pacelli is a full Jew."[49]

According to the March 4, 1939 entry in Joseph Goebbels' diary, Hitler considered abrogating the concordat in light of Pacelli's election as Pope.[50] A few weeks later, the German Reich's Chief Security Service issued a secret report which said:

> Pacelli has already made himself prominent by his attacks on National Socialism during his tenure as Cardinal Secretary of State, a fact which earned him the hearty approval of the Democratic States during the papal elections.... President Roosevelt said in his cable of congratulations: "With great joy I learned of your election to the papacy. I recall with pleasure our last conversation during your visit to the U.S.A." The *Humanité* writes, inter alia: "twenty days after the death of Pius XI the new pope is elected. It is Pius XII. In adopting his name, will he not also resume the work of that man whose collaborator as Secretary of State he has been in recent years? For in matters of the racial lunacy, the Nazi persecutions and the assaults of Fascism on the liberty of conscience and on human dignity, there was no separating Cardinal Pacelli from the Pope."[51]

Pacelli's election, however, would not dissuade the Nazis from their desired path.[52]

At the time Pacelli was elected, Germany had already annexed Austria, invaded Czechoslovakia, and was threatening Poland. Nevertheless, protocol required the new pope to send brief, personal messages to all heads of states with whom the Vatican had diplomatic relations,[53] and this note might provide an opportunity to advance the cause of peace.

Between his election and coronation, Pius XII met with the four German cardinals in an attempt to work toward the end of the Nazi persecution of the Church in Germany.[54] They all agreed to attempt a conciliatory approach in dealings with Germany.[55] There was, however, a limit. The new pope vowed: "We cannot sacrifice our principles. Once we have tried everything and if they still persist in their desire for war, then We will defend Ourselves. But the world should note that we have done everything to live in peace with Germany."[56] He then sent Hitler a letter which read as follows:

> To the illustrious Herr Adolf Hitler, *Führer* and Chancellor of the German Reich! Here at the beginning of Our pontificate We wish to assure you that We remain devoted to the spiritual welfare of the German people entrusted to your leadership. For them We implore God the almighty to grant them that true felicity which springs from religion. We recall with great pleasure the many years We spent in Germany as Apostolic Nuncio, when We did all in Our power to establish harmonious relations between Church and State. Now that the responsibilities of Our pastoral function have increased Our opportunities, how much more ardently do We pray to reach that goal. May the prosperity of the German people and their progress in every domain come, with God's help to fruition![57]

Although the letter was written in an attempt to reach an understanding with Germany, "not a single word could be construed as approbation of what Hitler stood for."[58] It was simply an attempt to end the hostilities. When Pius XII met with the German ambassador, however, it became clear that no accord would be possible. The meeting ended with Pius telling the ambassador that he was aware of Nazi abuses and would not tolerate them.[59]

Pius then made the first clear move to justify the faith that the Jewish press had placed in him. He appointed Cardinal Luigi Maglione as Secretary of State for the Vatican. As the *Zionist Review* (London) reported:

> Pope Pius XII has given the Nazis and Fascists another unpleasant surprise. On the eve of his coronation His Holiness announced the appointment of Cardinal Luigi Maglione as Secretary of State for the Vatican. Cardinal Maglione... is known as a staunch Liberal and as a friend of the democratic powers. His appointment confirms the view that the new Pope means to conduct an anti-Nazi and anti-Fascist policy.[60]

Along with Pope Pius XII, Msgr. Domenico Tardini,[61] and Msgr. Giovanni Montini (the future Pope Paul VI),[62] Cardinal Maglione played an important part in Vatican diplomacy and efforts to restore justice to the world until his death in 1944.

The coronation of Pope Pius XII took place on March 12, 1939. Due to the Vatican's dispute with Italy, there had not been a traditional ceremony in over a century. This coronation, however, was one of the most magnificent that Rome had ever seen. It was the first to be broadcast on radio, the first to be filmed in its entirety, and delegations were sent from almost every nation of the world.[63] The American Ambassador to England, Joseph P. Kennedy (accompanied by his son, the future President of the United States), was the first ever official representative of the United States at the coronation of a Pope.[64] Germany was the only major power that did not send a representative,[65] though the Ambassador to the Holy See did convey the congratulations of the Reich and its leaders.[66] (A memorandum by an official in the Reich Protocol Department pointed out that following the election of Pope Pius XI, German President Friedrich Ebert sent his "most cordial congratulations," but that in light of Pacelli's "well-known attitude" toward Germany, congratulations to the new Pope "are not to be conveyed in a particularly warm manner.")[67]

Hitler did not let problems with the Vatican slow down his aggression. On March 15, 1939, just three days after the coronation in Rome, and despite assurances to the world made only months earlier, Hitler invaded interior Czechoslovakia (beyond the area he had won in negotiations) and broke it into two states. This finally caused British Prime Minister Neville Chamberlain to abandon his appeasement stance and offer military alliances to the two countries now threatened by Germany (Poland and Romania) and to Greece, which was threatened by Italy.[68] (It was to honor the pledge to Poland that Britain went to war against Germany later in the year.) Unlike the German Czechs in the annexed Sudetenland, who were seen as Aryans and treated rather well, those who lived in the newly occupied protectorate states of Bohemia and Moravia (including six million Catholics) were treated quite harshly. As always, religious institutions were singled out for persecution.

Addressing the cardinals, Pius XII explained he would devote his papacy to the struggle for peace.[69] The Pope's supreme title, "*Pontifex maximus,*" means "the great builder of bridges." Pacelli had taken the name Pius (in Latin, meaning pious, kindhearted, and gentle; in Hebrew signifying conciliation) in honor of his predecessor, but clearly the outbreak of war was utmost in his mind. Even before the coronation, Pius developed his plan for peace. He selected as his coat-of-arms a dove holding an olive branch in his beak. His device was "*Opus Justitiae Pax*" ("the work of justice is peace"). His first message on Vatican radio was a pledge to work for unity and a plea for peace throughout the world.[70] Pius XII came to be called the "Herald of Peace," as he regularly prayed in public for matters such as eternal rest for all who died in the war, and comfort for the exiled, refugees, prisoners, the displaced, and all who suffered.[71]

Pius XII subscribed to the same doctrine of impartiality for the Holy See that was exercised by Pope Benedict XV during World War I.[72] Throughout the war, he tried to improve the conditions for prisoners of war, displaced persons, and those in concentration camps, regardless of their nationality. (Government officials in Germany and Russia so resented this activity that they dismissed the Vatican's representatives from occupied territories). Vatican diplomats distributed medicine, books, rosaries and other items—including Christmas presents—to prisoners of war in every country. They also spoke with the prisoners, took messages to concerned families, and tried to improve conditions for the interned of all nations. Most of all, Pius consistently struggled to bring peace to a world afflicted by war.

CHAPTER TEN

1939 AND THE OUTBREAK OF WAR

At the beginning of 1939, supposedly in response to a letter from the parents of a severely handicapped child, Adolf Hitler announced the formation of a special Reich Council to deal with "mercy death" for the severely handicapped.[1] In the spring, Nazi officials, doctors, and directors of several established institutions met to consider the creation of euthanasia centers. This was the beginning of the Nazi racial purification program.[2]

A "euthanasia" program had long been part of the Nazi plan. In 1929, at the Nazi convention in Nuremberg, Hitler had proposed the annual "removal" of 700,000 to 800,000 of the "weakest" Germans as a means of rapidly improving the overall health and capabilities of the German race.[3] He also wanted to eliminate millions among the "inferior races that breed like vermin."[4] This led to the creation of the "Reich Commission for the Scientific Registration of Hereditary and Constitutional Severe Disorders," and doctors soon began conducting the experiments which would lead to the gas chambers of World War II.[5]

One of the first steps was official recognition of the "right to die," which aroused only minimal opposition.[6] Then, in 1939, doctors began to give "mercy deaths" to the "incurably sick."[7] Carbon-monoxide chambers were built to carry out the euthanasia program. Next came deformed children, who were said to adversely affect the race and not to have very happy lives anyway.[8] At first, these children were identified while still very young (not more than three years old), but the age gradually edged up to seventeen and then to adulthood. Moreover, the standards also changed. Originally only the severely deformed were included in the program. Eventually, children with mis-shaped ears, bed wetters, and those who were found difficult to educate were marked for elimination.[9]

Between December 1939 and August 1941, about 5,000 children and 100,000 adults were killed by lethal injections or in gas chambers that were built to look like shower rooms.[10] The victims were all deemed to have a "life unworthy of living" because they were handicapped, retarded, deformed, or otherwise considered "undesirable."[11]

When word of the program leaked out to the German populace, widespread outrage led by religious leaders spread throughout the country. In December 1940, the Vatican condemned the program as "contrary to both natural and divine law."[12] On August 3, 1941, Bishop Clemens Count von Galen of Münster became the first prominent clergyman to denounce the program when he mounted the pulpit and asked:

> Do you or I have the right to live only as long as we are productive?...
> Then someone has only to order a secret decree that the measures tried out on the mentally ill be extended to other "nonproductive" people, that it can be used on those incurably ill with a lung disease, on those weakened by aging, on those disabled at work, on severely wounded soldiers. Then not a one of us is sure anymore of his life....
> Woe to humanity, woe to our German people, when the sacred commandment "Thou shalt not kill" is not only violated, but when this violation is tolerated and carried out without punishment![13]

When these sermons were brought to the attention of Pope Pius XII, he wrote to Galen in a letter dated September 1, 1941, that they had brought him "a consolation and a satisfaction which We have not experienced for a long time as We walk down a sorrowful path with the Catholics of Germany."[14]

Although the euthanasia program took on a much lower profile in late 1941,[15] at almost this same time, the Nazis began a similar program on a vastly greater scale in Poland.[16] (In fact, according to one account, the euthanasia program in Germany only appeared to slow down because the killing resources were redirected to Jewish victims.)[17] Euthanasia continued throughout the war. In the autumn of 1941, the staff at Hadamar, one of the euthanasia centers, celebrated the cremation of its 10,000th corpse with a special ceremony, followed by music, dancing, and drinking.[18]

The execution techniques that were developed in these euthanasia hospitals would soon be adapted for use on those who were deemed racially valueless.[19] The euthanasia doctors would move on to their new patients. The "scientific" techniques they had developed were refined and perfected until, in the gas chambers of Auschwitz, it would be possible for these doctors to eliminate thousands of people in one day.

Hitler was confident enough of his ability to eliminate the Jewish race that on January 30, 1939, in a speech before the Reichstag commemorating the sixth anniversary of his coming to power he announced:

> Today I will once more be a prophet: if the international Jewish financiers in and outside Europe should succeed in plunging the nations once more into a world war, then the result will not be the Bolshevizing of the earth, and thus the victory of Jewry, but the annihilation of the Jewish race in Europe![20]

No one then knew how close he would come to carrying out this threat.

*****

Ahmed Zog was elected president of the Albanian republic early in 1925. The National Assembly proclaimed him King in 1928. Under his leadership, Albania strengthened its ties with Italy. By the late 1930s, however, the relationship was strained. In early 1939, the two nations were engaged in peace negotiations, but King Zog balked at Mussolini's demand that the Italian navy be given permanent access to Albanian harbors and that military garrisons be established along Albania's Greek and Yugoslavian borders. When Mussolini could not win these concessions at the bargaining table, he decided to take them by force.

On Good Friday, April 7, 1939, Italy invaded Albania, citing the need to protect Italians residing there from roving armed bands. The invaders gave no notice and faced almost no resistance. King Zog was driven into exile, and Albania became an Italian protectorate.

On Easter Sunday, April 9, Pius XII condemned both the Italian attack on Albania and the German invasion of Czechoslovakia. He blamed the current state of war on those who neglect justice: "How is peace possible in this world, if acknowledgment of just interest as well as unanimous efforts toward social progress are lacking? If solemnly given promises are broken without any hesitation?"[21]

Mussolini at first said that Pius could "go ahead and protest, if only to save his own soul...."[22] By July, however, he sent Count Ciano to present an ultimatum to the papal nuncio. In his diary, Ciano recorded: "Either [*L'Osservatore Romano*] will cease its subtle propaganda against the Axis or we shall prohibit its circulation in Italy. It has become the official organ of the anti-Fascists."[23]

Pius, who was deeply concerned about the Hitler-Mussolini pact,[24] wanted desperately to avoid another big war. Thus, he did not negotiate in a public forum. Instead, less than two months after he had been coronated, Pope Pius XII asked Germany, Italy, France, and Britain to attend peace talks at the Vatican. Rumors soon circulated that Pius wanted Warsaw to soften its stand against German demands on Danzig and the Polish corridor.[25] The talk became so widespread that Secretary of State Maglione wrote to Lord Halifax assuring that Pius never intended to take "the initiative in proposing to the two governments a concrete solution of the problem," but had merely urged the parties to treat it calmly and with moderation."[26] Peace talks never took place, however, at least in part because French and Polish leaders were afraid that the only way to attain peace would be to make concessions to Germany.

*****

On May 22, Italy and Germany signed a new ten year agreement, the "Pact of Steel," which—according to Hitler—created "an invincible block of 300 million people." The agreement bound the two nations economically, politically, and militarily. It also attracted world-wide attention. Britain called an extra session of Parliament to discuss it. The Vatican saw it as a dangerous sign of the forthcoming war. In an address to the Cardinals on June 2, 1939, Pius XII said:

> The Church is not dominated by the interests of one party. She will not become embroiled in the dangerous temporal conflicts of the States but, with the anxiety of a mother, she will attempt to secure peace in moments of great danger, to quiet the frenzied passions of the fighting parties. She will do everything possible in order to stop the war now threatening the world and to forestall its disastrous consequences.[27]

Throughout the war, the Pope would abide by this plan, which he had laid out prior to Germany's invasion of Poland.

*****

Despite the limitations imposed by the Versailles Treaty, Hitler spent much more money ($50 to $100 billion) on the German military machine in the 1930s than other nations spent on their military.[28] As a dictator, Hitler did not need to gather political support for his programs, and he did not worry about the economic consequences of the huge deficits he ran up. British and French leaders were unable to convince a majority of the need for similar spending in those nations.[29] As such, by 1939, Germany was far better prepared for war than were most other nations. Still, the combined might of England and France might have been able to dissuade Hitler from his ambitious plans, if only they had reached an agreement with the Soviets. The Germans, however, beat them to the punch.

On August 23, 1939, Hitler put together the final piece of his plan for a military invasion of Poland. He had been held in check because he feared that the Soviets, who would not like an aggressive German army right at their border, would strike back if he invaded Poland. He got the assurance he needed by signing a non-aggression pact with Stalin. The pact was supposed to assure peace between the two nations for five years. All it really did was assure Germany's invasion of Poland.

Since one of Hitler's primary goals was the containment of Bolshevism, Stalin might naturally have sided with the Western Allies. They, however, would have demanded that he agree to protect Poland. Not only did Hitler ask less of the Soviets, he was willing to give Stalin a prize. After the war it was disclosed that the non-aggression agreement had a secret additional protocol, that assigned to the Soviets a "sphere of influence" which included Finland, Estonia, Latvia, part of Romania, and eastern Poland—despite a non-aggression agreement that the Soviet Union had with Poland.[30]

Stalin appears to have intended to honor the agreement with Hitler. Over the course of the next year, the Soviet Union sent many supplies and raw materials to Germany. Hitler, however, never intended to honor his pledge. He later admitted that this was simply a way of stalling for time; he breached the agreement with a massive invasion of the Soviet Union less than two years later.

Recognizing the dangerous world situation, Pius broadcast appeals for peace on Vatican Radio on August 19 and August 24, 1939. Speaking to "you leaders of peoples, politicians, men of arms, writers and broadcasters" he pleaded: "The danger is tremendous, but there is still time. Nothing is lost by peace; all is lost by war." He urged "by the blood of Christ... the strong [to] hear us that they may not become weak through injustice... [and] if they desire that their power may not be a destruction."[31] As he made his appeals, the new Pope clearly identified the cause of the current state of world affairs; Pius "was pointing the finger at Hitler."[32]

On the afternoon of August 31 the Pope sent identical notes to the governments of Germany, Poland, Italy, France, and Great Britain "beseeching, in the name of God, the German and Polish Governments... to avoid any incident."[33] He begged the British, French and Italian governments to support his appeal and added, "The Pope is unwilling to abandon hope that pending negotiations may lead to a just pacific solution."[34] Unfortunately, other nations did not see this as a realistic alternative.[35]

A year earlier, Hitler had said that he would have no more territorial demands and that he understood Poland's need for a port, but ever since he had railed against the Polish corridor that separated East Prussia from the rest of Germany (and provided Poland with its only access to the sea). Poland already permitted German trains and cars free transit across the corridor, but that did not satisfy the German dictator. The free city of Danzig, under the protection of the League of Nations, had a heavy German population. It had been "torn from the Fatherland," Hitler argued. (Privately, he also thought that Poles were an inferior race that needed to be eliminated.) He began a propaganda campaign to convince his nation that the Germans in this area were being mistreated by the Poles.[36]

Previously Hitler had encountered world leaders who were willing to accommodate him. Chamberlain was only the most visible proponent of appeasement. Now, however, Hitler ran up against people who were determined to make no concessions. Poland had been restored as an independent nation following the First World War. At that moment in time, neither Russia nor Germany were great powers. As those nations grew in power over the next twenty years, Polish leaders became concerned. They now felt that Poland's only chance was to behave defiantly.[37]

In the early morning hours of September 1, 1939, German forces staged an incident along the border of the two nations. Hitler took to the airwaves to denounce the "Polish attack" (and to announce the annexation of Danzig to the Reich).[38] At that very time, German planes began a massive bombing assault, as German tanks rumbled across the border.[39] This *Blitzkrieg* (Lightening War) attack came with a speed unparalleled in earlier warfare. For two weeks German mechanized troops smashed through Polish towns and villages, reducing them to rubble as Poles on horseback charged modern tanks.

Luigi Cardinal Maglione, Vatican Secretary of State, telephoned the pontiff to tell him of the invasion of Poland. After answering in his customary manner, *"E'qui Pacelli"* ("Pacelli here") and hearing the news, the Pope retreated to his chapel, fell to his knees and poured out his grief in prayer.[40] After he regained his composure, Pius telegraphed Nuncio Paccini in Warsaw and instructed him to try to organize Polish Jews for a passage to Palestine.[41] Meanwhile, Pius had the Apostolic Delegate in Istanbul, Angelo Roncalli (the future Pope John XXIII), prepare thousands of baptismal certificates for arriving Jews in the hope that such papers would permit passage into the country.[42]

The Poles were almost powerless to resist aggression by the world's finest fighting machine. Screaming dive bombers terrorized Polish cities. Much of the Polish Air Force was destroyed in the first few hours. Long columns of German tanks smashed the Polish cavalry. Hundreds of thousands of Poles were captured, injured, or killed. Though civilians rallied to defend their country, German victory in Poland was assured from the outset as German forces used military bases in Czechoslovakia so that the attack could come from the north and the south. Within weeks much of Poland was occupied; German victory took only twenty-eight days. At a fairly small cost, Hitler had acquired twenty-one million more subjects and vast agricultural and industrial resources.[43]

The Nazis built almost all of their death camps in Poland. Jews from all over Europe were sent here in cattle cars to be eliminated. About six million Jews died in these camps. Other groups were also marked for extermination, particularly Gypsies and Poles. It is estimated that three million Catholic Poles died in the Nazi concentration camps, and another two million were sent to Germany as slave labor for the Reich.[44]

The campaign against Christian Poles is often overlooked, but Hitler's first prisoners and victims in Poland were thousands of intelligentsia, members of the resistance, and clergy.[45] As Hitler's private secretary, Martin Bormann, explained:

All Polish intelligentsia must be exterminated. This sounds cruel, but such is the law of life.... [Polish priests] will preach what we want them to preach. If any priest acts differently, we will make short work of him. The task of the priest is to keep the Poles quiet, stupid, and dull-witted.[46]

"There probably isn't a Polish family that hasn't lost someone close at Auschwitz or at another camp."[47] These were the leaders who might pose a threat to the occupation forces. Thousands of Polish priests were sent to the concentration camps by the Nazis; two-thirds of them—about 2,500—died there.[48] The primate of Poland, Cardinal August Hlond, was forced overseas along with the Polish government in exile. When he attempted to return home, the German ambassador sent a note to the Vatican saying that Hlond was an enemy of Germany and did not have permission to return to his diocese.[49] Archbishop Adam Stefan Sapieha soon took on the role of leader of the Polish Church within the occupied nation. [50]

On September 3, 1939, two days after the invasion and in compliance with mutual defense treaties they had signed with Poland, the nations of Great Britain, France, New Zealand, and Australia all declared war on Germany. Within a week, Canada would also declare war and the United States would declare its neutrality. It was too late for Poland, but the days of appeasement were over. Hitler found himself in a much larger war than he had expected.[51]

*****

As German troops continued their advance into Poland from the west, to the surprise of everyone except Hitler, Soviet troops marched in from the east. There were occasions of confusion, with Poles thinking that perhaps the Soviets were there to support them in the war against Germany, but such was not the case. Seven hundred Soviet soldiers and thousands of Poles were killed in the fighting.[52] The Polish government and high command escaped into exile on September 18, but the fighting continued. Hour after hour, Warsaw radio broadcasted the Polish National anthem. Finally, on September 27, it went silent.

Germany and the Soviet Union divided Poland between themselves. The Soviets were ruthless in their occupation of the eastern half of Poland. Anyone who might be able to rally civilians to revolt, including military officers, intellectuals, politicians, and priests, was systematically eliminated. Poland once more disappeared from the map. John F. Kennedy, writing in 1945, reflected the brutality of the

Soviets, and perhaps an ignorance of German brutalities, when he wrote: "In many ways, the 'S.S.' were as bad as the Russians."[53]

The Soviet Union's expansionist plans were not limited to Poland. Pursuant to their secret agreement with Hitler, the Soviets demanded the right to establish naval and military bases in the republics of Estonia, Latvia, and Lithuania.[54] Those nations were invaded in October.[55] (The following year, these three nations were incorporated into the Soviet Union as constituent republics).[56]

Finnish authorities refused to permit Soviet military bases, so on November 30, without a declaration of war, about one million Soviet troops invaded Finland.[57] The Soviets were particularly brutal towards Finnish civilians. President Roosevelt sharply condemned "this dreadful rape" and referred to Stalin's regime as "a dictatorship as absolute as any other dictatorship in the world."[58] The League of Nations expelled the Soviet Union, making it the only country ever expelled from the League for aggression.[59]

By the following March, the Finns had to accept the Red Army's treaty terms and cede territories in southern and eastern Finland to the Soviet Union. The Finnish President bitterly remarked, as he signed the treaty, "Let the hand wither that is forced to sign such a treaty."[60] A few short months later he suffered a stroke and was paralyzed on his right side.[61]

*****

While the prospect of fighting for Hitler was troubling for many Germans, national loyalty was seen as something separate from Nazism. The idea of refusing military service simply did not occur to most people, with the exception of Jehovah's Witnesses.[62] At the beginning of the war at least, it seemed possible to be respectable soldiers. A document called the "Ten Commandments of the German Soldier" was printed in the payment books. The Commandments included such instructions as a prohibition on plundering and instructions that civilians and unarmed prisoners should be treated decently. Later in the war, however, Hitler had that page torn out of the books.[63]

After the coronation of Pope Pius XII, at least some Nazi leaders thought that a *modus vivendi* with the Church might be possible.[64] With the outbreak of aggression, however, such hope evaporated, and

Hitler even briefly recalled his ambassador to the Vatican.[65] Theodor
Groppe, a general who was dismissed from the German army because
he opposed Nazi propaganda against the Catholic Church, warned
Pius that Hitler had vowed: "I will crush Christianity under my heel
as I would a toad."[66]

Early in the war, the German bishops issued a pastoral letter calling on Catholics soldiers to do their duty "full of the spirit of self-sac-
rifice."[67] They also called on "all devout Catholics in civilian life to
pray that God's Providence may bring the war to a victorious conclusion, with a peace beneficial for *Volk Und Vaterland*."[68] This was
never the Vatican's attitude, and it did not take long for the bishops
to change their minds. In 1941, they issued another pastoral letter
condemning the continued persecution of the Church in Germany.[69]
Nazi authorities recognized this second letter as a direct attack on
their authority. One high-ranking Nazi (Reinhard Heydrich) even
went so far as to comment, "Here we see what a bitter and irreconcilable enemy we have in the Catholic Church."[70]

*****

In a report dated December 10, 1939, Cardinal Hlond informed Pope
Pius that numerous priests had been killed, imprisoned or deported;
Catholic schools, hospitals and orphanages were closed; priests were
compelled to say a prayer for Hitler after Sunday Mass (the only day
Mass was permitted); Church money was confiscated; and many
churches were closed "under the pretext of being unsafe for use."[71]
He concluded by saying "In a word, the finest Polish dioceses with
their seven million Catholics are doomed to be lost to the Faith."[72]
The Cardinal's second message to Pius was even more clear as to the
intent of the Nazis:

> It goes without saying that the Nazi aim is to de-Christianize as rap-
> idly as possible these countries which are attached to the Catholic
> faith and the results are as follows: 95 percent of the priests have
> been imprisoned, expelled, or humiliated before the eyes of the faith-
> ful. The Curia no longer exists; the Cathedral has been made into a
> garage... the bishop's palace into a restaurant; the chapel into a ball-
> room. Hundreds of churches have been closed. The whole patrimo-
> ny of the Church has been confiscated, and the most eminent
> Catholics executed....
>   Apparently, it has to be admitted, Hitlerism has succeeded in its
> designs.[73]

Reports also informed the Pontiff about the Nazis' treatment of Polish citizens, noting specifically mass executions and the imprisonment of tens of thousands of Poland's civilian leaders.[74]

From the earliest weeks of the war, the Allies (especially the French and Polish governments) asked the Holy See to condemn both Nazi and Soviet aggression in Poland.[75]

Many Polish priests, including the primate of Poland, also called for a condemnation of the occupying forces.[76] The first papal response came in a speech presented in French to the Belgian Ambassador to the Vatican on September 14. Pius decried the invasion of Poland as "an immeasurable catastrophe," pleaded for civilian populations, and warned against the use of "poison and asphyxiating gases."[77] In an address to a group of Poles at Castel Gandolfo on September 30, in the presence of Polish Cardinal Hlond, Pius again expressed his anguish over the tragedy of Poland and his conviction that it would rise again.[78]

Most of the world learned of Pius XII's feelings towards the Nazis the following month with the release of his first encyclical, *Summi Pontificatus* (*Darkness over the Earth*), on October 20, 1939. In it, Pius wrote of "a world in all too dire need of help and guidance... a world which, preoccupied with the worship of the ephemeral, has lost its way and spent its forces in a vain search after earthly ideals."[79] He condemned the "Godless State" and deplored "the forgetfulness of that law of human solidarity and charity which is dictated and imposed by our common origin and by the equality of rational nature in all men, to whatever people they belong."[80] His reference to an "ever-increasing host of Christ's enemies"[81] was a clear swipe at both Germany and the Soviet Union. He went on to condemn racists, dictators, and treaty violators.[82]

Like most of Pius XII's statements, the words were guarded, but there was no question about the nations he was discussing. Poland was identified by name, and the other nations were easy to identify. Nazi authorities in Germany restricted the publication of *Summi Pontificatus*. "This Encyclical," wrote Heinrich Mueller, head of the Gestapo, "is directed exclusively against Germany, both in ideology and in regard to the German-Polish dispute; How dangerous it is for our foreign relations as well as our domestic affairs is beyond dispute."[83] Goebbels wrote in his diary on October 28, 1939 that it was "partly very aggressive toward us, though covertly."[84] Reinhard

Heydrich, leader of the S.S. Security Office in Warsaw, wrote: "this declaration of the Pope makes an unequivocal accusation against Germany."[85] Von Bergen, the German ambassador to the Holy See, was told that Pius had ceased being neutral.[86] In occupied Poland, Nazi police destroyed a monument to Pope Pius XI which had been on the Cathedral.[87] Eventually the Nazi military in Poland reprinted the encyclical, but they changed the wording, substituting "Germany" for "Poland."[88]

The western powers certainly saw this encyclical as an endorsement. A report from the British Legation to the Holy See noted that *Summi Pontificatus* contained a "frank condemnation of statolatry and its consequences" similar to the condemnation of Nazism that was found in *Mit brennender Sorge*.[89] The minutes of a meeting of the British high command report:

> The Encyclical itself is perhaps, in some ways, the most important document the war has yet produced and the wider its circulation the better from all points of view.
>
> ***
>
> I am strongly in favor of instructing Mr. Osborne to convey, if possible to the Pope himself, an expression of H.M. Government's appreciation of the sentiments expressed in the Encyclical. To this might be added a personal message from the Secretary of State.[90]

A headline in the London *Daily Telegraph* on October 28 read: "Pope condemns Nazi theory."[91] *The American Israelite* reported on the Pope's "denunciation of Nazism."

The President of France praised the new Pope's encyclical,[92] and Cardinal Hlond wrote from Poland to offer his thanks:

> This official and solemn statement, together with the unforgettable paternal allocation of September 30, will be greatly treasured by Poles. It will also be, for the rising generation, a source of the great strength in the Faith and the traditional attachment to the Holy See, especially when it is seen in the light of the many and far-reaching works of relief that Your Holiness has initiated, and conducts with papal generosity on behalf of the Polish people, condemned even in their own country to extermination by misery, hunger and disease.[93]

Later, French planes dropped thousands of copies of this encyclical over western Germany in a propaganda battle.[94]

Pius sought to unite Catholics throughout the world in a crusade of prayer for peace. He also called upon them to provide money, food, and clothing to help the victims of the war. He said that whatever money was given to him would be spent to relieve the poor and needy, and that is what he did. During the war there was no heat in the papal apartment. Pius felt that, since the poor lacked coal, he too would make a sacrifice.[95] In a November 1939 radio address, he explained that "when Catholics are not aware of their duty with regard to the non-Catholics throughout the world, this is a defect in their Catholic mentality."[96]

Yitzhak Isaac Halevy Herzog, Chief Rabbi in the Holy Land, sought an audience with Pius XII in 1939 on "certain matters of a non-political nature which are of most vital importance to Jewry."[97] The Pope did not meet with Rabbi Herzog, but he did arrange for the rabbi to have an audience with the Cardinal Secretary of State.[98] The rabbi's concern was forwarded to the Pope, who established committees to help Catholic-Jewish refugees, and he also attempted to organize the emigration of some 3,000 Catholic-Jews to Brazil.[99] After the war, Rabbi Herzog offered his thanks for Pius XII's "life-saving efforts on behalf of Jews during the Nazi occupation."[100]

Shortly after the outbreak of war, Pius XII established the Pontifical Relief Commission, with agencies in Norway, Denmark, France, Belgium, The Netherlands, Greece, and Yugoslavia. An office was also established in Lisbon for the purchase and distributions of supplies from the United States.[101] These agencies worked throughout the war to help alleviate suffering. The Vatican's efforts to provide food and clothing to people in occupied countries was frequently hindered by Allied or Axis efforts to avoid providing any benefit to the enemy.[102] Thus, the Allies refused to lift the blockade against Germany and argued that the occupying nation had the responsibility to provide for the needs of those in the occupied countries.[103] Similarly, when the Vatican tried to send money and supplies to occupied Poland, the effort was derailed by German authorities. Later, when the Germans agreed to allow the American Commission for Polish Relief to send supplies to Poland, the Vatican was able to funnel in supplies.[104]

Pius opened the Vatican Information Bureau in September 1939, based on a similar organization formed by Benedict XV during World War I.[105] It started when a Polish family requested the Vatican Secretary of State to find family members who had been deported. The volume of requests for information grew as the war spread. The office was originally staffed with only a handful of clerks, but the

bureau had to hire many more people to handle the increasing number of requests. Soon, the office was receiving a thousand letters per
day asking for help in locating prisoners and other war victims.
Eventually, as many as 600 people were hired to answer the correspondence. Vatican Radio sent out up to 27,000 messages per month
trying to locate missing persons.[106] After the war, the Vatican offered
a similar information service, providing the name and addresses of
German prisoners to their families.[107]

*****

In late 1939, with Poland fully under control, Hitler turned his attention to the West and began preparing for war. Many in the German
populace, however, feared that Hitler would lead Germany to ruin.
Some of them began considering ways to thwart him.[108]   One of
Hitler's most serious threats came from the High Command of the
German Armed Forces, which began plotting to overthrow him and to
put a new government in place.[109]

The reaction by other nations to an anti-Hitler coup was a serious
concern to these conspirators. If they were to stage a revolt the
British and French might take military advantage of it, occupy
Germany, and mete out harsh justice to the German people even
though they had deposed Hitler. It was therefore necessary to reach
an understanding with the Allies.

There was only one leader of a neutral government who was trusted by the German resistance: Pope Pius XII.[110] Although the leaders
of the planned coup, Colonel Hans Oster, General Ludwig Beck, and
Major Hans Dohnanyi, were Protestants, they recruited Dr. Josef
Mueller, a leading Munich lawyer and a devout Catholic, to travel to
the Vatican to ask the Pope to broker a peace agreement between
Britain and the anti-Nazi Germans.[111]

Mueller was well connected inside the Vatican, and he succeeded
in convincing the Pope to serve as an intermediary. Although he was
not anxious to get involved in the matter,[112] Pius said that "the
German opposition must be heard in Britain," and the voice would be
his.[113] Word of this spread quickly among the conspirators, and the
conspirators used papal cooperation to convince other Germans to
join in the conspiracy.[114]

Oster and Dohnanyi were members of the German Intelligence Service, and they inducted Mueller into that organization so that he could explain the many trips that he would be making to Rome.[115] Mueller then set up a chain of communication (through Fr. Robert Leiber, long time private secretary and confidant to Pius XII) in order to avoid drawing suspicion.[116] Over the course of several months, the Pope relayed messages between Mueller and the British Minister to the Holy See, Sir Francis D'Arcy Osborne.[117] On several occasions Mueller also brought messages to Pius from sources inside Germany concerning military plans and movements.[118] Pius forwarded these warnings to the threatened governments.[119] As others have noted, "Never in all history had a pope engaged so delicately in a conspiracy to overthrow a tyrant by force."[120]

The Pope's involvement in this clandestine work was prompted by his distrust of Nazism and his perception of its bitter attitude toward Christianity. He specifically told the British ambassador that "the German principals are in no way connected with the Nazi Party."[121] On December 4, 1939, the French ambassador to the Holy See was received by Pius XII in a private audience. The ambassador later reported: "The religious situation in Germany preoccupied him more than ever. Anti-Christianity was apparently congenital to Nazism (he said), incorporated in it."[122]

On January 12, 1940, in a private letter to Lord Halifax, Osborne wrote that the Pope had been approached by an intermediary who said that a German offensive was planned for February, but that a group of German generals were prepared to overthrow Hitler and reach a peace settlement if they were assured of certain terms.[123] Those terms included "restoration" of Poland and Czechoslovakia, but retention of the *Anschluss* with Austria. Osborne reported that the Pope felt it his duty to pass on this information, but that he was not expressing any personal opinion on the terms of the proposal.[124]

The British were cautious about the message from Germany. (Osborne reported that "the whole thing was hopelessly vague.")[125] They had previously received false messages of this sort, designed by the Nazis to determine whether any Germans were cooperating with the British.[126] Osborne reported back to the Pope that the British wanted more assurances regarding the overthrowing of Hitler. Pius seemed to understand that the British could not take the rather nebulous and uncertain proposals very seriously unless there were more details from inside Germany.[127]

In the first week of February 1940, Pius arranged for a secret meeting with Osborne. Osborne was told not to dress in formal wear, but to be in his normal work clothes.[128] He was discretely led to the Pope's personal apartment. The Pope reported that he had again been approached by the German intermediary and that the Germans once again proposed overthrowing Hitler. This time, however, there were more details. The proposal was to establish a military dictatorship for a period of time, to be replaced by "a democratic, conservative and moderate government," decentralized and federal in nature.[129] The Rhineland and Westphalia would remain united to Prussia; Austria would be within the federation, but Poland and non-German Czechoslovakia would be independent. The Germans wanted to use this plan as the basis for future negotiations.[130]

The Pope again made it clear that he was not recommending this proposal. In fact, he expressed intense dislike at having to pass on the message.[131] He recognized the risk and urged absolute secrecy (even to the point of not informing his own Secretary of State).[132] He thought, however, that this was an important matter, and he was willing to do whatever was necessary to bring about peace.[133]

The British leadership, like the Holy See, was very concerned that a coup might lead to a Communist takeover in Germany.[134] Nevertheless, they replied that if they were certain that the principals behind this offer were capable of carrying out the plan, they would be willing to consider the proposal after consultation with French leaders.[135]

Unfortunately, the conspirators came to fear that Nazi officials had caught wind of their plot, and they were reluctant to reveal their identities to the British officials.[136] Additionally, Hitler's early and impressive military campaigns made it much more difficult to gather support inside of Germany for his overthrow.[137] On March 30, 1940, Pope Pius told Osborne that he had heard no more from the Germans since passing on the last message. Osborne reported that Pius seemed considerably disillusioned, but that he seemed to understand the reasons why the British were skeptical of German intentions.[138] As others have observed: "The plot thickened for some five months and ultimately failed only because of a lack of trust between the

British and the German plotters, not because of any hesitancy on the part of Pius XII to take part in so dangerous a conspiracy."[139]

In the following years there were several times when the Nazis almost uncovered the Pope's involvement in this plot, and the Vatican expected that this would happen.[140] In such a case, "the pope certainly would have been a hunted (if not dead) man, and terrible retaliation would likely have been visited on the Vatican and Catholics throughout Europe."[141] In the autumn of 1942, a Munich businessman was arrested for smuggling foreign currency across the border into Switzerland. He told Himmler's men about Mueller's trips to the Vatican and the plot to get rid of Hitler, but the whole truth was not known by the Reich leaders until late 1944.[142] Certainly this sealed Hitler's view of Pope Pius XII.[143]

Pius might have supported a proposed coup, but would not have supported a bombing, especially in the early years when the Pope still hoped to persuade world leaders toward a path of peace. He sent Hitler a letter congratulating him for surviving an attempt on his life in 1939.[144] Some commentators have looked to this letter as a sign of pro-Nazi sympathy. Hitler, however, did not see it the same way. "He would much rather have seen the plot succeed," Hitler said.[145] When his aids pointed out that Pius XII had been a friend to Germany when he was nuncio, Hitler responded, "that's possible, but he's no friend of mine."[146]

*****

Relations between the Vatican and the United States government, though informal, were very good at the time the war broke out. Pius XII (then Secretary of State Pacelli) met President Roosevelt on his 1936 trip to the United States, and the two men had become friends.[147] Their wartime correspondence reveals a deep and mutual respect. At Christmas time 1939, Roosevelt named Myron C. Taylor as his "personal representative" to Pope XII (not an ambassador to the Vatican).[148] This was a compromise for the formal diplomatic relations that Pius wanted, but which might have been seen in America as giving preference to one religion over another.[149]

In his letter to the Pope suggesting this arrangement, Roosevelt said that this would help "our parallel endeavors for peace and the alleviation of suffering."[150] In Pius XII's return letter to Roosevelt, he said that the President's pledge to join the Vatican's struggle for peace

was "an exemplary act of fraternal and hearty solidarity between the
New and the Old World in defiance against the chilling breath of
aggressive and deadly godless and antichristian tendencies, that
threaten to dry up the fountain head whence civilization has come
and drawn its strength."[151] This language, so close to that used in
Summi Pontificatus to indicate the Nazis, must be read in the same
light. In fact, the American Ambassador to Italy reported back on
Christmas Eve 1939 that:

> The Pope today after referring to a violation of "international and
> divine laws" told the Sacred College of Cardinals that he was deeply
> gratified by the appointment of Myron C. Taylor.... The Pope
> remarked "This is Christmas news which could not be more welcome
> since it represents on the part of the eminent head of a great and
> powerful nation a worthy and promising contribution to our desires
> to a just and honorable peace and for a more effective work toward
> alleviating the sufferings of the victims of the war."[152]

Roosevelt and Pius saw some things differently when it came to the
best way to bring about ultimate peace, but they always agreed as to
the unjust nature of Hitler's aggression.[153]

Throughout the war, Taylor carried written and verbal messages
between these two world leaders. (Mussolini, in fact, later came to
blame Taylor for a network of military intelligence in which he thought
the clergy participated.)[154] Following Roosevelt's death, Truman reap-
pointment Taylor, and he stayed in his position until his resignation
on January 18, 1950.[155] Following the war, Pius wrote that the "solution of urgent problems, the interchange of important information,
[and] the organization of American relief," would have been "unthinkable and almost impossible" but for this relationship which permitted
President Roosevelt and the Pope to coordinate their efforts on so
many projects.[156]

*****

The Pope gave the world a five-point peace program in his 1939
Christmas address. Pius called on Catholics the world over, and
especially in comparatively comfortable America, to care for and share
with the needy and alleviate the suffering of refugees and war victims.
He also blamed the hostilities on the way treaties and commitments
were violated. He said the "unlawful use of means of destruction,
even against non-combatants and fugitives, against old people,

women, and children, and the utter contempt for human dignity, liberty, and human life result in deeds which call for the vengeance of God."[157] He would spend the remaining years of the war attempting to alleviate the suffering.

CHAPTER ELEVEN

1940 AND THE NAZIS PRESS ON

By January 1940, approximately 15,000 civilians had died in Nazi-occupied Poland, though the Germans tried to conceal the real situation. As word of Nazi atrocities began to leak to the outside world there was much denial and disbelief. The Holy See, however, was well informed. It knew that innocent people were being subjected to severe abuse (though the "Final Solution" had not yet begun). Mussolini was one of the few world leaders who also knew of the horrible abuses by the German military, and he knew only because the Vatican told him.[1]

On January 19, Pope Pius told Mngr. Giovanni Battista Montini, the future Pope Paul VI, that Vatican Radio must broadcast a report on the conditions of the Catholic Church in German-occupied Poland.[2] The first report, broadcast in German, took place on January 21.[3] Two days later, the Manchester *Guardian* reported: "Tortured Poland has found a powerful advocate in Rome.... [Vatican Radio has warned] all who care for civilization that Europe is in mortal danger."[4] On January 26, Vatican Radio broadcast in English that "Jews and Poles are being herded into separate ghettos, hermetically sealed and pitifully inadequate for the economic subsistence of the missions designed to live there."[5] The report confirmed that "the horror and inexcusable excesses committed on a helpless and a homeless people have been established by the unimpeachable testimony of eyewitnesses."[6]

These broadcasts created a great deal of controversy. In the west, newspapers editorialized that Vatican Radio had set forth "a warning to all who value our civilization that Europe is under a mortal danger."[7] The Germans, on the other hand, sent a representative to the Holy See to file a protest and warn that such broadcasts could lead to "disagreeable repercussions."[8] In fact, the Germans ultimately decided that due to the hostile and anti-German attitude of the Vatican's press and radio, Catholic priests and members of religious orders in occupied Poland would be prohibited from leaving that country.[9]

Pius had condemned German abuses in his first encyclical, *Summi Pontificatus,* and he was behind the radio broadcasts, but he wanted to be more outspoken. He maintained a lower profile, however, because he thought that was his duty. On February 20, 1940, Pius wrote: "When the Pope would like to shout out loud and clear, holding back and silence are unhappily what are often imposed on him; where he would like to act and help, it is patience and waiting (that are imposed on him)."[10] Nevertheless, it was clear by now that the Church was strongly opposed to Hitler's National Socialism. On January 26, an American Jewish newspaper reported: "The Vatican radio this week broadcast an outspoken denunciation of German atrocities in Nazi [-occupied] Poland, declaring the affronted the moral conscience of mankind."[11] This same month, the *United Jewish Appeal for Refugees and Overseas Needs* donated $125,000 to help with the Vatican's efforts on behalf of victims of racial persecution.[12]

In March 1940, Hitler sent his foreign minister, Joachim von Ribbentrop, to meet with Mussolini. *Il Duce* told Ribbentrop that the Church was not a particularly useful friend and that the Pope was not really dangerous. He went on, however, to explain that he knew from personal experience that the Pope's enmity could be unpleasant.[13] Ribbentrop decided to request an audience with the Pope.

The Vatican was not anxious to grant the request, but as Pius explained to the Archbishop of Breslau:

> To avoid the danger of any policy being misunderstood and despite the perplexities existing in many respects, We granted a private audience, allowing Ourselves to be guided here by the consideration that a personal conversation with one of the *Führer's* closest collaborators might offer Us the possibility of establishing a useful contact for restoring the best living conditions for the Catholic Church in Germany and also for the future of the war and of peace.[14]

A caravan made its way to the Vatican. The German cars were adorned with papal colors and Nazi swastikas. Vatican cars had neither.

Ribbentrop, dressed in his Nazi uniform, marched into the Pope's office and gave the Pope a lecture on German might and the folly of the Vatican having sided with the democracies.[15] Pius then pulled out a ledger and—in perfect German—recited a long list of outrageous abuses by the Nazis in Poland, giving the precise date, time, and details of each. *The New York Times* reported that "the Pontiff, in the burning words he spoke to Herr Ribbentrop... came to the defense of the Jews in Germany and Poland."[16] Ribbentrop did not satisfy the Pope's request for assurances of better treatment in the future, but he did promise to take the matter under consideration.[17] Pius then terminated the audience. Ribbentrop reportedly felt faint as he left.[18]

On April 9, 1940, German troops swept across the Danish border. Danes, including King Christian X, Catholic bishops, priests and students, demonstrated solidarity with the Jews by wearing the yellow star in public.[19] Privately, the Danes hid and eventually smuggled almost the entire Jewish population of 8,000 to safety.[20] The Catholic Church played an important role in this rescue, and Pius XII was noted for his contribution to the effort.[21]

It was clear that Hitler was not satisfied. On April 19, Roosevelt's envoy, Myron Taylor was sent from his residence in Florence to Vatican City to discuss ways to keep Mussolini out of the war. Cardinal Maglione suggested that Roosevelt write to Mussolini. Taylor then suggested that Pius might also play a role. He gave Maglione two questions and waited in Rome for an answer from the Pope. The following day, at three in the afternoon, Taylor cabled the response back to the States:

> 1. Is it necessary to send at this moment a message from the president to Mussolini?
> —*The reply was that such a message should be sent immediately.*
> 2. Should a parallel endeavor be undertaken by the Holy See?
> —*The response was affirmative. He added that the two steps, one taken by the pope and the other by the president, should remain independent and not appear as linked together.*[22]

Unfortunately, the joint effort could not stop Hitler from invading the threatened nations,[23] but the Vatican did play an important role in helping the Allies prepare for a German offensive.

The German coup which had been planned in late 1939 had never come to fruition, but some of the conspirators still believed that Hitler had to be stopped. Although they were Protestants, they again turned to the neutral world leader in whom they had the most confidence, Pope Pius XII.

These anti-Hitler Germans sent a message to the Vatican concerning the German plans to invade Holland, Luxembourg, and Belgium. When Pius learned of the message, he agreed to pass it on to the Allies. With his consent, it was sent by coded radio signals to the nuncios in Brussels and the Hague, then was forwarded to the Allied leaders in London and Paris.[24] On May 3, 1940, Cardinal Maglione sent two identical telegrams, one each to the nuncio in Brussels and to the internuncio at the Hague. (The following month, the Germans expelled the nuncios in Brussels and The Hague.)[25]

The telegrams from the Holy See read: "From a source that can be considered trustworthy, we have learned that, unless something prevents it or happens in the meantime, an offensive will shortly occur on the western front; it will also affect Holland, Belgium, and perhaps Switzerland."[26] A similar report was verbally given to Charles-Roux, the French Ambassador to the Vatican. On May 6, he telegraphed his government: "Once again the pope and Msgr. Montini informed me and my counselor that, according to information coming to them from a foreign country, the Germans will unleash an offensive to the western front within a very short time (a week)."[27] He added in a letter of the same date that the offensive would be simultaneously launched against France, Belgium, and Holland.[28] The British representative to the Vatican also sent a similar message back to his home office on May 6, though he mentioned that he gave it little credence.[29]

Although the warnings reached the Allies about one week before the Nazi invasions took place, they were unable to capitalize on the information. On May 10, 1940, German troops moved into the Low Countries (The Netherlands, Belgium, and Luxembourg). Luxembourg was occupied without any significant resistance. The Dutch mined bridges, blocked roads, and flooded large areas, but it was too little, too late. German tanks moved rapidly and parachutists dropped on the Dutch countryside as infantry troops pushed forward. The Dutch were overwhelmed in five days. Their government fled to England.

The Belgians lasted only two weeks longer than the Dutch. King Leopold III ordered his troops to cease resistance and to lay down their arms in unconditional surrender on May 28, 1940. For this action he was condemned by French Premier Paul Reynaud (who knew that France was vulnerable to attack through Belgium),[30] but the King had been relying on British support. When the support was not forthcoming, the Belgian King had little choice.

The invasion of these small, neutral nations deeply offended the Pontiff. On the very night of the invasions, he personally drafted three messages which were then sent, via telegrams, to the Queen of

Holland, the King of Belgium, and the Grand Duchess of Luxembourg.[31] The telegrams were also printed on the front page of *L'Osservatore Romano* on May 12.[32] (All 180,000 copies were either sold or confiscated shortly after they were delivered to the news-stands; news carriers were savagely beaten.)[33] Though these messages were primarily expressions of condolences, there was little doubt about where the Pope stood. For instance, in the message to King Leopold of Belgium the Pope wrote:

> At a time when the Belgian people, for the second time and contrary to its will and its law, see its territory exposed to the war's cruelties, We, profoundly moved, send to Your Majesty and to your whole beloved country assurances of Our paternal affection; in asking God that this difficult trial come to an end through the reestablishment of Belgium's full liberty and independence. From the bottom of our heart We grant Your Majesty and your people Our apostolic blessing.[34]

Similarly, the telegram to Queen Wilhelmina of Holland asked "the supreme arbiter of the destiny of nations, to hasten with his all-powerful help the reestablishment of liberty and justice."[35] As French Ambassador Charles-Roux later wrote, the messages were "a public affirmation of the guilt and the responsibility of the German government."[36]

Italian code-breakers intercepted and decoded the Pope's messages to the invaded nations.[37] Mussolini took it as a serious personal affront.[38] He called the Papacy "a disease wasting away the life of Italy," and promised to "rid himself of this turbulent priest."[39] The Fascist newspaper *Regime Fascista* declared that Pius XII had incited "the Catholic King of the Belgians to cause the blood of his people to flow, in order to help the Jews, the Freemasons, and the bankers of the City of London."[40] Myron Taylor, Roosevelt's representative to the Pope, wrote to the President that "the Pope is under fire from the political forces in Italy. The *Osservatore Romano* is assailed openly and even the Pope since his three messages... has been openly attacked. It is true that he needs all the support that can be given him...."[41]

Mussolini's ambassador, Dino Alfieri, personally filed an official protest on May 13, charging that Pius had taken sides against Italy's ally, Germany.[42] The Pope responded that his conscience was at ease, saying: "We are not afraid to go to a concentration camp."[43] He added:

> The Italians are certainly well aware of the terrible things taking place
> in Poland. We might have an obligation to utter fiery words against
> such things; yet all that is holding Us back from doing so is the
> knowledge that if We should speak, We would simply worsen the
> predicament of these unfortunate people.[44]

As he frequently explained to the German bishops, while he was neutral, he was not indifferent to violations of justice. The American Jewish press noted, "Pope Pius XII has been moving cautiously for this is a time of war—when heads of religions and states must act with calm and consideration," but now he was taking actions that were "obviously a rebuke to Italian anti-Semitism."[45]

Relations between Italy and the Holy See were now severely strained.[46] A headline in the *New York Times*, dated March 14, 1940, proclaimed: "Pope is Emphatic About Just Peace... Jews' Rights Defended." Fascist youths protested his stance.[47] A group of fascist youths even mobbed Pius XII's limousine shouting "death to the Pope!" as he was traveling to a Roman church for Mass.[48] By the end of May, 1940, the French ambassador to Italy reported: "Pius XII did not conceal from me that he had used up all his credit; the Duce refused to listen to him and no longer reads his letters."[49] Italian Minister of Foreign Affairs, Galeazzo Ciano, wrote in his diary on May 12, 1940:

> The telegrams sent by the Pope to the rulers of the three invaded
> states have incensed Mussolini, who would like to curb the Vatican,
> and is inclined to go to extremes. In these last few days he often
> repeats that the papacy is a cancer which gnaws at our national life,
> and that he intends, if necessary, to liquidate this problem once and
> for all. He added: "The Pope need not think that he can seek an
> alliance with the monarch, because I am ready to blow both of them
> up to the skies at the same time."[50]

The next day's entry in Ciano's diary indicates that Pius XII had been approached by one of Mussolini's representatives, but the Pope refused to cooperate. "[H]e is even ready to be deported to a concentration camp, but will do nothing against his conscience....He cannot be accused of cowardice or indifference to human suffering."[51]

*****

On the day after the Dutch surrendered, the Germans began turning their attention to northern France. Nazi propaganda had been favorably received in France, perhaps because Hitler had only authorized an expurgated French translation of *Mein Kampf*.[52] Robert d'Harcourt was one of the few voices warning the French about the dangers to be found in Hitler's teachings.[53] In the late 1930s, he published several pamphlets explaining Hitler's tactics and his aims. As Secretary of State, Pacelli sent him a handwritten note thanking him for taking these actions.[54] In general, however, the French did not know what lay in store.

Marshal Henri Pétain, a French World War I hero, succeeded Reynaud as Prime Minister of France on June 16, 1940, two days after the fall of Paris. The Nazis installed a friendly government on July 1, in the town of Vichy in central France. France was thus split into the occupied north and unoccupied Vichy France further south. Former Under-Secretary of Defense, General Charles de Gaulle, exiled in England, called on his compatriots to resist the Germans.

On October 24, 1940, Marshal Pétain met with Hitler. One week later, he proclaimed that "It is with honor, and in order to maintain French unity... that in the framework of an activity which will create the European new order I today enter the road of collaboration."[55] Pétain was attracted to the notion of a strong, authoritarian government. He stood for the protection of private property, social harmony, and order.[56] Believing that France had been overwhelmed through "moral decadence," he asked for and received full executive and legislative powers, without restriction. This was at first greeted with widespread support from the public.[57]

All but five or six of the nation's seventy-six bishops embraced Pétain's National Revolution, which promised a return to the spiritual and moral values espoused by the Church. Religious instruction, outlawed since the separation of church and state in 1905, was revived in public schools. Teachers were instructed to teach morality and spiritual values. Pétain replaced the familiar socialist-sounding device, "*Liberté, Fraternité, Egalité*" (Liberty, Brotherhood, Equality), with the more conservative: "*Travail, Famille, Patrie*" (Work, Family, Homeland).[58] The Vichy government also provided support for religious education, and crucifixes were hung on all public buildings.

Shortly after the Vichy government came into being, Cardinal Pierre Gerlier, Archbishop of Lyons, reflected the feeling of many French people when he said that "if [France] had remained victorious, we would possibly have remained the prisoners of our errors.

Through being secularized, France was in danger of death."[59] This did not reflect the attitude of the Pope. "From the very first day... the opposition between the orientation of the Vichy government and the thought of Pius XII was evident."[60] Shortly after the Germans took over, Pius XII sent a secret letter to Catholic bishops of Europe entitled *Opere et Caritate* (*By Work and by Love*). In it, he instructed the bishops to help all who were suffering racial discrimination at the hands of the Nazis.[61] They were instructed to read the letter in their Churches in order to remind the faithful that racism is "incompatible with the teachings of the Catholic Church."[62] Perhaps due in part to this letter, Cardinal Gerlier later became an outspoken critic of Vichy and part of the French resistance.[63]

From the summer of 1941 on, foreign Jews were rounded up and deported from Vichy, with the full cooperation of Vichy officials.[64] The highest dignitaries of the Church immediately denounced the deportations and the treatment of Jews. Nuncio Valeri contacted Pétain, demanding that the deportations end. Pétain reportedly said: "I hope that the Pope understands my attitude in these difficult circumstances." The nuncio replied: "It is precisely that which the Pope cannot understand."[65] Vatican Radio condemned "this scandal... the treatment of the Jews."[66] The Papal Secretary of State, Cardinal Maglione, told the French Ambassador to the Vatican "that the conduct of the Vichy Government toward Jews and foreign refugees was a gross infraction" of the Vichy Government's own principles, and was "irreconcilable with the religious feelings which Marshal Pétain had so often invoked in his speeches."[67]

On July 16, 1942, at 3:00 in the morning, French police officers spread out through Paris, rounded up 13,000 Jews, and locked them in a sports facility known as the *Vélodrome d'Hiver*. The French bishops issued a joint protest which stated:

> The mass arrest of the Jews last week and the ill-treatment to which they were subjected, particularly in the Paris *Vélodrome d'Hiver,* has deeply shocked us. There were scenes of unspeakable horror when the deported parents were separated from their children. Our Christian conscience cries out in horror. In the name of humanity and Christian principles we demand the inalienable rights of all individuals. From the depths of our hearts we pray Catholics to express their sympathy for the immense injury to so many Jewish mothers.[68]

Never, however, did mere words deter the Nazis from their goals. In fact, the statements of protest from Catholic leaders in France angered Laval, and he reaffirmed his decision to cooperate in the deportation of all non-French Jews to Germany.[69] On August 6, 1942, a *New York Times* headline proclaimed: "Pope is Said to Plead for Jews Listed for Removal from France."[70] Three weeks later, a headline in the same paper told the story: "Vichy Seizes Jews; Pope Pius Ignored."[71]

The Pope issued a formal protest to Pétain, instructed the nuncio to issue another protest, and recommended that religious communities provide refuge to Jewish people.[72] In fact, the American press reported that the Pope protested to the Vichy government three times during August 1942,[73] but Vichy officials tried to keep this from the public. This same month, Archbishop Jules Gerard Saliége, from Toulouse, sent a pastoral letter to be read in all churches in his dioceses. It said: "There is a Christian morality that confers rights and imposes duties.... The Jews are our brothers. They belong to mankind. No Christian can dare forget that!"[74] *L'Osservatore Romano* praised Saliege as a hero of Christian courage, and as soon as the war was over, Pope Pius XII named him a cardinal.[75]

According to the *Geneva Tribune* of September 8, 1942, Vichy ordered the French press to ignore the Pope's protest concerning the deportation of Jews. Despite this order, word spread rapidly due to the courageous attitude of members of the French resistance, who knew that they had the blessing of Rome.[76] *The Canadian Jewish Chronicle*, referring to Vichy leader Pierre Laval, ran the following headline on September 4, 1942: "Laval Spurns Pope—25,000 Jews in France Arrested for Deportation."[77] In an editorial dated August 28, 1942, *The California Jewish Voice*, called Pius "a spiritual ally" because he "linked his name with the multitude who are horrified by the Axis inhumanity."[78] In a lead editorial, *The Jewish Chronicle* (London) said that the Vatican was due a "word of sincere and earnest appreciation" from Jews for its intervention in Berlin and Vichy.[79]

The Archbishop of Lyons, Cardinal Gerlier, who had earlier welcomed the Vichy government, now wrote protests which were read from pulpits throughout his diocese and were broadcast throughout the nation despite Nazi censorship.[80] The cardinal declared that the French State and Church were now divided, and he refused to bless those who volunteered to fight for Vichy forces or to say mass for those who died fighting for that cause.[81]

Archbishop Saliége of Toulouse also protested against the deportations. He wrote a stirring letter which was read from all the pulpits in his diocese and broadcast over Vatican Radio:

> It has been reserved to our time to witness the sad spectacle of children, of women, of fathers and mothers, being treated like a herd of beasts; to see members of the same family separated one from another and shipped away to an unknown destination....Jews are men. Jewesses are women....They cannot be maltreated at will....They are part of the human race. They are our brethren as much as are so many others. A Christian cannot forget that.[82]

Late in June, 1943, the Vatican Radio warned the French people that "he who makes a distinction between Jews and other men is unfaithful to God and is in conflict with God's commands."[83]

A statement by Bishop Pierre Théas of Montauban, read in all the churches of his diocese, was representative of the attitude of the Catholic leadership:

> Hereby I make known to the world the indignant protest of Christian conscience, and I proclaim that all men, whether Aryan or non-Aryan, are brothers because they were created by the same God; and that all men, whatever their race or religion, have a right to respect from individuals as well as from States.[84]

Many Catholic priests sheltered Jews and urged their parishioners to do the same. When the Nazis discovered this, the priests were arrested for their efforts (and typically sent to concentration camps where many died).[85]

The widespread bravery of Catholic priests in their opposition to Nazism was illustrated in a wartime book written by a member of the French underground. Because the book, *Paris Underground*, came out in 1943, the author changed the names of the people involved, but she attested that the basic facts were "a matter of record."[86] One of the important characters was a Catholic priest, Fr. Christian. According to the book, he was very involved in underground work, including passing information to Britain and hiding refugees. At one point, he was found by a German officer in a private home where he had been hiding British soldiers. He invented a cover story, and the Nazi believed it. The officer then offered the priest a ride in his car.

> "Thank you, Captain," Father Christian answered, "but I am afraid my parishioners would not understand if they saw me arrive with a German officer. You realize, of course, how they feel."

"Yes, indeed," said Captain Weber stiffly. "They do not yet understand that we have come to save their country from degradation."[87]

Not only did the priest refuse to ride with the Nazi officer, but the officer also understood why the ride was declined: French people knew that the Catholic Church was opposed to what the Nazis were doing.[88]

As it did in other nations, the Church in France helped produce thousands of false documents that were used to deceive the Germans, and special efforts were made to protect Jewish children.[89] Working with Jewish groups, French Christian organizations saved an estimated 7,000 Jewish children in France.[90] At one point, a force of Protestant and Catholic social workers broke into a prison in Lyon and "kidnapped" ninety children who were being held with their parents for deportation.[91] The parents were deported the next day. The children were sheltered in religious institutions under the protection of Cardinal Pierre Gerlier, with the assistance of Father Pierre Chaillet, a member of the cardinal's staff. When Cardinal Gerlier refused an order to surrender the children, Vichy leaders had Chaillet arrested. He served three months in a "mental hospital" before being released.[92] On April 16, 1943, the *Australian Jewish News* ran an article quoting Gerlier to the effect that he was simply obeying Pius XII's instruction to oppose anti-Semitism.[93]

Father Marie-Benoît of Marseilles, a Capuchin priest, turned his monastery into a veritable rescue factory. Inside, he and his workers printed passports, identification cards, certificates of baptism, and employers' recommendation letters for Jews.[94] Outside, he helped smuggle many Jewish people into Spain and Switzerland. Eventually he earned the name "Father of the Jews."[95]

In July 1943, Marie-Benoît was summoned to Rome by the Italian government. He took advantage of the trip to present a plan to Pius XII. After thanking the Holy Father for his work on behalf of French Jews, and forwarding "the appreciation they feel toward the Catholic Church for the charity it has shown them,"[96] he proposed a plan to offer more help. Marie-Benoît wanted the Church to gather information on the whereabouts of Jews deported from France, particularly to Auschwitz; obtain more humane treatment of Jews in French concentration camps; work for the repatriation of Spanish Jews who were residing in France; and transfer some 50,000 French Jews to North Africa where they would be safe. The Pope readily agreed, and helped

Marie-Benoît obtain pledges of support from Britain, the United States, and Jewish organizations in the Allied nations.

Unfortunately, Marie-Benoît's project failed. With the surrender of the Italian forces to the Allies, German troops swept into the Italian zone of France, ruining any chance for cooperation with occupying forces. That was not, however, the end of his efforts. As thousands of Jews fled across the Alps to safer countries, Marie-Benoît again approached the Vatican. With its help, he convinced the Spanish government to authorize its consuls in France to issue entry permits to all Jews who could prove Spanish nationality. In case of doubt about nationality, the final decision rested with Marie-Benoît.[97]

In 1942, French forces in North Africa disregarded orders from Vichy and sided with Allied forces led by General Dwight D. Eisenhower, thus joining in the struggle against the Axis. This led to the German occupation of the whole of France in November 1942. The Vichy government was forced by the German authorities to move first to eastern France and finally, as virtual captives, into Germany.[98] In the face of the onslaught, the Vichy regime finally disintegrated.[99]

Even before France's liberation in August 1944, Charles de Gaulle was named president of the new provisional government of France (after having served as commander-in-chief of the Free French forces). On May 29, he sent a handwritten note to Pope Pius XII:

> Dear Holy Father:
> Placed at the head of the French Republic's provisional government, I am happy to bring Your Holiness assurances of our people's filial respect for and their attachment to the Apostolic See.
> The trial endured by France for many years now, the suffering of each of its children, have been lessened by the witness of your fatherly affection. We foresee an end to the conflict.... In accord with what you have taught us, we believe that the most underprivileged deserve our greatest care.
> We are resolved to save [the French people], and we very much hope to do so while benefitting from the special kindness that Your Holiness indeed wishes to extend to France.
> May Your Holiness deign to bless our undertakings as well as the faith of the French people whose witness I place at Your feet.[100]

In June, de Gaulle visited Vatican City for a meeting with the Pope to discuss the future of Europe, France, Germany, and Italy. The Vatican recognized that Vichy would soon disappear, and de Gaulle was treated as the head of the French government (resulting in a protest from the ambassador from Vichy).[101]   As de Gaulle later described it:

> The Holy Father received me. Under the kindness of the welcome and the simplicity of the moment, I was grasped by how sensible and powerful was his thinking. Pius XII judges everything from a perspective that surpasses human beings, their undertakings and their quarrels.... This is why the Pastor had made the church a domain reserved to himself personally and where he displays the gifts of authority, of influence, of the eloquence given him by God. Pious, compassionate, political–such does this pontiff and sovereign appear to me because of the respect that he inspires in me.[102]

De Gaulle returned to Paris in August 1944. As part of the new government's procedures, all diplomats who had represented their countries to the Vichy government, including Bishop Valerio Valeri, the Vatican's nuncio, were expelled.[103] De Gaulle, however, made it clear that he appreciated the nuncio and the Holy See's efforts during the occupation, going so far as to grant Valeri an audience.[104] De Gaulle informed the former nuncio that he was aware of all the good things that he had done for France and he regretted his departure, which was "solely due to events that unfolded during these past years."[105] He awarded Valeri the Grand Cross of the Legion of Honor and had military honors paid to the departing diplomat.[106] Despite sending Valeri home, de Gaulle had no desire to sever relations with the Holy See.[107] Valeri was replaced by Pius XII's personal choice, Monsignore Angelo Roncalli, the future Pope John XXIII.[108]

*****

As war spread throughout Europe, the Pope became especially concerned about protecting his people and his nation—the Church and Vatican City. During the early months of the war, Mussolini remained neutral, but when France was about to fall he decided to join the Nazis and claim some of the spoils. On June 10, 1940, Italy declared war on France and Great Britain and invaded southern France.[109] Speaking of Italy, President Roosevelt said, "The hand that held the dagger, has stuck it into the back of its neighbor."[110] Then, citing "the almost incredible events of the past two weeks," he asked Congress for more than a billion dollars in additional defense appropriations. He also called for the annual production of 50,000 warplanes.[111]

Three days after Italy's entrance into the war, Pius XII issued the encyclical *Saeculo Exeunte Octavo* (*On the Independence of Portugal*). In it, he again emphasized his vision of the Church's role during the war:

> Following in the footsteps of Him who "went about doing good and healing" and obeying the command of Him who said, "heal the sick" and "make disciples of all nations," the missionary not only speaks learnedly and wisely of the Kingdom of God, but also attempts to heal bodies infected with disease and misery.[112]

The provisions of the Lateran Treaty were supposed to assure the freedom and neutrality of the Vatican, but the war would not be kept from Rome. Pius XII gave up his annual vacations during the war, abandoning his summer home so that he could stay in Vatican City.[113]

When his efforts to keep Italy out of the war failed, Pius next sought assurances from both sides that the Vatican's neutrality would be respected. Since Italy was allied with Germany, one of the Pope's first concerns was securing a promise that Allied forces would not bomb Rome.[114] Because Axis powers stored great quantities of munitions in Rome, it was a likely Allied target. There were also many important military targets on the outskirts of Rome, including three air fields and a munitions plant. As such, the Allies promised to respect the Vatican's neutrality, but did not promise to avoid Rome altogether.[115] Germany was more certain in its pledge to try to avoid damaging Italian cities.[116] Of course, there would have been little reason for Germany to plan an attack of Italy early in the war. (Later, German forces would occupy and ultimately threaten to raze the city.)

During the war, the Vatican provided sanctuary to Jewish people, German deserters, Poles conscripted by the German army, anti-fascist Italians, and diplomats from nations at war with Italy.[117] This caused the Vatican to be the possible target of bombings or other military action. Despite the promises from the Allies and Germany, Pius was worried that Vatican City would be bombed. All Vatican apartments were fitted with heavy curtains for blackouts. Vatican firemen made inspections each night. Air raid sirens went off several times a day, and the Vatican had many blackouts to avoid being bombed by one side or the other.[118] (Pius refused to enter the shelters during these times).

President Roosevelt wrote Pius and told him that British aircraft and weapons captured by Axis powers were being saved for the purpose of attacking the Vatican while placing the responsibility on the Allies.[119] The Vatican built several anti-air raid shelters as well as a steel armored room to protect rare books and manuscripts. (These precautions paid off when bombs did fall on the Vatican later in the war).[120]

Allied diplomats in Italy, including the ambassadors from France, Great Britain, Poland, and Belgium, all moved into Vatican City after Italy declared war. German intelligence suspected that the Allies used the Vatican as a secure base for espionage. In order to avoid a breach of neutrality, the diplomats were forbidden from having political discussions in public, their mail was read, their phone calls were monitored, they could not receive visitors without permission, and they were not permitted to leave Vatican City. Interestingly, in June 1944, when Italy threw in with the Allies, the German ambassador to Italy moved into the Vatican as the French, British, Polish, and Belgian representatives returned to their embassies in Rome.[121]

The Vatican was an important vehicle for uncensored information during the war. *L'Osservatore Romano*, the official Vatican newspaper, became the most widely read source of news in Italy. It had a circulation of about 20,000 before the war, but it increased to about 150,000 by 1940.[122] (Fascist persecution of those who purchased it would result in circulation dropping back down to around 10,000 later in the war).[123] The newspaper was criticized by the Nazis and the Fascists, who charged that it was the "evident mouthpiece of the Jews," that its primary readers were Jews and Masons, and that it, like the Vatican, had "joined the cause of the Allies."[124]

Vatican Radio was also an important source of uncensored information. In 1931, Secretary of State Pacelli hired Guglielmo Marconi, the inventor of wireless broadcasting, to install a 10-kilowatt transmitter on the highest point in Vatican City. It was refurbished and its power greatly enhanced in 1937. During the war, its steel tower became a symbol of hope for freedom and justice. Listening to it was a criminal offense in Germany.[125]

Vatican Radio was especially effective at rapidly responding to false claims put out by Axis leaders. Not long after the fall of Poland, Vatican Radio began making broadcasts concerning the atrocities that were taking place in that county. Polish Cardinal August Hlond, exiled in Rome, delivered a broadcast on September 28, 1939, in which he condemned aggression against his country and proclaimed,

"Martyred Poland, you have fallen to violence while you fought for the sacred cause of freedom.... On these radio waves... I cry to you. Poland, you are not beaten."[126] When Hitler proposed a "new order" with a federation of European states under the control of Germany and Italy, a Vatican Radio broadcast said, "[i]t is a world order which is as dry as the desert, an order which is the same order as the order of the desert. It is being achieved by the exploitation of human life. What these falsehoods call life is no life. It is dissolution—it is death."[127]

Vatican Radio was able to target its four short-wave bands to areas that were the focus of German propaganda. Thus, when the Germans flooded Spain with the claim that National Socialism was compatible with Christianity, Vatican Radio reduced the number of English broadcasts and increased Spanish broadcasts to tell the Spaniards about the religious conditions in Poland, Austria, and Germany.[128] The broadcast of November 20, 1940, for instance, was a response to an editorial in the Madrid newspaper, *Alcazar*, which had said that "National Socialism is primarily a religious movement based on Christian principles."[129] In response, Vatican Radio reviewed Nazi attacks on Christianity, the Catholic Church, religious leaders, Church doctrine, religious education, and also discussed other matters such as the closing of monasteries in Austria and the confiscation of religious property.[130] Part of the broadcast went as follows:

> With violence and with singular ability this [Nazi] literature has attacked Christianity and the Catholic Church both as a whole and in its personnel and institutions. It has even attacked the most essential dogmas of the Church. This attack has been carried out with the greatest possible efficiency while the Church has been hindered from the self-defense it should properly have employed. As to the education situation, if National Socialism is a Christian movement as the *Alcazar* alleges, what is the explanation of the fact that, whereas in 1933 almost the entire Catholic Youth was educated in Catholic schools, the whole magnificent school organization is now practically nonexistent?[131]

The broadcast went on to note the closing of monasteries in Austria, the deportation of priests in Poland, and the refusal to recognize the validity of Church wedding services.

On October 25, 1940, in response to German news reports concerning the Church in Poland, Vatican Radio revealed that 115 parishes had been deprived of their clergy, 200 clergy from the Poznan diocese had been placed in concentration camps, the cathedrals of Poznan and Gniezno had been closed, most larger seminaries had been taken over, and the Catholic University of Lublin had been closed (with many members of the theology faculty being suppressed).[132] The broadcast concluded by reporting: "The Catholics of Poland have grave need of the Catholics of the whole world to sustain them in their trial."[133] On November 2, the Nazis filed a protest with the Vatican complaining that recent transmissions were "against Hitler, against Nazism" and "in contrast with neutrality."[134]

During the war it was not known how involved the Pope was with Vatican Radio.[135] These broadcasts were so strongly worded and partisan that they regularly prompted vigorous protests from Mussolini and the German Ambassador to the Holy See.[136] (Later, the Polish bishops would complain that papal statements created problems for them by infuriating the Nazis.)[137] Vatican officials responded that Vatican Radio was run by the Jesuits as an independent concern.[138] Recently, however, the Vatican opened many of its wartime records. The researchers discovered that the Pius XII personally authored many of the intensely anti-German statements beamed around the world. In other cases, directives were found from the Pope regarding the content of the broadcasts.[139] The late Father Robert A. Graham, one of the people assigned to go through the Vatican's wartime records, told *The Washington Post*: "I was stupefied at what I was reading. How could one explain actions so contrary to the principle of neutrality?"[140]

In Germany, Bishop Rarkowski published a pastoral letter on the first anniversary of the outbreak of war. In it, he supported the German war effort. Vatican Radio immediately broadcast a response pointing out the discrepancy between his position and that of the Holy See. Vatican Radio reported that "Hitler's war unfortunately is not a just war" and that "God's blessing therefore cannot be upon it."[141]

While neither the Vatican newspaper nor the radio broadcasts were censored, the newspaper was subject to confiscation and radio broadcasts were sometimes jammed.[142] Both were regularly misquoted. When Vatican Radio engaged in counter-propaganda, the Nazis sometimes made threats to the Vatican. Nonetheless, the Vatican press played a very important role throughout the war.[143]

*****

In addition to using Vatican Radio and *L'Osservatore Romano* to spread the truth about the Nazis, Pope Pius XII played an interesting role in the publication of a book in 1940. As discussed earlier, in late 1939 and early 1940, Dr. Josef Mueller carried messages back and forth from anti-Hitler conspirators to the Pope.[144] Mueller also brought messages to Pius from sources inside Germany concerning military plans and movements.[145] Pius forwarded this information to the threatened governments.[146] In fact, on February 28, 1940, Pius met with the American Ambassador to Italy for forty five minutes and conveyed potentially useful military information about the situation as he knew it in Germany.[147]

In addition to smuggling information about the proposed coup and German military movements out of Germany, Mueller brought information with him regarding the persecution of the Catholic Church in Germany by the Nazis. This included information dating back well into the 1930s, and it clearly revealed the contempt that the Nazis had for the Catholic Church. Gestapo spies observed sermons and reported them back to the Nazi Party.[148] Catholic books were suppressed for containing pro-Jewish messages.[149] Members of the "German Faith Movement," who seemed to have the backing of the Nazi party, called the Catholic Church satanic, dangerous, and fraudulent.[150] Jesus was dismissed as a "Jewish Reformer," and Hitler declared to be the one true Lord.[151] If Pius had any delusions about the relationship between Hitler's followers and the Church in Germany, this information cleared them up. In fact, Pius had the information smuggled to London and assisted in having it published.[152] The Pope's efforts to see that this information was made known in the nation that was actively engaged in war with Germany is a clear indication of his true sympathies.

*****

In September 1940, Hitler traveled to the French town of Hendaye to meet with Spanish leader, General Francisco Franco. Hitler wanted Spain to enter the war, and he offered Franco arms, raw materials, and colonies. Spain, however, had not yet recovered from its civil war; it did not need a new foreign one. Besides, Franco's revolution had been against Communism. How could he now side with Hitler, who was cooperating (and soon would be allied) with the Soviet Union? Hitler did not give up easily, but Franco would not budge. Hitler ended up ranting about Franco and his "Jesuit swine" foreign minister.[153] (Later in the war, Franco opened Spain's border to Jews who were fleeing Nazi persecution. Pope Pius XII was able to help thousands reach safety in Spain.)[154]

In November, Hitler met with Soviet Premier Vyacheslav Molotov in Berlin. This resulted in the Soviets signing an accord with the Axis powers, a highly ironic result given the fact that the original purpose of the Axis was to stop the spread of Communism. (Mussolini, though Hitler's truest ally, was unable to prevent him from signing the short-lived treaty.)[155] The two nations had already signed a non-aggression pact and divided Poland, so it was not a big step to formalize their military agreement. Hitler, however, was primarily concerned with securing his eastern front, until he was ready to attack. Like many others, the Soviets reached an accord with Hitler, only to find that he never intended to carry through with his promises.

In December, *L'Osservatore Romano* published an article in response to a brochure that was then being circulated in Italy. The brochure, entitled *Germans and the Catholic Faith in Poland*, claimed that the German authorities had not interfered with religious activities in Poland, that church buildings remained open, and that the Nazis had even assisted in the building of some new Church buildings.[156] The Vatican newspaper, however, pointed out that at least one bishop had been exiled, numerous clergy had been imprisoned, the religious press (including publishers of prayer books) had been restricted, secondary schools and universities had been shut down, Poles were either prohibited from or at least limited in the times and places where they could enter churches, and even *German* Catholics in some areas were completely prohibited from taking part in religious services.[157] Clearly, the Vatican was incensed with the treatment of the Church by the Nazis. The cover of *Time* magazine, dated December 23, 1940, said: "Martyr of 1940; In Germany only the cross has not bowed to the swastika."[158]

On Christmas Eve, Pius XII took to the radio to condemn once more the evils in the world. He said:

> We find ourselves faced with actions as irreconcilable with the prescriptions of positive international law as they are with natural law

and even with the most elementary sentiments of humanity, actions which show us into what a polluted, chaotic circle the juridical sense, led astray by purely utilitarian considerations, can sink. It is in this category that we place: premeditated aggression against a small, hardworking and peaceful people under the pretext of a nonexistent danger that they neither intended nor were capable of; atrocities...; illegal use of destructive force even against noncombatants, fugitives, the elderly and children; a contempt for human dignity, freedom and life that gives rise to actions that cry out for vengeance before God; anti-Christian and even atheistic propaganda.... The memory of the short-lived duration of negotiations and agreements in the end paralyzes any effort capable of leading to a peaceful solution.[159]

There is no doubt but that these were references to Hitler's aggression.[160] Hitler, however, was not interested in a peaceful solution (though he did prevent this message from reaching people in occupied areas).[161]

In Poland, German troops began herding Warsaw's Jewish population into an area behind an eight-foot wall in the city's ghetto district. Nazis claimed that this would give the Jews a new life and also protect Poles from diseases spread by war. In reality, this was simply preparation for the Final Solution.

CHAPTER TWELVE

1941 AND NEW ENEMIES

Nazi occupying forces were very tough on Catholic churches. Prior to the German invasion of Yugoslavia (April 6, 1941), the diocese of Maribor consisted of 654,000 members, 254 parishes, 474 members of the secular clergy, and 109 members of the regular clergy. Within three months of the German invasion, the Gestapo arrested, killed, or expelled eighty-five percent of the clergy. Of the original 254 parishes, only 91 remained, each headed by a single priest. The others were closed or taken over by German authorities. The district of Ptuj originally had thirty parishes and fifty-seven priests. It was left with just one active and two retired priests to minister to 80,000 Catholics. Similarly, in the diocese of Lubliana, the area occupied by the Germans had 128 parishes. By the end of June, 1941, 137 priests had been killed, 74 were expelled and 37 others had fled. That left only nine priests to minister to 215,000 Catholics.[1] As Pope Pius wrote in February 1941, in a letter to the Bishop of Limburg: "The statements about the 'new order' for the Church that have been propagated by a certain party show that it has as its aim the equivalent of a death sentence for the Catholic Church in Germany."[2]

In his Easter message of April 13, 1941, broadcast from the Vatican, the Pope again called for peace and just treatment of the people in all of the occupied nations.[3] He began with a profession of his belief in prayer:

> In this tempest of misfortunes and perils, of afflictions and fears, our most powerful and safest haven of trust and peace is found in prayer to God, in whose hands rests not only the destiny of men but also the outcome of their most obdurate dissensions.
>
> ***
>
> Yes, let us pray for early peace. Let us pray for universal peace; not for peace based upon the oppression and destruction of peoples but peace which, while guaranteeing the honor of all nations, will satisfy their vital needs and insure the legitimate rights of all.[4]

Importantly, it was not just any peace, but "peace that will be just, in accordance with human and Christian norms."[5]

As he did throughout the war, the Pontiff expressed confidence in the ultimate success of prayer. "[U]nder the vigilant providence of God and armed only with prayer, exhortation and consolation, we shall persevere in our battle for peace in behalf of suffering humanity." He asked that "the blessings and comforts of heaven descend on all victims of this war."[6] He then asked the occupying powers to respect the occupied nations:

> With all due esteem we ask the powers which occupy the foreign territories during this war to treat the population in these countries according to the voice of their conscience and their own sense of honor. Be just, humane and cautious. Do not impose on them burdens which you, in similar circumstances, would think unjust. The glory and the pride of prudent commanders is helpful charity; the treatment of the prisoners of war and of the population in the occupied countries is the safest criterion and a most definite characteristic of the height of civilization among persons and peoples. Remember that God may, perhaps, bless or curse your own motherland according to your behavior toward those who fell the victims of your victory.[7]

Clearly, it was an instruction directed at the Axis powers, particularly Germany. In fact, German and Italian representatives criticized the Pope, the Gestapo confiscated printed copies of the remarks, and Goebbels vowed to silence Vatican radio,[8] which the Nazis called the "Voice of the Pope."[9] British officials acknowledged that "the independent stand taken by the Vatican radio is of the greatest importance to our propaganda generally and to our appeal to German Catholics in particular."[10]

British propagandists used Pope Pius XII's Easter statement for military purposes.[11] Rather than simply repeating the Vatican broadcast, British authorities "reinforced" and re-transmitted it from London, while giving the impression that it was coming from and on behalf of the Vatican. (More than once during the war, the Vatican had to warn people that statements being attributed to it—from both sides—were not valid).[12] In addition, British intelligence put out the word that a Christian-oriented radio station that broadcasted Allied propaganda into Germany was actually an arm of Vatican Radio.[13] This, of course, had at least the appearance of being a breach of the Vatican's promises and agreements it had made with Italy and Germany. It also put the Vatican in jeopardy without the Pope's consent.

Bishops in Poland reported that these broadcasts were causing the Nazis to increase the persecution of their victims, especially Catholics.[14] As a result, Pius directed that Vatican Radio be perfectly objective, and broadcasts regarding Germany were suspended.[15] The British government, which lost "a formidable source of propaganda,"[16] issued a protest to the Holy See:

> The sudden silence on a subject of imperative concern to Catholics can only be attributed to successful pressure on the Vatican by German authorities, and his majesty's government cannot but regard the decision of the Vatican to yield to this pressure as highly regrettable and inconsistent with the best interests of the Holy See and the Catholic Church. There can be no doubt that with the United States, the Allied cause will prevail, and the Christian ideal triumph over pagan brutality. What then will be the feeling of the Catholics of the world if it may be said of their Church that, after at first standing courageously against Nazis paganism, it subsequently consented, by surrendering silence, the rights and the principles on which it is based and by which it lives.[17]

There were also some complaints filed by priests who had previously broadcast their sermons but were now prohibited from doing so.

The Vatican's response to the British charge was threefold. First, Pope Pius assured the British Minister to the Holy See, Sir D'Arcy Osborne, that there was no agreement between the Vatican and the Germans concerning future broadcasts. The Pope also, however, explained that he could not ignore the persecution of innocent Catholics that these broadcasts always seemed to prompt. Finally, Pius complained about the British use of his proclamations for propaganda purposes, to the detriment of Catholics in Germany.[18]

Despite these answers, there was some concern in the Vatican that the suspension of radio broadcasts might be seen as some sort of alignment with the Nazis.[19] As such, the Secretary of State prepared a long memorandum, which was personally reviewed and corrected by Pius XII, for distribution to the Holy See's representatives in France, Switzerland, Spain, Argentina, Brazil, and the United States. It pointed out that in those areas occupied by the Germans, Catholic schools and churches were closed, religious houses were invaded and searched, priests were arrested, bishops were kept away from the people, and religious teaching and worship was impeded in a thousand ways.[20] With this type of treatment being accorded Catholics in Nazi-occupied areas, and with a defiant attitude at the upper echelons of the Holy See, it is not surprising to find that by January, Vatican Radio was again broadcasting anti-Nazi messages.[21]

*****

In June 1941, Hitler breached the neutrality agreement he had signed two years earlier and invaded the Soviet Union to seek "living space" for the German people. Hitler believed that Providence intended for Slavs to be servants of the godlike Aryans. (Medieval Latinists had used the word *sclavus* for both slaves and Slavs).[22] In order to make conquered areas of Russia "fit" for German settlers, Jews, Poles, Gypsies, Russians, and Ukrainians convicted of offenses were not to receive normal sentences; they were to be executed.[23] Educated Slavs, like the clergy, were a potential threat and had to be eliminated.

Vyacheslav M. Molotov, Vice Premier of the Soviet Union, broadcast an address in which he said, "This war has been forced upon us, not by the German people, not by German workers, peasants and intellectuals, whose sufferings we well understand, but by the clique of bloodthirsty Fascist rulers of Germany who have enslaved Frenchmen, Czechs, Poles, Serbians, Norway, Belgium, Denmark, Holland, Greece and other nations."[24] Of course, none of the Nazi's earlier aggression seemed to matter to the Soviets until their nation was invaded.

Hitler said the attack was necessary to combat the Russian-British threat to Europe and called it the biggest military attack in the history of the world. He wanted the Pope's blessing on the invasion. He claimed that it was a "crusade" into the godless Soviet Union.[25] (Msgr. Domenico Tardini, head of the Vatican foreign office and an outspoken opponent of Hitler, replied: "Nazism has conducted a veritable persecution against the church and continues to do so. Consequently the swastika is not the cross of a crusade.")[26]

Volunteer regiments of Frenchmen, Spaniards, Italians, Croatians, Hungarians, and Slovenians signed on to go with the German troops for the invasion. A sizeable contingent of priests from the Vatican's Russian seminary in Rome also planned to accompany the German troops, with the hope of opening long-closed churches in the Soviet Union.[27] French Cardinal Boudrillart traveled to Rome to ask a papal blessing for French volunteer soldiers (many of whom were Catholic). The Cardinal said their task was "to free the Russian people." Pius, however, demanded an immediate withdrawal of the request for a blessing and ordered Cardinal Boudrillart to make no further public statements on the war whatsoever.[28]

Although Communism was an open and acknowledged enemy of the Church, Pius XII refused to support the invasion by the Axis powers.[29] Minutes from the British high command, dated September 10, 1941, state: "His Holiness is heart and soul with us in the struggle against Nazism, and his attitude as regards the 'anti-Bolshevist Crusade' leaves nothing to be desired."[30]

In an address Pius gave in late June 1941, he denounced the suffering of "old people, women, children, the most innocent, the most peaceful, the most defenseless."[31] He also spoke of religious persecutions "which the very concern for those who suffer does not allow one to reveal in all their painful and moving detail."[32] Mussolini was furious at the Pope's refusal to support the Axis.[33] In Berlin, a report on intercepted Vatican documents said "the pro-Polish attitude of the Pope and of his secretary of state are clearly seen—an attitude which has been at least insinuated in his public declarations."[34] An intelligence report on Pius XII's June 21 address stated: "A few days after the outbreak of Germany's struggle against the Bolsheviks, the Pope had not one word to say against them. This fact alone shows clearly that his words in this allocution do not refer to Bolshevism but are directed exclusively against National Socialist Germany."[35] The British representative to the Vatican later sought and obtained permission from Pius to report on the Pope's refusal to support Hitler's "crusade." That the Pope had maintained neutrality even against atheistic Bolshevism, it was thought, "would make an excellent impression in London."[36]

With German tanks advancing, Stalin turned to Churchill for help. In a radio address to his people little more than a week after the German invasion, Stalin praised Churchill and other heroes of the West, without mentioning typical Soviet heroes. He re-opened the churches and called up fifteen million men for "The Great Patriotic War." Churchill said that Britain would help the Soviets in any way possible to obliterate the "blood-thirsty guttersnipe." He stated his "one single, irrevocable purpose... to destroy Hitler and every vestige of the Nazi regime."[37] The two nations signed a "Mutual Assistance" agreement on July 12.

Despite their history of abuse and oppression, the Soviets were invited to sign the Atlantic Charter.[38] That document's first point declared that signatories "seek no aggrandizement, territorial or other." It did not matter that the Soviet Union had already annexed the Baltic states, divided Poland with Hitler, and had been expelled from the League of Nations for its invasion of Finland; the Soviets were to be full-fledged partners with the Western Allies.

Pius XII now found himself in the awkward position of privately siding with atheistic Soviet Russia, overwhelmingly Protestant Britain (with its vast, mainly non-Christian Empire), and the predominantly Protestant United States, against Hitler's largely Catholic "Fortress Europe." Moreover, the Pope's predecessor, Pius XI, had written in *Divini Redemptoris (On Atheistic Communism*, 1937) that no one who wanted to save Christian civilization could collaborate with Communists.[39] Yet, here it was: the Allies had made the Soviet Union a full partner in the war against Hitler's National Socialism.

The Pontiff's preference for the Allies over the Axis is reflected in a top secret message, dated September 17, 1941, to the German Foreign Ministry. In it was a translation of the Italian Ambassador to the Holy See's report on a meeting that he had with the Pope a day earlier. When Ambassador Attolico brought up the subject of the Soviet Union, Pius cut him off:

> But if I should talk of Bolshevism—and I would be fully prepared to do so, continued Pius XII, should I then say nothing about Nazism? The situation in Germany, he told me, has become infinitely worse since the day of his departure from Berlin. Even if the *Führer* has ordered the "suspension" of the persecutions, this does not mean that Christ has been readmitted to the schools from which He was removed... or that the German children will no longer be made to recite that parody of the Our Father in which they thank Hitler for their daily bread.[40]

The secret message went on to quote a serious question that Pope Pius asked of the Italian ambassador:

> I was told long ago that in Germany they already had it in mind to do away with the Vatican, because there was no place for it in the new European order, etc., etc. Now, I am assured that even in his meeting with Mussolini the *Führer* stated that it was necessary to "put an end to" the Vatican. Is that true?[41]

The Italian ambassador issued a firm denial and said that this "seemed to make the Pope feel good and almost relieved, thus showing how much his conviction, I might say almost his nightmarish fear, of new and more ruthless persecutions weighs on his mind...."[42] The ambassador went on to explain that the Pope thought that he might one day "be driven out of Rome. But—mark me—he does not speak it out of fear."[43]

Regarding the German request that Pius make a statement about the evils of Communism, the Pope explained that if he were one day to speak, he would condemn not only Bolshevism, but also the events in Germany. Recognizing the papal enmity toward Hitler's Germany, the Italian ambassador reported: "I have never realized as well as I did this time that the state of the relations with Germany affects the general attitude of the Vatican, even to some extent as far as we are concerned, and undoubtedly a great deal as far as the war is concerned."[44] The ambassador expected the Vatican to side with Italy and anti-Communist nations, but Pius refused to do so.

The United States was officially still neutral, but the lend-lease trade law essentially extended credit to Great Britain. American Catholics were very concerned about extending a similar benefit to a Communist nation.[45] President Roosevelt wanted Pope Pius to help change their minds. On September 30, 1941, he wrote to Pius:

> In so far as I am informed, churches in Russia are open. I believe there is a real possibility that Russia may as a result of the present conflict recognize freedom of religion in Russia, although, of course, without recognition of any official intervention on the part of any church in education or political matters within Russia. I feel that if this can be accomplished it will put the possibility of the restoration of real religious liberty in Russia on a much better footing than religious freedom is in Germany today.[46]

The Americans summoned the apostolic delegation in Washington to the White House to offer assurances that the United States was only doing what was necessary to fight the Nazis and was not changing in its fundamental distrust of communism.[47] Roosevelt's representative to the Pope, Myron Taylor was sent back to Rome. He pleaded with the pontiff to clarify (if not change) Catholic teaching regarding the propriety of cooperating with the Soviets, especially as that teaching was reflected in Pius XI's encyclical, *Divini Redemptoris*.[48]

Myron Taylor argued that in order to avoid a deep split among Catholics in the United States, the Holy See would have to come out with a statement on *Divini Redemptoris*.[49] Cardinal Maglione answered that "The Holy See has condemned and still condemns

Communism. It had never uttered a word, and it cannot do so, against the Russian people. It has also condemned Nazism."[50] Maglione did not think that the Pope needed to further clarify this matter, but he promised to assure the apostolic delegation in Washington that they did not need to worry about supporting Roosevelt in the war against Hitler.[51]

In a letter dated September 20, 1941, the Vatican Secretariat of State explained to the apostolic delegate in Washington, Archbishop Amleto Cicognani who later became the Vatican's Secretary of State, that in *Divini Redemptoris* Pius XI had condemned atheistic Communism, but "not the Russian people to whom, in the same document, he sent expressions of good wishes and compassion."[52] The apostolic delegate was instructed to have one or more respected bishop make the following public statement:

> The attitude of the Holy See with regard to the Communist doctrine is and remains what it always has been. However, the Holy See has nothing whatsoever against the Russian people. It is now the Russian people which has been unjustly attacked and is suffering greatly as a consequence of this unjust war. This being so, Catholics should not have any objections to collaborating with the United States government to help the Russian people by giving the latter such help as they need.[53]

This fit well with the American position that Soviet dictator Joseph Stalin was opening the way to religious freedom in Russia and helped dissolve American Catholic opposition to extending the lend-lease program.[54]

In keeping with the same public neutrality that he had advanced prior to the Soviet/German conflict, Pius XII refused Roosevelt's request to make a statement that he regarded Nazism as a greater threat to the world than Communism. One of his closest aides, however, reported that she joined the Pontiff in a daily prayer for Allied victory.[55]

The position of most people in the Vatican (which was shared with the future President of the United States, Harry S. Truman)[56] was summed up by the Assistant Secretary of State, Monsignor Tardini, who said it was "one devil chasing out the other."[57] Camille M. Cianfarra, a correspondent for the *New York Times*, wrote that "the Vatican was hoping that the German-Soviet War would give the British Empire and the United States time to increase their military preparedness."[58] Winston Churchill might have been thinking of the

Church's concerns when he said, "I have only one purpose, the destruction of Hitler.... If Hitler invaded Hell, I would make at least a favorable reference to the Devil in the House of Commons."[59]

Pius was well aware that the Soviet Union was capable of everything Hitler had done to this point, and more. Moreover, the Soviets had been doing these bad things longer and had publicly identified their aim of destroying religion. From 1928-1953, the period when Stalin headed the Soviet Union, most historians estimate that he was responsible for twenty million deaths.[60] This includes victims who were shot, who died in the Gulag, and those who died in man-made famines. Stalin was responsible for starving to death about five million Ukrainian peasants in 1932-33, the extermination of perhaps six and a half million kulaks (well-off peasants), the execution of one million Party members in the Great Terror of 1937-38, and the massacre of all Trotskyists in the Gulag.[61] In other words, Joseph Stalin killed more, perhaps millions more people than did Hitler. He also had conducted an all-out effort to rid his country of the Catholic Church.

Throughout its entire existence, the Soviet Union suppressed religion, primarily in countries that had been highly Catholic. It was the first nation in history to make a "dogma of the non-existence of God."[62] The Holy See warned the British and the Americans that Stalin had not changed his goal of elimination of religion just because the Soviet Union had joined in with the Allies. (Hitler, by contrast, was much more circumspect in his dealings with the Church. His attitude was that Catholicism must be eliminated after the war was won, but he never had an open and announced policy of eliminating religion).[63]

The Vatican's concern about the Soviets caused some observers to speculate that Pius XII favored Germany over the Soviet Union.[64] Germany had several predominantly Catholic regions, and the area under Hitler's control was now overwhelmingly Catholic.[65] A wartime correspondent located in the Vatican, however, quoted "a high prelate who cannot be further identified" as to why—on a philosophical level—the Vatican could not support the Axis, even in a war against Communism:

Atheist Bolshevism is less preoccupying for the reason that, although it has forcibly eliminated God, man cannot live without believing in a superior being. On the other hand, Nazism has replaced God with a pagan theory which, though it does not meet his spiritual needs, yet gives him something to look up to. When the time of reconstruction comes, it will be more difficult for the Church to eradicate the false Neo-pagan theory of the Nazis from the consciousness of the masses than to instill in the soul of the atheist the belief in God, for this belief will answer a natural craving of man's soul, while the Neo-pagan masses may not feel it equally strongly.[66]

Pius himself said that Germany had changed and that it was "infinitely worse" than when he had been there as nuncio.[67] It has also been suggested that he saw Hitler as a greater threat than Stalin because Germany's military might meant that Nazism could more easily be imposed on other nations.[68] During the war, however, the Vatican officially remained neutral.[69]

Pius did go along with one Allied request. The Allies did not want the Pope to bring up Stalin's persecution of the Church, and Pius agreed not to, probably because by bringing it up he would have openly appeared to be taking sides. However, this "silence" caused him great concern. Pius wrote to Myron C. Taylor, Roosevelt's personal representative to the Pope:

> [A]t the request of President Roosevelt, the Vatican has ceased all mention of the Communist regime. But this silence that weighs heavily on our conscience, is misunderstood by the Soviet leaders who continue the persecution against churches and faithful. God grant that the free world will not one day regret my silence.[70]

Ironically, he would later come to be attacked for a different silence.

*****

On December 2, a powerful naval attack force received orders from Japan to proceed with their plans. The undetected force arrived off the Hawaiian Islands on the morning of December 7, 1941. Sunday was selected because the Japanese leadership expected the Americans to be less prepared on their day of rest and worship.[71] They hit Pearl Harbor in two successive waves of more than 350 Japanese bombers, torpedo planes, and fighters. Altogether, eighteen American ships were sunk or disabled. In less than two hours the Japanese dealt the United States the single most staggering blow in its military history. Fortunately, the American aircraft carriers—Japan's true target—were on missions elsewhere, and the attack failed to destroy any of them. The Japanese lost only twenty-nine planes.

On the day following the attack, President Roosevelt told a joint session of Congress that December 7 was a date "which will live in infamy."[72] He requested a declaration of the existence of a state of war between Japan and the United States. Congress immediately voted in favor of the declaration. Almost simultaneously, Japanese naval and air forces attacked Wake Island, Guam, British Malaya, Singapore, the Dutch East Indies, Burma, Thailand, and the Philippines. On December 11, Germany and Italy declared war on the United States.

*****

In his Christmas address of 1941, presented to the Sacred College of Cardinals on December 24, 1941, Pope Pius XII greatly expanded on the plan for peace that he had set forth in 1939:

> In a new order founded on moral principles, there can be no place for (1) open or subtle oppression of the cultural and language character-istics of national minorities, (2) contraction of their economic capaci-ties, (3) limitation or abolition of their natural fecundity. The more conscientiously the state respects the rights of its minorities, the more safely and effectively it can demand from its members loyal observance of their civil rights which are equal to those of other citi-zens.[73]

The Pope argued for respect of the minorities within a state and for respect of the state by the minorities. Once each side showed such respect, he argued, peace would naturally follow. Understood in the context of the time, the Pope was advocating the preservation of four national rights of minorities that were being threatened by National Socialism: culture, language, economic capacity, and the right to rear children.

As Hitler was announcing his need for more land and raw materi-als, the Pope condemned the "narrow, selfish considerations which tend to monopolize economic wealth and raw materials in general use, to the exclusion of nations less favored by nature."[74] Property, the Pope argued, is a right *and* a duty. Private rights had to be limited by the public good, and these same principles must be applied to inter-national relations. As Hitler longingly eyed resources that might be captured militarily, the Pope explained that selfish economic policy was at the heart of the world's current economic problems. Similarly, as Germany was arming itself for aggression, Pius urged disarma-ment, both physically and spiritually. He wanted people to forgo not only their weapons, but also their *wish* for weapons. While Hitler was breaking treaties and violating concordats, Pius explained that true peace could take place only when international obligations were fully respected (through the establishment of an effective international organization).[75]

Commenting on this message, the Reich's ambassador noted that it was directed at both Hitler's Germany and Stalin's Soviet Union.[76] Mussolini was angered because, as Count Ciano recorded in his diary on Christmas Day 1941, "he found that out of the five points it contains at least four are directed against the dictatorships."[77] As the *New York Times* editorialized on Christmas Day, 1941, the Pope had placed himself squarely against Hitlerism:

> *The voice of Pius XII is a lonely voice in the silence and darkness enveloping Europe this Christmas.* The Pope reiterates what he has said before. In general, he repeats, although with greater definiteness, the five-point plan for peace which he first enunciated in his Christmas message after the war broke out in 1939. *His program agrees in fundamentals with the Roosevelt-Churchill eight-point declaration.* It calls for respect for treaties and the end of the possibility of aggression, equal treatment for minorities, freedom from religious persecution.... The Pontiff emphasized principles of international morality with which most men of good-will agree. He uttered the ideas a spiritual leader would be expected to express in time of war. Yet his words sound strange and bold in the Europe of today, and we comprehend the complete submergence and enslavement of great nations, the very sources of our civilization, as we realize that *he is about the only ruler left on the Continent of Europe who dares to raise his voice at all.* The last tiny islands of neutrality are so hemmed in and overshadowed by war and fear that no one but the Pope is still able to speak aloud in the name of the Prince of Peace....
>
> In calling for a "real new order" based on "liberty, justice and love," to be attained only by a "return to social and international principles capable of creating a barrier against the abuse of liberty and the abuse of power," *the Pope put himself squarely against Hitlerism.* Recognizing that there is no road open to agreement between belligerents "whose reciprocal war aims and programs seem to be irreconcilable," *he left no doubt that the Nazi aims are also irreconcilable with his own conception of a Christian peace.* "The new order which must arise out of this war," he asserted, "must be based on principles." And that implies only one end to the war.[78]

Pope Pius XII would say and do even more the following year.

CHAPTER THIRTEEN

1942 AND THE FINAL SOLUTION

At the beginning of 1942, the Vatican faced a demand from the German government that it make no further appointments of bishops, archbishops, or other high administrative dignitaries in Reich-occupied areas without consulting the German government. In response, the Vatican's Secretary of State not only itemized a long list of treaty violations by the Germans, he also attacked the Nazi government for acting "contrary not only to existing Concordats and to the principles of international law ratified by the Second Hague conference, but often—and this is much more grave—to the very fundamental principles of divine law, both natural and positive."[1] As such, the Church under Pius XII would not agree to the Nazi demands. Later in the year, Hitler considered recalling his ambassador to the Vatican.[2]

On January 20, 1942, Reinhard Heydrich, second in command of the S.S., convened a conference in the Berlin suburb of Wannsee. At the meeting, fifteen top Nazi bureaucrats and members of the S.S. met to decide on the resolution of the "Jewish Question."[3] Persecution was already widespread, but now the "Final Solution"—extermination of the entire race—was made official policy. Poland, the European nation with the greatest Jewish population, was already under Nazi control.[4]

On January 22, 1942, Vatican Radio broadcasted a dramatic description of German atrocities in Poland, and reported that Poland was in a state of terror and barbarism. Two days later, the *New York Times* reported: "Vatican City radio station made two broadcasts today, adding many details to the atrocities that supposedly are being committed in German-occupied Poland. It is now clear that the papacy is throwing the whole weight of its publicizing facilities into an exposé of conditions which, yesterday's broadcast said, 'profoundly pained' the Pope."[5]

This broadcast is noteworthy in that the Pope had expressly toned down radio condemnations of the Nazis in Poland following his broadcast on the preceding Easter,[6] but he did not hesitate to tell the world what the Vatican had learned about the Nazis and their treatment of Polish victims. The Germans threatened reprisals if broadcasts like this continued.[7]

German-occupied Poland was where 4,600,000 inhabitants, primarily Jews and Catholics, bore the brunt of the Nazi's plans for the future. The Wartheland area (*Warthegau* - derived from the river Warta which flows through the region), was annexed outright by Germany. In addition to being the first place where Jews would face mass extermination, this was an experimental area for Hitler's plan to eliminate Christianity.[8]

The Nazi plan for Christianity in Wartheland was set forth in a document dated March 14, 1940 (though this document did not come to light until more than a year later).[9] In a thirteen-point plan, the Nazis proposed to reduce all churches to the status of corporations. In other words, religious associations would be permitted, but not churches. Only adults could become members of these associations; there would be no youth groups. Germans and Poles could not meet together, and the Catholics could have no relations with the Holy See. The minimum age for marriage was fixed at twenty-eight for men and twenty-five for women, and for Polish workers deported to Germany, marriage was not authorized.[10]

In 1941, the government announced the formation of the "Roman Catholic Church of German Nationality in the Reich District Wartheland." This church would face government control of finances, Gestapo regulation of worship times, and radical alteration of the status of the Church in the region.[11] Of course, the Nazis had to undertake some drastic measures in order to implement such plans.

By early October 1941, more than half of the 2,000 pre-war clergy in the Wartheland had been imprisoned, deported, or expelled, and the arrests were continuing.[12] At least 700 priests were incarcerated at Dachau, and more than 400 nuns were interned in a special camp at Bojanowo.[13]

The Vatican was prohibited from having a nuncio in Wartheland,[14] but the extent of Nazi abuse is reflected in Charge No. seventeen against Governor-General of Poland Hans Frank at the war crimes trials. Submitted by the Polish government, the charge provided in part:

>   11. The general situation of the clergy in the Archdiocese of Poznan in the beginning of April 1940....
>   5 priests shot,

27 priests confined in harsh concentration camps...,
190 priests in prison or in [other] concentration camps...,
35 priests expelled into the Government General,
11 priests seriously ill in consequence of ill-treatment,
122 parishes left entirely without priests.

12. In the diocese of Chelmno, where about 650 priests were installed before the war, only 3 percent were allowed to stay, the 97 percent of them were imprisoned, executed or put in concentration camps.

13. By January 1941 about 7000 priest were killed, 3000 were in prison or concentration camps.[15]

In addition, three Polish bishops died in German concentration camps.[16]

Wartheland was a test case for what Nazis would do everywhere if they won the war.[17] All Catholic clubs and organizations were dissolved; all cultural, charitable and social organizations were abolished; there was no longer a Catholic press, not even a single Catholic bookstore.[18] Those who lived under these conditions were only too aware that mere words would have no positive effect on the Nazis. For instance, Bishop Carl Maria Splett of Danzig was entrusted with the interim administration of the Polish diocese of Kulm.[19] Upon learning of calls for resistance that came from these leaders in exile, Splett wrote to Pius:

> At my inquiry the Gestapo told me that Cardinal Hlond had called for resistance among the Polish population over the Vatican radio station, and the Gestapo had to prevent him... They say that Cardinal Hlond called the Polish people to rally round its priests and teachers. Thereupon, numerous priests and teachers were arrested and executed, or were tortured to death in the most terrible manner, or were even shipped to the far east.[20]

The lesson was that strong words from the pulpit meant only more suffering for those in need of help.[21]

*****

In January 1942, Japanese officials contacted the Holy See with the intent of establishing diplomatic relations.[22] The Vatican's positive response upset American leaders, who filed a protest.[23] The Vatican Secretary of State, Cardinal Maglione, explained that the Asian territories overrun by Japan contained 18 million Catholic people. As such, the Holy See felt that it needed to have diplomatic relations with the Japanese government. It was simply a reflection of the role of a neutral church in the time of war.[24] (Moreover, the Vatican's presence in Japan eventually proved helpful to the Allies when its contacts were used to provide relief to British civilian internees.)[25] After a meeting with Cardinal Spellman of New York, President Roosevelt announced that the Holy See really had no alternative in this matter.[26]

In April 1942, American forces in the Pacific suffered a serious defeat at Bataan. The Americans responded with bombing raids over Tokyo and other Japanese cities. Bombing of British cities continued, and Allied forces intensified their air raids over Germany. In May, the first RAF 1,000-bomber raid was directed against Cologne, destroying much of the city. In the summer the United States Army Air Corps joined in the operations. The German Luftwaffe, which might have provided some defense for the German cities, had declined in effectiveness since the Battle of Britain.[27]

This expansion of the war into civilian areas particularly concerned the Pope. In his message of May 13, 1942, to the warring nations, Pius condemned cruelty and violence, pleading for the protection of civilian populations. Unfortunately, the warring nations did not listen to the Pope's words. As Pius later mentioned to the British chargé d'affairs, the Nazis noted the significance of this statement by suppressing it in Germany.[28]

*****

On June 9, 1942, in German-occupied areas of the Soviet Union, the Nazis enacted a new law on "religious tolerance."[29] Despite its name, it was actually a measure designed to regulate religion and restrict churches. Hitler told his inner circle: "The formation of unitary churches for larger parts of the Russian territory is... to be prevented. It can [only be] in our interest if each village has its own sect which develops its own image of God."[30] German authorities not only reviewed sermons for proper subject matter but also censored the texts.[31] All religious organizations were required to register with the German district commissar. The commissar was given the right to remove any priest suspected of political unreliability. Religious organizations had to limit their activities or they could face penalties ranging anywhere from fines up to the dissolution of the church community.[32] It was similar to what was happening in Poland, and it reflected Hitler's eventual intent for all areas under his control.

*****

Edith Stein was born on Yom Kippur 1891, in the Prussian town of Breslau (now Wroclaw, Poland). Although she was brought up in a Jewish family, she quit practicing her faith by her teenage years and considered herself an atheist. She attended the University of Breslau, then transferred to the University of Göttingen to continue her studies in philosophy. It was the study of philosophy that brought her to Christianity.

In 1921, at the age of twenty-nine, Edith read the autobiography of St. Teresa of Avila, founder of the Carmelite Order of Catholic nuns. St. Teresa's grandfather had been a Jewish Spanish convert to Catholicism, and Edith felt a kinship. Edith joined the Catholic Church 1922 and eventually became a leading voice in the Catholic Woman's movement in Germany.

By the early 1930s, Edith was well known in the German academic community. While on a trip during Holy Week 1933, she stopped in Cologne at the Carmelite convent for the Holy Thursday service. It was here when she decided to relinquish her life as an author and lecturer to become a nun in the Carmelite Order. She later wrote:

> I told [the Lord] that I knew it was His cross that was now being placed upon the Jewish people; that most of them did not understand this, but that those who did would have to take it up willingly in the name of all. I would do that. At the end of the service, I was certain that I had been heard. But what this carrying of the cross was to consist in, that I did not yet know.[33]

On October 15, 1934, Edith Stein took the name Teresa Benedicta of the Cross and entered the Carmel of Cologne.[34]

After *Kristallnacht*, when Nazis in Germany terrorized so many Jews, Edith moved to a convent in Holland to spare her sister Carmelites possible trouble over her Jewish origin. (Her sister followed shortly thereafter). When Holland fell to the Nazis and the deportations started in the Netherlands, converts to Christianity were exempted. Nevertheless, the leaders of all the churches in Holland, Protestant and Catholic, agreed to read a public protest against the deportation of Jews. The Nazis replied that the holy men should keep quiet or things would get worse.[35]

The Catholic Archbishop of Utrecht ignored this warning and had a letter read in all of the Catholic churches on July 26, 1942, condemning the treatment of the Jews.[36] The letter stated, in part:

> Ours is a time of great tribulations of which two are foremost: the sad destiny of the Jews and the plight of those departed for forced labor... all of us must be aware of the terrible sufferings which both of them have to undergo, due to no guilt of their own.... we have learned with deep pain of the new dispositions which impose upon innocent Jewish men, women and children, the deportation into foreign lands....the incredible suffering which these measures cause to more than 10,000 people is in absolute opposition to the Divine Precepts of Justice and Charity....let us pray to God and for the intercession of Mary... that He may lend His Strength to the people of Israel, so sorely tried in anguish and persecution.

Rather than making things better, this statement caused the Nazis to end the exemption for Jewish converts to Catholicism.[37]

On July 30, 1942, a memorandum from the S.S. declared: "Since the Catholic bishops—without being involved—have interfered in these affairs, the entire population of Catholic Jews will now be sent off this week yet. No intervention will be considered."[38] On August 2, the Nazis began deporting those Jews who had converted to Catholicism. Seventy-nine percent of the total Jewish population was deported from Holland to the death camps; more than from anywhere else in the west.[39] "If the Catholic clergy can thus ignore negotiations, then we in turn are forced to consider the Catholic full-blooded Jews as our worst opponents and to take measures to ship them off to the East as quickly as possible," read the official announcement from the *Reichskommissar* in the *Deutsche Zeitung in den Niederlandern*.[40] (Since Protestant leaders had refrained from reading the letter, Protestant Jews were not deported).[41]

Edith Stein and her sister, along with 600 other Catholic "Non-Aryans," including 3 other nuns and 2 brothers from religious orders, were ordered to pack their belongings for deportation to Auschwitz on the first day of the new policy. When it was suggested that she might be able to use her position to avoid the gas chambers, she declined to accept any special treatment. On the trip, various eye-witnesses recall her comforting and consoling others. When her sister became disoriented, Edith told her, "Come, Rosa. We go for our people."[42]

She was last seen with her sister, both of them praying and smiling. No survivors reported on her final moments. She was put to death at Auschwitz on August 9, 1942, along with her sister and at least six other German nuns.[43] She was canonized as St. Teresa Benedicta of the Cross by Pope John Paul II in October 1998.[44]

*****

In the summer of 1942, the situation in Warsaw was getting worse. In July, the first deportations from the ghetto to concentration camps took place, and the Treblinka camp was opened. The Polish underground, which was strongly influenced by the Catholic Church,[45] was in full swing. Nuns carried secret messages and priests conducted special Masses behind closed doors.[46] In at least one case, a member of the underground who was about to go on a dangerous mission attended a secret Mass at which the priest, in violation of normal Catholic practices, presented him with a consecrated host. The Priest said: "I have been authorized by those in whom the authority of the Church is vested, to present you, soldier of Poland, with Christ's Body to carry you on your journey.... If danger approaches, you will be able to swallow it."[47]

Zofia Kossak-Szcaucka, a well-known writer of historical novels, was also a Catholic and a member of a Catholic organization known as FOP. In the name of that organization, Kossak-Szcaucka wrote an illegal leaflet that was posted around Warsaw. It described the horror of life and death in the ghetto, and called upon those who could not undertake actions to at least raise a protest:

> We have no means actively to counteract the German murders; we cannot help, nor can we rescue anybody. But we protest from the bottom of our hearts filled with pity, indignation, and horror. This protest is demanded of us by God, who does not allow us to kill. It is demanded by our Christian conscience. Every being calling itself human has the right to love his fellow man. The blood of the defenseless victims is calling for revenge. Who does not support the protest with us, is not a Catholic.
> *****
> Whoever does not understand this, and whoever dares to connect the future of the proud, free Poland, with the vile enjoyment of your fellow man's calamity is, therefore, not a Catholic and not a Pole.[48]

Kossak-Szcaucka followed this document up with a request to establish an underground organization to save the Jews. By the end of

1942, the Council for Aid to Jews had been established.   Later, Kossak-Szczucka was caught and sent to Auschwitz.   She was released after about one year and resumed her underground activity, focusing especially on sheltering Jewish children in convents and other institutions run by the Catholic Church.

*****

In September 1942, a report from the Inter-Allied Information Committee claimed that the Nazis had killed 207,373 people in occupied territories, 200,000 of them in Poland.[49]   The committee suggested that many more may have been put to death by Hitler, but these numbers could not be officially confirmed.

Up until this time, the Pope had continued to receive leading members of the National Socialist Party.[50]   Now, however, Pius began to follow the lead of Bishop Konrad von Preysing of Berlin, who was a recognized opponent of Nazism.[51]   Not only did the Pope send a message congratulating Preysing for his defense of the rights of all people, he also took Preysing's advice when selecting episcopal candidates, avoiding those whom Preysing felt were sympathetic toward the Nazis.[52]

On September 19th, an American delegation had an audience with Pius XII.   They explained the irrevocable determination of America to "obliterate" Nazism, and to do so in concert with the Soviet Union.   The Allies informed the Pope that he must drop any idea of a negotiated settlement.   The Americans were concerned that the Vatican would support the Axis in an attempt to seek a peace without suffering a defeat.   The Americans made it clear that they would accept nothing short of a an unconditional surrender.[53]

The Holy See was still concerned about the ultimate aims of Soviet Communism, including the elimination of religion.[54]   The Vatican argued that the Communists had not changed just because Stalin had been forced to form an alliance with the western democracies.[55]   Roosevelt, however, argued that Nazism was a worse menace, at least in the short term, than Communism, and that the Allies were justified in cooperating with Stalin in order to defeat Hitler.[56]   Pius XII seemed to accept the Allies' position, and he became even more critical and outspoken against the Nazis.[57]   On October 26, 1942, a coded telegram to the British War Cabinet from the Madrid Offices reported:

"Suner in his visit to the Pope said that the Germans would win the war and that the Vatican and Spain should adapt their policy accordingly. The Pope replied 'if the Germans win, it will mean the greatest period of persecution that Christians have ever suffered.'"[58]

The Axis leaders recognized Pius XII's bias against their cause. The editor of the Fascist publication *Regime Fascista* wrote in October 1942. "The Church's obstruction of the practical solution of the Jewish problem constitutes a crime against the New Europe."[59] According to the *London Tablet* of October 24, out of disgust at the number of Jews that were released from Nazi-occupied areas due to Vatican pressure, the Third Reich circulated ten million of copies of a pamphlet saying that Pius XII inspired a lack of confidence in the Catholic world.[60] The pamphlet argued that earlier Popes had not been friendly to Jews, but this "pro-Jewish" pope—Pius XII—is the only one who has "found it necessary to make interventions on behalf of Jews."[61] Mussolini, too, was venting displeasure over the "anti-dictatorial darts" that appeared in *L'Osservatore Romano*.[62]

In September 1942, President Roosevelt sent a message to the Pope detailing reports from the Warsaw ghetto and asking whether the Vatican had any information that would tend to confirm or deny the reports of Nazi crimes.[63] In mid-October, the Holy See replied, stating that it, too, had reports of "severe measures" taken against the Jews, but that it had been impossible to verify the accuracy of the reports. The statement went on, however, to note that "the Holy See is taking advantage of every opportunity offered in order to mitigate the suffering of non-Aryans."[64]

At their annual meeting in November 1942, in Washington, D.C., the U.S. Bishops released a statement:

> Since the murderous assault on Poland, utterly devoid of every semblance of humanity, there has been a premeditated and systematic extermination of the people of this nation. The same satanic technique is being applied to many other peoples. We feel a deep sense of revulsion against the cruel indignities heaped upon Jews in conquered countries and upon defenseless peoples not of our faith.... Deeply moved by the arrest and maltreatment of the Jews, we cannot stifle the cry of conscience. In the name of humanity and Christian principles, our voice is raised.[65]

For his part, in late 1942, Pius sent three letters of support to bishops in Poland. The letters were intended to be read and distributed by the bishops to the faithful. The bishops all thanked the Pontiff, but responded that they could not publish his words or read them aloud, because that would lead to more persecution of Jews and of Catholics.[66]

*****

With the Vatican having recognized Nazi atrocities earlier than many other nations and having assisted western powers early during the hostilities, Allied leaders sought to have the Pope join in a formal declaration concerning the atrocities taking place in Germany and in German-occupied areas. In a message dated September 14, the Brazilian ambassador, Ildebrando Accioly, wrote: "It is necessary that the authorized and respected voice of the Vicar of Christ be heard against these atrocities."[67]   On that same day, British Ambassador D'Arcy Osborne and American representative Harold H. Tittmann requested a "public and specific denunciation of Nazi treatment of the populations of the counties under German occupation."[68] Interestingly, neither Tittmann nor Accioly mentioned the treatment of Jews by the Nazis in any of their documents.[69] British Ambassador Osborne, who did mention the treatment of Jewish people in his request to the Pope, reported back to London that the coordinated requests to the Pontiff looked like an effort to involve the Pope in political and partisan action.[70] Pius was non-committal in response to these requests, and a few weeks later President Roosevelt's representative, Myron Taylor, renewed the request on behalf of the Allies.[71] American representatives ultimately reported back that the Holy See was convinced that an open condemnation would "result in the violent deaths of many more people."[72]

The Allies went ahead with a declaration that was signed by the three main Allies and the governments of eight occupied countries. It pointed specifically at the German government's "intention to exterminate the Jewish people in Europe," and it condemned "in the strongest possible terms this bestial policy of cold-blooded extermination." It affirmed that "the necessary practical measures" would be taken to insure that those responsible for the crimes would be brought to retribution. It was the strongest statement concerning atrocities against Jews to be issued by the Allied powers during the war. Furthermore, it committed the United States, Britain, and the

Soviet Union for the first time to postwar prosecution of those responsible for crimes against the European Jews.

The Pope did not join in this statement, perhaps because as a *New York Times* editorial concluded, the joint statement was "an official indictment."[73] Pius did not want to breach the Church's official neutrality by joining in a declaration made by either side, and he was concerned that the Allies' statement would be used as part of the war effort (as happened with some of his earlier statements). He did, however, make his own statement.

In his 1942 Christmas statement, broadcast over Vatican Radio, Pope Pius XII said that the world was "plunged into the gloom of tragic error,"[74] and that "the Church would be untrue to herself, she would have ceased to be a mother, if she were deaf to the cries of suffering children which reach her ears from every class of the human family."[75] He spoke of the need for mankind to make "a solemn vow never to rest until valiant souls of every people and every nation of the earth arise in their legions, resolved to bring society and to devote themselves to the services of the human person and of a divinely ennobled human society."[76] He said that mankind owed this vow to all victims of the war, including "the hundreds of thousands who, through no fault of their own, and *solely because of their nation or race*, have been *condemned to death or progressive extinction*."[77] In making this statement, Pius used the Latin word "*stirps,*" which means race, but which had been used throughout Europe for centuries as an explicit reference to Jews.[78]

Pius also condemned totalitarian regimes and acknowledged some culpability on the part of the Church: "A great part of the human race, and not a few—We do not hesitate to say it—not a few even of those who call themselves Christians, bear some share in the collective responsibility for the aberrations, the disasters, and the low moral state of modern society." He urged all Catholics to give shelter wherever they could.[79]

The Pope considered his statement to have been "clear and comprehensive in its condemnation of the heartrending treatment of the Poles [and] Jews in occupied countries."[80] Others shared this view. The Polish ambassador thanked the pontiff, who "in his last Christmas address implicitly condemned all the injustices and cruelties suffered by the Polish people at the hands of the Germans. Poland acclaims this condemnation; it thanks the Holy Father for his words...."[81] British records reflect the opinion that "the Pope's condemnation of the treatment of the Jews & the Poles is quite unmistakable, and the message is perhaps more forceful in tone than any of his recent statements."[82] A Christmas Day editorial in the *New York Times* praised Pius XII for his moral leadership:

> No Christmas sermon reaches a larger congregation than the message Pope Pius XII addresses to a war-torn world at this season. *This Christmas more than ever he is a lonely voice crying out of the silence of a continent.* The Pulpit whence he speaks is more than ever like the Rock on which the Church was founded, a tiny island lashed and surrounded by a sea of war. In these circumstances, in any circumstances, indeed, *no one would expect the Pope to speak as a political leader, or a war leader, or in any other role than that of a preacher ordained to stand above the battle, tied impartially, as he says, to all people and willing to collaborate in any new order which will bring a just peace.*
>
> But just because the Pope speaks to and in some sense for all the peoples at war, *the clear stand he takes on the fundamental issues of the conflict* has greater weight and authority. When a leader bound impartially to nations on both sides condemns as heresy the new form of national state which subordinates everything to itself: when he declares that whoever wants peace must protect against "arbitrary attacks" the "juridical safety of individuals:" when he assails violent occupation of territory, the exile and persecution of human beings for no reason other than race or political opinion: when he says that people must fight for a just and decent peace, a "total peace"–the "impartial judgment" is like a verdict in a high court of justice.
>
> Pope Pius expresses as passionately as any leader on our side the war aims of the struggle for freedom when he says that those who aim at building a new world must fight for free choice of government and religious order. They must refuse that the state should make of individuals a herd of whom the state disposes as if they were a lifeless thing. [83]

The editorial was wrong about one thing: some now do condemn him for not speaking the way a political or war leader would.

To the Axis leaders the Pope's Christmas message was not hard to decipher. Mussolini was greatly angered by the speech.[84] The German ambassador to the Vatican complained that Pius had abandoned any pretense at neutrality and was "clearly speaking on behalf of the Jews."[85] An American report noted that the Germans were "conspicuous by their absence" at a Midnight Mass conducted by the Pope on Christmas Eve for diplomats.[86] One German report stated:

In a manner never known before, the Pope has repudiated the National Socialist New European Order.... It is true, the Pope does not refer to the National Socialist in Germany by name, but his speech is one long attack on everything we stand for... God, he says, regards all people and races as worthy of the same consideration. Here he is clearly speaking on behalf of the Jews... he is virtually accusing the German people of injustice toward the Jews, and makes himself the mouthpiece of the Jewish war criminal.[87]

German Ambassador Bergen, on the instruction of Foreign Minister Ribbentrop, immediately warned the Pope that the Nazis would seek retaliation if the Vatican abandoned its neutral position. When he reported back to his superiors, the German ambassador stated: "Pacelli is no more sensible to threats than we are."[88]

Chapter Fourteen

1943 and Turning Tides

In January 1943, the Pope met with Nicholas Kallay, the Hungarian Premier. According to Kallay, Pius "condemned the system and the methods of the Germans, which independently of the war were inhuman and brutal, especially towards the Jews."[1] Pius further explained that the Church could never cooperate with governments like those in Germany and in the Soviet Union. He had long known about the brutality of Russian Bolshevism, but had been painfully surprised to learn that the Germans were capable of the same anti-Semitism and brutality.[2]

This same month, Pius wrote a letter to President Roosevelt in which he expressed his gratitude for the support he had received from the President in his efforts to bring about peace and alleviate suffering. He promised to continue

> to recall to men's minds... those higher principles of justice and Christian morality without which there is no salvation, and to draw men's spirits anew towards those sentiments of charity and brotherhood without which there can be no peace.
>   In the ceaseless furtherance of this, Our program, We feel certain that We may count upon the efficacious comprehension of the noble American people and upon the valid collaboration of Your Excellency.[3]

As the year went on, Pius expressed confidence that a new spirit of collaboration among men and nations would unite men after the war, and despite official neutrality, he conveyed to the American President, the leader of a belligerent state, his desire to continue with parallel endeavors for the alleviation of suffering and for peace.[4]

In terms of the war the most important development of January 1943 was that President Roosevelt, Prime Minister Churchill, and Charles de Gaulle concluded a ten-day meeting in Casablanca. (Stalin, angry that the Allies had not yet started a second European front, refused to attend.) Out of this conference the Allies established a seven-point plan to coordinate their efforts for future military action in the Mediterranean. This included the union of British and American operations in North Africa and an invasion of Sicily. They also agreed that strategic bombing of German industry would be intensified. The decision with the greatest impact on the duration of the war, however, was probably the demand for unconditional surrender.

As soon as the policy was announced, critics voiced their objections: unconditional surrender would lengthen the war; it would intensify the German fighting force; it would also delay the ultimate peace settlement. Some have argued that once Germany was on the run, the main obstacle to peace was this self-imposed barrier.[5] The German Ambassador to the Holy See later reported: "I told every official quarter in Rome to which I had access that this formula would cost the lives of many more Allied soldiers."[6] Hitler did not miss the chance to use this demand as propaganda to motivate the German people. In his campaign of "strength through fear," Goebbels focused on unconditional surrender.[7] The German people, he said, had no choice but to fight or face obliteration."[8]

Perhaps the most valid criticism of Pius XII would be that he was too willing to compromise in order to achieve peace. As such, the unconditional surrender policy was much to his disliking.[9] Years later, his housekeeper, Sister Pascalina, complained about this policy:

> How unfair that His Holiness was forced to suffer so much blame... the self-righteous Allies—particularly Roosevelt, who would accept nothing short of unconditional surrender, even though it meant prolonging the Holocaust—were devious enough to shift responsibility. The Allies blamed Pius for his so-called "silence" to escape the world's criticism for their disgraceful hypocrisy.[10]

In fairness to the Allied leaders, it should be noted that a conditional surrender had not held up after World War I.[11] In addition, British and American policy-makers were concerned that the Soviet Union might seek a separate peace with Germany, and unconditional surrender seemed the best insurance against such an eventuality.[12]

Another decision at Casablanca was perhaps less controversial at the time, but in retrospect may have cost more lives. This was the directive calling for the progressive destruction and dislocation of the German military, industrial, and economic system and the undermining of the morale of the German people. In other words, the directive called for the strategic bombing of civilian targets.

In 1922, three years after World War I had ended, the major powers met at the Washington Arms Limitation Conference. There they adopted rules of warfare which reflected the view that some restraints ought to apply, even in times of war.[13] Article 28 of these rules stated: "The area of bombardment for the purpose of terrorizing the civilian population, destroying or damaging civilian property not of a military character, or injuring non-combatants is prohibited." Both Prime Minister Churchill and British Air Marshal Arthur Harris, however, believed in the effectiveness of bombing civilian targets.[14] The years when the Allies controlled the air (1944-45), were the peak years in terms of the sheer tonnage of bombs dropped. The Allies emphasized area bombing in population centers and working class neighborhoods. This bombing, it was thought, would weaken the German will to fight and reduce German war production. The Americans also applied this tactic in Japan. Pius, as always, strongly opposed the introduction of warfare into civilian areas.[15] (The Germans even asked him to intervene and try to stop the bombing of civilian populations in Germany.)[16]

*****

In early 1943, the Vatican received information from the nuncio in Berlin about the deportation and execution of Jewish people. Bishop Preysing of Berlin urged Pius to speak out against this treatment,[17] but the Pope felt that he had said all that he could publicly say in his 1942 Christmas address.[18] Thus, he declined to make a further statement. In late April, Pius wrote to Preysing, explaining:

> In Our Christmas message We have already said something about what is now being done against the non-Aryans in the area of German domination. This was short, but was well understood. We do not now need to give assurances that Our paternal love and paternal care is due in increased measure to the non-Aryan or half-Aryan Catholics who are children of the Church like all the others, now during the collapse of their exterior existence and in their spiritual distress. With the situation such as it is at the moment, We can unfortunately provide them with no effective help except our prayers. We are determined, however, to raise Our voice again on their behalf, according to what the circumstances demand or permit.[19]

Regarding efforts on behalf of Jewish people, Pius explained: "To the extent it was able, the Holy See has in fact given charitable aid to non-Aryan Catholic and to members of the Jewish religion.... The principal Jewish organizations have expressed to the Holy See their warmest appreciation for its relief efforts."[20] He added that "It was for us a great consolation to learn that Catholics, in particular those of your Berlin diocese, have shown such charity towards the sufferings of the Jews."[21]

One effort that Pius did make in 1943 was to have his nuncio in Berlin, Cesare Orsenigo, approach Hitler directly in order to discuss the treatment of Jews in Germany and in occupied areas. Orsenigo reported:

> A few days ago I finally was able to go to Berchtesgaden, where I was received by Hitler; as soon as I touched upon the Jewish question, our discussion lost all sense of serenity. Hitler turned his back on me, went to the window and started to drum on the glass with his fingers... while I continued to spell out our complaints.
>
> All of a sudden, Hitler turned around, grabbed a glass off a nearby table and hurled it to the floor with an angry gesture. Faced with this kind of diplomatic behavior, I thought my mission was over.[22]

As others have noted, "the correspondence and documents of the Holy See during the War reveal a growing sense of helplessness and frustration in the face of the persecution of the Jews in Germany and in Poland."[23] The Spanish ambassador, Domingo de las Barcenas, reported on a conversation he had with the Pope in the spring of 1943. "His Holiness... said with great emphasis that it must be kept in mind that communism is not the only enemy. I cannot tell you in writing the terms he used in speaking of the *Nazi menace*. He strictly forbade me to do so."[24]

In 1941, before the Final Solution had become official policy, Pius expressed a "special love" for the Germans. He held audiences with German soldiers often, Protestants as well as Catholics. He said that he had "nothing against" Germany, which he "loved and admired." Regarding Hitler's regime, Pius said it had caused him profound sadness, especially "certain measures" which it had taken, but he still hoped that matters would improve.[25] By 1943, however, his feelings had changed. He expressed great doubt about any eventual improvement of Germany's religious policies. "Personally," Ambassador Barcenas said, "the Pope, contrary to what is generally believed, in spite of his professed affection for the German people," is angry at the regime.[26] The ambassador reported that the Pope

> believes that this [anti-religion] policy is fundamental to the regime; that it is more dangerous than any previous persecution; and that its application to Poland went to inconceivable extremes. He gave me to understand that any indication that Italy might help remedy the situation was hopeless and that there was no hope for change as long as [Hitler and his top advisors] remain in charge.[27]

Pius warned, "do not underestimate the danger that Rome will be in if the Nazi menace spreads all over Europe."[28]

The Pope's feelings about Nazism were well known inside the German leadership. In the spring of 1943, a group of German officials, including Marschall von Biberstein (an official of the German foreign ministry), Martin Luther (director of the German agency that handled certain domestic affairs), and Walter Schellenberg (a German intelligence officer), hoped to overthrow foreign minister Joachim von Ribbentrop and negotiate a peace treaty with the Allies.[29] They indirectly approached Pius XII, seeking to have him encourage a negotiated peace. The Pope then addressed an open letter to the Vatican's Secretary of State, Luigi Maglione, in which he called for prayer for peace, especially from the children. The anti-Ribbentrop movement stalled however, when Ribbentrop learned of their plans and had Luther sent to a concentration camp and other members sent to the front.[30]

That same Easter, the Protestant community in Munich submitted a petition to their bishop, Hans Meiser. The petitioners, perhaps emboldened by their anonymity, denounced the policy of anti-Semitism and by implication the regime which had approved that policy. "We can as Christians no longer bear it that the church in Germany remains silent regarding the persecutions of the Jews."[31] The duty of the Church, according to the petition, was to attest that "the Jewish question is primarily an evangelical and not a political question." The "politically irregular and singular existence and identity of the Jews" existed because God had chosen them as the instrument of his revelation. The Church was obliged to bear witness to this by assisting the Jews who "fell among thieves" under the Third Reich. It must also oppose "that 'Christian' anti-Semitism" which speaks of "the 'deserved' curse against Israel." Even more important, the

Church must denounce the State's attempt "to destroy Judaism" with its "homemade political gospel."[32]

The petition, like all such statements during the war, had no beneficial effect on the Nazis; the brutality continued. In fact, the Nazis were by now so secure in their power that they viewed the petition as unimportant. They did not even make any effort to identify and punish those who were behind it.

*****

As Germany began to suffer military defeats, it also faced increasing difficulties from underground resistance in occupied nations. At first, resistance was modest, perhaps because many believed the Nazis to be invincible, but after some early Axis setbacks, anti-Nazi activity increased, even in Germany.

One of the best known opposition groups was centered at the University of Munich and went by the name of the White Rose. It was led by philosophy professor Kurt Huber and two students, Hans and Sophie Scholl (who were brother and sister). The group was genuinely high-minded, recklessly daring, and "profoundly Catholic."[33] They often made reference to their Christian faith as they opposed the Nazis.

The White Rose published four pamphlets in quick succession in June and July 1942. The first one, which contained the first German account of mass slaughter by the Nazis, told of German troops killing 300,000 Polish Jews. It urged readers to: "Offer passive resistance—*resistance*—wherever you may be, forestall the spread of this atheistic war machine before it is too late...."[34] Other pamphlets were even more bold:

> Every word that comes from Hitler's mouth is a lie. When he says peace, he means war, and when he blasphemously uses the name of the Almighty, he means the power of evil, the fallen angel, Satan. He is the foul-smelling maw of Hell, and his might is at bottom accursed.[35]

They promised: "We will not be silent. We are your bad conscience. The White Rose will not leave you in peace!"[36]

The group distributed the leaflets throughout Germany, traveling by train with suitcases full of documents. They would hand them out at night or mail them from addresses that could not be traced. They were so successful that a branch of the White Rose was opened in Hamburg; it ended up surviving the original group.

On February 19, 1943, (the same day that Vatican Radio condemned deportations and forced labor, saying "the curse of God" will fall on those who do these things),[37] the regional Nazi commissar made a presentation at the University of Munich. The students in attendance were primarily women and unfit men. He told the men that they would be put to some "more useful" work; he told the women that they would better serve their country by having babies than by pursuing a higher education. He was shouted down, and the students took their protest out to the street. It was the first openly anti-Nazi protest in Germany.[38]

The White Rose published a new pamphlet following the protests. It said: "For us there is but one slogan: fight against the party....The name of Germany is dishonored for all time if German youth does not finally rise up, take revenge, and atone, smash its tormentors, and set up a new Europe of the spirit."[39] Hans and Sophie distributed it personally at the university, but they were betrayed by a janitor. The Gestapo reacted immediately.

One hundred fifty people were arrested for membership in the White Rose. The leaders were tortured and interrogated by the Gestapo for three days, tried by the People's Court, and beheaded at the guillotine on the day they were found guilty. All told, eighteen members of the White Rose died at the hands of the Nazis, and dozens were imprisoned until the end of the war. (The Hamburg leaders were executed in 1945.) Today, the main square outside the University of Munich is called *Geschwister-Scholl-Platz* in their honor.[40]

The leaders of the White Rose made a statement for God and for their consciences, but the Nazis were not deterred one bit. The persecution continued unabated.

*****

Pope Pius XII recognized that the Church had influence in some nations and therefore could accomplish more than in others. The nation of Slovakia (carved out of the defunct Czechoslovakia), for example, came under Nazi rule on March 16, 1939. The Nuremberg race laws were introduced to that country on September 9, 1941. Two days later Monsignor Giuseppe Burzio, the papal Nuncio in Bratislava (the capital of Slovakia), went to see Slovak President Josef Tiso (a Catholic priest and professor of theology) in order to stress "the injustice of these ordinances which also violate the rights of the Church."[41] Shortly thereafter, Slovakia's representative to the Vatican received a written protest from the Holy See that these laws were "in open contrast to Catholic principles."[42] Several other protests followed.[43]

When Jews were deported from Slovakia in 1942, the Vatican Secretary of State immediately filed a protest with the Slovakian government.[44] On March 21, 1942, a pastoral letter, inspired by Rome, was read by episcopal order in all Slovak churches. The letter spoke of the "lamentable fate of thousands of innocent fellow citizens, due to no guilt of their own, as a result of their descent or nationality."[45] Under direct orders from Pius XII, the Slovak Minister to the Holy See was summoned and requested to take immediate action with his Government. The Vatican also instructed the nuncio in Bratislava personally to contact President Tiso of Slovakia and seek relief.[46]

Pope Pius XII himself weighed in on the matter with a letter, dated April 7, 1943, to the Slovak government:

> The Holy See has always entertained the firm hope that the Slovak government... would never proceed with the forcible removal of persons belonging to the Jewish race. It is, therefore, with great pain that the Holy See has learned of the continued transfers of such a nature from the territory of the republic. This pain is aggravated further now that it appears... that the Slovak government intends to proceed with the total removal of the Jewish residents of Slovakia, not even sparing women and children. The Holy See would fail in its Divine Mandate if it did not deplore these measures, which gravely damage man in his natural right, mainly for the reason that these people belong to a certain race.[47]

The following day, a message went out from the Holy See instructing its representative in Bulgaria to take steps in support of Jewish residents who were facing deportation.[48] Shortly thereafter, the secretary of the Jewish Agency for Palestine met with Archbishop Roncalli, the future Pope John XXIII, "to thank the Holy See for the happy outcome of the steps taken on behalf of the Israelites in Slovakia."[49]

On September 19, 1944, the Vatican again instructed its representatives in Bratislava (provincial capital of Slovakia) to intervene for the Jews.[50] That same month, the *Jewish Chronicle* (London) editorialized that "The Pope's action is... a striking affirmation of the dictum of one of the Pope's predecessors that no true Christian can be an anti-Semite."[51] Jewish communities around the world soon recognized that the Vatican was an advocate in favor of Jews in Slovakia.[52]

By October 1944, deportations were back underway, and many Jews were in hiding. Tiso reported to the Vatican on October 26: "In spite of all protests the German security forces continue transfer of Jews to Germany."[53] A telegram drafted under the name of the acting Secretary of State bears corrections in Pius XII's handwriting. It directed the nuncio to:

> Go at once to President Tiso and, informing him of His Holiness's deep sorrow on account of sufferings which very large numbers of persons—contrary to principles of humanity and justice—are undergoing in that nation *on account of their nationality or race*, in the name of the August Pontiff bring him back to sentiments and resolutions in conformity with his priestly dignity and conscience.[54]

Between 1941 and 1944, the Vatican sent four official letters of protest and made numerous oral pleas and protests regarding the deportation of Jews from Slovakia.[55]

In November 1944, the Holy See sent a note expressing "deep sorrow" and hope that the Slovak government would assure that "Jews who are still in the territory... may not be subjected to even more severe sufferings." The note concluded:

> The Holy See, moved by those sentiments of humanity and Christian charity that always inspire its work in favor of those who are suffering, *without distinction of religion, nationality or race*, will continue also in the future, in spite of the growing difficulties of communications, to follow with particular attention the fate of the Jews of Slovakia, and will do everything in its power to bring them relief.[56]

Tiso ultimately managed to slow down the deportation of Slovakian Jews,[57] but due to his collaboration with the Nazis (albeit under pressure from Hitler), the Slovaks hanged him after the war.

*****

Hans Frank, the Nazi *Gauleiter* (governor) of occupied Poland, declared in 1941, "I asked nothing of the Jews except that they should disappear." His forces then set about trying to accomplish just that: The Nazis refused to allow enough food into the ghetto to keep the Jews healthy, forcing most to try to survive for a whole day on a bowl of soup. Soon, several hundred were dying each day from starvation and disease. By July of 1942, about 80,000 Jews had perished. That month, the S.S. began a massive "resettlement," taking the Jews out of the ghetto to extermination camps (mainly Treblinka) where they were to be gassed. In just two months, a total of 310,322 Jews were sent to their deaths. By the end of the year only 60,000 Jews remained.[58]

On April 19, 1943, Jewish residents of Warsaw staged a desperate uprising in the ghetto. The Nazis countered with a block-to-block search, but they found it difficult to kill or capture the small battle groups of Jews, who would fight, then retreat through cellars, sewers, and other hidden passageways. On the fifth day of the fighting, Himmler ordered the S.S. to comb out the ghetto with the greatest severity and relentless tenacity. S.S. General Juergen Stroop decided to burn down the entire ghetto, block by block. Many victims burned or jumped to their death, rather than permit themselves to be caught by the Nazis.[59]

The Jews in Warsaw resisted for a total of twenty-eight days. On May 16, General Stroop reported that "the former Jewish quarter of Warsaw is no longer in existence. The large scale action was terminated at 2015 hours by blowing up the Warsaw synagogue....Total number of Jews dealt with 56,065, including both Jews caught and Jews whose extermination can be proved."[60] (About 20,000 Jews were killed in the streets of Warsaw and another 36,000 in the gas chambers.) Polish sources estimated that 300 Germans were killed and about 1000 were wounded.

Not only in Warsaw, but throughout Poland, Jewish people were in hiding. About 200 convents hid more than 1,500 Jewish children, mainly in Warsaw and the surrounding area. This was especially difficult, because Polish nuns in German-occupied areas were often persecuted and forced into hiding themselves.[61] Nuns who lived in Soviet-occupied areas did not have it much better. They were sent to work for the Soviets, in areas as far away as Siberia. As such, the courage of the priests and nuns who provided shelter to Jewish people was truly admirable.

The case of Fr. Père Jacques of Jesus (of the Carmelite order) illustrates the risks that clergy took when they hid Jewish people from the Nazis. Fr. Jacques was headmaster at a boys school in Avon, France, when the Nazis invaded. As the deportations began, he agreed to hide Jews, seminarians facing deportation, and Resistance fugitives.

When he was questioned about taking such chances, he said: "If by chance I were shot, I would be leaving my pupils an example worth more to them than all the instruction I could give." In January 1944, the Gestapo conducted a raid. When Fr. Jacques and three Jewish boys were being taken away, he called to the remaining children, "*Au revoir, les enfants!*"[62] He died in German custody, having spent his final days comforting other prisoners.[63]

On May 5, 1943, the Vatican secretariat issued a memorandum expressing the reaction of the Roman authorities:

> The Jews. A dreadful situation. There were approximately four and a half million of them in Poland before the war; today the estimate is that not even a hundred thousand remain there, including those who have come from other countries under German occupation. In Warsaw a ghetto had been established which contained six hundred and fifty thousand of them; today there would be twenty to twenty-five thousand. Some, naturally, have avoided being placed on the list of names. But there is no doubt that most have been liquidated. The only possible explanation here is that they have died.... There are special death camps near Lublin (Treblinka) and Brest-Litovsk. It is said that by the hundreds they are shut up in chambers where they [are] gassed to death and then transported in tightly sealed cattle trucks with lime on their floors.[64]

On August 30, the United States Secretary of State expressed doubt, sending a message that "there exists no sufficient proof to justify a statement regarding executions in gas chambers."[65]

*****

In 1940, the Germans decided to put all priests from the concentration camps into one location where they could be tightly controlled. They were kept together in Dachau Barracks 26, 28, and 30 (later they were squeezed into barracks 26 and 28 which had room and beds for 360, even though there were rarely fewer than 1,500 priests interred there).[66] These barracks were ringed with a barbed-wire fence, which restricted the ability of priests to minister to other prisoners during their few free hours.[67]

These Dachau priests worked in the enormous S.S. industrial complex immediately to the west of the camp, but the Nazis had other uses for them as well. Some were injected with pus so that the Nazi doctors could study gangrene; others had their body temperature lowered to study resuscitation of German fliers downed in the North

Atlantic; one German priest was crowned with barbed wire and a group of Jewish prisoners was forced to spit on him.[68] Fr. Stanislaus Bednarski, a Pole, was hanged on a cross.

As the tide of the war began to turn, and the Germans needed to get all the labor possible out of the prisoners, the S.S. decided to use these generally well-educated prisoner/priests as secretaries and managers. With priests in the offices where they could manipulate labor schedules, they were able to engage in forms of sabotage. Thus, a planned gas oven at Dachau never became functional due, at least in part, to the efforts of these imprisoned Catholic priests.[69]

The deportation and execution of priests from occupied countries created some very difficult personal dilemmas. For instance, if Nazis were deporting priests, soldiers would be charged with finding them, and the whole community would often help protect them. One technique that the Germans used to uncover those in hiding was to pretend to seek counsel so that the person being sought would come out of hiding.[70] On occasion, however, a Catholic German soldier (or even a Nazi official) would actually seek spiritual counseling from a priest. How would the community decide whether the request to see a priest was real, and how much courage did it take for the priest to come out of hiding to counsel those who might be hunting him? The priests usually did come out to provide counsel,[71] which might help account for the high number of priests who were sent to the concentration camps.

On June 2, 1943 (the feast day of St. Eugenio), in an address to the cardinals which was broadcast on Vatican Radio and clandestinely distributed in printed form within Poland, the Pope expressed in new and clear terms his compassion and affection for the Polish people and predicted the rebirth of Poland:[72]

> No one familiar with the history of Christian Europe can ignore or forget the saints and heroes of Poland... nor how the faithful people of that land have contributed throughout history to the development and conservation of Christian Europe. For this people so harshly tried, and others, who together have been forced to drink the bitter chalice of war today, may a new future dawn worthy of their legitimate aspirations in the depths of their sufferings, in a Europe based anew on Christian foundations.[73]

Pius XII assured his listeners that he regarded all people with equal good will. He then, however, provided a bit more insight into his thoughts.

[D]o not be surprised, Venerable Brothers and beloved sons, if our soul reacts with particular emotion and pressing concern to the prayers of those who turn to us with anxious pleading eyes, in travail *because of their nationality or their race*, before greater catastrophes and ever more acute and serious sorrows, and destined sometimes, even without fault of their own, to exterminating constraints.[74]

The Pope warned the cardinals to be cautious about what they said. "Every word we address to the competent authority on this subject, and all our public utterances, have to be carefully weighed and measured by us in the interests of the victims themselves, lest, contrary to our intentions, we make their situation worse and harder to bear."[75]

Leaders of the Catholic Church in Poland, including some who had asked the Pope to make a statement on behalf of the victims of the Nazis, were very grateful for the address. On June 11, Cardinal Hlond sent his thanks for the "historic words" of the Pope, saying that "the Poles needed this, and they anxiously awaited this statement which put an end to the fables of Hitler's propaganda that the Holy See had simply given up in regard to the situation in Poland."[76] Archbishop Sapieha wrote from Cracow that: "the Polish people will never forget these noble and holy words, which will call forth a new and ever more loyal love for the Holy Father... and at the same time provide a most potent antidote to the poisonous influences of enemy propaganda."[77] He also said that he would try to publicize the speech as much as possible by having copies printed, if the authorities would permit it.[78]

*****

The Catholic Pope is also the bishop of Rome. As such, the safety of Rome was always very close to Pius XII's heart. He had several communications with Roosevelt, seeking assurance that the Allies would not bomb Rome.[79] On May 18, 1943, Pius wrote to Roosevelt:

The assurance given to Us in 1941 by Your Excellency's esteemed Ambassador Mr. Myron Taylor and spontaneously repeated by him in 1942 that "America has no hatred of the Italian people" gives Us confidence that they will be treated with consideration and understanding; and if they have had to mourn the untimely death of dear ones, they will yet in their present circumstances be spared as far as possible further pain and devastation.[80]

In response, on June 16, Roosevelt wrote:

> Attacks against Italy are limited, to the extent humanly possible, to military objectives.... This may be an opportune time to warn Your Holiness that I have no reason to feel assured that Axis planes would not make an opportunity to bomb Vatican City with the purpose of charging Allied planes with the outrages they themselves had committed.
>
> My country has no choice but to prosecute the war with all force against the enemy until every resistance has been overcome.... Any other course would only delay the fulfillment of that desire in which Your Holiness and the governments and peoples of the United Nations—I believe the people of Italy likewise—are joined—the return of peace on earth.[81]

This was followed within a month by a telegram in which President Roosevelt said "Churches and religious institutions will, to the extent that it is within our power, be spared the devastations of war during the struggle ahead. Throughout the period of operations the neutral status of the Vatican City as well as of the Papal domains throughout Italy will be respected."[82]

Despite the Pope's pleas, on the morning of July 19, 1943, the Allies bombed Rome. As he did whenever there was an air-raid, Pius XII refused to go to a shelter. Instead, he watched the two and a half hour raid from a window in his study.[83] More than 500 American bombers dropped 1200 tons of explosives on Rome. The Basilica of St. Laurence Outside-the Walls, first built in the sixth century by Pope Pelagius, was partially demolished, as was the cemetery of Campo Verano, where the remains of the Pope's parents were blown from their graves. It was estimated that "well over 1000" people were killed.[84]

As soon as the all-clear was sounded, the Pope withdrew the cash reserves in the Vatican Bank and drove into the city. He said prayers, gave comfort to the injured, and distributed about two million lira.[85] About dawn, Pope Pius returned to the Vatican and composed a letter to President Roosevelt. It said:

> We call on God, Our sole stay and comfort, to hasten the dawn of that day when His peace will erect the glorious temple built of living stones, the nations of the earth, wherein all members of the vast human family will find tranquillity, security in justice, and freedom and inspiration to worship their Creator and to love their fellow men. It is the day, as Your Excellency says, longed for by all men of good will.... We avail Ourselves of this occasion to renew Our good wishes,

while we pray God to protect Your Person and the people of the United States.[86]

He also sent an open letter to the Cardinal-Vicar of Rome, in which he expressed great disappointment at his failure to persuade Allied leaders not to bomb Rome,[87] and he wrote the Italian government to verify whether they had kept their promise to remove all military targets from the city.[88]

Memories of this day would haunt the Pontiff for years thereafter. In 1948 he recorded his thoughts:

> That day will be known in history as the most sorrowful for the Eternal City during the Second World War. Seldom perhaps have the Shepherd and the faithful of the Bishopric of Rome been as closely united as in the common mourning of July 19. The air attack had devastated a peaceful section of Rome; the tombs of the cemetery of San Lorenzo were destroyed; the roof, the vestibule, the facade and one of the walls of one of Rome's oldest basilicas had been razed. This day, however, gave us an opportunity to come in close contact with the suffering and frightened population of our beloved native town. Up to the last day of our life we will still remember this sorrowful meeting.[89]

One month after this attack the district of San Giovanni was bombed, and the Pope was again among the first on the scene.[90]

The Axis leaders expressed great concern over the bombing and offered their condolences to the Holy See. According, however, to a telegram from the American Ambassador in Switzerland:

> Many Fascists are shedding "crocodile tears." In their hearts they are rejoicing that Papacy has after all proved itself unable protect Rome since loss prestige which they believe Pope will suffer as result will tend to strengthen their own political position with masses. The Germans as well, I understand, have been quick to recognize propaganda possibilities for them.[91]

Vatican Radio countered German propaganda in a broadcast on the night of July 24, which reported (in German) that the Pope did not protest to Roosevelt, did not summon American representatives to his office, and did not question the good faith of the American aviators.[92]

Around this time Pius was reportedly told that Hitler had ordered his capture and given instructions that the Pope should be shot if he resisted.[93] Pius was urged to move the papacy to a neutral nation, but he resolved to stay in Rome and do what he could to alleviate the suffering. About six months earlier he had said to the rector at the

Gregorian University that the Nazis "want to destroy the Church and crush it like a toad. There will be no place for the Pope in the new Europe. They say that he is going to America. I have no fear and I shall remain here."[94]

In June 1943, Pius released his encyclical *Mystici Corporis Christi* (*On the Mystical Body*). At least one of his advisors reportedly urged him to name Hitler as the "barbaric butcher behind the Holocaust," but the draft as released contained no express references to Hitler or the Nazis.[95] Still, it was an obvious attack on the theoretical basis of National Socialism. As Pinchas E. Lapide, the Israeli consul in Italy, wrote: "Pius chose mystical theology as a cloak for a message which no cleric or educated Christian could possibly misunderstand."[96]

In *Mystici Corporis Christi*, Pius wrote: "the Church of God... is despised and hated maliciously by those who shut their eyes to the light of Christian wisdom and miserably return to the teachings, customs and practices of ancient paganism."[97] He wrote of the "passing things of earth," and the "massive ruins" of war, including the persecution of priests and nuns.[98] He offered prayers that world leaders be granted the love of wisdom and expressed no doubt that "a most severe judgment" would await those leaders who did not follow God's will.[99]

Pius appealed to "Catholics the world over" to "look to the Vicar of Jesus Christ as the loving Father of them all, who... takes upon himself with all his strength the defense of truth, justice and charity."[100] He explained, "Our paternal love embraces all peoples, whatever their nationality or race."[101] Christ, by his blood, made the Jews and Gentiles one, "breaking down the middle wall of partition... in his flesh by which the two peoples were divided."[102] He noted that Jews were among the first people to adore Jesus.[103] Pius then made an appeal for all to "follow our peaceful King who taught us to love not only those who are of a different nation or race, but even our enemies."[104]

In as much as these words were contained in the middle of an encyclical on Church doctrine, Pius XII's critics are probably correct when they suggest that the message was not widely disseminated. However, in June, Vatican Radio followed up with a broadcast that expressly stated: "He who makes a distinction between Jews and other men is unfaithful to God and in conflict with God's commands."[105] On July 28, 1943, a Vatican Radio broadcast followed up on the Pope's denunciation of totalitarian forms of government and support for democratic ideals. It said:

> The life and activities of all must be protected against arbitrary human action. This means that no man has any right on the life and freedom of other men. Authority... cannot be at the service of any arbitrary power. Herein lies the essential differences between tyranny and true usefulness.... The Pope condemns those who dare to place the fortunes of whole nations in the hands of one man alone, a man who as such, is the prey of passions, error and dreams.[106]

Adolph Hitler's name was not used, but there was no doubt to whom the Pope was referring.

Jewish organizations had taken note of Pius XII's efforts, and they turned to him in times of need. In June, Grand Rabbi Israel Herzog wrote to Cardinal Maglione on behalf of Egyptian Jews, expressing thanks for the Holy See's charitable work in Europe, and asking for assistance for Jews being held prisoner in Italy.[107] The following month he wrote back thanking Pius for his efforts on behalf of the refugees that "had awoken a feeling of gratitude in the hearts of millions of people."[108] On August 2, 1943, the World Jewish Congress sent the following message to Pope Pius:

> World Jewish Congress respectfully expresses gratitude to Your Holiness for your gracious concern for innocent peoples afflicted by the calamities of war and appeals to Your Holiness to use your high authority by suggesting Italian authorities may remove as speedily as possible to Southern Italy or other safer areas twenty thousand Jewish refugees and Italian nationals now concentrated in internment camps... and so prevent their deportation and similar tragic fate which has befallen Jews in Eastern Europe. Our terror-stricken brethren look to Your Holiness as the only hope for saving them from persecution and death.[109]

Later that same month, *Time* magazine reported: "...no matter what critics might say, it is scarcely deniable that the Church Apostolic, through the encyclicals and other Papal pronouncements, has been fighting totalitarianism more knowingly, devoutly, and authoritatively, and for a longer time, than any other organized power."[110]

In September, a representative from the World Jewish Congress reported to the Pope that approximately 4,000 Jews and Yugoslav Nationals who had been in internment camps were removed to an area that was under the control of Yugoslav partisans.[111] As such, they were out of immediate danger. The report went on to say:

I feel sure that the efforts of your Grace and the Holy See have brought about this fortunate result, and I should like to express to the Holy See and yourself the warmest thanks of the World Jewish Congress. The Jews concerned will probably not yet know by what agency their removal from danger has been secured, but when they do they will be indeed grateful.[112]

In November, Rabbi Issac Herzog again wrote to Pius expressing "his sincere gratitude and deep appreciation for so kind an attitude toward Israel and for such valuable assistance given by the Catholic Church to the endangered Jewish people."[113] Jewish communities in Chile, Uruguay, and Bolivia also sent similar offers of thanks to the Pope.[114]

*****

The Allied leaders met in Washington in May 1943, to discuss strategy. Freed from the battles in Africa, Allied troops could look to the north. Churchill wanted to attack Italy "the soft underbelly of the Axis." President Roosevelt agreed. The next month the Allies began their long awaited attack on Sicily.

The German forces in Italy put up dogged resistance, and the Italian front soon was marked by the most bitter and bloody fighting of the European war. Italian cities, which contained some of the most precious memorials of European culture, were ravaged by the prolonged fighting. The Italian people, however, were no longer ready to be led to slaughter by Mussolini. The invasion of Italy was the last straw.

By this time, there were several movements to rid Italy of Mussolini. The Vatican was asked to participate in his ouster, but Pius was concerned that this would be interfering in internal affairs.[115] Nevertheless, he was anxious to take whatever action he could to help shorten the war, and on May 12 he wrote a note encouraging Mussolini to pursue a separate peace with the Allies.[116] Mussolini thanked the Pope, but replied that "under present condition there is no alternative, and Italy will continue to wage war."[117]

By now the Americans were certain of ultimate victory. Roosevelt had already asked the Vatican to keep him informed of governmental changes within Italy.[118] On May 29, Myron Taylor sent a message to the Vatican in which the Holy See was urged to tell "whoever has the means for acting" that Italy now had to separate itself from Germany and form a new government.[119] The only other alternative was utter devastation.

In early June Pius agreed to draft a message to the Italian King. Before it was sent, Roosevelt made the information public. He announced in a press conference that the Italian people had to oust the Fascist regime and rid itself of Nazis. If that were done, Italy could choose its own government and join the family of nations. Otherwise Italy had to brace for intensive warfare.[120] On June 17, Pius sent his nuncio to see King Emmanuel and confirm that the United States had sent a substantially similar message to the King through the Vatican's diplomatic offices.[121] The king was not ready to move at that time, but Mussolini did not remain in power much longer.

Following the bombing raid on Rome that took place on July 19, King Emmanuel scheduled a meeting at which Mussolini would face the Fascist Grand Council. It took place on the night of July 24.[122] When it was over, Mussolini went out to his car, but it was gone. He was directed to a shaded area of the King's Villa. Mussolini found himself surrounded by secret police who ordered him into an ambulance. He asked where he was being taken and was told that he would be safe. Without saying anything more, Mussolini got into the vehicle and was driven to a place of imprisonment. He was replaced by Marshal Pietro Badoglio.[123]

Even though the King pledged to continue fighting alongside the Germans, the change in Italian leadership concerned Hitler's high command. They were worried that Badoglio might defect and take sides with the Allies.[124] To prevent this, the Germans seized strategic centers, preparing to occupy an allied nation. Pius, for his part, urged the new Italian government to declare Rome an open city. On July 31, the Badoglio government informed the Vatican that Rome would, in principle, be free and asked the Vatican to forward that message to Washington.[125]

When the news spread that Mussolini had been overthrown, most Italians were delighted.[126] He had led Italy into the war and was blamed for much of the suffering that came with it. On the other hand, as long as Mussolini was in power and the Vatican maintained relations with Italy, he could be counted on to provide some protection to the Jews who lived in Italy. With him in charge, Italians did not agree to deportation of Jews from Italy, Italian-occupied France, or Italian-occupied Croatia.[127] (Some top German leaders blamed the

200 HITLER, THE WAR, AND THE POPE

influence of the Catholic Church for the Italian resistance to Jewish deportation.)[128]   Now, however, German troops were going to be in charge.   "Suddenly the future seemed at risk not only for the 43,000 Italian Jews whom Mussolini had protected from deportation, but also for many thousand more Jews who lived, or had found refuge, in [Italian-occupied areas]."[129]

Hitler learned of Mussolini's downfall over the radio.   (It was reported that Mussolini had suddenly resigned for health reasons.) He believed that Pius had been involved in Mussolini's ouster, and he blamed the Pope for Italy's capitulation to the Allies.[130]   Napoleon Bonaparte had kidnaped Pope Pius VII in 1809,[131] and Hitler considered doing the same.[132]   When someone suggested that this would create a public relations problem,[133] Hitler at first dismissed the concern.   Minutes of a meeting that took place that night quote him as saying:

> That doesn't matter, I'll go right into the Vatican.   Do you think I worry about the Vatican?   We'll take that right off.   All the diplomatic corps will be hiding in there.   I don't give a damn; if the entire crew's in there, we'll get the whole lot of swine out.   Afterward, we can say we're sorry.   We can easily do that.   We've got a war on.[134]

People living in the Vatican kept their bags packed, fearing that the Germans would enter.   They also all used false names, just in case.[135] (Pius told Cardinal Nasalli Rocca, "If the Nazis decide to kidnap me, then they're going to have to drag me away by force.   Because I'm staying here.")[136]

There was even a joke that made the rounds in Vatican City concerning German occupation and Air Marshall Hermann Goering's well-known fondness for uniforms and decorations.   According to the story, he had been sent to Rome by Hitler.   Shortly thereafter he wired back: "Have placed the Holy See under German protection.   All prelates in concentration camp.   Pope has fled.   Vatican in flames. Cardinal's robe suits me beautifully."[137]   Fortunately, wiser counsel prevailed.[138]   Rome was not stormed by Panzer divisions, and the Vatican was never invaded, but Hitler did send his troops into Rome. They took the city after just two days of fighting.

As soon as it became clear that German troops would occupy Rome, Pius tried to help Jews evacuate the city and made plans for feeding the city's residents.[139]   Rome's population was swollen to almost double its size by refugees drawn by what they thought was the protection of an open city. It was, according to one account, "a city of spies, double agents, informers, torturers, escaped war prisoners, hunted Jews, and hungry people."[140] Pius also had the Vatican Secretary of State write to the leaders of all religious orders and ask them to help refugees in any way they could.[141]

Upwards of 60,000 German soldiers entered Rome.[142] They ringed the Vatican, supposedly to protect the Holy Father and the Eternal City.[143] They then established a line of demarcation by painting a white line on the pavement between the Vatican and Rome. German soldiers patrolled outside the ring, and the Swiss Guard stood inside it. (London Radio used the posting of guards to broadcast that the Pope was being held hostage.)[144] At first, people could pass freely into Vatican City, but when the Nazis realized that the Pope was offering shelter to Jews and other refugees, they began checking identification. The Church countered by providing fake identification for people wanting to enter the Vatican. Later still, many people made mad dashes to safety after dark.[145]

*****

The Allies bombed Rome on August 19, 1943, and two days later they sent a message to the Holy See. Why, they wondered, had the new Italian government not separated itself from the Germans, and were they being forced to continue the war?[146] There was some hesitation on the part of the Holy See with regard to the propriety of answering, but ultimately the Pope decided to reply.[147] A return cable, sent on August 21, said that Italian cooperation with the Germans was not freely given, but was forced.[148] This information helped the Allies with their next major move in the war.

On September 3, 1943, British and American forces moved across the Strait of Messina to the Italian peninsula. At Algiers, on the same day, the Badoglio regime secretly signed an armistice with the Allies.[149] The Italian capitulation was announced on September 8th.[150] The very next day, the newspaper *Il popolo di Roma* reported that the Holy See had an important role in bringing the armistice about, though this was subsequently denied to Nazi authorities.[151] Within a month, southern Italy was under Allied control, and on October 13 the new anti-Fascist government declared war on Germany.

Even before the anti-Fascist Italians declared war, Hitler began moving troops into Italy. This is when the Church undertook a relief effort which has been called "probably the greatest Christian program in the history of Catholicism."[152] Pius sent a letter by hand to the bishops instructing them to open all convents and monasteries throughout Italy so that they could become safe refuges for Jewish people.[153] All available Church buildings—including those in Vatican City—were put to use.[154] One hundred and fifty such sanctuaries were opened in Rome alone. Castel Gandolfo, the Pope's normal summer home, was used to shelter about 500 Jews, and several children were born in his personal apartment which was converted to a temporary obstetrical ward.[155] St. Peter's Basilica itself was also made available.[156] As the Nazis intensified their persecution, the Church also placed Jews in monasteries, parish houses, and private homes.[157] Almost 5,000 Jews, a third of the Jewish population of Rome, were hidden in buildings that belonged to the Catholic Church.[158] Even more were hidden outside Rome. Deserting German soldiers were also given sanctuary. (The pontiff even granted audiences to German soldiers, many of whom suffered from guilty consciences, until an order from the German High Command prohibited them from entering the Vatican.)[159]

Catholic hospitals were ordered to admit as many Jewish patients as possible, even if their ailments were fictitious.[160] Pius took away the ceremonial halberds of his Swiss guard and replaced them with machine guns. Guards were also placed at the extraterritorial buildings around Rome where Jewish people were being sheltered. Pius even ordered that the papal seal be carved on the entrance gate of Rome's Great Synagogue.[161] The Church's neutrality, he hoped, would prevent the Nazis from overrunning it.[162] The chief rabbi of Rome reported:

> No hero in history has commanded such an army; an army of priests works in cities and small towns to provide bread for the persecuted and passports for the fugitives. Nuns go into canteens to give hospitality to women refugees. Superiors of convents go out into the night to meet German soldiers who look for victims.... Pius XII is followed by all with the fervor of that charity that fears no death.[163]

Because of this leadership, Pope Pius XII's actions accomplished much more than empty words ever could have.

Those receiving shelter were required to pledge that they did not have weapons, that they would act in accordance with the Vatican's official neutrality, and that they would follow any rules that were necessary to preserve that neutrality. Jewish religious articles presented particular problems, as they would be sure give-aways if they were discovered by the Germans. There are, however, records of Catholic clergy saving sacred books and copies of the Torah for their Jewish "guests."[164]

Convents were normally closed to outsiders. The rules were very strict and could not have been violated without instructions from high Church authorities. At first, refugees were kept in common areas, out of the cloistered rooms, but as more and more people sought protection from the Germans, all rooms were opened.[165] Still, however, everyone in the convents and monasteries had to abide with strict separation of the sexes rules. As a result, most Jewish families were split up. Priests sometimes had to play "postmen," carrying messages between husband and wife. In very rare occasions, Church officials would bend the rules to accommodate married couples.[166] Catholic authorities also made provisions for Kosher food and tried to provide decent burials when Jewish people were killed in the war.[167]

Blank and forged documents were freely handed out by Church authorities. Many Jews used these to show that they had been baptized into the Catholic faith, and—because of the provisions of the concordat—Germans would usually leave them alone. Pius also assisted Jewish people as they emigrated to safe nations.[168] Many Jewish people with these documents were transported to safety in Spain or Switzerland, but as the border became better secured by the Germans, relocation became more dangerous. On the Pope's instructions, many Jews were dressed in clerical garb and taught to chant the liturgy.[169] (Some survivors recall switching in mid-prayer from the Hebrew *Shema* to the Latin *Ave Maria* when a stranger approached.)[170] Catholic priests then began personally escorting these "monks and nuns" across the Allied lines. Even later, some were sent in trucks disguised as food delivery vehicles.

As the Pope placed himself in danger and sacrificed much to save others, the world Jewish community took note. A note from the Israelite Central Committee of Uruguay to the papal nuncio reported:

> We deem it a high honor to make known to Your Excellency our
> fondness and support of His Holiness, Pius XII, who already directly
> suffers the consequences of the actual conflict that strikes the world.
> [T]he Community that we represent has always followed the
> news... of the situation of the Vatican and the August person of His
> Holiness.. And from the depths of their hearts the Israelites of
> Uruguay pray [for]... news that assures the cessation of the danger
> that threatens His Holiness, Pius XII, ardent defender of the cause of
> those who are unjustly persecuted.[171]

The Germans had a list of priests who had given shelter to Jews, and
they tried to capture these priests and send them to concentration
camps. As the Nazis moved into Italy, many "listed" priests moved
into the Vatican, and they did not re-emerge until the Allies had liberated the city. In Northern Italy, where the priests had more difficulty hiding out, the Nazis executed many of them.

On September 20, a representative from Mussolini's new government in northern Italy approached Archbishop Ildefonso Schuster of
Milan, to demand 6,000 Jewish "hostages" in exchange for six
German soldiers who were killed at a hospital.[172] The Pope's close
advisor, Giovanni Battista Montini, the future Pope Paul VI, filed an
objection with German Ambassador Ernst Von Weizsäcker.[173]
Weizsäcker, who was sympathetic to the Church and Jewish victims
of the Nazis,[174] said that he did not want to speak of the Vatican when
he communicated with Berlin. "At headquarters they are not thinking about the Holy See, and I am afraid that to talk about hostages in
the name of the Holy See would provoke grave repercussions against
the Holy See," he said.[175] Montini rejected this line of argument in the
name of the Pope, saying "the pope is the common father of the faithful, and he can intervene to defend them at any time and in any
way."[176] Eventually, however, Weizsäcker persuaded Montini to trust
him. Montini wrote: "He is a man with a heart, and knows that we
must make every effort to dam the flood of hate that threatens to
drown the peoples."[177] Eventually the Germans dropped their
demand, but Weizsäcker warned that similar cases were likely to follow, and one did within a week.[178]

On September 27, S.S. officials summoned representatives of
Rome's Jewish community and demanded fifty kilograms of gold (or
the equivalent in dollars or sterling) within thirty-six hours.[179]
Otherwise, the Nazis would send 200 Jews to the concentration
camps.[180] In his 1954 memoir, Rabbi Eugenio Zolli gave his account

of when a representative of the Jewish community approached him to seek help:

> The Community had succeeded in gathering together only around thirty-five kilograms of gold. Would I, he asked, go to the Vatican and try to obtain a loan of fifteen kilograms of gold? "Right away," I replied.
>
> Dr. [Giorgio] Fiorentino arrived with a car. "I am dressed like a beggar," I remarked. "We shall go in by one of the back doors," he replied. "The Vatican is always guarded by the Gestapo. A friendly person will be waiting for you, and so that you can avoid showing personal documents stamped 'Hebrew Race,' you will be presented as an engineer, called to examine some walls that are being constructed."
>
> ***
>
> The Vatican had already spent millions in aiding fugitive Jews to reach safety. I said, "The New Testament does not abandon the Old. Please help me. As for repayment, I myself shall stand as surety, and since I am poor, the Hebrews of the world will contribute to pay the debt."[181]

The Vatican officials retreated to speak to Pope Pius XII. After just a few minutes, they returned and offered to lend money for the ransom. The time for re-payment was left open; there was no interest charge; and everyone knew that it could not be repaid anytime soon.[182]

According to most accounts, sufficient funds were collected from other sources so the Vatican did not actually make the loan.[183] Nevertheless, the Pope's charitable offer was not forgotten. Rabbi Zolli expressed his thanks to the Pope on behalf of the Jewish community. Following the war, Rabbi Zolli even converted to Catholicism, and he adopted the Christian name Eugenio to honor the man who had done so much to protect others during the war.[184]

The ransom paid to the Germans merely bought a bit of time. The very next day German troops entered the main synagogue in Rome and took a complete list of Roman Jewish families.[185] Less than a month later, on Saturday October 16, the Gestapo launched an attack on those Jews who had not yet left the city or found safe refuge.[186] Unfortunately, many who might have otherwise left were persuaded to stay due to the earlier ransom payment.[187] Thus, within a short time, 1,259 Jews were captured.[188] A distress call was placed to Italian Princess Enza Pignatelli, who went to the Pope to seek help.[189] As she later reported, Pius was "furious" when he learned of the roundup.[190] "Let's go make a few phone calls," he said.[191]

Pius immediately filed a personal protest with German Ambassador Weizsäcker, demanding that the Germans "stop these arrests at once."[192] The British representative to the Holy See sent a secret telegram back to the Foreign Office in which he reported: "As soon as he heard of the arrests of Jews in Rome Cardinal Secretary of State sent for the German Ambassador and formulated some [sort] of protest."[193] The result, according to British records, was that "large numbers" of the Jews were released.[194] When the British representative to the Holy See asked whether he could report on the Vatican's efforts, he was told that a report strictly to the Foreign Office would be acceptable, but that it could be used "on no account for publicity, since any publication of information would probably lead to renewed prosecution."[195]

Cardinal Maglione's demand that Ambassador Weizsäcker intervene on behalf of the Jews for the sake of "humanity and Christian charity,"[196] was received with embarrassment. Weizsäcker said to Maglione: "I always expect you to ask me, 'So why then are you staying in your position?'"[197] Maglione, who knew of Weizsäcker's efforts to help the Jews, replied:

> No, I simply tell you: Excellency, you have a soft and good heart. Try to save these innocent ones. It is painful to the Holy father, painful beyond measure, that in Rome itself and under the eyes of the father of us all so many people are made to suffer for the simple reason that they are members of a particular race.[198]

Weizsäcker promised to respect the sanctity of the Holy See's buildings, and he sent a message to the generals in charge of German troops.[199] He also assured Cardinal Maglione that "a good number" of Jews had been released, but he cautioned that this information was strictly confidential.[200] Any indiscretion would be likely to result in further persecutions. Weizsäcker later explained: "Any protest by the Pope would only result in the deportations being really carried out in the thoroughgoing fashion. I know how our people react in these matters."[201] At the end of the meeting, Weizsäcker asked Maglione for permission not to report this conversation back to his superiors, lest it lead to retaliation. The Cardinal replied: "Your Excellency has informed me that he is attempting to do something for the unfortunate Jews. I thank him for this. As to the rest, I leave it to his judgement."[202]

The next day, Weizsäcker wired to Berlin that "The Curia is particularly shocked that the action took place, so to speak, under the pope's windows. This reaction would be perhaps softened if the Jews could be used for military work in Italy."[203] That same day, Pius sent his nephew, Carlo Pacelli, to see the rector of the National German Church in Rome, who was known to have close ties to German government officials. Ignoring Weizsäcker's advice, the young Pacelli warned the Nazis to suspend all actions against the Jews or risk public condemnation.[204] The rector then forwarded the message on to the military governor of Rome.[205]

The Nazis stopped large-scale roundups in Rome following the Vatican's protest.[206] For one of the few times during the war, it appeared that words had actually impacted Nazi behavior. The Chief Rabbi of Rome at the time, Israel Zolli explained:

> With regard to the probability of persecution in Rome, there was this to be said: the influence of the Vatican was great, and open persecution was certain to produce a great outcry from the Pope. The number of Jews was small, and the Germans had little to gain from their elimination. It was known that the German army was opposed to persecution on political grounds. But reason had little hold on the S.S.[207]

The real reason why Vatican complaints seem to have had an impact, however, was that a German official completely minimized them in his report back to Berlin.

Ambassador Weizsäcker was constantly worried that Hitler would order an invasion of the Vatican.[208] "From the time he arrived in Rome, Weizsäcker was determined that his policy would be to avoid any rupture between his government and the Holy See."[209] As such, he played a "subtle double game,"[210] and sometimes censored messages from the Vatican or sent "tactical lies" to persuade the Nazis that Pius was not a threat.[211] Rather than just forwarding messages to Berlin, he would even occasionally reword them. In fact, Weizsäcker sometimes sent one set of comments to Berlin, while recording a different version in his private notes.[212]

On October 25-26, 1943, the Vatican newspaper printed a major article under the headline: *The Charitable Work of the Pope.*[213] It said: "The charity of the pope is universal and fatherly. It knows no frontiers—of nationality, of religion, of race. The pope's continual activity has been increased in these last days because of the sufferings which have fallen upon so many unfortunates."[214] Concerned that Berlin

would be upset by this clear statement of support for the Jews,
Weizsäcker sent a notorious telegram to his superiors on October 28.
It said:

> Although the Pope is said to be importuned from various quarters, he
> has not allowed himself to be carried away making any demonstra-
> tive statements against deportation of the Jews. Although he must
> expect our enemies to resent this attitude on his part, he has never-
> theless done all he could in this delicate question as other matters,
> not to prejudice relationships with the German government. Since
> further action on the Jewish problem is probably not to be expected
> here in Rome, it may be assumed that this question, so troublesome
> to German-Vatican relations, has been disposed of. On 25 October
> *L'Osservatore Romano*, moreover, published a semi-official commu-
> nique on the Pope's charitable activities in which the statement was
> made, in the style typical of this Vatican newspaper–that is to say,
> involved and vague–that the Pope extends his paternal solicitude to
> all men without distinction of nationality and race. There is no need
> to raise objections to its publication, since hardly anyone will under-
> stand the text as referring specifically to the Jewish question.[215]

Despite what the telegram said, Weizsäcker understood the Pope's
message.[216] He knew that thousands of Roman Jews were being sheltered in Church buildings that had been opened at the instruction of
Pius XII, and he knew that the Church had provided many Jews with
falsified documents showing them to have been baptized as
Catholics.[217] His telegram helped dissuade the Nazi leadership from
invading the Vatican, and the Nazis did not again attempt a large-
scale roundup,[218] but the telegram also misled historians studying
this era.[219]

*****

In providing forged documents to victims of the Nazis, the neutral
Vatican was actually violating the Geneva Convention. As such, this
activity brought occasional complaints from groups such as the
International Red Cross, because a compromise of neutrality could
jeopardize that organization's ability to carry out its work.[220] Another
problem for the Pontiff was that Allied planes routinely machine-
gunned trains and cars in German-occupied Italy. In August 1943,
the British government refused the Vatican's request for permission
to pass into areas occupied by the Axis powers. The British informed
the Vatican, "so long as the Germans have no hope of obtaining sup-

plies through the blockade they are obliged in their own interest to maintain a minimum standard of nourishment from the resources at their disposal in order to prevent the economic collapse of the occupied countries."[221] Thus, the Vatican was prohibited from carrying out its humanitarian work so that the Allies could further their military objectives.

Difficulties presented by either side of the warring nations did not prevent the Pope from offering assistance to both sides. A communique published by the Vatican in October 1943, explained:

> The August Pontiff... has not desisted for one moment from employing all the means in His power to alleviate the suffering which, whatever form it may take, is the consequence of this cruel conflagration. With the augmentation of so much evil, the universal and paternal charity of the Supreme Pontiff... knows neither boundaries nor nationality, neither religion nor race.[222]

That same month, President Roosevelt announced at a press conference that the Allied campaign in Italy was a crusade to free Rome, the Vatican, and the Pope from Nazi domination.[223] London Radio had already broadcast that the Pope was being held captive,[224] and the Germans were upset by the combination of these stories. Foreign minister Joachim von Ribbentrop sent Weizsäcker to see the Pope with a statement affirming that the German government had fully respected the sovereignty of Vatican City.[225] The Germans wanted the Pope to issue a similar statement. Eventually they agreed on a statement that appeared in *L'Osservatore Romano* on October 30. It clarified the information that had been set forth by the Allies and stated that the neutral status of Vatican City had indeed been respected by the Germans.[226] Unfortunately, such a statement could not have been made just a short time later.

After the armistice with the Allies, many Italian soldiers were taken as prisoners to Germany. Because of the changing alliances, these soldiers were regarded as "military internees," not prisoners of war. As such, they did not have rights under the Geneva Red Cross Convention, and the Allies would not allow the passage of material assistance destined for them. The Pope filled the void by making sure that the soldiers were well cared for by his agents who were already inside Germany.[227]

As the tension in the city increased, Pius became increasingly apprehensive that the Roman citizenry would rebel. Again and again he appealed to the people to refrain from such activity because of the reprisals that would be sure to follow. All the while, he was sending truckload after truckload of food and clothing from Vatican warehouses to the convents and other buildings where Jewish people were being sheltered.[228]

*****

Mussolini, under guard since his arrest in the summer, had been moved from place to place by his Italian captors so that the Germans would not discover his whereabouts. Hitler, however, named a special S.S. unit to the task of finding and rescuing him.[229] In early September, just after the occupation of Rome, German commandos located Mussolini in a small mountain hotel near the Gran Sasso. On September 13, 1943, in a carefully scripted rescue, 120 S.S. soldiers flew into the area on gliders. One glider crash-landed, three failed to land in the correct area, but eight succeeded in landing. That was enough to do the job. The Italians guarding Mussolini were surprised and overcome without a single shot being fired. Mussolini was skirted off in a small aircraft which was capable of taking off in a limited area.

On September 23, 1943, Mussolini was put in charge of the new "Italian Social Republic" in the northern part of Italy.[230] From this time until the end of the war, Italy was a divided country. The two governments—one on the side of the Axis, the other on the side of the Allies—each claimed to represent the people. Mussolini was now, however, little more than a Nazi puppet supported with German troops and money. He argued that the Vatican should continue to recognize his Fascist regime due to the Lateran Treaty. The Vatican however, replied that it made concordats with nations, not with particular governments-in-power.[231] He was no longer recognized by the Vatican.

The weakness of Mussolini vis-a-vis Hitler was reflected in January 1944, when Hitler forced Mussolini to execute his son-in-law, Count Ciano, former Italian Ambassador to the Vatican. Hitler believed Ciano to be guilty of betraying the Axis cause by seeking a separate peace through the mediation of Pope Pius XII.[232] Accordingly, he pressured Mussolini to arrest and execute his daughter's husband.[233]

According to one wartime account, when Hitler learned that the Pope was hiding Jews in the Vatican, he encouraged Mussolini to send men to investigate.[234] *Il Duce* was not in a position to refuse. Unlike the disciplined German troops, his new men were vicious renegades. They entered Rome and soon began to brutalize anyone who gave them trouble.[235] As they approached Vatican City, the Pope ordered all of the Jewish people within the Vatican to take sanctuary in St. Peter's Basilica. Then, for the first time in history, the doors to the Basilica were sealed during the daytime hours.[236] Mussolini's men would have to fight their way in.

The Swiss Guards were stationed along the white line that the Germans had painted on the pavement to separate the Vatican from Rome. The guards were normally armed with traditional herberds (part pike, part battle-axe, mounted on six foot handles), but with the Nazi occupation, Pius had ordered them to get out their machine guns. The Fascists marched up to the line, face-to-face with the Swiss Guards. The Black Shirts and the Swiss Guard were both armed, but neither side crossed the white line.[237] German Field Marshall Albert Kesselring, sensing a terrible public relations nightmare that would result from an armed confrontation, overrode the Italian commander and called off the troops.[238]

*****

On November 5, 1943, at around eight in the evening, a plane dropped four small bombs on Vatican City. The Germans wanted the Holy See to suspect the Allies (or perhaps be intimidated into embracing the Axis), but the plane is thought to have belonged to an Italian man who was angry at Pius XII for having sided with the Allies.[239] One of the bombs hit the glass roof over the workshop of mosaics. Others smashed holes in the walls of the Vatican railroad station and other nearby buildings. Windows were broken in many buildings.[240]

The German high command offered to enter the Vatican and "investigate the whole matter," but Pius turned them down. The Germans next urged Pius to let them escort him to a neutral country in the interest of his "personal safety." He also declined this offer.[241] President Roosevelt labeled Nazi military exploitation of Rome as "an affront to all religions."[242] For the time being, however, the threat of a Nazi invasion of the Vatican had passed.

On December 3, the Vatican's newspaper ran an article strongly protesting the way Jews were being treated by the Nazis, calling it unChristian and inhuman.[243] The following day, the German-controlled press responded by saying that Jews were considered foreigners and therefore were potential enemies and subject to deportation to concentration camps.[244] *L'Osservatore Romano* responded that same day, arguing that no decree issued by a political party can change the status of an Italian-born citizen, and in any case, the old, infirm, women, and children would be exempt from deportation.[245] The following day the newspapers reported on the murder of the Fascist commander in Florence and the ten anti-Fascists who were killed in retaliation.[246]

The Pope's efforts on behalf of Jewish people were beginning to be noticed. On December 30, the following message was sent to Pius XII:

> With profound gratitude, the Israelite families, fraternally sheltered by the Institute of "Our Lady of Zion," turn their moved thoughts to Your Holiness, who deigned to show them a new proof of benevolence.
>
> And while they express their gratitude for the attentive response to the call for help not in vain directed to Your Christian charity, they wish above all to show their confidence and faith for the spiritual comfort received from the Apostolic Blessing paternally imparted to them.[247]

Even more blessings would be needed in the year to come.

CHAPTER FIFTEEN

1944 AND THE ALLIES INVADE

Under the terms of the Lateran Treaty, only a limited number of Church buildings were entitled to extraterritorial status. The Italians, however, treated all Church property in Rome as if it were off-limits. When German forces moved into Rome, they initially followed that same approach. Before long, however, they learned that these buildings were being used to shelter Jews and other refugees. In February 1944, the Republican (Fascist) Roman police broke into the extraterritorial Basilica of St. Paul's Outside-the Walls. They found that the monastery was a shelter for Jews, former members of the dissolved *Carabinieri* (military police), and various men avoiding military service with the Fascist army.[1] If such raids were to continue, the results would be disastrous. Almost the entire National Committee of Liberation was hidden in the Roman Seminary at St. John Lateran, only "a few paces" from the headquarters of the Gestapo Police Chief.[2] The Vatican immediately protested to Italian and German authorities, and issued condemnations on Vatican Radio and in *L'Osservatore Romano*.[3]

Many German officials could now see the writing on the wall. Soon they would be forced out of Rome, and unless things changed, the Allies would be victorious. In an effort to win Vatican support in brokering a separate peace with the Western Allies, the German ambassador to the Holy See, Ernst Von Weizsäcker, met with Cardinal Maglione in January 1944. Weizsäcker cautioned the cardinal that "if Germany, a bulwark against Bolshevism, should fall, all Europe will become Communist."[4] Maglione replied: "What a misfortune that Germany, with its antireligious policy, has stirred up concerns as serious as these."[5]

As the fighting came closer to Rome, the German high command informed the Pope that if forced to leave the city, they would practice a "scorched earth" policy, leaving behind only ruins.[6] The Nazis made it clear that the risk to Vatican City was very real, but they offered him safe refuge in Germany. He immediately declined the offer and registered a protest against any violence.[7]   Pius then called together all of the cardinals in the Vatican and explained the German threat. Since he had asked bishops in war-torn areas to stay in place as long as possible, he was determined not to leave his post. Others, however, might have felt differently. According to some accounts, the Pope released the cardinals from their obligation to stay with him in Rome. Not one accepted the offer.[8]

Pius was also concerned about the impact of war on civilian populations in Rome. The *New York Times* reported in 1944 that Rome's population grew during Nazi occupation because:

> in that period under the Pope's direction the Holy See did an exemplary job of sheltering and championing the victims of the Nazi-Fascist regime. I have spoken to dozens of Italians, both Catholics and Jews, who owe their liberty and perhaps their lives to the protection of the church. In some cases anti-Fascists were actually saved from execution through the Pope's intervention.[9]

The article went on to explain that "none doubts that the general feeling of the Roman Curia was anti-Fascist and very strongly anti-Nazi."[10]

On February 10, bombs once again fell on Rome and the Vatican's sacred shrines. They nearly demolished Castel Gandolfo, the Pope's summer residence, where thousands of refugees were being sheltered. More than 500 people were killed.[11] On February 15, bombs fell on the abbey of Monte Cassino, reducing it to rubble and killing an unknown number of people who had sought refuge there.[12]   On March 1, bombs again fell on Vatican City, causing minor damage. Shortly thereafter Pius XII gave his first public address since the Nazi occupation of Rome. He blasted both the Allies and the Axis for turning Vatican City into a battle zone. His words did little good.

On March 24, the Nazis conducted a massive roundup and execution, which was prompted when the group GAP (*Gruppi di Azione Patriottica*), comprised mainly of Communist students, decided that the time had come for a major gesture.[13] On March 23, GAP planted a bomb which exploded as a German unit was marching down Via Rasella in Rome.[14] Thirty-three German soldiers were killed. The High Command in Berlin ordered the immediate execution of ten Italians for every soldier who had been killed.[15] According to the order, issued in Hitler's name, the reprisal was to be completed within twenty-four hours.[16] By noon the next day, a convoy that included Jews, Catholic priests, women, and two fourteen-year-old boys—none of whom had anything to do with the bomb—was directed to some man-made caves on the outskirts of Rome, among the catacombs of the Appian Way.[17] Under the direction of S.S. Lt. Col. Herbert Kappler, these 335 Italians were shot and killed. German engineers then blew up the entrances to the caves, sealing the evidence inside. Months passed before the identities of all the victims were known.

The only record of these executions that has surfaced in the archives of the Vatican Secretariat of State is a memo written by a Vatican secretary reporting a call received at 10:15 a.m. on the day after the explosion. The caller described the bombing and reported that: "Counter measures are still not known; it is thought, however, that for every German killed, ten Italians will be executed."[18]

When Pius learned of the arrests, he put his head in his hands and moaned: "It is not possible, I cannot believe it."[19] He sent his special liaison officer, Fr. Pancratius Pfeiffer, S.D.S. Superior General, to plead with the German command.[20] Pius may also have sent his nephew, Prince Carlo Pacelli, to investigate. Unfortunately, the Vatican officials were unable to learn what had happened until it was too late to intercede.[21] The German diplomatic corps withdrew into discreet silence, and on March 29 the German ambassador's office said that inquiries about persons taken by the Germans should be addressed to the headquarters of S.S. Lt. Col. Herbert Kappler, the Nazi chief of police in Rome. As Kappler confessed years later, it was a waste of time to come to him; by then the people had all been killed.[22]

*****

In April 1944, two young men, Rudolf Vrba and Fred Wetzler, escaped from Auschwitz and wrote a very detailed report to warn others of what was going on in that camp ("the Auschwitz Protocol"). The report said that 1,750,000 Jews had already been exterminated, and the killings were continuing.[23] In his book, *I Cannot Forgive,* Vrba explained that he gave the report to Jewish officials in Budapest, but that nothing seemed to have come of it. Then one day, several weeks later, he was asked to meet with Monsignor Joseph Burzio, nuncio in Bratislava.[24]

Burzio "cross-examined" Vrba for six hours to confirm what he had written in the protocol. "He went through the report line by line, page by page, returning time after time to various points until he was satisfied that I was neither lying or exaggerating."[25] Finally, the Vatican official found himself weeping. He told Vrba: "I shall carry your report to the International Red Cross in Geneva. They will take action and see that it reaches the proper hands."[26]

Burzio did indeed take the report to the International Red Cross immediately after he presented it to Pope Pius XII.[27] While informed sources had heard rumors, and many probably had good information about the death camps, this report confirmed the worst to the whole world. Before long leaders from all the Allied nations were citing the figures set forth in this report. Not only did the Vatican play a significant role in spreading this information to others, Pius also later used this information to put pressure on the Regent of Hungary to end the deportation of Jews from that country.[28]

On June 2, 1944 (the feast day of St. Eugenio), the Pope spoke about his war-related efforts: "To one sole goal our thoughts are turned, night and day: how it may be possible to abolish such acute suffering, coming to the relief of all, without distinction of nationality or race."[29] On June 4, the Allies finally made their way to Rome. It had little strategic value, but it had great psychological value. It was the capital of one of the original Axis powers and the first European capital to be liberated from the Nazis. Pius feared that it would suffer great damage in battle. He said, "Whoever dares to raise his hand against Rome will be guilty of matricide in the eyes of the civilized world and in the eternal judgement of God."[30] He had also urged the Germans to leave peacefully so as to avoid a terrible battle in the city.[31] Fortunately, despite Hitler's earlier warnings (and Mussolini's call for street-fighting),[32] as the Allies entered on one side of Rome, the Germans left quietly from the other side.[33] In fact, the Germans had moved their military equipment out of Rome in April, and they informed the Allies of this (and the consequent reason to stop bombing Rome) via the Vatican.[34] The German Ambassador to the Holy See, Ernst Von Weizsäcker, in discussing the peaceful exchange that took place in Rome, gave "chief credit to the ceaseless quiet activity of the Pope."[35]

With the Germans on the point of entering Rome, both the Italian King and the Prime Minister had fled to safety in Brindisi, a city in southern Italy. Mussolini was still in northern Italy. As such, during the occupation and at the time of liberation, the Pope was the only authority figure in Rome. Thousands who had been in hiding ran out into St. Peter's Square for the first time in nine months and embraced the soldiers.[36] That evening, families joined other families in a massive, joyous march up to Vatican City to thank God (and Pope Pius) for bringing them through the war.[37]

The Romans considered Pius "their bishop."[38] They proclaimed him *Defensor Urbis Civitatis* (Urban Defender).[39] These people had no doubts about where the Pope stood. Books had already been written and speeches had been made documenting the Vatican's support of the Allies and work with the Jewish victims of the Nazis.[40] Crowds streamed into the square and called for *Papa Pacelli*, who appeared on the loggia. He thanked God for saving Rome.[41] "Every phrase of his was punctuated with thunders of applause.... He said that whereas yesterday Rome was still fearful for the fate of her children, today she rejoiced...."[42] He gave a blessing to the crowd and left the balcony. The crowd continued to acclaim him.[43] Mussolini, who had sided with the Nazis, would receive a very different reception the following year.

A few days after the liberation, United States Lieutenant General Mark Clark, Commander of the 5th Allied Army, came to pay his respects to the Pope. One of the first things he said was, "I am afraid you have been disturbed by the noise of my tanks. I am sorry." Pope Pius XII's face lit up with a bright smile as he replied, "General, any time you come to liberate Rome, you can make just as much noise as you like."[44]

The Pope's standing with Jewish soldiers from the United States is reflected in the bulletin put out by the "Jewish Brigade Group" (U.S. 8th Army). The June 1944 edition carried a front-page editorial which proclaimed: "To the everlasting glory of the people of Rome and the Roman Catholic Church we can state that the fate of the Jews was alleviated by their truly Christian offers of assistance and shelter."[45] The Jewish chaplain of the Fifth American Army explained: "If it had not been for the truly substantial assistance and the help given to Jews by the Vatican and by Rome's ecclesiastical authorities, hundreds of refugees and thousands of Jewish refugees would have undoubtedly perished before Rome was liberated."[46] The Committee on Army and Navy Religious Activities of the American Jewish Welfare Board wrote to the Pope:

> Word comes to us from our army chaplains in Italy telling of the aid and protection given to so many Italian Jews by the Vatican and by priests and institutions of the Church during the Nazi occupation of the land. We are deeply moved by these stirring stories of Christian love, the more so as we know full well to what dangers many of those exposed themselves who gave shelter and aid to the Jews hunted by the Gestapo.
>
> From the bottom of our heart we send to you, Holy Father of the Church, the assurance of our unforgetting gratitude for this noble expression of religious brotherhood and love.[47]

Davar, the Hebrew daily of Israel's Federation of Labor, quoted a Jewish Brigade officer shortly after Rome's liberation: "When we entered Rome, the Jewish survivors told us with a voice filled with deep gratitude and respect: 'If we have been rescued; if Jews are still alive in Rome come with us and thank the pope in the Vatican. For in the Vatican proper, in churches, monasteries and private homes, Jews were kept hidden at his personal orders.'"[48]

On July 31, 1944, in front of 50,000 people at Madison Square Garden, Judge Joseph Proskauer, the President of the American Jewish Committee said, "We have heard... what a great part the Holy Father has played in the salvation of refugees in Italy, and we know... that this great Pope has reached forth his mighty and sheltering hand to help the oppressed of Hungary."[49] Today, in Vatican City, where one enters the porticos of the Congregation for Bishops just off St. Peter's Square, is a square called "The Square of Pius XII, the Savior of the City."[50] "Savior of the world," is the way some Jewish survivors have preferred to describe him.[51]

In the weeks following Rome's liberation, the Holy Father was to grant daily audiences to large groups of Allied soldiers of every religious persuasion. One of the frequent themes of his presentations was captured in a filmed statement. In English, the Pope said: "You have had experience now of the danger and uncertainty of life in the midst of a war. Make one thing certain–that you keep always close to God."[52] Another film shows him addressing Allied soldiers and saying, "It is a real joy for Us to welcome you all here, within the very old home of the common Father of the Christians...."[53]

At the conclusion of one small audience held for Allied servicemen, an overjoyed American lieutenant called out, "Okay! Let's really hear it for His Holiness," and then led his men in a loud rendition of *For He's a Jolly Good Fellow*.[54] Another time, excited Polish soldiers, after presenting the Pope with a beautifully decorated shield, sought permission to carry him on the *sedia gestatoria*.[55] Later in the year, Pius announced that he would say a Midnight Mass at St. Peter's Basilica on Christmas. The Vatican received terrorist threats that it would be bombed, but Pius would not cancel. Some seventy thousand persons, mostly Allied soldiers, were in attendance, and it came off without incident.[56]

Pius appreciated the thanks and the blessings that he received immediately after the war, but it was not yet time to celebrate. For a while yet, Allied troops might have to be stationed in Rome. Just before Rome's liberation, the British ambassador to the Vatican, Francis D'Arcy Osborne, cabled to England that "the pope hoped that no allied colored troops would be among the small number that might be garrisoned at Rome after the occupation."[57] Actually the Pope's concern was not about "colored troops," but French Moroccan troops who were known to the Vatican to have engaged in acts of violence. As reflected in an American intelligence report of the time, this misunderstanding stems from a report the Pope received about French Moroccan troops that had committed acts of violence in other areas where they were stationed.[58] As bishop of Rome, he did not want those soldiers in his city (or elsewhere). Pius expressed his concerns about these men (not "colored troops") to Osborne, who broadened the statement in his cable back to London, perhaps in order to avoid insulting French allies.[59]

In the months following Rome's liberation, the Germans retreated from one defensive line to another as Allied troops pushed north through Italy. In fact, the Germans in Italy did not surrender until May 1, 1945. With many Jewish prisoners still in the hands of the Axis powers, the Holy See still had much left to do. Fortunately, due to the Church's efforts and the reluctance of the Italians to enforce racial laws, the Jews in Italy had a far higher survival rate under Nazi occupation than was the case in most other occupied nations.

On June 22, 1944, Rabbi Andre Zaoui wrote to Pius to thank him for saving so many Jewish people: "What a magnificent manifestation of fraternity, so great in its intimate simplicity. Israel will not forget you. Side by side you continue to accomplish your mission, practicing and teaching the law of love of God and neighbor." That same month, the chief Rabbi of Rome, Israel Zolli, held a service which was broadcast on radio, to publicly express the gratitude of Italian Jews to Pius.[60] The synagogue in Rome was even ordained with a plaque thanking Pius XII for assisting in their defense.[61]

The American Jewish Welfare Board wrote in July 1944 also expressing its appreciation for the protection that the Pope had given to the Jews during Germany's occupation of Italy.[62] An editorial in the July 27 edition of *The American Israelite* entitled *True Brotherhood* discussed Vatican efforts in Rome and Pope Pius XII's efforts in Hungary and concluded "we feel an immeasurable degree of gratitude toward our Catholic brethren." In August, Pulitzer Prize-winning writer Anne O'Hare McCormick issued a dispatch for the *New York Times* from Rome indicating that Pius enjoyed an "enhanced" reputation because during the occupation, he made "hiding someone 'on the run' the thing to do," and he had given Jewish people "first priority."[63]

*****

Pietro Boetto, the Cardinal Archbishop of Genoa, gave his whole-hearted support to the Jewish rescue group DELASEM and its clandestine operations in Genoa on behalf of Jewish people. Boetto asked the Vatican for help in this endeavor, and Pope Pius XII answered by having Monsignor Giovanni Battista Montini (the future Pope Paul VI) send money. Later estimates put the number of Jewish lives saved by Boetto at 800. An article in the Italian paper *Il Nuovo Cittadino*, dated February 3, 1946, called Boetto "the Cardinal of the Jews."[64]

In Rome, Monsignor Hugh O'Flaherty was known for his work on behalf of the Jews and Allied soldiers hiding in Rome. Under Pius XII's direction, he was in charge of a network of hundreds of people that rescued thousands of Jews from the Nazis. Gestapo officer Herbert Kappler was in charge of the German occupation forces. When the Allies liberated Rome, Kappler was captured and sentenced to life imprisonment for war crimes. In the years that followed, he had only one regular visitor, Monsignor O'Flaherty. O'Flaherty and Kappler had been bitter enemies during the occupation, but the priest's compassion following the war impressed the German. In 1959, O'Flaherty baptized Kappler into the Catholic faith.[65]

Pope Pius recognized Fr. O'Flaherty's work on Easter Sunday, 1945, by calling together a number of priests who had worked with him during the war. The Pope then offered a deep and sincere tribute to Fr. O'Flaherty and his assistants for all that they had done to help the Jewish victims who were "particularly dear to my heart." O'Flaherty was also honored by Australia, Canada, and by the United States (as a recipient of the Medal of Freedom).[66]

*****

In March 1944, Germany invaded Hungary on the pretext of safeguarding communications, and the last great nightmare of the war began. Hungary had been a haven for refugee Jews.[67] The Nazis immediately issued anti-Jewish decrees. After several oral protests, the papal nuncio, Monsignor Angelo Rotta, was the first foreign envoy to submit a formal note expressing Pope Pius XII's protest.[68] Shortly thereafter, Rotta received a letter of encouragement from Pius XII in which the Pope termed the treatment of Jews as "unworthy of Hungary, the country of the Holy Virgin and of St. Stephen."[69] From then on, acting always in accordance with instructions from the Holy See and in the name of Pope Pius XII, Rotta continually intervened against the treatment of the Jews and the inhuman character of the anti-Jewish legislation.[70]

The Vatican had direct contact with Jewish organizations, and it agreed to assist the War Refugee Board (a newly created organization linking all Jewish organizations) in its effort to help Jews in Hungary.[71] Shortly after the deportations started, the War Refugee Board urged five neutral nations (Sweden, Spain, Portugal, Switzerland, and Turkey), the Vatican, and the International Red Cross to assign additional diplomatic personnel to Hungary. It was thought that foreign observers might act as a restraining influence on the Germans. Sweden and the Vatican complied very quickly. The International Red Cross, fearful that it might antagonize Germany and find itself excluded from its important work for war prisoners, hesitated to intervene, but it eventually complied. Spain, Portugal, Switzerland, and Turkey did not.[72]

Almost from the first day, Nuncio Rotta worked to help improve the treatment of the Jews. He issued baptismal certificates and passports that enabled thousands of Jews and converted Jews to leave Hungary.[73] The Vatican also informed other nations about the conditions in Hungary, and this brought international pressure on the

Hungarian government. In June 1944, the British News Service representative in Switzerland, at the request of the Vatican, sent a telegram outlining the brutal treatment of Jews in Hungary and their deportation to Auschwitz. Using abbreviated language to minimize the per-word telegraph charge, it reported: "Dramatic account one darkest chapters modern history revealing how 1,715,000 Jews put death annihilation Camp Auschwitz, Birkenau and Harmansee... where also awful destiny HungJews today fulfilling itself."[74] The message ended with the following language: "Absolute exactness above report unquestionable and diplomat Catholic functionaries well-known Vatican desire widest diffusion worldwide."[75]

Sometimes Church officials were embarrassed about how quickly they would convert Jews to Catholicism for the purpose of avoiding persecution. One small church in Budapest averaged about four or five conversions a year before the occupation. In 1944, those numbers shot up dramatically. Six were converted in January, 23 in May, 101 in June, over 700 in September, and over 1,000 in October. Three thousand Jews became Catholics at this one small church in 1944.[76] The Nazi occupying forces soon recognized that these conversions were being done only to avoid deportation, so they started persecuting the "converts."[77] Since it no longer assured protection, the flood of conversions dried up.

By mid-summer, despite the Church's efforts, 437,000 Jews had been deported from Hungary. Then, on June 25, just days after he had seen the Auschwitz Protocol, Pius XII sent an open telegram to the Regent of Hungary, Admiral Nicholas Horthy:

> Supplications have been addressed to Us from different sources that We should exert all Our influence to shorten and mitigate the sufferings that have for so long been peacefully endured on account of their national or racial origin by a great number of unfortunate people belonging to this noble and chivalrous nation. In accordance with our service of love, which embraces every human being, Our fatherly heart could not remain insensible to these urgent demands. For this reason We apply to your Serene Highness appealing to your noble feelings in the full trust that your Serene Highness will do everything in your power to save many unfortunate people from further pain and suffering.[78]

Hungarian authorities also received protests from the nuncio, the King of Sweden, the Swiss press, and the International Red Cross.

In addition to the telegram to Admiral Horthy, Pius sent an open telegram to Hungarian Cardinal Justinian Seredi, asking for support from the Hungarian bishops:

> We would forfeit our moral leadership and fail in our duty if we did not demand that our countrymen should not be handled unjustly on account of their origin or religion. We, therefore, beseech the authorities that they, in full knowledge of their responsibility before God and History, will revoke these harmful measures.[79]

The telegram was read publicly in many churches before all copies were confiscated by the government. Nuncio Rotta informed Seredi of Pius XII's desire "that the Hungarian episcopate should publicly take a stand... on behalf of their compatriots who are unjustly hit by racist decrees."[80] Two days after this telegram, Pius requested that Hungarian bishops "intercede publicly on behalf of Christian principals and to protect their fellow citizens, especially Christians, unjustly affected by racial regulations."[81]

On June 28, Archbishop Francis J. Spellman of New York broadcast a strong appeal to Hungarian Catholics deploring the anti-Jewish measures, which he said, "shocked all men and women who cherish a sense of justice and human sympathy."[82] These measures were, he said, "in direct contradiction of the doctrines of the Catholic Faith professed by the vast majority of the Hungarian people."[83] He called it incredible "that a nation which has been so consistently true to the impulses of human kindness and the teachings of the Catholic Church should now yield to a false, pagan code of tyranny...."[84] *Time* magazine reported: "This week listeners at Europe's thirty-six million radio sets might have heard New York's Archbishop Francis Joseph Spellman preaching civil disobedience. The Archbishop's broadcast (his first)... eloquently urged Hungary's nine million Catholics to disobey their government's new anti-Semitic decrees."[85] The Allies dropped printed copies of it over Hungary.[86] Spellman later confirmed what most observers had thought: he had made the statement at the express request of Pope Pius XII.[87]

Admiral Horthy complained to the Germans that he was being bombarded with telegrams from the Vatican and others and that the Nuncio was calling on him several times each day.[88] In the face of these protests, Horthy withdrew Hungarian support from the deportation process, making it impossible for the Germans to continue. Horthy's reply cable to the Pope provided: "It is with comprehension and profound gratitude that I receive your cable and request you to be convinced that I shall do all within my power to make prevail the demands of Christian humanitarian principles."[89]   More than 170,000 Hungarian Jews were saved from deportation on the very eve of their intended departure.[90]

Horthy agreed to work against the deportations and he even signed a peace agreement with the Allies. For once it appeared that Pius XII's words might actually have had a positive effect.   The Apostolic Delegate in London wrote to the representative of the World Jewish Congress: "At this moment I have a telegram from the Holy See.   The Holy Father has appealed personally to the Regent of Hungary... on behalf of your people, and has been assured that the Regent will do all possible to help."[91] The Germans, however, would not be dissuaded by mere pleas.

The Germans arrested Horthy in October, put Hungary under the control of a group of Hungarian Nazis known as the Arrow Cross, and the deportations resumed. The Pope and his representatives then made many more protests to German authorities, issued a report documenting the Vatican's work with the Jews of Hungary, and encouraged Catholics to help the victims.[92] In October, Pius joined in an effort to raise money to support Hungarian refugees, urging all the faithful to redouble their efforts on behalf of all victims of the war, regardless of their race.[93] Almost every Catholic Church in Hungary provided refuge to persecuted Jews during the autumn and winter of 1944.[94]

On November 10, 1944, Nuncio Rotta protested to the German foreign ministry, saying "from a humanitarian perspective but also to protect Christian morality, the Holy see protests the inhumane attitude adopted toward the Jews."[95] When Nazi officials suggested that Jews were merely being sent to Germany to work, not for any evil purpose, Rotta responded:

> When old men of over seventy and even over eighty, old women, children and sick persons are taken away, one wonders for what work these human beings can be used?... When we think that Hungarian workers, who go to Germany for reasons of work, are forbidden to take their families, we are really surprised to see that this great favor is granted only to Jews.[96]

Such sarcasm is quite rare in official communications from the Vatican.

The nunciature in Budapest had been bombed and half destroyed; communications with the Vatican were extremely difficult, and the lives of those Catholic officials still in the city were in constant danger. Nuncio Rotta sent a message to Rome asking what to do. The reply from Pope Pius was: "If it is still possible to do some charity, remain!"[97] Accordingly, Rotta stayed in Budapest, providing help to the Jewish victims of the Nazis.

The Germans were finally forced out of Budapest two days before Christmas, December 23, 1944. Despite the terrible losses that had taken place during their occupation, most of the Jews in Budapest were saved from the gas chamber, at least in part as a result of the combination of strong protests made by the Pope, the nuncio, and the Hungarian bishops to a government that was willing to listen. On May 25, 1945, Nuncio Cassulo informed the Vatican:

> [Chief] Rabbi Safran has expressed to me several times... his gratitude for what has been done for him and for the Jewish community. Now he has begged me to convey to the Holy Father his feelings of thankfulness for the generous aid granted to prisoners in concentration camps on the occasion of the Christmas festivities. At the same time, he told me he had written to Jerusalem, to the Chief Rabbi (Herzog), and also elsewhere, in America, to point out what the Nunciature has done for them in the time of the present difficulties.[98]

Rabbi Safran also told other Jewish leaders about the Catholic Church's efforts to protect Jewish people.[99] On September 27, 1944, Safran published an article in the newspaper *Mantuirea* under the title: "The apostolic nuncio has seen to it that the deportation of Jews to Transnistrie has been halted. May God reward him for what he has done."[100]

On October 31, President Roosevelt's representative to the Pope, Myron Taylor, transmitted a report to the director of the Committee for Refugees in Washington:

> I also want to pay tribute to many non-Jewish groups and individuals who have shown a true Christian spirit in their quick and friendly reaction in support of the helpless of Europe.... The record of the Catholic Church in this regard has been inspiring. All over Europe, Catholic priests have furnished hiding places and protection to the persecuted. His Holiness, Pope Pius XII, has interceded on many occasions in behalf of refugees in danger. In this country too, we have received help from many Catholic leaders.[101]

The World Jewish Congress, on December 1, 1944, at its war emergency conference in Atlantic City, sent a telegram of thanks to the Holy See for the protection it gave "under difficult conditions to the persecuted Jews in German-dominated Hungary."[102] Similarly, the American Jewish Committee sent an expression of deep thanks to Pius and Cardinal Maglione for having helped stop the deportations from Hungary.[103]

*****

In August 1944, British Prime Minister Winston Churchill traveled to the Vatican to meet with Pope Pius XII for a discussion of problems in Germany, Poland, Italy, and the Soviet Union.[104] According to Churchill, "The Pope received me... with the dignity and informality which he can so happily combine." With the war against Germany drawing near an end, both men were very concerned about the danger of Communism. Churchill informed Pius of Stalin's famous quote, "How many divisions has the Pope?" Pius responded: "When you see Joseph Stalin again, tell him that he will meet our divisions in heaven."[105] Churchill would later write, "I have always had the greatest dislike of [Communism]; and should I ever have the honour of another audience with the Supreme Pontiff I should not hesitate to recur to the subject."[106]

The same month that Pius received Churchill, an attempt was made, through the Pope, to save the Jews in German-occupied northern Italy. Sir Clifford Heathcote-Smith, the Intergovernmental Committee's delegate in Italy, and Myron C. Taylor, President Roosevelt's representative to Pius XII, spoke with the Pope.[107] They asked him to urge the German government to stop the deportations from Italy and to release the Jews to the Allied part of the country. The Pope immediately agreed. He told Heathcote-Smith that neither his conscience nor history would forgive him if he did not make the effort. Unfortunately, his approach, made through the Nuncio in Berlin, brought only an evasive response from the Germans.[108]

August 1944 was also the month when a group of Roman Jews came to thank Pius for having helped them during the period of Nazi occupation. In response, the Pontiff reaffirmed his position: "For centuries, Jews have been unjustly treated and despised. It is time they were treated with justice and humanity. God wills it and the Church wills it. St. Paul tells us that the Jews are our brothers. They should also be welcomed as friends."[109]

*****

On the eastern front, as the Soviet Army followed the retreating Germans, it advanced along an 800-mile front and did not stop at the national border. By mid-July 1944 the Soviets swept across the Ukraine and Poland and up to the gates of Warsaw. With the Soviets approaching, the exiled Polish government called for an insurrection to liberate Warsaw from Germany, similar to the one that led to the liberation of Paris. On July 21, a Polish Committee of National Liberation, set up in the recently liberated town of Chelm, put into operation plans for the reconstruction of their war-devastated country. On August 1, underground units of the Polish Home Army began an insurrection. Almost the entire city fought against the Nazis.

The Germans were ruthless in putting down the insurrection. The only way for it to succeed was with Soviet support. The British and Americans urged Stalin to help, as Eisenhower did in Paris. The Soviets, however, refused to go along. Stalin argued that the insurrection had begun without any prior coordination with the Soviet command.[110]

In August, Pius received a message from a group of women in Poland asking for prayers and moral support. The message went as follows:

> Most Holy Father, we Polish women in Warsaw are inspired with sentiments of profound patriotism and devotion for our country. For three weeks, while defending our fortress, we have lacked food and medicine. Warsaw is in ruins. The Germans are killing the wounded in hospitals. They are making women and children march in front of them in order to protect their tanks. There is no exaggeration in reports of children who are fighting and destroying tanks with bottles of petrol. We mothers see our sons dying for freedom and the Fatherland. Our husbands, our sons, and our brothers are not considered by the enemy to be combatants. Holy Father, no one is helping us. The Russian armies which have been for three weeks at the gates of Warsaw have not advanced a step. The aid coming to us from Great Britain is insufficient. The world is ignorant of our fight. God alone is with us. Holy Father, Vicar of Christ, if you can hear us, bless us Polish women who are fighting for the Church and for freedom.[111]

Pius responded to the president of the Polish Republic, expressing his desire to neglect nothing in his effort to save lives.[112] The message from the Polish women was then forwarded on to the American and British representatives with the request that it be brought to the attention of their governments.[113] It was also published in *L'Osservatore Romano* on September 15.[114]

Unfortunately the Pope's efforts did not stop the flow of blood. On October 2, the insurgents gave up. Overall, about 216,000 Poles and 2,000 Germans were killed. Hitler ordered the population removed from the city, the insurgents taken prisoner, and most of Warsaw destroyed.[115]

*****

Nazi persecution of Catholic priests continued, and 1944 was an especially bad year for the Jesuits in Germany. It was said that Jesuits were, first and foremost, enemies and adversaries of the Reich.[116] From the early days of Nazi rule, Jesuits attacked the intellectual basis of Nazism in their publications.[117] This, however, led to severe reprisals, including the Gestapo's publication in 1935 of a document entitled "Safeguarding against the Jesuits" that called the attention of local Nazi leaders to the Jesuit opposition.[118] Finally, Nazi presure led to the closing of the Jesuit presses.[119] The persecution of Catholic priests did not, however, come to an end. In Dachau alone over 2,000 Catholic priests were murdered or died from the treatment they received. In November 1944, three priests were executed "not because they were criminals," as one judge stated, "but because it was their tragedy that they were Catholic priests."[120]

In October, Mussolini denounced Pius XII as a renegade Italian who had sided with the enemies of his country.[121] In November, the Vatican sent a letter demanding that the Germans release some Jewish prisoners (sick, elderly, women and children) and guarantee humane treatment for the rest.[122] Although nothing directly came of it, the people closest to the situation were well aware of the Pontiff's support for Jewish victims.

By February 1943, the Jewish community in Romania had already twice sent its gratitude to the Holy Father for assistance given by the Church during the war.[123] The Holy See once again, however, sent a large donation to Romania "for those civilian internees, excluding the

Polish Aryans."[124] About that same time, Dr. Safran, the chief rabbi in Bucharest sent Pius "the loving respect and the sincere an gracious wishes of the whole community whose members are well aware that the august pontiff regards them with fatherly solicitude."[125] Almost two years later, Safran declared that his "permanent contact with and spiritual closeness to" the Pope's representative "were decisive for the fate of my poor community."[126] Rabbi Herzog of Palestine also expressed thanks to the Vatican on behalf of the Jewish community for the Church's effort in helping Romanian-Jewish orphans escape to Istanbul.[127] Chief Rabbi Herzog wrote:

> The people of Israel will never forget what his Holiness and his illustrious delegates inspired by the eternal principles of religion which form the very foundations of true civilization, are doing for us unfortunate brothers and sisters in the most tragic hour of our history, which is living proof of divine Providence in this world.[128]

After the war, Herzog sent "a special blessing" to the Pope for "his life-saving efforts on behalf of the Jews during the Nazi occupation of Italy."[129] The intermediary, Harry Greenstein, who would later go on to become Executive Director of the Associated Jewish Charities of Baltimore, reported a reaction that was quite similar to the final scene of the motion picture *Schindler's List:* "I still remember quite vividly the glow in [Pope Pius XII's] eyes. He replied that his only regret was that he was not able to save many more Jews."[130]

*****

Pius XII's 1944 Christmas address was entitled "Democracy and Peace." In it, he thanked the personal representative of President Roosevelt (Myron C. Taylor), for "the vast work of assistance accomplished, despite extraordinary difficulties."[131] Pius then expressed his confidence in a democratic future:

> A healthy democracy, based upon the principles of the natural law and of revealed truth, will resolutely oppose the corrupt notion which attributes to State legislation an authority beyond limit or restraint, and which, despite deceptive appearances to the contrary, will transform even a democratic régime into a system of absolutism pure and simple.[132]

Pius also offered support and suggestions for the democratic ideals of liberty and equality.[133]

As for the leaders of the Axis powers, Pius foresaw what lay in store. In a section entitled "War criminals," he did not defend them, but said:

> As for those who have taken advantage of the war to commit real and proved crimes against the law common to all peoples, crimes for which supposed military necessity may have afforded a pretext but could never offer an excuse–no one, certainly will wish to disarm justice in their regard.[134]

Pius added that only those individuals who were guilty of these offenses should be punished, not "whole communities."[135]

CHAPTER SIXTEEN

1945 AND THE END OF WAR

On January 12, the Soviets initiated a major assault on the German lines in the east. Within five days they took Warsaw and two days later captured Krakow. On the 27th, they reached Auschwitz and discovered 220,000 starving prisoners and evidence of the extermination of millions of "undesirable" people. The gas chambers and crematoria had been blown up by the retreating Nazis, but the Germans had kept records, including times and dates of executions, up until the very end.

In all, the Nazis exterminated approximately six million Jews and close to as many non-Jews in their concentration camps.[1] The victims included Poles and Slavs (characterized in Nazi Germany as *Untermenschen* or sub-humans), Gypsies, mentally ill people, politicians, intellectuals, ministers, priests, and anyone else who might have been a threat to the occupying Nazi forces. Had the Nazis won the war, all of the concentration camp victims would have eventually faced the gas chambers. As it was, some survived, and Pius was recognized by the Jewish community for his part in helping them.[2]

In February, Roosevelt, Stalin, and Churchill met at the Yalta Conference to consider the fate of Europe after the conclusion of hostilities. They decided that all territories annexed by the Nazis between 1938 and 1940 would be returned to their former Austrian, Czechoslovakian, or French owners. Germany itself was to be divided into zones, which would be administered by the United States, Great Britain, France, and the Soviet Union. The Soviets promised to establish provisional democratic governments and hold free elections in the eastern European areas as soon as possible. In return for their cooperation in Europe, the Soviets were promised an even bigger piece of Poland than Hitler had offered prior to the war.[3] Land from Germany would be used to compensate the Poles. The Soviet Union was also to receive islands in the Pacific.

Pius was not pleased with the results of Yalta.[4] In his wartime correspondence with President Roosevelt, Pius indicated a desire to have the Allies isolate Russia. He also condemned the partition of the world between the great powers and pointed to the failure of settlements in the past based on the distinction between victor and vanquished, rather than true justice. In one filmed statement, he said:

> Do we have peace, true peace? No, merely a post-war period. How many years will it take to overcome the moral suffering? How much effort will it take to heal so many wounds? Today, as the reconstruction begins, mankind is beginning to realize how much care, honesty and charity will be required to rescue the world from physical and spiritual ruin, and to lead it back to the paths of peace and righteousness.[5]

His objections to the post-war plans of the Allies, however, had little more effect than did his objections to the wartime activities of the Axis powers.

*****

As the end of the war drew near, President Roosevelt became the first of the major leaders from the warring nations to pass away, though both Mussolini and Hitler would come to their end in that same month. Roosevelt had suffered bad health for a long time; he died from a cerebral hemorrhage while resting up at Warm Springs, Georgia. Pope Pius sent telegrams to Eleanor Roosevelt and Harry Truman:

> The unexpected and sorrowful word of the passing of the President brings to Our heart a profound sense of grief born of the high esteem in which We held this renowned Statesman and of the friendly relations which he fostered and maintained with Us and with the Holy See.
>   To the expression of Our condolences We join the assurance of Our prayers for the entire American people and for their new President to whom We extend Our fervent good wishes that his labors may be efficacious in leading the Nations at war to an early peace that will be just and Christian.[6]

Roosevelt was replaced by Vice President Harry Truman, who—in just a few months—would have to make one of the most difficult and controversial decisions of the war.

The death of Roosevelt raised some issues about continued relations between the Holy See and the United States. Myron Taylor, after all, had been the personal representative of the president to Pope

Pius, not an official ambassador. When the United States expressed a desire to continue relations through Taylor, since he had been sent by the office of the President, not by Franklin Roosevelt himself, the Vatican reply was that the reasoning was not very persuasive, but the news was very good.[7]

*****

While the Soviets were making their final drive to Berlin, Allied troops liberated numerous concentration camps. In April they reached Buchenwald and Belsen, where they found 40,000 inmates barely alive and 10,000 unburied corpses. The camp at Dachau revealed even greater horrors. Shock and revulsion ran through the entire world as the reality of Hitler's Final Solution became known. German civilians, many of whom claimed not to have known what took place in the concentration camps, were escorted through to see the evidence.

As the Axis military power in Europe was collapsing, American, British, and Russian armies were destroying the will of the aggressors and encouraging resistance movements. On April 27, Mussolini and several other Fascists tried to make their escape to Switzerland. Having been once deposed and then made a puppet, Mussolini was only a shadow of his former self. While the Italian people celebrated Pius XII for his brave resistance to Hitler and the Nazis, Mussolini was despised.

The group of Italian Fascists traveled in a column of vehicles toward the Swiss border, but they were stopped by Italian partisans. Mussolini, disguised in a German coat and helmet, was recognized and taken prisoner. He and his mistress, Claretta Petacci, were shot, and their bodies were taken to Milan, the city where Fascism had first taken root. They were hung from their heels in the public square and then dragged through the street, with people kicking and spitting on them. One hysterical woman fired five shots into Mussolini's body, screaming, "Five shots for my five murdered sons."[8]

In April 1945, Pius issued the encyclical *Communium Interpretes Dolororum* (An Appeal for Prayers for Peace), in which he encouraged the faithful to pray for peace and to return to Christian morals. As was his style, he appealed to the spiritual side of life, not the secular:

> Change the heart and the world will be changed. Eradicate cupidity and plant charity. Do you want peace? Do justice, and you will have peace. If therefore you desire to come to peace, do justice; avoid evil and do good. This is to love justice; and when you have already avoided evil and done good, seek peace and follow it.[9]

The Holy Father specifically asked his followers to pray for those who had fallen victim to the war:

> We desire moreover that those who heed Our exhortation, also pray for those who are fugitives banished from their homeland and longing to once again see their own homes; also for those in captivity who wait for their liberation after the war; and finally those who lie in numberless hospitals.[10]

Around this time, the Vatican heard rumors that the Germans intended to execute all foreigners under their control (estimated at 600,000 Jews). The Pope and other Church officials "worked feverishly" to prevent this massacre.[11]

*****

On April 30, just days after Mussolini's capture and execution, Hitler and his long-time mistress, Eva Braun, were married. Early in the war he had lived high in the mountains, in his "Eagle's Nest." Now he lived in a Berlin bunker, emerging only when necessary for meetings or to walk his dog, Blondie. After the wedding, the newlyweds committed suicide rather than face the world in defeat. Their bodies were then taken outside, burned, and buried in a shallow grave. The Nazi propaganda machine announced that he had died fighting with his last breath for Germany and against Bolshevism.[12]

German Admiral Karl Doenitz, Hitler's successor, tried desperately to arrange a surrender to the Western Allies instead of the Soviets, but Eisenhower refused all attempts to put conditions on surrender.[13] Finally, on May 7, representatives of Germany's armed forces capitulated to the Allies at Eisenhower's headquarters in Reims. The formal unconditional surrender came the next day in Berlin, May 8th, V-E Day. Hitler's "thousand-year" Third Reich had come to an end. Eisenhower declared: "We come as conquerors but not as oppressors."[14] Stalin had a different view. Three and a half million German soldiers were marched off to the Soviet Union. Half of them were never seen again.[15]

In an allocution to the Sacred College on June 2, 1945, which was also broadcast on Vatican Radio, Pius noted the death of about 2,000 Catholic priests at Dachau and described National Socialism as "the arrogant apostasy from Jesus Christ, the denial of His doctrine and of His work of redemption, the cult of violence, the idolatry of race and blood, the overthrow of human liberty and dignity."[16] With "the satanic apparition of National Socialism" out of the way,[17] Pius expressed his confidence that Germany would "rise to a new dignity and a new life." He went on to point out that Nazi persecution of the Catholic Church both in Germany and occupied nations had been continuous, and that he had been aware of Nazism's ultimate goal: "its adherents boasted that once they had gained the military victory, they would put and end to the Church forever. Authorities and incontrovertible witnesses kept Us informed of this intention."[18]

The German threat was now over, and by mid-summer 1945 Japan was on the verge of collapse. Since January, Vatican officials had been in contact with Japanese leaders, hoping to reach a negotiated settlement.[19] Unfortunately, as the Vatican representatives realized, Japan's demands were beyond anything that the Allies would accept. The war would have to end in some other manner.[20]

Back in August 1939, Leo Szilard wrote President Roosevelt asking him to consider the use of atomic energy in war. Albert Einstein, the most renowned scientist in the world, added his name to the letter, even though he was known as an ardent pacifist.[21] He had come to believe that only military might could stand up to Hitler. Over the next six years, the American government sponsored a secret two billion dollar operation known as the Manhattan Project. On April 25, 1945, Secretary of War Henry Lewis Stimson told President Truman, "Within four months we shall in all probability have completed the most terrible weapon ever known in human history, one bomb of which could destroy a whole city." When Winston Churchill was informed that the Americans had developed the bomb, he said: "This is the Second Coming, in wrath."[22]

On July 26, without mentioning the bomb, Truman, Churchill, and Chiang Kai-shek issued an ultimatum. Surrender had to be complete, include the return of all Japanese conquests since 1895, and provide for Allied occupation of Japan until "a peacefully inclined and responsible government" was established. The alternative was to face "the utter devastation of the Japanese homeland."[23] Surrender, however, was not forthcoming. On July 28, the Japanese Prime Minister, in a statement designed for domestic consumption, pronounced the Allies' ultimatum "unworthy of public notice."[24]

Two years earlier, Pope Pius XII, in an allocution to the Pontifical Academy of Science, warned against the destructive use of nuclear energy.[25] Despite that warning, on August 6, 1945, from an altitude of 31,600 feet, the American B-29 *Enola Gay* dropped a bomb with an explosive force greater than had ever been known. The bomb destroyed five square miles in the center of the Japanese city of Hiroshima. At least 78,000 people (including the entire Japanese Second Army) were killed outright, 10,000 more were never found, and more than 70,000 were injured. Almost two-thirds of the city was destroyed.[26]

On August 9, another atomic bomb was dropped on Nagasaki. About 40,000 people were killed, and about the same number were injured. On August 10, Japan sought peace on the condition that the emperor retain his position as sovereign ruler. The Allies responded that the future status of the emperor would be determined by them. On August 14, Japan accepted the Allies' terms, and a cease fire was ordered the following day.

*****

In terms of loss of life, World War II was the costliest war in history. More than 15 million military personnel were killed in action. Of the Axis powers, Germany lost about 3.5 million soldiers in battle, Japan lost 1.5 million, and Italy lost 200,000. Among the Allies, the Soviet Union had the heaviest battle casualties, with about 7.5 million dead; China lost 2.2 million soldiers; the British lost more than 300,000 military personnel; the United States suffered 292,000 losses; and France lost 210,000.[27]

Civilian casualties were even worse, numbering perhaps twenty million. The Soviet Union lost more than ten million civilians, China lost at least six million, France lost 400,000, the United Kingdom 65,000, and the United States 6,000. On the Axis side, Germany lost about 500,000 civilians, Japan lost 600,000, and Italy 145,000.

There were other costs as well. Expenditures for war materials and armaments were enormous. The United States spent about $300 billion on the war effort; Germany spent about $231 billion. Japan, the Soviet Union, Italy and Britain also each spent billions. Added to these costs was the tremendous material damage done to property of all kinds, including priceless historical sites, art, and buildings.[28]

Most notoriously, an estimated 6,000,000 Jews, mostly from eastern Europe, were killed by the Nazis. Before the Final Solution, there were approximately 9,000,000 Jews north of Spain in continental Europe. By 1945, two-thirds of them had been murdered or died because of the conditions in the German concentration camps. In Germany, Austria, the Baltic countries, and Poland, ninety percent of all Jews were killed.[29] Several million non-Jewish Nazi victims (estimates range as high as 6,000,000) also lost their lives in the death camps.

Many Germans had to face the question of their own role in the course of Nazism,[30] but most of them were also victims of the war. A majority of German families lost members at the front, and most of the rest lost relatives, homes, or possessions in the bombing raids on German cities or on the refugee treks from the east at the end of the war. Many Germans left their country following the war;[31] those who remained suffered from severe hunger. The average caloric intake from 1945 to 1947 was less than 70 percent of that which was deemed adequate.[32] Many took to looting and fighting in the streets. Germany was called "a country where men had lost all hope and women all shame."[33]

The Vatican, too, suffered greatly during the war. Thousands of priests and nuns had been killed; millions of Catholics had died.[34] This all put an enormous strain on Pius. Associates worried about his ability to survive the eighteen-hour days he put in during the war.[35] By the end of the war, he was emaciated. Although he was more than six feet tall, he weighed only one hundred and thirty pounds. He had witnessed terrible suffering up close, and had been unable to stop it. Additionally, the Pontiff was not pleased about what the future held. He feared that the spread of Communism and Soviet influence would bring the Church and its people throughout the world to their knees.[36]

*****

The last Allied wartime conference was held at Potsdam, Germany, in July and August 1945. Roosevelt had died in April, so President Truman represented the United States, but Churchill and Stalin were both there for at least part of the conference (Churchill was defeated by Clement Attlee in an election for Prime Minister that took place during the conference). The Allies also agreed at Potsdam that they would prosecute Nazi Party and German military leaders for crimes against humanity and world peace.

Potsdam, like Yalta, called for the Soviet Union to have a very significant role in post-war Europe. This was seen by many (including most people in the Holy See) as a betrayal of the ideals for which the Allies had fought.[37] The Soviet Union emerged from the war with 262,533 more square miles of territory, 22,162,000 more people, and satellite states in Poland, East Germany, Lithuania, Latvia, Estonia, Romania, Bulgaria, Czechoslovakia, and Albania.[38] Ambassador William C. Bullitt said of the Yalta agreement: "No more unnecessary, disgraceful, and potentially disastrous document has ever been signed by a President of the United States."[39] Arthur Bliss Lane, U.S. Ambassador to Poland in 1944-47 called the Yalta agreement: "a capitulation on the part of the United States and Great Britain to the views of the Soviet Union on the frontiers of Poland and the composition of the Polish Provisional Government...."[40] Even Winston Churchill ended up calling the results of Yalta "a tragedy on a prodigious scale."[41] The problem with these agreements was not how they were negotiated. Like so much that took place in the war, it had to do with differing ethics and morality. The Yalta and Potsdam agreements "were based on the fallacy that the golden rule would work on the Russian government, which regarded Christian ethics as outmoded."[42]

From the Vatican's perspective, the world was perhaps less stable than ever. Uneasy alliances were falling apart, weapons of incalculable power were aimed at key targets around the globe, and governmental power was dangerously centralized. The Soviets, in particular, seemed intent on expanding their influence, by force if necessary. In March 1946, Winston Churchill, speaking at Westminster College in Fulton, Missouri, said: "From Stettin in the Baltic to Trieste in the Adriatic, an Iron Curtain has descended across the Continent."[43]

CHAPTER SEVENTEEN

POST-WAR POPE

The end of the war saw Pius XII hailed as "the inspired moral prophet of victory,"[1] and he "enjoyed near-universal acclaim for aiding European Jews through diplomatic initiatives, thinly veiled public pronouncements, and, very concretely, an unprecedented continent-wide network of sanctuary."[2] With the end of hostilities, he concentrated on trying to help people recover from the ravages of war.[3] As late as 1947, he was feeding an average of a quarter of a million people per day.[4] Papal money was sent to every war-torn nation and distributed without regard to race, creed, or nationality. With his two personal assistants, Monsignor Giovanni Montini (the future Pope Paul VI) and Domenico Tardini, the pontiff personally helped to feed and reconstruct western Europe. Shipments of food, clothing, and medicine continued until June 3, 1966.

One of Pius XII's biggest post-war projects was helping displaced children and families through the Pope's Children War Relief program. More than 10,000 children from Austria, Hungary, Germany, Italy, and Switzerland obtained release papers, transatlantic passage, and admission into the United States thanks to this project.[5] Pius also established the International Committee of Catholic Charities. This organization coordinated local and national efforts to assist victims of war and to help return displaced persons to their homes.[6]

Following the war, Pius received numerous guests from the world of entertainment and films, the aristocracy, politics, and religion. Some sought counsel; others merely paid their respects. Among the distinguished groups which were granted audiences shortly after the war were many American officials, including the House of Representatives' Foreign Affairs Committee and more than 200 senators and congressmen. (Said Indiana Congressman Samuel B. Pettengill: "I am far from being a Roman Catholic, but it sometimes seems to me that the present Pope is the most sane and sagacious leader on the stage of action at this time.")[7]

In 1945, the Chief Rabbi of Romania, Dr. Alexander Safran, expressed the gratitude of the Jewish community for the Vatican's help and support for prisoners in the concentration camps.[8] Pinchas E. Lapide, the Israeli consul in Italy, wrote:

> The Catholic Church saved more Jewish lives during the war than all other churches, religious institutions and rescue organizations put together. Its record stands in startling contrast to the achievements of the International Red Cross and the Western Democracies.... The Holy See, the nuncios, and the entire Catholic Church saved some 400,000 Jews from certain death.[9]

The Grand Rabbi Issac Herzog of Jerusalem sent a message to Msgr. Angelo Roncalli (the future Pope John XXIII), expressing thanks for actions taken by Pius XII and the Holy See on behalf of Jewish people.[10] The World Jewish Congress also expressed thanks and donated two million lira (about $20,000) to Vatican charities.[11] The *New York Times* reported that the gift was given in recognition of the work of the Holy See in rescuing Jews from Fascist and Nazi persecution. The National Jewish Welfare Board wrote to Pius: "From the bottom of our hearts we send to you, Holy Father of the Church, the assurance of our unforgetting gratitude for your noble expression of religious brotherhood and love."[12] Dr. Joseph Nathen, a representative of the Hebrew Commission, expressing thanks for support during the Holocaust, said: "Above all, we acknowledge the Supreme Pontiff and the religious men and women who, executing the directives of the Holy Father, recognized the persecuted as their brothers and, with great abnegation, hastened to help them, disregarding the terrible dangers to which they were exposed."[13]

In a letter sent to major newspapers and published in the *Jewish Newsletter*, William Zukerman called "the rescue of thousands of Jewish Nazi victims by the Vatican... one of the greatest manifestations of humanitarianism in the 20th century as well as a new, effective method of fighting anti-Semitism."[14] On April 5, 1946, the Italian Jewish community sent a message of thanks to Pope Pius XII:

> The delegates of the Congress of the Italian Jewish Communities, held in Rome for the first time after the Liberation, feel that it is imperative to extend reverent homage to Your Holiness, and to express the most profound gratitude that animates all Jews for your fraternal humanity toward them during the years of persecution when their lives were endangered by Nazi-Fascist barbarism. Many times priests suffered imprisonment and were sent to concentration

camps, and offered their lives to assist Jews in every way. This demonstration of goodness and charity that still animates the just, has served to lessen the shame and torture and sadness that afflicted millions of human beings.[15]

Cecil Roth, the leading English authority on the history of Italian Jewry, also paid tribute to the Church's uncompromising stand against racism in his *Encyclopedia Judaica*.[16] The Protestant publication, *Christian Century*, wrote an editorial on Pius stating that "it is to be regretted that no equally impressive Church statesmanship, no equally commanding message, has as yet come to this post-war world from any other authoritative body or leadership."[17]

Dr. Herman Datyner, a member of the Inter-Allied Conference for Refugees and special representative of Italian Jewish refugee groups and organizations, was granted an audience with Pius XII to thank him for assistance during the war. He memorialized some of the Pontiff's comments. Regarding Jewish suffering, the Pope said:

> Yes, I know, my son, all the sufferings of you Jews. I am sorry, truly sorry, about the loss of your family. I suffered a great deal,... knowing about Jewish sufferings, and I tried to do whatever was in my power in order to make your fate easier.... I will pray to God that happiness will return to you, to your people. Tell them this.[18]

Tributes and kind words, as well as acts of charity, continued for years following the war.[19]

In 1947, King Gustav V of Sweden honored Pius XII with the annual Prince Carl medal, given to the person who has done the most outstanding work in the field of charity. The citation said it was for his "tireless work in relieving the misery of the war victims."[20] The War Refugee Board, representing the united effort of various American Jewish organizations, publicly acknowledged its close relationship with the Holy See and the good work of the Church.[21] Maurice Edelman, President of the Anglo-Jewish Association, visited Pius XII to thank him for his help. According to Edelman, papal intervention "was responsible during the war for saving the lives of tens of thousands of Jews."[22] When the Pope received a large delegation of Roman Jews in the Vatican, he ordered that the Imperial steps be opened for them to enter. This was an honor usually reserved for crowned Heads of State. Noting that his visitors seemed uncomfortable in the Sistine chapel, he came down from his throne and warmly welcomed them, saying: "I am only the Vicar of Christ but you are His very kith and kin."[23]

In 1955, when Italy celebrated the tenth anniversary of its liberation, Italian Jewry proclaimed April 17 as "The Day of Gratitude." That year, thousands of Jewish people made a pilgrimage to the Vatican to pay their thanks for the Pope's wartime solicitudes. The Israeli Philharmonic Orchestra even gave a special performance of Beethoven's ninth symphony in the Papal Consistory Hall as an expression of gratitude for the Catholic Church's assistance in defying the Nazis.[24] Before the celebration, a delegation approached Archbishop Montini, the director of Vatican rescue services who later became Pope Paul VI, to determine whether he would accept an award for his work on behalf of Jews during the war. He was extremely gratified and visibly touched by their words, but he declined the honor: "All I did was my duty," he said. "And besides I only acted upon orders from the Holy Father. Nobody deserves a medal for that."[25] Angelo Roncalli (the future Pope John XXIII), war time apostolic delegate in Istanbul, made a very similar statement concerning his efforts to save Jewish lives: "In all these painful matters I have referred to the Holy See and simply carried out the Pope's orders: first and foremost to save Jewish lives."[26] In fact, when the truth finally came out, it was clear: the driving force behind rescue operations carried out by papal representatives all around the world was Pope Pius XII.[27]

Despite the accolades he received, and the high hopes he had for the United Nations,[28] Pius was not pleased with the way the post-war world was shaping up. After the war, more than 2,000,000 Soviet refugees in Western Europe, primarily prisoners of war and slave laborers taken by the Germans, were forcibly repatriated with the assistance of British and American troops.[29] Poles were forced to evacuate those areas of Poland that had been claimed by the Soviet Union. In return, Poland was given parts of Germany. Seven million Germans disappeared from those regions awarded to Poland; many were killed, many fled, and the rest were driven out. Later, more than 3,000,000 Germans were expelled from Czechoslovakia.[30] Pius viewed all of this as a continuation of the human rights abuses that had taken place during the war.[31]

All along, Pius had feared that a Soviet victory would mean that eastern Europe would fall to Communism, and much of it did. The Soviets quickly established satellite states—governments that were beholden to (if not dominated by) Moscow—in Poland, East Germany, Lithuania, Latvia, Estonia, Romania, Bulgaria, Czechoslovakia, and Albania. In light of the Church's history with Communism in Russia, China, and Mexico, Pius was afraid that the spread of Soviet influence would bring the Church to its knees, and in many places it did.[32] He actively worked to limit the Communist influence in Western Europe, especially in Italy. Fortunately, the Church emerged from World War II with enhanced strength and prestige within Italy. In fact, the immediate post-war years may have seen the Catholic Church at its most influential since the Reformation.[33] As such, it was able to have a substantial impact on political issues, particularly in the 1948 Italian elections, when the Pope helped fight off a possible Communist take-over.[34]

*****

For Pius, reminders of the war years were particularly disheartening. Not only did the war reveal humans at their most evil, but the suffering was not confined the way it had been in previous wars. World War II was, unlike others before it, a war between entire nations. Women and children figured very high among the death rolls. Pius was, however, proud of how the Church had maintained its dignity during the war. In his speech at the 1946 consistory, he pointed to the crucial role played by the Church in preserving the civil values that had been so threatened by the war.[35] Speaking to delegates from the Supreme Council of the Arab People of Palestine on August 3, 1946, Pius said: "It is superfluous for me to tell you that we disapprove of all recourse to force and violence, from wheresoever it comes, just as we condemned on various occasions in the past the persecutions that a fanatical anti-Semitism inflicted on the Hebrew people."[36] When it seemed that concerns for humanity were lacking throughout the world, the Church was one entity that continued to exhibit charity and compassion.

As for questions about his "silence," he had done what he believed to be correct with full knowledge of the possible consequences. He would not now turn to words for redemption. (Though he did once state: "If only peace could be had by the crying: 'Peace, peace.' But no....")[37] Besides, throughout his life, accolades were far more common than questions. Only after he had been dead for several years did questions about the Pope's alleged silence become widespread.

*****

Although the elderly Pope Pius XII was frail and spiritual in appearance, he served thirteen post-war years, reigning in a style reminiscent of the grand centuries of the papacy. Until failing health forced him to restrict his activities, Pius XII was an extraordinarily accessible Pope. He celebrated more public Masses and held more private audiences than any of his recent predecessors had, and each week he held a special audience just for newlyweds.[38] *Life* magazine considered him *"Life's* first Pope."[39] He also used television and radio to reach out directly to the people.

Pius XII was more willing than his predecessors to see positive elements in the ecumenical movement. In December 1949, shortly after the formation of the World Council of Churches, he formally recognized the ecumenical movement and permitted Catholic scholars to dialogue with non-Catholics on matters of faith. That same year, the Holy Office issued a decree, with papal approval, stating that actual incorporation into the Catholic Church was not necessary for salvation.[40] He also encouraged Catholic nuns to study theology, scripture, and psychology.[41]

Pius even considered calling a council which might have completely changed the face of the Church.[42] He went so far as to have preliminary studies made, but he ultimately decided against proceeding in that direction. His work, however, encouraged his successor, Pope John XXIII, to convene Vatican II.[43] John's reformation of the curia followed along the lines set forth by his patron, Pius XII, over a decade earlier.[44] As others have concluded: "However the pontificate of the Pacelli pope was to be evaluated, it has to be acknowledged that, without him, John's achievement would have been unthinkable."[45]

Vatican II led to the release of the "Declaration on the Relation of the Church to Non-Christian Religions." That declaration "commends mutual understanding and esteem" between Christian and Jews, rejects anti-Semitism, and specifically states that God has neither rejected nor cursed the Jews.[46] *The Jewish Post,* explained that Pope

Pius XII had set the stage for a new understanding between Jews and Christians:

> Organized and institutionalized Christianity realized that the old religious bitterness and hatred between Christians and Jews no longer had meaning or reason and that the failure to remove them in time had almost brought Judeo-Christian civilization to its end. It is to the credit of Pope Pius XII that he, a great leader of Christianity, not only recognized this truth in time, but also that he visualized a positive method of acting upon it in a grand manner: Instead of merely preaching Christianity, he and (other church leaders) practice Christian principles and set an example by their acts and lives, as did the founder of Christianity. This was the uniqueness of the achievement of Pope Pius XII.[47]

Increasing ill health in his later years caused Pius to turn to a life of comparative solitude, and this in turn enhanced the air of mystery which surrounded him. Though he had been a very social diplomat early in his life, he now lived more monastically. He was not, however, in isolation (except for one hour every day, which he reserved for prayer and meditation). As tradition dictated, he ate alone (except for ceremonial dinners).[48] While he ate, however, secretaries handed him dispatches from around the world. At the same time, another secretary laid out important documents on his desk so that when he returned to his office no time would be lost.[49] He also enjoyed tending to his pet canaries which flew around the room while he ate (sometimes perching on his shoulder).

In December 1954, Pius fell seriously ill, and his physicians feared for his life. Cardinals packed their bags; diplomats prepared memos; and journalists speculated about a successor, but he recovered his strength and returned to work.[50] During this illness, Pius reported an apparition of Jesus.[51] He also claimed to have had mystical experiences at other times in his life, such as a vision of Mary while walking in the Vatican gardens.[52] While this caused some to question his mental stability, the crowds drawn to him grew even larger.

During his pontificate, Pius expanded and internationalized the Church by creating fifty-seven new bishoprics, forty-five of them in America and Asia. This allowed the percentage of Italians in the college of cardinals to drop to less than half, paving the way for the eventual election of a non-Italian Pope. (One of the first new cardinals following the war was German Count von Galen, Bishop of Münster and a noted opponent of Hitlerism).[53]

In 1958, at Castel Gandolfo, Pius XII summoned his last ounce of energy for the necessary paperwork that included nominations for six new auxiliary bishops in Poland. One of the openings was in the Kraków archdiocese. On July 8, Pius XII signed the nomination of Karol Wojtyla to be the titular Bishop of Ombia (an honorary title) and auxiliary bishop in Kraków. The signing of this nomination fundamentally altered the future of the Church and of Fr. Wojtyla, who would go on to become Pope John Paul II. It was Pius XII's final great historic act.

*****

On October 3, 1958, the first word of the Pope's illness was released. Eight days later, at the age of eighty-two, Pope Pius XII died peacefully in his sleep. With church bells ringing, a Jesuit priest read the final bulletin: "The supreme pontiff is dead. Pope Pius XII, the most esteemed and venerated man in the world, one of the greatest pontiffs of the century, with sanctity passed away at 3:52 today, October 9, 1958."[54] He had served for nineteen and a half years, the longest pontificate since Pius IX (1846-1878). Four days after his death, on Friday, October 13, Pius XII began his final trip to his beloved Rome.

Last rites for Pius XII were marked by splendor and reverence that was unusual even for the Vatican. Ceremonies continued for nine days.[55] Hundreds of thousands of tearful people lined the route as the cortege (itself, two miles long) slowly made its way through the Roman countryside and entered the city through the St. John Gate, past the house where Eugenio Pacelli had been born, to the Basilica of St. John Lateran (the cathedral church of Rome) where a contingent of the Swiss Guard led the way to the papal altar. Fifty-three nations sent representatives to the requiem mass in his honor.[56]

The fallen pontiff's last will and testament provided: "I am aware of the failures, of the sins, committed during so long a pontificate and in so grave an epoch. Sufficient it is that my remains should be laid simply in a sacred place–the more obscure the better."[57] He was laid to rest in the Sacred Grotto beneath the basilica, close to the tomb of St. Peter, near most of the 261 Popes who had preceded him.[58]

Even at the time of his death, Pius's activity in World War II was the primary focus of attention.[59] Then Israeli representative to the United Nations and future Prime Minister of Israel, Golda Meir, said:

"During the ten years of Nazi terror, when our people went through the horrors of martyrdom, the Pope raised his voice to condemn the persecutors and to commiserate with their victims."[60] Nahum Goldmann, President of the World Jewish Congress, said: "With special gratitude we remember all he has done for the persecuted Jews during one of the darkest periods of their entire history."[61] Rabbi Elio Toaff, who would later become Chief Rabbi of Rome, said: "More than anyone else, we have had the opportunity to appreciate the great kindness, filled with compassion and magnanimity, that the Pope displayed during the terrible years of persecution and terror, when it seemed that there was no hope left for us."[62] As *The Jewish Post* (Winnipeg) reported in its November 6, 1958 edition:

> It is understandable why the death of Pope Pius XII should have called forth expressions of sincere grief from practically all sections of American Jewry. For there probably was not a single ruler of our generation who did more to help the Jews in their hour of greatest tragedy, during the Nazi occupation of Europe, than the late Pope.[63]

In New York, virtually every major rabbi offered praise for Pius ("an example for all religious leaders" and "man at his highest").[64] President Dwight D. Eisenhower said: "The world is a poorer place with the death of Pius XII."[65] The Anti-Defamation League, the Synagogue Council of America, the Rabbinical Council of America, the American Jewish Congress, the New York Board of Rabbis, the American Jewish Committee, the Central Conference of American Rabbis, the National Conference of Christians and Jews, and the National Council of Jewish Women all expressed sorrow at his passing and thanks for his good works.[66] Israel sent an official delegation to his funeral, and many people in Israel wrote to newspapers suggesting that a forest in the Judean hills be established in his name.[67]

The cardinals went into conclave sixteen days after Pius XII's death, and Cardinal Angelo Giuseppe Roncalli of Venice (who had been recommended by Pius XII)[68] was elected pope three days later, taking the name of John XXIII. Pope John would soon launch Vatican Council II. From that council would come the Church's teaching that:

> With respect to the fundamental rights of the person, every type of discrimination, whether social or cultural, whether based on sex, race, color, social condition, language or religion is to be overcome and eradicated as contrary to God's intent.[69]

*****

In 1963, Pope John XXIII passed away and was succeeded by Pope Paul VI (Cardinal Giovanni Battista Montini). In 1965, Pope Paul VI proposed that "his great model," Pius XII, be considered for saint-hood.[70] He has been declared "Servant of God," and the cause of his beatification is still underway.

CHAPTER EIGHTEEN

THE QUESTIONS AND ANSWERS

With all of the accolades given to Pope Pius XII after the war and even at the time of his death, why do people today question his behavior in World War II? Clearly, the Pope neither sympathized with the Nazis, nor was he indifferent. Just as earlier Popes had avoided designating the aggressor when consoling the victims, Pius did not expressly name Hitler.[1] Nevertheless, his meaning was plain enough for any-one who read or listened to his words.[2] Indeed, in Nazi circles throughout the war, it was "axiomatic" that Pius XII "sympathized with the Allies and covertly assisted their cause."[3]

While the charge that Pius XII was overly tolerant of the Nazi regime had been leveled earlier (particularly by some of the post-war Communists who were trying to discredit the Church),[4] most people trace the issue of Pius XII's reputation to a play, *The Deputy* (*Der Stellvertreter*),[5] written by Rolf Hochhuth, a German playwright who helped found a dramatic movement known as "Theater of Fact."[6] *The Deputy* opened on February 23, 1963, which coincided closely in time with the Second Vatican Council, the publication of Anne Frank's Diary, and the trial and execution of Adolf Eichmann. It was a scathing indictment of the Pope's alleged indifference to the Holocaust. Ever since, his role in the war has been a matter of spec-ulation.[7]

The Deputy is a seven-hour play, with Pius XII as the central, sta-tionary figure. It is "historical fiction based on scant documenta-tion."[8] Pius is not developed as a tragic figure, since he is neither tragically indecisive nor torn by his alternatives. Not only does this Pius lack Christian charity, but also simple human decency.[9] "The characterization of Pacelli as a money-grubbing hypocrite is so wide of the mark as to be ludicrous."[10] Unfortunately, the depiction of Pius as an unprincipled politician, possessed of an aristocratic coolness and eyes that have an "icy glow," so shaped the perception of Pius that it has become an "unshakable axiom of popular mythology that Pope

Pius XII was, if not actually a crypto-Nazi, at least guilty of criminal cowardice and insensitivity in the face of the Holocaust."[11]

"Perhaps never before in history have so many human beings paid with their lives for the passivity of a single statesman,"[12] Hochhuth wrote. While recounting the events of the fall and winter of 1942, including the Allies' December 17 announcement, Hochhuth ignored the Pope's 1942 Christmas message. Regarding the Pope's statements in general, Hochhuth described them as:

> carefully insipid, flowery, vaguely moralizing and generalizing speeches, or rather assemblages of clichés about the events of the war. In none of them did he ever specifically name a statesman, a country–aside from Poland–or even the fact of the deportations which had been going on for years.[13]

Despite the very negative depiction, Hochhuth claimed to have offered a "better opinion of Pius XII than may be historically justified, and a better one than I privately hold."[14]

Hochhuth criticized Pius for everything from having makeup applied to his face when he appeared in a film,[15] to being sympathetic to Hitler because he had negotiated the concordat,[16] to not being seriously disturbed when Hitler persecuted priests who spoke out against Nazism.[17] He also faulted the Church for profiting from both sides by continuing to trade with them during the war.[18] Ignoring Nazi persecution of Catholic clergy, Hochhuth argued that Himmler concentrated his policy of extermination on Jews, Slavs, Gypsies, Jehovah's Witnesses, and Communists because this would not damage relations with the Holy See.[19]

According to Hochhuth, the "main thesis" of *The Deputy* was "that Hitler drew back from the extermination program as soon as high German clerics... or the Vatican... forcibly intervened."[20] He went on to argue that he was not sure that Pius could have stopped Hitler's persecution of the Jews, but as "Vicar of Christ," he had a moral obligation to try.[21] He suggested that Pius XII's statements led to the end of the deportation of Jews from Hungary, "prov[ing] again how high the Pope's credit stood."[22] Hochhuth said that after the United States entered the war, the Church was the only authority that Hitler continued to respect.[23] Hochhuth defended the historical accuracy of his play, but he also argued that it had a moral truth of its own, separated from historical truth.[24]

Immediately after *The Deputy* premiered Church officials respond-ed, as did Protestant and Jewish leaders.[25] They advanced the argu-ments that as a neutral nation the Vatican could not choose sides, that any provocation would have made it even harder on Hitler's vic-tims, and that Pius had done much to support the Allied war effort.[26] Some writers and commentators have supported this view.[27] Jeno Levai, the leading scholar of the Jewish extermination in Hungary observed that it was a "particularly regrettable irony that the one per-son in all of occupied Europe who did more than anyone else to halt the dreadful crime and alleviate its consequences is today made the scapegoat for the failures of others."[28] Others, of course, joined in support of Hochhuth.

Hochhuth condemned Pius XII's moral cowardice.[29] In more tem-perate language, historian Guenter Lewy wrote:

> Finally one is inclined to conclude that the Pope and his advi-sors... did not view the plight of the Jews with a real sense of urgency and moral outrage. For this assertion no documen-tation is possible, but it is a conclusion difficult to avoid....All things told, did not the murder of several million Jews demand a "candid word"?[30]

Rabbi Marvin Hier, dean of the Simon Wiesenthal Center in Los Angeles, has described Pius XII as the "Pope of silence."[31] He said that during the war, "Pope Pius XII sat on the throne of St. Peter in stony silence."[32] Hier acknowledged that, "in late 1943 and early 1944, [Pius XII] undertook private initiatives to aid Jews," but he went on to add that "by that time 4.5 million Jews had been murdered and Germany was clearly on the road to defeat."[33]

In 1965, Pope Paul VI proposed that Pius XII be considered for sainthood, and the Church is still in the process of considering that proposal.[34] Fr. Paul Molinari, the Church-designated advocate for sainthood (the Postulator General of the Cause), has written that he has "an excellent case."[35] Fr. Peter Gumpel, relator for the beatifica-tion of Pius XII with the Congregation for the Causes of Saints,[36] has called Pius XII's case one of the strongest he has seen in four decades of working on saints' causes.[37] Rabbi Hier has responded that, "granting sainthood to Pius XII desecrates the memory of my ances-tors and the millions of martyrs by allowing the world to think that a saint was enthroned nearby, in Rome, while they were being taken to the crematoria without even an echo of protest."[38]

Defenders of Pius, like those who attacked him, have set forth their interpretations of his behavior, advancing theories that are sometimes inconsistent with one another and often flat-out wrong. Thus, some have argued that Pius was very well informed and able to provide assistance to persecuted Jews, while others argued that he did not know enough about the abuses to make a statement. Similarly, some have argued that he was several times on the verge of coming out with a strong condemnation of Hitler, but was dissuaded by some particular act, while others have argued that he was true to his (correct) vision throughout the war.

Many of Pope Pius XII's defenders have argued that he needed "to preserve the Church from the temporal quarrels in order to preserve its eternal mission."[39] According to one, "Pius XII undoubtedly believed, at least originally, that he would inevitably forfeit any claim to the role of peacemaker if he once modified his position of neutrality and as time went on felt unable to condemn the atrocities committed by one side without condemning those committed by the other.... In sum, Pius XII was a diplomat who thought it his duty to keep silent... to avoid greater evils."[40] While many of these explanations are reasonable, and some are partially correct, they are incomplete. They do not answer all of the questions.

Pope Pius XII played a controversial role in World War II. The first step in assessing his performance is to look at the world situation as it appeared to him in those years. At the conclusion of that process, one is left with a picture of Pius XII that permits an accurate evaluation of his leadership of the Church in the war years. In order to carry out that evaluation, one must take the knowledge gained from the first part of the assessment (which was carried out in the preceding chapters of this book), and apply it to the issues that have arisen since the end of the war. This can be accomplished by addressing ten questions.

1. Was the Pope Anti-Semitic?

The close work of the Vatican, local bishops, and papal nuncios with Jewish groups belies any claim that the Pope discriminated against any race or religion.[41] The Catholic Church saved more Jewish lives than all the other churches, religious institutions, and rescue organizations put together. The 1943-1944 *American Jewish Yearbook* reported that Pius XII "took an unequivocal stand against the oppression of Jews throughout Europe." The head of Italian Jewry's wartime Jewish Assistance Committee, Dr. Raffael Cantoni, who subsequently became the President of the Union of all Italian Jewish communities, reported: "The Church and the papacy have saved Jews as much and in as far as they could save Christians.... Six millions of my coreligionists have been murdered by the Nazis, but there could have been many more victims, had it not been for the efficacious intervention of Pius XII."[42] Even Pope Pius XII's most severe critics acknowledge that he was personally involved in saving Jewish victims.[43] *The Deputy* has no imputation of anti-Semitism, because Hochhuth felt there was no evidence that Pius was an anti-Semite.[44]

If any restraint on the part of the Vatican were to be attributed to an anti-Semitic attitude on the part of the Pope, then one would expect to see the Church behave in a different manner when a similar situation involving Christians arose. By late in the war most of the Jews in Poland had been eliminated, and Hitler was concentrating on other victims, the vast majority of whom were Catholic.[45] The Pope did not become more vocal or behave differently in these cases than he had when the victims were primarily Jewish.

No one who was around the Pontiff during the war has ever imputed any anti-Semitic attitudes to him. Father Leiber, the Pope's private secretary and personal confidant during the war years seems to have put this issue to rest with one brief statement: "The Pope sided very unequivocally with the Jews at the time. He spent his entire private fortune on their behalf....Pius spent what he inherited himself, as a Pacelli, from his family."[46] Clearly, anti-Semitism did not affect Pius XII's actions during the time of Hitler.[47]

A related issue is the impact of the general anti-Semitic attitude that permeated much of Christianity, including the Catholic Church, prior to the war. After the war, the World Council of Churches issued the following statement: "We have failed to fight with all our strength the age-old disorder which anti-Semitism represents. The churches in the past have helped to foster an image of the Jews as the sole enemies of Christ which has contributed to anti-Semitism in the secular world."[48] In 1998, the Vatican released a fourteen-page document entitled *We Remember: A Reflection on the Shoah* which acknowledged that centuries of anti-Jewish attitudes in the Church may have contributed to Christians' lack of resistance to Nazi policies. "We deeply regret the errors and failures of those sons and daughters of the

Church. This is an act of repentance, since, as members of the Church, we are linked to the sins as well as the merits of all her children."[49] The document was somewhat controversial,[50] however, because in a long footnote, it defended the "wisdom of Pope Pius XII's diplomacy."[51]

Granting that Hitler perverted Christian concepts, is it possible Christian teaching concerning the "people who rejected Jesus" made it easier for him to develop his extreme racial views or for the German public to accept his ideas? Of course. In a meeting that took place between Hitler and German church officials in 1933, Hitler essentially justified his policies by citing Catholic traditions.[52] Religious differences often create deep divides; however, the evidence for Christianity having shaped Hitler's racial views is weak.[53]

The Final Solution entailed two elements that were fundamentally new and clearly did not evolve from Christian theology: the view of racial Jewishness, which rendered baptism irrelevant, and the commitment to extermination of the Jewish people.[54] Because of this, Christian leaders who proclaimed the worst anti-Semitic teaching of their faith still were unable to embrace the extreme teachings of the Nazis.[55]

If anti-Jewish teachings from Christian churches were the cause of the persecution of Jews, how does one account for the persecution of Gypsies and Catholic Poles? Similarly, there was no religious basis for the euthanasia program of the 1930s; Christian Germans were subjected to it. Church teachings also cannot account for persecution of Jehovah's Witnesses or—for that matter—of the bourgeois in Communist nations. These things happened independently of religion, not because of it.

There is no record of Hitler having attended church services at any time after his childhood.[56] Ernst von Weizsäcker, German Ambassador to the Holy See during the war, wrote that Hitler "had from his youth been an enemy of the Church."[57] In 1939, Joseph Goebbels wrote:

> The *Führer* is deeply religious, though completely anti-Christian. He views Christianity as a symptom of decay. Rightly so. It is a branch of the Jewish race. This can be seen in the similarity of religious rites. Both (Judaism and Christianity) have no point of contact to the animal element, and they, in the end, will be destroyed.[58]

In 1934 Hitler told a group of Protestant church leaders that he was glad to have been brought up Catholic, because it helped him attract votes, but inwardly he felt closest to the Evangelical (Protestant) Church.[59] Privately, he was opposed to any form of Christianity.[60]

Hitler's strong anti-Semitic feelings are thought to have developed in his teens and twenties, after he quit attending Mass. His first known anti-Semitic writing came after the end of World War I, and after he had attended the army's program for veterans, which taught anti- Semitism. The essential premise of Nazism is drawn from non-Christian, Darwinian racial and biological theories. While one can never be certain when re-creating a "what if" scenario, it is completely possible (and perhaps even reasonable) to argue that Hitler would never have developed his extreme views if only he had continued attending church services into his adulthood.

A distinction should be drawn between antipathy toward the Jewish race (anti-Semitism) and differences with the Jewish faith (sometimes called anti-Judaism). Catholic teaching, like most Christian teaching, says that acceptance of Jesus is the road to salvation. Members of the Jewish faith reject Jesus as savior, but people of Jewish heritage are always welcome and encouraged to join the Catholic Church. Thus, Hitler's concept of a lesser race (as opposed to a different faith) is clearly distinct from (and in opposition to) the Catholic Church's teaching.

The Catholic Church was so open to Jewish converts that some have argued that during the war this was the Church's primary interest.[61] Many Jews were quickly converted for the purpose of avoiding Nazi persecution. Undoubtedly Church leaders would have been glad to welcome converts to Christianity. However, in a great many more cases, false baptismal documents were provided so that Jewish people could avoid persecution, even though they had not actually converted. This indicates compassion for the human suffering, regardless of religion.[62]

A slant on this claim relates to children, particularly those under the age of six. The surest way to protect such young children from the Nazis was by actually baptizing and indoctrinating them, in case they were ever challenged. This practice could create resentment among some surviving Jews, especially when Christian clergy encouraged the children to adopt this outward behavior. This probably varied from location to location, but the evidence suggests that most clergy did not undertake these conversions lightly:

[I]t is clear that conversion of Jewish children was undertaken cautiously and often only after special permission was granted by parents or guardians. Moreover, Catholics close to the process explained
that, after baptism, Jewish children were more likely to feel Christian
and, therefore, had a better chance of avoiding giving themselves and
their rescuers away.[63]

In fact, classes were established to let the children study their own
religion.[64] (In parts of France and Belgium, Church officials forbade
the actual baptism of Jewish children. Outward appearances were
thought sufficient to deceive the Nazis.)[65]

The Secretary General of the World Jewish Congress reported on
a meeting with Pius XII after the war to thank him for helping hide
Jewish children.[66] Pius promised to cooperate with returning the
children to their communities. Chief Rabbi Herzog of Palestine also
announced that he had the Vatican's promise of help in bringing
"converted" Jewish children back into the Jewish fold. In 1964, Dr.
Leon Kubovitzky, who directed this project, reported that there were
almost no cases of Catholic institutions resisting the return of Jewish
children.[67]

Perhaps the question of anti-Semitism affecting the Pope's wartime performance can best be answered by Jewish leaders who knew
of his efforts during the war. Grand Rabbi Isaac Herzog of Jerusalem
wrote:

I well know that His Holiness the Pope is opposed from the depths of
his noble soul to all persecution and especially to the persecution...
which the Nazis inflict unremittingly on the Jewish people....I take
this opportunity to express...my sincere thanks as well as my deep
appreciation...of the invaluable help given by the Catholic Church to
the Jewish people in its affliction.[68]

After the war, Rabbi Herzog visited the Vatican to thank Pius and the
Holy See for "manifold acts of charity" on behalf of the Jews.[69] Thus,
if anti-Semitic prejudice existed within the Catholic Church, it did not
affect Pius XII's behavior during the war.

2. Was the Pope Blinded by His Hatred of Communism?

Some have argued that Pius XII's hatred of Communism caused
him to turn a blind eye to the Nazis and their Jewish victims. The
Vatican certainly had viewed Communism as the Church's greatest

threat from the early 1920s until at least the late 1930s. Many British leaders also thought that Communism was a greater threat than Nazism.[70] The Soviet Union not only killed millions of peasants, but made it a policy to persecute the Church and drive religion out of the country. Many Church leaders feared that if Germany were thoroughly de-Nazified, the Communists would take over. The prospect of a communistic Germany was of deep concern to the Catholic hierarchy (as well as Protestant leaders).[71]

Long before Pacelli became Pope, Hitler and Mussolini were seen by many world leaders (including some officials of the Holy See) as the best defense against the spread of Communism.[72] Of course, this was before the Nazis began their reign of terror (and right in the middle of the Soviet terror). Moreover, Church leaders were right to fear Communism. After the Allied victory, the Soviets expanded their sphere of influence (and their persecution of the Church) throughout most of eastern Europe, including half of Germany.[73]

Despite his concern over the spread of Communism, Pius recognized that Nazism presented a similar threat. He continued to condemn Communism, but as an observer of that time noted, "[w]ith it he bracketed Nazism in the same breath, for it strikes, no less ruthlessly, at the individuality of the home, the very heart of religion. Both are tyrannically pagan."[74] In 1942, Pius told a Jesuit visitor, "the Communist danger does exist, but at this time the Nazi danger is more serious. They want to destroy the Church and crush it like a toad."[75] When the Allies sought to have him speak out against Nazi Germany, he said he was unwilling to do so without also condemning the atheistic government of the Soviet Union, but he also refused Axis requests to bless their attack on the Soviet Union.[76] In fact, by cooperating with Roosevelt's request that he encourage American Catholics to support extending the lend-lease program to the Soviets, Pius actually gave economic and military aid to the Soviets.[77]

In the British Public Records Office, there is a short message dated May 10, 1943, from the British Embassy in Madrid. It reports on a message that had been forwarded by a member of the Spanish Ministry of Foreign Affairs. According to this report, "In a recent dispatch the Spanish Ambassador reported that in conversation with the Pope, the latter informed him that he now regarded Nazism and Fascism, and not Communism, as he used to, as the greatest menace to civilization and the Roman Catholic Church."[78] Others were also aware of the Pope's view. According to a post-war interrogation of Nazi official Joachim von Ribbentrop, Hitler thought that the Catholic Church sometimes worked with the Communists.[79]

Before the war, Pius identified a specific role that he would play in the war. In that role, he was aggressive in countering Hitler's Nazism. He actively worked to undermine Nazi deportation of Jews, he frequently prompted Mussolini to complain about his opposition to everything that Hitler stood for, he helped those who were suffering, and he passed military information to Allied leaders when he could. Pius quite clearly put himself and the Church at risk by giving aid and comfort to the Jews, and he helped provide information to the Allies. He even went so far as to cooperate in at least one plan to overthrow Hitler, who rightly saw the pontiff as an enemy. As such, the record simply does not support the conclusion that hatred of Communism blinded Pius XII to the evils of Nazism.[80]

3. Did the Pope Come Under the Influence of Hitler?

As a former nuncio to Germany for thirteen years, fluent in the German language, and well known to many German leaders, Pius certainly had close connections to the Axis powers. He also held the German people in great esteem. (He was, however, once quoted as having said: "I have lived for too long among Germans not to value highly social relations with Frenchmen.")[81] Some critics have used this relationship with Germany to charge that the Pope was sympathetic to the German war effort. Even though Pacelli never met Hitler,[82] in the sidelights on history which follow *The Deputy*,[83] Hochhuth accused Pius of being influenced by Hitler because as Secretary of State he negotiated the concordat with Germany.[84]

Many people did fall under the influence of Hitler. Some religious leaders at that time thought that the churches were not socialistic enough. They hoped to reform Socialism and retain a political (and national) identity. This is what Hitler offered—National Socialism.[85] Thus, many religious people supported Nazism. Pius, however, understood that Hitler, who wanted to create national "popes" and replace the existing churches with a German Nazi church, was no friend to the Holy See.[86] It is totally at odds with all of the evidence, including the Pope's public pronouncements, all that is known about his wartime activities, and his pre-war attitude, to think that Pius was attracted to Hitlerism. In fact, General Erich Ludendorff, a German national hero and one of Hitler's earliest supporters wrote: "Pacelli was the live spirit which stood behind all the anti-German activities of Rome's policy."[87] John Cornwell, a severe critic of Pius XII, has noted that Pacelli's "hatred of Hitler was sufficient to allow him to take grave risks with his own life—and...the lives of a great many others."[88]

As for the concordat, this was a common diplomatic procedure. Pius XI viewed the concordat process as the best way to safeguard and defend the freedom of worship of the Catholic faithful (especially in countries where they were in a minority) and to defend and safeguard essential elements of Catholic life (such as Catholic schools and Catholic associations). Pacelli was at that time Secretary of State for the Vatican. Certainly he had significant input into the Vatican's international policies, and he probably agreed with the approach, but the ultimate decision to sign the concordat was not his. The Holy See had sought such an agreement with Germany for well over ten years. Moreover, although the Nazis immediately began a pattern of ignoring the concordat, on paper it seemed very favorable to the Vatican. Had the Vatican turned it down, the Catholic Church certainly would have been criticized for having bypassed an opportunity to restrict the Nazis. A few years after the concordat, the Vatican released the encyclical *Mit brennender Sorge*, which was a clear condemnation of the Nazis. As such, the concordat provides no basis to conclude that Pius XII or the Vatican fell under the influence of Hitler.[89]

4. Would a Statement by the Pope Have Diminished Jewish Suffering?
This is perhaps the most important question, and yet it is also the one most difficult to answer. Holocaust survivor Elie Wiesel, accepting the Nobel Peace Prize, said: "Take Sides. Neutrality helps the oppressor, never the victim. Silence encourages the tormentor, never the tormented." There are, however, certain assumptions inherent in this observation, and not all of them are applicable to the situation during World War II.

Reading accounts of "rescuers" and resistance fighters in occupied nations, one is struck by how often the people were in their teens or late twenties. There might be several explanations for this: older rescuers have died so we do not hear their stories, younger people traditionally are more willing to challenge authority, and younger people are better able to take whatever physical risks that accompany this work. It might also be that as people move into adulthood and assume obligations to others, they are much more reluctant to risk retaliation because of the impact that it might have on others, especially their children.

Pius was not in the situation of a teenager; he was more like the parent of a very large family.[90] He knew well that any of his acts or comments might bring retaliation—not against him, but against Catholic clergy and laity in Germany and every occupied nation.[91] As one bishop who was imprisoned at Dachau reported:

> The detained priests trembled every time news reached us of some protest by religious authority, but particularly by the Vatican. We all had the impression that our wardens made us atone heavily for the fury these protests evoked...whenever the way we were treated became more brutal, the Protestant pastors among the prisoners used to vent their indignation on the Catholic priests: "Again your big naive Pope and those simpletons, your bishops, are shooting their mouths off... why don't they get the idea once and for all, and shut up. They play the heroes and we have to pay the bill."[92]

With concerns like this, Pope Pius XII had to weigh carefully the force of his words. This threat might not be justification for maintaining neutrality if a different course of action would have saved more lives, but that is far from certain.

Hochhuth suggested that Pius XII could have made 35,000,000 Germans "hostile to the state," perhaps causing the Nazi leaders to rethink their actions.[93] For this to be true, however, the Pope's message would have to reach receptive listeners. That probably would not have happened.

Clearly, the Vatican held no sway with the Nazis.[94] Pius made several private protests to the German leaders, but they had no lasting impact on Nazi activities.[95] "Hitler showed no respect at all for the intervention of the Pope and the nuncios on behalf of the Jews."[96] Public denunciations of totalitarian regimes tended not only to be useless, but—as in the case of protests by the Dutch bishops—they provoked retaliation. Pius knew that a breach of neutrality might lead to great damage to the Church, but it would probably not have any impact on the functioning of the Third Reich.[97] In fact, at times German occupation authorities believed that an immediate papal protest might work in their favor.[98] The few times when German authorities were concerned about a public denunciation, such as after the invasion of Rome in 1943, Pius used the threat of a statement to convince the Nazis to reduce persecution of Jews.[99] Rabbi Steven S. Wise, who has been called the foremost Jewish leader in America during the war years, agreed that Pius could not wield any real authority when it came to the Nazis.[100]

At the Nuremberg trials, German Field Marshal Albert Kesselring testified: "If [Pius XII] did not protest, he failed to do so because he told himself, quite rightly: If I protest, Hitler will be driven to madness; not only will that not help the Jews, but we must expect that they will then be killed all the more."[101] The U.S. Deputy Chief of Counsel at the Nuremberg War Crimes Trials,[102] Dr. Robert M.W. Kempner, wrote, "[e]very propaganda move of the Catholic Church against Hitler's Reich would have been not only 'provoking suicide,'... but would have hastened the execution of still more Jews and Priests."[103] Fr. Robert Leiber, who worked closely with Pope Pius XII for many years, said "During the war the thought never entered anybody's head that Pope Pius XII could have been able to put a stop to the annihilation of the Jews by means of public protest."[104]

Pius XII's words would have provoked retaliation from the Nazi leaders, but what would the impact have been on the citizenry? Hochhuth argued that the Pope would have been believed by the masses, whereas pronouncements from the Allies were "shrugged off" as propaganda.[105] In all likelihood, however, condemnation would have been kept from the German public by the Nazis. The idea of a free press came to an end in Germany in 1933,[106] and expression was suppressed everywhere else the Nazis went. As others have written: "The very evil to be condemned was sufficiently evil to be able to prevent its condemnation."[107] As one of the Pope's most vocal critics has acknowledged: "Pacelli had only limited scope for action. His cables and messages to nuncios around the world could be intercepted. His newspaper could be stopped at the gates of the Vatican. His radio station could be jammed. An encyclical aimed at Germany could be destroyed or altered before publication."[108] Pius himself was aware of these limitations, writing in a letter dated March 1, 1942: "Whereas Our Christmas radio message found a strong echo in the world... We learn with sadness that it was almost completely hidden from the hearing of German Catholics."[109] In private conversations, too, he expressed dismay at the limited impact of his words.[110]

According to the U.S. Deputy Chief of Counsel at the Nuremberg War Crimes Trials, the Nazi hierarchy sent their ambassadors a "guideline on silencing the Vatican" which made clear that the Nazi propaganda machine would be put in gear to counter any statements from the Vatican.[111] Such efforts were effective where they were employed. In occupied France, for instance, the media put forth only censored versions of the Pope's proclamations, including his Christmas messages. No outside news reached Poland during the occupation.[112] Thus, when the Allies invaded southern France, General Eisenhower said: "You see this country has suffered an intellectual blackout ever since the fall of France. The people have heard only what the Germans and Vichy wanted them to hear."[113]

Had a statement gotten through, it is very questionable as to whether it would have prompted the citizens of Germany to abandon their allegiance to Hitler. He was wildly popular, and few civilians would have wanted to become martyrs.[114] More likely, German Catholics would have left the Church. After all, the Vatican's efforts to win freedom for its bishops and priests imprisoned in Dachau were all frustrated.[115] That being the case, it is unreasonable to think that the Pope could have been more effective helping Jews. In fact, "in the expert hands of a Goebbels, a pontifical speech could become a choice weapon against Christianity."[116] Author Guenter Lewy concluded that once the inability of the Pope to motivate the faithful into a decisive struggle against the Nazis is accepted as a fact, it may well be that a statement would only have made things worse.[117] As the Pope said in 1942:

> Every word we address to the competent authority on this subject, and all our public utterances, have to be carefully weighed and measured by us in the interests of the victims themselves, lest, contrary to our intentions, we make their situation worse and harder to bear.[118]

In 1963, Dr. Joseph L. Lichten, Director of Intercultural Affairs for the Anti-Defamation League of B'nai B'rith, wrote an appraisal of the Vatican during the War. He quoted a German Jewish couple whom Pius XII helped escape through Rome to Spain:

> None of us wanted the Pope to take an open stand. We were all fugitives, and fugitives do not wish to be pointed at. The Gestapo would have become more excited and would have intensified its inquisitions. If the Pope had protested, Rome would have become the center of attention. It was better that the Pope said nothing. We all shared this opinion at the time and this is still our conviction today.[119]

Ernst von Weizsäcker, German ambassador to the Vatican during the war, expressed this same sentiment when he informed the Holy See that any protest by the Pope would only make things worse on the Jews:

> A "flaming protest" by the Pope would not only have been unsuccessful in halting the machinery of destruction but might have caused a great deal of additional damage—to the thousands of Jews hidden in the Vatican and the monasteries, to the *Mischlinge*, the Church, the territorial integrity of the Vatican City, and—last but not least—to the Catholics in all of Germany-occupied Europe.[120]

As the official representative of the Nazi government, Weizsäcker's advice would have been very influential.[121] Moreover, this is the same advice that Pius received from his bishops in occupied nations.[122]

It is impossible to reconstruct history and determine what would have happened if only a minor change were made. As such, Pius XII's behavior during the war will always be subject to speculation. We do know that the "survival rates for Jews in Catholic countries were almost invariably higher than for Jews who found themselves under Nazi occupation elsewhere."[123] "Suppose that Pacelli had... made visible and vocal statements condemning Nazism, excommunicated all Catholic Nazis, even died a martyr's death in a concentration camp. What then? Almost certainly, more Jews would have perished than was actually the case."[124] While speculating about what might have been, it is possible to look at the assistance—in terms of information, lines of communication, and influence within Italy—given by the Vatican to the Allies and conclude that if the Pope had spoken, and the German war machine had retaliated, the very outcome of the war would have been adversely affected.

Pius XII's decision to use pastoral action instead of political posturing was neither ill-informed, shaped by prejudice or bias, nor made without serious consideration of the consequences. Perhaps more important, as expressed in his encyclical *Summi Pontificatus*, Pius felt that what he was doing was the appropriate thing for the Church to do. All evidence shows that he believed his approach would best serve Jewish victims of the Nazis. This was what most Jewish leaders had advised,[125] as well as Polish Archbishop Adam Sapieha,[126] almost all German religious leaders,[127] the International Red Cross,[128] and several Jewish rescue organizations. A fair evaluation of the evidence suggests that they (and the Pope) were right.[129]

5. Was the Pope Afraid of Retaliation Against Himself or the Church?

On August 11, 1995, the Arts and Entertainment Television Network broadcast an edition of *Investigative Reports* entitled "The Pope and the Nazis." Hosted by Bill Kurtis, the episode began with Kurtis posing the question, "Was he a pragmatic hero, or a moral coward?"[130] Some have suggested that the Pope was not more vocal in his Nazi condemnation due to fear of retaliation. The Vatican, of course, is located within Italy, Germany's first ally and signatory to the "Pact of Steel."[131] Pius was well aware of the Church's vulnerability with regard to the Italian Fascist state, which could violate the Lateran Treaty at any time, treat the Vatican as a subordinate state rather than an equal, and establish national Catholic churches apart from the Vatican.[132] He was especially concerned about the ability of the Holy See to provide for the needs of the Church and the people if the Vatican were under the control of a Fascist government.

The Nazis had warned the College of Cardinals that they were not happy with the election of Pius XII. If he were to provoke the Axis powers to a greater degree than he did, Catholics and Jews in the Vatican and throughout Europe might have suffered, and he would have had no way to defend them. If he kept silent to protect the persecuted, it would not necessarily be an act of cowardice, but perhaps an act of compassion.

A concern like this is reflected in the Pope's letter of June 2, 1943, to German Bishop von Preysing.[133] Pius wrote:

> We are leaving to the pastors, according to each location, the care of evaluating if, and in what measure, the danger of reprisals and pressure, as well as perhaps other circumstances due to the length and psychology of war, warrant restraint—despite the reasons for intervening—so as to avoid greater evils. This is one of the reasons for which We ourselves are imposing limits in Our declarations.[134]

Pius recognized that his words would likely lead to greater persecution of innocent people. Restraint in such a situation certainly cannot be said to reflect moral cowardice.

The possibility of a German invasion of Vatican City was very real.[135] Napoleon had done this in 1809, capturing Pope Pius VII at bayonet point and taking him away.[136] Hochhuth rejected the notion that Pius XII feared "violence against himself or, say, against St. Peters,"[137] but even he admitted that Hitler considered invading the

Vatican. In fact, Hitler spoke of wanting to enter the Vatican and "pack up that whole whoring rabble."[138]

In addition to minutes from a meeting on July 26, 1943, in which Hitler discussed invading the Vatican,[139] Ernst von Weizsäcker, the German Ambassador to the Vatican, wrote that he heard of Hitler's plan to kidnap Pius XII.[140] Weizsäcker regularly cautioned Vatican officials not to provoke Berlin.[141] Written statements by the German Ambassador to Italy, Rudolf Rahn, also describe the plot and attempts by him and other Nazi officials to head it off.[142] "The fact of [the plan's] existence and its target is solidly anchored in my memory," reported Rahn.[143] Albrecht von Kessel, Weizsäcker's closest aide, explained, "All we could do... was to warn the Vatican, the church, and the Pope himself against rash utterances and actions."[144] Karl Otto Wolff, a German general who was the S.S. chief in Italy toward the end of the war, also testified to such a plan.[145] He reported the following conversation from 1943:

> HITLER: Now, Wolff, I have a special mission for you, with significance for the whole world, and it is a personal matter between you and me. You are never to speak of it with anyone without my permission, with the exception of the Supreme Commandant of the S.S. [Himmler], who is aware of everything. Do you understand?
> WOLFF: Understood, *Führer!*
> HITLER: I want you and your troops, while there is still a strong reaction in Germany to the Badoglio treachery, to occupy as soon as possible the Vatican and Vatican City, secure the archives and the art treasures, which have a unique value, and transfer the Pope, together with the Curia, for their protection, so that they cannot fall into the hands of the Allies and exert a political influence. According to military and political developments it will be determined whether to bring him to Germany or place him in neutral Liechtenstein. How quickly could you prepare this operation?[146]

Wolff said that it would take four to six weeks in order to come up with a plan. Hitler replied: "That's far too long. It's crucial that you let me know every two weeks how you are getting on. I should prefer to take the Vatican immediately."[147]

Early in December 1943, Wolff informed the *Führer* that he had completed his preparations for the plan against the Vatican. He went on, however, to express his opinion that the Italian people would defend their Church at all costs and any action against the Church would make occupation all the more difficult. In light of this advice, Hitler told Wolff that he would drop the kidnaping plan.[148]

Hochhuth diminished the threat of an invasion by saying that Hitler made his comment "among his intimates" and suggesting that it was not serious. Hochhuth then went on to discuss "feverish diplomatic activity" on behalf of the Vatican.[149] This would be natural, especially since thousands of Jewish people were being hidden from the Nazis in the Vatican. It would also indicate that the Vatican took the threat very seriously.

Sir Francis D'Arcy Osborne, British Minister to the Holy See from 1936 to 1947, came to know the Pope quite well during the war years. He denied any cowardice on the part of the Pontiff:

> Pius XII was the most warmly humane, kindly, generous, sympathetic (and, incidentally, saintly) character that it has been my privilege to meet in the course of a long life. I know his sensitive nature was acutely and incessantly alive to the tragic volume of human suffering caused by the War and, without the slightest doubt, he would have been ready and glad to give his life to redeem humanity from its consequences.[150]

John Cornwell, a severe critic of Pius, charged him with "almost foolhardy valor" due to his involvement with the plan to topple Hilter.[151] Similarly, the Chief Rabbi in Rome during the German occupation, Israel Zolli, said that "no hero in all of history was more militant, more fought against, none more heroic, than Pius XII."[152] Giovanni Battista Montini said, "it is utterly false to tax Pius XII with cowardice."[153]

He may not have made repeated public pronouncements, but Pius took affirmative action when there was some chance to make a lasting difference, even though he risked retaliation. He was not afraid of being taken prisoner or of having the Vatican invaded, and he did not hesitate to put himself in jeopardy.[154] Mussolini's ambassador filed a protest that Pius had taken sides against Germany by sending telegrams of support to the leaders of Belgium, Holland, and Luxembourg after they had been invaded by Hitler's forces. Pius replied that his conscience came first and he was "not afraid to go to a concentration camp."[155] It should also be noted that Pius did not change his approach even after the Allies had liberated Rome, Germany was in retreat, and the Vatican was safe. Thus, it cannot be said that cowardice kept Pius from being open about the German abuses.

6. *Did the Pope Know of the "Final Solution" Before the End of the War?*

The general public did not become aware of the extent of Nazi atrocities until after the war. Even today it is hard to comprehend. Recent surveys have indicated that up to 25 percent of the American populace think that the Holocaust might never have happened. Because of the difficulty in understanding the magnitude of this evil, several of Pius XII's defenders have speculated that he did not know of the Holocaust in time to raise a protest. They have even made a pretty good case.

In early 1940, the Vatican began receiving reports of the forced deportation of German Jews, the slaughter of Jews in Slovakia, and abuse of Jews in Romania. There was not, however, a clear pattern of deadly Nazi violence toward the Jews at this time. The Final Solution did not come into being until early 1942. The World Jewish Congress in Geneva first noted an increase in persecutions in March of 1942.[156] A Jewish official reported this to the Vatican in August, and about this same time priests also began reporting the massive extermination of Jews by the Nazis.[157] When this was reported to the United States, President Roosevelt sought confirmation from the Vatican, but the Vatican was unable to confirm those reports until late 1942.[158]

As the Allies began to send information about the Nazi abuses to the Vatican, there was reason to question it. The Soviets certainly did not have a good reputation for veracity, and the Vatican would need strict proof of their allegations. In addition, the Germans tried to disguise the extent of their crimes, and they were successful. The Holy See had witnessed Mussolini's activity up close, and Jews in Italy were not subject to the abuses reported from Germany and Poland.[159]

The only problem with the theory that the Vatican did not have good information about the Holocaust is that it is almost certainly wrong. During the war the Vatican had diplomatic representatives in Berlin, Vienna, Lisbon, Madrid, Rome, and Washington. Priests returning from various countries brought with them accounts of the events that were taking place everywhere the Nazis went. In addition, the Vatican had innumerable ecclesiastics on both sides of the conflict who reported to Rome via friends or acquaintances and through underground operatives in the various resistance movements.[160] In fact, the Church was widely regarded as one of the best informed sources in the world and had the reputation as the listening post of

Europe. German intelligence, which was convinced that the Catholic Church was a world-wide intelligence organization, had radio operators monitoring Vatican transmissions 24 hours per day.[161]

Exactly when the Vatican recognized the pattern of treatment carried out against the Jews is unclear. As early as May 1940, Pius confided in a private conversation to a senior Italian diplomat that "terrible things" were occurring in Poland.[162] There was no set extermination plan at this time, however. In all likelihood, the Vatican learned of the plan shortly after the Nazis themselves decided on it. In February 1942, Archbishop Hlond of Warsaw (who had fled Poland and was not living under Nazi rule) informed the Vatican that prisoners in Nazi concentration camps "were deprived of all human rights, handed over to the cruelty of men who have no feeling of humanity. We live in terror, continually in danger of losing everything if we attempt to escape, thrown into camps from which few emerge alive."[163] In 1943, a bishop wrote a memo urging the Pope to intervene in the matter, but it was then retracted by Adam Sapieha, the Archbishop of Krakow, who was still in Poland.[164]

It is, of course, possible–even likely–that not all of the reports were believed when they were first heard. Many Allied agencies doubted the earliest reports.[165] It is virtually certain that most people, hearing the reports for the first time, thought they were exaggerated.[166] It makes no sense, however, to contend that Pius was unaware of the abuses until after the war. He did what he thought was most appropriate as the spiritual leader of his people.

7. Was the Pope Too Willing to Compromise to Achieve Peace?

Prior to the outbreak of the war, many world leaders were willing to compromise with Hitler to avoid further aggression; British Prime Minister Neville Chamberlain was only the most prominent. The League of Nations also followed this course rather than confront Mussolini after his conquest of Ethiopia. The minor sanctions let Hitler know that there was no need to fear retaliation for his early conquests. When Hitler annexed Austria and threatened Czechoslovakia, leaders from France and England agreed to transfer the Sudetenland region of Czechoslovakia to Germany. In return, Hitler assured them that the rest of the country would not be invaded. Hitler was given everything he wanted.

Prior to the war, most Vatican leaders followed the appeasement line. Pius XII was also attached to this policy, at least early in the war. He believed that the continuance of the war was a greater evil than the horrors committed during it.[167] His willingness to negotiate in order to win peace is often portrayed as a willingness to accommodate the aggressive tendencies of Hitler and Mussolini. It must be noted, however, that in a 1942 message to the United States government, he expressly stated that

> despite what any propaganda may say to the contrary, We have never thought in terms of a peace by compromise at any cost. On certain principles of right and justice there can be no compromise. In our Christmas allocutions of 1939, 1940, and 1941 the world may read some of these essential principles expressed in unmistakable language, We think they light the path along which We walk and will continue to walk unswervingly.... We shall never approve of, much less further a peace, that gives free rein to those who would undermine the foundations of Christianity and persecute Religion and the Church.[168]

Moreover, while it is certainly true that Pius wanted to bring the war to an end as quickly as possible, that end would also have brought an end to the Holocaust.[169] While appeasement might have been an unwise policy for a warring nation to advance, it was—as modified by Pius XII in the above quoted message—a completely understandable position for a man of God in search of peace.

8. *Should the Pope Have Made a Statement for the Sake of Appearances?*

This question certainly has the appearances of being a straw-man, but Hochhuth suggests that the Pope *should* have considered the impact of his actions on the Church. "The Pope must surely have realized that a protest against Hitler... would have elevated the Church to a position it has not held since the Middle Ages."[170] Pius XII's dilemma was this:

> Was his own moral reputation more important than the life of a single Jew, or is the life of even one Jew more valuable than justifying his conscience in the eyes of the world? If Pius XII had spoken in this context, no doubt the case against him would have been that, by issuing moral platitudes, he had threatened the lives of others.[171]

Of course, there could have been no more outrageous sin for the Pope than to sacrifice his ideals and compassion for the persecuted in order to advance the stature of himself or the Church.[172] Such an action would have gone against everything that is known about Pope Pius XII. "Nothing was more opposed to the pope's intentions than to use human suffering as an opportunity to increase his prestige and power."[173]

One time Pius speculated that a record of his personal actions in helping the Jews might have given him a better place in history. He said, "No doubt a protest would have gained me the praise and respect of the civilized world, but it would have submitted the poor Jews to an even worse fate."[174] Any statement of his compassion would be, he thought, "superfluous."[175] Thus, with full knowledge of the consequences, Pius elected to work behind the scenes, instead of making grand pronouncements, though he knowingly risked, and subsequently did incur, much condemnation. Doing what he believed to be right was more important than appearing to do what others thought was right, especially when it might cause others to suffer.

9. *Can Responsibility be Diminished by Pointing to the Failings of Others?*

The evil that Hitler symbolizes is so hard to comprehend that there is a desire to find other culprits to share the blame.[176] Thus, there are those who would spread the blame not only to Pius, but also to Roosevelt, the Allies, other churches, and various world organizations and officials.[177] Hochhuth said that Jews could not expect the same help from the Vatican, the Red Cross, or any other nation (with the possible exception of the Danes) that non-Jews would receive.[178] He also blamed the Allies for not acting sooner against the gas chambers in Austria and Poland, asserting that they knew of the atrocities in 1942.[179]

It is not unusual for observers to praise one entity by contrasting it with other institutions. Thus it has been argued that the Christian churches showed a greater resistance to Hitler and the Nazis than did the judiciary, the universities, or German trade unions.[180] Similarly, a former Israeli Consul in Italy stated that, "the Catholic Church saved more Jewish lives during the war than all the other Churches, religious institutions and rescue organizations put together. Its record stands in startling contrast to the achievements of the International Red Cross and the Western Democracies."[181] Pulitzer Prize winning author John Toland called the Holy See's silence "deplorable," but he also said that the record of the Allies was far more shameful.[182] Toland argued that the British and Americans, despite lofty pronouncements, not only avoided taking any meaningful action but gave sanctuary to few persecuted Jews.[183]

In 1944, Secretary of the Treasury Henry Morgenthau confronted President Roosevelt concerning the government's reluctance to provide aid to European Jews. Ultimately, the President created the War Refugee Board, which helped rescue tens of thousands of Jewish people from Europe.[184] Those who wish to spread Hitler's blame, have called it "the great shame" that Roosevelt did not act earlier and rescue American's reputation.[185] Others have condemned the United States Congress for its reluctance to open up immigration limitations or the Allies, particularly Roosevelt, for the unconditional surrender demand.

In all of these cases, people have tried to shift blame away from Hitler and the Nazis by pointing to others. More often than not, Pius receives the blame when people do this. Some, however, have used this technique in an effort to defend Pius. In other words, they defend him by saying that he is not the only one who treated the Jews improperly.

There is, for instance, no indication that the Holy See was intentionally involved in trying to help Nazis escape justice following the war.[186] Nevertheless, some commentators point to Nazi abuse of the Church's post-war relocation program as evidence of Vatican sympathy for the Nazis.[187] The International Red Cross, however, has similarly been identified as having helped Nazis escape from justice.[188] One could defend Pius by pointing to the Red Cross, but that would simply be making false accusations against another entity.[189] It is inconceivable that the Nazis revealed their background to the Church or Red Cross officials. It is even less likely that any such information would have reached the upper echelons of these organizations. The logistics of the massive relocation programs simply made it impossible to investigate most individuals who sought help. The Church and the Red Cross were interested in ending suffering, and those in need received assistance, with few questions asked. This made it easy to abuse the program, but it was put in place to help the victims, not the perpetrators.[190]   (The Vatican, in fact, cooperated with the prosecution at the Nuremberg Trials.)[191]

If Pius XII's actions had been wrong, blaming others would not lessen his sin. It is, however, interesting to note how many individuals and groups have been blamed for the Nazis' actions. The evil is so great that people keep looking for another culprit. Hitler and his top advisors, however, deserve the vast majority—if not all—of the blame. Others who are sometimes named may have in some way contributed to the evil, but action or inaction on their part does not affect the proper allocation of the blame. Similarly, the failings of others would not excuse Pius if he had acted with improper motives.

10. Should the Pope Have Excommunicated Hitler?

Hitler was born and baptized into the Catholic faith, so some have suggested that excommunication would have been an appropriate sanction for him and some of the other Nazi leaders. Some critics have argued that Hitler might have backed down under this threat. Reportedly, Pius was urged to threaten excommunication in the 1942 Christmas address.[192] In a note from the Pope that was smuggled to Polish priests, Pius said he had considered excommunication and greater condemnation of the Nazis, but he had concluded that it would only create more fury against the Jews, multiplying acts of cruelty.[193]

It should be noted that excommunication from the Catholic Church is not akin to the process of shunning, where a community turns its back on an individual. Excommunication from the Catholic Church means that the person is prohibited from receiving sacraments.[194] In cases where this is important to the individual, a mere threat can have a significant impact. Hitler, however, had not been a practicing Catholic since his childhood, and he "hated the Christian religion in which he was reared."[195] In fact, Mussolini himself said that appeals to Christianity were meaningless when it came to the Nazis "because they are true pagans."[196] (The events surrounding his suicide make clear that the Catholic religion had no influence over him, even at the time of his death.)[197] He did not receive communion as an adult and had essentially excommunicated himself.[198] As such, a papal announcement of excommunication would have amounted to simply making a statement for public consumption, with no positive benefits for Hitler's victims and potentially tragic consequences.[199] As one commentator has written:

> To criticize the Pope for failing to excommunicate Hitler is unrealistic since the action would have triggered greater evils. And to criticize Pius XII for his alleged failure to condemn the murderous actions of the Nazis fails to take into account that he had actually done this and that his words had already fallen upon deaf ears.[200]

Pius XII's decision not to excommunicate Hitler not only is in keeping with his approach to the war effort, but is also completely understandable.

The Real Answer

In his first encyclical, *Summi Pontificatus* (*Darkness over the Earth*), released in 1939, Pope Pius XII set forth his position on Hitler, the war, and the role that he would play. He made reference to "the ever-increasing host of Christ's enemies" (paragraph 7), and noted that these enemies of Christ "deny or in practice neglect the vivifying truths and the values inherent in belief in God and in Christ" and want to "break the Tables of God's Commandments to substitute other tables and other standards stripped of the ethical content of [Christianity]." In the next paragraph, Pius charged that Christians who fell in with the enemies of Christ suffered from cowardice, weakness, or uncertainty.

In paragraph thirteen, Pius wrote of the outbreak of war. "Our paternal heart is torn by anguish as We look ahead to all that will yet come forth from the baneful seed of violence and of hatred for which the sword today ploughs the blood-drenched furrow." In the next paragraph, he wrote of the enemies of Christ (an obvious reference to Hitler's National Socialists) becoming bolder.

Paragraphs twenty-four through thirty-one laid out the Pope's belief that prayer (not public condemnation) was the only appropriate response for the Bishop of Rome. Obviously, Pius viewed this as an important act of faith. Moreover, it was the lack of Christianity that he identified as the cause of the "crop of such poignant disasters." Faith and prayer were the things he could contribute to the world at that time, not political or military strength.

Pius also expressed his belief in redemption. Thus, even though the enemies of Christ were committing horrible atrocities, it was still possible for even these very evil people to be redeemed. It was fundamental to the Pope's faith that anyone could ask and be forgiven.

Paragraphs forty-five to fifty of the encyclical deal with racial matters and expressed the Pope's belief that the Church could not discriminate against any given race of people. This would have to be seen as a slap at the racial policies in both Germany and Italy. Pius expressly stated that all races and nationalities were welcome in the Church and had equal rights as children in the house of the Lord. In paragraph forty-eight, he put meaning to those anti-racist statements by naming new bishops of different races and nationalities. Moreover, he expressly said that the Church must always be open to all:

> The spirit, the teaching and the work of the Church can never be other than that which the Apostle of the Gentiles preached: "putting on the new (man) him who is renewed unto knowledge, according to the image of him that created him. Where there is neither Gentile nor Jew, circumcision nor uncircumcision, barbarian nor Scythian, bond nor free. But Christ is all and in all" (Colossians iii. 10, 11).

The equating of Gentiles and Jews would have to be seen as a clear rejection of Hitler's fundamental ideology.

Paragraphs fifty-one to sixty-six seem to be Pius XII's view of a just society. Here he asserts that the first reason for the outbreak of war is that people have forgotten the law of universal charity. The second reason is the failure to put God above civil authority. He argues that when civil authority is placed above the Lord, the government fills that void, and problems develop. This is exactly what Hitler had done. (This analysis would likely also apply to Pius XII's view of the Soviet Union—which at that time had an agreement with Hitler.)

Pius said that nations must have a religious basis. He wrote that the goal of society must be development of the individual, not the power of the state. Again, this was a slap at Hitler's dismantling of religious institutions and development of the state in Germany. In fact, paragraph sixty was a direct answer to Hitler's view of the state as set forth in *Mein Kampf*:

> To consider the State as something ultimate to which everything else should be subordinated and directed, cannot fail to harm the true and lasting prosperity of nations. This can happen either when unrestricted dominion comes to be conferred on the State as having a mandate from the nation, people, or even a social order, or when the State arrogates such dominion to itself as absolute master, despotically, without any mandate whatsoever.

Similarly, Pius presented an answer to Hitler's views of the family and of education in this section of the encyclical.

Pius made note of how "powers of disorder and destruction" stand ready to take advantage of sorrow, bitterness, and suffering in order to make use of them "for their dark designs." This would seem to be a description of how Fascists in Italy and Nazis in Germany took advantage of the chaos following the First World War to rise to power. Pius also responded to the demands of Hitler and Mussolini (and, for that matter, Stalin) for stronger central governments. While acknowledging that there may be difficulties that would justify greater powers being concentrated in the State, the Pope also said that the moral law requires that the need for this be scrutinized with greatest rigor. The State can demand goods and blood, but not the immortal soul.

Paragraphs seventy-three to seventy-seven, dealt with the Pope's ideas relating to international relations. Here, he wrote:

> Absolute autonomy for the State stands in open opposition to this natural way that is inherent in man... and therefore leaves the stability of international relations at the mercy of the will of rulers, while it destroys the possibility of true union and fruitful collaboration directed to the general good.

Pius stressed the importance of treaties and wrote of an international natural law which requires that all treaties be honored. With Hitler having recently breached several treaties and the concordat, this must be seen as another swipe at the Nazi leader.

Interestingly, in paragraph eighty-five, Pius accurately described the challenges he would face, and he set forth the code of conduct that he followed throughout the rest of the war:

> And if belonging to [the Kingdom of God], living according to its spirit, laboring for its increase and placing its benefits at the disposition of that portion of mankind also which as yet has no part in them, means in our days having to face obstacles and oppositions as vast and deep and minutely organized as never before, that does not dispense a man from the frank, bold profession of our Faith. Rather, it spurs one to stand fast in the conflict even at the price of the greatest sacrifices. Whoever lives by the spirit of Christ refuses to let himself be beaten down by the difficulties which oppose him, but on the contrary feels himself impelled to work with all his strength and with the fullest confidence in God.

In paragraphs ninety-three to ninety-five, Pius expressed the importance that he attached to the spirit as opposed to the physical world. Here he made clear that the most important thing would be to open people to Christ. He said that the Church must be protected so that it can fulfill its role as an educator by teaching the truth, by inculcating justice, and by inflaming hearts with the divine love of Christ. Indeed, throughout the war, he would protect the Church so that it could carry out its life and soul-saving functions.

Paragraphs 101 to 106 drew distinctions between the Vatican and other secular nations and explained the Church's special role in the world. The Church "does not claim to take the place of other legitimate authorities in their proper spheres." Instead, Pius wrote, the Church should be a good example and do good works. The Church

> spreads it maternal arms towards this world not to dominate but to serve. She does not claim to take the place of other legitimate authorities in their proper spheres, but offers them her help after the example and in the spirit of her Divine Founder Who "went about doing good" (Acts x. 38).

This same thought was expanded upon when Pius wrote "render therefore to Caesar the things that are Caesar's." In other words, the Church plays an important, but limited role in resolving disputes in the secular world. His obligation was to pray for peace and offer comfort to the afflicted.

Pius expressed his confidence that the Church would always prevail in the long run. Any structure that is not founded on the teaching of Christ, he wrote, is destined to perish. Read in context, this was a promise of the ultimate failure of Nazism. In fact, he expressly foresaw that Poland would be resurrected:

> This... is in many respects a real "Hour of Darkness,"... in which the spirit of violence and of discord brings indescribable suffering on mankind.... The nations swept into the tragic whirlpool of war are perhaps as yet only at the "beginnings of sorrows,"... but even now there reigns in thousands of families death and desolation, lamentation and misery. The blood of countless human beings, even non-combatants, raises a piteous dirge over a nation such as Our dear Poland, which, for its fidelity to the Church, for its services in the defense of Christian civilization... has a right to the generous and brotherly sympathy of the whole world, while it awaits, relying on the powerful intercession of Mary, Help of Christians, the hour of a resurrection in harmony with the principles of justice and true peace.

The reference to Poland resolved any doubts about to whom Pius was referring.

In paragraphs 107 to 112, Pius wrote that it was his duty to try for peace, and that duty had to be fulfilled even if it meant that the Church was misunderstood in the effort:

> While still some hope was left, We left nothing undone in the form suggested to us by Our Apostolic office and by the means at Our disposal, to prevent recourse to arms and to keep open the way to an understanding honorable to both parties. Convinced that the use of force on one side would be answered by recourse to arms on the other, We considered it a duty inseparable from Our Apostolic office and of Christian Charity to try every means to spare mankind and Christianity the horrors of a world conflagration, even at the risk of having Our intentions and Our aims misunderstood.

He encouraged people to keep faith that good will prevail, and he once again expressed his faith in the ultimate triumph of God's will.

This encyclical shows that Pius did not waver in his approach to Hitler and the Nazis. In 1939 he laid out his vision, which he followed for the rest of the war. Thus, it was not a matter of fear, nor did Pius change after he learned of the Nazi abuses. All along he thought that the best way to assure peace was through prayer. Moreover, his primary concern was with the eternal soul, which was always subject to redemption.

Ironically, but perhaps fittingly for Pius XII, even *Summi Pontificatus* has become a point of controversy. It turns out that in June 1938, more than a year before the outbreak of World War II, when Pacelli was still the Vatican Secretary of State, Pope Pius XI commissioned an American priest, Father John LaFarge, to draft an encyclical attacking racism and anti-Semitism. LaFarge worked on the document for several months, with help from two other Jesuit priests, German professor Gustaf Gundlach and French Father Gustave Desbuquois, and submitted the manuscript to his Jesuit Superior General in Rome, Polish Count Wlodimir Ledóchowski. Ledóchowski did not think that the document was in publishable form, so he worked with others trying to improve it as Pius XI slipped into increasingly fragile health. The draft was later found among Pius XI's papers, but it had no notations by Pius XI (nor any by Pius XII).[201] Apparently the ailing Pope, who died in February 1939, received the text too late to take action on these issues.[202]

Pacelli was elected Pope in March 1939 and published his first encyclical, *Summi Pontificatus,* on October 20, 1939. Written with the help of Father Gundlach (who worked with LaFarge and would continue to work with Pius XII), the new encyclical drew heavily on LaFarge's draft. (The *New York Times* reported on the connection between the two documents when *Summi Pontificatus* was released.)[203] Missing, however, were the sections on racism and anti-Semitism, which would be very offensive by today's standards. (Many have expressed the opinion that it is good for the Church that this draft remained unpublished).[204]

By the time Pacelli released his encyclical, many things had changed. Relations between the Vatican and the Axis powers had deteriorated; racial laws were now being enforced in Italy; all of Czechoslovakia had been occupied; Poland had been invaded; and World War II had broken out. It was, therefore, harder for a neutral nation to be as blunt about matters that had taken on an international flavor. If Pius lost his neutral position in his first proclamation, it would have ruined the plan that he was then actively pursuing of having the warring nations come to Rome and negotiate a peaceful resolution. Thus, his encyclical was less adamant than the draft prepared for his predecessor, but with good reason. Nevertheless, the differences between Pius XII's encyclical and the draft prepared for Pius XI have added to the controversy surrounding this issue.[205]

In the end, perhaps one must acknowledge the different roles that various agencies play in times of crisis. The Jewish rescue groups did not speak out during the war. Rather, they did their work in relative silence. The same goes for humanitarian groups like the International Red Cross. In order to have any effectiveness in their chosen role, these agencies had to maintain a fairly low profile. The same was true for Pius XII. He chose a role for the Church and carried it out in the best way possible. Condemnations from the pulpit would likely have had no effect on the Nazis, and would almost certainly have resulted in Hitler putting an end to the Vatican's charitable works and the Holy See's efforts to end the war. As others have written, "if Pope Pius had said anything, the impact would have lasted a day and the Vatican would have lasted thirty minutes."[206]

Pius saw his obligation as a Christian to ease suffering where he could, but he recognized that there were different roles for the spiritual realm and the secular world. He bravely chose to do what he knew was right, even though it might subject him to great criticism. Any suffering that he would endure paled in comparison to the suffering that he would cause to others if he did anything else.

It was written during the war that, "Pius XII is the Peacemaker who God raised up for this world."[207] The Bible says, "Blessed too the peacemakers; they shall be called sons of God." (Matthew 5:9).

EPILOGUE

HITLER'S POPE

After this manuscript was substantially completed, *Hitler's Pope: The Secret History of Pius XII,* by British journalist John Cornwell, was released by Viking Press. That book created quite a splash in the popular press and therefore merits some discussion. As the title suggests, it presents a very cynical portrait of Pope Pius XII.[1] Cornwell's thesis is that Eugenio Pacelli was a single-minded Vatican lawyer and diplomat who, from the earliest part of his career, set out to establish the absolute authority of Rome over Europe's Catholic populations. According to Cornwell, Pacelli was vain, beady-eyed, and an overwhelmingly ambitious careerist who dominated Vatican policy long before he was elected Pope. Cornwell concludes that Pius XII "was the ideal Pope for Hitler's unspeakable plan. He was Hitler's pawn. He was Hitler's Pope."[2] Rather than a saint, Cornwell believes that Pius XII was a "deeply flawed human being from whom Catholics, and our relations with other religions, can best profit by expressing our sincere regret."[3]

To reach his conclusions, Cornwell disregards much recent scholarship and provides quirky interpretations of well-known facts.[4] As one reviewer (himself a critic of Pius) explained: "Throughout the book Cornwell insists on interpreting every decision and action of Pacelli in a way most inimical to him. The author is so committed to demonstrating or proving everything prejudicial to Pacelli, that he weakens, almost to the point of destruction, his own basic argument."[5] Those who read only Cornwell's book (as did far too many reviewers in the popular press) may think that he has established his case.[6] A fair evaluation of the facts, however, reveals that he has not.[7]

Before delving into a full analysis of Cornwell's work, brief mention must be made of the claims that he put forth regarding his faith and motivation as he worked on his book Having raised these issues to bolster his credibility, and having made these claims an important part of his work, he has invited such scrutiny.

Cornwell claims that he decided to write on Pius after a conversation with some students "several years ago."[8] He says that he wanted to write a new defense of Pius XII. He was convinced of Pius XII's evident spirituality and thought that the full story would vindicate him.[9] So, assuring Church officials that he was on the Pope's side,[10] Cornwell claims to have obtained permission to look at the Vatican's archives, including previously "unseen material."[11] Then, "for months on end I sat in a windowless dungeon beneath the Borgia Tower in Vatican City while a silent factotum brought me Pacelli's files, which had been hidden from view for decades."[12] By the middle of 1997, after studying the Vatican files, Cornwall claims to have found himself in a "state of moral shock."[13] He was now convinced that Pius XII had a soaring ambition for power and control that had led the Catholic Church "into complicity with the darkest forces of the era."[14] He concluded that Pacelli was "an ideal Pope for the Nazis' Final Solution."[15]

One is always reluctant to comment on another person's beliefs, but Viking Press has marketed this book as having been written by a practicing Catholic who started out to defend Pius XII. Most reviewers took delight in calling Cornwell a good, practicing Catholic determined to defend his Church. Earlier accounts of Cornwell's background, however, paint a very different picture.

According to a 1989 report in the *Washington Post*, Cornwell "was once a seminarian at the English College in Rome and knows the Vatican terrain, [but] he has long since left the seminary and the Catholic faith, and thus writes with that astringent, cool, jaundiced view of the Vatican that only ex-Catholics familiar with Rome seem to have mastered."[16] At that time he described himself as a "lapsed Catholic for more than 20 years."[17] In *The Hiding Places of God* (1993) he wrote of his days in the seminary: "I took delight in attempting to undermine the beliefs of my fellow seminarians with what I regarded as clever arguments; I quarreled with the lecturers in class and flagrantly ignored the rules of the house." He declared that human beings are "morally, psychologically and materially better off without a belief in God." He also said that he had lost his "belief in the mystery of the real presence of Christ in the Eucharist." Reviews of that book called Cornwell an agnostic and former Catholic.[18]

Cornwell claims that the Vatican assisted him with his research for *Hitler's Pope* both because of his professed desire to defend Pius XII and because of his 1989 book, *A Thief in the Night*, which he says was favorable to the Holy See. It is true that Cornwell rejected rumors of a papal poisoning conspiracy in that book, but it was not friendly to the Vatican.[19] One reviewer of *A Thief in the Night*, wrote:

> Cornwell lets his private journalistic ambition sully his integrity as a writer of supposed "history." This man has a clear agenda: vilify the Vatican in every possible way, cast aspersions on those who cannot defend themselves, and where possible make the Catholic Church generally and the Vatican "establishment" in particular look like a bunch of powerhungry egomaniacs and a den of thieves.[20]

George Weigel, Pope John Paul II's biographer, wrote that *A Thief in the Night* provided a "skewed picture" of the Holy See.[21] Cornwell himself wrote: "The Vatican expected me to prove that John Paul I had not been poisoned by one of their own, but the evidence led me to a conclusion that seems to me more shameful even, and more tragic, than any of the conspiracy theories."[22] It was hardly the kind of book that would win friends in high Vatican circles.

Perhaps more revealing about Cornwell's intent as he began this important project is the brief mention of Pope Pius XII in *A Thief in the Night*. On page 50 Cornwell mentions the "alleged anti-Semitism" of Pius without offering any defensive comment. Then, on page 162, he seemingly mocks Pius, saying that he was "totally remote from experience, and yet all-powerful—a Roman emperor." He goes on to call Pius an "emaciated, large-eyed demigod." In a 1995 article in London's *Sunday Times*, Cornwell described Pius as a diplomat, a hypochondriac and a ditherer.[23] The next year, when he was supposedly working on his defense of Pius XII, Cornwell wrote in the *New York Times* of "Pius XII's silence on Nazi atrocities" as an example of a failing by the Catholic Church.[24] In light of this evidence, his claim to have had nothing but the highest regard for Pius XII when he began his research for Hitler's Pope is "difficult to accept."[25]

When I was shopping my manuscript around in 1998, I received a polite rejection letter from Viking Press. It said that they agreed that this was an important topic. In fact, the letter said that they had a book on the topic under contract. The letter went on to note that the book had been under contract for two years. This suggests to me that Cornwell submitted a proposal to Viking in 1996 or earlier. If he intended to defend Pius at that time, the proposal should make that clear.

Cornwell's other books have also been unfriendly to the Church. His 1993 novel, *Strange Gods*, is about Father Nicholas Mullen, a Jesuit priest in his late forties who keeps a mistress on whom he lavishes caviar and champagne, goes on golfing holidays in Barbados, and takes lithium for manic-depressive swings. He supports his lifestyle by absolving a wealthy Catholic benefactor from his own sins of the flesh. Although unhappy with his emotional, sexual, and spiritual lot, Fr. Mullen lacks the courage and imagination to do anything about it. *The Independent* (London) called the priest "a cut-out model of a sexually tortured Catholic."[26] Driven by fear and desperation, he deserts his pregnant mistress in favor of a dangerous, immoral venture in an obscure part of Latin America. There, he encounters Father Christian O'Rourke, an Irish Jesuit whose fanatical attempts to indoctrinate natives into the One True Faith are by turns comical and sinister. Ultimately, Mullen returns to England, his faith transformed into what one reviewer called "a soggy Christian humanism."[27]

None of this material concerning Cornwell's anti-Catholic background and prior hostility towards Pope Pius XII serves by itself to undermine Cornwell's research. It does however raise serious questions about his credibility. Moreover, as one studies his work, it becomes apparent that *Hitler's Pope* was not a work of honest scholarship, but a book that was written to justify a conclusion that was reached in advance.

The first cause for suspicion is on the cover of Cornwell's book.[28] The dust jacket of the British edition shows Nuncio Pacelli leaving a reception given for German President Hindenburg in 1927. The photograph, a favorite of those who seek to portray Pius XII in an unfavorable light,[29] shows the nuncio dressed in formal diplomatic regalia (which could easily be confused with papal garments), as he exits a building. On each side of him stand soldiers of the Weimar republic. In front of him stands a chauffeur saluting and holding open the square-looking door, typical of automobiles from the 1920s. Those who do not recognize the differences in uniform details could easily confuse the Weimar soldiers with Nazi soldiers because of their distinctive helmets associated with Nazi-era German soldiers.

Use of this photograph, especially when coupled with a provocative title such as "Hitler's Pope," gives the impression that Pope Pius XII is seen leaving a meeting with Hitler.[30] Making matters even worse is the caption from inside the rear cover of the dust jacket on early British editions of the book. This caption says that the photograph is from March 1939.[31] By this time, Hitler was Chancellor of Germany, and this was the month Pacelli was made Pope. A fair-minded person reading the caption could easily conclude that

Cardinal Pacelli paid a visit to Hitler immediately prior to or just after being elected Pope.

The American version of *Hitler's Pope* never had the wrong date, but—given that the date might have been an honest error—it is far more revealing about the intentional mis-information that went into the marketing of this book. The U.S. edition uses the same photograph as the British edition, but it is cropped to eliminate two important points of reference: The soldier nearest the camera and the square door of the automobile. Both of those images provide clues to the true date of this photo (1927), and author apparently did not want that known.[32] Even more telling is the intentional blurring of the background. Looking at this cover, Nuncio Pacelli is in focus, but the soldier to his left and the chauffeur are both badly blurred. They are so badly blurred that it is impossible even for a well-trained observer to recognize that the soldier wears a Weimar uniform rather than a Nazi uniform. The chauffeur, due to the blurring and cropping that eliminates the car door, takes on the appearance of a saluting S.S. officer. Even a civilian in the background could seem to be a military (Nazi) official.[33]

Since none of the images on the British edition are blurred, and since Nuncio Pacelli is in focus on the U.S. cover, but the other images are blurred, the only logical conclusion is that Viking Press intentionally altered the photograph to support the author's thesis. Unfortunately, this is not the only dishonest aspect of the book.

Not long after the release of *Hitler's Pope,* the Vatican issued a statement on Cornwell's work in Rome. It denied Cornwell's claim to have been the first person to have access to the archives that he used, denied his claim that he had worked "for months on end" in these archives, denied his claim that a letter he had found had been kept secret prior to his efforts (noting that it had been published in full several years earlier), and stated that these falsehoods had been revealed "to put readers on guard about Cornwell's claims."[34]

It seemed to me that there was enough of a question about Cornwell's credibility to justify contacting the Vatican for details about his work and the "special assistance" he claimed to have received. I faxed a letter to the *relator* of the cause for Pope Pius XII's sainthood,[35] Fr. Peter Gumpel S.J., of the Congregation for the Causes of Saints in Vatican City.[36] I told Gumpel of my work and asked him about Cornwell's assertions. Just a few days later, I received a call from him.

Gumpel specifically denied that Cornwell saw any secret files. The
Vatican has always insisted that all relevant documents relating to
World War II have been published in the *Actes et Documents* collection.[38] Cornwell's supposed "new information" came from the pre-
1922 archives in the Vatican's Secretary of State office.[39] Moreover,
any competent scholar can obtain access to the archives to do scholarly research without saying anything about being "favorable" or
"unfavorable" to any pontiff or ecclesiastic. As for a desire to help
Cornwell because he said he wanted to defend Pius XII, "I am not as
naive as he portrays me," Gumpel said at least twice. He was
adamant about Cornwell's distortions of the truth.

Gumpel invited me to visit Rome and inspect the files that
Cornwell had used. My publisher encouraged me to accept Gumpel's
offer, and I traveled to Rome in early December 1999. For two days,
Gumpel and I went over my manuscript (which he had already read),
some of his writings, and issues that were highlighted by Cornwell's
book. On the third day he provided me with an office on Vatican property and gave me all of the documents that I wanted to review, including Pius XII's beatification deposition transcripts.[40]

Cornwell claimed that these beatification deposition transcripts
were "unseen materials,"[41] but other scholars had seen them.[42] More
revealing was that he called the files' "explosively critical matter"[43]
and "a priceless biographical resource"[44] that Gumpel had made
available to him "at great risk."[45] In fact, he said that "in the absence
of a devil's advocate [the testimony of Pacelli's younger sister,
Elisabetha] should be heeded."[46] I at least expected to find controversy in the materials. However, as I began to plow through the nine-
ty-eight deposition transcripts (not seventy-six, as Cornwell writes),[47]
I found them not at all controversial. No witness gave "shocking" testimony, but each witness provided positive testimony about Pope Pius
XII. Many spoke of his concern for and help given to Jewish people,
both before and after he became Pope.

I thought that perhaps I was simply overlooking specific points
that Cornwell had found, so I looked at his endnotes and cross-refer-
enced them with the deposition transcripts. I first noted how few citations there were. The original transcripts take up just over 1700
pages which are spread over seven volumes; the two volume printed
set is just over 900 pages (not a thousand pages, as Cornwell says).[48]
Yet, Cornwell has only 30 citations to this material, in which he references only 12 of the 98 witnesses. More telling, however, are the

contents of the testimony that he found so devastating.

Cornwell was able to uncover a bit of disharmony between the Pope's housekeeper and his sister (who wanted to be his housekeeper), but other than some petty jealousy—not on the part of Pius, mind you—the testimony is not in the slightest negative. Much of it relates to matters such as Pius XII's height, weight, health problems, etc.[49] Cornwell attempts to present these transcripts as controversial by quoting statements favorable to the Pope, then arguing against them. The testimony itself, however, is not at all negative. In fact, the clear message from each and every witness is that Eugenio Pacelli—Pope Pius XII—was an honest, holy, and charitable man—even saintly.[50]

On pages 289-90 is a chart that covers all of Cornwell's citations to the deposition transcripts. Listed is the witness and a thumbnail sketch of the testimony. Not only did each of these witnesses have favorable things to say about Pope Pius XII, even the portions of testimony cited by Cornwell are not actually critical of Pius (despite Cornwell's arguments to the contrary).[51] The testimonies "are without any exception, positive with regard to the life, activity, and virtue of Pius XII."[52]

While Cornwell has only thirty citations to the deposition transcripts, he has about twice that many citations to the writings of Klaus Scholder.[53] As the New York Times reported: "Footnote after crucial footnote refers to Mr. Scholder."[54] In fact, Cornwell says that his "greatest debt, and indeed homage, is to the magisterial scholarship of the late Klaus Scholder."[55]

According to Cornwell, Scholder's reputation as a church historian is "unchallenged in German scholarship,"[56] but he has been overlooked by the Vatican. On both counts, he is clearly wrong. Cornwell reports that in a conversation, Gumpel admitted "that not only had he not read Klaus Scholder's extensive and crucial scholarship on the Reich Concordat, but that he was unaware of its existence."[57] Gumpel, of course, has read Scholder's writings. He attributes Cornwell's error to a misunderstanding that took place when Cornwell visited Rome. "He has a very bad pronunciation of German," Gumpel explained. "He may have asked whether I knew of Scholder's work, but mispronounced the name so badly that I did not recognize it."[58] Gumpel has even explained why Cornwell relies so heavily on Scholder: "Scholder's work relating to the various concordats is 'largely surpassed' by other standard works, but Scholder better supports Cornwell's thesis."[59]

Despite Cornwell's claim, Scholder is certainly not unchallenged. He has been most seriously challenged by Konrad Repgen. In several works, Repgen has particularly contested Scholder's assertion that there was a connection between the dissolution of the Center Partyand the concordat negotiations in 1933.[60] Ludwig Volk's work, though published prior to Scholder's, refutes the latter's contentions, in particular Scholder's claim that the initiative for the concordat came from the Vatican.[61] Other scholarship also undercuts Scholder's claim that the push for the concordat came from the Vatican instead of the Germans.[62]

Perhaps more surprising than Cornwell's trust in Scholder is his reliance on Robert Katz. Cornwell says Katz provides "the most authoritative account" of the roundup of Roman Jews in October 1943.[63] Cornwell goes on to explain that Katz was sued by Pacelli's sister and nephew (actually it was his niece) for libel, but he incorrectly reports that the case was ultimately ruled "inconclusive."[64] In Rome, I was provided with a copy of the Italian Supreme Court's decision on this matter. The case actually was based on a film made from one of Katz's books. The Court ruled that "Robert Katz wished to defame Pius XII, attributing to him actions, decisions and sentiments which no objective fact and no witness authorized him to do."[65] Katz was fined 400,000 Lire and given a 13-month suspended prison sentence.[66] Someone truly interested in the truth about Pius XII would have been dissuaded from relying on any of Katz's work.

Cornwell begins his analysis of Eugenio Pacelli's life by looking at his childhood. Because he is trying to build a case for calling Pacelli anti-Semitic, he does not mention Eugenio's friendship with a Jewish schoolmate.[67] Instead, he tells an incorrect story about the young boy's teacher. According to Cornwell, the headmaster of Eugenio's school "was in the habit of making speeches from his high desk about the 'hard-heartedness of the Jews.'"[68] Cornwell cites for this proposition N. Padellaro, *Portrait of Pius XII*, the English translation.[69] The original Italian version of this work, however, provides the true quotation about young Pacelli's headmaster: he scolded "not against hard-hearted Jews, but against block-headed pupils."[70] An error in translation completely changed the meaning of the whole incident.

Another mistake about young Pacelli's schooling relates to an essay he wrote while enrolled in a secular school. According to Cornwell, "For an essay assignment on a 'favorite' historical figure, Pacelli is said to have chosen Augustine of Hippo, prompting sneers

Hitler's Pope Chapter	Note #.in Hitler's Pope	Vatican Transcript Page	Witness	Subject Matter of Testimony
Intro		229	Carlo Pacelli (nephew)	Height and Weight of Pius.
1	7	30	Gugliemo Hentrich (professor)	No heat in Pacelli's childhood home
1	14	109	Pascalina Lehnert (sister)	Young Pacelli had unusual sense of control over self.
1	20	3	Elisabetha Pacelli (sister)	Family brought him food when he was in seminary.
2	4	255-56	Maria Teresa Pacelli (cousin)	Young cousin felt that she could confide in him.
2	5	256	Maria Teresa Pacelli	Older, the same cousin found him open, modest, humble, reserved but cheerful, and marked by simplicity
5	26	6	Guglielmo Hentrich	1920s problems between members of Nuncio Pacelli's domestic staff.
5	27	6	Guglielmo Hentrich	Pacelli pleased when accusations of a romance between him and his housekeeper were disproved.
5	28	69	Suora Ignazia Caterina Kayser (member of religious order)	Priest/Assistant thought Nuncio Pacelli should fire his housekeeper.
6	18	54	Hans Struth (journalist)	Pacelli blessed crowds as he left Germany.
7	12	6	Elisabetha Pacelli	Domestic quarrel between housekeeper and staff.
11	13	12	Guglielmo Hentrich	Pacelli's nephew took photo of housekeeper in an embarrassing position with a man.
15	3	31	Guglielmo Hentrich	Pius slept no more than 4 hours/night during the war.
16	22	85	Pascalina	Pius decides to burn notes of condemnation due to news of persecution of Baptized Jews in Holland.
17	31	831	Gen. Carlo F. Wolff (SS Comander)	Wolff talks with Hitler about occupation of Vatican
17	32	832-33	General Carlo F. Wolff	Hitler makes "dark threats" against Vatican

17	33	832	Gen. Carlo F. Wolff	Hitler orders occupation of Vatican, kidnaping of Pope.
17	34	834	Gen. Carlo F.Wolff	Wolff tries to thwart Hitler's plans.
17	35	836-37	Gen. Carlo F.Wolff	Wolff urges Hitler to drop plans against Vatican.
18	14	340	Quirino Paganuzzi (worked in Vatican)	Pius got on knees and apologized to priest with whom he had been sharp.
20	3	102	Pascalina Lehnert	Pius says that a Pope must be perfect, but not others.
20	4	334	Quirino Paganuzzi	Pius stayed up late to return books and files to their proper place.
20	8	89	Pascalina Lehnert	Companion did not share the vision seen by Pius.
20	10	219	Carlo Pacelli	There was a rumor that Pius XII's housekeeper interrupted an important meeting.
20	13	37	Guglielmo Hentrich	Pius did not think beauty contests were good for women.
20	14	249	Virginio Rotondi (journalist)	Pius rejected a candidate for sainthood due to his use of obscene language.
20	15	210	Giacomo Martegani (radio and newspaper man)	Pius warned priests to avoid temptation by avoiding trips with young women.
20	23	229	Carlo Pacelli	Pius had dental problems.
20	26	276	Cesidio Lolli (newspaper writer)	Pius XII's health problems.
20	27	227	Carlo Pacelli	Pius changed doctors.

from his classmates. When he attempted to expand a little on the history of Christian civilization, a theme absent in the curriculum, his teacher chided him...."[71] Cornwell offers no citation for this incident with the authoritarian teacher, but German scholars have written on this matter. The teacher involved is Professor Della Giovanna. Cornwell, however, got the story wrong. The professor Giovanna did not chide young Eugenio; rather, Della Giovanna praised the young boy for his willingness to stand up for his beliefs.[72]   The event was precisely the opposite of what Cornwell would have his readers believe.

These errors relating to Pacelli's schooling would seem rather trivial, but Cornwell builds them up significantly. He argues that as a young boy, Pacelli saw anti-Semitism and authoritarianism in the men he respected and goes on to argue that "the impressions gained by small children are never lost."[73] As it turns out, however, Pacelli had good teachers, and the impressions made on him as a boy were indeed never lost.

Cornwell criticizes Pacelli for his efforts on a project that he worked on shortly after his ordination. In 1903, Pope Pius X assigned the young Pacelli to a team charged with codifying Church canon law. For the next decade and a half, he served as a research aide in the office of the Congregation of Ecclesiastical Affairs helping take Church law which had been built up over a thousand years and reducing it to a single code which could easily be referenced. This was much more manageable than the edicts, papal encyclicals, instructions, decrees, regulations, and precedents which were confused and perhaps even contradictory. In fact, "most theologians view centralization as a vast improvement over what went before."[74] Cornwell, however, argues that this code is what eventually led to the rise of Hitler, and he argues that the blame should fall to Pacelli.[75]

As an initial matter, codification projects reduce various pronouncements into a single code, but they do not create fundamentally different rules.[76] The rules in the code were fully in force prior to being codified. Certainly a junior prelate like Pacelli had no authority to write new law. Not only did the codification team have to agree that the new code reflected existing Church law, the code also had to be approved by the Holy See.[77] Pope Pius X commissioned the process, and Pope Benedict XV received and approved what became known as the 1917 Code of Canon Law. To assert that Pacelli, who was nothing more than a promising young diplomat at the time, rewrote Church law in this process is to credit him with far more authority than he (or any other individual) actually had.[78]

Cornwell elaborates his argument by saying that Pacelli spent the rest of his life trying to impose the code on Catholic churches throughout the world by reaching agreements with civil governments. As these concordats were signed, according to Cornwell, local priests and bishops lost the ability to complain about injustices that they saw. "Political" disputes were instead handled through Rome. The first concordat about which Cornwell complains was signed by the Vatican and Serbia in 1914.

Cornwell argues that Pacelli was the driving force behind the 1914 concordat, and he further suggests that this concordat led to World War I. Cornwell argues that the Serbian concordat "implied the abrogation of the ancient protectorate rights of the Austro-Hungarian Empire over the Catholic enclaves in Serbia's territories."[79] He explains that this threatened the influence of Emperor Franz Josef.[80] He goes on to report that "Vienna reacted to news of the concordat with outrage."[81] He quotes opposition newspapers *Die Zeit* and *Arbeiterzeitung* expressing the anger that, according to Cornwell, led to the First World War.[82] Cornwell, however, leaves out some important details.

Cornwell ominously suggests that all of the various materials were "once in the keeping of Eugenio Pacelli."[83] Of course they were. Pacelli was a junior member of the Vatican team, and his primary obligation was to take minutes at the negotiations. This does not suggest that he was an important participant in setting terms of the agreement. In fact, it tends to suggest the opposite. As one reviewer wrote, blaming Pacelli for what took place is tantamount to blaming the "minute taker for the minutes."[84] More importantly, however, as even critics of the Vatican have concluded, the Serbian concordat was absolutely irrelevant to the outbreak of war.[85]

For his authority, Cornwell cites a secondary source,[86] but in the Vatican archives, in a fascicle that was signed out to John Cornwell while he was researching his book,[86] is a hand-written letter from the nuncio in Vienna back to the Vatican Secretary of State in Rome, where negotiations for the concordat were taking place. That letter, dated June 24, 1914, reports that Vienna had no displeasure with the negotiations for the concordat. According to that dispatch, the opposition press argued that this concordat was a defeat for Austria/Hungarian diplomacy (these are the newspapers Cornwell cites in his book), but the "serious press" agreed that this was the only solution to the difficult problems regarding religious interests in Serbia.[88] The nuncio went on to explain that the Austria/Hungarian government has from the very beginning been informed about the negotiations in Rome and has followed them with "benevolent interest."[89] The conclusion of the concordat is what Austria/Hungary has wanted for Catholics and, as was published in the government's newspaper, was in accord with the government's wishes.[90] In fact, the government issued a publication noting the praiseworthiness of the proposed concordat.[91] The thesis that a power-driven Pacelli forced this concordat despite the risk of war is a wild accusation that is completely contradicted by the evidence.[92]

Cornwell writes of Pacelli's 1917 departure to become the nuncio in Munich that: "not only had Pacelli commandeered his own private compartment, but an additional sealed carriage had been added to the train to transport sixty cases of groceries to ensure that his troublesome stomach would not be affected by the food of wartime Germany."[93] For his authority, Cornwell cites the diary of Carlo Monti, which was published by the Vatican in 1997.[94]

Monti reported the facts, as outlined above, to Pope Benedict shortly after Pacelli's departure. Monti wrote that the Pope was scandalized.[95] However, the introduction to the diary explains that Pacelli had angered Monti sometime prior to the 1917 departure by refusing to meet with him. At that time, Monti complained to Pope Benedict, hoping that he would rebuke Pacelli. The Pope, however, sided with Pacelli. Now, as Pacelli was leaving Rome, Monti again sought to have the Pontiff rebuke Pacelli. Had Benedict truly been scandalized, he certainly would have rebuked the new nuncio. He did not do so, however, because he well knew that Pacelli—who would later go on a war-rations diet though he had food—was actually taking the food to provide for the war-torn city, prisoners of war, and others.[96] This is explained in the very text that Cornwell cites.[97] The Pope ignored the scandalous claim by Monti with good reason. Anyone who was really interested in finding the truth—instead of just creating a scandal—should also have seen through this absurd charge.

Cornwell argues that Pacelli, as nuncio and Secretary of State, withdrew support from the Catholic Center Party in Germany, transferring power to the Holy See. In particular, Cornwell faults Pacelli for having negotiated the 1933 concordat with Germany. This agreement, according to Cornwell, silenced political priests and bishops who might have held Hitler in check.

The Holy See's concordat with Germany has long been a matter that critics use to cast aspersions. Cornwell's twist is that he admits that Pacelli had no sympathy for the Nazi regime. "He didn't like Hitler," Cornwell says. "He didn't like the Nazis. He hated them. But he was enthralled with the notion of power and control from the center."[98] According to Cornwell, Pacelli (not Pope Pius XI) agreed to the concordat in the interest of imposing papal absolutism on the Church in Germany.

As an initial matter, it should be noted that the 1917 Code applied to German Catholic churches before the concordat was signed. The Code, being a compilation of Church teaching over the years, was binding as soon as it was approved by the Holy See. In fact, the contents of the Code (which came from papal statements, encyclicals, and other authoritative teachings) was binding even before the Code itself was completed. Thus, contrary to Cornwell's claim that the Code was at the heart of this agreement, the concordat itself does not even mention the 1917 Code.

The concordat did exclude the German clergy from party politics, but it imposed no such restrictions on the Catholic laity. The relevant provision, paragraph 32 of the concordat, said: "the Holy See will prescribe regulations which will prohibit *clergymen and members of religious institutes* from membership in political parties and from working on their behalf"(emphasis added).[99] The supplemental protocol relating to this paragraph said: "The conduct enjoined upon the pastors and members of religious institutes in Germany does not entail any limitation of the prescribed preaching and interpretation of the dogmatic and moral teachings and principles of the Church."[100]

Cornwell argues that direct political involvement by the Church could have held Hitler in check, but that Pacelli, the 1917 Code, and the concordat all served to restrict this possibility in order to centralize the Vatican's authority. This criticism is based upon four assumptions: 1) that Pacelli made the decision, not Pius XI; 2) that the party would have remained viable; 3) that the party would have opposed Hitler; and 4) that the concordat effectively silenced the German bishops. Three of these four assumptions are demonstrably false, and the fourth is far from certain.

As for the assumption that Pacelli was the driving force behind the concordat, Cornwell again credits (or blames) Pacelli for decisions that were far beyond his control. Cornwell seems to think that Pacelli was the instigator of all the international moves that took place while he was Secretary of State.[101] That is not, however, the way that diplomats saw it at the time. Reporting back to London on the prospects of the 1939 papal election, the British Minister to the Holy See, Francis D'Arcy Osborne, wrote that "it was always [Pacelli's] task to execute the policy of the late Pope rather than to initiate his own."[102]

In fact, Osborne reported that Pacelli had not garnered the ill will typically found between the Secretary of State and other cardinals precisely because he only carried out Pius XI's objectives.[103] Contrary to what Cornwell would have us believe, Secretary of State Pacelli took pride in executing the will of his Pope, Pius XI. The Pontiff himself said, "Cardinal Pacelli speaks with my voice."[104] Either young Pacelli dominated the Church's international policies years before he had any true authority (as Cornwell asserts) or he carried out the will of his superiors (as Pope Pius XI and others who actually knew Pacelli said). Cornwell's argument is at odds with all relevant evidence.[105] .

As to Cornwell's assumption that the Catholic Center Party in Germany would have remained viable but for the concordat, it too must fail. Hitler's power was sufficiently secure, and his means sufficiently brutal, that by March 1933 no religious institution could really stand up to him.[106] Moreover, neither the concordat nor Church doctrine prohibited Catholic laypersons from being involved in politics.[107] That was not, however, the Nazis' plan. They alone, not the concordat, brought down the Center Party.

The Catholic Center Party was seriously weakened and almost eliminated by the Nazis in March 1933.[108] For the next three months, the Nazis brutalized the remaining members of the Center Party as well as other Catholics. On July 5, 1933, two weeks before the concordat was signed, the party membership decided to dissolve voluntarily in the hope that his would stop the persecution.[109] Again, Cornwell has blamed Pacelli for decisions that were not his to make.

Even Cornwell's assumption that the Catholic Center Party would have opposed Hitler but for the concordat is subject to question. "The party was split and many Roman Catholics were attracted by the early achievements of the Nazis, as were most Germans."[110] Today one wonders how this could have been possible. At the time, however, Hitler promised to provide economic prosperity, free Germany from the Treaty of Versailles, end daily street fighting, and promote a form of social justice.[111] While all of these points were popular with German people, the term "social justice" had particular meaning to Catholics. This term was used in the United States by both social activist Dorothy Day (whose political leanings were clearly to the left) and Fr. Charles Coughlin (whose anti-New Deal radio broadcasts were sometimes associated with Fascism).[112] When Hitler's socialistic programs seemed to help people who had been in need, and he used a term that Catholic leaders across the political spectrum sometimes used, it is easy enough to see how some Catholics might have been attracted to his policies.[113]

Cornwell argues that the concordat created an opening for Hitler by withdrawing support from clergy participation in the political parties. It must be noted, however, that only one party remained in Germany—the National Socialists. The concordat provided Catholic clergy with a reason to decline membership in that party. Many Protestant ministers, not protected by a concordat, were coerced into joining the Nazis.

Cornwell's assumption that German bishops would have been outspoken against the Nazi regime but were silenced by the concordat, is wrong. The German bishops voted to ask Pacelli to ratify the concordat without delay.[114] They understood, as Cornwell does not, that they would not be silenced by the concordat. The supplemental protocol relating to paragraph 32 of the concordat made clear that the German clergy was not prohibited or even limited in preaching about "the dogmatic and moral teachings and principles of the Church." As such, the concordat set forth traditional Church teaching about politics and the clergy. Priests and bishops are not supposed to take sides on matters of economics and politics unless they deal with human dignity or the right and ability of the Church to carry out her mission. When it comes to those matters, however, the clergy are free to speak, even if that means talking about politics.[115] The concordat, in fact, did no more than assert traditional Church teaching (predating the 1917 Code of Canon Law) when it limited the participation of clergy in party politics.[116]

Throughout the book, Cornwell condemns Pacelli for matters that were beyond his control. Perhaps nowhere is this better illustrated than when Cornwell discusses the so-called "hidden encyclical." This episode has been cited by many critics of Pius XII, but Cornwell presents a new twist. The traditional story told by critics of Pius XII (as set forth in Chapter 18) is that Pius XI was prepared to make a strong anti-Nazi statement, but he died too soon. His successor, Pius XII, then buried the draft.

One of the problems with the traditional story is that the original draft contained some anti-Semitic statements. Critics of Pius XII usually are reluctant to attribute such sentiments to Pius XI. Cornwell resolved this problem by accusing Pacelli of having written the original draft of the encyclical when he was Secretary of State, then burying it when he was Pope.[117] (In fact, Cornwell even suggests that he suppressed the encyclical while he was still Secretary of State, during Pius XI's illness.)[118] Thus, Cornwell criticizes Pius twice. It is really too great a stretch of logic to be considered legitimate. There is, in fact, no evidence that either Pope ever saw the original draft, and there is absolutely no evidence that Pacelli had anything to do with the drafting of this text.

The ability of Pacelli to dominate the policy of the Holy See, long before he held any real position of authority, is central to Cornwell's thesis.[119] As *The New York Times* reported on October 2, 1999:

> If Pius XII was "Hitler's pawn," as Mr. Cornwell writes, then everyone else was Pacelli's pawn. No one seems to act from motives or principles, virtues or vices, independent of his, not the German bishops, the Center Party leaders or even Pius's predecessor, Pius XI. One chapter describes the young Pacelli's hand in the negotiation of a June 1914 concordat with Serbia, and the reader ends up wondering whether this man did not also start World War I![120]

Certainly Cornwell, who described Pope Pius XI as "bossy," "an autocrat," and "one of the most self-willed pontiffs in the recent history of the papacy,"[121] knows that Pacelli was unable to dominate the Vatican as Secretary of State, much less as nuncio. In fact, Cornwell himself notes that some cardinals opposed elevating Pacelli to the papacy because he might "prove too weak after serving under such a forceful Pope."[122]

Another fundamental point in Cornwell's overall thesis is the claim that Pacelli was an anti-Semite.[123] This is a rare allegation, even for critics of Pius XII, but Cornwell claims to have found two pieces of evidence to support his claim. They come from 1917-19, when Eugenio Pacelli was a nuncio in Munich. Cornwell looks at these two events in the worst light possible and concludes that they are consistent with anti-Semitism. That conclusion, however, is farfetched. In fact, putting these two minor points up against a lifetime of work, it is clear that Pius was not anti-Semitic.[124]

The first of the two supposedly new discoveries is a letter written in 1917. It seems that a rabbi requested Pacelli's assistance in obtaining palm fronds from Italy to be used in a synagogue festival. Pacelli apparently offered to try, but—in the middle of a nation torn by World War—it was not easy to comply, especially since the Vatican did not have diplomatic relations with Italy at that time. In fact, with Italy and Germany at war, such assistance would have been in direct violation of Italian dictates.[125] In his report back to Rome, Pacelli said that he declined to offer help because the assistance sought was not in a matter pertaining to "civil or natural rights common to all human beings," but rather in a matter pertaining to the ceremony of a "Jewish cult."[126] Pacelli also noted that the rabbi understood the difficulty and thanked him for his efforts.[127]

As in initial matter, Cornwell completely overlooks the importance of Pacelli's qualification. In the report to Rome, Pacelli clearly indicated his belief that if this matter had pertained to civil or natural rights (e.g. "human rights"), he would have been obliged to offer help. He did not, however, see any similar duty to help another religion conduct a ceremony.

Another difficulty with this letter is the pejorative meaning that is today associated with the word "cult." The actual Italian word used by Pacelli was "culto." The first three meanings for this word in *Webster's 3rd International Dictionary* all deal with religious rites and worship. The Vatican still uses the word to refer to the Church's own rites and worship, such as "the cults of the saints" and "the cult of the Virgin Mary." Thus, the word does not carry any derogatory connotation.[128] Cornwell is well aware of this non-pejorative meaning, as he uses the term several times himself.[129] To stretch the word to include an anti-Semitic sentiment really reflects Cornwell's ill-disguised motive. In fact, the Rabbi's willingness to approach Pacelli for help like this would seem to indicate that Pacelli had a reputation for being friendly to Jews.

A more controversial letter was written in 1919. That year, Bolshevik revolutionaries temporarily took power in Bavaria. Most foreign dignitaries left Munich, but Pacelli decided to stay at his post, and he became a target of Bolshevik hostility.[130] As Cornwell himself acknowledges, one time a car sprayed Pacelli's residence with machinegun fire.[131] Another time, a small group of Bolsheviks broke into the nunciature, threatened Pacelli with pointed revolvers, and tried to rob him.[132] Yet another time an angry mob descended on Pacelli's car, yelling blasphemies and threatening to turn the car over.[133] In the last two episodes, Pacelli directly addressed the gangs and convinced them to abandon their assault.

The Bolsheviks were not, however, dissuaded from occupying the royal palace in Munich. In a letter to Rome, sent over Pacelli's signature, the occupation of the palace was described as follows:

A gang of young women, of dubious appearance, Jews like the rest of them, hanging around in all the offices with lecherous demeanor and suggestive smiles. The boss of this rabble was a young Russian woman, a Jew and a divorcee (while their chief) is a young man of about 30 or 35, also Russian and a Jew. Pale, dirty, with vacant eyes, hoarse voice, vulgar, repulsive, with a face that is both intelligent and sly.[134]

For Cornwell the use of the words Jew and Jews, together with unflattering descriptions of the revolutionaries, gives an impression of "stereotypical anti-Semitic contempt."[135]

Pacelli's letter is six pages long, but Cornwell quotes only two paragraphs describing a chaotic incident at a former royal palace taken over by revolutionaries. While these lines do read badly, "the trouble is that it seems to be largely true. The 1919 Munich terror was led by Russian Jewish Bolsheviks. They did murder people. They were very frightening."[136] Moreover, as Cornwell himself explains, Pacelli had not witnessed the scene he described in this letter. His assistant, Monsignor Schioppa, is the one who actually went to the palace. Pacelli did no more than relate Schioppa's description.[136]

The choice of words in the letter would certainly have to be considered offensive by today's standards, but the disrespect reflected in the language does not stem from racial or even religious differences, but from the Bolshevik activity in Munich. There was clear animosity between the Church and the revolutionaries, and those revolutionaries are the focus of the comment, not all Jewish people.[138] It should also be noted that the message was written fourteen years before Hitler came to power and the Jewish persecution began. The language used to describe a similar event in 1943 might well have been very different.[139]

When one considers all of these factors put together (it was an actual description, written by another, who was mad at the revolutionaries because they had attacked the Church, and the anger was directed at a small group, not Jews in general, etc.) anti-Semitism is hardly even a debatable point. Going further, however, and stacking this up against the rest of Pacelli's life, there is simply no case for anti-Semitism.

Rather than focusing on indirect evidence from the World War I era and fabricating an argument, one could look to direct, on-point evidence from that same period. On December 15, 1915, the

American Jewish Committee of New York petitioned the Vatican for a statement on the "ill-treatment" suffered by Jewish people in Poland.[140] The response came from the office of the Secretary of State, where Eugenio Pacelli was working hand-in-hand with Cardinal Gasparri.[141] It said:

> The Supreme Pontiff... as Head of the Catholic Church, which, faithful to its divine doctrine and to its most glorious traditions, considers all men as brothers and teaches them to love one another, he never ceases to inculcate among individuals, as well as among peoples, the observance of the principles of natural law and to condemn everything which violates them. *This law must be observed and respected in the case of the children of Israel, as well as of all others, because it would not be conformable to justice or to religion itself to derogate from it solely on account of religious confessions.* The Supreme Pontiff at this moment feels in his fatherly heart... the necessity for all men of remembering that they are brothers and that their salvation lies in the return to the law of love which is the law of the Gospel.[142]

This is clearly a much better indication of Pacelli's understanding of Catholic teaching on anti-Semitism and the proper relation that should exist between Catholics and Jews. Unfortunately for Cornwell, it disproves his point.

On a related matter, Cornwell suggests that the deportation of Jews from Rome on October 16, 1943, did not sufficiently concern Pius XII. The details of this matter are discussed in Chapter 14 of this book, but one point needs to be mentioned here. Part of the "evidence" cited by Cornwell is a message sent from U.S. official Harold Tittmann to the State Department regarding a meeting he had with Pius.[143] The message is dated October 19, and reports not the Pope's outrage at the Nazis roundup a few days earlier, but his concern that "Communist bands" might "commit violence in the city."[144] If things were actually as Cornwell reports them, Pius would indeed appear indifferent to this Nazi abuse of Jewish people. Such, however, is not the case.

The Vatican keeps very precise records of audiences given by the Pope. The transcribed message to Washington from Harold Tittmann is dated October 19th, but this is a mistake. Vatican records show that the meeting between Pius and Tittmann took place on October 14.[145] In fact, *L'Osservatore Romano* of October 15/16, 1943 reports on page one that Tittmann was received by the Pope in a private audience on October 14, 1943.[146] Apparently a handwritten 4 was misread as a 9 when the documents were typed. The Pope did not mention the roundup of Jews because it had not yet happened! His concern was that a group of Communists would commit a violent act and this would lead to serious repercussions. Of course, he proved exactly correct the following spring.[147]

My work in Rome did cause me to re-think one aspect of my analysis. Up until this point in time I had not placed much faith in an event regularly cited by supporters of Pius XII, namely the anti-Hitler statement that he is supposed to have burned upon learning of the deportation of Catholic Jews in Holland (including Edith Stein)[148] in retaliation for the protest by Catholic bishops.[149] I had discounted this for two reasons. The first is that I believe Pius XII determined the course he would take very early in his Pontificate, and an express condemnation of any party would represent a departure from that course. The second reason was that this story is usually attributed solely to Sr. Pascalina. The book *La Popessa* purports to give her story, but it seems rather far-fetched in many respects.[150] Accordingly, when I read Cornwell's arguments against the validity of this story, I was pleased to find that I had only two brief references to it in my manuscript and they were both in endnotes. My opinion about this event began to change, however, when I got to Rome.

Although the book *La Popessa* is subject to criticism, Pascalina's German autobiography, *Ich durfte ihm dienen: Erinnerungen an Papst Pius XII,* is much better accepted. Moreover, she testified under oath to this event at the Vatican, and in Rome I was able to review the transcript of that testimony and speak to people who knew her.[151] They all vouched for her veracity. More importantly, I discovered that another witness, Maria Conrada Grabmair, also testified to the same event.[152] Pascalina and Grabmair were both domestic workers who claim that they saw Pius XII burn some paper on which he had been writing. Pascalina testified that the Pope said that "if the letter of the bishops has cost the lives of 40,000 persons, my own protest... could cost the lives of perhaps 200,000 Jews," and that statement is the focus of Cornwell's criticism. Grabmair did not claim to hear any such statement.[153]

Grabmair worked in the Pope's kitchen. She testified that Pius brought two pieces of paper over to the stove and watched them burn completely. This was unusual because at other times when he wanted to dispose of papers, he would hand them to her and leave. This time he burned them himself and stayed until he knew then were completely destroyed.[154] Grabmair testified that she later was told by

Sr. Pascalina and by Fr. Robert Leiber that this was a draft of a document that Pius decided to burn after he was informed about the disastrous consequences of the public protest by the bishops of Holland against the deportation of Jews from that nation.[155] While such "hearsay" evidence would not be conclusive by itself, it strongly supports Pascalina's testimony and makes the entire event more believable.

The burning of this paper is important in this respect: Since the Nazis decided on the Final Solution in early 1942, and word began filtering to Rome in the spring and summer of 1942, it is at least possible (giving the Vatican time to confirm reports) that this was the Pope's first serious consideration of an express denunciation of the Nazi treatment of the Jews. The exact date of the incident is lost, but since the deportation of Catholic Jews in Holland occurred in midsummer, it probably took place in the autumn of 1942.

These witnesses do not claim to have seen the contents of the document. They only state that the Pope said he wanted to publish it in *L'Osservatore Romano*. This could have been similar to the other anonymous statements that were published in the paper during the war. Alternatively, it might have been similar to the type of statement that Pius made later this same year in his Christmas address. In fact, this might have been an early version of that Christmas address.

Cornwell correctly notes that the numbers cited by Sr. Pascalina could not be correct.[156] The Pope might have had incorrect information. There was no nuncio in Holland at the time, since he had been expelled by the Nazis, so Pius learned of these events from newspapers and radio accounts. According to some people I spoke with in Rome, numbers like this were reported in news broadcasts. Alternatively, he might have meant 40,000 people altogether (which is what he said, not 40,000 Jews as others sometimes assume), he might have made a misstatement since he was off-the-record and speaking only to his household help, Pascalina may have misunderstood what he said (she is the only witness who claims to have heard these numbers), or her memory may have failed before she testified. The fact remains that open condemnation by the Catholic bishops led to greater persecution in Holland, and the Pope knew that a statement from him would have had a magnified effect. The truth of the logic stands, regardless of the precise numbers involved, and I now believe that there is more validity to this story than I had previously supposed.

The only occupied nation to merit a full chapter in Cornwell's book is Croatia. This is not surprising since the activities of the Church in opposing Nazism in Germany, Italy, Austria, Czechoslovakia, France, Poland, Holland, Denmark, and elsewhere are well documented. As such, many modern critics have had to turn to Croatia—where details from the war era are less well established—to raise questions about the Church's relationship with the Nazis.

Croatia came into being during the war. On March 25, 1941, Italy, Germany, and Yugoslavia signed an agreement bringing Yugoslavia into the Axis. Two days later, a group of Serbian nationalists seized control of Belgrade and announced that they were siding with the Allies.[157] As a result, Hitler invaded Yugoslavia. Croat Fascists then declared an independent Croatia. The new Croat government was led by Ante Pavelic and his group, the Ustashe.

There had been a long history of hatred in this part of the world between Croats (predominantly Catholic) and Serbs (mainly Orthodox). The Ustashi government exacted revenge against the Serbs for years of perceived discrimination.[158] According to some accounts, as many as 700,000 Serbs were slaughtered.[159] Among the charges against the Catholic Church in Croatia are that it engaged in forcible conversions, that Church officials hid Croat Nazis after the war, that Nazi gold made its way from Croatia to the Vatican, and that Catholic leaders in Croatia supported the government's brutality toward the Serbs.

While some of these charges are recent in origin (and from suspect sources), there is no credible evidence that the Pope or the Vatican behaved inappropriately. For instance, the Vatican expressly repudiated forcible conversions in a memorandum, dated January 25, 1942, from the Vatican Secretariat of State to the Legation of Yugoslavia to the Holy See (addressing conversions in Croatia).[160] In August of that year, the Grand Rabbi of Zagreb, Dr. Miroslav Freiberger, wrote to Pius XII expressing his "most profound gratitude" for the "limitless goodness that the representatives of the Holy See and the leaders of the Church showed to our poor brothers."[161] In October, a message went out from the Vatican to its representatives in Zagreb regarding the "painful situation that spills out against the Jews in Croatia" and instructing them to petition the government for "a more benevolent treatment of those unfortunates."[162] In December 1942, Dr. Freiberger wrote again, expressing his confidence "in the support of the Holy See."

The Cardinal Secretary of State's notes reflect that Vatican petitions were successful in getting a suspension of "dispatches of Jews from Croatia" by January 1943, but Germany was applying pressure for "an attitude more firm against the Jews."[164] Maglione went on to outline various steps that could be taken by the Holy See to help the Jews.[165] Another instruction from the Holy See to its unofficial representatives (since there were no diplomatic relations) in Zagreb directing them to work on behalf of the Jews went out on March 6, 1943.[166]

Croatian Archbishop Alojzij Stepinac originally welcomed the Ustashe government, but after he learned of the extent of the brutality, and after having received direction from Rome,[167] he condemned its actions.[168] A speech he gave on October 24, 1942, is typical of many that he made refuting Nazi theory:

> All men and all races are children of God; all without distinction. Those who are Gypsies, Black, European, or Aryan all have the same rights.... for this reason, the Catholic Church had always condemned, and continues to condemn, all injustice and all violence committed in the name of theories of class, race, or nationality. It is not permissible to persecute Gypsies or Jews because they are thought to be an inferior race.[169]

The Associated Press reported that "by 1942 Stepinac had become a harsh critic" of that Nazi puppet regime, condemning its "genocidal policies, which killed tens of thousands of Serbs, Jews, Gypsies and Croats."[170] He thereby earned the enmity of the Croatian dictator, Ante Pavelic.[171] Although Cornwell argues that the Holy See granted de facto recognition to the Ustashi government,[173] in actuality the Vatican rebuked Pavelic and refused to recognize the Independent State of Croatia or receive a Croatian representative.[173] When Pavelic traveled to the Vatican, he was greatly angered because he was permitted only a private audience rather than the diplomatic audience he had wanted.[174] He might not even have been granted that privilege, but for the fact that the extent of the atrocities that had already begun were not yet known.

In 1944-45, Communist partisans under Josip Broz Tito conquered the Balkans, occupied Zagreb, and established the Socialist Federation of Yugoslavia. That government immediately undertook severe prosecution of the Catholic Church, confiscating property, closing seminaries and schools, banning Masses, and persecuting clergy. Before coming to power, the Communists had "used

Stepinac's speeches in their propaganda, as the Cardinal always spoke against the Nazi occupation and against the violation of human rights committed by Pavelic. Stepinac cried out against all injustice, especially against racism."[175] Now that they had power, however, Stepinac was a threat.

The Communists put Stepinac on trial for allegedly supporting the Ustashi government.[176] Pope Pius publicly protested the prosecution, noting that the cardinal had saved thousands of people from the Nazis. The president of the Jewish Community in the United States, Louis Braier, said that Stepinac was a "great man of the Church... [who] spoke openly and fearlessly against the racial law. After His Holiness, Pius XII, he was the greatest defender of the Jews in persecuted Europe."[177] (During the war, Meir Touval-Weltmann, a member of a commission to help European Jews, wrote a letter of thanks for all that the Holy See had done and enclosed a memorandum of thanks which stated: "Dr. Stepinac has done everything possible to aid and ease the unhappy fate of the Jews in Croatia.)[178]

Stepinac was sentenced to sixteen years of hard labor, but due to protests and indignation throughout the democratic world, and Jewish testimony as to the good work he had done, he was moved to house arrest in 1951. Almost immediately, Pope Pius XII raised him to the cardinalate. He died under house arrest in 1960.[179]

Croatia's Jewish community recently credited Stepinac with helping many Jews avoid Nazi persecution. In fact, one of the first acts of Parliament in the newly independent state of Croatia in 1992 was to issue a declaration condemning "the political trial and sentence passed on Cardinal Alojzij Stepinac in 1946."[180] Stepinac was condemned, declared the Parliament: "because he had acted against the violence and crimes of the communist authorities, just as he had acted during the whirlwind of atrocities committed in World War II, to protect the persecuted, regardless of the national origin or religious denomination."[181] He was beatified as a martyr on October 3, 1998, at which time Pope John Paul II described him as a man who had the strength to oppose the three great evils of our century—Fascism, Nazism, and Communism.[182]

Cornwell's problem with Croatia is simply that he has relied too strongly on post-war Communist propaganda. As more evidence comes to light, the situation in Croatia will look less and less like a problem for the Catholic Church and more like another case where the Church defied the Nazis.

Cornwell calls Pius XII a hypocrite for accepting praise following the war.[183] It is true that Pius received much praise from people who knew him best. Some have argued that these people did not know what Pius did during the war, and hence they were uninformed when they offered their thanks. But if "silence" was the shortcoming, how could people not have known about it? Did they think statements had been made, only to learn that they had not? No, they knew about the actions and behind-the-scenes maneuvers. That earned Pius their well-deserved appreciation.

The last chapter of Cornwell's book is entitled "Pius XII Redivivus." In it, Cornwell argues that John Paul II represents a return to a more highly centralized, autocratic papacy, as opposed to a more diversified Church.[184] He writes that there are early signs of a titanic struggle between the progressives and the traditionalists, with the potential for a cataclysmic schism, especially in North America.[185] Cornwell feels that John Paul II is leading the traditionalists as the Church moves toward this struggle, and he has argued that "canonization of Pius XII is a key move in the attempts to restore a reactionary papal absolutism."[186]

Cornwell decided that the easiest way to attack the Pope of today was to denigrate Pius XII.[187] If he can prove that Pius was deeply flawed, especially in the current process of canonization, then he can argue that popes can be politically motivated. If that is the case, then he can argue that John Paul II is politically wrong about celibacy, women priests, artificial contraception, abortion, and other matters. Importantly, if Cornwell undermines papal authority on matters such as political involvement of the clergy and the obedience of local prelates, he can argue that individual priests and bishops are free to engage in politics, even on matters unrelated to human dignity or the freedom of the Church. After all, according to Cornwell, Pius XII's greatest sin seems to have been restricting the freedom of local priests and bishops to become directly involved in politics.

In this final chapter, it becomes clear that Cornwell's understanding of Catholicism, politics, and especially Pope John Paul II is profoundly flawed. He has to deal with the fact that John Paul II played a pivotal role in the downfall of the Soviet Union. Cornwell's answer is that John Paul was directly involved in politics early in his pontificate (and that the "defining moment" of his pontificate came in 1979 when he encouraged Polish workers in their efforts that led to the eventual downfall of Soviet Communism),[188] but that he has retreated from politics, injuring the Church in the process.

Cornwell misses the important point that is so well explained in George Weigel's biography of Pope John Paul II, *Witness to Hope*. John Paul's political impact came about precisely because he did not primarily seek to be political, or to think or speak politically.[189] His strategy was culture-driven and evangelical.[190] The Pontiff's contribution to the downfall of the Soviet Union was that he launched an authentic and deep challenge to the lies that made Communistic rule possible.[191] He fought Communism in the same way that Pius XII fought Nazism: by challenging the intellectual foundation on which it was based.[192]

"One might argue that Weimar Germany possessed elegantly constructed democratic institutions. What it lacked was a public moral culture that held politics accountable to the higher standards, and ultimately to the higher sovereignty without which freedom cannot be sustained."[193] That made Germany vulnerable to an evil tyrant like Hitler. As nuncio, Secretary of State, and finally Pope, Eugenio Pacelli tried to bring about a "public moral culture" that would secure the future of Germany, Europe, and ultimately the world. Had he immersed the Church in secular politics without challenging the moral fabric of the ideology, his effort would have been in vain. As it was there was terrible suffering, but Pius XII planted seeds that are still bearing fruit.

Pope John Paul has recognized the parallels between his efforts and those of Pius XII, perhaps better than anyone else.[194] John Paul, of course, did not have a horrible war to contend with, nor was he threatened with the possibility of Vatican City being invaded, but given those differences, the approach each leader took was similar. As John Paul II has explained: "Anyone who does not limit himself to cheap polemics knows very well what Pius XII thought of the Nazi regime and how much he did to help countless people persecuted by the regime."[195]

John Cornwell recognized a division in the Catholic Church today, but rather than trying to discuss it honestly he has picked a target that he thought would be easy to attack, created a far-fetched theory, and ignored all evidence contrary to his thesis. Along the way, he has revealed a basic misunderstanding of modern history.[196] His book, which purports to be genuine scholarship, is unfortunately much less than that.[197]

AFTERWORD

BY ROBERT P. GEORGE

Since the German playwright Rolf Hochhuth in 1963 began the assault on the reputation of Eugenio Pacelli with a play (*Der Stellvertreter*) that depicted the war-time pope as indifferent toward Nazi atrocities, many decent people have innocently come to believe the myth that Pacelli, as Pope Pius XII, was "silent" in the face of the Holocaust, that he was an anti-semite and even a Nazi sympathizer (in the words of Martin Peretz "an enabler"), that he was, as the particularly vile title of a recent book labels him, "Hitler's Pope." Ronald Rychlak's patient and comprehensive historical study will, I'm sure, cause people of goodwill who read it, Jews and Christians alike, to revise their opinion of Pius XII. For them, the questions will become: Who created the myth? Why was it created? How did it come to be so widely credited?

Some say that these questions are best put aside. The important thing, they insist, is that Rychlak has buried the myth under an avalanche of facts and demonstrated that Pacelli's reputation deserves to be what it was during the war when the *New York Times*—more than once—praised him as "a lonely voice crying out of the silence of a continent," and after the war when Grand Rabbi Isaac Herzog of Jerusalem sent the Pope a special blessing for "his life-saving efforts on behalf of the Jews," and, at his death, when Golda Meir observed that "during the ten years of Nazi terror, when the Jewish people went through the horrors of martyrdom, the Pope raised his voice to condemn the persecutors and to commiserate with their victims." Those who would "table" questions of responsibility for the defamation of Pacelli say that dwelling on these questions will serve no useful purpose. They fear that it will impede the process of healing old wounds, particularly those arising from conflicts between "liberal" and "conservative" Catholics and between Jews and Christians.

I'm afraid that I cannot join those who would dispense with the demand for accountability. My reason is this: anti-Catholic bigots and anti-papal Catholics have a large stake in preserving the myth that Eugenio Pacelli was "Hitler's Pope." The myth is of enormous utility to their continuing efforts to undermine the credibility of the Catholic Church and the teaching authority (magisterium) exercised by the Pope and the bishops in communion with him. Consequently, they will almost certainly refuse to abandon the project of defaming Pius XII.

How will they deal with Rychlak? In all likelihood, they will ignore his work and hope that it goes unnoticed. If that strategy fails—if Rychlak's book is noticed—then I fear they will seek to defame him, just as they have defamed Pacelli. Who but an anti-semite, they will ask, would defend an anti-semitic pope? And the name "Rychlak"— doesn't that sound rather, well, Polish? And isn't Rychlak likely a Catholic himself? And aren't Polish Catholics congenital anti-sem- ites? I fear that bigotry will be deployed in the cause of false allega- tions of bigotry.

Indeed, the myth that Pius XII was "Hitler's pope" lives and breathes on anti-Catholic bigotry. It can do so for the simple reason that anti-Catholicism remains "the anti-semitism of intellectuals." Thus, as anyone who has spent time in the environment of a contem- porary American university can attest, anti-Catholicism can be expressed and practiced in elite circles without fear of the repercus- sions that attend manifestations of other forms of bigotry. The defam- atory falsehoods that have been spread about Pius XII—though many decent people have, as I say, innocently come to believe them—are not in their origins innocent errors. They originate in, and are to a large extent sustained as part of, a larger effort to undermine the credibili- ty and weaken the moral and cultural influence of the Catholic Church. Why? Because the Catholic Church—and, within the Church, the institution of the papacy—is the single most potent force on the side of traditional morality in cultural conflicts with commu- nism, utilitarianism, radical individualism, and other major secular- ist ideologies.

It goes without saying that the record of Catholic Christians, including some popes, is far from spotless. Indeed, throughout his- tory Catholics and other Christians—sometimes in the very name of Christianity—have behaved in grossly unChristian ways and brought dishonor on the Christian Church. Catholics have been guilty of their share of injustices. Often the victims of these injustices have been Jews. Bluntly confessing the historical reality and terrible conse- quences of anti-Jewish attitudes among Christians, and solemnly declaring all forms of anti-semitism to be gravely sinful, Pope John

Paul II has publicly—and, in my view, entirely rightly—acknowledged these offenses, taking particular note of the failure of many of the faithful to do what they could and should have done in the face of Hitler's atrocities.

As Rychlak shows, Eugenio Pacelli, though careful to preserve the Vatican's formal neutrality in the Second World War, was not among those who failed. Indeed, as Rychlak reports, long before John Paul II made his unprecedented visit to the Great Synagogue in Rome to declare that "the Jews are our brothers—indeed our elder brothers in faith"—Pius XII made the following remarks to a group of Roman Jews who came to thank him for having protected them from Nazi persecution:

> For centuries, Jews have been unjustly treated and despised. It is time they were treated with justice and humanity. God wills it and the Church wills it. St. Paul tells us that the Jews are our brothers. They should also be welcomed as friends.

Indeed, it is almost certainly true that Pius XII saved the lives of more Jewish and non-Jewish victims of Hitler's madness than any other human being. In the estimate of Israeli diplomat Pinchas Lapide, the Vatican and other Catholic institutions, acting at the Pope's express direction, saved the lives of more than 800,000 European Jews. Still, Pope John Paul II came in for criticism—even from people of goodwill—for not condemning his war-time predecessor for "indifference" to the plight of Hitler's Jewish victims—this despite the fact that no information has emerged that credibly does anything but confirm the judgment of Jewish leaders and organizations who, during and after the war, effusively praised Pius XII for his efforts to save Jewish lives.

In calling those responsible for the defamation of Pius XII to account, it is of supreme importance that Catholics avoid ascribing blame to Jewish people or organizations as such. Let us not forget that Jewish voices are well-represented among those who have praised and defended Pius XII. And if it is true that many Jews have today forgotten what Jewish leaders of the pope's own time in expressing their gratitude to him promised "never to forget," this failing of memory must be considered against the backdrop of a long history of all-too-well-founded suspicion and fear of Christians among Jews. Moreover, it would be a horrible sin, and a grave offense to the memory of Pius XII and his record of assistance to Hitler's Jewish victims, if the defense of his reputation against charges of anti-semitism became a cause or occasion of anti-semitism. Finally, let us be mindful that the defamation of Pius XII did not begin in the Jewish community, nor are those who most aggressively promote it today Jews. Far more often than not, they are disaffected Catholics whose real quarrel is with the Catholic theological principle of papal authority in matters of faith and morals.

Of course, there is a sense in which the dispute over Pius XII is inescapably a Jewish-Catholic issue. If the war-time pope was indeed a Nazi "enabler," how could the Jewish community not demand his repudiation? And how could the Catholic Church even consider his canonization? But in an even deeper sense, the dispute is internal to the Catholic Church. At issue is the nature and authority of the papal office. If Pius XII really was "Hitler's pope," it would be the duty of pro-papal Catholics to acknowledge and condemn his sins even as they insisted on the distinction between the authority of the office and the character of the man occupying it. It would be wrong for them to pretend that the pope was innocent in an effort to shore up support for the authority of the office. But, as Rychlak shows, the pope, in this case, was innocent. Indeed, in his remarkably successful efforts to save Jewish lives, Pius XII was truly Hitler's enemy. It will not do, then, for anti-papal Catholics to seek to undermine papal authority by defaming him. Their lies must be exposed. Rychlak has done more than anyone else to set the record straight.

A NOTE ON CITATION

Over the years, many books and articles have been written on this topic. Because they often contain conflicting accounts, or—more frequently—significant omissions, I have tried to provide citations for quotations and any controversial observations. This, I hope, will permit others who are so inclined to conduct further research.

The citation form is derived from the style used by lawyers. Endnotes refer to the work (usually by the name of the author) and typically provide the page where the relevant information is contained. By cross-referencing with the bibliography, it should be fairly simple to determine the source of the information. The date in the bibliography refers to the specific printing which I used.

ENDNOTES TO THE PREFACE

1. Tad Szulc, "An Interview with Pope John Paul II," *Parade Magazine*, April 3, 1994, at 6.

2. Chief Rabbi Herzog to Cardinal Maglione, May 1, 1939, *Actes et Documents*, vol. IV, p. 82-83 (no. 20).

3. Cardinal MacRory to Cardinal Maglione, May 19, 1940, in *Actes et Documents*, vol. VI, p. 306 (no. 201); Gaspari at 24; Blet, Chapter 9; Holmes at 154. Graham at 20.

4. Associated Press, "The Papal Visit: the Holocaust and Other Contentious Issues," *The New York Times*, September 12, 1987, section 1, page 8.

5. David Van Biema, "A Repentance, Sort Of; The Vatican issues a historic statement on the Holocaust but falls short of some Jewish hopes," *Time*, March 30, 1998, at 60.

6. Knight Ridder Newspapers, "Pope's silence during Holocaust debated," *Las Vegas Review-Journal*, March 22, 1998.

7. *Id.*

8. *Id.*

CHAPTER ONE
THE PAPACY AND THE WORLD

1. Vatican City also has a governor (during World War II this role was filled by Marchese Camillo Serafini). The governor is appointed by the Pontiff and is directly responsible to him. He has day-to-day control over the extensive gardens and technical services of Vatican City.

2. Korn at 125.

3. This dispute arose when Italian forces ousted the Pope from most of his temporal powers, claiming Church property for Italy. Due to his family's association with the Church, which was in conflict with the Italian government, young Eugenio encountered discrimination in school and elsewhere. Halecki & Murray at 8-11. More details are set forth in Chapter 4.

4. Hatch & Walsh at 32.

5. Apparently the young Pacelli was a handsome man. According to one account, "all the convent girls used to say–'Who could look at him and not love him!'" Cornwell at 33 (citing "Testimony of Maria Teresa Pacelli," before the Tribunal of the Vicariate of Rome, on the beatification of Pius XII).

6. While here, Pacelli served as an assistant lecturer in canon law. A young seminarian, Angelo Roncalli—the future Pope John XXIII—was impressed by his "understated brilliance" and felt that Pacelli was marked for

a bright future. Elliott at 32.

7. Church law had been built up over a thousand years of edicts, papal encyclicals, instructions, decrees, regulations, and precedents, each of which was applicable to its own era. By then they were confused and perhaps even contradictory. This project was designed to reduce the various pronouncements into a single code which could easily be referenced.

8. The ceremony took place on May 13, 1917, the same day that three young shepherd children in Fatima, Portugal reported their vision of Mary.

9. Deutsch at 109, n.14 (also noting Howard's distrust of Pope Benedict XV and his evaluation of Cardinal Gasparri as a charming but slippery old man).

10. Elliott at 73-74. Wilhelm did later, however, express his admiration for Pacelli's "distinguished sympathetic appearance, the high intelligence, and the impeccable manners." The Kaiser also called Pacelli "the prototype of a Roman prelate." Halecki & Murray at 37.

11. Hatch & Walsh at 77. The Vatican also proposed the exchange of war prisoners incapable of further military service. When that suggestion was favorably received, the Pope proposed including interned civilians who were unfit to serve in the armed forces. All these arrangements were negotiated through Pacelli's office, and it has been estimated that around 63,000 persons, chiefly from Belgium, Britain, France, and Germany, profited from such exchanges. Halecki & Murray at 29.

12. Halecki & Murray at 41-42; Hatch & Walsh at 74.

13. Cornwell at 60 (also noting that Pacelli "declined even a day's vacation" during the first three years of the war).

14. Benedict thought that impartiality would help the Vatican have some influence on the warring parties, so he resisted strong pressure to take sides. Cornwell at 60. The Italian government, still in conflict with the Vatican, pressured France, Great Britain, and Russia to keep the Holy See out of the post-war proceedings. Halecki & Murray at 27; Hatch & Walsh at 68.

15. Copeland at 352. French Premier Georges Clemenceau was not eager to provide Germany with much freedom. Regarding President Wilson's fourteen points, he said: "Why, God Almighty only had ten."

16. *Id.*

17. Not counting the territories annexed before and during World War II, Germany was at its largest just prior to the first World War. With the Treaty of Versailles, it lost significant territory to France, Poland, and Czechoslovakia.

18. The Italians also were not pleased with the peace proposal. They had wanted to be given certain lands as spoils of war, but the Allies did not agree. The Italian delegation left Paris in a rage. Though they returned to sign a treaty that did not give them the land they wanted, the incident disrupted the conference. It may also have shaped Italian attitudes about the Allied nations, giving Mussolini a reason to side with Germany in the next war. See generally Arno J. Mayer, *Politics and Diplomacy of Peacemaking: Containment and Counterrevolution at Versailles 1918-1919*, Harcourt (New York,1967).

19. The Weimar Constitution was widely acclaimed as one of the most democratic in the world. It featured universal adult suffrage; proportional representation; provisions for popular referenda, petition, and recall; and an extensive list of civil liberties. It created a dual executive: a chancellor as

head of government appointed by the president, and a directly elected president as chief of state. However, it also had a serious flaw: The president had the power to issue decrees in lieu of legislation if there was a state of emergency. This provision would be used before Hitler came to power, and that use would set the precedent for his abuse of power.

20. See M. Price at 155 (Hitler exhorts crowd to help Germany by hanging "the criminals of November 1918"). The majority of Jews in Germany at this time were Social Democrats and were identified with that part of the political spectrum. Friedlander (1997) at 75. This linkage of Jews with the group that had agreed to the 1918 surrender and accompanying penalties imposed on Germany may have been the final straw that sent Hitler over the edge and drove him to his fanatical beliefs.

CHAPTER TWO
HITLER AND THE POST-WAR WORLD

1. Alois & Klara were second cousins and therefore needed special dispensation from the Church to get married. Kershaw at 10.

2. Vienna of this era spawned "one of the most fertile, original and creative periods in art and architecture, music, literature and psychology, as well as in philosophy." Janik & Toulmin at 9. From this city came Sigmund Freud, Victor Adler, Arnold Schönberg, Adolf Loos, Oskar Kokoschka, Ernst Mach, and Ludwig Wittgenstein.

3. Kershaw at 57.

4. *Id.* at 44.

5. According to Hitler, Wagner "had really proclaimed the eternal tragedy of human destiny. He was not merely a musician and a poet; he was the supreme prophetic figure among Germans." Rauschning at 229 (also noting that Hitler attributed his vegetarianism to Wagner's writings on the subject).

6. Hitler would later say: "Whoever wants to understand National Socialist Germany must know Wagner." Shirer (1962) at 101. There is also some speculation that he became involved in certain occult activities, and that this is where he developed his extreme racial ideas.

7. Janik & Toulmin at 54.

8. Kershaw at 58; Lapomarda at 68.

9. Kershaw at 33-34, 58. Hitler came to believe that Schonerer had failed to achieve national prominence by openly opposing the Church and thereby antagonizing the people. Hitler would adopt the attitude, but try not to repeat the mistake.

10. Hannes Stein, "Return of the Gods," *First Things*, November 1999, at 34, 37,

11. *Id.*

12. *Id.*

13. *Id.*

14. *Id.*

15. Payne at 102, 166.

16. Hitler was not really a corporal in American terms. A U.S. Army corporal wears two stripes. Hitler's rank was *Gefreiter*; he had one stripe. Thus, he was the equivalent of a private first class. The British Army equivalent, however, is lance corporal, which accounts for the common assertion that he was a corporal.

17. Although he would maintain a largely German staff even after becoming Pope, none of them were compromised by German intelligence initiatives during the war. Alvarez & Graham at 175.

18. Pope Leo XIII's 1891 encyclical, *Rerum novarum*, remembered today primarily as the basis of Catholic social justice teaching, said that Marxism was incompatible with Catholicism.

19. Hatch & Walsh at 83. He did, however, briefly move to Switzerland, but he returned before the Bolsheviks were ousted. Cornwell at 73 (noting that he left no earlier than mid-November 1918 and was back by February 3, 1919 (if not sooner)).

20. Halecki & Murray at 46 (noting that others were home, but no one was hurt); Cornwell at 78 (noting that more than fifty bullet holes were found in the masonry of the building's facade).

21. Hatch & Walsh at 84. Whether their primary motive was to seek reprisal against the Church (as most reports have it), to steal a car (as Cornwell has it) or just to obtain food to feed their families (as "Judging Pope Pius XII," *Inside the Vatican*, June 1997, at 12, 14 has it) remains a matter of debate.

22. Hatch & Walsh a 84 (noting that Pacelli later gave the bent cross to Francis Cardinal Spellman of New York).

23. Halecki & Murray at 47.

24. *Id.* While most reports of the incident focus on Pacelli's bravery, his own account is much more modest. See Cornwell at 78.

25. Hatch & Walsh at 84-85; Halecki & Murray at 47-48.

26. Korn at 135; Duffy at 263; Stehlin at 41. Despite his obvious bravery, he was only human. His doctor later reported that Pacelli had recurring dreams about the car episode for the rest of his life. Cornwell at 76.

27. Hatch & Walsh at 85.

28. As a young man, Luther had been a champion of the Jews. When he failed to win them to the Gospel of Christ, however, he raged at them with violent language. Hitler misappropriated these writings for his own purposes, circulating them to counter Christian opposition to his Nazi theories.

29. The difficulty that the Catholic Church was having in the late 19th century caused Pope Leo XIII to issue an encyclical entitled *Iampridem* (*On Catholicism in Germany*, 1886). In it, Leo complained about how the relationship between Church and state was "thrown into sudden disorder" by certain laws which placed "Catholic citizens in such danger and distress."

30. Rauschning at 236 (Hitler said that anti-Semitism was beyond question the most important weapon in his propagandist arsenal). See also M. Price at 140-41 (discussing the anti-Semitism of emerging nationalist parties in post-war Germany).

31. Rauschning at 234 (among Nazi leaders, Hitler's racial doctrine was called "Adolf's bunkum").

32. Barnett at 15 (quoting Eberhard Bethge).

33. Hatch & Walsh at 81.

34. Even when he was a boy, Hitler was proud that his eyes were blue and his hair was then light brown. Toland (1997) at 298.

35. His girlfriend (and later, wife), Eva Braun, has been called the most envied woman in Germany. Nevertheless, she was hidden from the public so well that in 1945 *Newsweek* foreign editor Harry Kern sent a cable asking who she was. Some have speculated that she was hidden in order to keep German women interested in Hitler (he received thousands of love letters), but even some of those close to Hitler were uncertain as to whether he and Eva had a physical relationship. Even when he moved into his Berlin bunker in 1945, Eva had her own small suite next to Hitler's. O'Donnell at 29. There were, however, rumors of love affairs that Hitler had with other women, including film-maker Leni Riefenstahl.

Several of the women with whom Hitler was romantically involved, including Eva Braun in 1935, attempted suicide; at least one (his niece, Geli Rabble) succeeded. Bullock at 174 (suggesting that this was the true love of his life and that he may have killed her in the course of a jealous argument). Hitler told Eva that he could not marry because he did not have time for a wife and child. "Besides, I don't want children. The children of a genius have a hard time in the world. People expect such a child to be a replica of his famous father and don't forgive him for being average. Besides, it's common for them to be mentally deficient." Toland (1997) at 314; *id.* at 293.

36. The postcard is reproduced in Kershaw (photograph section). Himmler was also an animal lover who opposed hunting. Crankshaw at 18.

37. Toland (1997) at 311. Reportedly, he loved all jokes, except political or "dirty" ones.

38. Holmes at 101.

39. Akin at 14; Lapide at 118.

40. Holmes at 101.

41. Halecki & Murray at 59.

42. Holmes at 146-47.

43. Cheetham at 283. It should be noted, however, that Catholic political parties in Germany were subject to sudden shifts in political positions. See M. Price at 106. This is one of the reasons why the Holy See gradually withdrew support from Catholic political parties.

44. The Socialists probably would have agreed to an alliance with the Catholics, but the Pope rejected it as a compromise with the powers of evil. Moreover, the Pope made it clear to the priest/leader of the Socialist Popular Party, Father Don Sturzo, that he regarded Sturzo's political activity as incompatible with his priestly duties. Sturzo obediently resigned his leadership of the party and withdrew into exile.

45. According to a close war-time advisor, Mussolini delighted in calling himself "an unbeliever." *The Ciano Diaries* at 184. "For me," he declared, "Christmas is nothing more than the twenty- fifth of December. I am the man who in all this world feels least these religious anniversaries." *Id.* at 424-25.

46. Holmes at 40. Hitler pointed out that Fascism came to power despite the opposition of the Church. *Hitler's Secret Conversations* at 422.

47. See Chapter 18, question 6.

48. See Heller & Nekrich.

49. *Id.*

50. *Id.* at 137. In April 1923, Monsignor Konstantin Buchkavich, Vicar General of the Roman Catholic Church in Russia, was convicted on the charge of opposing the Soviet government. He was tried along with 18 other people for engaging in activities "detrimental to the proletarian revolution." Despite foreign protests, the monsignor was shot through the head in the cellar of the Moscow secret police building. *Chronicle* at 301.

51. *Controversial Concordats* at 2.

52. Cheetham at 284-86; Cornwell at 263.

53. Cheetham at 286.

54. *Divini Redemptoris*, paragraph 58.

CHAPTER THREE
THE SPREAD OF NATIONALISM

1. Halecki & Murray at 56-58.

2. Taylor at 121.

3. Payne at 154.

4. Meltzer at 18.

5. *Chronicle* at 307.

6. *Chronicle* at 314.

7. See Kershaw at 262-63, *Chronicle* at 323.

8. Stehlin at 148. The only problem with this plan, from the German perspective, was that the Danzig government was unprepared to pay the salary of its new Catholic leader, and there was concern that Poland might underwrite the costs and thereby gain influence over Danzig's Catholic administration. Therefore, the German Republic came up with more than 50,000 marks to help defray O'Rourke's living expenses and maintain the diplomatic advantage that it had gained with appointment of a German speaking administrator.

Later, on May 3, 1934, *L'Osservatore Romano* reported that if Danzig fell to the Nazis, Poland, Romania and the Balkans would fall shortly thereafter. Halecki & Murray at 97.

9. Hatch & Walsh at 87; Cornwell at 101.

10. O'Carroll at 31; Halecki & Murray at 63.

11. Ironically, after working so long to get Pacelli to move to Berlin, German leaders almost sent him away later that year. In November 1925, the nuncios in France and Brazil were recalled to Rome after completing their assignments. As is traditional, they were named to receive cardinals' hats at the next consistory. German leaders, while desiring to retain Pacelli in Berlin, became concerned that he had served longer than either of these other two nuncios, but he was not included on the list for elevation to the Sacred College of Cardinals. This omission was thought to be an indication that the Vatican did not regard the Berlin nunciature of equal stature with those of other nations. These concerns were brought to the Curia's attention, but the

Church was able to convince the Germans that this should not be seen as a slight.

12. Hatch & Walsh at 88-89. Foreign correspondent Dorothy Thompson later reported: "In knowledge of German and European affairs and in diplomatic astuteness the Nuncio was without an equal." Halecki & Murray at 63; see Cornwell at 101.

13. Conradt at 10.

14. Hitler at 114. See also Kershaw at 33-34; Janik & Toulmin at 58.

15. The German term *Kulturkampf* is derived from this struggle. This struggle is cited by some as motivation for the Church's 1933 agreement with Nazi Germany. Kevin E. Schmiesing, "Dealing with Dictators," *Crisis*, October 1999, at 47 (reviewing *Controversial Concordats: The Vatican's Relations with Napoleon, Mussolini, and Hitler*, Catholic University of America Press (Frank J. Coppa, ed., 1999)).

16. See Kershaw at 33-34, 58.

17. Kershaw at 262. Following Hitler's release from prison, some of his political opponents accused him of having given in to the international power of the Catholic Church. *Id.* at 263. In 1928, one rival even accused Hitler of being a tool of the Catholic Church. *Id.* at 298.

18. Hitler at 108.

19. *Id.* at 108-09.

20. *Id.* at 109. "[O]nly an ignoramus could fail to see that an offensive in favor of German interests was something that practically never occurred to the German clergyman." *Id.* at 109-10.

21. *Id.* at 109.

22. *Id.* at 112.

23. *Id.* at 113.

24. *Id.* at 119.

25. *Id.* at 113-14.

26. *Id.* at 100.

27. *Id.* at 562.

28. *Id.* at 561.

29. Taylor at 144.

30. Hitler at 562.

31. Rauschning at 239. Regarding Hitler's distrust of the Freemasons, he once said: "Ourselves or the Freemasons or the Church—there is room for one of the three and no more.... and we are the strongest of the three and shall get rid of the other two." *Id.* At 241.

32. *Id.* at 239.

33. Friedländer (1997) at 432.

34. Hitler at 459.

35. At the end of the war, as Germany's resources—including manpower—were being depleted, Hitler continued devoting significant man hours to the process of eliminating European Jews.

36. Hitler at 475.

37. Interestingly, Hitler condemned exactly the same thing that he was proposing: "Worst of all, however, is the devastation wrought by the misuse of religious conviction for political ends. In truth, we cannot sharply enough attack those wretched crooks who would like to make religion an implement to perform political or rather business services for them." Hitler at 268.

38. Rauschning at 239.
39. Martin at 183; Matheson at 72; Lapide at 108.
40. The Nazis, at one point, demanded that *Mein Kampf* replace the Bible in all German churches. See Shirer (1962) at 332.
41. Kershaw at 318-22; M. Price at 186.

CHAPTER FOUR
THE LATERAN TREATY

1. H. Stewart at 108.
2. Cianfarra at 69 (quoting a December 1934 writing by Mussolini).
3. Holmes at 45.
4. Pope Pius XI made reference to this in his encyclical *Quinquagesimo Ante*.
5. *Chronicle* at 372.
6. Hatch & Walsh at 94.
7. Halecki & Murray at 8-11; Hatch & Walsh at 95.
8. This is reprinted in *Controversial Concordats* at 193.
9. Hatch & Walsh at 95-96.
10. Article 34 of the concordat between Italy and the Vatican provided:

The Italian State, wishing to restore to the institution of marriage-basis of the family–a dignity in conformity with the Catholic tradition of its people, recognizes civil validity to the sacrament of marriage disciplined by canon law.

This provision was to cause controversy later, when Italy adopted racial laws that, *inter alia*, refused to recognize a marriage between a Jewish person and a non-Jewish Italian.

11. This provision caused some reporters to mistakenly report that the Lateran Treaty gave Mussolini equal say in the appointment of bishops and archbishops in Italy. Actually, bishops had been appointed by the Church subject to the approval of the state before the Lateran Treaty. After the new terms went into effect, the state's role was diminished to having the right to object to an appointee for political reasons only. See Benns at 230.
12. Cianfarra at 298.
13. P. Murphy at 99-100.
14. Hatch & Walsh at 96.
15. Holmes at 56.
16. Benns at 231.
17. Mussolini's burning desire to unite all of Italy also led him to neutralize the Mafia in Sicily. In fact, Mussolini's war against the Mafia caused many Italian Mafiosi, including the 19-year-old future Godfather Carlo Gambino, to leave Sicily for the United States of America.
18. Hoar at 149.
19. See Margo Hammond, "Masking the Realities of History," *St. Petersburg* (Florida) *Times*, May 15, 1994 at 1D (discussing positive images of

Mussolini by Gandhi, the Archbishop of Canterbury, and Thomas Edison); Jeffrey M. Landaw, "Gilbert, as in Sullivan: a Victorian Paradox," *The Baltimore Sun Company*, September 29, 1996 at 5E (George Bernard Shaw's positive feelings towards Mussolini); Hoar at 237, 240 (Churchill); Yosef Yaakov, "Roots of Fascism," *The Jerusalem Post*, February 24, 1995, at 23 (Freud). According to some reports, when the Germans invaded Austria in 1938, Mussolini intervened with Hitler and obtained permission for Freud to escape to England. Other reports have it that Freud used his contacts in the United States. Either way, he avoided the concentration camps, where three of his sisters died in the 1940s.

20. Payne at 235. See Jack Epstein, "Digging Up Former Nazis in Argentina, Some say it's finally time to expose war criminals," *The San Francisco Chronicle*, July 3, 1994, *Sunday Punch* at 3 (Hitler's and Peron's respect for Mussolini); Fest at 157 (Hitler's admiration for Mussolini).

21. Holmes at 58-59.

22. *Id.* at 58-59; Cheetham at 280.

23. Ray at 28-29.

24. Holmes at 58-59.

25. *Summi Pontificatus*, paragraph 17.

26. Nichols at 282. See also *The Catholic Church in World Affairs*, University of Notre Dame Press (W. Gurian & M.A. Fitzsimons, eds., Notre Dame, Ind. 1954) (discussing the relationship between the Vatican and Mussolini in light of the Lateran Treaty).

27. Kevin E. Schmiesing, "Dealing with Dictators," *Crisis*, October 1999, at 47 (reviewing *Controversial Concordats: The Vatican's Relations with Napoleon, Mussolini, and Hitler*, Catholic University of America Press (Frank J. Coppa, ed., 1999)).

28. *Id.*

29. Report from Osborne to London, British Public Records Office FO 371/24935 60675 (May 21, 1940).

30. Procacci at 356. The story making the rounds in Rome was that on the day after the agreement was signed, Cardinal Gasparri's car was stopped by a fight in the street. Looking at the two men, the cardinal commented, "I wonder how long ago they signed a concordat." Daniel-Rops at 305.

31. Barzini at 139-40. "It seemed beyond doubt that Mussolini himself had very little faith." Daniel-Rops at 306.

32. Darragh at 4; Daniel-Rops at 310 (Ratti was Pius XI's family name).

33. Daniel-Rops at 310.

34. The risk of Italian censorship of the printed press caused Pacelli to engage in a modernization program that included installation of a radio tower for Vatican Radio broadcasts. Hatch & Walsh at 108.

35. *Non Abbiamo Bisogno*, paragraph 44.

36. Holmes at 66-67; *Ciano's Diplomatic Papers* at 48 (Mussolini's 1936 statement that "since September 1, 1931, Catholic Action in Italy has practically ceased to exist").

37. Hatch & Walsh at 107.

38. Two months after the encyclical, the Italian leadership reached a compromise agreement with the Holy See. According to one commentator:

> What was at stake was the existence of Catholic Action and its independence of the secular power, and on both these points the

Pope obtained satisfaction. The Catholic organizations retained their unique position of freedom from control by the totalitarian machine, as well as the right to recruit members from the rising generation. It was for this principle that Pius XI had fought, and there seems to me no doubt that he saved it.

Darragh at 5 (quoting Daniel A. Binchy, *Church and State in Fascist Italy* at 529). Another commentator said "the Pope's arrows were barbed, they hurt; and moral victory easily lay with him." *Id.* at 4 (quoting Finer, *Mussolini's Italy* at 466). See also Daniel-Rops at 311.

39. In 1926, Pacelli consecrated a Jesuit bishop in Berlin, Fr. Michel d'Herbigny, "whose task it was to go into the USSR to consecrate several bishops secretly, to inform them officially of their appointments as apostolic administrators." Nichols at 280.

40. It was signed on June 14, 1929. Cornwell at 103.

CHAPTER FIVE
HITLER'S RISE TO POWER

1. Payne at 165.

2. O'Carroll at 33.

3. Leni Riefenstahl, perhaps the most talented female film-maker of the century, would later turn Nazi propaganda into an art form with films like *Triumph of the Will* and *Olympia*.

4. See Cornwell at 132.

5. *Chronicle* at 380.

6. Bullock at 178.

7. Halecki & Murray at 86 (also noting that Pacelli predicted at this time that Austria would be the first of Hitler's victims).

8. Hatch & Walsh at 101.

9. *Id.* at 90.

10. *Id.* at 90-91; see also Halecki & Murray at 63.

11. Pacelli was concerned that his work in Germany was not really done. He could see that Hitler and the National Socialists presented a serious threat. His housekeeper, Sr. M. Pascalina Lehnert, in her personal memoirs, recorded:

A distressing thought disturbed the Nuncio on his departure from Germany: The continuing progress of National Socialism. How perceptive he had been already at that time in judging Hitler and how many times he had warned the German people of the tremendous danger that threatened them! They did not wish to believe him. People of every rank and class let him know at the time of his departure what they expected of Hitler: the ascent and greatness of Germany.

On one occasion I asked the Nuncio if he did not think that this man could have some good in him, and that ... he [Hitler] could perhaps help the German people. The Nuncio shook his head and said:

I would be very, very much mistaken in thinking that all this could end well. This man is completely obsessed: all that is not of use to him, he destroys; all that he says and writes carries the mark of his egocentricity; this man is capable of trampling on corpses and eliminating all that obstructs him. I cannot understand how many in Germany, even among the best people, do not understand and are not able to draw the lesson from what he writes and says. Who among these has at least read his horrifying book *Mein Kampf?*

When, later on, one of Hitler's early followers came to Rome, he said to me: "How much moral misery; how much humiliation and how much shame we and the world would have been spared if at that time we had paid attention to Nuncio Pacelli!"

Translated from the original German edition: Sr. M. Pascalina Lehnert, *Ich durfte ihm dienen: Erinnerungen an Papst Pius XII,* Würzburg (4th ed. 1983) at 42-43.

12. Orsenigo was criticized for being too accommodating to the Nazis. Though he had been appointed by Pius XI, Pius XII could have removed him. At one point, Pius XII reportedly convened a meeting of the Cardinals of the Congregation for Extraordinary Ecclesiastical Affairs, and considered recalling Orsenigo. The Pope, however, determined that the Germans would break off all diplomatic relations if Orsenigo were removed, and they would be unlikely to accept a new nuncio. This would cut off the Vatican's best source of information on the Nazi activities in Germany, including the many acts of persecution against the Church. Holmes at 149; Alvarez & Graham at 161; O'Carroll at 138, 150-51; Blet, Chapter 3. Besides, Ernst Von Weizsäcker, the German Ambassador to the Holy See, later wrote that Orsenigo carried out his duties properly, but that his efforts to avoid angering Hitler caused him to appear more sympathetic to the Nazis than he really was. Weizsäcker at 282-83; see also Rhodes at 343. In fact, Orsenigo intervened with leaders in Berlin on behalf of Nazi victims at least 300 times, but it was almost all in vain. Lapomarda at 128.

13. Stehlin at 318.

14. Hatch & Walsh at 109; see Halecki & Murray at 65 ("closest possible co-operation").

15. Cornwell at 109.

16. Stehlin at 353.

17. The October 11, 1930, edition of *L'Osservatore Romano* declared: "Belonging to the National Socialist Party of Hitler is irreconcilable with the Catholic Conscience." Marchione (2000) (Background Documentation). This was reprinted in diocesan newspapers around the world, and especially in Germany.

18. Holmes at 101; Cornwell at 108-09. Several protests from bishops of this time period are reviewed in Lothar Groppe, "The Church's Struggle with the Third Reich," *Fidelity,* October 1983, at 24.

19. Cornwell at 109.

20. Stehlin at 353.

21. Holmes at 109-110.

22. *Id.*

23. *Id.*

24. Kershaw at 418-20.

25. *Id.* at 392.

26. This black and white animation is sometimes incorporated into documentaries about the Nazi era.

27. After several weeks of negotiations in Switzerland, the European Allies agreed not to punish Germany for this failure to meet its obligations.

28. See Eric Black, "A chilling choice," *Star Tribune* (Minneapolis, MN), February 7, 1993 at 23A.

29. *Chronicle* at 411.

30. See Kershaw at 500.

31. Palmer at 159; Lothar Groppe, "The Church's Struggle with the Third Reich," *Fidelity*, October 1983, at 24. Although von Papen ultimately played into Hitler's hands and helped his rise to power, von Papen was a devout Catholic and expressed many anti-Hitler sentiments. Hamilton Fish, *The Other Side of the Coin* 238 (1962).

32. *Office of United States Chief of Counsel,* vol. II, at 932.

33. *Id.*

34. On February 12, 1933, the Bavarian bishops' conference at papal urging, issued pastoral instructions to all their clergy which said in part: "Leading spokesmen of National Socialism put race before religion, rejecting the Old Testament and even the Mosaic Ten Commandments." All priests were ordered to explain to their congregations that "National Socialism has taken up a position of *Kulturkampf* irreconcilable with Catholic teaching" and to prohibit the attendance of Nazis in uniform or "with their flags at Divine services, lest people think that the Church has come to terms with National Socialism." Lapide at 98-99.

35. Mr. Kirkpatrick (The Vatican) to Sir R. Vansittart, August 19, 1933, *Documents on British Foreign Policy*, Series II, vol. V, London, 1956, no. 342, p. 524.

36. Sweeney at 260; Lapomarda at 240, n.36 (Pacelli viewed Hitler's victory as "more fatal than a victory of the socialist left.")

37. Rauschning at 49; Lothar Groppe, "The Church's Struggle with the Third Reich," *Fidelity*, October 1983, at 24.

38. Holmes at 102-103.

39. Cornwell at 138.

40. *Office of United States Chief of Counsel,* vol. II, at 932-3 (reprinting the full statement by the bishops). The earlier prohibition is reflected in the minutes of the Bishops' Conference in Fulda, of August 17, 1932. The relevant passage provides:

> All the gathered bishops have declared that membership in this Party is not allowed because: 1) Portions of its official program, the way they read and as they must be understood without reinterpretation, contain false doctrine; 2) Because the announcements of numerous leading representatives and journalists of the Party contain statements of a character which are opposed to faith, expressing a hostile attitude towards basic teachings and requirements of the Catholic Church, and these statements have not been denied or withdrawn on the part of the highest Party leadership....

Lothar Groppe, "The Church's Struggle with the Third Reich," *Fidelity*, October 1983, at 14.

41. Lothar Groppe, "The Church's Struggle with the Third Reich," *Fidelity*, October 1983, at 14.

42. Lapide at 99.

43. The filmed statement can be found in some documentaries on the Nazi era. See Kershaw at 470.

44. An entry in Goebbels' diary suggests that the burning of the Reichstag surprised Hitler's inner circle. *Time*, September 14, 1987, at 44.

45. *Chronicle* at 416.

46. *Id.* at 417.

47. Hamerow at 12.

48. Peter Hoffman, *Stauffenberg: A Family History, 1905-1944*, Cambridge University Press (Cambridge, 1995) at 61. The Catholic Center Party, including former Chancellor Heinrich Brüning, voted in favor of Hitler's Enabling Bill of 1933. Cornwell at 135-36. This is at least partially due to pressure from the Nazis, who seriously weakened and almost eliminated the Center Party in March 1933. On July 5, 1933, two weeks before the concordat was signed, the party voluntarily dissolved in an effort to stop Nazi brutality. Telegraph from Mr. Newton (Berlin) to Sir J. Simon, July 7, 1933, *Documents on British Foreign Policy 1919-1939*, Her Majesty's Stationary Office (E.L. Woodward, ed., London, 1956) (party members believe that dissolution will end arrests, sequestrations, and discrimination against the Catholic press); Peter Gumpel, "Cornwell's Cheap Shot at Pius XII," *Crisis*, December 1999, at 19, 21.

49. See Kershaw at 465-67.

50. *Chronicle* at 418.

51. Halecki & Murray at 72.

52. *Chronicle* at 417.

53. "The 1990s; A weekly countdown to the third millennium; 1933," *The Fort Worth Star-Telegram*, September 20, 1998 (Life section, p. 3).

54. *Chronicle* at 419.

55. *Id.*

56. Hamerow at 76.

57. *Chronicle* at 420.

58. *Id.*

59. *Id.*; Blet, Chapter 7.

60. C. Doyle at 31.

61. Rauschning at 49.

62. McCabeus at 20; Rauschning at 246.

63. McCabeus at 20; Rauschning at 246.

64. Rauschning at 49; McCabeus at 19.

65. Rauschning at 53; Barnett at 44.

66. McCabeus at 19.

67. *Id.* at 19; Rauschning at 52-53.

68. Bullock at 169; Rauschning at 223.

69. In fact, Hitler's official statements were always conciliatory toward the churches. For instance, in a message that he sent to Cardinal Bertram on April 28, 1933, Hitler wrote that the Reich government "does not desire conflicts with the two churches in Germany, but a sincere cooperation for the good of the state as well also for the good of the churches." *Documents of German Foreign Policy 1919-1945*, Series C (1933-1937), vol. I, no. 196.

Nevertheless, Hitler himself explained: "The fact that I remain silent in public over Church affairs is not the least misunderstood by the sly foxes of the Catholic Church, and I am quite sure that a man like Bishop von Galen knows full well that after the war I shall extract retribution to the last farthing." *Hitler's Secret Conversations* at 451. Reichsleiter Bormann suggested to Hitler that Galen be hanged in retaliation for his sermons, but instead 37 members of the clergy were arrested, ten of whom lost their lives. *Three Sermons in Defiance of the Nazis,* Church in History Information Centre (Birkenhead, U.K.) at 4-5.

70. Stehlin at 353.

71. Not long after coming to power, the Nazi authorities conducted a widely publicized campaign for the "purification" of public morals. Bars and cabarets featuring nudity were instructed to be more modest; commercialized vice became less conspicuous; plays and movies turned from social criticism and bedroom comedy to preaching and moralizing; and gay nightclubs and cafés were closed by order of the police.

72. Hamerow at 54.

73. *Id.*

74. *Id.* at 154-55.

75. *Id.* at 227.

76. *Id.* at 306-07.

77. *Id.*

78. *Id.*

79. *Id.*

80. *Id.*

81. *Id.*

82. *Id.* at 7-8, 307.

83. *Id.* at 364.

84. *Id.*

85. *Id.* at 20-23.

86. *Id.* at 73.

87. *Id.* at 54.

88. Lothar Groppe, "The Church and the Jews in the Third Reich," *Fidelity,* November 1983, at 20.

89. Hamerow at 54.

90. Lapide at 101.

91. Halecki & Murray at 72.

92. *Controversial Concordats* at 2.

93. The Germans considered Pacelli more "realistic" than Pius XI, who was said to "often create serious obstacles." "Confidential Telegram from the Ambassador to the Holy See to the Foreign Ministry, Oct. 16," in *Documents on German Foreign Policy, 1918-1945,* Series C (1933-1937), vol. II, no. 3, at 3.

94. The term "concordat" was important to Pope Pius XI, who preferred it to the word "treaty." Memorandum from Ambassador Bergen to Foreign Minister Neurath, July 3, 1933, in *Documents on German Foreign Policy 1919-1945,* Series C (1933-1937), vol. I, no. 351.

95. Giorgio Angelozzi Gariboldi, *Pius XII, Hitler e Mussolini: Il Vaticano fra le dittature,* Mursia (Milan, 1995) at 52.

96. Papen explained his thinking in a letter to the German ambassador to the Holy See:

When it became apparent in January, 1932 [sic] that the social collapse of Germany could be prevented only by calling Hitler to power, it was clear for anyone with insight into the situation that assumption of power by the National Socialist movement would necessarily raise a number of fundamental problems. It was clear, above all, that the attitude of the National Socialist movement toward German Catholicism would be one of active opposition. For political Catholicism had fought the movement most bitterly for the preceding ten years—with the important assistance of the authority of the bishops, at least some of whom had pronounced an anathema against the ideological content of the National Socialist doctrine and had moreover taken action against its followers with the most serious weapons of ecclesiastical disciplinary punishment.

It went therefore without saying that all energies had to be concentrated upon overcoming as far as possible the ideological differences between German Catholicism and the National Socialist movement. This was the basic conviction inspiring my ardent desire to reach as quickly as possible a new arrangement of affairs between the Reich and the Holy See....

Vice Chancellor Papen to Ambassador Bergen, April 7, 1934, in *Documents on German Foreign Policy, 1918-1945*, Series C (1933-1937), vol. II, no. 383.

97. On June 2, 1945, Pope Pius XII [Pacelli] said : "As the offer [to negotiate] came from the Reich Government, the responsibility of a refusal would have devolved upon the Holy See." Lapide at 101. Papen later claimed that the concordat was necessary to protect the Church from Hitler's aggression. *Office of United States Chief of Counsel*, vol. II, at 935-36 (indicating that the prosecutors did not completely believe him).

98. *Id.* at 102-03. During negotiations, Hitler put pressure on the Vatican by arresting 92 priests, searching 16 Catholic Youth Clubs, and shutting down nine Catholic publications, all within three weeks. R. Stewart at 17.

99. Mr. Kirkpatrick (The Vatican) to Sir R. Vansittart, August 19, 1933, *Documents on British Foreign Policy*, Series II, vol. V, London, 1956, no. 342, p. 524. See also John Jay Hughes, "The Pope's Pact with Hitler," 17 *Journal of Church and State* 63 (1975) (arguing that the Vatican had no real choice but to negotiate).

100. Telegram from the German Embassy in Italy to the Foreign Ministry, July 4, 1933, in *Documents on German Foreign Policy 1919-1945*, Series C (1933-1937), vol. I, no. 352.

101. Cornwell at 138.

102. Lewy at 77.

103. Cornwell at 143. In 1809, the Vatican signed such an agreement with Napoleon. See *Controversial Concordats: The Vatican's Relations with Napoleon, Mussolini, and Hitler*, Catholic University of America Press (Frank J. Coppa, ed., 1999).

104. In 1929, Pius XI said: "Where there is a question of saving souls, We feel the courage to treat with the Devil in person." Nichols at 282. See Kevin E. Schmiesing, "Dealing with Dictators," *Crisis*, October 1999, at 47 (reviewing *Controversial Concordats: The Vatican's Relations with Napoleon, Mussolini, and Hitler*, Catholic University of America Press (Frank J. Coppa, ed., 1999)) ("If anyone thought that the signing of concordats meant that the

Vatican thereby became a partner, or pawn, of the dictator in question, these essays conclusively demolish the idea.")

105. *Controversial Concordats* at 141. Holmes at 105; James Carroll, "The Holocaust and the Catholic Church," *The Atlantic Monthly,* October 1999, at 107, 109. The Vatican's position on this matter was known to historians during the war. See Daniel-Rops at 317.

106. *Mit brennender Sorge,* paragraph 3.

107. In June 1933, after negotiations for the concordat were well underway, the Archbishop of Munich, Cardinal Michael von Faulhaber, cautioned that Hitler wanted an agreement with the Vatican for propaganda purposes. He said that Hitler "sees what a halo his government will have in the eyes of the world if the Pope makes a treaty with him." He argued that Catholic people would not understand the Holy See making a treaty with the Third Reich when "a whole row of Catholic officials are sitting in prison or have been illegally ejected." Holmes at 107. Later, when Faulhaber learned all of the reasons why the Church had agreed to the concordat, he said: "With the concordat we are hanged, without the concordat we are hanged, drawn and quartered." "Let's Look at the Record," *Inside the Vatican,* October 1999, at X. Faulhaber became an outspoken opponent of Hitler, and support from Pius was cited as a reason for his outspokenness. Fabert at 36; Hamerow at 75-76; Gallin at 210.

108. This is in accord with the old rule of contract law, under which a breach by one party does not relieve the other of his or her obligations.

109. Lapide at 101.

110. Peter Gumpel, "Cornwell's Cheap Shot at Pius XII," *Crisis,* December 1999, at 19, 21. It had been largely worked out a few weeks earlier, but Pope Pius XI demanded restitution for acts of violence against the Church, and this held up the final agreement. Cornwell at 148-52.

111. See Mary Alice Gallin, *German Resistance to Hitler: Ethical and Religious Factors,* The Catholic University of America Press (Washington, 1961) (arguing that the concordat helped the Vatican by providing it with a legal basis for its arguments); John Jay Hughes, "The Pope's Pact with Hitler," 17 *Journal of Church and State* 63 (1975) (without the concordat, Hitler would have been able to persecute the Church without restriction).

112. Benns at 266.

113. Lewy at 77.

114. Secret Memorandum from Vice Chancellor Papen to Chancellor Hitler, July 2, 1933, in *Documents on German Foreign Policy 1919-1945,* Series C (1933-1937), vol. I, no. 347 (reporting on difficulty in negotiations and a promise that violence would end with the signing of the concordat).

115.

It is sometimes imagined that a Concordat is concluded by the Vatican only with those countries whose relations with her are particularly friendly.This is the precise opposite of the fact; a country which was on ideally good terms with Rome would not need to have a Concordat at all; and the existence of such a document implies that the two signatory parties are, in a more or less degree, distrustful of each other's intentions. It is an attempt to regularize a difficult situation by tying down either party, on paper, to a minimum of good behavior.... **Nothing could be more absurd than to represent [the**

Concordat of July 1933] as if it meant that the New Germany and the Vatican were working hand in hand.

Darragh at 15 (quoting Knox, *Nazi and Nazarene* at 9) (emphasis in original). See also Daniel- Rops at 308 (similar).

116. Mr. Kirkpatrick (The Vatican) to Sir R. Vansittart, August 19, 1933, *Documents on British Foreign Policy*, Series II, vol. V, London, 1956, no. 342, p. 524.

117. Because of this provision, when National Socialists argued that someone baptized into the Catholic faith remained a Jew, it was not just an assault on the Church's authority, it was a breach of the concordat. As such, the Church had a legal basis for its argument to the contrary.

118. Article 32 of the concordat provided:

> In consideration of the special situation existing in Germany, and in view of guaranty provided by this Concordat of legislation which will safeguard the rights and privileges of the Roman Catholic Church in the nation and its component states, the Holy See will prescribe regulations which will prohibit clergymen and members of conventual orders from membership in political parties and from working on their behalf.

The entire text of the concordat can be found in *Controversial Concordats* at 205 and in *The Persecution of the Catholic Church in the Third Reich* at 516.

119. The Belgian Ambassador in Rome reported that the party had not consulted Rome about its decision to dissolve, and that Pacelli was irritated about how it all took place, believing that the party had disappeared without dignity. Stehlin at 438. The leaders of the Center Party, however, felt that they had to dissolve or they would endanger the Church and risk major clashes with the Nazis, who had already used arrests and intimidation against the party. See Telegraph from Mr. Newton (Berlin) to Sir J. Simon, July 5, 1933, *Documents on British Foreign Policy 1919-1939*, Her Majesty's Stationary Office (E.L. Woodward, ed., London, 1956) (party members believe that dissolution will end arrests, sequestrations, and discrimination against the Catholic press). For details on the collapse of the Catholic Center Party, see Robert Leiber, *Reichskonkordat und Ende der Zentrumspartei, Stimmen der Zeit: Monatschrift für das Geistesleben der Gegenwart*, December 1960, at 213.

120. Cornwell at 128.

121. Telegraph from Mr. Newton (Berlin) to Sir J. Simon, July 5, 1933, *Documents on British Foreign Policy 1919-1939*, Her Majesty's Stationary Office (E.L. Woodward, ed., London, 1956); see Cheetam at 283-84; Kershaw at 478.

122. Stehlin at 438.

123. *Id.* at 46-47 (Pius X "believed the mixture of politics and religion to be the most hybrid and dangerous possible for the Church."). In 1931, Pius XI wrote an encyclical, *Quadragesimo Anno*, which asserted that the Church has the right and duty "to interpose her authority... in all things that are connected with the moral law." Regarding political issues unrelated to morality, however, Pius wrote: "the Church holds that it is unlawful for her to mix without cause in these temporal concerns." Modern Church teaching agrees with

him. The Second Vatican Council, in its *Pastoral Constitution on the Church in the Modern World* (*Gaudium et Spes*) said: "At all times and in all places, the Church should have the true freedom to... pass moral judgment even in matters relating to politics." The ability of the clergy—of the Church itself—to become involved in politics is limited, however, to situations in which "the fundamental rights of man or the salvation of souls requires it."

124. In 1988, John Paul II wrote:

> The Church does not have technical solutions to offer for the problem of underdevelopment as such....For the Church does not propose economic and political systems or programs, nor does she show preference for one or the other, provided that human dignity is properly respected and promoted, and provided she herself is allowed the room she needs to exercise her ministry in the world.

On Social Concerns (*Sollicitudo Rei Socialis*) (1988).

125. See generally Rhodes. On the other hand, internal German documents indicate that ending the Church's involvement in politics was a very important provision for the Germans. Secret Memorandum from Vice Chancellor Papen to Chancellor Hitler, July 2, 1933, in *Documents on German Foreign Policy 1918-1945*, Series C (1933-1937), vol. I, no. 347.

126. Pope Pius XI wrote *Quadragesimo Anno* in 1931. This was the first papal encyclical to use the term "social justice." Many modern Catholics equate that term with political action, but according to that encyclical, the Church has the right and duty "to interpose her authority... in all things that are connected with the moral law." This right and duty, however, is limited to issues of morality or natural law. Regarding political issues unrelated to morality, Pius wrote: "the Church holds that it is unlawful for her to mix without cause in these temporal concerns." Thus, two years before Hitler's rise to power, Pius XI set forth his thinking on the Church's political involvement.

127. "Once the war is over we will put a swift end to the Concordat. It will give me the greatest personal pleasure to point out to the Church all those occasions on which it has broken the terms of it. One need only recall the close co-operation between the Church and the murderers of Heydrich. Catholic priests not only allowed them to hide in a church on the outskirts of Prague, but even allowed them to entrench themselves in the sanctuary of the altar." *Hitler's Secret Conversations* at 449.

128. Kershaw at 488 ("it was an unqualified triumph for Hitler").

129. *Minutes From the Meeting of the Conference of Ministers*, July 14, 1933, in *Documents on German Foreign Policy 1918-1945*, Series C (1933-1937), vol. I, no. 362.

130. Hitler verbally attacked the German bishops at a mass rally in the Berlin *Lustgarten*. "The Church and the Jews in the Third Reich," *Fidelity*, November 1983, at 21. Article 16 of the concordat contained a pledge required of new bishops that they "swear and promise to honor the constitutional government and to cause the clergy of my diocese to honor it." Article 32 of the supplementary protocol, however made clear that the German clergy was not prohibited or even limited in preaching about "the dogmatic and moral teachings and principles of the Church." *The Persecution of the Catholic Church in the Third Reich* at 522 (reprinting the supplementary protocol). See

Controversial Concordats at 209; Lothar Groppe, "The Church's Struggle with the Third Reich," *IBW Journal* (Alan F. Lacy trans.)

131. The political restrictions, set forth in paragraph 32 of the concordat, apply only to "clergymen and members of conventional orders."

132. Cornwell at 172.

133. The Second Vatican Council, *Pastoral Constitution on the Church in the Modern World (Gaudium et Spes)*; see also Pius XI, *On Reconstruction of the Social Order (Quadragesimo Anno)* (1931).

134. In 1943, the German bishops issued a statement saying: "The extermination of human beings is *per se* wrong, even if it is purportedly done in the interests of society; but it is particularly evil if it is carried out against the innocent and defenseless people of alien races or alien descent." Saperstein at 43. Since this type of statement related to morality, it was not restricted by the terms of the concordat.

135. *Chronicle* at 422; Cornwell at 153.

136. See Cornwell at 153.

137. Benns at 266.

138. See Cornwell at 130-31.

139. Earlier that summer, while the negotiations were still pending, the Nazis had attacked and beaten Catholic youth at a Munich rally. Cornwell at 146.

140. *Office of United States Chief of Counsel*, vol. II, at 937.

141. Cornwell at 179 (calling this a "hollow exhortation").

142. *Id.*

143. *Id.* at 179-80.

144. Matheson at 48-49.

145. Holmes at 108; Cornwell at 180.

146. The Papal Secretary of State to the German Ambassador to the Holy See, Oct. 19, 1933, in *Documents on German Foreign Policy, 1918-1945*, Series C (1933-1937), vol. II, no. 17, at 23 (enclosure); *see Controversial Concordats* at 226.

147. Graham (1968) at 56. German bishops at one point considered mediation of the disputes with the Reich, but Secretary of State Pacelli insisted that the agreement was with the Holy See, not German bishops. Vice Chancellor Papen to Ambassador Bergen, Nov. 11, 1933, in *Documents on German Foreign Policy, 1918-1945*, Series C (1933-1937), vol. II, no. 61 (margin note). The likely reason for this insistence is concern that the Nazis would bully local clergy into compliance.

148. Lapide at 103-04; Holmes at 110. See Telegram from the Chargé d'Affaires of the Embassy to the Holy See to the Foreign Ministry, dated Sept. 12, 1933, in *Documents on German Foreign Policy 1918-1945*, Series C (1933-1937), vol. I, no. 425 (refusal to accept Catholics of Jewish descent as equal to Catholics of Aryan descent). One of the German officials at the Foreign Office complained that "the Nuncio used to come to me nearly every fortnight with a whole bundle of complaints." Weizsäcker at 282. In December 1933, the German ambassador to the Holy See wrote to German Foreign Minister Neurath that he considered a clash with the Curia quite possible and that the lack of response to the Vatican's charges would look bad to the world. Ambassador Bergen to Foreign Minister Neurath, Dec. 28, 1933, in

Documents on German Foreign Policy, 1918-1945, Series C (1933-1937), vol. II, no. 152.

149. Micklem at 80-82.

150. *Hitler's Secret Conversations* at 449.

151. Matheson at 47-48.

152. *Why the Churches Kept Silent.*

153. Original documents, as well as translations and commentary are available on the Internet at: watchtower.observer.org/.

154. *Id.*

155. *Why the Churches Kept Silent.*

156. See Gabriele Yonan, "Spiritual Resistance of Christian Conviction in Nazi Germany: The Case of the Jehovah's Witnesses," 41 *Journal of Church and State* 307 (March 22, 1999).

157. *Id.*

158. "Theological principles were adhered to; Witnesses remained 'neutral,' they were honest and completely trustworthy and as such, ironically, often found themselves employed as servants of the S.S." *Watchtower Magazine,* October 1, 1984, at 8.

159. *Why the Churches Kept Silent.*

160. Figures from the Watchtower's 1974 yearbook.

161. Holmes at 115.

162. Passelecq & Suchecky at 113.

163. Holmes at 109.

164. Cornwell at 161.

165. This filmed statement sometimes appears in documentaries on the Nazi regime.

166. Holmes at 108.

167. Benns at 266-67.

168. See The German Youth Leader to the Vice Chancellor, Feb. 20, 1934, in *Documents on German Foreign Policy, 1918-1945,* Series C (1933-1937), vol. II, no. 272.

169. Holmes at 108.

170. Barnett at 78.

171. Unsigned Memorandum, reporting on a meeting that took place on December 18, 1933, in *Documents on German Foreign Policy, 1918-1945,* Series C (1933-1937), vol. II, no. 133.

172. *Chronicle* at 425.

173. Holmes at 111.

CHAPTER SIX
WORLD UNREST

1. According to some reports, Himmler and Goering actually duped Hitler into killing all of *their* rivals within the party. See Shirer (1962) at 305.

2. Speer at 87-89.

3. Fest at 450-51.

4. The exact figure is unknown. It seems certain that more than one hundred, and perhaps several hundred, people were killed. Goldston at 80 (suggesting that there might have been more than 1,000 victims); Cornwell at 165-66 (putting the estimate at 85).

5. Kershaw at 348; *The Persecution of the Catholic Church in the Third Reich* at 314 (noting that Hitler claimed to have protected Roehm from violent attacks in the past).

6. Daniel-Rops at 320; Cornwell at 166.

7. Cornwell at 165.

8. *Id.*

9. Payne at 277-83.

10. *The Persecution of the Catholic Church in the Third Reich* at 336 (reprinting orders to leave the Church); Marchione (2000) (Overview).

11. Goldston at 81.

12. A German court reportedly once took children away from their parents because the parents refused to teach Nazi ideology. The parents were accused of creating an environment where the children would grow up to be "enemies of the state." The judge wrote, "the law as a racial and national instrument entrusts German parents with the education of their children only under certain conditions, namely, that they educate them in the fashion that the nation and the state expect."

13. The mass starvation that followed was no improvement on the Nazi death camps with their gas chambers disguised as showers. Heller & Nekrich at 233-38.

14. Hollander.

15. *Id.*

16. *Id.*

17. David Remnick, "Gorbachev, Vatican Aide Hold Talks; 'Good Atmosphere' Cited by Casaroli," *The Washington Post*, June 14, 1988, at A18.

18. Cornwell at 112 ("It became a crime to teach children under sixteen about God.").

19. *Id.* at 112-13.

20. See Joshua Rothenberg, "The Legal Status of Religion in the Soviet Union," in *Aspects of Religion in the Soviet Union 1917-1967*, Chicago/London (Richard H. Marshall, ed. 1971).

21. James P. Gallagher, "Catholic Church on Rise in Russia: Communism's End Unleashes Repressed Spirit," *Chicago Tribune*, Nov. 26, 1995.

22. Holmes at 94.

23. Hatch & Walsh at 109.

CHAPTER SEVEN
HITLER BATTLES THE CHURCHES

1. Many of the voters viewed Hitler as the best defense against the spread of Bolshevism. Kershaw at 546-47. Others may have been afraid to cast a ballot against a return for fear of what Hitler would do to them if they returned to Germany and he found out.

2. Kershaw at 547.

3. *Chronicle* at 442.

4. Hatch & Walsh at 110-11.

5. O'Carroll at 41.

6. *Standard American Encyclopedia,* vol. 12 ("Pacelli, Eugenio" heading). An internal German document from the Chargé d'Affaires in Great Britain to the Foreign Ministry indicated that the Nazi's "conflict with the Catholic Church and the dissensions within the Evangelical Church constitute the main bone of contention in German-British relations." *Documents on German Foreign Policy 1918-1945,* Series C (1933-1937) vol. I, no. 218 (Sept. 22, 1934).

7. *Controversial Concordats* at 173 (quoting *Pacelli to Schulte,* Vatican City, 12 March, 1935, in Volk, *Akten deutscher Bischöfe,* 2:113-17).

8. Bogle, *The Salisbury Review.*

9. Holmes at 141.

10. Hamerow at 196-97.

11. *Persecution of the Catholic Church in the Third Reich* at 275 (reprinting a speech from July 13, 1935).

12. *Id.* at 412.

13. Goldhagen at 118; Cornwell at 198.

14. *Persecution of the Catholic Church in the Third Reich* at 429.

15. *Id.*

16. *Id.* at 415.

17. *Id.* The following year, the S.S. newspaper, *Das Schwarze Korps,* published an article entitled: "Dear Vatican, We Beg a Little Greater Indignation!." It said:

> For us Westerners it is difficult to understand the tolerance which Rome shows towards a Bolshevism which disseminates universal destruction from the Kremlin.... They march separately in order to strike down, together, the real enemy of their theories, National Socialism.... Catholic Action has never been more closely in line with Bolshevism than today.... It does not matter whether one is Indian, Hottentot or Anglo-Saxon so long as all acknowledge the Church of Rome; all are equal and equally worthy of Heaven, to which a democratically elected Pope claims the keys....

The Persecution of the Catholic Church in the Third Reich at 415 (quoting *Das Schwarze Korps* of April 23, 1936).

18. *Id.*

19. Hamerow at 75-76.

20. *Id.*

21. *Id.* Support from Pacelli has been identified as one of the reasons for Faulhaber's outspokenness. Fabert at 36. Faulhaber did, however, praise the Nazis for their anti-drinking and anti-smoking policies. Cornwell at 187.

22. *Chronicle* at 446.

23. Taylor at 144.

24. Goldston at 89-90.

25. "Let's Look at the Record," *Inside the Vatican,* October 1999, at X.

26. See Goldston at 89-90; Kershaw at 563-65.

27. Matthew Berke, "Accomplices to Genocide?," *First Things,* Feb. 1998, at 42 (reviewing William D. Rubinstein, *The Myth of Rescue: Why the Democracies Could Not Have Saved More Jews from the Nazis*).

28. Rousmaniere at 116-17.

29. Polish Bishops, *The Victims of Nazi Ideology,* January 1995, reprinted in Secretariat for Ecumenical and Interreligious Affairs, National Conference of Bishops, *Catholics Remember the Holocaust,* United States Catholic Conference (Washington, 1998).

30. Marchione (1997) at 200.

31. *The Persecution of the Catholic Church in the Third Reich* at 19.

32. *Id.* at 421 (quoting Julius Streicher's *Stürmer*).

33. Richard J. Neuhaus, "The Public Square," *First Things,* Oct. 1997, at 75, 89.

34. Michaelis at 240.

35. Graham at 1.

36. Cianfarra at 112.

37. For a discussion of the economic maneuvers that Hitler was using to keep up appearances within Germany, see Kershaw at 576-78.

38. Goldston at 85.

39. Conradt at 12.

40. *Id.* at 50-51.

41. *Id.*

42. This was best expressed by Sir Neville Chamberlain as an "Anglo-German understanding" for "the two pillars of European peace and buttresses against Communism" (Sept. 13, 1938, in a letter to King George VI).

43. See Payne at 139.

44. See Horst J.P. Bergmeier & E. Lotz Rainer, *Hitler's Airwaves: The Inside Story of Nazi Radio Broadcasting and Propaganda Swing,* Yale University Press (1997).

45. *Id.* These inexpensive radios had great difficulty picking up broadcasts from outside of Germany. Whether by design or luck, this worked in Hitler's favor when he later wanted to suppress information from the Vatican and other nations.

46. *Chronicle* at 429.

47. *Id.* at 431.

48. Cornwell at 166.

49. *Chronicle* at 435.

50. Goldston at 98-99.

51. Charles Pichon, *The Vatican and its Role in World Affairs,* E.P. Dutton (New York, 1950) at 146.

52. *Id.* at 147.

53. *Chronicle* at 453.

54. Kennedy (1961) at 93-94. Kennedy suggests that this retooling problem put Britain two years behind Germany.

55. *Chronicle* at 452.

56. *Id.*

57. German troops received a warm welcome as they entered the Rhineland. Women placed flowers in the road and priests offered their blessings. Cardinal Schulte offered praise to Hitler for "sending back our army." Kershaw at 588.

58. Shirer (1962) at 402-03.

59. Hatch & Walsh at 129.

60. Hitler at 108-09.

61. Speer at 142.

62. *Id.* at 142-43.

63. *Id.* Hitler also said, "If we ever get rid of Christianity, then other nations can have it." Lothar Groppe, "The Church's Struggle with the Third Reich," *Fidelity*, October 1983, at 12, 13 (quoting the diary of Alfred Rosenberg).

64. Matheson at 43.

65. Shirer (1962) at 329.

66. Hitler at 213.

67. Saperstein at 38-39 (noting that in 1936 it was published under Nazi auspices and later excerpts from Luther's writings were printed in a pamphlet that was distributed by the Nazis).

68. Shirer (1962) at 326-27. Saperstein makes the point that Luther was calling for the destruction of synagogues, not people, but his choice of language (calling for good Christians to "act like a good physician who, when gangrene has set in, proceeds without mercy to cut, saw, and burn flesh, veins, bone, and marrow") made it easy for the National Socialists to exploit. Saperstein at 39.

69. Saperstein at 39 (quoting Luther, *On the Jews and Their Lies* at 275).

70. Lapide at 96 (noting that such comments appeared until Pope Pius XI put an end to them in 1938).

71. O'Carroll at 73-74.

72. "Nazi laws defining 'Jewishness' were carefully drawn to exclude both Jesus Christ and Adolf Hitler" (who may have feared that one of his grandparents was Jewish). Toland (1997) at 288.

73. In 1936, Himmler sent out a memorandum defining new holidays which were based upon paganism and Nazism. They included: Hitler's Birthday (April 20), May Day, Summer Solstice, Harvest Feast, The Beer Hall Putsch Anniversary (Nov. 9), and Winter Solstice. He also devised ceremonies that he hoped would one day replace Christian rituals (Naming Rites, for instance, were to replace Baptism).

74. Daniel-Rops at 316.

75. Cornwell at 164.

76. See Alvarez & Graham at 49 ("The Catholic Church, then, joined the Communists, Jews, and Freemasons as one of the 'Transnational Powers' (*Uberstaatliche Mächte*) which were the mortal enemies of the National Socialist state."); Kershaw at 560 (citing internal S.A. reports to the effect that Jews, Catholics, and capitalists were their ideological enemies); Daniel-Rops at 319.

77. Lapide at 104.

78. Speer at 143; Blet, Chapter 2 ("official catechism of the new Germanic religion").

79. Shirer (1962) at 332-33. In 1933, all German newlywed couples were presented with a copy of *Mein Kampf*. Sales were so brisk that Hitler renounced his salary as chancellor and lived on the royalties from the book. Daniel-Rops at 317.

80. Speer at 143; Shirer (1962) at 210.

81. Benns at 263.

82. *Id.* at 264. This accounts for the typical references to "the Protestant Church" in Germany.

83. *Id.*

84. *Id.*

85. Their first act was to issue a statement of guiding principles mirroring the Nazi position on German nationalism and race. Among the declarations were: "We see in race, folk, and nation orders of existence granted and entrusted to us by God....Faith in Christ does not destroy one's race but deepens and sanctifies it....We also demand that the nation be protected against the unfit and inferior." The statement's ninth principle provided:

> As long as the Jews possess the right of citizenship and there is thereby the danger of racial camouflage and bastardization, we repudiate a mission to the Jews in Germany. Holy Scripture is also able to speak about a holy wrath and a refusal of love. In particular, marriage between Germans and Jews is to be forbidden.

Most of the clergy in this new religion appeared in jackboots and Nazi party brown shirts. In 1933 the "German Christians" could claim 3,000 out of a total of 17,000 Protestant pastors in Germany, and the percentage of churchgoers was probably even greater. Shirer (1962) at 326; Rousmaniere at 118.

86. Benns at 264.

87. Shirer (1962) at 327-28.

88. *Id.* at 328.

89. *Id.*

90. Benns at 265.

91. Shirer (1962) at 325.

92. *Id.* at 326.

93 .Barnett at 91-92.

94. *Id.*

95. Benns at 265.

96. Barnett at 91-92.

97. The Barmen Confession was drafted by German-Swiss theologian Karl Barth. He had lost his professorship at the university in Bonn because he refused to sign the pledge to put the German state over his religious ideals.

98. Rousmaniere at 118-119; Matheson at 45-47.

99. Rousmaniere at 119.

100. Barnett at 84.

101. Hamerow at 207-09; Matheson at 58-62.

102. See Barnett at 84.

103. Matheson at 58-62.

104. McGarry, in *Introduction to Jewish-Christian Relations*, at 72.

105. Saperstein at 42; Hamerow at 228.

106. *Id.*

107. *Chronicle* at 456.

108. Darragh at 6; Hatch & Walsh at 115.

109. Daniel-Rops at 312.

110. Darragh at 7-8.

111. F. Murphy at 192.

112. *Id.*

113. Telegram from the Ambassador in France (Bullitt) to the Secretary of State, in *United States Department of State, Foreign Relations of the United States, Diplomatic Papers,* 1937, vol. I (General), United States Government Printing Office (Washington, 1954) at 89-91; Cornwell at 175.

114. Shirer (1962) at 410. Hitler was quoted at this time saying that Christianity was "the foundation of Western culture," but expressing his doubt as to whether "the Catholic Church was a God-established institution." Cornwell at 181.

115. Speer at 172-73; Deighton at 594.

116. Copeland at 513.

117. *Id.* at 522.

118. Michaelis at 226.

119. *Divini Redemptoris,* paragraph 4.

120. *Id.,* paragraph 58.

121. De Lubac at 28, n.10. Cardinal Faulhaber, Archbishop of Munich, also had a hand in drafting the encyclical. Duffy at 260.

122. Bogle, *The Salisbury Review*; Lapide at 111.

123. Duffy at 256; Gannon at. 177. Pacelli, who went to the top of the Empire State building, saw the Liberty Bell, drove to Mount Vernon, and met with President Roosevelt, also said, in an address to the National Press Club: "Glory belongs not only to those who triumph on the battlefield, but to those who safeguard tranquility and peace." Hatch & Walsh at 118. Pacelli avoided meeting with Roosevelt during his campaign for re-election, but they had lunch together after Roosevelt won. Leaving the Roosevelt's Victorian home in Hyde Park, Pacelli quipped, "I enjoyed lunching with a typical American family." *Id.* At 120. See also Letter from President Roosevelt to His Holiness, Dec. 23, 1939, in *Wartime Correspondence* at 4, 19 (letter in which Roosevelt calls Pius "a good friend and an old friend"). According to one account, Pacelli helped Roosevelt remove Father Charles Coughlin from the American airwaves. Cornwell at 176. Couglin, who acted under the banner of "social justice," was anti-New Deal, anti-Roosevelt, and anti-Semitic.

124. "It is enough to read the drafts, not only to confirm that Pacelli was one of the writers but (to see that) the original text has additions in his own handwriting." "World Press Unmasks Fallacies in Book Defaming Pius XII: Exclusive Interview with Reporter of Pacelli's Beatification Cause," *ZENIT News Service,* Oct. 3, 1999 (quoting Fr. Peter Gumpel).

125. *Mit brennender Sorge,* paragraph 8.

126. *Id.,* paragraph 11.

127. *Id.,* paragraph 42.

128. Maccarrone at 163.

129. Some authors have claimed that the encyclical was not actually read in many German churches. A telegram from the German Ambassador to the Holy See, dated March 23, 1937, however, reports that "the reading from the

pulpits in German churches proceeded without incident." *Documents on German Foreign Policy 1918-1945*, Series D (1937-1945), vol. I, no. 634. Ambassador Bergen went on to write that this encyclical and the way it was distributed "amount to an attempt at intimidation" by the Vatican. *Id.* The Reich and Prussian Minister for Ecclesiastical Affairs wrote to the German bishops complaining that this attack "against the welfare and interests of the German nation" was a violation of the concordat. *Documents on German Foreign Policy 1918-1945*, Series D (1937-1945), vol. I, no. 635.

130. De Lubac at 32. According to Dr. Duncan-Jones, the Anglican Dean of Chichester, the encyclical was of "shattering force." Darragh at 15 (quoting Duncan-Jones, *The Struggle for Religious Freedom in Germany*, at 225).

131. *Documents on German Foreign Policy 1918-1945*, Series D (1937-1945), vol. I, no. 633.

132. "Let's Look at the Record," *Inside the Vatican*, October 1999, at X (noting that Count Claus von Stauffenberg, who was later executed for his attempt to assassinate Hitler, read the encyclical and had his doubts about Nazism confirmed); Peter Hoffman, *Stauffenberg: A Family History, 1905-1944*, Cambridge University Press (Cambridge, 1995) at 317 (similar).

133. Cianfarra at 100; Holmes at 113; Lothar Groppe, "The Church and the Jews in the Third Reich," *Fidelity*, November 1983, at 21. Nazi official Reinhard Heydrich's belief that the Vatican was the archenemy of National Socialism was only strengthened with the release of *Mit brennender Sorge*. Alvarez & Graham at 64.

134. Eric A. Johnson, *Nazi Terror: The Gestapo, Jews, and Ordinary Germans*, Basic Books (New York, 1999).

135. Lapide at 110; Robert Martin, *Spiritual Semites: Catholics and Jews During World War Two*, Catholic League Publications (Milwaukee, 1983).

136. Lapide at 110.

137. *Id.*

138. "The Church and the Jews in the Third Reich," *Fidelity*, November 1983, at 21. German officials also complained about "the Vatican's harsh policy toward the Third Reich." *Documents on German Foreign Policy 1918-1945*, Series D (1937-1945), vol. I, no. 644. Göring gave his own two-hour harangue and announced the resumption of morality trials against Catholic clergy. Cornwell at 183.

139. Cornwell at 183.

140. Holmes at 101.

141. *Id.*

142. Bokenkotter at 370-71.

143. Holmes at 113.

144. The Pope wanted *Mit brennender Sorge* to be published in Spain, but this left Franco in a bind. If he allowed the encyclical to be published as was customary with papal documents, he might antagonize the German government upon which he was dependent for military support. On March 26, two weeks after the encyclical was issued, Pacelli sent a telegram asking if the document had been published in Spain's daily press. The nuncio in Spain responded that the only public notice of the encyclical was a strong attack on the Vatican's position by German radio. Pacelli, in an interview with the official Spanish agent, the Marqués de Magaz, said that Nazi racism was just as bad as atheistic Communism, and that both systems were lacking spirituali-

ty. The encyclical was not published in the diocesan bulletins until early the following year. The only periodical in Spain which published the document at the time was the Jesuit monthly, *Razón y Fe*. Sánchez at 369-70.

145. The third encyclical of March 1937, *Nos es muy conocido (It is Well Known to Us)*, dealt with the religious persecution of the Church in Mexico. Pius wrote: "only the teaching and the work of the Church, assisted as it is by its Divine Founder, can furnish a remedy for the very grave ills which burden humanity." One point of instruction is particularly relevant with regard to his successor, Pius XII. Speaking of living conditions for Mexican workers and peasants, Pius XI wrote: "it may be necessary at times to denounce and to blame boldly...; at the same time, however, care must be taken to guard against either making violence legitimate... [or] to effects which are more harmful than the evil itself which is intended to be corrected."

146. Kennedy (1961) at 80.

147. Lothar Groppe, "The Church's Struggle with the Third Reich," *Fidelity*, October 1983, at 14 (Alan F. Lacy trans.).

148. *Id.*

149. Lapide at 118-19.

150. Hatch & Walsh at 122.

151. Lapide at 119.

152. In 1935, Pope Pius XI organized a huge peace pilgrimage to Lourdes, just before the outbreak of the Ethiopian war. On April 28, Pacelli addressed 250,000 of the pilgrims and said of the National Socialists that they were in reality only miserable plagiarists who dress up old errors with new tinsel. It does not make any difference whether they flock to the banners of the social revolution, whether they are guided by a false conception of the world and of life, or whether they are possessed by the superstition of a race and blood cult. F. Murphy at 59; Hatch & Walsh at 116-17 (longer quotation); Cornwell at 172-73 (similar quotation). *The New York Times* called the address an "attack on both Hitlerism and communism." "Nazis Warned in Lourdes," *The New York Times*, April 29, 1935.

153. R. Stewart at 18.

154. F. Murphy at 59-60.

155. *Documents on German Foreign Policy 1918-1945*, Series D (1937-1945), vol. I, no. 672.

156. *Documents on German Foreign Policy 1918-1945*, Series D (1937-1945), vol. I, no. 673. But see Cornwell at 175 (suggesting that it was not a political speech).

157. F. Murphy at 60.

158. Micklem at 15.

159. Korn at 126.

CHAPTER EIGHT
THE VIOLENCE SPREADS

1. Stephen Schwartz, "Gertrude and the Führer," *The San Francisco Chronicle*, June 9, 1996 (noting that Stein also supported Marshal Philippe Pétain, head of the pro-Nazi French occupation regime during World War II); Peter S. Prescott, "The Great Barbarian," *Newsweek*, September 20, 1976 at 87.

2. Gilbert (1985) at 57.

3. About this time, the Nazis passed a law requiring Jews to wear a yellow Star of David on their clothing. German bishops tried to intervene on behalf of non-Aryan Catholics, *i.e.*, Jews who had been baptized into the Catholic faith. Bishops Heinrich Wienken and Wilhelm Berning both asked that their dioceses be exempt from the Star of David rule, but the Gestapo denied the request. Fogelman at 171.

4. *Documents on German Foreign Policy 1918-1945*, Series D (1937-1945), vol. I, no. 695.

5. Holmes at 73.

6. Pacelli left for Budapest, to speak at the International Eucharistic Congress on May 25. While there, in the wake of the Anschluss, he made a moving address in which he explained:

> Face to face with us is drawn up the lugubrious array of the military godless shaking the clenched fist of the Anti-Christ against everything we hold most sacred. Face to face with us spreads the army of those who would like to make all peoples of the earth and every individual human believe that they can find prosperity only by receding from the Gospel of Christ.

C. Doyle at 159-61. When Pacelli left the city, people lined the streets to honor him. *Id.* See also Levai at 7-16 (Levai personally witnessed Pacelli's presentations); id. at 18 (noting the Pope's early intervention following the occupation of Hungary). Hatch and Walsh at 127.

7. Daniel-Rops at 313.

8. Cianfarra at 120-22; Holmes at 73; Message from German Ambassador to the Holy See (Bergen) to the German Foreign Ministry, dated May 5, 1938, *Documents on German Foreign Policy 1918-1945*, Series D (1937-1945), vol. I, no. 706 (reporting that the Vatican press had not reported on Hitler's trip but had reported the Pope's anti-Nazi comments). According to some authors, the idea of closing the museums was Pacelli's. Hatch & Walsh at 128.

9. Holmes at 73; Message from German Ambassador to the Holy See (Bergen) to the German Foreign Ministry, dated May 5, 1938, *Documents on German Foreign Policy 1918-1945*, Series D (1937-1945), vol. I, no. 706 (relaying the anti-Nazi sentiments of the Pope).

10. Cianfarra at 111. At least some German officials felt that the Pope was offended by Hitler's refusal to meet with him, and that this is why he left town and closed the museums. Message from German Ambassador to the Holy See (Bergen) to the German Foreign Ministry, dated May 23, 1938,

Documents on German Foreign Policy 1918-1945, Series D (1937-1945), vol. I, no. 710.

11. Stille at 12; Lamb at 35 (noting that Jewish support for Mussolini survived the imposition of anti-Jewish laws in 1938).

12. Not only Italian writers (many of them Jewish) praised Mussolini, but Ezra Pound (who would broadcast Fascist propaganda during the war and later be indicted for treason), T.S. Eliot, W.B. Yeats, and Wyndham Lewis were all early supporters of Mussolini's Fascism.

13. Holmes at 73. In Turin, a Jewish banker published a Jewish Fascist newspaper, *La Nostra Bandiera.* Lamb at 38.

14. Holmes at 13. By 1939, 80 percent of Germany's Jewish population under the age of 40 had fled. Matthew Berke, "Accomplices to Genocide?," *First Things,* Feb. 1998, at 42 (reviewing William D. Rubinstein, *The Myth of Rescue: Why the Democracies Could Not Have Saved More Jews from the Nazis*).

15. Cianfarra at 126.

16. Daniel-Rops at 313.

17. Lothar Groppe, "The Church and the Jews in the Third Reich," *Fidelity,* November 1983, at 21.

18. *Id.*

19. Holmes at 116. Not long thereafter, Secretary of State Pacelli used this same language in a speech in Rome. Lapide at 118; R. Stewart at 21.

20. The Germans were, by now, less concerned about statements from the pulpit, because they knew that they could restrict the spread of information. On September 19, 1938, Rudolf Hess gave a speech in Nuremberg in which he not only called National Socialism "a God-ordained order and institution," but went on to explain:

> Who bothers any longer if, for example, pastoral letters are read from the pulpits of the Catholic churches—however packed they may be with concealed threats, attacks, distortions of the truth, and so on...? Their lordships can read out what they want as long as they have no access to the outside world.

Matheson at 75; see Lapide at 96. At this same time, Reich Leader Alfred Rosenberg said: "I am absolutely clear in my own mind, and I think I can speak for the *Führer* as well, that both the Catholic Church and the Evangelical Confessional Church, as they exist at present, must vanish from the life of our people." *The Persecution of the Catholic Church in the Third Reich* at 277.

21. *Ciano's Hidden Diary* at 190.

22. *Id.*

23. In Germany, the Nazis convinced most citizens to stay away from "enemies of the state." Persecution of church-goers drove a wedge between Christians and Nazis, and it was dangerous to side with the Church. In Italy, on the other hand, racial persecution was not nearly as significant. Millions of Christians did not regard their religion as incompatible with their political beliefs, at least until the 1938 laws were passed.

24. Stille at 230-31.

25. *Id.* at 73-75.

26. *Id.* at 75.

27. *Id.* at 73.

28. *Id.* at 134.

29. Hatch & Walsh at 126.

30. K. Doyle at 16.

31. On the day following that vote, an editorial in *Der Angriff*, a Nazi newspaper, said: "Radio Moscow and Radio Vatican have conducted full-scale electoral sabotage and vilified the laudable attitude of German Princes of the Church. But all in vain!" Lapide at 112.

32. Cornwell at 201.

33. Holmes at 114.

34. See Blet, Chapter 2.

35. Cianfarra at 220. See The Chargé in Austria (Wiley) to the Secretary of State, March 19, 1938, in *Foreign Relations of the United States, Diplomatic Papers*, 1938, vol. I (General), United States Government Printing Office (Washington, 1955) at 458 (priests arrested).

36. Goldston at 99-100.

37. The report, translated into English, was sent to Ambassador Joseph P. Kennedy by Cardinal Pacelli, who strongly disassociated it from the Vatican's position. Memorandum by the Vatican Secretary of State (Cardinal Pacelli) to the American Ambassador in the United Kingdom, April 19, 1938, in *Foreign Relations of the United States, Diplomatic Papers*, 1938, vol. I (General), United States Government Printing Office (Washington, 1955) at 474. According to a report from the American Chargé in Austria to the Secretary of State:

> Cardinal Innitzer... called in person upon Hitler in the Hotel Imperial and had a fifteen minute interview with him. Subsequently a statement appeared in the press on March 16 which stated that the Cardinal had expressed his joy to Hitler at the "reunion" of German Austria with the Reich.... [W]hile Cardinal Innitzer did sign a statement, the text of the one which appeared was not that which he had approved. The Nuncio added that Cardinal Innitzer was a weak man.

The Chargé in Austria (Wiley) to the Secretary of State, March 19, 1938, in *Foreign Relations of the United States, Diplomatic Papers*, 1938, vol. I (General), United States Government Printing Office (Washington, 1955) at 458.

38. Hatch & Walsh at 126; Cornwell at 202. Internal German records reflect that Nazi leadership wanted to "encourage Cardinal Innitzer and the Austrian bishops in their patriotic attitude." Message from German Ambassador to the Holy See (Bergen) to the German Foreign Ministry, dated April 2, 1938, *Documents on German Foreign Policy 1918-1945*, Series D (1937-1945), vol. I, no. 699 (also complaining about the Vatican Radio broadcast).

39. Cornwell at 201.

40. *Id.* at 202.

41. A German official in Rome, who saw Innitzer shortly after his meetings, reported: "I have the impression that the Cardinal, who seemed very exhausted from the conversations in the Vatican, had had a hard struggle there." Message from German Ambassador to the Holy See (Bergen) to the German Foreign Ministry, dated April 6, 1938, *Documents on German Foreign*

Policy 1918- 1945, Series D (1937-1945), vol. I, no. 701. The same official reported later the same day that the retraction of the earlier statements "was wrested from Cardinal Innitzer with pressure that can only be termed extortion." Id., no. 702.

42. Passelecq & Suchecky at 56. According to the British Minister to the Holy See, Sir D'Arcy Osborne, Innitzer "was severely hauled over the coals by the Vatican" and "told to go back and eat his words." *Confidential Letter to Oliver Harvey from D'Arcy Osborne*, February 26, 1947, British Public Record Office, FO 371/67917 60675.

43. Cianfarra at 142-43. The Innitzer matter is examined in the 1963 motion picture, *The Cardinal*, starring Thomas Tryon (screenplay by Robert Dozier, based on the novel: *The Cardinal* by Henry Morton Robinson). The motion picture presents Innitzer's letter welcoming Hitler, the Holy Father's efforts to have him reverse himself, Hitler's persecution of the Church, Innitzer's changed position, and the crowd storming his residence. The most serious factual flaw in the movie is that it shows Innitzer changing his mind after a meeting with Hitler, rather than after being called to the Vatican.

44. Cianfarra at 143; Holmes at 115.

45. *Chronicle* at 487.

46. Rousmaniere at 117.

47. *Id.*; Matthew Berke, "Accomplices to Genocide?," *First Things*, Feb. 1998, at 42 (reviewing William D. Rubinstein, *The Myth of Rescue: Why the Democracies Could not have Saved More Jews from the Nazis*).

48. Meltzer at 55.

49. At the announcement ceremony, John Paul II read a letter he had written for the event. For two days in a row, however, he omitted several paragraphs dealing with the Church's role in World War II, including the statement: "Anyone who does not limit himself to cheap polemics knows very well what Pius XII thought of the Nazi regime and how much he did to help countless people persecuted by the regime." The Vatican has explained that the written version stands as the official papal statement.

50. Lapide at 95.

51. *Id.*; Anti-Jewish laws were not officially lifted until January 20, 1944.

52. Some top German leaders blamed the influence of the Catholic Church for the Italian resistance to Jewish deportation. Michaelis at 322-23 (citing a note written by Obersturmführer S.S. Lieutenant Heinz Röthke).

53. Martínez at 26.

54. Michaelis at 181.

55. See *Chronicle* at 846-48.

CHAPTER NINE
PRE-WAR POPE

1. Korn at 140. Later, Pacelli, as Pope Pius XII, made similar statements. Hatch & Walsh at 233.

2. He predicted that Italy would lose the war. Cornwell at 203.

3. Lapide at 115.

4. Martinez at 26. The Pope, on April 13, 1938, had the Congregation of Seminaries and Universities send a letter to Cardinal Baudrillart, charging Catholic academic institutions to refute the Nazi theories of racism. Copies of this letter were sent to all European cardinals with instructions to act likewise. Lapide at 112.

5. Lapide at 115.

6. "Let's Look at the Record," *Inside the Vatican*, October 1999, at XI.

7. *Id.*

8. Lapide at 115.

9. This appeared in the *Jerusalem Latin Patriarch*, on February 12, 1939.

10. Duffy at 262.

11. Otto D. Tolischus, "A 'Political Pope' is Reich Comment," *The New York Times*, February 11, 1939.

12. Holmes at 116-17. A 1940 book published with the assistance of Pope Pius XII documented the persecution of the German Catholic Church in the 1930s. It reprinted the following poem, reporting that it had first been published in *Schwarze Korps*, the official publication of the S.S., on January 19, 1939.

> Go bury the delusive hope
> About His Holiness the Pope
> For all he knows concerning Race
> Would get a schoolboy in disgrace
> ***
> Since he regards both Blacks and Whites
> As children all with equal rights,
> As Christians all (whate'er their hues),
> They're 'spiritually' nought but Jews.
> ***
> The banner is at last unfurled"
> 'Chief Rabbi of the Christian World.'

The Persecution of the Catholic Church in the Third Reich at 426-27.

13. Lapide at 118.

14. F. Murphy at 57; Duffy at 261 ("stubborn old man"). Count Ciano reported in his diary on December 14, 1938, that Mussolini hoped for the Pope's death in the near future. *Ciano's Hidden Diary* at 204. On October 18, 1938, Mussolini said that all Popes named Pius have brought misfortune to the Church and that Pius XI "will leave behind him a larger heap of ruins than any Pope before him." *Id.* at 179.

15. *Chronicle* at 490.

16. F. Murphy at 59; see Cornwell at 166.

17. See *Report from the British Legation to the Holy See,* Feb. 17, 1939, British Public Record Office, F0 371/23789 (reporting on Pacelli's chances).

18. *Report from the British Legation to the Holy See,* Feb. 17, 1939, British Public Record Office, F0 371/23789.

19. Cianfarra at 22-23 (also identifying pressure from the Italian government); See *Report from the British Legation to the Holy See,* Feb. 17, 1939, British Public Record Office, F0 371/23789 (reporting that the Nazis were expected to oppose Pacelli). In 1903, the Italian and Austrian governments applied pressure to prevent the election of Vatican Secretary of State, Cardinal Rampolla, who was not elected. Halecki & Murray at 19; Hatch & Walsh at 58.

20. *Enclosure in Mr. Osborne's dispatch No. 37 of February 17th 1939,* British Public Record Office, FO 371/23789 57760.

21. See Otto D. Tolischus, "A 'Political Pope' is Reich Comment," *The New York Times,* February 11, 1939 (sub headlines: "Hitler Sends Message" and "Reich Holds Successor Should Be Man Who Understands 'Laws of These Times'"). According to at least one account, however, Pacelli was Bergen's personal favorite to become the new pope (due to his previous ties with Germany). Alvarez & Graham at 65.

22. *Message from the British Legation to the Holy See,* February 17, 1939, British Public Record Office FO 371/23789 57760 (also noting that the German ambassador had not appeared at any recent official functions "because of the present deadlock between the Holy See and the Reich government").

23. Alvarez & Graham at 65. "Members of the French and British foreign offices discussed the idea of attempting to influence the conclave in favor of Pacelli...." Cornwell at 206. The Spanish ambassador from Franco's regime also indicated that he hoped that the new Pope would not be as obsessed with Nazism as Pius XI had been. Sánchez at 373.

24. *Secret Message from Osborne to Ingram,* February 23, 1939, British Public Record Office FO 371/23789 57760.

25. *Message from the British Legation to the Holy See,* February 17, 1939, British Public Record Office FO 371/23789 57760.

26. Korn at 126. The literal translation is closer to "the Vicar of Christ on the ground." See also Hatch & Walshe at 18; Halecki & Murray at 93.

27. Holmes at 120.

28. Fabert at 37 ("The only vote cast against him was his own."); Cheetham at 285; see also Hatch & Walshe at 17 (reporting that Pacelli obtained a majority of votes in the second vote, but not the required two-thirds). Angelo Roncalli, the future Pope John XXIII, commented: "I am very pleased with this election, in which we can clearly see the Lord's hand." Elliott at 147.

29. Hebblewaite at 50. "He was elected, as everyone knew, to be pope in time of total war, a role for which everything about his career - his diplomatic skills, his gift of languages, his sensitivity and his intelligence - equipped him." Duffy at 263.

30. See Blet, chapter one.

31. Hebblewaite at 50; Deutsch at 108.

32. Korn at 140; Sweeney at 219; Hatch & Walshe at 20.

33. Cianfarra at 84.

34. *Id.* at 85.
35. F. Murphy at 58.
36. Elliott at 270. "Pacelli was everyone's idea of a Catholic saint." Duffy at 263. Mussolini might have preferred a friendlier Pope, but on March 3, 1939, he reportedly was "satisfied with Pacelli's election." *The Ciano Diaries* at 36. His "satisfaction," however, should be viewed in light of his statement on March 5: "I don't give a damn about the Pope, the Cardinal Secretary of State, or anybody who occupies such positions." *Id.* At 38.
37. See *Report from the British Legation to the Holy See,* Feb. 17, 1939, British Public Record Office, F0 371/23789 ("I should myself be very pleased to see Cardinal Pacelli elected Pope"). Osborne went on to report on "the saintliness of character of Cardinal Pacelli, who has been a politician in spite of himself. *Id.*
38. Smit at 125 (quoting *The New York Times*).
39. *The Canadian Jewish Chronicle* (Montreal), March 10, 1939.
40. *Id.*
41. *Palestine Post,* March 6, 1939.
42. That same edition of *The Jewish Chronicle* went on to note that "on January 22 [1939], the *Voelkischer Beobachter* published pictures of Cardinal Pacelli and other church dignitaries beneath a collective heading of 'Agitators in the Vatican against Fascism and National Socialism.' "
43. "Jews Express Pleasure at Selection of New Pope," *The Canadian Jewish Chronicle* (Montreal), March 10, 1939, at 2.
44. Michaelis at 241.
45. See Lapide at 122.
46. See Akin at 14.
47. Cornwell at 218.
48. *Id.* at 218.
49. Earlier that year, the *Voelkischer Beobachter* (January 22, 1939) published pictures of Cardinal Pacelli and other Church officials with the caption, "Agitators in the Vatican against Fascism and National Socialism." See *The Jewish Chronicle* (London), March 10, 1939, at 31.
50. *The Goebbels Diaries (1939-1941)* at 10.
51. Lapide at 121.
52. The paper of the French Communist Party, *L' Humanité*, happily reported on March 2, 1939, "The insolent veto against him [Cardinal Pacelli] lodged by the Fascist governments of Berlin and Rome, has received its proper response." On the next day, the *Humanité* added:

Pius XII. is a pope who is an adversary of the racial standpoint and a friend of freedom of conscience and human dignity...for Cardinal Pacelli and the (late) pope could not be separated when it was a matter of condemning the folly of racialism or the persecutions of the Third Reich....But for the Gestapo Pius XII was already "the pope of Moscow!" The election of Pius XII will undoubtedly be called by them "a Bolshevik machination."

See Lapide at 122. The weekly of the Communist International, *La Correspondance Internationale*, wrote that "In calling to succession the one who had demonstrated energetic resistance against the fascists totalitarian ideas that tend to eliminate the Catholic Church, (and) Pius XI's most direct collaborator, the Cardinals made a demonstrative gesture by placing, as head of the Church, a representative of the Catholic resistance movement." See "World Press Unmasks Fallacies in Book Defaming Pius XII: Exclusive Interview with Reporter of Pacelli's Beatification Cause," *ZENIT News Service*, Oct. 3, 1999.

53. Peter Gumpel, "Cornwell's Cheap Shot at Pius XII," *Crisis*, December 1999, at 19, 22.

54. Blet, chapter two.

55. *Id.*; *The Ciano Diaries* at 47 (reporting on March 18, 1939 that Pius XII "was most concerned about Germany and intends to follow a more conciliatory policy than Pius XI"); Deutsch at 110 (citing a German report of March 8, 1939, referring to "very strong hopes" that relations between Germany and the Vatican would improve).

56. Blet, chapter two.

57. O'Carroll at 49. It has been suggested that the new Pope thought that warm greetings might lead to an end to hostilities. Cornwell at 209.

58. Peter Gumpel, "Cornwell's Cheap Shot at Pius XII," *Crisis*, December 1999, at 19, 20.

59. Smit at 215. In fact, the Vatican leadership seriously discussed breaking off diplomatic relations with Germany. Cornwell at 209, 210.

60. "The New Secretary of State of the Vatican," *Zionist Review* (London), March 16, 1939, at 13.

61. Tardini served as the Deputy for the Congregation for Extraordinary Ecclesiastical Affairs (foreign relations).

62. At this time, Montini was the Deputy for the Congregation for Ordinary Affairs (domestic matters).

63. Cornwell notes that the coronations in 1878, 1941, and 1922 were essentially private affairs. Cornwell at 211. He neglects to point out, however, that these Popes (Leo XIII, Benedict XV, and Pius XI) considered themselves "prisoners" within the Vatican. *Chronicle* at 372.

64. The United States had not maintained a diplomat at the Holy See since 1867. Cornwell at 176.

65. Holmes at 121.

66. *Documents on German Foreign Policy 1918-1945*, Series D (1937-1945) no. 472 (March 5, 1939) (telegram from the German Ambassador to the Holy See to the Foreign Ministry, reporting on a warm meeting with Pius XII).

67. *Documents on German Foreign Policy 1918-1945*, Series D (1937-1945) no. 470 (March 2, 1939).

68. *Chronicle* at 491-92.

69. Smit at 127.

70. *Records and Documents* at 91.

71. Smit at 238-39. Reflecting on this period in a radio broadcast after the war, Pius said:

> The world was then still at peace, but what a peace, and how precarious! With Our heart full of anguish, in perplexity and prayer. We regarded that peace as a person would regard the bed of a dying man, fighting, against all the odds, to save him from the throes of death.

"The Catholic Church and the Third Reich: Pope Pius XII Surveys an Heroic History," *The Tablet* (London), June 9, 1945, at 268.

72. Korn at 105-06.

CHAPTER TEN
1939 AND THE OUTBREAK OF WAR

1. Barnett at 106.

2. *Id.*

3. *Id.* Hitler's ultimate goal was to create a "pure" volk. See Mary M. Penrose, 20 Pepp. L. Rev. 689 (1993)

4. Meltzer at 131; McGarry, in *Introduction to Jewish-Christian Relations* at 66.

5. Hoar at 154.

6. See "Assisted Suicide Bill," *Los Angeles Times*, June 4, 1999, Part B; Page 6 ("In Nazi Germany, the mentally retarded and other sick, who were called "useless eaters," were given involuntary euthanasia, as the "right to die became the duty to die.")

7. Hans Jonas, *The Right to Die*, Hastings Center Report 8, no. 4 (1978) at 31; Marvin Zalman et al, *Michigan's Assisted Suicide Three Ring Circus—An Intersection of Law and Politics*, 23 Ohio N.U.L. Rev. 863 (1997); Ingo M ller, *Hitler's Justice: The Courts of the Third Reich* (Deborah Lucas Schneider trans., 1991); Scott I. Davidson, *But, Why Do We Shoot Horses?: An Analysis of the Right to Die and Euthanasia*, 12 N.Y.L. Sch. J. Hum. Rts. 115 (Fall, 1994).

8. McGarry, in *Introduction to Jewish-Christian Relations* at 66.

9. Barnett at 106.

10. A total of 70,273 patients appeared on the official lists of those who had been murdered; the actual number is estimated at closer to 105,000. See Rousmaniere at 120.

11. *Id.*

12. Meltzer at 131; *Controversial Concordats* at 162 (citing *L'Osservatore Romano* of December 6, 1940).

13. Barnett at 117. Within a few years, Galen's outspokenness was well known throughout Germany, and during the war, Pius XII sent him encouragement. *Actes et Documents*, Vol. II, p. 306 (no. 101) (letter dated February 24, 1943, from Pius encouraging Galen's "open and courageous pronouncements" and telling him that two letters he had mailed to the Holy See laid the groundwork for the 1942 Christmas message). When his arrest seemed imminent, peasants came each morning to his residence and called for him to show himself at the window. Arvid Fredborg, *Behind the Steel Wall: Inside Report on Germany 1943*, Viking Press (New York, 1943), portions reprinted in *Reader's Digest*, Jan. 1944, at 125, 138-39. According to a wartime book, legends soon spread about his defiance of the Nazis. According to that account, the best known legend was that a Nazi official once stood up in church one day and shouted that those who did not contribute to Germany's struggle with their own flesh and blood, or that of their children, should remain silent. Galen reportedly scolded the official in a sarcastic manner: "I forbid anyone in this church, whoever it may be, to criticize the *Führer*." *Id.*

14. Blet, chapter three.

15. Levai at 108 (noting that Galen's comments were not really influential in this decsion); Cornwell at 199 ("the 'euthanasia' program was not entirely halted and there are reasons to suppose that Galen's intervention was not crucial to the reduction of deaths.")

16. Meltzer at 131.

17. Cornwell at 277. Based on interviews conducted by this author, one of the primary reasons that the program was driven underground was the impact that it had on morale in the military. Soldiers knew that they might lose a limb in war. If that then meant that they would be put to death, they might be less willing to fight for the Fatherland. When the Nazi hierarchy realized this, they tried to make it look like the program had ended.

18. Barnett at 118.

19. *Id.*

20. *The History Place: World War II in Europe*, on the Internet at: http://www.historyplace.com/worldwar2/timeline/threat.htm.

21. *Records and Documents* at 99, Smit at 205.

22. *The Ciano Diaries* at 98.

23. *Id.*at 111.

24. Cornwell at 229.

25. British authorities suggested that Pius could convince Poland to make certain concessions to Germany. Great Britain's Minister Osborne to the Secretariat of State, dated August 26, 1939, *Actes et Documents*, Vol. I, p. 251 (no. 134).

26. Cornwell at 230 (quoting Foreign Office Papers, in Public Record Office, Kew 371/23790/283).

27. *Records and Documents* at 151; Smit at 207-08.

28. Kennedy (1961) at 122, 179, 190-91.

29. *Id.* at 122.

30. *Chronicle* 494-500.

31. Shirer (1962) at 746; Hatch & Walsh at 146; Blet, chapter one.

32. Shirer (1984) at 434.

33. *Id.* at 746.

34. *Id.* at 746; Cianfarra at 167; Smit at 210; Blet, chapter one.

35. Telegram from the Ambassador in France (Bullitt) to the Secretary of State, May 9, 1939, in *Foreign Relations of the United States, Diplomatic Papers, 1939, vol. I (General),* United States Government Printing Office (Washington, 1956) at 182-83 (reporting on France's absolute rejection, Poland's reasons for resisting, and Britain's counter-proposal); The Under Secretary of State (Welles) to President Roosevelt, May 16, 1939, in *Foreign Relations of the United States, Diplomatic Papers, 1939, vol. I (General)* at 186-87, United States Government Printing Office (Washington, 1956) (the Pope's report on the negative reaction to his proposal).

36. Mazour & Peoples at 715-17; Morison at 992; Taylor at 162-63.

37. Taylor at 155.

38. "War! Bomb Warsaw!," *Chicago Daily Tribune*, September 1, 1939, at 1.

39. Mazour & Peoples at 717; Goldston at 121.

40. Hatch & Walsh at 147.

41. Martinez at 26.

42. *Id.*

43. See Keegan (1989) at 44-46.

44. Barnett at 176.

45. Polish Bishops, *The Victims of Nazi Ideology,* January 1995, reprinted in *Secretariat for Ecumenical and Interreligious Affairs,* National Conference of Bishops, *Catholics Remember the Holocaust,* United States Catholic Conference (Washington, 1998).

46. William J. O'Malley, *Priests of the Holocaust,* reprinted in *Pius XII and the Holocaust: A Reader* at 153.

47 Polish Bishops, *The Victims of Nazi Ideology,* January 1995, reprinted in *Secretariat for Ecumenical and Interreligious Affairs,* National Conference of Bishops, *Catholics Remember the Holocaust,* United States Catholic Conference (Washington, 1998).

48. Morrow at 34; Jim Skowronski, *So Others Will Never Forget,* Columbia, Sept. 1997, at 18; William J. O'Malley, *The Priests of Dachau, in Pius XII and the Holocaust: A Reader* at 143.

49. Polish Bishops, *The Victims of Nazi Ideology,* January 1995, reprinted in *Secretariat for Ecumenical and Interreligious Affairs,* National Conference of Bishops, *Catholics Remember the Holocaust,* United States Catholic Conference (Washington, 1998).

50. Weigel at 73, 74 (noting that Sapieha worked to help Jews escape Nazi persecution). After the war, Pius made Sapieha a cardinal. *Id.* at 78.

51. Todd & Curti at 671. So did France and Britain, both of which seriously underestimated Germany's military might. Tenen at 355-56.

52. Hoar at 196-97.

53. Kennedy (1995) at 58. Vatican Radio at this time reported:

In Poland, destitution and desolation are not confined to that part of the country under Russian occupation. Even more terrible are conditions in that part of Poland that has fallen to German administration.

54. Keegan (1989) at 47.

55. *Chronicle* at 499.

56. *Id.* at 510.

57. *Id.* at 500.

58. Blum at 726.

59. Mazour & Peoples at 720.

60. Deighton at 432.

61. *Id.*

62. Even the German Mennonites, traditionally pacifists, chose not to "exercise the principle of nondefense" at a meeting of elders and ministers on January 10, 1938. See John D. Thiesen, *Mennonite and Nazi? Attitudes Among Mennonite Colonists in Latin American, 1933-1945.*

63. Barnett at 163. Pius responded, through Cardinal Faulhaber, by instructing all priests and theology students drafted into the German army to "shun all ideas that are contrary to justice and Christian charity, to profess by action and when necessary also by word their Catholic convictions." Blet, chapter three.

64. *The Ciano Diaries* at 86.

65. Cianfarra at 101-02.

66. Lapomarda at 85, n.43.

67. Holmes at 148.

68. *Id.*

69. *Id.* at 149. On December 18, 1939, Count Ciano recorded: "The fight against Catholicism in Germany is being carried on pitilessly and idiotically." *The Ciano Diaries* at 180.

70. Holmes at 149 (quoting Reinhard Heydrich). "Heydrich seems to have had a pathological hatred of the Churches.... He sought to ruin them by discrediting them through a long and sustained campaign of slander, backed up by Gestapo action." Crankshaw at 85.

71. "First Report of Cardinal Hlond, Primate of Poland, to Pope Pius XII, on the Religious Situation in the Archdioceses of Gniezno and Pozan," reprinted in *The Persecution of the Catholic Church in German-Occupied Poland* at 1-35. Later reports noted the conversion of some Catholic churches into Protestant churches. See *id.* at 40-41.

72. *Id.*

73. "Second Report of Cardinal Hlond, Primate of Poland, to Pope Pius XII, on the Religious Situation in the Polish Dioceses of Chelmno, Katowice, Lodz, Plock, Wloclawek, and Others Incorporated in the Reich," reprinted in *The Persecution of the Catholic Church in German- Occupied Poland* at 37-65. This report also notes that priests were confined together with Jews in wooden huts, suggesting that Nazis viewed priests in the same manner that they viewed Jews.

74. Halecki & Murray at 142.

75. Graham (1968) at 29.

76. Blet, chapter three.

77. *The Tablet*, September 23, 1939, at 375.

78. Cornwell at 232 (noting that many Poles wanted a stronger condemnation of Russia and Germany).

79. Paragraph 3.

80. Paragraph 45. Less than two weeks after publication of *Summi Pontificatus*, in *Sertum Laetitae* ("On the Establishment of the Hierarchy in the United States"), Pius wrote of a "special paternal affection" for black Americans.

81. Paragraph 7.

82. In addition to being a dictator and a racist, one of Hitler's first actions after assuming power was to denounce and repudiate all treaties he deemed unfavorable to Germany.

83. O'Carroll at 53. The German-controlled Polish newspapers took advantage of the lack of communication with the outside world to distort and falsify the attitude of the Holy See. The encyclical *Summi Pontificatus* was circulated in corrupted versions which seemed to make the Pope blame the Poles for their own predicament. Graham (1968) at 34. *See* Holmes at 124.

84. *The Goebbels Diaries: 1939-1941* at 33.

85. SS Group Leader Heydrich to Reich Minister and Chief of the Reich Chancellery Lammers, Federal Archives (Germany), Koblenz, R 43 II/1504 c, typed copy with enclosure (June 22, 1940).

86. Cornwell at 234.

87. *The Persecution of the Catholic Church in German-Occupied Poland* at 59.

88. Cornwell at 234.

89. British Legation to the Holy See, January 7, 1941, British Public Record Office, FO 371/3073 56879.

90. Minutes of November 13, 1939, British Public Record Office no. FO 371/23791 56879. Minutes of the following meeting, November 16, 1939, reflect the decision not to thank the Pope, lest Mussolini find out and take offense. *Id.* FO 371/30173 56879 (similar report)

91. O'Carroll at 53.

92. Cornwell at 234.

93. Graham (1968) at 32-34; Blet, chapter three.

94. K. Doyle at 17; Blet (conclusion); Peter Gumpel, "Cornwell's Cheap Shot at Pius XII," *Crisis,* December 1999, at 19, 20 (88,000 copies). The Hitler Youth were ordered to collect these copies and destroy them. Meeting with Fr. Peter Gumpel, Rome, Italy, Dec. 5, 1999.

95. C. Doyle at 9. For similar reasons, he did not have a single cup of coffee during the war. Gaspari at 26.

96. Smit at 195.

97. Holmes at 154.

98. Cardinal MacRory to Cardinal Maglione, May 19, 1940, in *Actes et Documents,* Vol. VI, p. 306 (no. 201).

99. Holmes at 154.

100. Graham at 20. Tad Szulc wrote an article addressing Pius XII's refusal to meet with Rabbi Herzog prior to the war, but neglected to mention Herzog's later letter praising the Pope. Tad Szulc, "An Interview with Pope John-Paul II," *Parade Magazine,* April 3, 1994, at 6.

101. Holmes at 150-51.

102. See *Actes et Documents,* vol. VIII, no. 169 (message from Maglione to Osborne regarding distribution of provisions in Greece); *Actes et Documents,* vol. VIII, no. 200 (similar message from Orsenigo to Maglione).

103. Holmes at 150-51.

104. *Id.*

105. Cianfarra at 28.

106. Bokenkotter at 373.

107. Smit at 240.

108. Even later in the war, it was clear to many German leaders that peace would only be possible without Hitler. Weizsacker at 285.

109. "Probably the most feasible plot to depose Hitler during the war." Cornwell at 234.

110. Pius preferred not the term "neutrality," which could be confused with passive indifference, but "impartiality" that judges things according to truth and justice. Paci at 39.

111. Brown at 181; Alvarez & Graham at 24. The leaders might have been concerned that selection of a Protestant to broker the agreement would be seen as an attempt to advance their religion. Deutsch at 108. Mueller had previously carried out various assignments for the Vatican. *Id.* At 113.

112. Secret memorandum from the British Legation to the Holy See, January 12, 1940, British Foreign Office Document no. FO 371/24405 (Pius did not endorse or recommend the plan, but his conscience "would not be quiet easy" unless he sent it on).

113. Brown at 181.

114. Deutsch at 120; Alvarez & Graham at 27; Thomas J. Craughwell, "Pius Defenders," *The Latin Mass,* Winter 1998, at 36, 39.

115. Alvarez & Graham at 25. It was reported to Nazi authorities that Mueller went to the Vatican to collect information for German intelligence from his sources in the Vatican. Deutsch at 126. Later in the war, another member of German intelligence, Paul Franken, would keep Pius informed on anti-Hitler activity inside of Germany. Alvarez & Graham at 35-36.

116. Brown at 181-82; Alvarez & Graham at 25; Deutsch at 114. At the pontiff's request, he never met personally with Mueller. Deutsch at 122.

117. Secret memorandum from the British Legation to the Holy See, January 12, 1940, British Foreign Office Document no. FO 371/24405; Secret message from the British Legation to the Holy See, January 12, 1940, British Public Records Office F.O. 800/318; Personal and Confidential Message from the British Legation to the Holy See, February 7, 1940, British Public Record Office, FO 371/24405; Personal and Confidential Message from the British Legation to the Holy See, February 19, 1940, British Public Record Office, FO 371/24405. The first visit took place in September or October 1939. Deutsch at 119.

118. Deutsch at 144.

119. Secret message from the British Legation to the Holy See, January 12, 1940, British Public Records Office F.O. 800/318 (reporting on a planned German offensive); Personal and Confidential Message from the British Legation to the Holy See, February 7, 1940, British Public Record Office, FO 371/24405 (reporting on the planned attack on Belgium and future plans for an invasion of France). One of Mueller's reports concerned a speech Hitler made at the S.S. Ordensburg (youth leader training center) at Sonthofen, where he had screamed that he would crush the Catholic Church under his heel, as he would a toad. Deutsch at 110, n.1.

120. Lapomarda at 240, n.36 (quoting Owen Chadwick, *Britain and the Vatican During the Second World War,* Cambridge University Press (Cambridge, 1987) at 91). Pius begged the British diplomats to keep these matters "absolutely secret," lest the German generals have their lives put at risk. Secret memorandum from the British Legation to the Holy See, January 12, 1940, British Foreign Office Document no. FO 371/24405.

121. Secret memorandum from the British Legation to the Holy See, January 12, 1940, British Foreign Office Document no. FO 371/24405.

122. Lapide at 119-20.

123. Secret memorandum from the British Legation to the Holy See, January 12, 1940, British Foreign Office Document no. FO 371/24405. See also Personal and Confidential Message from the British Legation to the Holy See, February 7, 1940, British Public Record Office, FO 371/24405.

124. *Id.*

125. *Id.;* Secret message from the British Legation to the Holy See, January 12, 1940, British Public Records Office F.O. 800/318.

126. Secret message from Halifax to Osborne, February 17, 1940, British Public Record Office, FO 371/24405. See Cornwell at 237.

127. Woodward at 189 (citing British Foreign Office documents).

128. Personal and Confidential message from the British Legation to the Holy See, February 7, 1940, British Public Record Office, FO 371/24405.

129. *Id.*

130. A note from King George reflects that he was approached with this proposal on January 26, 1940. Handwritten note, February 2, 1940, British Public Records Office, FO 371/24405.

131. "Personal and Confidential message from the British Legation to the Holy See," February 7, 1940, British Public Record Office, FO 371/24405.

132. Id.

133. Shirer (1962) at 914. Even some of Pope Pius XII's closest advisors thought that "the Pope had gone much too far" and took a foolhardy risk by joining with forces in opposition to the Nazis. Deutsch at 121. Pius was likely encouraged to become involved in this attempt because both Prime Minister Chamberlain and Lord Halifax had assured him that Britain would welcome his cooperation in any peace efforts. Id.

134. Deutsch at 103.

135. See "Memorandum of February 15, 1940," British Public Record Office FO 371/24405 (discussing a counter-proposal).

136. In November 1939, two British intelligence officers were lured to the Dutch frontier by Nazi officers posing as conspirators. They were captured by the S.S. and dragged into Germany. Deutsch at 136. This set negotiations back and caused the British to demand assurances from the Pope. Fortunately, due to the "trust and admiration" that British representatives to the Vatican had for him, Pius was able to reassure British leaders and put the plan back in place. Id. at 137.

137. According to at least one report, the British negotiators demanded that Hitler be assassinated, and many of the conspirators were unwilling to go that far. O'Carroll at 55.

138. Woodward at 191.

139. Robert McClory, "Tunnel Visions," In These Times, December 12, 1999, at 40.

140. Robert A. Graham, "Foreign Intelligence and the Vatican," The Catholic World Report, March 1992, at 48, 51.

141. Robert McClory, "Tunnel Visions," In These Times, December 12, 1999, at 40.

142. Robert A. Graham, "Foreign Intelligence and the Vatican," The Catholic World Report, March 1992, at 48, 51.

143. After months of investigation the Gestapo acted. Numerous conspirators were arrested, and most were executed. Mueller was one of the few conspirators to avoid execution, even though he was arrested. Brown at 797-98. He endured 200 interrogations in Nazi prisons and concentration camps, but he did not betray the trust of his co-conspirators. This earned him the grudging admiration of his tormentors, who reported that he was "an unusually adroit man of the Jesuit school." Deutsch at 114. Reinhard Heydrich's personal conviction was that Mueller was actually a Jesuit priest in disguise. Id. At 114, n.32. After the war, Pius held an audience with Mueller. The Pontiff gave thanks for Mueller's survival, and reminded him: "We have contended with diabolical forces." Thomas J. Craughwell, "Pius Defenders," The Latin Mass, Winter 1998, at 36, 39.

144. This and the official greeting announcing his coronation are the only two messages Pius ever sent to Hitler. Both were sent in 1939.

145. Sigmund von Braun, a post-war German ambassador to the Vatican, has speculated that Pius probably would have liked to see an assassination attempt succeed.

146. Toland at 687.

147. Letter from President Roosevelt to His Holiness, Dec. 23, 1939, in *Wartime Correspondence* at 17, 19 (letter in which Roosevelt calls Pius "a good friend and an old friend").

148. Appointment by President Roosevelt of Myron C. Taylor as the President's Personal Representative to Pope Pius XII, in *Foreign Relations of the United States, Diplomatic Papers, 1939, vol. II (General, The British Commonwealth and Europe)*, United States Government Printing Office (Washington, 1956) at 869; Letter from President Roosevelt to His Holiness, Dec. 23, 1939, in *Wartime Correspondence* at 17.

149. The designation "personal representative" meant that this was something less than formal diplomatic relations. As such, Taylor's office was established in his apartment in Rome, not inside the Vatican. When, however, Italy declared war on the United States, the office was moved into Vatican City. *Wartime Correspondence* at 6.

150. Letter from President Roosevelt to His Holiness, Dec. 23, 1939, in *Wartime Correspondence* at 17, 19. Roosevelt, in internal documents, had also expressed his "personal belief that there will be, in all probability, more Christian refugees than Jewish refugees," and asked whether "the Vatican itself may not desire to take an active interest in helping the Catholic refugees to find homes in wholly new surroundings." Memorandum by President Roosevelt to the Secretary of State, Oct. 2, 1939, in *Foreign Relations of the United States, Diplomatic Papers, 1939, vol. II* (General, The British Commonwealth and Europe) at 870, United States Government Printing Office (Washington, 1956).

151. Reply of His Holiness to President Roosevelt, Jan. 7, 1940, in *Wartime Correspondence* at 23.

152. Telegram from the Ambassador in Italy (Phillips) to the Secretary of State, Dec. 24, 1939, in *Foreign Relations of the United States, Diplomatic Papers, 1939, vol. II (General, The British Commonwealth and Europe)*, United States Government Printing Office (Washington, 1956) at 874.

153. The Jewish press agreed. Upon Taylor's appointment, the *Jewish Advocate* editorialized:

> The agitation in some Protestant circles to have Myron Taylor recalled from the Vatican is to be deplored.... We can't see any possible infringement on the constitutional guarantees for separation of church and state in this matter; to the contrary we regard it as a personal effort on the part of the President to keep informed on the European situation, to exchange opinions with others who seek peace, and the explore the roads ahead for restoration of a sane world.

Gannon at 168 (quoting the *Jewish Advocate*, April 26, 1940).

154. O'Connell at 60; "A Vatican Visit," *The London Times*, October 1, 1942 (reporting on a rumor that Taylor was trying to get Pius to serve as a mediator for a possible peace settlement). Count Ciano recorded in his diary on October 26, 1942:

The Duce was irritated with Myron Taylor and with the Vatican. He attributes to the reports of the American envoy the heavy bombardments of our northern Italian cities. "This buffoon," he said, "went back to America to report that the Italians are on their last legs, and that with one or two hard blows they can easily be beaten." Anyway, "he learned those things from the Holy See, where information comes by way of parish priests. But," says the Duce, "there they don't see that the people who follow the priests are the least courageous, and the worst, always ready to weep and beg." In any case, he wanted me to let the Vatican know that "concordat or no concordat, if Myron Taylor tries to return to Italy he will be put in handcuffs."

The Ciano Diaries at 534.

155. Gannon at 168, 171.

156. *Wartime Correspondence* at xiii.

157. Marchione (1999) (Background Information). The Nazis recognized the Pope's anger at them. Joseph Goebbels wrote in his diary on December 27, "The Pope has made a Christmas speech. Full of bitter, covert attacks against us, against the Reich and National Socialism. All the forces of internationalism are against us. We must break them." *The Goebbels Diaries 1939-1941* at 75. The *Jewish Chronicle* (London) later (March 14, 1940) reported that the Pope's conditions for peace, especially for protection of racial minorities, were a "welcome feature," and it praised him for supporting the "rights of the common man."

CHAPTER ELEVEN
1940 AND THE NAZIS PRESS ON

1. Payne at 376.

2. Blet, chapter four.

3. *Id.*

4. "Let's Look at the Record," *Inside the Vatican,* October 1999, at XI.

5. "Vatican Radio Denounces Nazi Acts in Poland," *The Jewish Advocate* (Boston), January 29, 1940, at 1; Sánchez at 374; Gilbert (1987) at 40. The entire text of the broadcast of January 21-22, 1940, intended for American broadcast, can be found in *The Persecution of the Catholic Church in German-Occupied Poland* at 115-17. The story was reported in the January 23 edition of the *New York Times*, under the headline: "Vatican Denounces Atrocities in Poland; Germans Called Even Worse that Russians." A separate story in that same edition of the *Times* reported on a Soviet newspaper which had labeled Pius the "tool of Great Britain and France."

6. *Supra* note 5. This same month, Pope Pius XII ordered the publication of a large volume (565 pages) of eye-witness accounts of the German efforts to crush the Church. "Let's Look at the Record," *Inside the Vatican,* October 1999, at XI.

7. Blet, chapter four (quoting the *Manchester Guardian*).

8. *Id.*; Vatican Radio "attracted a flow of protest implying that the Holy See was continuously breaking the terms of the Reich Concordat." Cornwell at 227.

9. Blet, chapter four.

10. Paci at 43.

11. *The Jewish Advocate* (Boston, Mass.), January 26, 1940.

12. This was reported in the *Jewish Ledger* (Hartford, Conn), on Jan. 19, 1940, which called it an "eloquent gesture" which "should prove an important step in the direction of cementing bonds of sympathy and understanding" between Jews and Catholics.

A popular 1940 American encyclopedia reported that Hitler's regime was "marked by... constant conflict with Protestants and Catholics." *Standard American Encyclopedia*, vol. 9 ("Hitler, Adolf" heading). In fact, Allied authorities saw Christianity "as one of the most important instruments for the reorientation of German society." Barnett at 217.

13. *Ciano's Diplomatic Papers* at 349.

14. Message to the Cardinal Archbishop of Breslau, dated March 17, 1940, *Actes et Documents*, vol. II, no. 42.

15. *Id.*

16. "Pope is Emphatic About Just Peace; His Stress on Indispensable Basis for End of Hostilities Held Warning For Reich; Jews' Rights Defended; Pontiff in von Ribbentrop Talk Spoke on Behalf of Persecuted in Germany and Poland," *The New York Times*, March 14, 1940.

17. Memorandum from Undersecretary of State Sumner Welles, dated March 18, 1940, in *United States Department of State, Foreign Relations of the United States, Diplomatic Papers, 1940, vol. I (General)*, United States Government Printing Office (Washington, 1959) at 107 (discussing a meeting with Pope Pius XII and reporting, contrary to many other accounts, that Ribbentrop "had been exceedingly quiet and moderate in his manner"). Following the Undersecretary's meeting with Pius, he met with Cardinal Maglione, the Cardinal Secretary of State. Cardinal Maglione hinted that he was aware of a plan to topple Hitler from within Germany, and he asked Welles whether he knew anything of the plan. Welles essentially declined to answer. Memorandum from Undersecretary of State Sumner Welles, dated March 18, 1940, in *United States Department of State, Foreign Relations of the United States, Diplomatic Papers, 1940, vol. I (General)*, United States Government Printing Office (Washington, 1959) at 108.

18. Lapide at 185; Hatch & Walsh at 150-51; Office of the United States Chief of Counsel, Supp. B, at 1238 (Ribbentrop's testimony as to his desire to obtain a new agreement with the Vatican but that "things didn't come off").

19. During the war there were also "Catholic bishops, priests and students who wore the 'Jewish star' to declare their fellowship with the persecuted." John M. Oesterreicher, "As We Await *The Deputy*," *America*, November 9, 1963, at 570.

20. Rousmaniere at 121.

21. Marchione (1997) at 178.

22. Blet, chapter two.

23. According to British documents from 1940, Pius reported that the Germans did not reply to him, and he no longer felt that there were favorable

prospects for him to help bring about peace talks. Minutes of April 3, 1940, British Public Records Office FO 371/24407 65042; *Personal and Secret Message to the Secretary of State from Osborne*, April 3, 1940, British Public Records Office FO 371/24407 65042.

24. Gilbert (1981) at 59; Deutsch at 338-39.

25. Blet, chapter five. Similar treatment was given to nuncios in the Balkan States after the Soviet invasion. *Id.*

26. Blet, chapter two.

27. *Id.*

28. *Id.*

29. *Id.*

30. See *Chronicle* at 508.

31. Blet, chapter two.

32. *Id.*

33. Cianfarra at 226-27; Hatch & Walsh at 152; Cornwell at 243; Blet, chapter two.

34. Blet, chapter two.

35. *Id.*

36. *Id.*

37. Cornwell at 242.

38. *The Ciano Diaries* at 248; see *Special Distribution from Italy*, Public Records Office FO 371/24935 60675 (May 30, 1940) (noting strained relations between the Holy See and Italy).

39. Hatch & Walsh at 152; Cornwell at 241 (Mussolini called the Vatican the "chronic appendicitis of Italy.")

40. Holmes at 126; Blet, chapter two. The Belgians needed little incitement beyond that which was provided by Nazi brutality. See Jan-Albert Goris, "Lest We Forget III: We Shall Come Back," *Reader's Digest*, January 1945, at 69.

41. Telegram from Mr. Myron C. Taylor, Personal Representative of the President to Pope Pius XII, to President Roosevelt, dated May 17, 1940, in *Foreign Relations of the United States, Diplomatic Papers, 1940, vol. II* (General and Europe) at 705, United States Government Printing Office (Washington, 1957).

42. Blet, chapter two.

43. O'Carroll at 57-58; Cornwell at 243.

44. Blet, chapter two.

45. "Rome and Detroit," *The American Israelite*, March 14, 1940, at 4.

46. Cianfarra at 226-27.

47. Alvarez & Graham at 82.

48. *Id.*

49. Holmes at 126.

50. *The Ciano Diaries* at 248-49.

51. *Id.* at 249.

52. De Lubac at 15, 20.

53. *Id.* at 152-53, n.11.

54. *Id.*

55. R. Price at 259.

56. *Id.* at 253.

57. *Id.* at 255. Alfred Cardinal Baudrillart, the rector of the Catholic Institute in Paris, called Hitler's mission a noble and inspiring one.

58. *Id.* at 253-55.

59. *Id.* at 255.

60. De Lubac at 97. In the July-August 1999 issue of *Commentary*, Robert S. Wistrich made reference to a memorandum sent from the French ambassador to the Vatican back to the Vichy leaders, the so-called "Bérard Report." Wistrich used that memorandum to argue that the Vatican originally supported Vichy's anti-Semitic legislation, and when the "Vatican's posture shifted" and it started opposing anti-Semitic legislation, it was disregarded by Vichy leaders because of this earlier report.

De Lubac has two chapters about the Bérard Report in his book. De Lubac explains that Pétain was being pressured by the Catholic hierarchy in France to abandon the anti-Semitic laws, and Bérard wanted a statement from the Vatican that he could use to silence French Catholics. Thus, in a letter dated August 7, 1941, he asked for a report on the Holy See's attitude towards the new legislation.

The response came in a long memorandum, dated September 2, from Leon Bérard, French ambassador to the Holy See. The key phrase is as follows: "As someone in authority said to me at the Vatican, he will start no quarrel with us over the statute for the Jews." The ambassador was assured that "the Holy See had no hostile intention;" he was persuaded that it did not wish to "seek a quarrel."

Rather than providing the official position of the Holy See, Bérard cited the above-mentioned "someone in authority," and also gave a long justification for that position, based on Church history, including the writings of St. Thomas Aquinas. It seems highly suspect for a diplomatic report to go into historic Church teaching rather than relying on diplomatic sources. Moreover, the historic discussion omitted many much more recent authoritative statements on anti-Semitism. Authorative statements, however, would not have served Pétain's purposes.

It is certainly reasonable to conclude that Bérard drafted this memorandum to meet Pétain's needs, not to reflect the Church's actual position. As De Lubac says, "[i]f the ambassador had been able to obtain from any personage at all in Rome a reply that was even slightly clear and favorable, he would not have taken so much trouble to 'bring together the elements of a well-founded and complete report' obviously fabricated by himself or by one of his friends."

Bérard's report was dated September 2, 1941. On September 13, at a reception at the *Parc Hotel*, the apostolic nuncio, Bishop Valerio Valeri, criticized Vichy's anti-Semitic legislation. Pétain, citing the Bérard Report, replied that the Holy See found certain aspects of the laws a bit harsh, but it had not on the whole found fault with the laws. Valeri replied that the Holy See had made clear its opposition to racism, which was at the basis of this legislation. Pétain then suggested that the nuncio might not be in agreement with his superiors.

Bishop Valeri immediately wrote the Vatican's Secretary of State, Cardinal Maglione, and asked for more information. Then, around September 26, Valeri called upon Pétain and was shown Bérard's report.. The nuncio judged it to be "more nuanced" than Pétain had led him to believe, and he gave Pétain a note concerning the "grave harms that, from a religious perspective, can result from the legislation not in force." Blet, chapter eleven. Pétain replied that he too disagreed with some of the anti-Jewish laws, but that they had been imposed under pressure from the Germans. *Id.*

On September 30, Valeri wrote to Maglione, enclosing a copy of the Bérard Report. He explained the conversation at the *Parc Hotel* as follows: "I reacted quite vigorously, especially because of those who were present [ambassadors from Spain and Brazil]. I stated that the Holy See had already expressed itself regarding racism, which is at the bottom of every measure taken against the Jews...." *Id.*

The Secretary of State wrote back on October 31 explaining that Bérand had made exaggerations and deductions about Vatican policy that were not correct. He fully approved of the note that Valeri had given to Pétain and encouraged him to continue efforts designed to at least tone down the rigid application of the anti-Semitic laws. *Actes et Documents*, vol. 8, no. 189. Valeri then drafted a note of protest which he sent to Pétain.

As such, it is clear that if Pétain ever thought that Bérard's accounting of the situation was legitimate, the "shift" in the Vatican's position was *immediately* brought to his attention. As De Lubac concludes, "from the very first day... the opposition between the orientation of the Vichy government and the thought of Pius XII was patent."

61. "Let's Look at the Record," *Inside the Vatican*, October 1999, at XI.

62. *Id.*

63. Jesuit priests and their publications *Etudes* and *Témoinage Chrétien* were at the center of much of the French underground work. Lapomarda at 275-85.

64. Eventually, some 40,000 citizens were murdered and 60,000 more deported to concentration camps for "Gaullism, Marxism or hostility to the regime." One hundred thousand others were deported on racial grounds.

65. De Lubac at 161-62; Gilbert (1985) at 355.

66. Lacouture at 387 (footnote). A French Jesuit priest, Fr. Michel Riquet, who was imprisoned for his work in support of Jews later said: "Throughout those years of horror when we listened to Vatican Radio and the Pope's messages, we felt in communion with the Pope, in helping persecuted Jews and in fighting Nazi violence." R. Stewart at 9.

67. *The London Times*, Sept. 11, 1942.

68. Holmes at 164-65. See also George Kent, "Shepherds of the Underground," *The Christian Herald*, April 1945. Numerous other courageous statements from French bishops are set forth in Susan Zuccotti, *Pope Pius XII and the Holocaust: The Case in Italy*, in *The Italian Refuge*, at 257.

69. Blet, chapter eleven.

70. "War News Summarized," *The New York Times*, August 6, 1942. This protest has been questioned by some writers, but it is confirmed in a telegram sent from the German ambassador to France. *Ambassador Abetz in Paris to the Office of Foreign Affairs*, dated August 28, 1942, *Akten Zur Deutschen Auswärtigen Politik*, 1918-1945, Series E, Band III, Vandenhoeck & Ruprecht in Göttingen (1974) no. 242 (discussing a protest from the Nuncio regarding the treatment of the Jews, instructions from the Archbishop of Toulouse telling priests "to protest most vehemently from the pulpit against the deportation of the Jews," and Laval's protest to the Vatican). At about this same

time, Jewish leaders in American were also taking note of Pope Pius XII's actions.

> It appears to be more than rumor that his Holiness Pope Pius XII, urgently appealed through the Papal Nuncio to the Vichy Government to put an end to deportations from France and the appeal of the Pope is said to have been reinforced by petition and protect from the Cardinal Arch Bishops of Paris and Lyons... If such Papal intervention be factual, then Pius XII follows the high example set by his saintly predecessor, whose word in reprobation of anti-Semitism "spiritually we are all Semites," will never fade out of the memory of the people which does not forget but forgives.

Stephen S. Wise, *As I See It*, Marstin Press (New York, 1944) (reprinting an article from 1942).

71. *The New York Times*, August 27, 1942.

72. Holmes at 164; "Pope is Said to Plead for Jews Listed for Removal From France," *New York Times*, August 6, 1942.

73. Wymann at 34 (footnote); see "A Spiritual Ally," *California Jewish Voice*, August 28, 1942; "Vichy Seizes Jews; Pope Pius Ignored," *The New York Times*, August 27, 1942; and "25,000 Jews Reported Held in South France For Deportation by the Nazis to the East," *The New York Times*, August 28, 1942 (noting the Pope's support for appeals made to Vichy leaders by Catholic clergymen).

74. "Let's Look at the Record," *Inside the Vatican*, October 1999, at XII.

75. *Id.*

76. De Lubac at 143; *see* Shiber at 159.

77. "Laval Spurns Pope—25,000 Jews in France Arrested for Deportation," *The Canadian Jewish Chronicle*, September 4, 1942.

78. *The California Jewish Voice*, August 28, 1942.

79. "Christendom and the Jews," *The Jewish Chronicle* (London), Sept. 11, 1942. The editorial went on to say that the rebuke that Pius received from "Laval and his Nazi master" was "an implied tribute to the moral steadfastness of a great spiritual power, bravely doing its manifest spiritual duty." See Lothar Groppe, "The Church and the Jews in the Third Reich," *Fidelity*, November 1983, at 25 (quoting parts of the editorial).

80. A censorship order to the press said, "No mention is to be made of the Vatican protest to Marshal Pétain in favor of the Jews." Lothar Groppe, "The Church and the Jews in the Third Reich," *Fidelity*, November 1983, at 25.

81. Holmes at 164.

82. Goldhagen at 110; Lothar Groppe, "The Church and the Jews in the Third Reich," *Fidelity*, November 1983, at 25.

83. Joseph L. Lichten, "A Question of Judgment: Pius XII and the Jews," in *Pius XII and the Holocaust: A Reader* at 114-15.

84. David S. Wyman, *The Abandonment of the Jews: America and the Holocaust 1941-1945*, Pantheon Books (New York, 1984).

85. Gilbert (1987) at 333-50. According to one account, 162 French priests were arrested by the Gestapo, of which 123 were shot or guillotined. Marchione (1999) (Vatican Documents).

86. Shiber (Author's note).

87. *Id.* at 159.

88. Fr. Christian was later captured by the Nazis and sentenced to death for his work with the underground. He, however, escaped with the help of British intelligence. *Id.* at 312, 385.

89. Fogelman at 209. See also George Kent, "Shepherds of the Underground," *The Christian Herald*, April 1945.

90. Fogelman at 209. See also George Kent, "Shepherds of the Underground," *The Christian Herald*, April 1945.

91. Fogelman at 209; Graham at 23-24.

92. Fogelman at 209; Graham at 23-24.

93. *The Australian Jewish News*, April 16, 1943.

94. The Vatican provided papers indicating Latin American citizenship to many Jews in occupied France. When the papers were discovered to be illegal, the Latin American countries withdrew recognition of them. This made the Jews subject to deportation to the concentration camps. Pursuant to a request from the Union of Orthodox Rabbis of the United States and Canada, and working in conjunction with the International Red Cross, the Vatican contacted the countries involved and urged them to recognize the documents, "no matter how illegally obtained." Graham at 23-24; Blet, chapter eleven.

95. Blet, chapter nine.

96. *Id.*

97. Joseph L. Lichten, "A Question of Judgment:: Pius XII and the Jews" in *Pius XII and the Holocaust: A Reader* at 116-17. Later in the war, Marie-Benoît (operating under the name of Padre Benedetto) went to the International College of Capuchins in Rome where he worked with a Jewish rescue organization, the Delegation for Assistance to Jewish Emigrants (DELASEM). Beginning in April 1944, DELASEM operated from its headquarters in Marie-Benoît's residence, and he helped that organization keep in touch with the International Red Cross, the Pontifical Relief Commission, the Italian police, and other civil authorities. Marie-Benoît and others in Rome helped DELASEM manufacture false documents and establish contact with sympathetic Italian, Swiss, Hungarian, French, and Romanian officials. After the war, he received an award from the Italian Jewish Union for his work in protecting about 1,000 Jews in Rome. Holmes at 152-53. For further cooperation between DELASEM and the Catholic Church, *see* Lapomarda at 233-34.

98. *Chronicle* at 576.

99. R. Price at 268. Laval was executed, Pétain was sentenced to death (the sentence was later commuted and he was exiled), and a handful of other collaborators were imprisoned.

100. Blet, chapter eleven.

101. *Id.*

102. *Id.* (quoting de Gaulle's *War Memories*).

103. "The minister did not want the dean of the diplomatic corps, who once had presented Marshal Pétain with the customary greetings in addresses required by protocol, to offer similar greetings to General de Gaulle." *Id.*

104. *Id.* The Vatican Ministry of State made innumerable requests to foreign governments for exit and entry papers during the occupation of France. Vatican funds were used to help procure transit visas from other nations. The costs for these rescue operations was enormous, totaling in the millions of

dollars, and the primary source for this money was the Vatican. Blet, chapter seven.

105. *Id.*

106. *Id.*; De Lubac at 98.

107. Pope Pius XII reported that "it was with deep satisfaction that We heard of M. De Gaulle's desire not to allow any interruption in the happy relations between France and the Holy See." "The Task of France," *The Tablet* (London), May 19, 1945.

108. Fabert at 38-39.

109. Todd & Curti at 675.

110. Blum at 719. "The same dagger pierced the very heart of Pius XII." Hatch & Walsh at 153.

111. Blum at 719.

112. *Saeculo Exeunte Octavo*, paragraph 39.

113. Cianfarra at 228, 242.

114. "Letter from His Holiness to President Roosevelt," May 18, 1943, *Wartime Correspondence* at 89-90; *id.* at 91-92 (Roosevelt's reply, dated June 16, 1943).

115. Blet, chapter two (noting particularly Great Britain's reluctance to give assurances).

116. Graham at 16.

117. Prior to Italy's entry into the war, many European Jews fled to Italy. After it got involved in the war and Jews were put at risk, St. Raphael Verein, a Catholic Church organization which had long been active in helping emigrants leave Europe for the New World, received instructions from Pope Pius XII to give aid to Jewish refugees from Germany, Austria, Poland, Hungary and other European nations. Before long St. Raphael Verein had a well-run organization working for their protection. When open operations became impossible and the last plane carrying Jewish refugees left Rome on September 8, 1943, St. Raphael Verein turned to the task of assigning the Jews left behind to hiding places. By 1945, this organization had given assistance to some 25,000 Jews. Joseph L. Lichten, "A Question of Judgment: Pius XII and the Jews," in *Pius XII and the Holocaust: A Reader* at 123-24.

118. Blet, chapter five (noting that the British would have preferred that Vatican City remain lighted, as a beacon for British planes seeking out Rome).

119. "Reply of President Roosevelt to His Holiness," June 16, 1943, in *Wartime Correspondence* at 91-92.

120. Halecki & Murray at 182-83.

121. This diplomatic practice was done with the cooperation of Allied leaders. See *United States Department of State, Foreign Relations of the United States, Diplomatic Papers, 1944, vol. IV (Europe)*, United States Government Printing Office (Washington, 1966) at 1318-1327 (various communications regarding movement of diplomats in and out of the Vatican). Following the war, the Vatican requested that German diplomats be treated with normal diplomatic immunity. Telegram from Mr. Myron C. Taylor, Personal Representative of President Roosevelt to Pope Pius XII, to the Secretary of State, June 8, 1945, in *United States Department of State, Foreign Relations of the United States, Diplomatic Papers, 1945, vol. III (European Advisory Commission; Austria; Germany)*, United States Government Printing Office (Washington, 1968) at 787.

122. Cornwell at 241 (noting that its impact was magnified by the practice of priests reading it from the pulpit).

123. Cianfarra at 220, 227-28; Holmes at 127; Cornwell at 242. See *General Distribution from Italy,* British Public Records Office FO 371/24935 60675 (May 17, 1940) (vendors and purchasers beaten); *Report from Osborne to London,* British Public Records Office FO 371/24935 60675 (May 21, 1940) (report on the ban on the sale of the Vatican newspaper); *Special Distribution from Italy,* Public Records Office FO 371/24935 60675 (May 30, 1940) ("agreement has been reached on the circulation within Italy of the present emasculated *Osservatore*") .

124. Cianfarra at 220-21 (quoting Roberto Farinacci, editor of *Regime Fascista*); Cornwell at 242 (citing Farinacci).

125. "Let's Look at the Record," *Inside the Vatican,* October 1999, at XII. *Palazzo Pio,* Vatican Radio's production headquarters since 1970, is named after Pope Pius XII.

126. Alvarez & Graham at 142. Hlond's protests from afar brought complaints from Poles still in Poland. Bishop Carl Maria Splett of Danzig wrote to Pius XII:

At my inquiry the Gestapo told me that Cardinal Hlond had called for resistance among the Polish population over the Vatican Radio station, and the Gestapo had to prevent him.... They say that Cardinal Hlond called the Polish people to rally round its priests and teachers. Thereupon, numerous priests and teachers were arrested and executed, or were tortured to death in the most terrible manner, or were even shipped to the far east.

Lothar Groppe, "The Church's Struggle with the Third Reich," *Fidelity,* October 1983, at 15.

127. Cianfarra at 256.

128. Holmes at 129. Similar broadcasts were directed at other nations. Alvarez & Graham at 142 (discussing France).

129. Speaight at 25.

130. Cianfarra at 256-57.

131. Speaight at 25.

132. See Blet, chapter five (going into detail regarding the broadcasts and dispute of October 1940).

133. Speaight at 26. Throughout the war there were many similar broadcasts concerning German abuses, misrepresentations, and crimes against humanity. For instance, when *Das Schwarze Korps* published an article arguing that it was a crime against nature for the French army to permit black soldiers to fight against white [German] soldiers, Vatican Radio replied: "That it is sufficient for a black man to be a human being in order to be able to claim a human soul and human dignity." The report went on to note that Germany had made blacks fight in the previous war in East Africa and that there was a large movement of black people into the Catholic faith. Speaight at 27.

134. *Actes et Documents,* vol. IV, no. 140.

135. See Martinez at 26.

136. Speaight at 26; Alvarez & Graham at 143. See, *e.g., Actes et Documents,* vol. IV, no. 140.

368 HITLER, THE WAR, AND THE POPE

137. Bishop Stefan Sapieha of Kracow wrote a letter to Pius, dated October 28, 1942, in which he said: "It displeases us greatly that we cannot communicate Your Holiness' letters to our faithful, but it would furnish a pretext for further persecution and we have already had victims suspected of communicating with the Holy See."

138. *Actes et Documents*, vol. IV, no. 401; *Actes et Documents*, vol. IV, no. 140; *Actes et Documents*, vol. IV, no. 374. This was in keeping with the Pope's official instruction at the beginning of the war that Vatican Radio would be an independent, autonomous entity and not an organ of the Holy See. "Catholic Historian's Report Details Perils of 'Martyrs of Vatican Radio,'" *The National Catholic Register*, Feb. 1, 1976 (citing Robert Graham).

139. "Catholic Historian's Report Details Perils of 'Martyrs of Vatican Radio,'" *The National Catholic Register*, Feb. 1, 1976 (citing a directive dated Jan. 19, 1940, from the Pope ordering German language broadcasts on the state of the Church in Poland).

140. Martinez at 26.

141. Holmes at 129.

142. Report from Osborne to London, British Public Records Office FO 371/24935 60675 (May 21, 1940).

143. Some dispute does exist over the value of Vatican Radio broadcasts in Soviet-occupied areas. At least some people felt that broadcasts "had no effect other than to rile up the Soviet authorities against the church." Blet, chapter five.

144. This is discussed in chapter 10.

145. Deutsch at 144.

146. Secret message from the British Legation to the Holy See, January 12, 1940, British Public Records Office F.O. 800/318 (reporting on a planned German offensive); Personal and Confidential Message from the British Legation to the Holy See, February 7, 1940, British Public Record Office, FO 371/24405 (reporting on the planned attack on Belgium and future plans for an invasion of France). One of Mueller's reports concerned a speech Hitler made at the S.S. Ordensburg (youth leader training center) at Sonthofen, where he had screamed that he would crush the Catholic Church under his heel, as he would a toad. Deutsch at 110, n.1.

147. Telegram from the Ambassador in Italy (Phillips) to the Secretary of State, dated Feb. 28, 1940, in *United States Department of State, Foreign Relations of the United States, Diplomatic Papers, 1940, vol. I (General)*, United States Government Printing Office (Washington, 1959) at 126 (discussing the security of France and England, the mood in Germany and in the German military, Germany's resources in the event of a long war, and Italy's attitude towards war).

148. *The Persecution of the Catholic Church in the Third Reich* at 64.

149. *Id.* at 62-63.

150. *Id.* at 413.

151. *Id.*

152. O'Carroll at 55-56. The material was edited by W. Mariaux and published in 1940 by Burns & Oates under the title *The Persecution of the Catholic Church in the Third Reich*.

153. Deighton at 256-57.

154. Lapide at 174. Pius also urged his bishops in Spain to use their influence to try to keep Spain out of the war, much to the consternation of Nazi leadership. *The Goebbels Diaries 1942–1943* at 166 (the Pope "thereby gives expression to his enmity for the Axis.")

155. Earlier that year, when it had become obvious that Hitler was considering a treaty with the Soviet Union, Mussolini wrote him a letter urging him against it. Payne at 376.

156. Reprinted in *The Persecution of the Catholic Church in German-Occupied Poland* at 121-23.

157. *Id.*

158. Marchione (1999) (Overview).

159. De Lubac at 34-35.

160. British diplomats certainly thought so. See *Distribution B from Switzerland*, December 30, 1940, British Public Record Office, FO 371/30173 56879 (request from Osborne for permission to offer Pius "a personal message of appreciation").

161. *Id.* at 35.

CHAPTER TWELVE

1941 AND NEW ENEMIES

1. Cianfarra at 266.

2. *Message to the Bishop of Limburg (Antonius Hilfrich)*, dated February 20, 1941, *Actes et Documents*, vol. II, no. 65.

3. Pope Pius XII also sent President Roosevelt the following Easter greeting by means of telegram:

> We thank Your Excellency for the greetings which you have so kindly sent Us for Easter. In these festive days of joyful commemoration Our heart is particularly saddened by the thought of the massacre and widespread devastation which the present conflict is leaving in its wake....We have found unbounded sympathy and generous cooperation among Our beloved children of the United States. Not content with this We have felt and We feel it Our duty to raise Our voice, the voice of a Father not moved by any earthly interests but animated only by a desire for the common good of all, in a plea for a peace that will be genuine, just, honorable, and lasting; a peace that will respect individuals, families and nations and safeguard their rights to life, to a reasonable liberty, to a conscientious and fervent practice of religion, to true progress, and to an equitable participation in the riches which providence has distributed with largess over the earth; a peace whose spirit and provisions will tend to revitalize and reinvigorate through new and enlightened organization the true spirit of brotherhood among men today so tragically alienated one from another.

"Message from His Holiness to President Roosevelt," Easter-April 1941, *Wartime Correspondence* at 53.

4. Copeland at 525 (setting forth the entire speech); Smit at 227.

5. Copeland at 525.

6. *Id.*

7. *Id.*

8. Vatican Radio explicitly condemned "the wickedness of Hitler" on March 30, 1941, and "the immoral principles of Nazism" on April 5, 1941. Joseph M. McGowan, "Hitler's Pope' author drew flawed conclusions," *The Pantagraph* (Bloomington, IL.), December 7, 1999 at A10.

9. "Catholic Historian's Report Details Perils of 'Martyrs of Vatican Radio,' " *The National Catholic Register*, Feb. 1, 1976 (citing Robert Graham).

10. Holmes at 130.

11. Blet, chapter five. Allied propaganda often contained misleading information about the Church, the Vatican, or the Pope. Alvarez & Graham at 14.

12. Alvarez & Graham at 17. For a wartime account of British radio propaganda, see William D. Bayles, "England's Radio Blitz, Saturday Night, Jan. 29, 1944," reprinted in *Reader's Digest,* April 1944, at 61.

13. Alvarez & Graham at 144.

14. Martinez at 26. Certain Polish bishops, exiled in London, called for stronger statements by the pontiff. Those who remained in Poland, however, urged him not to speak. Paci at 41; Lamb at 48.

15. Blet, chapter five.

16. Martinez at 26. British diplomat Sir Alec Randall recorded in the minutes of a meeting dated July 21, 1941:

> The Vatican wireless has been of the greatest service to our propaganda and we have exploited it to the full. No other neutral power would, in the face of this, have persisted so long in furnishing us with useful material risking violent criticism from powers with which it is in ordinary diplomatic relations.
>
> ***
>
> For the future, I think we should keep a very careful watch on developments and take advantage of the Pope's assurance... that should specific occasion arise for denial of new Nazi propaganda lies the Vatican radio will be used. We can I think slightly expand that assurance, when we have really good material, into a request....

Minutes, July 21, 1941, British Public Record Office, INF 1/893.

17. Holmes at 130-31; Blet, chapter five.

18. Blet, chapter five; "Catholic Historian's Report Details Perils of 'Martyrs of Vatican Radio,' " *The National Catholic Register*, Feb. 1, 1976 (citing Robert Graham).

19. Diego von Bergen, the Reich's ambassador to the Holy See, described the situation as "a stabilization of tension, which at times could give an outsider the false impression of an approaching accommodation." Blet, chapter six.

20. Blet, chapter five.

21. Holmes at 128-29.

22. William J. O'Malley, "Priests of the Holocaust," reprinted in *Pius XII and the Holocaust: A Reader* at 153.

23. Gilbert (1987) at 362.

24. Copeland at 516.

25. Blet, chapter three. Later, Hitler wanted to back off from the "crusade" language, because it might mean that he would have to let Churches into occupied areas, and he did not want to do that. Cornwell at 261.

26. Blet, chapter six.

27. Few priests ended up accompanying the German troops. Not only had the Pope opposed their mission, German leadership also opposed them. The Germans feared that the Church might try to use the invasion to gain entry and do missionary work. In July 1941, Reinhard Heydrich circulated a report that the Vatican had a long term plan to proselytize Russia and encircle the Reich with hostile Catholic states. Hitler ordered that missionary activity was absolutely prohibited, and non-military priests were barred from entering occupied areas to the east of Germany. Alvarez & Graham at 12-13; 124. Most of the priests who did accompany the invasion were shot and killed as deserters or spies. Cornwell at 264.

28. Martinez at 26.

29. Internal German documents suggest that some German officials felt that Pius XII privately favored their side in the war with the Soviets. According to one 1941 report, Pius was about to condemn Nazi policies in Germany when the war with the Soviet Union broke out. The writer went on to speculate that Pius refrained from condemning Nazi policies so that he would not hurt the German cause in the war. *Documents on German Foreign Policy 1918-1945*, Series D (1937- 1945) no. 309 (Secret message from Counselor of Embassy Menshausen to State Secretary Weizsäcker, Sept. 12, 1941).

30. *Minutes dated September 10, 1941*, British Public Record Office, FO 371/30175 57750.

31. Gilbert (1987) at 362. A year earlier, Cardinal Maglione, the Vatican Secretary of State, was unable to disguise his aversion for the German government as he expressed the opinion that Communism would come to dominate Germany before too long. Memorandum from Undersecretary of State Sumner Welles, dated March 18, 1940, in *United States Department of State, Foreign Relations of the United States, Diplomatic Papers, 1940, vol. I (General)*, United States Government Printing Office (Washington, 1959) at 108.

32. Gilbert (1987) at 362. British leaders recognized the references to Poland and Germany. *Minutes of June 28, 1941*, FO 371/30175 57750.

33. Gilbert (1985) at 362.

34. O'Carroll at 132.

35. Robert A Graham, "A Return to Theocracy," *America*, July 18, 1964, at 70.

36. *Actes et Documents*, vol. V, no. 105. The British leadership used the Vatican's refusal to support the "crusade" for propaganda, even to the extent that they acknowledged "causing the Vatican some embarrassment." *Report from Mr. Osborne*, Sept. 29, 1941, British Public Record Office, FO 371/30175; *see also* British Public Records Office, INF 1/893 (secret telegram dated Oct. 26, 1942, to the British War Cabinet reporting on pressure being put on the Vatican to declare the German invasion a crusade).

37. *Chronicle* at 524.

38. The roots of the Atlantic Charter have been traced back to a peace proposal that Pius presented in an allocution to the cardinals on Christmas Eve, 1939. Hatch & Walsh at 150.

39. In addition, Pope Pius IX, in 1846, had referred to "that infamous doctrine of so-called Communism, which is absolutely contrary to the natural law itself, and if once adopted would utterly destroy the rights, property, and possessions of all men and even society itself." Similarly, Pope Leo XIII defined Communism as "the fatal plague which insinuates itself into the very marrow of human society only to bring about its ruin." Doyle at 46.

40. Memorandum form the Ambassador in Italy to the Foreign Ministry, Sept. 17, 1941, (Top Secret), enclosing The Royal Italian Embassy to the Holy See, Subject:: Taylor's Conversations at the Vatican, Rome, Sept. 16, 1941 (Secret), in *Documents on German Foreign Policy 1918-1945*, Series D (1937-1945) no. 330 (Sept. 22, 1934).

41. *Id.*

42. *Id.*

43. *Id.*

44. *Id.*

45. President Roosevelt "was shocked by a poll of American Catholic clergy which revealed that 90 per cent were opposed to US aid to Russia." Lamb at 47.

46. "Letter from President Roosevelt to His Holiness," Sept. 3, 1941, in *Wartime Correspondence* at 61-62. In reply, Pius wrote:

> We are endeavoring, with all the forces at Our disposal, to bring material and spiritual comfort to countless thousands who are numbered amongst the innocent and helpless victims. We should like, on this occasion, to express to Your Excellency Our cordial appreciation of the magnificent assistance which the American people have given, and continue to offer, in this mission of mercy.

Id. at 63-64 (Reply of His Holiness to President Roosevelt, Sept. 20, 1941). The Holy See at this time was only aware of two Catholic churches that were open in all of the Soviet Union. Blet, chapter six.

47. Alvarez & Graham at 11-12.

48. Langer & Gleason at 796; Blet, chapter six.

49. Blet, chapter six (noting Archbishop Mooney of Detroit's argument that American Catholics needed direction from Rome).

50. *Id.*

51. Blet, chapter six. The Auxiliary Bishop of Cleveland, Michael Ready, was assigned to head up the campaign to clarify *Divini Redemptoris* in the United States. Langer & Gleason at 796-97, vol. V, no. 63 (Tardini's notes: "These Americans–who in reality are already in the war against the Axis... should comprehend that the Holy See is in a very difficult situation.... As for religious liberty in Russia, it is clear that so far it was the most that was trampled upon....").

52. Blet, chapter six.

53. Peter Gumpel, "Cornwell's Cheap Shot at Pius XII," *Crisis*, December 1999, at 19, 25.

54. Martinez at 26. For an example of how the American popular press reported on religion in the Soviet Union, see "Up from the Russian

Catacombs," *Time,* December 27, 1943, reprinted in *Reader's Digest,* March 1944, at 94; *see also* William Philip Simms, "Give Us Your Hand, Russia," *New York World-Telegram,* Nov. 6, 1945 ("Our pulpits and platforms welcome pro-Soviet propagandists."); Terkel at 113-120 (American woman questions pro-Soviet propaganda). See also Blet, chapter twelve ("When *Collier's* magazine printed that about eighteen hundred Catholic churches remained open in Russia, it gave completely false information.")

55. P. Murphy at 224. Sister Pascalina reportedly made this claim. Another account reports that Pius prayed on a regular basis for exorcism of the evil that inhabited Hitler's soul. Cornwell at 273.

56. In 1941, when he was a senator, Truman described the ideal reaction of the still neutral America: "If we see Germany as winning, we ought to help Russia. And if we see Russia is winning, we ought to help Germany. And in that way, let them kill as many as possible." *The Chicago Tribune,* on September 17 of that year similarly wrote: "The Nazi-Communist War is the only one of the last century that civilized men can regard with complete approval. They hope it will persist until both brutal antagonists have bled to death." Langer & Gleason at 793.

57. Cheetham at 287; Blet, chapter six. Giuio Andreotti, the former Prime Minister of Italy, said the Pope had to choose "between the Plague and Cholera."

58. Blet, chapter six.

59. Blum at 726.

60. According to the head of the Soviet Parliamentary Commission on Rehabilitation, from 1929 to 1953, 21.5 million people were "repressed." Of these a third were shot, the rest were imprisoned (where many of them died). These figures do not include famine victims and deported ethnic groups. If the victims of politically induced famines and deportations are counted, the total number of Soviet victims is far greater than the Nazi victims. When it comes to the deliberate mass murder of civilians, the Communists are the "blood-stained world champions." Hollander, *National Review,* May 2, 1994.

61. Holmes at 138.

62. Gascoigne at 290.

63. Cheetham at 287-88. In December 1941, Hitler disclosed his thoughts on this matter:

> The war will come to an end, and I shall see my last task as clearing up the Church problem. Only then will the German nation be completely safe.... In my youth I had the view: dynamite! Today I see that one cannot break it over one's knee. It has to be cut off like a gangrenous limb.

Cornwell at 261.

64. Toland at 774.

65. Moreover, the German-allied countries of Italy, Slovenia, Slovakia, and Croatia were entirely Catholic, and Hungary was primarily Catholic. This led to several minor disputes between the Reich and the Holy See regarding the application of the concordat (and therefore the rights of the Church) in occupied areas. *Documents on German Foreign Policy 1918-1945,* Series D (1937- 1945) no. 241, 260 (memoranda concerning application of the concordat).

66. Cianfarra at 269-70.

67. Memorandum from the Ambassador in Italy to the Foreign Ministry, Sept. 17, 1941, (Top Secret), enclosing The Royal Italian Embassy to the Holy See, Subject: Taylor's Conversations at the Vatican, Rome, Sept. 16, 1941 (Secret), in *Documents on German Foreign Policy 1918-1945*, Series D (1937-1945) no. 330 (Sept. 22, 1934).

68. Cianfarra at 326.

69. Pius received even more pressure to resist Marxism as the war dragged on. Late in the war Nuncio Roncalli (the future Pope John XXIII) wrote to express "panic" at the Soviet offensive. In April 1944, the Prime Minister of Hungary came to Rome with a desperate plea for the Pope to put himself "at the head of a peace initiative capable of halting the Soviet advance that was about to engulf the Christian peoples of Europe." The Pope, however, refused to do anything to support the Axis.

70. Martinez at 26.

71. Deighton at 537.

72. The day that this statement was made, December 8, the first Jews were gassed at Chelmno, Poland. Rousmaniere at 113.

73. Pius XII presented Christmas messages asking for peace throughout the war. The 1942 message is the one most often cited. This 1941 message is discussed (among other places) in Cianfarra at 319-29.

74. Cianfarra at 319-29.

75. Hitler, of course, had pulled Germany out of the League of Nations.

76. Notes of the Legation Counsellor Haidlen, January 5, 1942, *Akten Zur Deutschen Auswärtigen Politik, 1918-1945*, Series E, Band I, Vandenhoeck & Ruprecht in Göttingen (1960), no. 95; Blet, chapter six.

77. *The Ciano Diaries* at 424. Ciano added that "This is unavoidable, in view of the anti-Catholic policy of the Germans." He also reported that "at the Vatican the Russians are preferred to the Nazis." *Id.*

78. See Cianfarra at 319-29 (emphasis added).

CHAPTER THIRTEEN

1942 AND THE FINAL SOLUTION

1. Office of the United States Chief Counsel, vol. I, at 279. Despite the tone of the rejection, the Vatican did express a desire to improve relations between the Holy See and Germany. *Id.*, vol. V, at 1009.

2. *Hitler's Secret Conversations* at 447. He also spoke of ending the concordat once the war was over. *Id.* at 448. One of his complaints was that "the Catholic Church strives always to seek advantage where we are the weakest by demanding the application to the whole Reich of those of the various Concordats which conform most closely to its aspirations." *Id.* at 448.

3. *Chronicle* at 542.

4. "This was where the majority of European jews lived and, therefore, such a Nazi crime could be better hidden from world public opinion in a country totally occupied and even partially annexed to the Third Reich." Polish

Bishops, *The Victims of Nazi Ideology*, January 1995, reprinted in Secretariat for Ecumenical and Interreligious Affairs, National Conference of Bishops, *Catholics Remember the Holocaust,* United States Catholic Conference (Washington, 1998).

5. Holmes at 128-29.

6. *Minutes, July 21, 1941*, British Public Record Office, INF 1/893.

7. Holmes at 129.

8. Lothar Groppe, "The Church's Struggle with the Third Reich," *Fidelity,* October 1983, at 14; see Matheson at 93-94. The Holy See refused to recognize the annexed portion of Poland as part of Germany. Because of this, when it attempted to protest the treatment of people in this area, the Germans refused to recognize the Holy See's standing to voice objection. R. Stewart at 29.

9. Graham (1968) at 18.

10. *Id.* These Poles in Germany also were prohibited from possessing Catholic prayer books in the Polish language. R. Stewart at 28.

11. O'Carroll at 132.

12. Graham (1968) at 20.

13. *Id.* (1968) at 20.

14. Robert A. Graham, "Author Questions Pope Pius XII's Vatican Diplomacy," *The Pilot* (Boston), Oct. 31, 1970, at 1, 16.

15. *Maltreatment and Persecution of the Catholic Clergy in the Western Provinces,* Office of the United States Chief of Counsel, vol. I, at 286. See also *A note of His Eminence the Cardinal Secretary of State to the Foreign Minister of the Reich about the religious situation in "Wartegau" and in the other Polish provinces subject to Germany,* March 2, 1943, in Office of the United States Chief of Counsel, vol. V, at 1018.

16. Graham (1968) at 22.

17. In the un-annexed part of German-occupied Poland (the General Government), the situation was not quite as severe, though religious persecution certainly existed. In Germany itself, where many Polish workers were sent, Poles were refused permission to enter churches that were conducting services intended for Germans, and they were not allowed to use the Polish language in confession. Graham (1968) at 20-21.

18. Lothar Groppe, "The Church's Struggle with the Third Reich," *Fidelity*, October 1983, at 14 (citing Walter Adolph, *Im Schatten des Galgens* (Berlin, 1953)).

19. This was necessary because the bishop from Klum had fled Germany (as had Cardinal Hlond).

20. Lothar Groppe, "The Church's Struggle with the Third Reich," *Fidelity*, October 1983, at 14 (citing Walter Adolph, *Im Schatten des Galgens* (Berlin, 1953)).

21. In protest of the treatment that the Polish Catholic Church suffered at the hands of the Nazis, the Vatican issued a memorandum on October 8, 1942, to the German Embassy:

> For quite a long time the religious situation in the *Warthegau* gives cause for very grave and ever increasing anxiety. There, in fact, the Episcopate has been little by little almost completely eliminated; the secular and regular clergy have been reduced to proportions that are absolutely inadequate, because they have been in large part deport-

376 HITLER, THE WAR, AND THE POPE

ed and exiled; the education of clerics has been forbidden; the Catholic education of youth is meeting with the greatest opposition; the nuns have been dispersed; insurmountable obstacles have been put in the way of affording people the helps of religions; very many churches have been closed; Catholic intellectual and charitable institutions have been destroyed; ecclesiastical property has been seized.

Office of the United States Chief of Counsel, vol. I, at 283; *id.,* vol. V at 1017. This and similar protests sent by Catholic officials failed to bring any relief. In fact, they tended to make things worse.

22. Blet, chapter six.

23. Telegram from the Chargé in Switzerland (Huddle) to the Secretary of State, Feb. 9, 1942, in *Foreign Relations of the United States, Diplomatic Papers, 1942, vol. III (Europe),* United States Government Printing Office (Washington, 1961) at 778. It should be noted, however, that Japan was widely perceived to be waging a war against Christianity. See Robert Bellaire, "'Christianity Must Go,' Says Japan: The Enemy fights the Christians as viciously as he fights us," *Collier's,* Nov. 20, 1943 ("Japan is as much at war with Christianity as with the United States.")

24. Holmes at 136. The Japanese were similarly concerned that the Vatican had established relations with Chiang Kai Chek's government. Blet, chapter six.

25. Darragh at 15; Blet, chapter twelve.

26. Blet, chapter six.

27. The Germans may have asked Pope Pius to intervene and try to stop the bombing of civilian populations. *The Ciano Diaries* at 523.

28. *Enclosure in Mr. Osborne's Despatch No. 111 of September 11th 1942,* British Public Records Office, FO371/334148[?] 56879.

29. Heller & Nekrich at 408.

30. *Id.* at 408; Barnett at 166. This is very similar to some of the ideas he had set forth almost twenty years earlier in *Mein Kampf.*

31. Heller & Nekrich at 409.

32. *Id.* at 408.

33. Garcia at 19.

34. This caused some difficulty with her mother, who felt that Christians were persecuting the Jews; Edith's sister Rosa was baptized as a Catholic only after their mother had died. Garcia at 19.

35. Lothar Groppe, "The Church and the Jews in the Third Reich," *Fidelity,* November 1983, at 23.

36. Dutch bishops had warned their followers about the dangers of Nazism as early as 1934, and in 1936 they ordered Catholics not to support Fascist organizations or they would risk excommunication. They forbade Catholic policemen from hunting down Jews, even if it meant losing their jobs. Fogelman at 172; Holmes at 165.

37. Cianfarra at 268. A similar letter concerning the situation in the Third Reich was sent by German bishops on July 6, 1941. One of its provisions was: "Never, and under no circumstances, may a man, except in the case of war and legitimate defense, kill an innocent person." O'Carroll at 116.

38. Lothar Groppe, "The Church and the Jews in the Third Reich," *Fidelity,* November 1983, at 23.

39. Lapide at 202.

40. Lothar Groppe, "The Church and the Jews in the Third Reich," *Fidelity*, November 1983, at 23.

41. Lapide at 200.

42. Garcia at 20.

43. Lapomarda at 261, n. 23.

44. Reportedly, Pius XII was considering having *L'Osservatore Romano* publish a protest against Nazism when the events from Holland were reported back to him. There was no nuncio in Holland at the time, since he had been expelled by the Nazis, so Pius learned of these events from newspapers and radio accounts. He is said to have picked up two pages of writing that he had been working on and to have burned them. *Testimony of Sr. Pascalina Lehnert*, Oct. 29, 1968–Jan. 24, 1969, before the Tribunal of the Vicariate of Rome, on the beatification of Pius XII (Eugenio Pacelli), Part I, page 77, 85; *Testimony of Maria Conrada Grabmair*, May 9, 1969–May 29, 1969, before the Tribunal of the Vicariate of Rome, on the beatification of Pius XII (Eugenii Pacelli), Part I, page 173, 174. See also the Epilogue of this book.

45. Karski at 129-30, 235, 257, 271-72, 387 (first-hand account of the Polish underground); Lapomarda at 132; Mazgaj at 62-63 (priest sent to Auschwitz due to work in Polish underground).

46. Karski at 167, 180, 352-53.

47. *Id.* at 354.

48. *Reprinted in* Tec at 110-112.

49. F. Murphy at 201-02.

50. Holmes at 139.

51. Blet, chapter three (reporting that Pius always was closer to Preysing).

52. Holmes at 149; O'Carroll at 89; Blet, chapter three.

53. Cheetham at 287.

54. Lamb at 47.

55. Monsignor Tardini to Ambassador Myron Taylor, dated September 26, 1942, *Actes et Documents*, vol. V, p. 727-29 (no. 492) (discussing suppression of religion in the Soviet Union).

56. *Letter from President Roosevelt to His Holiness*, Sept. 3, 1941, in *Wartime Correspondence* at 61-62.

57. Holmes at 139.

58. British Public Records Office, INF 1/893.

59. Lapide at 137.

60. *The Tablet* (London), October 24, 1942, at 202 (quoting the *Jewish Chronicle*).

61. *Id.*

62. *The Ciano Diaries* at 537, 538. According to Ciano, Mussolini wanted to "break a few wooden heads," but he had been dissuaded from doing so because "the prestige of the Church is very high." *Id.* At 538-39.

63. The President's Personal Representative to Pope Pius XII (Taylor) to the Cardinal Secretary of State (Maglione), Sept. 26, 1942, in *Foreign Relations of the United States, Diplomatic Papers, 1942, vol. III (Europe)*, United States Government Printing Office (Washington, 1961) at 775.

64. Telegram from the Minister in Switzerland (Harrison) to the Secretary of State, Oct. 16, 1942, in *Foreign Relations of the United States, Diplomatic Papers, 1942, vol. III (Europe)*, United States Government Printing Office (Washington, 1961) at 777 (going on to suggest that "there is little hope of

checking Nazi barbarities by any method except that of physical force coming from without."); *Actes et Documents,* vol. IIX, no. 507.

65. Reprinted in Secretariat for Ecumenical and Interreligious Affairs, National Conference of Bishops, *Catholics Remember the Holocaust,* United States Catholic Conference (Washington, 1998) at 17.

66. Bishop Stefan Sapieha of Kracow wrote a letter to Pius, dated October 28, 1942, in which he said: "It displeases us greatly that we cannot communicate Your Holiness' letters to our faithful, but it would furnish a pretext for further persecution and we have already had victims suspected of communicating with the Holy See." Paci at 41; Pius would later cite this experience in a letter to Bishop Preysing of Berlin:

> We leave it to the [local] bishops to weigh the circumstances in deciding whether or not to exercise restraint, *ad maiora mala vitanda* [to avoid greater evil]. This would be advisable if the danger of retaliatory and coercive measures would be imminent in cases of public statements by the bishop. Here lies one of the reasons We Ourselves restrict Our public statements. The experience We had in 1942 with documents which We released for distribution to the faithful gives justification, as far as We can see, for Our attitude.

Joseph L. Lichten, *A Question of Judgment: Pius XII and the Jews in Pius XII and the Holocaust: A Reader* at 118-19.

67. Blet, chapter six.

68. The British chargé d'affaires reported back to London that Pius felt that his broadcast of May 13 had already condemned the Nazis, and he had sent messages of consolation to various Polish priests. Pius did not see how he could do more. *Enclosure in Mr. Osborne's Despatch No. 111 of September 11th 1942,* British Public Records Office, FO371/334148[?] 56879; *Letter from Osborne to Mr. Howard,* July 12, 1942, British Public Records Office, FO371/33426 65042 (similar message).

69. Marchione (1999) (Church, Shoah, and Anti-Semitism).

70. See Telegram from the Minister in Switzerland (Harrison) to the Secretary of State, August 3, 1943, in *Foreign Relations of the United States, Diplomatic Papers, 1942, vol. III (Europe),* United States Government Printing Office (Washington, 1961) at 772 expressing concern over the lack of a statement).

71. Memorandum from Mr. Harold H. Tittmann, Assistant to the President's Personal Representative to Pope Pius XII, to the Cardinal Secretary of State (Maglione), Sept. 14, 1942, in *Foreign Relations of the United States, Diplomatic Papers, 1942, vol. III (Europe),* United States Government Printing Office (Washington, 1961) at 774. Taylor expressly denied having asked Pius to identify Hitler by name. Blet, chapter six.

72. Mr. Harold Tittmann, Assistant to the President's Personal Representative to Pope Pius, to the Secretary of State, Oct. 6, 1942, in *Foreign Relations of the United States, Diplomatic Papers, 1942, vol. III (Europe),* United States Government Printing Office (Washington, 1961) at 776.

73. Wyman at 76. See Marchione (1999) (Church, Shoah, and Anti-Semitism) (suggesting that the Pope would have been reckless to have joined in the statement).

74. *The Rights of Man*, broadcast of Pope Pius XII, Christmas 1942, reprinted in *Pius XII: Selected Encyclicals and Addresses* at 277.

75. *Id.* at 278.

76. *Id.* at 295.

77. *Id.* at 294 (emphasis added).

78. Marchione (1999) (Overview).

79. O'Carroll at 86.

80. Telegram from the Minister in Switzerland (Harrison) to the Secretary of State, Jan. 5, 1943, in *Foreign Relations of the United States, Diplomatic Papers, 1943, vol. II (Europe)*, United States Government Printing Office (Washington, 1964) at 91.

81. This message was delivered on February 20, 1943. Blet, chapter four.

82. British Public Records Office, FO 371/34363 59337 (January 5, 1943) (the same document reflects the desire of some other officials for a more forceful statement). A secret British telegram from this same time period reported on an audience with the Pope:

> His Holiness undertook to do whatever was possible on behalf of the Jews, but His Majesty's Minister doubted whether there would be any public statement. The Pope informed the Unites States Minister to the Vatican that he considered his recent broadcast to be clear and comprehensive in its condemnation of the heartrending treatment of Poles, Jews, hostages, etc. And to have satisfied all recent demands that he should speak out.

Outward Telegram, FO 371/34363 59337 (January 10, 1943). See also *Political Distribution from Switzerland from Berne to Foreign Office*, January 5, 1943, FO 371/34363 59337 (similar).

83. *The London Times* also ran an editorial expressing similar sentiments about the Pope's statements since his coronation:

> A study of the words which Pope Pius XII has addressed since his accession in encyclicals and allocutions to the Catholics of various nations leaves no room for doubt. He condemns the worship of force and its concrete manifestation in the suppression of national liberties and in the persecution of the Jewish race.

"A Vatican Visit," *The London Times*, October 11, 1942.

84. *The Ciano Diaries* at 558-59.

85. Duffy at 264.

86. *Telegram from the Minister in Switzerland (Harrison) to the Secretary of State*, Jan. 5, 1943, in *Foreign Relations of the United States, Diplomatic Papers, 1943, vol. II (Europe)*, United States Government Printing Office (Washington, 1964) at 91.

87. Holmes at 140; Blet, chapter seven.

88. *Telegram from the German Ambassador (Bergen) to the Reich Minister*, dated January 26, 1943, NARA, T-120, Roll 361, at 277668-70; Holmes at 140.

CHAPTER FOURTEEN

1943 AND TURNING TIDES

1. Kallay at 169.
2. Cianfarra at 301.
3. *Reply of His Holiness to President Roosevelt,* Jan. 5, 1943, in *Wartime Correspondence* at 81- 82.
4. *Explanatory Note* by Myron Taylor, in *Wartime Correspondence* at 69-70.
5. Hart at 587-88.
6. Weizsäcker at 297.
7. Toland at 1163; Majdalany at 194-95.
8. In February 1945, General Eisenhower said: "The policy of unconditional surrender faced the German high command with the choice of being hanged or jumping into a cluster of bayonets. Dupuy & Dupuy at 1016.
9. Blet (conclusion) (noting that he did not press the point with the Western Allies because he thought that it would "only offend the U.S. representative and make any further steps impossible"); Alvarez & Graham at 8.
10. P. Murphy at 229.
11. President Roosevelt explained:

The trouble is that the reassuring [of conditional surrender] presupposes reconstituting a German state which would give active co-operation apparently at once to peace in Europe. A somewhat long study and personal experience in and out of Germany leads me to believe that the Germany philosophy cannot be changed by decree, law or military order. The change in German philosophy must be evolutionary and may take two generations. To assume otherwise is to assume, of necessity, a period of quiet followed by a third World War.

Ziemke at 31.
12. Blum at 749. The possibility of a separate peace with the Soviets had been discussed in high Italian in January 1943. *The Ciano Diaries* at 565.
13. *Other Soviet Affairs; Japanese claim to islands disputed in Diet,* BBC Summary of World Broadcasts, March 14, 1979.
14. In 1943, Air Marshal Harris said: "Every ton of bombs dropped on Germany's industires will save the lives of ten United Nations soldiers when the invasion comes." Allan A. Michie, "Germany was Bombed to Defeat," *Skyways,* August 1945, reprinted in *Reader's Digest,* August 1945, at 77.
15. *The Rights of Man,* broadcast of Pope Pius XII, Christmas 1942, reprinted in *Pius XII: Selected Encyclicals and Addresses* at 277. Blet, chapter ten.
16. *The Ciano Diaries* at 523.
17. Preysing, in fact, suggested that the Holy See should terminate relations with Germany. R. Stewart at 27.
18. Marchione (1999) (Church, Shoah, and Anti-Semitism).

19. Holmes at 167.

20. Blet, chapter nine.

21. Marchione (1999) (Background Information).

22. "Book Claims Vatican Official Confronted Hitler on Persecution," *National Catholic Register*, July 5-11, 1998, at 6 (quoting Monica Biffi, *Msgr. Cesare Orsenigo: Apostolic Nunciao in Germany (1930-46)*). See also R. Stewart at 11; Rhodes at 343 (relating the same event).

23. Holmes at 166. On February 20, 1941, Pius wrote to the German bishops: "When the pope wanted to cry aloud in a strong voice, waiting and silence were unhappily often imposed...." Blet (conclusion). Similarly, on March 3, 1944, he wrote: "frequently it is with pain that a decision is made as to what the situation demands; prudent reserve and silence or, on the contrary, candid speech and vigorous action." *Id.* His protest to German leaders about the conditions in Poland, mailed one day earlier, went unanswered. R. Stewart at 23.

24. Sánchez at 375.

25. *Id.* at 374.

26. *Id.*

27. *Id.* at 375.

28. *Id.* at 375.

29. Apparently several Nazi leaders had problems with Ribbentrop. Weizsäcker at 278, 284 ("his lust for war showed me how dangerous he was, and I honestly hated him").

30. Alvarez & Graham at 41 (noting that Schellenberg avoided punishment).

31. Hamerow at 310.

32. *Id.*

33. K. Doyle at 16; Keegan (1994).

34. Scholl at 73, 74.

35. *Id.* at 85-86.

36. *Id.* at 86; Gill at 183-95.

37. "Let's Look at the Record," *Inside the Vatican,* October 1999, at XII.

38. Moshe Kohn, "Remember the White Rose," *The Jerusalem Post,* July 9, 1993.

39. Scholl at 91, 92.

40. Gill at 183; Ari L. Goldman, "Anti-Hitler German Students Lauded," *The New York Times,* June 30, 1985.

41. Lapide at 138. In the Vatican, the secretary of the Congregation for Extraordinary Ecclesiastical Affairs (Msgr. Domenico Tardini) recorded in his notes of October 21 and 23, 1941, that if the pro-Nazi statements attributed to Tiso were actually made by him, the Holy Father wanted his name to be removed from a list of prelates designated for special praise. *Actes et Documents,* vol. V, no. 123.

42. Lapide at 138. See *Actes et Documents,* vol. VIII, no. 305 (Vatican Secretary of State's concern over expulsion of Jews from the Slovak Republic).

43. *E.g., The Apostolic Delegate (Cicognani) to the Acting Secretary of State,* Feb. 26, 1944, in Foreign Relations of the United States, Diplomatic Papers, 1944, vol. I (General) at 995, United States Government Printing Office (Washington, 1966).

44. While Catholics did not face the same fate as Jews, the post-war Czechoslovak *Official Report for the Prosecution and Trial of Major War Criminals* documented Nazi efforts to suppress Catholicism in this area:

> At the outbreak of war, 487 Catholic priests were among the thousands of Czech patriots arrested and sent to concentration camps as hostages. Venerable high ecclesiastical dignitaries were dragged to concentration camps as hostages.... Religious orders were dissolved and liquidated, their charitable institutions closed down and their members expelled or else forced to compulsory labor in Germany. All religious instruction in Czech schools was suppressed. Most of the weeklies and monthlies which the Catholics had published in Czechoslovakia, had been suppressed from the very beginning of the occupation.... To a great extent Catholic church property was seized for the benefit of the Reich.

Office of United States Chief of Counsel at 283.

45. Lapide at 141.

46. See *Actes et Documents,* vol. IX, no. 87 (Vatican direction to impede the deportation of 20,000 Jews from Slovakia).

47. Holmes at 159-60; See *Actes et Documents,* vol. VII, no. 346 (Maglione's notes reflecting protests by the Holy See regarding "measures directed against the Jews.")

48. *Actes et Documents,* vol. IX, no. 141.

49. Blet, chapter nine.

50. *Id.,* chapter eight.

51. *The Jewish Chronicle* (London), Sept. 11, 1942.

52. *Actes et Documents,* vol. X, no. 60 (requests from the World Jewish Congress); *Actes et Documents,* vol. X, no. 159 (similar).

53. Lapide at 147.

54. Robert A. Graham, *Pius XII's Defense of Jews and Others: 1944-45 in Pius XII and the Holocaust: A Reader* at 65-66 (emphasis added). The Vatican's message to Tiso stated: "The grave news has caused profound pain to the Holy Father.... He felt deep anguish at the sufferings of numerous persons, inflicted against all principles of humanity and justice–solely for reason of their descent...." Lapide at 147.

55. O'Carroll at 106.

56. Robert A. Graham, *Pius XII's Defense of Jews and Others: 1944-45 in Pius XII and the Holocaust: A Reader* at 66 (emphasis added).

57. Michaelis at 373. The survival of nearly 25% of the Slovakian Jews has been attributed to Vatican pressure on Tiso. Lapide at 144.

58. See Gunther Deschner, *Warsaw Rising,* Ballatine Books (New York, 1972).

59. *Id.*

60. *Id.*

61. In a small town near Mir, Poland, the Nazis executed 12 nuns in one day for suspicion of harboring Jews.

62. His story was later made into a motion picture entitled *"Au revoir, les enfants!"*

63. Patricia Treece, "Joyful Martyr," *Crisis,* July/August 1997.

64. Blet, chapter seven.

65. *Id.*

66. William J. O'Malley, *The Priests of Dachau*, reprinted in *Pius XII and the Holocaust: A Reader* at 143. As part of their war against the Church, the Nazis were deporting a rising number of senior prelates. Archbishop Juliusz Nowowiejski of Plock died in a concentration camp in May 1941, followed by his suffragan bishop, Leon Wetmaski. Archbishop Michael Kozal of Wloclawek was killed in Dachau. Szulc at 119.

67. In all camps, one of the primary fears of those who were not immediately executed was that of contracting a disease. Diarrhea, enteritis, edema, and typhus all raged through the camps the two final winters, with two to three hundred prisoners dying each day. When the S.S. refused to enter the contagious wards, priests volunteered to bathe and care for the victims (which included removing the bodies of those who died).

68. Father Andreas Rieser impressed his S.S. captors, because it was so difficult to break his spirit. One day, after Rieser had been severely beaten, an S.S. guard looked at the bruised, sweating priest, picked up a length of barbed wire and ordered him to braid a crown. The guard then hammered the crown onto the priest's head and forced some nearby Jews to spit on him.

69. William J. O'Malley, *The Priests of Dachau*, reprinted in *Pius XII and the Holocaust: A Reader* at 143.

70. See Zolli at 156.

71. See Francesca Bierens, "Encounter on a Wartime Night," *Catholic Digest*, July, 1996, at 74.

72. Graham (1968) at 48; Blet, chapter two (noting that this statement was made at the request of Polish Archbishop Sapieha).

73. Toland at 864; Holmes at 132; O'Carroll at 131; Blet, chapter four.

74. This section was suppressed in Italy and Germany. *The Tablet* (London), June 12, 1943, at 282, n.1 (reprinting the Pope's words).

75. Toland at 864; Holmes at 132; O'Carroll at 131; Blet, chapter four.

76. Graham (1968) at 49; Blet, chapter four.

77. Graham (1968) at 50.

78. Blet, chapter four.

79. See generally *Appeals of the Vatican to the American and British Governments that they Refrain from Bombing Rome,* in Foreign Relations of the United States, Diplomatic Papers, 1942, vol. III (Europe) at 791-800, United States Government Printing Office (Washington, 1961); *Appeals of the Vatican to the American and British Governments that they Refrain from Bombing Rome,* in Foreign Relations of the United States, Diplomatic Papers, 1943, vol. II (Europe) at 910-961, United States Government Printing Office (Washington, 1964).

80. Letter from His Holiness to President Roosevelt, May 18, 1943, in *Wartime Correspondence* at 89.

81. *Id.* at 91 (reply of President Roosevelt).

82. The answer from the British was similar. *The Ciano Diaries* at 552. This prompted Pius to ask Mussolini to remove military commands from Rome. The Italian King favored such a move, and at one time agreed to do it, but as the demands from the Allies grew, the Italian leaders found it impossible to comply. *Id.* At 552, 554, 555, 558-59.

83. Halecki & Murray at 182-83.

84. Telegram from the Minister in Switzerland (Harrison) to the Secretary of State, July 28, 1943, in Foreign Relations of the United States, Diplomatic Papers, 1943, vol. II (Europe) at 935-36, United States Government Printing Office (Washington, 1964). More recent estimates put the number of dead at 1,500 (Blet, chapter ten) or at 500 (Cornwell at 298).

85. Smit at 231.

86. Reply of His Holiness to President Roosevelt, July 19, 1943, in *Wartime Correspondence* at 95-97.

87. This was reprinted in *L'Osservatore Romano*, July 20, 1943.

88. Blet, chapter ten.

89. Smit at 230 (quoting *L'Osservatore Romano*, June 21, 1948). The object of the attack was the depot of San Lorenzo, with its military trains and storehouses. *Id.* The German Ambassador to the Holy See wrote: "For us Rome had become a German garrison." Weizsäcker at 290.

90. Blet, chapter ten.

91. Telegram from the Minister in Switzerland (Harrison) to the Secretary of State, July 27, 1943, in Foreign Relations of the United States, Diplomatic Papers, 1943, vol. II (Europe) at 934-35, United States Government Printing Office (Washington, 1964). In fact, Italian authorities shortly thereafter announced several steps that they were taking to make Rome a less likely target. Memorandum from The Apostolic Delegation at Washington to the Department of State, in Foreign Relations of the United States, Diplomatic Papers, 1943, vol. II (Europe) at 946-47, United States Government Printing Office (Washington, 1964).

92. Telegram from the Minister in Switzerland (Harrison) to the Secretary of State, July 28, 1943, in Foreign Relations of the United States, Diplomatic Papers, 1943, vol. II (Europe) at 935-36, United States Government Printing Office (Washington, 1964).

93. See Testimony of Karl Otto Wolff, before the Tribunal of the Vicariate of Rome, on the beatification of Pius XII (Eugenii Pacelli) at 827-851.

94. O'Carroll at 60; Lothar Groppe, "The Church's Struggle with the Third Reich," *Fidelity*, October 1983, at 12 (Alan F. Lacy trans.) (noting that Pius XII was aware of this statement).

95. P. Murphy at 212.

96. Lapide at 251.

97. *Mystici Corporis Christi*, paragraph 3.

98. *Id.*, paragraph 4.

99. *Id.*, paragraph 105.

100. *Id.*, paragraph 6.

101. *Id.*

102. *Id.*, paragraph 32.

103. *Id.*, paragraph 110.

104. *Id.*, paragraph 96.

105. Marchione (1999) (Overview) (noting that this statement was quoted in the *American Jewish Yearbook, 1943-1944*).

106. Cianfarra at 315-16.

107. *Actes et Documents,* vol. IX, no. 247. The Rabbi, in asking for assistance, noted that Jews of the world consider the Holy See their "historic protector in oppression." See also *Actes et Documents,* vol. IX, no. 270, at 403-

06 (The Grand Rabbi Herzog to Cardinal Maglione, July 19, 1943) (offering thanks and seeking help for the Jews in Poland).

108. Blet, chapter nine.

109. *Actes et Documents,* vol. IX, no. 282.

110. Darragh at 1 (quoting Time, August 16, 1943).

111. Blet, chapter nine.

112. *Actes et Documents,* vol. IX, no. 346.

113. Blet, chapter nine.

114. *Id.*

115. *Id.,* chapter ten

116. *Id.* Later, Mussolini did try to negotiate an armistice through Archbishop Schuster of Milan. Barzini at 162.

117. Blet, chapter ten.

118. *Id.*

119. *Id.*

120. *Id.*

121. *Id.*

122. *Id.;* Cornwell at 298.

123. Blet, chapter ten.

124. *Actes et Documents,* vol. VII, no. 316. Weizsäcker at 289. According to some accounts, the new Italian leadership did try to reach a settlement with the Allies, but they refused to accept the demanded unconditional surrender. Katz at 5.

125. Blet, chapter ten.

126. Procacci at 368.

127. Lamb at 35-39; Cornwell at 303 ("the overwhelming evidence is that they did all in their power to hamper and thwart [deportations]"). Goebbels wrote in his diary on December 13, 1942: "The Italians are extremely lax in their treatment of Jews. They protect Italian Jews both in Tunis and in occupied France and won't permit their being drafted for work or compelled to wear the Star of David." *The Goebbels Diaries 1942–1943* at 241; see Crankshaw at 188 ("Many Jews in Italy and the south of France owe their lives to the flat refusal of the Italian Fascist authorities, civil and military, to co-operate with Eichmann, and to their ingenuity in frustrating his plans"); Chadwick (1977) at 183 (the Vatican was less pleased with Mussolini's overthrow than was the rest of Rome).

128. Michaelis at 322-23 (citing a note written by Obersturmführer S.S. Lieutenant Heinz Röthke); Cornwell at 254.

129. Gilbert (1981) at 152.

130. Alvarez & Graham at 86. In his diary on July 26, 1943, Joseph Goebbels wrote that "the Pope is said to be playing an important role in the development of this crisis." *The Goebbels Diaries 1942–1943* at 405. The next day he wrote, "the Vatican is developing feverish diplomatic activity. Undoubtedly it is standing behind the revolt [against Mussolini] with its great world-embracing facilities. The *Führer* at first intended, when arresting the responsible men in Rome, to seize the Vatican also, but Ribbentrop and I opposed the plan most emphatically." *Id.* at 409.

131. Schom at 458.

132. Lamb at 45. See Blet, chapter ten ("the Italian government feared an attack upon the city, even an invasion of the Vatican"). The German

Ambassador to the Holy See seems to have taken pride in his efforts to preserve Rome, noting that the German occupying forces were reduced to a "ridiculously small minimum." Weizsäcker at 289, 291-93.

133. As Joachim von Ribbentrop explained in an interrogation during the Nuremberg war trials, maintaining good relations with the Vatican was an important part of the German foreign policy. Bad relations with the Vatican would negatively impact on Germany's relations with other nations, particularly in South America. Office of the United States Chief of Counsel, Supp. B, at 1236. Ribbentrop's concern over relations with the Vatican is reflected in a telegram he sent in January 1943. *Secret Telegram From Ribbentrop to the German Ambassador (Bergen)*, dated January 13, 1943, *Akten Zur Deutschen Auswärtigen Politik, 1918-1945*, Series E, Band V, Vandenhoeck & Ruprecht in Göttingen (1978) no. 123.

134. Toland at 851; Payne at 485; *Hitler Directs His War* at 53. See *Testimony of Karl Otto Wolff*, before the Tribunal of the Vicariate of Rome, on the beatification of Pius XII (Eugenii Pacelli) at 827-851.

135. At other times, Hitler made similar threats about the Catholic Church in Germany. Consider the following statement made by Hitler in mid-July, 1941:

> The ideal situation would be to leave the religions to devour themselves....The heaviest blow that ever struck humanity was the coming of Christianity. Bolshevism is Christianity's illegitimate child. Both are inventions of the Jew. The deliberate lie in the matter of religion was introduced into the world by Christianity....

Hitler's Secret Conversations at 6; Cornwell at 261. Similarly, Goebbels wrote in his diary on November 1–2, 1941, that "The Catholic Church... has not lost contact with its Jewish origin." *The Goebbels Diaries 1942–1943* at 117.

136. Paci at 40; *see* Lamb at 45 (similar quote).

137. Cianfarra at 219.

138. "We agreed that carrying out such a plan would have had tremendous consequences and that it had to be blocked at all costs," wrote Ambassador Rahn. As a result, he was instructed to draft a note stating that it was Hitler's wish that "nothing whatever be undertaken against the person of the Pope, the integrity of his entourage and the inviolability of Vatican institutions." Haberman, *New York Times*.

139. The Pope set up a Catholic refugee committee which helped thousands of Jewish people by providing baptismal certificates, financial aid, and support as they fled European Nazism.

140. Katz at 6.

141. Graham at 14; Marchione (1997) at 130.

142. Blet, chapter ten.

143. *Id.*

144. *Id.*

145. Hatch & Walsh at 168.

146. Blet, chapter ten.

147. *Id.*

148. *Id.*

149. *Id.*

150. *Id.*

151. *Id.*; Chadwick (1977) at 185 (noting that the denial appeared in *L'Osservatore Romano* on September 10).

152. P. Murphy at 203.

153. Susan Zuccotti, "Pope Pius XII and the Holocaust: The Case in Italy," in *The Italian Refuge,* at 269; Zolli at 141; Holmes at 152. Pius was in charge of the overall relief effort. Zolli at 141; Holmes at 152. Years later, when the Israeli press asked why Christian rescuers had risked their lives for others, they frequently referred to Vatican orders issued in 1942 "to save lives by all possible means." Lapide at 134-35. Pius could have obtained credit for opening the buildings if he had made an announcement, but the almost certain reaction of Hitler's Nazis would have been to invade the buildings and seize those being protected.

154. Blet, chapter ten.

155. Jason Berry, "Papal Lives: Biographies of Pius XII and John Paul II examine 2 of the century's most controversial men of the cloth," *The Chicago Tribune,* October 24, 1999, section 14, p.1.

156. Information from Germany described Vatican City as a refuge for politicians, Jews, and soldiers. *Actes et Documents,* vol. IX, no. 387 (noting Montini's denial).

157. Holmes at 152; Fogelman at 172. A list of 155 religious houses used to shelter can be found in *Actes et Documents,* vol. IX, no. 548.

158. See Lapomarda at 234-35, n. 17 (referring to a list of 4,447 Jews who had been sheltered by religious groups).

159. In his diary, on April 5, 1942, Joseph Goebbels wrote that he urged the *Führer* to forbid German soldiers from visiting the Pope because Pius was using these opportunities for propaganda that was in conflict with Nazi aims. *The Goebbels Diaries 1942–1943* at 161.

160. This rarely noted act was reported by Senator Adriano Ossicini, founder of the "Christian Left" in Italy, who was arrested in 1943 due to his opposition to the Fascist regime. "More Echoes on Pope Pius XII, Nazi Holocaust," *Catholic World News,* June 27, 1996 ("On the eve of one massive police sweep... the hospital received direct orders from Pope Pius XII to admit as many Jews as possible immediately.")

161. Zolli at 141; Holmes at 152; Korn at 148; Martinez at 26.

162. Rabbi Zolli, like many Roman Jews had done earlier, took shelter in one of nearly two hundred Catholic institutions in and around Rome that housed thousands of Jewish fugitives. He had, however, offered himself as hostage in exchange for the Jews that the Germans had already taken. A.B. Klyber, "The Chief Rabbi's Conversion," *The Liguarian,* August 1945, reprinted in Zolli (Introduction).

163. Zolli at 187; Lapide at 132-33.

164. Marchione (1997) at 73.

165. Blet, chapter ten.

166. Stille at 270.

167. *Id.* at 270-71.

168. Lamb at 39.

169. Holmes at 153.

170. Mary DeTurris, "The Vatican and the Holocaust," *Our Sunday Visitor,* May 18, 1997.

171. *Actes et Documents,* vol. IX, p. 501-02 (no. 364).

172. *Actes et Documents*, vol. VII, no. 410; Chadwick (1977) at 187.

173. Weizsäcker replaced von Bergen, the German ambassador earlier in July 1943. *Actes et Documents*, vol. VII, no. 277.

174. Weizsäcker lived a double life, politically. Outwardly he conformed to the requirements of a loyal Nazi diplomat, but inwardly, as his confidants testified, he was determined to sabotage and resist. See *Actes et Documents*, vol. IX, no. 368; Chadwick (1977) at 190-91; Robert Graham, *La strana condotta di E.von Weizsäcker ambasciatore del Reich in Vaticano*, Indice Pelle Materie, Vol. II, Del 1970; see also Weizsäcker at 277-78. When he learned that German troops would take over Rome, Weizsäcker expressed depression at the thought of it. Chadwick (1977) at 183- 84. One priest reported that when others tried to report the names and places were Jews were being sheltered, Weizsäcker turned them away. Chadwick (1977) at 199. When several conspirators were arrested in a failed coup attempt, they were questioned by Nazi officials as to whether Weizsäcker was involved in the plot. Weizsäcker at 295-96. Weizsäcker, though he was a Protestant, asked for the Vatican post because he thought that would give him the best opportunity to work for peace. Weizsäcker at 286. He would have liked to have followed custom and have a priest attached to his Embassy, but German authorities offered him only a priest who had left the Church. "I had no difficulty in deciding between this plan and not having an ecclesiastical advisor at all." Weizsäcker at 288. See Hatch & Walsh at 166; Katz at 12 ("Weizsäcker... was considered by the Vatican and others, including himself, to be secretly anti-Nazi"). He was convicted at the post-war Nuremberg trials, but was released from prison after only 18 months. Chadwick (1977) at 181.

175. *Actes et Documents*, vol. VII, no. 410; Chadwick (1977) at 187.

176. *Actes et Documents*, vol. VII (appendix), no. 410; Chadwick (1977) at 187.

177. Chadwick (1977) at 187.

178. *Actes et Documents*, vol. VII (appendix), no. 410.

179. This demand was the brainchild of S.S. Major Kappler, who was in charge of the occupation of Rome. According to at least one hypothesis, he was afraid that deportation of Jews would make occupation harder, so he invented this ransom idea to convince his Nazi superiors in Berlin not to order deportation. Lamb at 40-41. He refused payment in lira, saying: "I could print as many of them as I like." Chadwick (1977) at 187-88.

180. Michaelis at 355. Apparently, such a demand was not unprecedented. See Mazgaj at 71 (similar demand in Polish town of Klimontow in 1942)

181. Zolli at 160-61.

182. *Id.* at 161, 206; Holmes at 155; Michaelis at 355; Bogle, *The Salisbury Review*. It was a point of pride for the Jews to pay their rescuers if they could afford to do so, though many could not. Marchione (1997) at 22.

183. O'Carroll at 95; Chadwick (1977) at 188.

184. While many Jewish people converted to Catholicism as a sign of gratitude for support during the war, Zolli always explained that his conversion was a matter of faith, not an effort to thank the Pope or the Catholic Church. Zolli at 185.

185. Lamb at 41.

186. Scrivener at 38 (diary account of what took place).

187. Chadwick (1977) at 188.

188. Susan Zuccotti, "Pope Pius XII and the Holocaust: The Case in Italy," in *The Italian Refuge*, at 254. Zuccotti speculates that Pius knew of the roundup before it took place.

189. Blet, chapter ten.

190. See Chadwick (1977) at 190 ("The pope was obviously surprised. He said that the Germans promised that they would not hurt the Jews, and knew of the 50 kilograms of gold.")

191. *L'Osservatore Romano* reported on October 25-26 that "With the augmentation of so much evil, the universal and paternal charity of the Supreme Pontiff has become, it might be said, ever more active; it knows neither boundaries nor nationality, neither religion nor race." See Susan Zuccotti, "Pope Pius XII and the Holocaust: The Case in Italy," in *The Italian Refuge*, at 255.

192. *Actes et Documents*, vol. IX, no. 368; Gilbert (1981) at 157; Marchione (1997) at 16; Scrivener at 38. An editorial in *The Jewish Chronicle* (London) of October 29, 1943, entitled "Jewish Hostages in Rome: Vatican Protests," said: "The Vatican has made strong representations to the German Government and the German High Command in Italy against the persecution of the Jews in Nazi occupied Italy."

193. *Diplomatic (Secret) Telegram from Osborne to Foreign Office*, October 31, 1943, British Public Record Office, FO 371/37255 56879.

194. *Id.* ("Vatican intervention thus seems to have been effective in saving a number of these unfortunate people.") But see Cornwell at 308 ("Robert Katz's research has conclusively discredited" the Vatican's efforts).

195. *Diplomatic (Secret) Telegram from Osborne to Foreign Office*, October 31, 1943, British Public Record Office, FO 371/37255 56879.

196. Cornwell at 304.

197. Blet, chapter ten.

198. *Id.*

199. On the order of Pius XII, the German military commander of Rome, Brigadier General Rainer Stabel, was persuaded to telegram Hitler. In that telegram, Stabel argued that a crackdown on Roman Jews could create difficulties for his effort to keep supply lines open to German troops south of Rome. The German leaders agreed and stopped the massive raids. Peter Gumpel, "Cornwell's Cheap Shot at Pius XII," *Crisis*, December 1999, at 24. See also Robert A. Graham, *La strana condotta di E. von Weizsäcker ambasciatore del Reich in Vaticano*, Indice Delle Materie, Vol. II, del 1970, at 455. Weizsäcker, who often shaded his reports to help protect the Vatican from Hitler's wrath, later reported back to Berlin that the Pope had not intervened in this matter. *Id.*

200. Blet, chapter 10 (also noting that the Vatican undertook efforts to help the Jews who were not returned); Lamb at 42. Reportedly, 282 Jews were released. Cornwell at 308, 310 (arguing that Vatican officials had no part in obtaining these releases).

201. Weizsäcker felt that "if it were possible to do anything at all for peace, it could be done at or through the Vatican." Weizsäcker at 277. German occupation authorities were convinced that Pius was bound to protest sooner or later, and they thought an immediate public protest might work in their favor. Cornwell at 316.

202. Blet, chapter 10; Chadwick (1977) at 191.

203. Chadwick (1977) at 194.

204. Blet, chapter 10.

205. *Id.*

206. Peter Gumpel, "Cornwell's Pope: A Nasty Caricature of a Noble and Saintly Man," *ZENIT News Service*, Sept. 16, 1999; Cornwell at 310 (noting that initiatives on behalf of Pope Pius XII "halted the further persecution of Rome's Jews, but only temporarily"). Henceforth there were no further massive roundups, but there still were individual arrests. *Id.*

207. Zolli at 140.

208. Robert A. Graham, "A Return to Theocracy," *America*, July 18, 1964, at 72; Chadwick (1977) at 195. When the Nazis first occupied Rome, he sent his second-in-command, Albrecht von Kessel, into the Vatican so that he would be able to calm things down if German troops should invade. *Id.* at 185.

209. Blet, chapter 10.

210. Cornwell at 312.

211. Holmes at 156; Blet, chapter 10.

212. Holmes at 156.

213. See Chadwick (1977) at 196.

214. *Id.*

215. Holmes at 157-58.

216. Weizsäcker, Ribbentrop's former under-secretary at the Foreign Office, had long served in Germany's diplomatic service, and probably knew Pius XII's attitudes toward Nazism better than anyone else in the German government. He had no doubt about where Pius stood. He said to Hitler on the day he left for Rome as German Ambassador to the Vatican: "I am actually leaving for enemy country." Lapide at 123. On January 25, 1940, while he was the German Secretary of State in the foreign office, Weizsäcker wrote to the ambassador from the Holy See, "To be sure the Vatican does express itself in general terms, but it is totally clear who is meant." Lothar Groppe, "The Church and the Jews in the Third Reich," *Fidelity*, November 1983, at 25.

217. Holmes at 158. Between 1942 and December 1943, the Pope's Palatine Guard increased in number from 300 to over 4,000, "not due to any militarist expansion, but [as] a means of distributing Vatican passports to refugees." Gerald Warner, "Twisted Interpretation of History Blames Pius XII for the Plight of the Jews," *Scotland on Sunday*, Sept. 26, 1999. After the war, Father Marie-Benoît of Marseilles was given an award by the Italian Jewish Union for his work in protecting about 1,000 Jews in Rome. Upon receiving his gold medal from the Italian Jewish Union, Fr. Marie-Benoît paid tribute to Ambassador Weizsäcker, "who undoubtedly knew that the institutions of Rome were packed with Jews," but did not reveal this to his superiors. *Id.* at 152-53.

218. There were, however, several small raids that caused Jews to be taken prisoner. Blet, chapter ten.

219. As others have noted, "it is ironical that Pius XII became the unintended victim... of this maneuver that saved the lives of thousands of Roman Jews." Robert A. Graham, "A Return to Theocracy," *America*, July 18, 1964, at 72. Chadwick calls this "the very nub of the problem." Was Weizsäcker

really telling the truth or trying to dissuade the Nazi leadership in Berlin from invading the Vatican? He ultimately concludes that it was the latter. Chadwick (1977) at 194 ("This telegram did as much as any other single document to lower the post-war reputation of Pius XII. Looked at in terms of the reign of terror, and of Weizsäcker trying to do what he could for the Jews, it was beautifully drafted.")

220. Holmes at 163-64.

221. *Id.* at 151.

222. Michaelis at 370 (quoting *L'Osservatore Romano*, Oct. 25-26, 1943).

223. Blet, chapter ten.

224. *Id.*

225. *Id.*

226. *Id.*

227. Graham at 10-11.

228. The Vatican was supplying up to 100,000 meals per day to the people hardest hit by food shortages. Cornwell at 320. Pius asked for assistance from the Allies in feeding the Roman population, but the Allies took the position that this was the responsibility of the Germans. Blet, chapters ten and eleven. They were concerned that if they sent goods into occupied areas, the Germans would hoard them. *Id.*, chapter eleven. Pius then demanded that the Germans provide for the city's needs. *Id.*, chapter ten. Later in the war, the Vatican was able to convince the Allies to authorize a shipment of 8,000 tons of grain into Greece. *Id.*, chapter eleven.

229. Gilbert (1987) at 447.

230. *The Italian Refuge* at 6.

231. Holmes at 134.

232. Pius had encouraged Mussolini and King Victor Emmanuel III to abandon Germany and seek a separate peace agreement with the Allies. Blet at 17. Later, Mussolini tried to negotiate an armistice through Archbishop Schuster of Milan. Barzini at 162.

233. Shirer (1962) at 1306.

234. Cianfarra at 219.

235. Hatch & Walsh at 167.

236. Cianfarra at 219.

237. Pius had ordered his Swiss Guard not to offer any resistance if German troops were to enter Vatican City. Alvarez & Graham at 84.

238. P. Murphy at 221-22. Kesselring's concern about publicity and public relations is reflected in the request he made to Pius shortly after the Nazis entered Rome. In exchange for his promise to respect Vatican neutrality and not invade its buildings, Kesselring requested that the Pope let the world know that German troops were behaving "correctly." Hatch & Walsh at 166. At that time, even Jewish shopkeepers were giving good reports on the Germans. Susan Zuccotti, "Pope Pius XII and the Holocaust: The Case in Italy," in *The Italian Refuge*, at 265.

239. On November 9, 1943, Joseph Goebbels wrote in his diary:

The dropping of some enemy bombs on Vatican City still creates a world sensation. Under the pressure of commentary in the neutral press the English have been compelled to deny any guilt and to attempt to blame us. They are doing that, however, in such a clumsy and transparent manner that nobody will believe them. Their lies are too transparently foolish....

Unfortunately the *Osservatore Romano* assumes only a very moderate attitude concerning this event. Obviously the Pope does not want to forego the possibility of acting as mediator between the Reich and the western enemy powers, at least not for the present, although there isn't the slightest occasion for such mediation at the moment.

The Goebbels Diaries 1942–1943 at 503. A few days later, Goebbels complained about the Germans' inability to use the Vatican's complaint to their political advantage. *Id.* at 514.

240. Smit at 233.

241. Korn at 145. When the Germans again urged Pius to leave Rome in 1944, he said, "If Rome really is an open city, why don't you leave?" Hatch & Walsh at 176.

242. Korn at 146.

243. Lapomarda at 235, n.18 (citing *L'Osservatore Romano*); Scrivener at 65.

244. Scrivener at 66.

245. *Id.*

246. *Id.*

247. *Actes et Documents,* vol. IX, no. 490, at 636 (Some Jewish families to Pope Pius XII, Dec. 30, 1943).

CHAPTER FIFTEEN

1944 AND THE ALLIES INVADE

1. Scrivener at 106 (quoting a dispatch from *Popolo di Roma*).

2. Graham (1987) at 12.

3. Scrivener at 106.

4. *Id.*

5. *Id.*

6. In October 1943, the Department of State urged President Roosevelt to try to avoid destroying Rome when liberating it from the Germans. Memorandum by the Under Secretary of State (Stettinius) to President Roosevelt, Oct. 7, 1943, in *Foreign Relations of the United States, Diplomatic Papers, 1943, vol. II (Europe)*, United States Government Printing Office (Washington, 1964) at 948.

7. Smit at 234.

8. Smit at 234-35; O'Carroll at 70; Hatch & Walsh at 173-74. But see Robert A. Graham, "Author Questions Pope Pius XII's Vatican Diplomacy," *The Pilot* (Boston), Oct. 31, 1970, at 1, 16 (suggesting that this is an apocryphal story).

9. Herbert L. Mathews, "Happier Days for Pope Pius: Shadows of war are lifting for a Pontiff whose greatest interest is world peace," *New York Times,* Act. 15, 1944, at 8.

10. *Id.*

11. The Vatican had received word that the Allies might bomb in and around Castel Gandolfo, so in mid-February, 1944, the Apostolic Delegate in Washington contacted the United States Secretary of State to assure the American government that "no German soldier was ever admitted within the precincts of the Pontifical Villa and that no German military whatsoever are now within the villa." The Apostolic Delegate in Washington (Cicognani) to the Secretary of State, Feb. 16, 1944, *United States Department of State, Foreign Relations of the United States, Diplomatic Papers, 1944, vol. IV (Europe),* United States Government Printing Office (Washington, 1966) at 1277; see *id.* at 1279.

12. The Americans bombed the Abbey of Monte Cassino at the insistence of General Bernard Freyburg. General Mark W. Clark later wrote:

> I say that the bombing of the Abbey... was a mistake–and I say it with full knowledge of the controversy that has raged around this episode. The official position was best summed up, I suppose, in a State Department communication to the Vatican's undersecretary of State on October 13, 1945, saying that "there was unquestionable evidence in the possession of the Allied commanders in the field that the Abbey of Monte Cassino formed part of the German defensive system."
>
> I was one of the Allied commanders in the field and the one in command at Cassino, and I said then that there is irrefutable evidence that no German solider, except emissaries, was ever inside the Monastery for purposes other than to take care of the sick or to sightsee.

Gannon at 228-29.

13. The abbreviation is sometimes shortened to GAPO. Blet, chapter ten.

14. Cornwell at 320.

15. According to Vatican officials that I spoke to in 1999, Hitler originally ordered a hundred-to-one reprisal, but he was talked into the more traditional ten to one. Some of those executed were people who had already been condemned to death for other offenses.

16. See O'Carroll at 242.

17. Blet, chapter ten.

18. *Id.*

19. Cornwell at 321.

20. *Id.*; Carroll at 242.

21. This event was later depicted in an Italian motion picture entitled *La Rappresaglia* (1973), which was highly critical of Pope Pius XII. In 1974, a niece of Pius XII sued the writer, producer, and director of the film alleging calumny. Testimony established that the killings were carried out within twenty-four hours of the bombing and were done in complete secrecy. There was no opportunity for intervention by the pontiff. The court held in favor of the plaintiff, requiring the defendants to pay fines and handing out one (suspended) prison sentence. See O'Carroll at 242.

22. Graham (1987) at 12; Cornwell at 321. This explanation has not sat-isfied some critics, who argue that the Pope intentionally avoided making a protest. See Katz at 218 (citing Rolf Hochhuth's play, *The Deputy*). Following the war, the German generals who ordered the executions were tried for war crimes, found guilty, and sentenced to death. *Id.* at xii. See also the discus-sion of this matter in the epilogue.

23. Blet, chapter seven.

24. Graham (undated) at 9-12.

25. *Id.*

26. *Id.*

27. Burzio had protested against Nazi treatment of the Jews as early as September 11, 1941. Lapomarda at 104, n.34.

28. Graham (undated) at 9-12; Blet, chapter seven.

29. Robert A. Graham, "How to Manufacture a Legend: The Controversy over the Alleged 'Silence' of Pope Pius XII in World War II," in *Pius XII and the Holocaust: A Reader* at 22. Pius also took this opportunity to caution against the problems associated with unconditional surrender, which displeased President Roosevelt. Blet, chapter twelve; *id.* (conclusion).

30. *Perspectives on History: Pope Pius XII*, a 1963 made-for-television biography, hosted by Mike Wallace, which was re-broadcast on The History Channel on December 26, 1997.

31. Blet, chapter ten.

32. Cornwell at 321.

33. According to one account, this was the result of an order from Hitler. *Id.* The German Ambassador to the Holy See tried to approach the Allies though the Vatican to coordinate the transfer. He presented his proposal to the Vatican the night before the Allies moved into Rome. Weizsäcker at 292. See Smit at 237.

34. Blet, chapter ten.

35. Weizsäcker at 293. "Although he failed to obtain any formal bilater-al agreement, he did inspire both sides, as Weizsäcker wrote, with a type of reverential respect for Rome." Blet, chapter ten.

36. Scrivener at 201.

37. *Id.*at 202 (placards all around town read: "Come to St. Peter's at six o'clock to thank the Pope.") German Ambassador Weizsäcker noted how no one thought of the King of Italy. Chadwick (1977) at 183.

38. Nichols at 136.

39. Blet, chapter ten.

40. See Cianfarra at 7; Marchione (1999) (Church, Shoah, and Anti-Semitism) (quoting John W. Pehle, executive director of the United States War Refugee Board).

41. Blet, chapter ten.

42. Scrivener at 203.

43. *Id.*

44. Hatch & Walsh at 179. After the liberation of Rome, Pius is said to have hastened to the Jewish cemetery to pray there in private. Cornwell at 316.

45. Lapide at 131; see Weizsäcker at 297.

46. Marchione (1999) (The Jewish Community).

47. *Actes et Documents,* vol. X, p. 358 (no. 272).

48. Lapide at 131. The *Jewish News* (Detroit) reported on July 7, "It is gradually being revealed that Jews have been sheltered within the walls of the Vatican during the German occupation of Rome." An editorial in the July 14 edition of the *Congress Weekly*, the official journal of the American Jewish Congress, noted that the Vatican had provided kosher food.

49. Dimitri Cavalli, *How Pope Pius XII was made a villain*, Riverdale Press (Bronx, N.Y.), July 16, 1998, at A11. See also *Actes et Documents*, vol. X, no. 295, at 378 (Cicognani, the Apostolic Delegate to Washington, [writing] to Cardinal Maglione, August 9, 1944) (expressing thanks from the American Jewish Committee and the Committee to Save Jews in Europe to "the Holy Father and Your most Reverend Eminence for the decided improvement obtained in Hungary.... [T]he aforementioned committees recognize that everything is owed to the Holy Father").

50. In addition, as one enters St. Peter's Basilica, to the right just beyond Michelangelo's *Pietá*, stands a large statute of Pius XII.

51. Korn at 151. On October 29, 1944, elder survivors from a concentration camp in Ferramonti, Italy presented Pius a letter which said, in part:

> Now that the victorious Allied troops have broken our chains and liberated us from captivity and danger, may we, the Jewish internees of Ferramonti, be permitted to express our deepest and devoted thanks for the comfort and help which Your Holiness deigned to grant us with fatherly concern and infinite kindness throughout our years of internment and persecution.
>
> Your Holiness has as the first and highest authority upon earth *fearlessly raised his universally respected voice*, in the face of our powerful enemies, in order to defend openly our rights to the dignity of man.... When we were threatened with deportation to Poland, in 1942, Your Holiness extended his fatherly hand to protect us, and stopped the transfer of the Jews interned in Italy, thereby saving us from almost certain death. With deep confidence and hope that the work of Your Holiness may be crowned with further success, we beg to express our heartfelt thanks while we pray to the Almighty: May Your Holiness reign for many years on this Holy See and exert your beneficent influence over the destiny of the nations.
>
> [signed] The President and community of Jewish internees of the former camp at Ferramonti-Tarsia.

Lapide at 129-30. See also *Actes et Documents*, vol. VIII, no. 294 (Vatican efforts on behalf of the internees at Ferramonti); *Actes et Documents*, vol. IX, no. 55 (Vatican concern over internees at Ferramonti); *Actes et Documents*, vol. IX, no. 228 (Vatican concern over Yugoslavian Jews interned in Italy). See also Blet, chapter seven.

52. *Perspectives on History: Pope Pius XII*, a 1963 made-for-television biography, hosted by Mike Wallace, which was re-broadcast on The History Channel on December 26, 1997.

53. Joseph "Ducky" Medwick, a former outfielder with the fabled St. Louis Cardinals "Gashouse Gang," told Pius at an audience for Allied servicemen: "I, too, used to be a Cardinal." John M. McGuire, "Play on Words Paul Dickson's Books are a Feast of Slang, Lingo and Great Quotations," *Everyday Magazine, St. Louis Post-Dispatch*, July 18, 1991, at 1E.

54. Korn at 151.

55. O'Carroll at 140. The *sedia gestatoria* is the portable papal throne used in certain pontifical ceremonies. It consists of a richly-adorned, silk-covered armchair, fastened on a platform, which twelve footmen (*palafrenieri*) in red uniforms typically carry on their shoulders.

56. Doyle at 34.

57. Cornwell at 95.

58. "Criminal Excesses," *L'Osservatore Romano*, July 28, 1944 (report of brutality by Moroccan troops against women). Monsignor Tardini to the Nuncio in France, Roncalli, February 26, 1945, *Actes et Documents*, vol. X at 410: "It is known here that the French government has planned to occupy...northern regions of Italy with Moroccan troops. The Holy See has been sincerely asked to intervene...on account of the acts of violence already done by the above-mentioned troops in various parts of southern and central Italy." In fact, Pius did not want any troops to engage in unlawful activities. He was similarly critical of atrocities committed by white troops on both sides of the war. *E.g.* O'Carroll at 18-19, 134-36. See *infra* note 65.

59. The Pope's concern about these specific French Moroccan troops is made clear in a now-declassified confidential memorandum from the Office of Strategic Services, Washington, DC, dated November 4, 1944, and a message sent from the Vatican to its representative in France. Monsignor Tardini to the Nuncio in France, Roncalli, February 26, 1945, *Actes et Documents*, vol. X at 410. None of these documents make reference to race, just the Pope's concern over these specific French Moroccan troops. The lack of any other records relating to the request confirm that this was not a racist matter, especially when considered in light of the Pontiff's statements, actions, and appointment of minority bishops. For instance, when *Das Schwarze Korps* published an article arguing that it was a crime against nature for the French army to permit black soldiers to fight against white [German] soldiers, Vatican Radio replied: "That it is sufficient for a black man to be a human being in order to be able to claim a human soul and human dignity." The report went on to note that there was a large movement of black people into the Catholic faith. *The Tablet* (London), October 5, 1940 at 269; Speaight at 27. In paragraph 45-50, of his first encyclical, *Summi Pontificatus* (On the Unity of Human Society) Pius dealt with racial matters and expressed his belief that the Church could not discriminate against any given race of people. He expressly stated that all races and nationalities were welcome in the Church and had equal rights as children in the house of the Lord. In paragraph 48, he put meaning to his anti-racist statements by naming new bishops of different races and nationalities. Two weeks later, in *Sertum Laetitae* (*On the Establishment of the Hierarchy in the United States*), Pius wrote of a "special paternal affection" for black Americans.

60. Later Zolli (who had approached the Pope to obtain gold to pay the Nazi's ransom in 1943) converted to Catholicism (along with his wife), asked Pope Pius to be his godfather, and took Eugenio as his Christian name in honor of the Pontiff. *Popes of the Twentieth Century* at 53; see generally Zolli. Recently, Zolli's daughter, Myriam Zolli, in an interview published in the Italian daily, *Il Giornale*, made a statement regarding Pius XII, in which she said "the world's Jewish community owes him a great debt." EWTN Vatican Update, March 31, 1998.

61. "The Jews, Pius XII and the Black Legend," *Zenit News Service*, Dec. 8, 1998.

62. Holmes at 158.

63. See K. Doyle at 17.

64. See Lapide at 134.

65. This story is told in the Gregory Peck motion picture, *The Scarlet and the Black* (1992, LIVE Home Video) and in the book *The Scarlet Pimpernel of the Vatican*, by J.P. Gallagher. See also Hatch & Walsh at 170-72.

66. *Id.*

67. O'Carroll at 97.

68. Lapide at 151; Graham (undated) at 14 (footnote). See *Actes et Documents*, vol. X, no. 412 (letter expressing the Holy Father's "deep pain" and enclosing money to support Rotta's work on behalf of the persecuted).

69. Lapide at 151.

70. Graham (1987) at 5 (quoting Eugene Levai). See *Actes et Documents*, vol. X, no. 133 (delegating "intervention by the Holy See" to Rotta and instructing him to "judge which further steps are possible and opportune to achieve at the moment."); *Actes et Documents*, vol. X, no. 365 (asking Rotta to inform the Vatican concerning the threat to the Jews).

71. Almost as soon as the Nazis moved into Hungary, organizations began asking the Vatican for help. See, *e.g.*, *The World Jewish Congress to Cardinal Maglione,Act es et Documents*, Vol. X, p. 359 (no. 273) (thanking the Pope for help in other areas, and asking for more assistance in Hungary); *The British Legation to the Secretariat of State*, April 1, 1944, *Actes et Documents*, Vol. X, p. 205, n.1 (no. 132); *Archbishop Griffen of Westminster to Cardinal Maglione*, July 3, 1944, *Actes et Documents*, Vol. X, p. 341 (no. 253).

72. Wyman at 237; Graham at 25. The Board also appealed to the five neutral nations to grant protective citizenship documents to Hungarian Jews who had family or business ties to their countries. Turkey did not participate, but the cooperation of the other four countries helped save thousands of Jews. Wyman at 237.

The War Refugee Board sent a message to the Vatican in June 1944, in which it acknowledged that Pius "has labored unceasingly to reinculcate a decent regard for the dignity of man," and the "tireless efforts of His Holiness to alleviate the lot of the persecuted, the hunted and the outcasts." Telegram from the Secretary of State to the Consul General at Naples (Brandt), June 13, 1944, in *Foreign Relations of the United States, Diplomatic Papers, 1944, vol. I (General)*, United States Government Printing Office (Washington, 1966) at 1068-69.

73. Lapide at 159; O'Carroll at 99. The official records indicate that 4,770 Jews were baptized in Budapest during this time, but that 80,000 baptismal certificates were distributed. Graham (undated) at 17; O'Carroll at 104.

74. Gilbert (1981) at 248-49 (quoting Jeno Levai, *Zsidosors Europaban*, Budapest 1948, pp. 68- 72).

75. *Id;* Harmansee is a village in Poland that served as a farm labor-camp annex for the Auschwitz Camp. *Id.* at 248, n.4.

76. *Investigative Reports* (Bill Kurtis, A&E Network).

77. This was a direct affront to the Church. On May 14, the Nuncio wrote to the Hungarian Prime Minister and the Foreign Ministry, arguing:

The very fact of persecuting men merely on account of their racial origin is a violation of the natural law. If God has given them life, no one in the World has the right to take it from them or refuse them the means of preserving it, unless they have committed crimes. But to take anti-Semite measures, not taking into account at all the fact that many Jews have become Christians through reception of baptism, is a serious offense against the church and in contradiction with the character of the Christian state, such as Hungary is proud to profess itself, even today.

Graham (1987) at 26.

78. Holmes at 162; Graham (1987) at 29-30.

79. Holmes at 163.

80. Lapide at 153-54.

81. Levai at 68

82. Memo by Monsignor Tardini, dated October 18, 1944, *Actes et Documents,* vol. X, p. 446, n.4 (no. 357); Graham (undated) at 5-6 and footnote.

83. Graham (undated) at 5-6 and footnote.

84. *Id.*

85. *Time,* July 3, 1944.

86. Memo by Monsignor Tardini, dated October 18, 1944, *Actes et Documents,* vol. X, p. 446, n.4 (no. 357).

87. Graham (undated) at 5-6 and footnote. See also, Roger Butterfield, "Cardinal Spellman," *Life,* January 21, 28, 1946 (Spellman "became the Pope's radio expert"). According to the Italian periodical *Regime fascista,* Spellman was an "agent of American Jews, someone who sends any amount of dollars to the Vatican in exchange for an anti-fascist policy approved by the Holy See." Blet, chapter five. Anne O'Hare McCormick complained about "moral surrender" to the Nazis. "The worst thing the Germans could do," she wrote, "is to dehumanize other people and silence the voices that protest against cruelty and injustice." She was concerned that if the Nazis were to "stifle moral indignation," they would "win their war against the spirit of man." She encouraged others to remain strong by noting that "the Pope does not think it is hopeless." Anne O'Hare McCormick, *The New York Times,* July 15, 1944.

88. Gilbert (1981) at 266 (citing Report of Veesenmayer to Ribbentrop, 6 July 1944, Nuremberg Trial Documents, NG 6584).

89. Lapide at 153.

90. Gilbert (1987) at 50; Blet, chapter nine.

91. Lapide at 156. Rabbi Maurice Perlzweig, also of the World Jewish Congress, wrote to apostolic delegate to Washington, Amleto Cicognani on February 18, 1944, as follows:

It is scarcely necessary for me to assure Your Excellency that the repeated interventions of the Holy Father on behalf of Jewish communities in Europe has evoked the profoundest statements of appreciation and gratitude from Jews throughout the world. These acts of courage and consecrated statesmanship on the part of His Holiness will always remain a precious memory in the life of the Jewish people.

Actes et Documents, vol. X, p. 140 (no. 67).

92. Graham (1996) at 163; Graham (undated) at 19-22.

93. Blet, chapter nine.

94. Lapide at 161.

95. Blet, chapter nine.

96. Lapide at 152.

97. *Id.* at 159.

98. Blet, chapter nine; Robert A. Graham, *Pius XII's Defense of Jews and Others: 1944-45* in *Pius XII and the Holocaust: A Reader* at 61. Rabbi Herzog later wrote to the nuncio, saying:

> The people of Israel will never forget what His Holiness and his illustrious delegates, inspired by the eternal principles of religion which form the very foundations of true civilization, are doing for us unfortunate brothers and sisters in the most tragic hour of our history, which is living proof of divine Providence in this world.

Id.

99. To the entire international Jewish community, on December 3, 1944, Rabbi Safran declared:

> My permanent contact with, and spiritual closeness to, His Excellency the Apostolic Nuncio, the Doyen of the Diplomatic Corps of Bucharest, were decisive for the fate of my poor community. In the house of this high prelate, before his good heart, I shed my burning tears as the distressed father of my community, which was hovering feverishly between life and death.

Graham at 20.

100. Blet, chapter nine.

101. Memo by Monsignor Tardini, dated October 18, 1944, *Actes et Documents*, vol. X, p. 446, n.4 (no. 357).

102. Lapide at 161.

103. Blet, chapter nine (noting that the Nazis, who later overthrew Horthy, resumed surreptitious deportations). Unfortunately, the Soviets followed the Nazis, and they persecuted the Church and its leaders in Hungary, particularly Cardinal Jozsef Mindszenty. Cornwell at 333.

104. Blet, chapter twelve.

105. Hatch & Walsh at 184.

106. Churchill (1953) at 115-16.

107. Taylor had spent the summer trying to persuade the Holy See that the Soviet Union was more open to religion than generally thought and trying to alleviate the Vatican's concerns over the demand for unconditional surrender. Blet, chapter twelve.

108. See Telegram from the Ambassador in the United Kingdom (Winant) to the Secretary of State, Aug. 14, 1944, in in *Foreign Relations of the United States, Diplomatic Papers, 1944, vol. I (General)*, United States Government Printing Office (Washington, 1966) at 1123; *id.* at 1140.

109. Joseph L. Lichten, *A Question of Judgment: Pius XII and the Jews* in *Pius XII and the Holocaust: A Reader* at 127; R. Stewart at 60.

110. Heller & Nekrich at 415-16.

111. Churchill (1953) at 143.

112. Blet, chapter twelve.

113. *Id.*

114. *Id.*

115. Stalin said that the uprising's failure was to be blamed on the Polish leadership in London, but it was ultimately beneficial to his political goals. There are even some reports that he called for the uprising. Hoar at 209. The Soviets had installed their own Polish government as they had pushed into Poland, but the Polish government-in-exile planned to take control after the war. The uprising, however, greatly weakened the exiled government, and made it easier for the Soviets to claim Poland after the war. The Allies suppressed information about Stalin's actions because it did not fit with the current pro-Soviet propaganda. See Terkel at 113-120. Privately, however, Churchill was becoming increasingly concerned over the spread of Soviet power, as were the many in the Vatican. Blum at 741; Holmes at 137; F. Murphy at 63; DeSchner at 151.

116. Holmes at 146. See Lapomarda at 38, n.5 ("One can note that no Jesuit was ever a member of the Nazi party.") Lapomarda also lists the names of 152 Jesuit priests who were killed by, or died as result of, the Nazis. *Id.* at 313-18. Himmler, who admired certain aspects of the Jesuit order, also considered them to be one of the Nazis' most formidable enemies. Matheson at 72. He told the wife of Germany's ambassador to the Holy See that the National Socialists "would not rest until we have rooted out Christianity." Weizsäcker at 281. Late in the war, German Jesuits had the following stamp on their identification papers: "Jesuit: not fit for military service." Similar imprints were put on the identification cards of Jews and other dangerous undesirables. C. Ryan at 25. The Gestapo reportedly had plans to round up all German Jesuits and send them to concentration camps. Alvarez & Graham at 51.

117. Lapomarda at 11-12.

118. *Id.* at 12.

119. *Id.* at 11-12.

120. Holmes at 142, 145.

121. Michaelis at 425.

122. Graham (1987) at 11.

123. Blet, chapter nine. See also *Actes et Documents,* vol. IV, no. 15 (noting efforts made on behalf of Romanian Jews).

124. *Actes et Documents,* vol. IX, no. 53.

125. Blet, chapter nine.

126. Graham (1987) at 20 (December 3, 1944). Earlier, Rabbi Safran paid tribute to the Catholic Church's activities on behalf of Romanian Jews in a letter to the papal nuncio, in which he wrote:

> In these harsh times our thoughts turn more than ever with respectful gratitude to what has been accomplished by the Sovereign Pontiff on behalf of Jews in general and by Your Excellency on behalf of the Jews of Romania and Transnistria.
>
> In the most difficult hours which we Jews of Romania have passed through, the generous assistance of the Holy See, carried out by the intermediary of your high person, was decisive and salutary. It is not easy for us to find the right words to express the warmth and consolation we experienced because of the concern of the supreme Pontiff, who offered a large sum to relieve the sufferings of deported Jews,

sufferings which had been pointed out to him by you after your visit to Transnistria. The Jews of Romania will never forget these facts of historic importance.

Joseph L. Lichten, *A Question of Judgment: Pius XII and the Jews* in *Pius XII and the Holocaust: A Reader* at 130. See also *Actes et Documents*, vol. X, no. 88 (request from the Grand Rabbi of Jerusalem regarding the fate of 55,000 Jews concentrated in Transnistria).

127. Blet, chapter nine. In April 1942, the Romanian minister to the Holy See informed the Vatican that the number of Jews being baptized into Catholicism was too great, and it was drawing attention. *Id.* The Pope, however, rejected the suggestion that further conversions be suspended until the end of the war. *Id.* In February 1943, the Jewish community in Romania asked Archbishop Cassulo to send their gratitude to Pius XII for the help of the Vatican and its nunciature. Joseph L. Lichten, *A Question of Judgment: Pius XII and the Jews* in *Pius XII and the Holocaust: A Reader* at 112.

128. Graham (1987) at 20.

129. Joseph L. Lichten, *A Question of Judgment: Pius XII and the Jews* in *Pius XII and the Holocaust: A Reader* at 128.

130. *Id.*

131. Reprinted in *Pius XII, Selected Encyclicals and Addresses*, at 317.

132. *Id.* at 310.

133. The suggestions offered by Pius, including suggestions about the qualities required of rulers in a democracy, are reminiscent of the writings of the founders of the United States.

134. Reprinted in *Pius XII, Selected Encyclicals and Addresses*, at 315.

135. *Id.*

CHAPTER SIXTEEN

1945 AND THE END OF WAR

1. Barnett at 176.

2. On January 1, 1945, Joseph Hertz, the Grand Rabbi of the British Empire, wrote to Msgr. William Godrey, Papal Nuncio in the United Kingdom as follows:

All the deeper is our appreciation of the sympathy that His Holiness the Pope, and all those associated in the leadership of the Vatican, have shown in the fate of our doomed brethren. The whole House of Israel will be ever mindful of the many and persistent efforts that have been made by Roman Catholic authorities to rescue Jews threatened with barbarous murder.

Actes et Documents, vol. X, p. 513 n.6 (no. 419); *United States Ambassador Taylor to the Secretariat of State*, November 15, 1944, *Actes et Documents*, vol. X, p. 484, n.6 (no. 396) (referencing this message).

402 HITLER, THE WAR, AND THE POPE

3. Hoar at 206-07.

4. Blet, chapter twelve.

5. This filmed statement is included in some documentaries relating to the Church and the war.

6. Message from His Holiness to President Harry S. Truman, April 13, 1945, in *Wartime Correspondence* at 125.

7. *Id.* In fact, Taylor was better received at the Vatican than were ambassadors from some nations. *Id.* (conclusion).

8. Mussolini's widow lived quietly in Italy until her death in October 1979.

9. *Communium Interpretes Dolororum*, paragraphs 2 & 3.

10. *Id.*, paragraph 7.

11. Graham (1987) at 32-33; Blet, chapter twelve.

12. Hitler's propaganda minister from 1933 on, Joseph Goebbels, also committed suicide. He remained hidden in Hitler's bunker until May 1, 1945, when he poisoned his six children before he and his wife took their own dose of cyanide. Soviet forces later found all of the bodies.

13. Morison at 1041. One of the last messages between the warring parties to pass through the Vatican was a memorandum from the German Ambassador to the Holy See to President Roosevelt recommending a new democratic and federal constitution and suggesting that only American and British troops occupy Berlin. "That Allied armies should all advance to meet in Berlin was, I said, politically undesirable." Weizsäcker at 298.

14. Proclamation to the German People, September 28, 1944, reprinted in Snyder at 389.

15. See Keegan at 533.

16. Office of the United States Chief Counsel, vol. I, at 285-86; Shirer (1962) at 324-25 (footnote).

17. Lukacs at 265. Lukacs criticizes Pius for attributing National Socialism to an "apparition," thereby diminishing human (and Catholic) responsibility. Had Lukacs quoted the whole statement, however, his criticism would have been harder to support.

18. Paci at 43. An unofficial translation of this whole speech, as it was broadcast on Vatican Radio, can be found in "The Catholic Church and the Third Reich: Pope Pius XII Surveys an Heroic History," *The Tablet* (London), June 9, 1945.

19. Memorandum by the Director of the Office of Far Eastern Affairs (Ballantine) to the Under Secretary of State (Grew), Jan. 30, 1945, in *United States Department of State, Foreign Relations of the United States, Diplomatic Papers, 1945, vol. VI (The British Commonwealth; The Far East)*, United States Government Printing Office (Washington, 1969) at 475.

20. Japan demanded retention of Hong Kong and Hainan, an independent Phillippines, and more.

21. Einstein also wrote, in a declaration that was published in *Time* magazine on December 23, 1940:

> Only the Church stood squarely across the path of Hitler's campaign for suppressing truth. I had never any special interest in the Church before, but now I feel a great admiration because the Church alone has had the courage and persistence to stand for intellectual truth and moral freedom. I am forced thus to confess, that what I once despised, I now praise unreservedly.

22. Morison at 1044.

23. Morison at 1043. The American position was that war was not being waged on civilians, but that this was the only way to destroy Japan's ability to build planes and make war. Frederick C. Patton, "Why We Must Bomb Japanese Cities," *Reader's Digest,* May 1945, at 82; Thomas M. Johnson, "Doom Over Japan," *The American Mercury,* August 1945, reprinted in *Reader's Digest,* August 1945, at 89.

24. Blum at 756; Mazour & Peoples at 740.

25. Cornwell at 331.

26. The next day, the Soviets entered into the war against Japan, giving them standing to demand certain post-war concessions.

27. A comprehensive accounting of the damage, costs, and death caused by World War II can be found in *World War II,* Encyclopedia Americana/CBS News Audio Library (Print Material at 169-71) (1974).

28. See Lewis F. Gittler, "Life in a German City," *The American Mercury,* October 1945, reprinted in *Reader's Digest,* October 1945, at 25 (describing the devastation of most German cities).

29. Rousmaniere at 113.

30. Allied leaders forced this issue by making civilians go view the camps. Prittie at 60.

31. Jürgen Moltmann, "Wrestling with God: A Personal Meditation," *The Christian Century,* August 13-20, 1997, at 726.

32. Conradt at 16. The caloric intake of almost everyone in post-war Europe, including Allied soldiers, was limited. Vida at 57. See "Europe: From Freedom to Want," *Fortune,* May 1945 ("liberated Europe is fed, clothed and sheltered worse even than under German occupation").

33. Prittie at 54.

34. According to Blet, "it is estimated that 4 bishops, 1996 priests, 113 clerics, and 238 female religious were murdered; sent to concentration camps were 3642 priests, 389 clerics, 341 lay brothers, and 1117 female religious." Blet, chapter three.

35. He rarely slept more than four hours. Cornwell at 270.

36. Other officials had similar concerns. The Charge in the Soviet Union (Kennan) to the Secretary of State. Feb. 8, 1945, in *United States Department of State, Foreign Relations of the United States, Diplomatic Papers, 1945, vol. V (Europe),* United States Government Printing Office (Washington, 1967) at 1119-21 ("How this anti-Catholic tendency will affect Soviet policy in Poland, Hungary and Croatia is however still not apparent."); *The Apostolic Delegate Ciognani in Washington to Monsignor Tardini,* March 9, 1945, *Actes et Documents,* vol. X, p. 557-59 (no. 466) (enclosing Archbishop Sapieha's appeal concerning Soviet occupation).

37. Protestant religious leaders in the United States opposed Vatican involvement in the post-war peace process. Gannon at 169.

38. Hoar at 203. See Demaree Bess, "Will Europe Go Communist After the War?," *The Saturday Evening Post,* Jan. 22, 1944 (American concern over Soviet expansion).

39. Hoar at 208.

40. *Id.* The word "Yalta" became a pejorative term, resulting in boos and hisses when mentioned at certain events. Morison at 1049. See Frederic

Sondern, Jr., "We Are Bungling the Job in Germany," *Reader's Digest,* February 1946, at 87, 89 (criticizing the Potsdam Protocol).

41. Hoar at 208.

42. Morison at 1049.

43. *Chronicle* at 609.

CHAPTER SEVENTEEN

POST-WAR POPE

1. F. Murphy at 64.

2. K. Doyle at 16.

3. He supported the Marshall Plan to rebuild Europe by sanctioning a positive article that appeared in *L'Osservatore Romano.* Cornwell at 330.

4. Hatch & Walsh at 182.

5. Benzinger (preface).

6. Holmes at 150. One of the particular difficulties related to the many victims who had been exposed to tuberculosis and were therefore not welcome in most countries. Vida at 112.

7. C. Doyle at 48, 62. The Pope also shared words of concern about world peace with Connecticut Congresswoman Clare Boothe Luce. Hatch & Walsh at 184.

8. Graham at 20.

9. Holmes at 158. Lapide later increased his estimate of Jewish lives saved to between 800,000 and 860,000.

10. Gaspari at 24; Blet, chapter nine.

11. Lapide at 226. In a letter dated October 27, 1945, Msgr. Montini (the future Pope Paul VI) gave a detailed account of a private audience between Pius XII and Leo Kubwitsky, then-secretary general of the World Jewish Congress. Kubwitsky expressed his gratitude to the pontiff for his work in support of persecuted Jews. *Corriere della Sera,* August 1999. See also M. Perlzweig to the Apostolic Delegate in Washington, *Actes et Documents,* vol. X, p. 140 (no. 140) (World Jewish Congress representative expresses gratitude for "the repeated interventions of the Holy Father on behalf of Jewish communities throughout the world. These acts of courage and consecrated statesmanship on the part of His Holiness will always remain a precious memory in the life of the Jewish people.")

12. The National Jewish Welfare Board to Pope Pius XII, July 21, 1944, *Actes et Documents,* vol. X, p. 358-59 (no. 272).

13. Marrgherita Marchione, "Pope Pius XII and the Jews," *Crisis,* January 1997, at 20, 23; John Thavis, "Many Jews Once Defended Pius and Documentary Evidence Supports Him," *Inside the Vatican,* April 1998, at 30.

14. Marchione (1999) (The Deputy).

15. Marchione (1999) (The Jewish Community) (citing *L'Osservatore Romano*, April 5, 1946).

16. See also Michaelis at 243.

17. C. Doyle at 62.

18. Joseph L. Lichten, *A Question of Judgment: Pius XII and the Jews* in *Pius XII and the Holocaust: A Reader*, at 100.

19. At a conference in St. Louis, on March 16, 1946, William Rosenwald, chair of the United Jewish Appeal for Refugees, Overseas and Palestine, said: "I wish to take this opportunity to pay tribute to Pope Pius for his appeal in behalf of the victims of war and oppression. He provided aid for Jews in Italy and intervened in behalf of refugees to lighten their burden."

20. Smit at 247 (citing *L'Osservatore Romano*, March 1 and March 2, 1947). Even today, one of the highest awards that a Catholic Boy Scout can receive is the Pope Pius XII medal. Among the things that this award is intended to stimulate is an examination of how being a Christian affects daily life in the real world.

21. Telegram from the Secretary of State to the Consul General at Naples (Brandt), June 13, 1944, in *Foreign Relations of the United States, Diplomatic Papers, 1944, vol. I (General)*, United States Government Printing Office (Washington, 1966) at 1068-69.

22. P. Murphy at 208.

23. Bogle, *The Salisbury Review*.

24. K. Doyle at 16; O'Carroll at 108-09. According to the *Jerusalem Post* of May 29, 1955, "Conductor Paul Klecki had requested that the Orchestra on its first visit to Italy play for the Pope as a gesture of gratitude for the help his church had given to all those persecuted by Nazi Fascism."

25. Lapide at 137.

26. O'Carroll at 20; Lapide at 316.

27. O'Carroll at 104.

28. As early as 1944, Pope Pius XII expressed interest in joining the "International Organization." Telegram from Mr. Myron C. Taylor, Personal Representative of President Roosevelt to Pope Pius XII, to the Secretary of State, Oct. 6, 1944, in *Foreign Relations of the United States, Diplomatic Papers, 1944, vol. I (General)* United States Government Printing Office (Washington, 1966) at 963.

29. The Holy See tried to intervene and prevent repatriation of citizens of these areas who did not want to come under Soviet domination. Confidential Note from the Assistant to the President's Personal Representative at Vatican City (Tittmann) to the Secretary of State, July 5, 1945, in *United States Department of State, Foreign Relations of the United States, Diplomatic Papers, 1945, vol. I (The Conference of Berlin)*, United States Government Printing Office (Washington, 1960) at 797 (discussing the Vatican's efforts on behalf of Ukrainians who were in Germany); Telegram from the Acting Secretary of State to the United States Political Adviser for Germany, July 13, 1945, in *United States Department of State, Foreign Relations of the United States, Diplomatic Papers, 1945, vol. II (General: Political and Economic Matters)*, United States Government Printing Office (Washington, 1967) at 1176. Pius also issued an appeal in favor of a group of German internees who were being sent back to Germany (from the United States) rather than to Costa Rica, where their families were. The Apostolic Delegate (Cicognani) to the Secretary

of State, in *United States Department of State, Foreign Relations of the United States, Diplomatic Papers, 1945, vol. IX (The American Republics)*, United States Government Printing Office (Washington, 1966) at 281.

30. Taylor at 192.

31. See Blet, chapter twelve.

32. All over Soviet-dominated Europe, Christian people suffered for their allegiance to Rome. Church schools were closed, all Christian teaching outside church services forbidden, seminaries starved of funds or students, or closed altogether, key clergy targeted as anti-social or treacherous. There was a series of spectacular show-trials. Duffy at 266.

33. Conradt at 32; Douglas Woodruff, "Mediterranean Enquiry: The Church in Italy," *The Tablet* (London), June 9, 1945. See F. Murphy at 14, 64.

34. F. Murphy at 14, 64.

35. *Id.* at 64-65.

36. Cornwell at 297.

37. C. Doyle at 49.

38. Cheetham at 291; Pepper at 178; C. Doyle at 29; Hatch & Walsh at 210-11 (calling him the "least stuffy" of Popes).

39. Dora Jane Hamblin, *That Was the Life*, George J. McLeod Ltd. (Toronto, 1977) at 38.

40. Fogarty, in *The Papacy and the Church in the United States* at 126.

41. With this encouragement, more and more religious women earned advanced degrees. In many cases, this led to a broadened sense of service, causing many nuns to become active in the Civil Rights struggle in the United States and similar struggles elsewhere. Briggs at 26, 78.

42. His statement, "the laity are the Church," emerged as a major theme of Vatican II. See Weigel at 553-54.

43. F. Murphy at 67, 79.

Pius XII was the real architect and promoter of Vatican Council II. He was the one who created the Commission that was to prepare the sessions, but the situation had not matured and Pacelli was already ill. In any event, suffice it to read the Council's minutes to discover that, after Sacred Scripture, Pius XII is the most quoted author. In his encyclicals and addresses he focused on all the problems that would later be addressed by Vatican Council II.

"World Press Unmasks Fallacies in Book Defaming Pius XII: Exclusive Interview with Reporter of Pacelli's Beatification Cause," *ZENIT News Service*, Oct. 3, 1999 (quoting Fr. Peter Gumpel). Regarding the importance of Pope Pius XII's writings during Vatican II, see R.P. Paolo Molinari, *La Presence de Pie XII, au Concile Vatican II*, in *Pie XII et la cite: La Pensée et l'action politiques de Pie XII*, Presses Universitaires d'Aix-Marseille (Jean Chelini & Joël-Benoît d'Onorio, eds., 1988). But see Nichols at 132, 257 (Pius XII's teaching paved the way for Vatican II, but he "would never have called a Council.")

44. *Id.* at 106. The annotation to the documents of Vatican II contains over 200 references to Pius XII's works, more than for any source other than the Bible. O'Carroll at 182, n.8 (also noting that there are many other quotations from Pius XII's writing that were not attributed to him); *id.* at 226,

n.20; see generally *Pie XII et la Cite: Actes du Colloque de la Faculte de Droit d'Aix-en-Provence*, Tequi Presses Universitaires d'Aix-Marseille (Jean Chelini & Joël-Benoît d'Onorio, eds. 1988).

45. F. Murphy at 71; see also O'Carroll at 174 (similar quotation from Cardinal Bea, head of the Rome Biblical Institute).

> Without the Christmas messages of Pius XII during the war years, and particularly those of 1941 and 1942 and that of 1944 on democracy, without the same pope's profound reflections on the state, economic and social affairs, the encyclical *Pacem in Terris* would be scarcely thinkable. There is a clear line of continuity between Pius XII and John XXIII.

Francois Refoule, *The Church and the Rights of Man*, The Seabury Press (New York, 1979) at 78-79.

46. See generally, Committee for Religious Relations with the Jews, *Guidelines on Religious Relations with The Jews* (N.4), December 1, 1974.

47. *The Jewish Post* (Winnipeg), November 6, 1958.

48. Cornwell at 216. This tradition existed for centuries until Pope John XXIII changed it. Kuehnelt-Leddihn at 192.

49. C. Doyle at 12, 56.

50. Hebblethwaite at 51. It has been reported that he was never the same man after this illness. Elliot at 221. While many today consider Pius to have been a very conservative Pope, Elliot suggests that after his illness certain members of the Curia took over and gave the Vatican its conservative slant.

51. For details of the vision and the Pontiff's amazing recovery from illness, see Hatch & Walsh at 235, 238-39.

52. F. Murphy at 69.

53. See *Actes et Documents,* vol. II, p. 306 (no. 101) (Letter from Pius encouraging Galen: "It is always a comfort to Us when We learn of an open and courageous pronouncement on the part of a single German bishop or all of the German bishops together.")

54. Elliott at 1.

55. Cornwell reports that Pacelli's body began to decompose prematurely. Cornwell at 358. A first-hand account, which includes a photograph of the body lying in state, mentions no similar problem. Dora Jane Hamblin, *That Was the Life*, George J. McLeod Ltd. (Toronto, 1977) at 38-39.

56. Elliott at 2; Korn at 154.

57. Marchione (1999) (Death of Pius XII).

58. Elliott at 2. In St. Peter's Basilica, about halfway down to the left, is an ornate grillwork above his crypt which pays homage to the former pontiff. His crypt is immediately to the left as one files down the stairs from within the basilica.

59. Numerous tributes are collected in Marchione (1999) (Death of Pius XII).

60. Joseph L. Lichten, *A Question of Judgment: Pius XII and the Jews* in *Pius XII and the Holocaust: A Reader* at 129. Field Marshall Bernard Law Montgomery, a staunch Anglican and son of an Anglican bishop, wrote: "He was a good man, and I loved him." *Sunday Times* (London), October 12, 1958. In fact, Montgomery kept two photographs in his bedroom: one of his father

and one of Pius XII. Peter Gumpel, "Cornwell's Pope: A Nasty Caricature of a Nobel and Saintly Man," *ZENIT News Service,* Sept. 16, 1999.

61. Akin at 17 (citing Pinchas E. Lapide, *Three Popes and the Jews* 118 (1967)).

62. Joseph L. Lichten, *A Question of Judgment: Pius XII and the Jews* in *Pius XII and the Holocaust: A Reader* at 129. Roman Jews also hung a plaque in their synagogue in honor of Pius XII's efforts to save them. "Interview: 'The Jews, Pius XII and the Black Legend' A Book Tells the Story of Jews Saved from the Holocaust," *Zenit News Agency,* December 8, 1998.

63. Similarly, *The Jewish Chronicle* (London), in its October 10, 1958, edition said:

> Adherents of all creeds and parties will recall how Pius XII faced the responsibilities of his exalted office with courage and devotion. Before, during, and after the Second World War, he constantly preached the message of peace. Confronted by the monstrous cruelties of Nazism, Fascism, and Communism, he repeatedly proclaimed the virtues of humanity and compassion.

64. K. Doyle at 16. According to one account, when Pius died, nearly a thousand letters of gratitude from Jewish survivors of the Holocaust poured into the New York archdiocese. George Sim Johnston, "The 'Hitler's Pope' Canard," *The New York Post,* Sept. 21, 1999.

65. Cardinal Thomas Winning, "Pius XII - friend of the Jews and Hitler's foe," *The Daily Telegraph* (London) October 5, 1999. Former President Harry Truman said: "I'm sorry to hear of the passing of Pope Pius XII, whom I consider the greatest statesman in the Vatican in 200 years." William Doino, Jr., "John Paul II: 'Read Father Blet,' " *Inside the Vatican,* October 1999, at XX. Former President Herbert Hoover said: "The world has lost a great man. I have reason to know the breadth of his spiritual leadership. This world has been better for his having lived in it." *Id.* Secretary of State John Foster Dulles said: "The passing of this great spiritual leader, who has ever been in the forefront of the defense of Christian civilization, is a profound loss for all peoples of the world." *Id.* Adlai Stevenson said: "All of mankind feels, with the oneness he helped give it, an overpowering loss at this saintly man's being gone." *Id.*

66. Rabbi Theodore L. Adams, President of the Synagogue Council of America, said: "The late pontiff, throughout his long career, ceaselessly fought the forces of racism and bigotry." William Doino, Jr., "John Paul II: 'Read Father Blet,' " *Inside the Vatican,* October 1999, at XX. Rabbi Jacob P. Rudin, President of the Central Conference of American Rabbis, said: "His broad sympathy for all people, his wise social vision and his compassionate understanding made his a prophetic voice for righteousness everywhere." *Id.* Dr. Israel Goldstein, Chairman of the Western Hemisphere Executive of World Jewish Congress wrote: "In Rome last year, the Jewish community told me of their deep appreciation of the policy which had been set by the Pontiff for the Vatican during the period of the Nazi-Fascist regime, to give shelter and protection to Jews wherever possible." *Id.* Rabbi Joachim Prinz, National President of the American Jewish Congress, said: "The Pontiff will be remembered wherever men of good will gather for his profound devotion to the cause

of peace and for his earnest efforts in the rescue of thousands of victims of Nazi persecution, including many Jewish men, women and children." *Id.*

67. Memorial forests were planted for Winston Churchill, King Peter of Yugoslavia, and Count Bernadotte of Sweden. The proposal was that Pius XII's forest would have 800,000 trees one for each Jewish life he was credited with having saved. Graham at 34. This number was based upon the testimony of the post-war government of the State of Israel, and it is a larger total than all other European Jewish relief organizations combined. Akin at 17. "The Catholic Church, under the pontificate of Pius XII, was instrumental in saving at least 700,000, but probably as many as 860,000 Jews." Lapide at 269.

68. Bernstein & Politi at 111; Roncalli had likewise been very pleased when Pacelli became Pope Pius XII. Elliott at 147.

69. *Declaration of the Attitude of the Church towards Non-Christian Religions*, reprinted in Lapide, at 344-49.

70. During the war, Pius XII and Montini (the future Pope Paul VI) were "intimate friends" in daily contact with one another. Fabert at 13, 87. In fact, they had a father-son relationship, and it was thought by many that Pius was grooming Montini to one day become Pope. *Id.* at 37, 45, 48. The two had somewhat of a falling out over political matters in 1954, however, and Pius appointed Montini archbishop of Milan without naming him a cardinal. See *id.* at 46-52. Nevertheless, upon his election, it was said that Paul VI was closer to Pius XII, intellectually and emotionally, than he was to Pope John XXIII, his immediate predecessor. *Id.* at 66.

CHAPTER EIGHTEEN

THE QUESTIONS AND ANSWERS

1. In fact, the Vatican had a "long-standing papal practice in wartime of not condemning wartime atrocities by name and only in general terms. The reasons for this practice are... based on experience." Robert A. Graham, reviewing *Vatican Diplomacy and the Jews During the Holocaust: 1934-1943* (by John F. Morley), in *America*, August 9, 1980, at 56, 57. Myron Taylor, President Roosevelt's representative to Pope Pius XII early in the war apparently understood this. He denied having asked Pius to identify Hitler by name. Blet, Chapter 6.

2. Many anti-Hitler intellectuals in Germany chose the same indirect technique for criticizing Hitler. Knowing that a direct attack would only result in further oppression, they would write about Cromwell, Robespierre, Philip of Macedon, or Napoleon and still "hit the target." *The United States at War: The Audio Classics Series.* See also *The Ciano Diaries* at 493 (an article in *L'Osservatore Romano* was expressly written about Greek philosophy, but "the real purpose was evident" to Mussolini, who became "very hostile to the

Vatican"); *id.* at 497-98 (Mussolini considers arresting the director of *L'Osservatore Romano* due to articles which contain "a subtle vein of poison against the regime.")

3. Alvarez & Graham at xi. According to these authors, their study shows "that the Nazis considered the Catholic Church in general and the Vatican in particular to be their archenemies beyond any hope of accommodation, let alone collaboration." *Id.* at xii.

4. Cornwell at 322. According to some accounts, Communists in the 1950s put out a story similar to this in order to discredit Pius (who was active in opposing Communism).

5. In England the title is usually translated as *The Representative*, but sometimes as *The Vicar*.

6. Hochhuth was a disciple of Erwin Piscator, founder a the school of drama known as "Political Theatre," whose method was to put living or recently deceased political person on stage for either pillorying or praise. Robert A. Graham, lecture delivered to the Theological College, the Catholic University of America, Oct. 10, 1989, reprinted in the *Catholic League Newsletter* 11, vol. 16, no. 12, December 1989.

7. A 1963 made-for-television biography of Pius XII, narrated by Mike Wallace (rebroadcast on the History Channel as part of the "Perspectives" series on December 26, 1997), contains no discussion of any controversy relating to Pius and the Jews. The only reference to these matters is that he paid more than 100 pounds of gold to the Germans so that Roman Jews would be spared. The perception of Pius during the war has so changed that one could hardly imagine a post-1963 biography that did not discuss this controversy.

8. Cornwell at 375.

9. A number of war-time diplomats publicly rejected Hochhuth's characterization of Pope Pius XII, including Wladimir d'Ormesson (a member of the French Academy), Sir Francis D'Arcy Osborne (British Minister to the Holy See during the war), Ambassador Grippenberg (from Finland), Ambassador Gunnar Haggelof (from Sweden), and Minister Kanayama (from Japan). In 1963, Albrecht von Kessel, aide to the German Ambassador to the Holy See during the war, wrote:

> We were convinced that a fiery protest by Pius XII against the persecution of the Jews would have in all probability put the Pope himself and the Curia into extreme danger, but *would certainly not have saved a single Jew*. Hitler, like a trapped beast, would react to any menace that he felt directed against him, with cruel violence.

Die Welt, April 6, 1963 (emphasis added); O'Carroll at 21, 81.

10. Cornwell at 375.

11. Graham at 1. This depiction of Pius XII as having a physical emptiness about him is reflected in the writings of many of his critics. *See* Passelecq & Suchecky at ix ("As he goes toward the papal chamber, a famous countenance glides by him, all sunken eyes and cheeks–Eugenio Pacelli"). In reality, prior to the war Pacelli was a diplomat and brilliant conversationalist. Until his last few years, when he became very ill and nearly died, he was far from the isolated figure often depicted.

12. Hochhuth at 304.

13. *Id.* at 349.

14. *Id.* at 350.

15. *Id.* at 351.

16. *Id.* at 296.

17. *Id.* at 305.

18. *Id.* at 350.

19. *Id.* at 306.

20. *Id.* at 328.

21. Cardinal Pole said at the Council of Trent in 1545, "We are responsible for the words we ought to have said and did not. For the things we ought to have done and did not."

22. Hochhuth at 300. It was true, of course, that protests from the Vatican did stop the deportations in Hungary for a while by convincing Admiral Horthy to stop them. Before long, however, the Nazis ousted Horthy and resumed deportations. Vatican pressure had no impact on the German leadership.

23. Hochhuth at 301.

24. Ward at 47; *id.* at 142 ("he has continually stressed that his plays are works of art—not reportage"). In 1967, Jenö Levai, who testified as an expert witness in the Adolf Eichmann trial, released his book *Hungarian Jewry and the Papacy: Pope Pius XII Did Not Remain Silent.* Levai was outraged that Hochhuth had cited him as a source, and criticized what he thought was a dishonest use of historical sources. Dimitri Cavalli, *How Pope Pius XII was made a villain,* Riverdale Press (Bronx, N.Y.), July 16, 1998, at A11.

25. Rhodes at 351. An article by the Archbishop of Milan, Giovanni Battista Montini, written shortly before he became Pope Paul VI, was published in the London *Tablet* on June 29, 1963. In it, he wrote:

> For my part I conceive it my duty to contribute to the task of clarifying and unifying men's judgment on the historical reality in question —so distorted in the representational pseudo-reality of Hochhuth's play.
>
> ***
>
> Let some men say what they will, Pius XII's reputation as a true Vicar of Christ, as one who tried, so far as he could, fully and courageously to carry out the mission entrusted to him, will not be affected.

Montini's letter was received in London an hour after he became Pope. Rhodes at 352, n.28. Giuseppe Saragat, who was Italian Foreign Minister at the time, wrote:

> I, myself, am convinced Pius XII was a great Pope and that the campaign against him is orchestrated for partisans. So many years after his death, this is unacceptable not just for Catholics, but for all men of good will.... Innumerable episodes reveal the spirit behind Pius XII's activity, especially here in Rome... where there is living testimony from all citizens on Pius XII's work; moreover, instead of going to a safe place protected by Allied troops... he stayed in his place, in the middle of the storm, giving aid to neighborhoods stricken by the fury of the war, and trying to pry innocent victims away from Nazi barbarism.... In any event, the controversy that has broken out over the memory of Pius XII is not a cultural debate; it is founded on

calumnies and lies that have nothing to do with historical and cultural research. In the debates against Pius XII we see the cold, cal-
culating propaganda of those trying to excuse Nazism from horrific
crimes by making the Roman Catholic Church co-responsible.

"Additional Evidence of Pius XII's Help to Jews: Church Saved One Million
Jews from Certain Death," *Zenit News Agency*, March 15, 1999.

26. Ward at 43-44.

27. "I would like to say quite plainly that I regard *The Deputy* as a shame-
less and inexcusable attack upon a defenseless dead man who, in view of the
laws operative in most 'civilized states,' cannot be given protection against the
calumny of this theatrical web of lies." Kuehnelt-Leddihn at 184-85. "This
portrait of a callous, money-minded, cynical and selfish man is contradicted
by everything in the German and British Foreign Office documents." Rhodes
at 351.

28. Gerald Warner, "Twisted Interpretation of History Blames Pius XII for
the Plight of the Jews," *Scotland on Sunday*, Sept. 26, 1999.

29. In 1978, in a Norwegian newspaper, Hochhuth dismissed Pius as "a
common coward." Lothar Groppe, "The Church and the Jews in the Third
Reich," *Fidelity*, November 1983, at 18.

30. Lewy at 305.

31. Christopher Reed, "Jewish fury over plan for 'St. Pius'," *The Observer*,
July 18, 1999; Tom Tugend, "Jewish group protests proposed Pius XII canonization," *The Jerusalem Post*, February 21, 1993.

32. Tom Tugend, "Jewish group protests proposed Pius XII canonization,"
The Jerusalem Post, February 21, 1993.

33. *Id.*

34. The beginning of this process is an exhaustive canonical investigation. After this step, Church authorities must determine that God has worked
an authentic miracle through the candidate's intercession. Only then can the
candidate be considered for canonization. *Id.* At this point, the Church had
gathered more than 100 depositions from people who knew Pius personally.
Gaspari at 26.

35. Lewy at 305.

36. A further description of this position is contained in the Epilogue.

37. "Judging Pope Pius XII," *Inside the Vatican*, June 1997, at 12. More
recently, Fr. Gumpel said, "After reading 100,000 pages of the documents for
the process of beatification, I am more and more convinced that Pius XII was
a saint." *Cardinal Cassidy:* "We Cannot Be Chained to the Past," EWTN News,
March 25, 1999.

38. Tom Tugend, "Jewish group protests proposed Pius XII canonization,"
The Jerusalem Post, February 21, 1993.

39. Palmer & Colton at 991.

40. Michaelis at 377.

41. "In the final analysis, what the nuncios and bishops as well as the
priests, nuns and other religious did for the Jews had the approval and support of the Pope himself as the acts and documents of the Holy See... testify."
Lapomarda at 306. "It would have been impossible for the hundreds of
priests and nuns to carry forward their work of mercy and rescue if their Pope
had forbidden it." Id. at 310, n.6 (quoting Abram L. Sachar, *The Redemption
of the Unwanted*, St. Martin's Press (New York, 1983) at 97). The Nazis were

at least suspicious that Pius was behind the various activities of the bishops. One report to Hitler, giving the details of an interview with Cardinal Szeptyckyj, the Catholic Ukrainian Archbishop, said: "his ideas are the same as the French Bishops, the Belgian Bishops and the Dutch Bishops, just as if they all received identical instructions from the Vatican." R. Stewart at 12.

42. Lapide at 133.

43. Cornwell, for instance, criticizes Pius for failing to help enough Jews, not for failing to help any Jews.

44. Hochhuth at 331. Pius also had a life-long Jewish friend, Dr. Guido Mendes, of Ramat Gan, Israel. "A Jewish Boyhood Friend," *Inside the Vatican*, October 1999, at XXIV.

45. Nearly as many Catholic Poles died at the hand of the Nazis as did Jewish Poles. In fact, it seems clear that Poles were marked by the Nazis for eventual extermination. Lapomarda at 151, n.84 (noting that 400 nuns, mostly Polish, died in concentration camps). For an interesting account, *see* Richard C. Lukas, *The Forgotten Holocaust: Poles Under German Occupation, 1939-1944* (1986). Lukas argues that Hitler's hatred of Poles was quite similar to his feeling toward the Jews, and that until 1942, Christian Poles in German-occupied Poland were treated worse than Jewish Poles. From the very beginning, Polish bishops, priests and nuns were arrested and tortured. *Id.*; *The Victims of Nazi Ideology*, January 1995, reprinted in Secretariat for Ecumenical and Interreligious Affairs, National Conference of Bishops, *Catholics Remember the Holocaust*, United States Catholic Conference (Washington, 1998); Blet, Chapter 4.

46. Lapide at 168. This was apparently not an insubstantial amount. According to one account, the future Pope inherited $100,000 in the mid-1930s. Cornwell at 178.

47. One author claims to have uncovered evidence of anti-Semitism early in Pius XII's life. Cornwell at 70-75. This matter is addressed in the Epilogue.

48. Rousmaniere at 123.

49. This is reprinted in Secretariat for Ecumenical and Interreligious Affairs, National Conference of Bishops, *Catholics Remember the Holocaust*, United States Catholic Conference (Washington, 1998).

50. See *id.*, at 68.

51. *Id.*, footnote 16. Releasing the document, Cardinal Edward Idris Cassidy explained: "As for Pope Pius XII, it is our conviction that in recent years his memory has been unjustly denigrated." *Reflections Regarding the Vatican's Statement on the Shoah*, reprinted in *id.*, at 61, 72. Archbishop Oscar Lipscomb, Chair of the U.S. Bishops' Committee on Ecumenical and Interreligious Affairs, wrote: "Pope Pius XII maintained this teaching of his predecessor [as reflected in *Mit brennender Sorge*] throughout his pontificate.... The American, French, and other bishops of the world who joined the condemnations of Nazi genocide believed themselves to be following the lead of the Holy Father." *Commemorating the Liberation of Auschwitz*, January 1995, reprinted in Secretariat for Ecumenical and Interreligious Affairs, National Conference of Bishops, *Catholics Remember the Holocaust*, United States Catholic Conference (Washington, 1998).

52. *Documents on German Foreign Policy 1918-1945*, Series C (1933-1937), vol. I, no. 188.

53. "The intellectual origins of Nazi antisemitism are to be found in pseudo-scientific racist and mystical-romantic-traditionalist ideologies of the nineteenth century, not in the teachings of Augustine, Innocent III or even Martin Luther." Saperstein at 40-41.

54. *Id.* at 41.

55. *Id.* In fact, a 1940 book commissioned by Pope Pius XII and designed to analyze the treatment of the German Catholic Church by the National Socialists concluded that religious persecution "is determined and actuated by the *very nature and essence of the National Socialist totalitarian system.*" *The Persecution of the Catholic Church in the Third Reich* at 515 (emphasis in original).

56. Hitler is only known to have attended one church service in his adulthood—a funeral for Polish Marshal Pilsudski at the Berlin Cathedral..

57. Weizsäcker at 281. During the war, Lenin, Hitler, and Mussolini were noted for their similar intense dislike of religion. H. Stewart at 108. A number of Hitler's closest accomplices shared his hatred toward the Church and his desire to destroy it. The best known among them were Bormann, Himmler, Heydrich, Rosenberg and Goebbels. In fact, "Himmler's profession became destroying Jews, liberals and priests." Lothar Groppe, "The Church's Struggle with the Third Reich," *Fidelity*, November 1983 (Alan F. Lacy trans.), quoting Gerhard Reitlinger, *Die SS-Tragödie einer deutschen Epoche*, (Munich, 1977) at 29.

58. *The Goebbels Diaries 1939–1941* at 77. See also Sigrid Schultz, "Germany's Part-Time Brides," *McCall's Magazine*, April 1946 (quoting a German woman: "Nazism freed me of the fetters of Christian inhibitions. I'm through with that Christian stuff; I'm going to bring up my children according to my own ideas.")

59. Matheson at 43. "He said it was downright horrifying that a religion could ever have been possible which literally gobbled up its God in communion." Lothar Groppe, "The Church's Struggle with the Third Reich," *Fidelity*, October 1983, at 12, 13 (quoting the diary of Alfred Rosenberg).

60. *Hitler's Secret Conversations* at 49 (on October 19, 1941, Hitler says: "I didn't know that Julian the Apostate had passed judgement with such clear-sightedness on Christianity. You should read what he says on the subject."); *id.* at 52 (similar); *id.* at 274 (Feb. 8, 1942: "The evil that's gnawing our vitals is our priests, of both creeds.")

61. Graham at 34 (citing John F. Morley, *Vatican Diplomacy and the Jews During the Holocaust 1939-1943* (1980)). In a Papal Allocution of October 6, 1946, relating to judicial authority in the church and state, Pope Pius addressed the charge that the Church had engaged in "forced conversions." He found the best evidence to be a memorandum, dated January 25, 1942, from the Vatican Secretariat of State to the Legation of Yugoslavia to the Holy See. The Pope read from that document:

> According to the principles of Catholic doctrine, conversion must be the result, not of external constraint, but of an interior adherence of the soul to the truths taught by the Catholic Church.
>
> It's for this reason that the Catholic Church does not admit to her communion adults who request either to be received or to be readmitted, except on condition that they be fully aware of the meaning and consequences of the step that they wish to take.

If an episcopal committee was at once established with the charge of considering and deciding all questions concerning this matter, that was done precisely for the purpose of guaranteeing that the conversion should be, in conformity to the principles of Catholic doctrine, the fruit of conviction and not of constraint.

62. There is also evidence of the effectiveness of this approach. According to statistics put forth by a Catholic charity organization shortly after the war, 7,200 of 8,000 "Catholic" Jews in Vienna survived the war. Only 4,000 of the 152,000 other Jews survived. Vida at 73. See generally Marchione (2000) (Overview) (the Church historically was oppressive in its effort to convert Jews, but it always taught that it was wrong to harm or kill Jewish people).

63. Tec at 187 (noting that most Jewish survivors who had been sheltered by the Catholic Church "derived much comfort from the Catholic religion").

64. Marchione (1997) at 84; Stille at 262.

65. Even when parents requested the baptism, it was recognized that this was simply a matter of duress. Lapide at 210.

66. During the winter of 1943-44, the Jewish Agency in Jerusalem, under the patronage of the High Commander for Palestine, sponsored a memorial evening to recognize and honor the Pontiff's efforts on behalf of Jewish children. Dignitaries from throughout the city, including the apostolic delegation, were in attendance. Michael Wahbeh, "Incompatible Efforts," *The Jerusalem Post*, July 13, 1995.

67. Lapide at 209-10.

68. *Actes et Documents*, vol. IX, p. 575 (no. 436).

69. Cardinal MacRory to Cardinal Maglione, May 19, 1940, in *Actes et Documents*, vol. VI, p. 306 (no. 204); Gaspari at 24; Blet, Chapter 9; Holmes at 154. Graham at 20.

70. Kennedy (1961) at 62-63.

71. Barnett at 221.

72. Cianfarra at 99.

73. The treatment of Polish citizens by the Soviets after Poland (a predominantly Catholic country) was "liberated" also seems to justify any hesitation the Vatican may have felt about siding with the Soviet Union. See Deschner at 7.

74. Van Hoek at 90.

75. Cornwell at 261.

76. Minutes of August 7, 1941, British Public Records Office FO 371/30175 57760 (giving Pius "a good mark" for refusing "to say a single word in favour of Hitler's 'anti-Communist Crusade'").

77. Robert A. Graham, lecture delivered to the Theological College, the Catholic University of America, Oct. 10, 1989, reprinted in the *Catholic League Newsletter* 11, vol. 16, No. 12, December 1989. See also Pope Pius XII to Myron Taylor, dated September 26, 1942, *Actes et Documents*, vol. V, p. 724-25 (no. 489) (concern for Soviet prisoners).

78. Message from the British Embassy in Madrid, May 10, 1943, British Public Records Office, FO 3711 37538.

79. Office of the United States Chief of Counsel, Supp. B, at 1233. In his diary, on May 28, 1943, Joseph Goebbels wrote that Roosevelt was mediating between the Vatican and the Soviets, and that "Stalin is at present pursuing

a very realistic policy with reference to the church question, quite the opposite of ours." *The Goebbels Diaries 1942–1943* at 400.

80. At least some authors have traced contrary conclusions to Soviet propaganda. *See* Lapomarda at 172, 195, n.8.

81. Lapide at 120, quoting Erich Ludendorff, *General and Cardinal-On the Policy of the New Pope Pius XII 1917-1937* at 64.

82. Lapide at 118.

83. Forty-five closely printed pages of historical sidelights are appended on the printed text of the play–to show that the author of the drama allowed his imagination only so much freedom as was needed to shape the material. Forty-five pages of demonstration and proof! But the quantity is deceptive. The materials are all mixed up higgledy-piggledy; seldom are we told precisely where the arguments and quotations come from. "Solid collections of sources are mentioned only in isolated instances; but evidence and witnesses of dubious value are mentioned frequently.... The work is based on second and third-hand evidence, on popular books which do not even claim to provide a final clarification...."

Levai at 5-6 (quoting Albert Wucher, *Der Stellvertreter und die historische Wirklirhkeit*, in the *Süddeutsche Zeitung*, Munich 19.4.1963).

84. Hochhuth at 296.

85. On October 11, 1930, *L'Osservatore Romano* editorialized that membership in the National Socialist Party was "incompatible with the Catholic conscience, just as it is completely incompatible with membership in socialist parties of all shades." Cornwell at 116.

86. According to the *London Tablet*, Nov. 29, 1941, the head of the Gestapo in Yugoslavia told a priest: "Don't you know that our *Führer* wishes to stamp out all Jews and priests? I suppose you know how priests are treated at [the camp at Begnnje], like dogs." See Lapomarda at 209, n. 6.

87. Lapide at 120, quoting Erich Ludendorff, *General and Cardinal-On the Policy of the New Pope Pius XII 1917-1937* at 64. See also Duffy at 265.

88. Cornwell at 240.

89. There is a further discussion of this matter in the Epilogue.

90. A person may take martyrdom and death upon himself—often a man is obliged to do so—and this is a personal act; but no man may decree that another bear testimony in blood, especially if he himself is exempt. Only a tyrant would do that, but never a *Papa*, a true father.

Kuehnelt-Leddihn at 190.

91. Pius XII could easily have made this gesture, *at no risk at all to himself.* The Nazis had learned... not to lay hands on the bishops and archbishops. It was the little people - simple priests, monks, nuns, laymen - who had to pay the price of "freedom" enjoyed by the hierarchy under the swastika. Hitler, whose hatred of Christianity and especially of the Catholic Church knew no bounds, knew exactly how to attack: *he did not want heads to roll, but to cut away the roots.*

Kuehnelt-Leddihn at 189. Bishop Clemens August, Count von Galen was well known for three outspoken sermons he gave against National Socialism. He was, however, "deeply dejected" when the result was that 37 members of the clergy were arrested in retaliation, and ten of them lost their lives.   *Three Sermons in Defiance of the Nazis*, Church in History Information Centre (Birkenhead, U.K.) at 4-5.

92. O'Carroll at 127.

93. Hochhuth at 298.

94. "Everyone knows that the Holy See cannot bring Hitler to heel." *Notes of Monsignor Tardini*, July 13, 1942, *Actes et Documents*, vol. VIII, no. 426, p. 598. In a public letter addressed to Cardinal Maglione on August 5, 1943, Pius wrote: "since no heed is paid to the words which We have with trepidation uttered, We raise our heart and Our eye to the Father of Mercy." "The Church and the Italian Crisis," *The Tablet* (London), August 14, 1943, at 76.

95. G.M. Gilbert at 39 (Ribbentrop, during a recess from the Nuremberg Trials, admitted that there were several protests from the Vatican, but Hitler ignored them. Goering confirmed Ribbentrop, saying: "But that was our right! We were a sovereign State and that was strictly our business."). See *Actes et Documents*, vol. IX, no. 325 (notes dated September 6, 1943, reflecting German opposition to the Holy See's right to protest on behalf of Jews). See also Susan Zuccotti, *Pope Pius XII and the Holocaust: The Case in Italy*, in *The Italian Refuge*, at 258. While very critical of Pope Pius XII's "silence," Zuccotti acknowledges that "the Nazis never would have released Jews already caught or ceased future arrests."

96. Levai at 30. Those times when protests had some success were situations where the German S.S. had not yet fully taken over. *Id.* at 111-12.

97. Robert M.W. Kempner, the Deputy Chief U.S. Prosecutor at the Nuremberg war trials, explained that a public protest against prosecution of the Jews could only lead to partial success when "it was made at a politically and militarily opportune moment." He further explained that Pius made such protests through the nuncios in Slovakia and Romania when the time was opportune. Similar protests would not have been effective with Hitler. Levai at xi (Kempner's prologue). *Testimony of Cardinal Stefano Wyszynski*, October 18 & 25, 1968, before the Tribunal of the Vicariate of Rome, on the beatification of Pius XII (Eugenio Pacelli), Part II, page 574, 578 (no international authority would have been able to deter the Nazis).

98. Cornwell at 316.

99. This is explored in more detail in Chapter 14.

100. Wyman at 47, 69.

101. Hochhuth at 326 (suggesting that this testimony was false). "When Clemens August von Galen, bishop of Münster, wanted to speak against the persecution of the Jews in Germany, the Jewish elders of his diocese begged him not to because it would only damage them." Peter Gumpel, "Cornwell's Cheap Shot at Pius XII," *Crisis*, December 1999, at 19, 224-25.

102. One of the counts charged against the defendants at the Nuremberg trials reflected the Allies' view of the relations between the Vatican and the Nazis.

> The Nazi conspirators, by promoting beliefs and practices incompatible with Christian teaching, sought to subvert the influence of the Churches over the people and in particular over the youth of Germany....They avowed their aim to eliminate the Christian churches in Germany and sought to substitute therefor Nazi institutions and

Nazi beliefs and pursued a programme of *persecution of priests, clergy, and members of monastic orders* which they deemed opposed to their purposes, and *confiscated church property*.

O'Carroll at 138 (suggesting that a memorandum authorized by Pius XII influenced the terms of this charge).

103. Graham at 36 (quoting Dr. Robert M.W. Kempner).

104. "History on the Stage: Could Pius XII Have Stopped Hitler Killing the Jews?," *The London Tablet*, March 16, 1963.

105. Even during the war, many people in the Nazi-dominated areas knew that the civilized world would never believe their horror stories. Karski at 322-23. This included many American soldiers. See Richard Joseph with Waverly Root, "Why So Many GIs Like the Germans Best," *Reader's Digest*, March 1946, at 5, 6 9 ("many an American soldier carried his defense of the Germans to the point of accusing the American authorities of having invented the atrocity stories").

106. Cornwell at 195.

107. Holmes at 168.

108. Cornwell at 244.

109. Blet, Chapter 3.

110. Pius made a similar private statement during the war to a chaplain who reported to him on the conditions in Poland:

> Please tell everyone, everyone you can, that the Pope suffers agony on their behalf. Many times I have thought of scorching Nazism with the lightning of excommunication and denouncing to the civilized world the criminality of the extermination of the Jews. We have heard of the very serious threat of retaliation, not on our person but on the poor sons who are under the Nazi domination. We have received through various channels urgent recommendations that the Holy See should not take a drastic stand. After many tears and many prayers, I have judged that a protest of mine not only would fail to help anyone, but would create even more fury against the Jews, multiplying acts of cruelty.

Robert Martin, *Spiritual Semites: Catholics and Jews During World War Two*, Catholic League Publications (Milwaukee, 1983), quoting Father Scavizzi, in *La Parrochia*, June 15, 1964.

111. Graham at 35 (quoting a letter to *Commentary*, June 1964, from Dr. Robert M.W. Kempner).

112. Testimony of Cardinal Stefano Wyszynski, October 18 & 25, 1968, before the Tribunal of the Vicariate of Rome, on the beatification of Pius XII (Eugenio Pacelli), Part II, page 577.

113. See De Lubac at 24 (and footnote).

114. But see Falconi at 100 (if Pius had made a statement "at the right moment, it would probably have been very effective indeed–possibly even a determining factor in the war.")

115. Lapomarda at 97 (making this same argument).

116. Blet (conclusion).

117. Lewy at 304-05.

118. Toland at 864; Holmes at 132; O'Carroll at 131; Blet, Chapter 4.

119. Joseph L. Lichten, *A Question of Judgment: Pius XII and the Jews,* in *Pius XII and the Holocaust: A Reader* at 99.

120. Michaelis at 372 (footnote omitted).

121. Another time, discussing the Vatican and the International Red Cross, Weizsäcker said: "It is a matter of course and everybody knows it, that these two agencies of world significance and reputation and world-wide influence would have undertaken any possible step that they considered feasible and useful to save the Jews. O'Connell at 80.

122. O'Carroll at 129.

123. William D. Rubinstein, "Books in Review: *The Devil's Advocate,*" *First Things,* January 2000, at 39, 40.

124. *Id.*

125. F. Murphy at 70; *How to Manufacture a Legend: The Controversy over the Alleged "Silence" of Pope Pius XII in World War II,* in *Pius XII and the Holocaust: A Reader* at 18-19.

126. Early in the war, Sapieha had asked the Pope for a forceful statement, but he later changed his mind and recalled his letter. See Blet, Chapter 4; Paci at 41.

127. Lutheran pastor Dietrich Bonhoeffer was executed for his part in trying to eliminate Hitler. He is often used to contrast Pacelli's "silence." However, during the war, "Bonhoeffer never gave public condemnations of the Nazis. On the contrary he feigned public approval. The reason–not to draw attention to illegal activities–is the same reason given by Pacelli." Charles Ford, "Invidious Comparisons," *First Things,* January 2000, at 67.

128. The Geneva Red Cross decided that a public protest would have no beneficial effect and would compromise what good the Committee was already doing for the internees. Robert A. Graham, *How to Manufacture a Legend: The Controversy over the Alleged "Silence" of Pope Pius XII in World War II,* in *Pius XII and the Holocaust: A Reader* at 20.

129. An article by the Archbishop of Milan, Giovanni Battista Montini, written shortly before he became Pope Paul VI, was published in the London Tablet on June 29, 1963. In it, he wrote: "If Pius had made a public condemnation, Hochhuth could have written another play condemning the Pope for making a grand theatrical gesture which meant certain death for many."

130. One of the points noted in the *Investigative Reports* program was that when the Allies bombed Rome and the Pope went to inspect the damage, it was a very rare opportunity for the people of Rome to see the Pope since "he spent almost the entire war inside the Vatican." The implication seemed to be that he was hiding. In truth, Pius spent most of his time in the Vatican, even during times of peace. He normally traveled away from the Vatican during the summer, but during the war he decided to stay in the Vatican year-round, even though he knew Rome was subject to attack. The saying in Rome was: "The Pope is our best anti-aircraft." Hatch & Walsh at 176. When bombs did fall on Vatican City, Pius refused to enter the air-raid shelter. Thus, he placed himself at greater risk. In fact, there were many who had urged him to relocate and get out of harm's way, but Pius refused.

131. It was reported early in the war that Pius approved and blessed a day of national prayer for an Italian victory. However, British documents clarify that February 2 was appointed in the Rome Vicariate as a day of prayer for

the protection of Italian soldiers, and there was no mention of a papal bless-ing. *Outward Telegram Distribution B to Switzerland,* February 3, 1941, British Public Records Office FO 371/30173 56879.

132. Paci at 40. During the war, 27 of the 46 cardinals were Italian. Rhodes at 355.

133. Pius encouraged Preysing in his resistance work. De Lubac at 145; O'Carroll at 89. In fact, Pius was the only world leader who took the resist-ance seriously. Charles Ford, "Invidious Comparisons," *First Things,* January 2000, at 67.

134. De Lubac at 121-22, n.12; O'Carroll at 89.

135. On July 5, 1998, an article in the Milan newspaper *Il Giornale* reported on the discovery of a letter in the archives of the Archdiocese of Milan dated September 26, 1944, from Paolo Porta, the Fascist leader in Como, to Vincenzo Costa, the Fascist leader in Milan. In that letter, Porta cited a high S.S. official to the effect that in December 1943, Hitler personally delegated Himmler and Gestapo head Heinrich Müller to study and execute a plan to eliminate the Pope. The plan called for Germans dressed as Italian partisans to attack the Vatican. German troops would then come to the "rescue," with the hope that Pius would be killed in the foray. If he were not killed, he would be sent to Germany for "protection." After the attack, "the persecution of the Catholic Church would begin with mass deportations to Germany of all eccle-siastics in Italy and throughout the world. They are to be considered the cause of ignorance, of domination, of conspiracies...." The reason for the attack was identified as "the papal protest in favor of the Jews." See also Marchione (2000) (Hitler's Plan).

136. Schom at 458.

137. Hochhuth at 351. American documents from 1943 suggest that most people in the Vatican at that time felt that Germany would not invade the Vatican unless Hitler had "a sudden outburst of anger against the church" and he overruled wiser counsel. The same report also noted that a minority was completely convinced that Hitler would invade the Vatican. Telegram from the Minister in Switzerland (Harrison) to the Secretary of State, Oct. 29, 1943, in *Foreign Relations of the United States, Diplomatic Papers, 1943, vol. II (Europe),* United States Government Printing Office (Washington, 1964) at 951-52.

138. Haberman, *New York Times.* Goebbels recorded in his diary on July 27, 1943, that Hilter at first intended to seize the Vatican, but decided against it when Ribbentrop and Goebbels pointed out the impact that such actions would have on world opinion. *The Goebbels Diaries 1942–1943* at 409.

139. This is reported in Chapter 14. The meeting took place after Mussolini was deposed.

140. Weizsäcker at 291; *Actes et Documents,* vol. IX, no. 355 & 474.

141. See Chadwick (1977) 187-88, 195.

142. Holmes at 155-56.

143. Haberman, *New York Times.*

144. Michaelis at 377.

145. Testimony of Karl Otto Wolff, March 14, 1972, before the Ecclesiastical Tribunal of Munich, on the beatification of Pius XII (Eugenio Pacelli) at 825. In 1944, when the Allies liberated Rome, Wolff approached Pius XII to discuss a possible peace treaty. At that time Wolff provided Pius

with documents regarding Hitler's plans to invade the Vatican. *Id.* The documents are reprinted along with Wolff's testimony. *Id.* at 831. Peter Gumpel, S.J., the relator of the cause for Pope Pius XII's sainthood, told me that General Wolff was instrumental in freeing Gumpel's mother in 1938 when she was arrested by the Nazis.

146. Testimony of Karl Otto Wolff, March 14, 1972, before the Ecclesiastical Tribunal of Munich, on the beatification of Pius XII (Eugenio Pacelli) at 832.

147. *Id.*

148. *Id.* at 836-37.

149. Hochhuth at 324.

150. *The Times* (London), May 20, 1963; see Confidential Letter to Oliver Harvey from D'Arcy Osborne, February 26, 1947, British Public Records Office, FO 371/67917 60675. See also Tardini at 83 ("Pius was strong. He did not fear criticism, opposition, complaints, or accusations. We saw him go along the road that God and his conscience pointed out for him.")

151. Cornwell at 380.

152. Zolli at 187; Lapide at 132-33.

153. O'Carroll at 69. See Telegram from the German Ambassador (Bergen) to the Reich Minister, dated January 26, 1943, NARA, T-120, Roll 361, at 277668-70 ("Pius XII is as little susceptible to threats as we ourselves."); Lapomarda at 232, n. 9 ("Pius XII was fearless in the face of hostile threats from both the Fascists and the Nazis.")

154. F. Murphy at 70-71; Paci at 39.

155. O'Carroll at 58.

156. Gerhart M. Riegner, "The Holocaust and Vatican Diplomacy," *Reform Judaism*, Fall 1984, at 42.

157. *Id.*

158. See *id.* ("The Vatican understood only very late the full extent of the catastrophe.")

159. *Id.* at 80 (noting the difficulty the author had in 1945 convincing other Vatican officials of the extent of Nazi abuse).

160. F. Murphy at 61-2.

161. Kahn at 192, 473; Alvarez & Graham at 142-43. Axis intelligence suspected that Vatican Radio was transmitting intelligence information to the Allies, and apparently it was. Cornwell at 228; Alvarez & Graham at 136, n.1. Some members of the German intelligence believed that Pius XII was personally involved in intelligence work. *Id.* At 61.

162. Szulc at 104.

163. *Id.* at 104.

164. Certain Polish bishops, exiled in London, called for stronger statements by the Pontiff. Those who remained in Poland like Archbishop Sapieha, however, urged him not to speak. Paci at 41.

165. It is probable that no one in the Vatican knew about the "slaughter on an industrial scale" that the Holocaust actually turned out to be. Paci at 42. *Testimony of Cardinal Stefano Wyszynski*, October 18 & 25, 1968, before the Tribunal of the Vicariate of Rome, on the beatification of Pius XII (Eugenio Pacelli), Part II, page 578 (arguing that no one knew Hitler's intent at first).

166. Rhodes at 346. This is made clear in Jan Karski's *Story of a Secret State*. John Cornwell criticizes Pius for diminishing the number in his 1942

Christmas statement. Pius referred to hundreds of thousands of victims, instead of millions. Surely no responsible party in the free world knew that the victims numbered in the millions by 1942. In fact, the Allied statement that Pius refused to join in also referred to "hundreds of thousands," not millions.

167. Of course, some writers have suggested that if the Allies had been willing to go along with the peace plans supported by the Pope, there would have been a favorable end to the war in 1943. John Dombrowski, *The Greatest War Crime*, Culture Wars, December 1997.

168. *Pope Pius XII to Myron Taylor*, dated September 22, 1942, *Actes et Documents*, vol. V, p. 692-94 n.6 (no. 476).

169. O'Carroll at 74 (discussing how Hitler's theory required war to justify the killing of Jews and noting that without the war fewer Jews would have come under his control).

170. Hochhuth at 351.

171. Holmes at 168.

172. Would history have judged Pius differently if he had hurled anathemas at Hitler's regime, and wallowed martyr-like in the blood of his own people and the Jewish people?

Would it truly have been a sign of goodness to put his own reputation before the lives of men, women and children? There can be only one answer to these questions–questions which commentators and best-selling authors, in recent years have, alas, chosen not to ask themselves.

Cardinal Thomas Winning, "Pius XII–Friend of the Jews and Hitler's Foe," *The Daily Telegraph* (London) October 5, 1999.

173. Blet (conclusion).

174. Graham at 2-3 (quoting Pius XII).

175. Marchione (1997) at 155.

176. "The crime is too great to be attributed to a relatively small number of people." Mazgaj at 20.

177. For too many historians, the Nazis appear in accounts of the Holocaust as some inexplicable force of nature whose destructive powers it is pointless to question, while criticism focuses on the alleged inadequacies of those who could not prevent the slaughter. That this is utterly unfair should be evident, yet library shelves are filled with works on the "failures" of the Allies, as they are with works critical of Pacelli. At the very best such books deflect attention from the real criminals; at worst they imply a moral equivalency between mass murderers and those who tried, whether effectively or not, to stop them.

William D. Rubinstein, "Books in Review: *The Devil's Advocate*," *First Things*, January 2000, at 39.

178. Hochhuth at 317. Minister Louis Farrakhan of the Nation of Islam even blamed Jewish financiers for the Holocaust.

> German Jews financed Hitler right here in America.... International bankers financed Hitler, and poor Jews died while big Jews were at the root of what you call the Holocaust....Little Jews dying while big Jews made money. Little Jews being turned into soap while big Jews washed themselves in it....Jews playing music while other Jews [were] marching into the gas chamber.

NBC News Transcripts, April 13, 1997. Minister Farrakhan also spoke of "Jews that perished in Germany while ... Pope Pius XII looked the other way and the government of America looked the other way." *Id.*

179. Hochhuth at 315, 316.

180. Holmes at 141.

181. *Id.* at 158.

182. Toland (1976) at 687, 689, 865.

183. *Id.* at 865.

184. The War Refugee Board sent a message to the Vatican in 1944, in which it acknowledged that Pius "has labored unceasingly to reinculcate a decent regard for the dignity of man," and the "tireless efforts of His Holiness to alleviate the lot of the persecuted, the hunted and the outcasts." Telegram from the Secretary of State to the Consul General at Naples (Brandt), June 13, 1944, in *Foreign Relations of the United States, Diplomatic Papers, 1944, vol. I (General)*, United States Government Printing Office (Washington, 1966) at 1068-69.

185. Waters, *Newsweek* (quoting historian David Wyman).

186. Cornwell at 267. *See Declaration on Nazi Refugees After World War II*, Vatican Information Service, Feb. 14, 1992 (denying any intent to assist war criminals).

187. Adolf Eichmann is one of the former National Socialist leaders who allegedly escaped Europe with a Vatican passport. As head of the Gestapo's Jewish section from 1939 until 1945, he was responsible for the murder of millions of Jews during the war. After the war, using papers that had been obtained from the Catholic Church, he fled to Argentina where Hitler's friend, President/Dictator Juan Perón (best known today in the United States as the husband of "Evita"), welcomed the Nazis. Eichmann was captured by the Israeli Secret Service in 1960, deported to Israel, tried, convicted, and executed. But see Lapomarda at 234, n.16 (dismissing allegations that the Vatican was involved in the moving of Nazis).

188. Dr. Josef Mengele, notorious for his genetic experiments at Auschwitz, is thought to have escaped from Germany with papers from the International Red Cross. Like Eichmann, he moved to Argentina where he found employment for a period of time working as an abortionist. Mengele died under an assumed name without ever being brought to justice.

189. A Department of State, Office of American Republic Affairs memorandum dated July 14, 1947 (Top Secret, declassified in 1988; USNA:RG59; FW 800-0128/5-1547), entitled *Illegal Emigration Movements in and Through Italy*, identified the Vatican as the largest single organization involved in the illegal movement of emigrants. "Jewish Agencies and individuals" were identified as the second largest group. The memo, however, made clear that all of the agencies, including the International Red Cross, worked in collaboration with one another. It also made clear that identification procedures were such that anyone could take advantage of these programs. In fact, the memo indi-

cated that the Church was interested in sending anti-communist people around the globe, but that "no less than 10% of all illegal emigrants passing through Italy are Russian agents," because the Church had no way to identify the politics of the people in the program. Moreover, the memo reported that Vatican and Red Cross passports were easily and commonly falsified by changing the pictures on them.

190. Robert A. Graham, "Another Phony Chapter on 'Pius and the Nazis,'" *Columbia Magazine,* May 1984, at 4. The moral issue of aiding Nazis who might be persecuted by Allied forces following the war is raised in a very fascinating way in the Gregory Peck movie, *The Scarlet and the Black* (Avid Home Entertainment, 1983). In this account, based on the true story of the Nazis' occupation of Rome, Gestapo officer Herbert Kappler, in charge of the Roman occupation asks Monsignor Hugh O'Flaherty, a leader of Vatican resistance, to help relocate his family as the Allies are entering Rome. When the priest balks, the German accuses him of being a hypocrite because he had promised to help anyone in need.

191. Pius put at the disposal of the prosecution an important collection of documents dealing with the persecution of the Church by the Nazi regime. Louis J. Gallagher, *Edmund A. Walsh, S.J., Founder of the Foreign Service School, Georgetown University,* Benziger Brothers (New York, 1959). See also O'Carroll at 138 (suggesting that a memorandum authorized by Pius XII influenced the terms of one charge).

192. See "Nazi Reprisal Against Jews Held Fear of Pope Pius XII," *Religious News Service,* May 20, 1963 (report of comments by Pius to a chaplain who had been stationed with the Italian troops along the Russian front).

193. Robert Martin, *Spiritual Semites: Catholics and Jews During World War Two,* Catholic League Publications (Milwaukee, 1983), *quoting* Father Scavizzi, in *La Parrochia,* June 15, 1964. See Marchione (1997) at 54. According to some sources, however, he did pray for an exorcism of the evil being that inhabited Hitler's soul. Cornwell at 273.

194. Excommunication was possible, but it is normally reserved for a crime against the Church. Sin directed against another person or entity is usually not the basis for excommunication in a church that looks to the immortal soul and the possibility of redemption.

195. Morison at 988. Hitler "never allowed a member of the clergy to a Party meeting or to the burial of a member of the Party.... He said it was downright horrifying that a religion could ever have been possible which literally gobbled up its God in communion." Lothar Groppe, "The Church's Struggle with the Third Reich," *Fidelity,* October 1983, at 12, 13 (quoting the diary of Alfred Rosenberg).

196. *Actes et Documents,* vol. V, no. 130.

197. His wedding ceremony was carried out by a justice of the peace, not a priest. In addition, suicide has always been in violation of Catholic doctrine, and would have meant almost certain damnation to a devout Catholic. In 1945, cremation was also in clear violation of the Church's teaching. Moreover, despite his planning and the numerous directions that were left for others to carry out, Hitler made no arrangements for the last rites or any type of Christian burial. If the Catholic faith had meant anything to him, he certainly would have made some type of arrangement along these lines.

198. The Catholic Church has two forms of excommunication. The self-executing *latae sententiae* applies without official Church decree, based simply on the acts of the individual. Some have argued that Hitler actually did suffer this form of excommunication. Bogle, *The Salisbury Review* ("Hitler was already excommunicated *ipso facto* for a whole range of crimes and could only have returned to the Catholic faith, even assuming that he would ever have wanted to, by having his excommunication lifted"); Michael Schwartz, "Are Christians Responsible?," *The National Review*, August 8, 1980, at 956 (noting that Hitler incurred this type of excommunication under the canon law then in force when he served as best man in Goebbels' wedding, which took place in a Protestant church. According to Schwartz, the two men appealed to the tax office to be relieved of their obligation to pay church taxes due to their excommunication); Marchione (2000) (Overview) (citing Canons 2332 and 2342 of the Code of Canon Law that was then in effect). It would not have been drawn to anyone's attention unless he sought to receive one of the sacraments, but there is no record of him having done that. Thus, the 1917 Code of Canon Law, which the young Eugenio Pacelli helped prepare, actually set forth the terms of Hitler's excommunication.

199. Excommunication can backfire. See Rhodes at 342-43. Had the occasion arisen, Hitler almost certainly would have been denied a Christian burial. Michael Schwartz, "Are Christians Responsible?," *The National Review*, August 8, 1980, at 956, 957.

200. Lapomarda at 47, n.28. "People are deluding themselves if they think that the halberds of the Swiss Guard or a threat of excommunication would have stopped the *Wehrmacht* in its tracks." Cardinal Thomas Winning, "Pius XII–Friend of the Jews and Hitler's Foe," *The Daily Telegraph* (London) October 5, 1999 (quoting Pierre Blet).

201. Without any real evidence, one author suggests that Pacelli had a role in drafting the document for Pius XI. Cornwell at 189-91.

202. Hager, at 11-12.

203. Passelecq & Suchecky at 88.

204. The draft said that Jews were responsible for their own fate because God chose them to make way for Christ's redemption, but they rejected him and killed Christ. "Blinded by their dream of worldly gain and material success," they deserved the "worldly and spiritual ruin" that came down upon them. Cornwell at 191.

205. LaFarge himself wrote glowingly about *Summi Pontificatus* in *America* magazine, calling it "dangerous" because it obviously addressed the racism that was spreading across Europe. See Kevin M. Doyle, "The Moral Challenge of the Holocaust in 1998," *New Oxford Review*, July- August 1998, at 20, 22

206. Peter T. Farrelly Jr., "The Vatican and the Allies," *Our Sunday Visitor*, May 18, 1997 (quoting William Simpson, author of *A Vatican Lifeline* (1997)).

207. Van Hoek at 5.

ENDNOTES FOR THE EPILOGUE

1. One can take issue with many of Cornwell's assertions. Cornwell, for instance, reports that Pope Pius XI and Secretary of State Pacelli were determined that "no accommodation could be made with Communism, anywhere in the world." Cornwell at 114. The Vatican tried, however, (through Pacelli) to obtain a concordat with the Soviet Union in the mid-1920s, and it did conclude one with the predominantly Socialist government of Prussia in 1929. Pius also cooperated with President Roosevelt's request that he try to change the American-Catholic attitude toward extension of the lend-lease law to the Soviet Union, and he did what he could to help Soviet prisoners of war. In addition, in 1926, Pacelli consecrated a Jesuit bishop in Berlin, Fr. Michel d'Herbigny, "whose task it was to go into the USSR to consecrate several bishops secretly, to inform them officially of their appointments as apostolic administrators." Nichols at 280.

On pages 259, 281, and 376-77, Cornwell refers to a memorandum from Gerhard Riegner for transmission to the Holy See, dated March 18, 1942. It described Nazi persecution of Jewish people, and Cornwell points out that this memorandum was not published by the Vatican in its collection of wartime documents (*Actes et Documents*). By the same token, the letter of thanks that Riegner sent to Nuncio M. Philippe Bernadinion April 8, 1942 was also not published. In that letter, Riegner stated:

> We also note with great satisfaction the steps undertaken by His Excellence the Cardinal Maglione, with authorities of Slovakia on behalf of the Jews of that country, and we ask you kindly to transmit to the Secretariat of State of the Holy See the expression of our profound gratitude.
>
> We are convinced that this intervention greatly impressed the governmental circles of Slovakia, which conviction seems to be confirmed by the information we have just received from that country....
>
> It appears... that the Slovak Government finds it necessary to justify the measures in question. One might therefore conclude that it might be induced–in the application of these measures–to conform more closely to the wishes expressed by the Holy See which desired to revoke the recent measures against the Jews.
>
> In renewing the expressions of our profound gratitude, for whatever the Holy See, thanks to your gracious intermediation, was good enough to undertake on behalf of our persecuted brothers, we ask Your Excellency to accept the assurance of our deepest respect.

The reason that neither the memo nor the letter of thanks were printed in the *Actes et Documents* collection is that they were classified as "unofficial." Moreover, the memo was rather long and did not report a definite source of information, but reported on persecutions that were "more or less known to the public at large." "Judging Pius XII," *Inside the Vatican*, February 2000, at 61, 66 (quoting Fr. Blet, who noted that the memorandum had been published in a well-known book prior to the Vatican's collection being published). Riegner's memo is, however, mentioned in the *Actes et Documents* collection.

Le nonce à Berne Bernardini au Cardinal Maglione, March 19, 1942, *Actes et Documents,* vol. VIII, no. 314, p. 466. In fact, a footnote was added just to draw attention to receipt of the memo. It was certainly never hidden, concealed, or missing.

Many of Cornwell's other errors are minor to the point of being trivial, or they are discussed in earlier chapters of this book. For a few examples: *Mit brennender Sorge* is properly translated as *With Burning Anxiety*—not *With Deep Concern*; Cornwell completely misrepresents Pacelli's visit to Budapest to speak at the International Eucharistic Congress in 1938; Pius was not silent during September 1939; he intervened early—not late—in France, Hungary and every occupied nation; during the war foreign diplomats used the same doctor as did the Pope; Myron C. Taylor had nothing but the highest praise for Pope Pius XII after the war; the German ambassador to the Vatican did not plead for a public condemnation, precisely the opposite; Nicholas Horthy was not president but regent of Hungary, and he was a Calvinist not a Catholic, and Pacelli did appeal to him to stop the deportations; the motion picture filmed in 1942 (*Pastor Angelicus*) was completed at the request of Catholics around the world (particularly the United States) who had never seen the Pontiff, not in order satisfy his ego; no one with whom I spoke in Rome took calls from Pius on his or her knees (certainly there was no instruction to do so and it was not a widespread practice); and Pius XII's 1942 Christmas address was demonstrably more than "a paltry statement." For an answer to the allegation of racism by Pius XII following the liberation of Rome, see Chapter 15 at endnotes 57-59.

2. Cornwell at 297.

3. *Id.* at 384.

4. "Most of his sources are secondary and written by Pacelli's harshest critics. Errors of fact and ignorance of context appear on almost every page. Cornwell questions Pacelli's every motive, but never doubts those who tell a different story." Kenneth L. Woodward, "The Case Against Pius XII: A new biography is scalding–and deeply flawed," *Newsweek International,* September 27, 1999.

> It is difficult to know where to begin to criticize this work because it is replete with innuendo, guilt by the most tenuous association, cleverly phrased non sequiturs and blatant use of any work critical of Pius. He used those works that make Pius look bad, or silly, or imperious, or whatever suits his argument at the moment, even to the extent of repeating the hoary canard that "Vatican officials took phone calls from [Pius] upon their knees" presumably because Pius ordered them to do so.

José M. Sanchez & Kelly Cherry, "Pacelli's Legacy," *America,* October 23, 1999, at 25. See Cornwell at 324 ("Vatican officials took telephone calls from Pacelli upon their knees").

5. John F. Morley, "Pacelli's Prosecutor," *Commonweal,* November 5, 1999, at 27, 28. Another reviewer wrote: "Hitler's Pope is a malign exercise in defamation and character assassination. The author has, in my view, consistently misread and misunderstood both Pacelli's actions and the context in which they occurred." William D. Rubinstein, "Books in Review: *The Devil's Advocate,*" *First Things,* January 2000, at 39.

6. "Cornwell, a serious Catholic author who has written many books sympathetic to the Vatican and who once studied for the priesthood, set out to disprove the accusation that Pius XII was soft on Nazism." *The Sunday Herald* (London), September 19, 1999.

Cornwell's great achievement is to make it impossible any longer for Pacelli's defenders to say that it is only Jewish historians with axes to grind who have put their hero in the dock. Cornwell is himself a Catholic, but he has gone where the documentary evidence has taken him, having originally thought that Pacelli was unfairly criticized.

Frank Mclynn, "A Far from Pious World View: A Biography Which Reveals The Shameful History of the Wartime Pope," *The Herald* (Glasgow), September 23, 1999.

7. One reviewer concluded that, his charges "should be laughed out of the court of public opinion." "Cornwell's Popes," *Commonweal*, November 5, 1999, at 5, 6 (lead editorial).

8. Cornwell at vii.

9. *Id.* at viii.

10. *Id.*

11. *Id.* Cornwell now admits that he saw no "secret" documents. "Vatican Chronicles: A Different Read," *Brill's Content*, April 2000, at 60, 120.

12. John Cornwell, "Hitler's Pope: The Fight to reveal the secrets that threaten the Vatican," *The Sunday Times* (London) Sept. 12, 1999, at 1. Cornwell repeated this claim in "Hitler's Pope," *Vanity Fair*, October 1999, at 170. Actually, the archive is not a dungeon, just an underground vault where files are stored. These files were from the years 1912-1922 and therefore contained nothing about Hitler, the Nazis, or the Holocaust. Moreover, as Cornwell later had to admit, he spent only three weeks in those archives. John Cornwell, "Reply to the Vatican (Letters)," *The Tablet* (London), November 27, 1999, at 1613.

13. Cornwell at viii.

14. *Id.*

15. Cornwell later claimed that the Catholic Church tried to sabotage the project. "A campaign to boycott and denigrate the book started in North America," he wrote. "My publisher in the United States began to receive threatening and abusive emails and phone calls from traditionalist Catholics. Meanwhile, in Rome, without having read the manuscript, two Jesuit professors at the Gregorian University denounced the book as a travesty of the truth." John Burns, "Book exposes the Pope who 'helped Hitler'," *Sunday Times* (London), September 12, 1999. Actually, while in Rome I saw the heavily marked and underlined galley proofs that one of those Jesuit professors (Fr. Peter Gumpel) had read prior to his criticism of Cornwell's work. I have it on good authority that the other Jesuit professor also read a copy of the galley proofs prior to his criticism.

16. Michael Novak, "Death Comes For the Pontiff," *The Washington Post*, December 24, 1989 (Final Edition). Cornwell's writing has not changed much. As one generally positive review of Hitler's Pope noted:

So unsympathetic is the portrait of Pius XII–among other things,

Cornwell portrays him as a spiritual egotist–that it's hard to believe the author was ever much of an admirer of the man. Hitler's Pope is informed by a view of the Church that shows every sign of being long held, and the book uses the case of Pius XII, who reigned from 1939 to 1958, primarily to bolster that view.

Philip Marchand, "Hitler's Pope: unsympathetic portrait of Pius XII," *The Toronto Star*, October 8, 1999.

17. Michael Novak, "Death Comes For the Pontiff," *The Washington Post*, December 24, 1989 (Final Edition).

18. The term "Catholic agnostic," was used by the British writer Graham Greene to describe himself in an interview that he gave to John Cornwell in 1989. William Tuohy, "Reflections; The Author's View of Graham Greene; A 1989 Discussion Revealed Much About How The Leading British Writer, Who Died Last Week, Felt About Religion, Sex And Death," *Los Angeles Times*, April 9, 1991. Greene, while typically described as a "Catholic writer," was rebuked by the Vatican for some of his work (Cornwell at 347), and much of his later work seems to have taken on a "liberation theology" slant, which left him at odds with his Church. Robert Royal, "The (Mis)Guided Dream of Graham Greene," *First Things*, November 1999, at 16.

As late as 1996, Cornwell called himself a "Catholic agnostic," who did not believe in the soul as an immaterial substance. Christian Tyler, "A Philosopher's Tale: Science critic finds U.S. trial raises deeper moral questions," *The Financial Post* (Toronto), September 28, 1996. See also Ian Thomson, "Possession: ninetenths of the lore; The mysterious visions and spooks which led John Cornwell to travel the world in search of supernatural," *The Independent* (London), November 16, 1991 (Cornwell proclaims himself an "agnostic investigator"). The importance of this is that Cornwell claims to have spent six years researching Pius XII. Victoria Combe, *The Daily Telegraph* (London), September 17, 1999. Since his book came out in 1999, he must have had his dinner with the students and decided to defend Pius XII by 1993 at the latest. Thus his claim to have been a practicing Catholic intending to defend the Church is at odds with what he said at the time. The logical conclusion is that he concocted a story to add credibility to his work.

19. David Yallop had written a book entitled *In God's Name,* which contained allegations that Pope John Paul I had been murdered by insiders. Cornwell's book, *A Thief in the Night*, showed that "the smiling Pope" had not been murdered, but it went on to blame the death on Vatican ineptness and infighting. Cornwell argued that no one properly cared for the Pope and he died alone in the heart of a cynical, uncaring power structure.

20. This review was available on the Amazon.com website in late 1999.

21. George Weigel, "Not by the hand of conspirators," *The Washington Times*, November 23, 1989.

22. "Nonfiction in Brief," *Los Angeles Times*, December 10, 1989.

23. See Felicity O'Brien, "Looking Back on Pius XII," *Newsweek* (International), October 25, 1999, at 18.

24. John Cornwell, "Outfacing his critics," *Sunday Times* (London), October 6, 1996.

25. Kenneth Woodward, "The Case Against Pius XII," *Newsweek* (International), September 27, 1999, at 66. "The spin Cornwell puts on all

this tends to contradict his claim to evenhanded, objective scholarship. Virtually everything Pius XII did, said or thought about is skewed to portray him as a Machiavellian schemer, a moral coward and a pompous hypocrite. Even the most neutral reader would be hard pressed to stifle the suspicion that Cornwell doth protest too much." Robert McClory, "Tunnel Visions," *In These Times*, December 12, 1999, at 40.

26. Mary Loudon, Book Review / The missionary's position; 'Strange Gods', *The Independent* (London), August 29, 1993.

27. Piers Paul Read, "To Hell and back through the faith jungle," *Mail on Sunday* (London), July 18, 1993, at 45.

28. Of course, the title itself is "a grotesque exaggeration even of Cornwell's own arguments." William Rees-Mogg, "The Vatican's holy failure," *The Times* (London), October 4, 1999.

29. This photograph was used to illustrate James Carroll, "The Silence," *The New Yorker*, April 7, 1997 and James Carroll, "The Holocaust and the Catholic Church," *The Atlantic Monthly*, October 1999, at 107.

30. Although Cornwell never claims that Pius XII met with Hitler, some reviewers of his book did make that assertion. Linda Massarella, "Book Paints WWII Pope as Hitler Ally–Author: Vatican Files Show Pius Hated Jews," *The New York Post*, September 7, 1999, at 12. See Ronald J. Rychlak, "Cornwell's Errors: Reviewing Hitler's Pope," *Catalyst*, December 1999, at 8.

31. The error has been corrected in later versions of the dust jacket. "It was only after repeated protests that the publisher provided a new dust jacket for the books not yet sold." Peter Gumpel, "A Journalist Purporting to be a Scholar," *Die Furch*, January 6, 2000, at 1.

32. I originally attributed this matter to the publisher, but Cornwell has admitted that he approved the photograph. "Vatican Chronicles: A Different Read," *Brill's Content*, April 2000, at 60, 120.

33. In Rome I learned that the Vatican has received angry letters from people who saw this photograph and thought the Pope was being saluted by Nazi soldiers.

34. This statement was published in the Vatican newspaper, *L'Osservatore Romano*, on October 13, 1999:

> Mr. Cornwell states that he has been the first and only person to have access to this archive. This statement is completely false. In fact, numerous persons have had access to this archive, even before Mr. Cornwell consulted it. It must be stressed that Mr. Cornwell's research was limited to two series of documents: Bavaria (1918-1921) and Austria (Serbia, Belgrade: 1913-1915). Obviously, neither the author of the book nor others have ever had access to documents referring to the period which is not yet open to the public (1922 to the present).
>
> Mr. Cornwell stated that he worked for "months on end," in said archive. This statement does not correspond absolutely to truth, either. In fact, in that archive precise annotations are made about the purpose of the day, and the period of time (hours and minutes) that each person employs to carry out his consultation. From these data, it is deduced that Mr. Cornwell was admitted to the archive from May 12 to June 2 of 1997, therefore, not for 'months on end,' but for a period of close to three weeks.
>
> Moreover, in this very limited time, Mr. Cornwell did not come

every day; and on the days he did come, often his stay was for very brief periods of time.

Moreover, in open contrast to the truth, Mr. Cornwell stated that the documents he found had been kept strictly secret until he made his research. In this context, he refers specifically to a letter, sent on April 18, 1919, by the then Nuncio in Bavaria, Archbishop Pacelli, to the Secretariat of State. In connection with this document, he said this letter had remained secret in the Vatican Archive "like a time-bomb." But, in fact, said letter (of which Cornwell only quotes some limited phrases...), had already been published in 1992; in other words, seven years before the publication of Cornwell's book. The full text of this document appeared in E. Fattorini's book, *Germany and the Holy See: The Pacelli Nunciatures between the Great War and the Weimar Republic*,Il Mulino, Bologna, 1992, pp. 322-325.

It was important to point out the above facts to put readers on guard, who might otherwise be surprised by what is said in Mr. Cornwell's publication about the materials kept in the Archive in question.

The same announcement was reported on Vatican Radio.

35. The *relator* is an autonomous and independent Vatican Judge, charged with the supervision of the "*Positio*" (Position on Life and Heroic Virtues) to be presented to the Congregation for the Causes of Saints. The *relator* has the authority to stop a cause (which Gumpel has done when warranted in the past), but the ultimate decision to name a saint is not his.

36. This was my first contact with anyone at the Vatican. I had, of course, read the published documents, but I felt that working directly with the Holy See might cause me to slant my research. I instead tried to focus my original research on documents from American, British, German, and (published) Vatican archives, the Nuremberg trials, and various newspaper and magazine accounts from that time. To do what Cornwell claims to have originally intended (deciding on an outcome and seeking special treatment in exchange for that promised outcome), strikes me as dishonest.

37. According to Gumpel, the Secretariat of State authorized Cornwell to consult the archive of the section on Relations with States, which he did for some three weeks. The topic of his research was relations with Bavaria (1918-1921); Austria, Serbia and Belgrade (1913-1915). He had no access to the "closed period," beginning in 1922. Marcel Chappin, Professor of History at the Gregorian University and archivist of the Vatican Secretariat of State, has also confirmed that Cornwell was neither the first nor the only one to consult the archives of those years.

38. Frankly, my impression when I first heard Cornwell's charges was that he proved the Vatican's claim that all relevant documents from the war era were already public. The discovery of these two new "smoking guns," pop-guns though they be, actually helps confirm what Fr. Blet and others have long claimed: the wartime documents are already public. As a reviewer favorable to *Hitler's Pope* confessed, Cornwell's impact comes "not as a result of the publication of new documents but rather... [from] Cornwell's interpretation of existing evidence." Saul Friedlander, "Silence is Consent: Did Pope Pius XII Acquiesce in the Nazi Extermination of the Jews?," *Los Angeles Times*, October 10, 1999. Cornwell covers the war years in just 96 pages of his 371 page book.

39. This would account for the only "new" pieces of evidence offered in his book, both of which are dated before 1920.

40. This refers to the transcript of testimony given by 98 witnesses between the years 1967 and 1974. There are two "original" files containing these documents, but edited versions have been typed, indexed, and printed. Gumpel gave me one original and one printed version. Cornwell's citations, like mine, refer to the printed version.

41. Cornwell at vii.

42. See Kenneth Woodward, "The Case Against Pius XII," *Newsweek* (International), September 27, 1999, at 66 ("I have seen [the files] myself"); Felicity O'Brien, "Looking Back on Pius XII," *Newsweek*, October 25, 1999, at 18 ("In the late 1980's I studied the sworn testimonies gathered for the Canonization Cause of Pius XII in Rome"). Gumpel explained that deposition transcripts are kept secret only while testimony is actively being taken, so that later witnesses are not "tainted" by hearing the testimony of witnesses who came earlier. Once depositions are ended, the files are no longer secret. More recently Cornwell has modified his claim, saying only that his "access to and exploitation, for publication, of Pius XII's beatification depositions were unprecedented." "Reply to the Vatican," *The Tablet*, (London), November 27, 1999, at 1613.

43. John Cornwell, "Hitler's Pope: The Fight to reveal the secrets that threaten the Vatican," *The Sunday Times* (London) Sept. 12, 1999, at 1.

44. *Id.*

45. *Id.*

46. John Cornwell, "Look at the Facts: John Cornwell Replies," *The Tablet* (London), September 25, 1999.

47. Cornwell at 372-73.

48. *Id.*

49. One might wonder why such information would be relevant to Cornwell's point. Actually, "much of the last chapters consists of tittle-tattle aimed at demonstrating Pacelli's 'eccentricity,' 'narrow[ness]... in outlook, 'hypochondria,' and other weaknesses." William D. Rubinstein, "Books in Review: *The Devil's Advocate*," *First Things*, January 2000, at 39, 43. Of course, even if any of this is true (in Rome I was told that the dentist severely criticized by Cornwell was actually a very well respected professional who had served as the official dentist of the Italian Court), it has nothing to do with Pacelli's handling of the Church during World War II.

50. Peter Gumpel, "Cornwell's Cheap Shot at Pius XII," *Crisis*, December 1999, at 19, 25. "The half-dozen references" in Cornwell's book that are actually negative to Pius do not come from these depositions, but "come second- or third-hand from people who wanted to use the pope for propaganda or other purposes." Robert Royal, "Anti-Papal Whoppers," *Crisis*, November 1999, at 57.

51. One need not view the deposition transcripts to verify this summary. Just look at Cornwell's citations and compare them with his text.

52. Peter Gumpel, "Cornwell's Cheap Shot at Pius XII," *Crisis*, December 1999, at 19, 25.

53. Cornwell relies heavily on Klaus Scholder's two volumes on *The Churches and the Third Reich* (Fortress Press, 1988).

54. Peter Steinfels, "Beliefs; In a new book, a British journalist joins the

contentious debate concerning the relationship between Pope Pius XII and Nazi Germany," *The New York Times*, October 2, 1999, at A11.

55. Cornwell at 373.

56. John Cornwell, "Look at the Facts: John Cornwell Replies," *The Tablet* (London), September 25, 1999.

57. Cornwell at 383.

58. Scholder and Cornwell both rely on the memoirs of Heinrich Brüning, who criticizes Ludwig Kaas for his role in the enabling act and the concordat. See Heinrich Brüning, *Memoiren, 1918-1934, Stuttgart: Deutsche Verlags-Anstalt* (1970). Cornwell, though not Scholder, largely exonerates Kaas, lumping the blame on Pacelli. Brüning's memoirs, particularly those portions that Cornwell has used, have been questioned by other scholars. See William L. Patch, Jr., *Heinrich Brüning and the Dissolution of the Weimar Republic*, Cambridge University Press (Cambridge, 1998) at 302 ("Brüning was unfair to accuse Pacelli of betraying the Center Party."); *id.* at 189, 327 (similar).

59. Peter Gumpel, "Cornwell's Pope: A Nasty Caricature of a Noble and Saintly Man," *Zenit News Service*, Sept. 16, 1999 (also discussing Cornwell's "blind faith" in the suspect memoirs of Heinrich Brüning). In a different piece, Gumpel notes in particular Ludwig Volk's work as being "far more reliable" than Scholder's work. Peter Gumpel, "Cornwell's Cheap Shot at Pius XII," *Crisis*, December 1999, at 19, 20. Perhaps one of the reasons that Scholder supports Cornwell's thesis is that other German scholars have noted his anti-Catholic bias. See Heinz Hürten, *Deutsche Katholiken* 1918-1945, Ferdinand Schöningh (Paderborn, München, Wien & Zürich 1992) at 575, n. 5.

60. A brief summary of Repgen's work can be found in *Controversial Concordats* at 236-38. His works include: Konrad Repgen, *Das Ende der Zentrumspartei und Entstehung des Reichskonkordats, Militärselsorge*, 2 (1970), and later reissued in *Historische Klopfsignale für die Gegenwart*, Münster: Verlag Aschendorff, (1974) (concluding that the Center Party was not traded for the concordat); Konrad Repgen, *Dokumentation. Zur Vatikanischen Strategie beim Reichskonkordat, Vierteljahrshefte für Zeitgeschichte* 31 (1983) (the prohibition of clergy from party politics took place after the dissolution of the party); Konrad Repgen, *Hitlers Machtergreifung und der deutsche Katholizismus. Versuch einer Bilanz, in Katholische Kirche im Dritten Reich*, edited by Dieter Albrecht, Mainz: Matthias-Grünewald-Verlag (1976) (absolving Ludwig Kaas and the Vatican of initiating concordat negotiations and of making a deal to vote for the enabling act); Konrad Repgen, *Uber Umlaut! die Entstehung der Reichskonkordats-Offerte im Frühjahr 1933 und die Bedeutung des Reichskonkordats, Vierteljahrshefte für Zeitgeschichte* 25 (1978) at 499-534 (providing a detailed critique and refutation of Scholder's thesis that concordat negotiations influenced the Center Party's vote for the enabling act).

61. Ludwig Volk, *Das Reichskonkordat vom 20. Juli 1933*, Mainz: Matthias-Grünewald-Verlag (1972). See *Controversial Concordats* at 241-42 (calling this book "the most scholarly study of the subject" and briefly summarizing Volk's other work).

62. Alfons Kupper, *Staatliche Akten über die Reichs konkordatsverhandlungen* (1933) (Mainz, 1969) (collection of documents showing that the initiative for the concordat came from the Reich government); John Jay Hughes, "The Pope's Pact with Hitler," 17 *Journal of Church and State* 63 (1975). See

Controversial Concordats at 233-34 (synopsis of Kupper).

63. Cornwell at 406, n 4.

64. *Id.* at 379-80.

65. Peter Gumpel, "Cornwell's Pope: A Nasty Caricature of a Noble and Saintly Man," *Zenit News Service*, Sept. 16, 1999. See O'Carroll at 242.

66. Robert A. Graham, "A Valiant Lady's Struggle on a Matter of Honor," *Columbia Magazine*, December 1983, at 6.

67. "A Jewish Boyhood Friend," *Inside the Vatican*, October 1999, at XXIV (special insert).

68. Cornwell at 16-17.

69. Nazareno Padellaro, *Portrait of Pius XII*, J.M. Dent & Sons (London, 1956).

70. "*Il Sinai del signor Marchi, su cui saliva per tuonare non contro ebrei duri di cuore, ma contro ragazzi duri di testa.*" Nazareno Padellaro, *Pio XII*, Editrice S.A.I.E. (Torino, 1956) at 21.

71. Cornwell at 18.

72. Ilse-Lore Konopatzki, *Eugenio Pacelli: Pius XII, Kindheit und Jugend* in *Dokumenten,* Universitätsverlag Anton Pustet, Salzburg und München (Salzburg, 1974) at 146.

73. Cornwell at 17, quoting R. Leiber, S.J., "Pius XII As I Knew Him," *The London Tablet*, December 13, 1958. In a similar vein, Cornwell argues that Pacelli might have read certain anti-Semitic articles and been influenced by them. "On such evidence of association, no one would escape conviction." William Rees-Mogg, "The Vatican's holy failure," *The Times* (London), October 4, 1999.

74. José M. Sánchez & Kelly Cherry, "Pacelli's Legacy," *America*, October 23, 1999, at 25.

75. Cornwell at 45, 84-87.

76. As with all codification projects, the 1917 Code did slightly amend and clarify existing law. This is necessary to resolve conflicts and fill in gaps. An example is that prior to this code lay people were able to hold various offices such as tribunal judge. Following the code there was a strong distinction in the law between laity and clergy. However, this was a movement that long preceded this project and was in the direction of prior legislation.

77. The codification was carried out with a very large group of bishops and canonists all working on various portions, with a review committee of cardinals. It was then approved by the Pope and his closest advisors. If the 1917 Code reflects any personality, it is that of the Pope in office at the time of promulgation, Benedict XV.

78. See Cornwell at 338, 84, 41-45.

79. Cornwell at 49. Under this agreement, Serbia granted control over the Catholic regions in the new areas of the Balkans directly to the Vatican, rather than granting Austria extraterritorial control over Catholic property within Serbia. Certainly if Austria had been granted the authority over these new areas, Serb nationalists would have been enraged. See William D. Rubinstein, "Books in Review: *The Devil's Advocate*," *First Things*, January 2000, at 39, 40.

80. Cornwell at 50.

81. *Id.*

82. *Id.*

83. *Id.* at 48.

84. Sir Owen Chadwick, *The Tablet* (London), September 25, 1999, at 1284.

85. Falconi at 102; William D. Rubinstein, "Books in Review: *The Devil's Advocate*," *First Things*, January 2000, at 39, 43 ("It is, to put it mildly, extremely doubtful that the Serbian Concordat had a significant role in the outbreak of war. One wonders, for instance, if Britain's leaders even so much as heard of the Serbian Concordat. Cornwell's view of the role of the Concordat is simply absurd.")

86. On page 50, Cornwell cites Rhodes, *The Power of Rome* at 224, for the proposition that Pacelli had been warned by the papal nuncio in Vienna of the risk posed by the concordat. He does not cite the original document that he signed out while doing research at the Vatican, which directly contradicts his secondary source.

87. These records are kept in the Vatican archives. I have a copy of the particular record in question.

88. Vatican SS [Segreteria di Stato] SRS [Sezione per i rapporti con gli stati]: Austria-Ungheria (1913-14), Fasc. 454, folios 21-22.

89. *Id.*

90. *Id.*

91. *Id.*

92. Even if the concordat led to some unrest that increased pre-war tension, neither Pacelli nor anyone else in the Vatican had grounds to think anything other than what the nuncio reported.

93. Cornwell at 62.

94. *La Conciliazione Ufficiosa: Diario del barone Carlo Monti "incaricato d'affari" del governo italiano presso la Santa Sede (1914-1922),* Vatican Press (Antonio Scotta, ed. 1997, Vatican City) at 51 (vol. I) (introduction by Giorgio Rumi).

95. Cornwell at 62.

96. *La Conciliazione* at 49-50 (vol. I).

97. The food was destined for the the nunciatures of Munich and Vienna. Id.

98. Philip Marchand, "Hitler's Pope unsympathetic portrait of Pius XII," *The Toronto Star*, October 8, 1999 (quoting John Cornwell).

99. See Chapter 5.

100. The entire concordat is reprinted in *Controversial Concordats* at 205. According to one scholar, "Pacelli insisted that [a ban on clergy participation in party politics] was appropriate only in predominantly Catholic countries, and the Vatican resisted firmly on this point until the dissolution of the trade unions." William L. Patch, Jr., *Heinrich Brüning and the Dissolution of the Weimar Republic,* Cambridge University Press (Cambridge, 1998) at 302.

101. According to Cornwell, Pacelli dominated everyone around him, except for Sr. Pascalina, who allegedly controlled him.

102. See Report from the British Legation to the Holy See, Feb. 17, 1939, British Public Record Office, F0 371/23789.

103. *Id.* "To Cornwell, Pius XII was too authoritarian, too monarchical, too powerful. It may be argued that the very opposite was true. Pius XII was not sufficiently confident of his power and of his situation." John Lukacs, "In Defense of Pius," *National Review*, November 22, 1999.

104. Hatch & Walsh at 109; see Halecki & Murray at 65 ("closest possible co-operation").

105. Not only was the ultimate decision to move clergy out of politics attributable to Pius XI (not Pacelli), Popes since at least Pius X (1903-1914) had been withdrawing the clergy from direct political involvement. Cornwell at 46-47 (Pius X "believed the mixture of politics and religion to be the most hybrid and dangerous possible for the Church."). Pius XI felt that Catholic interests were better protected by lay organizations such as Catholic Action than they were by political parties. He forbade clergy from direct participation in Italian politics in 1929, when Pacelli was still in Germany (the Italian Catholic party had disappeared by 1927), and he did the same with France in the mid-1920s. Cornwell at 172.

In 1931, Pius XI wrote an encyclical, *Quadragesimo Anno*, which asserted that the Church has the right and duty "to interpose her authority... in all things that are connected with the moral law." Regarding political issues unrelated to morality, however, Pius wrote: "the Church holds that it is unlawful for her to mix without cause in these temporal concerns." Secretary of State Pacelli echoed this thought in 1938, when he explained "the Church is not called to take sides in purely earthly matters and expedients, between the various systems and methods which may come into question for the solution of the needs and problems of our time." Levai at 10.

The Second Vatican Council, in its Pastoral Constitution on the Church in the Modern World (Gaudium et Spes) said: "At all times and in all places, the Church should have the true freedom to... pass moral judgment even in matters relating to politics." (emphasis added) The document further explained that it is not usually legitimate for the clergy–the Church itself–to become involved in politics, except when "the fundamental rights of man or the salvation of souls requires it."

Pope John Paul II set forth a similar formula regarding political involvement by the Church in his 1988 encyclical, *Sollicitudo Rei Socialis*: "The Church does not have technical solutions to offer for the problem of underdevelopment as such.... For the Church does not propose economic and political systems or programs, nor does she show preference for one or the other, provided that human dignity is properly respected and promoted, and provided she herself is allowed the room she needs to exercise her ministry in the world." See also Cornwell at 367

106. Testimony of Cardinal Stefano Wyszynski, October 18 & 25, 1968, before the Tribunal of the Vicariate of Rome, on the beatification of Pius XII (Eugenio Pacelli), Part II, page 578; *Controversial Concordats* at 136. See Cornwell at 132 (Hitler given authority to suspend civil liberties).

107. Pope Pius XI preferred dealing with political matters through the lay organization, Catholic Action. Under this approach, the role of the clergy, especially of the bishops, is one of teaching. The clergy are the teachers of tradition and of social justice. That teaching remains on a theoretical level and does not descend to concrete situations and cases. These are left to the laity whose task it is to put the theory into practice. This definition comes from Archbishop Rembert Weakland of Milwaukee, Wisconsin. See Philip J. Murnion, *Commonweal*, September 11, 1992, at 23.

108. Peter Gumpel, "Cornwell's Cheap Shot at Pius XII," *Crisis*, December 1999, at 19, 21.

109. *Id.* See Cheetam at 283-84; Kershaw at 478; R. Leiber, *Reichskonkordat und Ende der Zentrumspartei, in Stimmen der Zeit: Monatschrift für das Geistesleben der Gegenwart, Verlag Herder-Freiburg im Breisgau,* 1960/61, at 213; Telegraph from Mr. Newton (Berlin) to Sir J. Simon, July 7, 1933, *Documents on British Foreign Policy* 1919-1939, Her Majesty's Stationary Office (E.L. Woodward, ed., London, 1956) (party members believe that dissolution will end arrests, sequestrations, and discrimination against the Catholic press). The documents show that it was only at this point that the Vatican gave up on its position of defending the right of clergy to participate in party politics. *Controversial Concordats* at 135 (citing Konrad Repgen, *Dokumentation. Zur Vatikanischen Strategie beim Reichskonkordat, Vierteljahrshefte für Zeitgeschichte* 31 (1983), 529-33).

110. William Rees-Mogg, "The Vatican's holy failure," *The Times* (London), October 4, 1999. See Cornwell at 135-36.

111. See Balint Vazsonyi, *America's 30 Years War: Who is Winning?*, (Regnery Press, 1998) at 58, 148.

112. It is hard to describe the politics of either Day or Coughlin in a brief paragraph. The point here is simply that Hitler used terminology that was very similar to that used by these two influential Catholic voices.

113. Cornwell himself notes that the Vatican could not control the party and that many German Catholics left the Center Party and joined the National Socialists. Cornwell also notes that the Catholic Center Party, including former Chancellor Heinrich Brüning, voted in favor of Hitler's Enabling Bill of 1933. Cornwell at 135-36. That hardly suggests that they were willing to battle Hitler to the end. See *id.* at 144, 197.

114. See *id.* at 158.

115. The German bishops were not silenced by the concordat. They spoke out more brazenly than any other group in Germany. Lothar Groppe, "The Church's Struggle with the Third Reich," *IBW Journal* (Alan F. Lacy trans.).

116. See Second Vatican Council, *Pastoral Constitution on the Church in the Modern World* (*Gaudium et Spes*).

117. Cornwell at 189-92.

118. *Id.* at 192.

119. This is crucial to Cornwell's thesis. Cornwell acknowledges that "a free press–still in operation in Bismarck's era–came to an end in 1933." Cornwell at 195. Accordingly, for a statement to have any effect within Germany, it would have had to take place prior to 1933. On September 27, 1999, on The O'Reilly Factor, a news program on the Fox News Network, Cornwell admitted that by the time Pacelli had become Pope, it was too late to effectively counter the Nazis with words:

O'REILLY: ...If Pope Pius XII had come out against Hitler, he would have – the Vatican would have been effectively shut down. Mussolini or Hitler himself would have moved in troops, shut them down. Pius probably would have been arrested or maybe even executed. He knew that. He knew that the whole power of the church was going to be destroyed if he came out and said anything anti-Axis, anti-Mussolini, or anti-Hitler. Isn't that true?
CORNWELL: Well, that would have been just too bad, but just think...

O'REILLY: Wait, wait, wait.

CORNWELL: There were 25 million Catholic Germans.

O'REILLY: Just too bad?

CORNWELL: Well, just think about it. Twentyfive million Catholic Germans who simply laid down and accepted Hitler...

O'REILLY: Do you believe they would have risen up if Pope Pius XII said, "Hitler's a bad guy. You should get him." I don't believe that for a second.

CORNWELL: Well...

O'REILLY: Not with the Gestapo and the SS already entrenched. No way.

CORNWELL: Yeah, but we're talking about 1933, long before the police state came into I accept your argument totally by 1938. That would have been true.

Pacelli, of course, became Pope in 1939.

120. Cornwell suggests that Pacelli was responsible for the First World War. Cornwell at 48-51.

121. Cornwell at 98, 217 (quoting D'Arcy Osborne).

122. *Id.* at 206. In fact, Cornwell reports that one French Cardinal, discussing Pacelli as a possible Pope, said he was "indecisive, hesitant, a man more designed to obey orders than to give them." *Id.* at 207. D'Arcy Osborne, the British Minister to the Holy See, had only one question about Pacelli as a Pope. Osborne said he was "not quite sure how strong a character [Cardinal Pacelli] is, working as he did under an autocrat like Pius XI." *Id.* at 217. This is in accord with the British records from 1939 relating to possible replacements for Pius XI. Minutes, February 1939, British Public Records Office, FO 371/23789 57760.

123. Cornwell at viii, 295-97.

124. According to historian Father Pierre Blet, one of the four men to have compiled the Vatican's wartime documents for publication, Cornwell has not presented "much to base accusations of anti-Semitism on." *Time,* September 20, 1999. "He ignores a great deal of material which doesn't fit his theory and makes grave accusations without supplying the evidence." *Id.*

125. Peter Gumpel informed me of this during my visit to Rome in December 1999, and he later reminded me of it in writing.

126. Cornwell at 70.

127. *Id.* at 70-71.

128. Eugene Fisher, Director of Ecumenical and Interreligious Affairs of the National Conference of Catholic Bishops, has explained that the word "cult" as used by Pacelli "was not a pejorative term." Marilyn Henry, "How pious was Pius XII?," *The Jerusalem Post,* October 1, 1999, at 7B. "It has nothing to do with personal animosity toward Jews." *Id.*

129. Cornwell at 174 (Cult of St. Thérèse); *id.* at 344 (cult of the Assumption and cult of the Virgin Mary); *id.* at 345 (the Fátima cult); *id.* at 382 (noting that beatification "indicates that the Pope has sanctioned a local cult of the individual's sainthood").

130. Cornwell at 78; Hatch & Walsh at 83.

131. Cornwell at 77; Halecki & Murray at 46 (noting that no one was hurt).

132. Pacelli had no food or money, having given it all to the poor of the city. Hatch & Walsh at 84.

133. Hatch & Walsh at 84-85; Halecki & Murray at 47-48.

134. Cornwell at 74-75.

135. Cornwell at 75. Even worse were press reports that Pacelli described "Jews" (not a specific group of revolutionaries) as "physically and morally repulsive, worthy of suspicion and contempt." Cathy Lynn Grossman, "Catholic scholar casts Pius XII as 'Hitler's Pope,'" *USA Today*, September 7, 1999. He certainly did not do that. See generally Ronald J. Rychlak, "Cornwell's Errors: Reviewing *Hitler's Pope*," *Catalyst*, December 1999, at 8.

136. William Rees-Mogg, "The Vatican's holy failure," *The Times* (London), October 4, 1999. See Cornwell at 74 (noting the kidnapping of "middle class" hostages, censorship, requisitioning of food, homes, and possessions).

137. Cornwell at 74-75.

138.
It is no safer to assume from this letter that Pacelli was a lifelong anti-Semite, than to assume that I must be a lifelong Germanophobe because in 1940, when they were bombing Bristol, I cursed the Luftwaffe pilots as bloodthirsty hounds. After an IRA atrocity, rude things come to be said about the Irish. Lifelong anti-Semitism is a charge which requires some lifelong proof; there is plenty of counter evidence in Pacelli's case.

William Rees-Mogg, "The Vatican's holy failure," *The Times* (London), October 4, 1999.

139. "Pacelli's description of communist Jews, while not especially enlightened, was hardly uncommon 80 years ago." Alessandra Stanley, "Debate rages over papal response to Holocaust," *The Plain Dealer*, November 25, 1999, at 17E.

140. "Cardinal Gasparri, Secretary of State, Replies to the Petition of the American Jewish Committee of New York," February 9, 1916, in *Principles for Peace: Selections from Papal Documents, Leo XIII to Pius XII*, National Catholic Welfare Conference (Harry C. Koenig, ed., Washington, 1943) at 198-99.

141. Cornwell continually argues that Pacelli was responsible for matters done in the name of Gasparri. See Cornwell at 31 (they worked in tandem); *id.* at 38 (Gasparri was Pacelli's "boss and close confidant"); *id.* at 41 (Gasparri and Pacelli were "principal architects" of the Code of Canon Law); *id.* at 44 (an idea "became clear to Gasparri and Pacelli"); *id.* at 46 (Gasparri referring to Pacelli: "one of my trusty staff in the Secretariat of State, in whom I had particular confidence"); *id.* at 55 ("Gasparri, Pacelli's guide and mentor"); *id.* at 56 (Pacelli as Gasparri's "protégé"); *id.* at 61 ("Gasparri would not hear of Pacelli's leaving Rome until the new code had been published.").

142. "Cardinal Gasparri, Secretary of State, Replies to the Petition of the American Jewish Committee of New York," February 9, 1916, in *Principles for Peace: Selections from Papal Documents, Leo XIII to Pius XII*, National Catholic Welfare Conference (Harry C. Koenig, ed., Washington, 1943) at 198-99. The reference to "religious confessions" instead of "race" reflects the traditional Catholic view, adhered to throughout World War II, that what defines a person as being "Jewish" is his or her faith, not an ethnic identity.

143. Cornwell at 309 (citing Katz, *Black Sabbath* at 259).

144. *Id.*

145. This is made clear in the diary of the Maestro di Camera (master of the chamber), which was shown to me when I traveled to the Vatican. The Maestro di Camera arranges audiences and pontifical ceremonies, and he keeps very detailed records of these matters. See also Note de Mgr. Tardini, *Actes et Documents*, vol. VII, p. 678, note 1 (noting Tittmann's mistake); *Actes et Documents*, vol. IX, p. 489-90 (noting the meeting on the 14th).

146. "Tittmann Received," *L'Osservatore Romano*, October 15, 1943, at 1.

147. See Chapter 14.

148. In an article entitled "The Saint and the Holocaust," in the June 7, 1999 edition of *The New Yorker* magazine, former priest James Carroll argued that by declaring Edith Stein a saint, the Catholic Church elevated her death above the deaths of six million Jews, and in the process may have "subverted" the value of Edith Stein's life.

Carroll makes a major point of the fact that in 1933, Stein wrote to Pope Pius XI requesting an audience to plead for an encyclical condemning Nazism. He goes on to complain that she never was granted a personal audience, though she was invited to a ceremonial audience with the Pope. Incredibly, however, Carroll never mentions the 1937 encyclical *Mit brenender Sorge*, which did exactly what Stein asked the Pope to do.

Carroll argues that Stein was killed because she was Jewish. This is true. Had she not been Jewish the Nazis would not have deported her at that time. However, if Carroll had quoted the Nazi statements, which he did not, he would have had to acknowledge that Stein was deported due to her Catholicism as well.

To make his point, Carroll reports that on her way to Auschwitz, Edith was supposedly offered the opportunity to use her baptism as a shield from deportation. She declined the offer, according to Carroll, saying: "Why should there be an exception made in the case of a particular group? Wasn't it fair that baptism not be allowed to become an advantage?"

This decision to decline an offer of freedom (and, indeed, life itself) seems particularly noble, even saintly. Carroll, however, gives this act of selflessness an unusual interpretation, arguing that in declining this offer, Edith was not being selfless and noble. Rather, Carroll would have us believe that she was rejecting her baptism and the Catholicism that she had adopted twenty years earlier and had fully devoted her life to for the previous nine years. This is a strained interpretation of her reported words. Perhaps more telling is Carroll's willingness to use this statement at all, much less to build a central argument around it.

Carroll acknowledges that the story came forth years after Edith had been deported and killed and that it came from a Dutch official who claimed to have met Stein in a transit camp on her way to Auschwitz. It is reasonable to be suspect of any unconfirmed, self-serving memory that is asserted years after the fact, but there is an even greater reason to be suspicious in this case.

The focus of Nazi deportation at this time was on Jews who had been baptized into the Catholic Church. Therefore, it is very unlikely that someone would have asked ask whether one of the numerous Catholic Jews would want to use her *baptism* in order to avoid deportation. Far more likely is the account given by some other sources, that Stein was offered the opportunity to use her status as a *nun* to avoid the concentration camp. That story, however, would not have fit with the premise that Stein was rejecting her religion.

Relating a story about his study of Edith Stein when he was a young seminarian, Carroll says "it never occurred to us then that there could be something offensive to Jews in our honoring her as a young woman in search of the truth." He now suggests that there is something wrong with honoring this young woman who went in search of the truth. The only real reason he has given for that is that she was born Jewish.

149. This point is addressed in greater detail in Chapter 13.

150. Robert A. Graham, "Will the Real Sister Pascalina Please Step Forward," *Columbia Magazine*, November 1983, at 9 (questioning the validity of this book).

151. Testimony of Sr. Pascalina Lehnert, Oct. 29, 1968 - Jan. 24, 1969, before the Tribunal of the Vicariate of Rome, on the beatification of Pius XII (Eugenio Pacelli), Part I, page 77, 85.

152. Testimony of Maria Conrada Grabmair, May 9, 1969 - May 29, 1969, before the Tribunal of the Vicariate of Rome, on the beatification of Pius XII (Eugenio Pacelli), Part I, page 173, 174.

153. See Cornwell at 286.

154. Testimony of Maria Conrada Grabmair, May 9, 1969 - May 29, 1969, before the Tribunal of the Vicariate of Rome, on the beatification of Pius XII (Eugenio Pacelli), Part I, page 173, 174.

155. *Id.* Gumpel told me that Fr. Leiber died before he was able to testify before the tribunal.

156. Of course, Cornwell's suggestion (p. 287) that Pius may have intentionally overstated the number of victims in Holland in order to justify his response is asinine. Had that been his intent, he surely would have made the statement in front of more than one witness. Similarly, Cornwell's claim that Pius intentionally understated the number of victims in his 1942 Christmas statement ("He had scaled down the doomed millions to 'hundreds of thousands.'" Cornwell at 293) is too absurd to merit a response. See Owen Chadwick, *Britain and the Vatican during the Second World War*, Cambridge University Press (Cambridge, 1986) at 218 (noting that the Allied declaration referred to "hundreds of thousands").

157. *Chronicle* at 520-21.

158. Cornwell at 249.

159. Andrew Borowiec, "Croatian-run death site remains dark secret; Unlikely parties kept story of WWII camp suppressed," *The Washington Times*, July 5, 1994, at A10.

160. This is quoted in Chapter 18 (see endnotes).

161. *Actes et Documents*, vol. VIII, no. 441. See also *id.* vol. VIII, no. 537 (report on Vatican efforts to "alleviate the sad conditions of the Croatian Jews"); *id.* vol. VIII, no. 473 (efforts to find sanctuary for Croatian Jews in Italy); *id.* vol. VIII, no. 557 (insistence on "a benevolent treatment toward the Jews").

162. *Actes et Documents*, vol. VIII, no. 502.

163. See *Actes et Documents*, vol. VIII, no. 566.

164. *Actes et Documents*, vol. IX, no. 92 (Maglione's notes, dated March 13, 1943).

165. *Id.*

166. *Actes et Documents*, vol. IX, no. 81. On September 24, 1943, Alex Easterman, the British representative of the World Jewish Congress, contacted Msgr. William Godfrey, the apostolic delegate in London and informed him

that about 4,000 Jewish refugees from Croatia were safely evacuated to an island in the Adriatic Sea. "I feel sure that efforts of your Grace and of the Holy See have brought about this fortunate result," wrote Easterman.

167. *Actes et Documents*, vol. IV, no. 358.

168. The British Minister to the Holy See during the war years, Sir Francis D'Arcy Osborne, wrote that Stepinac always acted according to the "well-intended dictates of his conscience." Confidential Letter to Oliver Harvey from D'Arcy Osborne, February 26, 1947, British Public Records Office, FO 371/67917 60675.

169. Alain Finkielkraut, *"Mgr. Stepinac et les deux douleurs de l'Europe,"* *Le Monde* (Paris), October 7, 1998.

170. Rick Hinshaw, "Cardinal's Past," *Chicago Tribune*, October 17, 1998, at 26.

171. On March 10, 1999, with a group of 18 Croatian bishops making their *ad limina* visit to Rome, the Vatican newspaper published an 86- page special supplement in *L'Osservatore Romano* on the life of Alojzije Stepinac. Details about his life can be found in that report.

172. Cornwell at 252.

173. *Actes et Documents,* vol. IV, no. 400 ("Pavelic is furious... because... he is treated worse by the Holy See than the Slovaks").

174. Minutes of August 7, 1941, British Public Records Office FO 371/30175 57760 (noting that Pavelic was not given an audience with the Secretary of State).

175. "Vatican Book Justifies Cardinal Stepinac: Example of Opposition to Fascism, Nazism and Communism," *Zenit News Agency*, March 10, 1999 (quoting Gianpaolo Mattei, author of a book on Stepinac published by *L'Osservatore Romano*).

176. In 1985, Jakov Blazevic, the man who conducted Stepinac's trial, admitted that the cardinal had been framed. Rick Hinshaw, "Cardinal's Past," *Chicago Tribune*, October 17, 1998, at 26.

177. *Zenit News Agency*, March 10, 1999. "This great man was tried as a collaborator of Nazism. We protest this slander. He has always been a sincere friend of Jews and was not hiding this even in times of cruel persecutions under the regime of Hitler and his followers. He was the greatest defender of the persecuted Jews." Rick Hinshaw, "Cardinal's Past," *Chicago Tribune*, October 17, 1998, at 26 (quoting Breier).

178. Blet, Chapter 8. See Lapomarda at 210, n.13.

179. Recent testing suggests that he was slowly poisoned by his captors. See Bruce Johnston, "Pope to beatify archbishop 'murdered by Tito'," *The Daily Telegraph*, May 15, 1998, at 20.

180. Assembly Condemns Communist Treatment of Cardinal Stepinac and Andrija Hebrang, BBC Summary of World Broadcasts, February 17, 1992.)

181. *Id.*; Peter Hebblethwaite, "John Paul's uphill pilgrimage to Zagreb," *National Catholic Reporter*, September 23, 1994, at 7.

182. "Vatican Book Justifies Cardinal Stepinac," *Zenit News Agency*, March 10, 1999.

183. Cornwell at 287.

184. Cornwell at 366 ("Wojtyla [John Paul II] appears sympathetic to pluralism on the surface; underneath there is an intransigently absolutist cast

of mind."); id. at 370; Philip Marchand, "*Hitler's Pope* unsympathetic portrait of Pius XII," *The Toronto Star*, October 8, 1999.

185. Cornwell at 370; Philip Marchand, "*Hitler's Pope* unsympathetic portrait of Pius XII," *The Toronto Star*, October 8, 1999.

186. John Cornwell, "*Hitler's Pope:* The Fight to reveal the secrets that threaten the Vatican," *The Sunday Times* (London) Sept. 12, 1999, at 1.

187. Any doubt about Cornwell's intent to denigrate Pope John Paul II was resolved in March 2000, at the time when the Pontiff made an unprece dented and historic trip to the Holy Land. At that time, as Christians and Jews were coming closer together, Cornwell wrote an article in the London *Sunday Times*. Cornwell described the Pontiff as "aging, ailing, and desperately frail as he presides over a Vatican that is riven by cliques, engulfed in scandal, and subject to ideological power struggles." *Jerusalem Post*, March 23, 2000 (online edition). To Cornwell, the Vatican "is a nest of nepotism and corruption, sexual depravity, gangsterism, and even murder." *Id.* According to Cornwell, the reason for the "decay" is "the increasingly isolated and debilitated Pope John Paul II, suffering from the advanced stages of Parkinson's disease." *Id.* Quoting a Vatican insider, Cornwell described the Vatican as "a palace of gossipy eunuchs.... The whole place floats on a sea of bitchery." *Id.*

188. Cornwell at 363.

189. "If we persist in reading purely political significance in every papal move, arbitrarily prescinding from that which makes the Pope a Pope, we shall never arrive at that understanding and objectivity that is, or ought to be, the goal of every serious historian and every fair-minded, intelligent person." Marchione (2000) (Vatican Documents) (quoting Robert Graham).

190. See Weigel at 281-87, 440-42.

191. *Id.* at 397 *et seq.*

192. In an allocution to the Sacred College on June 2, 1945, Pius explained that his radio messages and his appeals for humane treatment of all were:

> for Us the most opportune–and We might even say the only–efficacious way of proclaiming before the world the immutable principles of moral law and of confirming, in the midst of so much error and violence, the minds and hearts of German Catholics, in the higher ideals of truth and justice.

Marchione (2000) (Appeal for World Peace). See also Message to the Cardinal Archbishop of Breslau, dated March 17, 1940, *Actes et Documents*, vol. II, no. 42. Following the war, Sir Francis D'Arcy Osborne tried to explain that

> the Pope and his advisers do not consider and resolve a problem solely in the light of its temporary and obviously apparent elements. Their approach and survey are by habit and tradition unlimited in space and time so that, for example, they can regard the Savoy dynasty as an interlude, and the Fascist era as an incident, in the history of Rome and of Italy. They reckon in centuries and plan for eternity and this inevitably renders their policy inscrutable, confusing and, on occasion, reprehensible to practical and time-conditioned minds.

Confidential Letter to Oliver Harvey from D'Arcy Osborne, February 26, 1947, *British Public Records Office*, FO 371/67917 60675 (also explaining that the Pope felt he had "specifically condemned Nazi war crimes in his public speeches during the war" and that the Vatican considered *Mit brennender Sorge* a continuing papal condemnation of totalitarian systems).

193. Richard John Neuhaus, "The Public Square: Majorities, Minorities, and What Makes Real Law," *First Things*, November 1999, at 90.

194. See generally Marchione (2000) (Pope John Paul II).

195. Alan Cowell, "Demonstrators and Devout Greet the Pope In Germany," *The New York Times*, June 24, 1996, Section A; Page 3.

196. As one reviewer wrote, "to place the ultimate blame for Hitler's coming to power on Pius's ascetical shoulders is an almost absurdly simplistic reading of events." "Cornwell's Popes," *Commonweal*, November 5, 1999, at 5 (lead editorial).

197. As one reviewer concluded, *Hitler's Pope* is simply a "polemical chronicle." "Cornwell's Popes," *Commonweal*, November 5, 1999, at 5, 6 (lead editorial). See also Kenneth L. Woodward, "The Case Against Pius XII: A new biography is scalding–and deeply flawed," *Newsweek International*, September 27, 1999 ("bogus scholarship, filled with nonexistent secrets aimed to shock").

BIBLIOGRAPHY

Aarons, Mark, & John Loftus. *Unholy Trinity: How the Vatican's Nazi Networks Betrayed Western Intelligence to the Soviets,* St. Martin's Press (New York, 1991).

Actes et Documents du Saint Siège Relatifs à la Seconde Guerre Mondiale, Volumes I-XI, Libreria Editrice Vaticana (Citta del Vaticano, 1965-81); English edition by Corpus Books (Washington, Gerard Noel, ed. 1967-77). Volume III is split in two books, thus some authors refer to 12 volumes instead of 11.

Akin, James. *The Church Versus the Nazis* (audiotape, Catholic Answers, San Diego).

Alvarez, David, & Robert Graham. *Nothing Sacred: Nazi Espionage Against the Vatican 1939-1945,* Frank Cass (London, 1997).

Appleton, Ted. *Your Guide to Poland,* Funk & Wagnalls (New York, 1968).

Atkinson, Rick. "Germany Honors Anti-Nazi Patriots," *The Washington Post,* July 20, 1994, at A24.

Barnett, Victoria. *For the Soul of the People: Protestant Protest Against Hitler,* Oxford University Press (Oxford, 1992).

Barzini, Luigi. *From Caesar to the Mafia: Sketches of Italian Life,* The Library Press (New York, 1971).

———. *The Italians,* Bantam Books, (New York, 1969).

Beckwith, Barbara. "It's Amazing That a Bird Can Sing Here," *St. Anthony Messenger,* August 1996, at 30.

Bemporad, Jack, & Michael Shevack. *Our Age: The Historic New Era of Christian-Jewish Understanding,* New City Press (Hyde Park, 1996).

Benet's Readers Encyclopedia, Harper & Row (New York, 3d ed. 1987).

Benns, F. Lee. *Europe Since 1914 in its World Setting,* Appleton, Century, Crofts (New York, 1949).

Benzinger, Mariel G. *Echoes Across the Alps* (1978).

Bernstein, Carl, & Marco Politi. *His Holiness: John Paul II and the Hidden History of Our Time,* Doubleday (New York, 1996).

Blazynski, George. *Pope John-Paul II,* Dell Books (New York, 1979).

Blet, Pierre. *Pius XII and the Second World War,* Paulist Press (Lawrence J. Johnson trans. Mahwah, N.J., 1999). At the time of my research, the English edition of this book was not yet in print. As such, reference is made to the chapter rather than to a page.

Blum, John M., et al. *The National Experience: A History of the United States,* Harcourt, Brace, & World (New York, 2d ed. 1968).

Boatner, Mark M.,III. *The Biographical Dictionary of World War II,* Presido Press (Novato, California, 1996).

Bogle, James. "The Real Story of Pius XII and the Jews," *The Salisbury Review,* Spring 1996.

Bokenkotter, Thomas., *A Concise History of the Catholic Church,* Doubleday & Company (New York, 1966).

Breitman, Richard. *Official Secrets: What the Nazis Planned, What the British and Americans Knew,* Hill & Wang (New York, 1998).

Briggs, Kenneth A. *Holy Siege: The Year that Shook Catholic America,* Harper (San Francisco, 1992).

Brown, Anthony Cave. *Bodyguard of Lies,* Harper & Row (New York, 1975).

Brown, Robert McAfee. *Observer in Rome: A Protestant Report on the Vatican Council,* Doubleday & Company, (New York, 1964).

Brüning, Heinrich. *Memoiren, 1918-1934,* Stuttgart: Deutsche Verlags-Anstalt (1970).

Bullock, Alan. *Hitler: A Study in Tyranny,* Bantam (Chicago, 1962).

Carell, Paul, *The Foxes of the Desert,* Bantam Books (New York, Mervyn Savill trans. 1962).

Carlen, Claudia C. *The Papal Encyclicals,* Pierian Press (Ann Arbor, 1990).

Carroll, James. "The Silence," *The New Yorker,* April 7, 1997.

Owen Chadwick, *A History of Christianity,* St. Martin's Press (New York, 1995).

Cadwick, Owen. "Weizsäcker, the Vatican, and the Jews of Rome," 28 *Journal of Ecclesiastical History* 179 (April 1977).

Cheetham, Nicolas. *The Keeper of the Keys: A History of the Popes from St. Peter to John Paul II,* Macdonald (London,1982).

Chronicle of the 20th Century, Chronicle Publications (Mount Kisco, N.Y., C. Daniel, ed. 1986).

Churchill: A Memorial Edition (Dell, 1965).

Churchill, Winston S. *Their Finest Hour,* Houghton Mifflin (Boston,1949).

Churchill, Winston S. *Triumph and Tragedy,* Houghton Mifflin (Boston, 1953).

Cianfarra, Camille. *The Vatican and the War,* Literary Classics, Inc., distributed by E.P. Dutton & Company (New York, 1944).

Ciano Diaries, The Doubleday & Company, Inc. (Garden City, N.Y. Hugh Gibson, ed. 1946).

Ciano's Diplomatic Papers, Oldhams Press Limited (Long Acre, London, 1948).

Ciano's Hidden Diary: 1937-1938, E.P. Dutton & Co., Inc. (Andreas Mayor trans., New York, 1953).

Collins, Larry & Dominique LaPierre, *Is Paris Burning?,* Simon & Schuster (New York, 1966).

"The Communist Party," *Readers' Digest,* May 1933.

Conradt, David P. *The German Polity*, Longman (New York, 1978).

Controversial Concordats: The Vatican's Relations with Napoleon, Mussolini, and Hitler, The Catholic University of America Press (Frank J. Coppa, ed. Washington, 1999).

Conway, John S. "The Vatican, Germany and the Holocaust," in *Age*, Praeger (Westport, Conn., Peter C. Kent & John F. Pollard, eds. 1994).

Copeland, Lewis. *The World's Great Speeches*, Garden City Publishing Co. (New York, 1942).

Cornwell, John. *Hitler's Pope: The Secret History of Pius XII*, Viking Press (New York, 1999).

Crankshaw, Edward. *Gestapo*, Pyramid Books (New York, 1959).

Daniel-Rops, Henri. *A Fight for God: 1870-1939*, E.P. Dutton and Co. (New York, 1965).

Darragh, James A. *The Pope and Fascism*, John S. Burns & Sons (Glasgow, 1944).

Deighton, Len. *Blood, Tears and Folly: An Objective Look at World War II*, Harper Collins (New York, 1993).

Dershowitz, Alan M. *Chutzpah*, Little, Brown & Co. (Boston, 1991).

Deschner, Gunther. *Warsaw Rising*, Ballatine Books (New York, 1972).

Deutsch, Harold C. *The Conspiracy Against Hitler in the Twilight War*, University of Minnesota Press (Minneapolis, 1968).

Doenitz, Karl. *Memoirs: Ten Years and Twenty Days*. Greenwood Press (Westport, Conn., R.H. Stevens trans. 1959).

Doyle, Charles Hugo. *A Day with the Pope*, Doubleday (Garden City, N.Y. 1950).

Doyle, Kevin M. "Robert Graham, S.J.," *First Things*, June/July, 1997, at 16.

Duffy, Eamon. *Saints & Sinners: A History of the Popes*, Yale University Press (New Haven, Conn. 1997).

Duffy, James P. & Vincent L. Ricci. *Target Hitler: The Plots to Kill Adolf Hitler*, Praeger (Westport, Conn. 1992).

Dunn, L.C. & Th. Dobzhansky. *Heredity, Race and Society*, New American Library (New York, rev. ed. 1952).

Dupuy, Trevor N. & R. Ernest Dupuy, *The Encyclopedia of Military History*, Harper & Row (New York, 1970).

Duranty, Walter. *62 More Executions in Soviet Purge*, New York Times, October 22, 1937.

Eade, Charles. *Winston Churchill's Secret Session Speeches*, Simon & Schuster (New York, 1946).

Elliott, Lawrence. *I Will Be Called John: A Biography of Pope John XXIII*, Berkley Publishing Corp. (New York, 1973).

Ellsberg, Edward. *The Far Shore*, Dodd, Mead (New York, 1960).

Erst, Anna Marie. *Discovering Our Jewish Roots*, Paulist Press (New York, 1996).

Fabert, Andre. *Pope Paul VI*, Monarch Books, Inc. (Derby, Connecticut, 1963).

Falconi, Carlo. *The Silence of Pius XII*, Little Brown (Boston, B. Wall trans. 1970).

Fattorini, Emma. *Germania e Santa Sede: Le nunziature di Pacelli tra la Grande Guerra e la Repubblica di Weimar*, Il Mulino (Bologna, 1992).

Ferguson, Niall. "Hitler's German Enemies," *The Sunday Telegraph*, July 10, 1994.

Fest, Joachim C. *Hitler*, Vintage Books (New York, 1974).

Flood, Charles B. *Hitler: The Path to Power*, Houghton Mifflin Co. (Boston, 1989).

Fogarty, George P. *The Vatican and the American Church Since World War II in The Papacy and the Church in the United States* (Bernard Cooke, ed. 1989).

Fogelman, Eva. *Conscience & Courage: Rescuers of Jews During the Holocaust,* Anchor Books (New York, 1994).

Friedländer, Saul. *Pius XII and the Third Reich*, Knopf (New York, C. Fullman trans. 1966).

———. *Nazi Germany and the Jews, Volume I: The Years of Persecution, 1933-1939*, Harper Collins (New York, 1997).

Furniss, Edgar S. "Soviet World Relations," *Current History,* April 1935.

Gallin, Mary Alice. *German Resistance to Hitler: Ethical and Religious Factors*, Catholic University of America Press (Washington, 1961).

Gannon, Robert I. *The Cardinal Spellman Story*, Doubleday & Company (Garden City, New York, 1962).

Garcia, Laura. "Edith Stein - Convert, Nun, Martyr," *Crisis,* June 1977, at 18.

Gascoigne, Bamber. *The Christians* William Morrow & Co. (New York, 1977).

Gaspari, Antonio. "Justice for Pope Pius XII," *Inside the Vatican*, June 1997, at 20.

Gilbert, G.M. *Nuremberg Diary*, New American Library, (New York, 1961).

Gilbert, Martin. *Auschwitz and the Allies,* Holt, Rinehart, and Winston (New York, 1981).

———. *The Holocaust: A History of the Jews of Europe During the Second World War,* Holt, Rinehart, and Winston (New York, 1985).

———. *The Second World War: A Complete History,* H. Holt (New York, 1987).

Gill, Anton. *An Honourable Defeat*, H. Holt (New York, 1994).

Goebbels Diaries: 1939-1941, G.P. Putnam's Sons (Fred Taylor trans., New York, 1983).

Goebbels Diaries: 1942-1943, Doubleday & Co. (Louis P. Lochner trans., Garden City, 1948).

Goldhagen, Daniel J. *Hitler's Willing Executioners: Ordinary Germans and The Holocaust,* Alfred A. Knopf (New York, 1996).

Goldston, Robert. *The Life and Death of Nazi Germany,* Fawcett Publications (Greenwich, 1967).

Gonella, Guido. *The Papacy and World Peace: A Study of the Christmas Messages of Pope Pius XII,* Hollis and Carter, Ltd. (London, 1945).

Graham, Robert A. *Pius XII's Defense of Jews and Others: 1944-45,* Catholic League Publications (Milwaukee, 1987). This is also reprinted in *Pius XII and the Holocaust: A Reader,* Catholic League Publications (Milwaukee, 1988).

———. *Pope Pius XII and the Jews of Hungary in 1944,* United States Catholic Historical Society (undated).

———. *The Pope and Poland in World War Two,* Veritas (London, 1968).

———. *The Vatican and Communism During World War II: What Really Happened?,* Ignatius Press (San Francisco, 1996).

———. "Vatican Radio Between London and Berlin, 1940-4," *Journal of English Jesuits,* April 1976.

Haberman, Clyde. "Magazine Says Hitler Planned to Abduct Pope," *The New York Times,* July 21, 1991, at sec. 1, p. 7.

Hager, June. "A Censored Letter?," *Inside the Vatican,* December 1995, at 11.

Halecki, Oscar & James F. Murray, Jr., *Pius XII: Eugenio Pacelli, Pope of Peace,* Farrar, Straus and Young, Inc. (U.S.A., 1954).

Hamerow, Theodore S. H. *On the Road to the Wolf's Lair: German Resistance to Hitler,* Belknap Press (Cambridge, Mass., 1997).

Handy, Robert T. *A History of the Churches in the United States and Canada,* Oxford University Press (Oxford, 1976).

Hart, B.H. Liddell. *History of the Second World War,* G.P. Putnam's Sons (New York, 1972).

Hatch, Alden & Seamus Walsh, *Crown of Glory: The Life of Pope Pius XII,* Hawthorn Books, Inc. (New York, 1957).

Hebblewaite, Peter. *The Next Pope,* Harper San Francisco (San Francisco, 1995).

Heft, James L S.M. *From the Pope to the Bishops: Episcopal Authority from Vatican I to Vatican II, in The Papacy and the Church in the United States,* Paulist Press (New York, Bernard Cooke, ed. 1989).

Heller, Mikail and Aleksandr Nekrich. *Utopia In Power: The History of The Soviet Union From 1917 To The Present,* Summit Books (New York, Phyllis B. Carlos trans. 1986).

Higham, Charles. *Trading with the Enemy: An Expose of the Nazi-American Money Plot 1933-1949,* Dell Publishing Co. (New York, 1984).

Historical Atlas of the Holocaust, Macmillan Publishing USA (New York, 1996).

Hitler, Adolf. *Mein Kampf*, Houghton Mifflin (Boston, Ralph Manheim trans. 1971).

Hitler Directs His War, Oxford University Press (Felix Gilbert, ed., New York, 1951).

Hitler's Secret Conversations 1941-1944, Octagon Books (New York, 1972).

Hoar, William P. *Architects of Conspiracy: An Intriguing History*, Western Islands Publishers (Boston and Los Angeles, 1984).

Hochhuth, Rolf. *The Deputy* (Winston trans. 1964).

Hoffmann, Peter. *German Resistance to Hitler*, Harvard University Press (Cambridge, Mass. 1988).

Hollander, Paul. "Soviet Terror, American Amnesia," *National Review*, May 2, 1994.

Holmes, J. Derek. *The Papacy in the Modern World 1914-1978*, Crossroad (New York, 1981).

Hughes, John Jay. "Jesus Named Him 'The Rock'," *Catholic Digest*, July 1995, at 108.

———. *Pontiffs: Popes Who Shaped History*, Our Sunday Visitor Books (Huntington, Indiana, 1994).

Hunnicutt, C.W. & Jean D. Grambs. *The Great Adventure*, W.L. Singer Co. (Syracuse, 1963).

The Italian Refuge: Rescue of Jews During the Holocaust, The Catholic University of America Press (Washington D.C., Ivo Herzer, ed.1989).

James, Clive. "Blaming the Germans: The much lauded revisionist study of the Holocaust goes too far," *The New Yorker*, April 22, 1996, at 44.

James, Ed. *Book Review Digest* (1938-1939) (reviewing Ivan Soloenvich, *Russia in Chains*).

John Paul II. *Crossing the Threshold of Hope*, Alfred A. Knopf (New York, 1994).

———. *On Social Concerns* (*Sollicitudo Rei Socialis*) (1988).

Johnston, George Sim. "Pope Pius Helped Jews," *Newsday*, April 13, 1994, at 34.

———. "The Holocaust and the Vatican," *The Wall Street Journal*, April 24, 1997.

Kahane, Meir. *Never Again! A Program for Survival*, Pyramid Books (New York, 1972).

Kahn, David. *Hitler's Spies: German Military Intelligence in World War II*, Macmillan (New York, 1978).

Kallay, Nicolas. *Hungarian Premier: A Personal Account of a Nation's Struggle in the Second World War*, Greenwood Press (Westport, Conn. 1970).

Karski, Jan. *Story of a Secret State*, Houghton Mifflin (Boston, 1944).

Katz, Robert. *Massacre in Rome*, Ballantine (New York, 1973) (originally released as *Death in Rome*).

Keegan, John. *The Second World War,* Penguin Books (New York, 1989).

———. "When the Price of One's Conscience is too Dear," *The Daily Telegraph,* July 16, 1994.

Kennedy, John F. *Prelude to Leadership: The European Diary of John F. Kennedy, Summer 1945,* Regnery Publishing (Washington DC, 1995).

———. *Why England Slept,* Dolphin Books (Garden City, N.Y., 1961).

Kershaw, Ian. *Hitler: 1889-1936 Hubris,* W.W. Norton & Company (New York, 1998).

Kertzer, David I. *The Kidnapping of Edgardo Mortara,* Alfred A. Knopf Press (New York, 1997).

Korn, Frank. *From Peter to John Paul II: An Informal Study of the Papacy,* ALBA House (New York, 1980).

Kuehnelt-Leddihn, Erik von. *The Timeless Christian,* Franciscan Herald Press (Quincy, Illinois, 1969).

Küng, Hans. *The Church* (Ockenden trans. 1967).

Lacouture, Jean. *Jesuits: A Multibiography Counterpoint* (Jeremy Leggatt trans., Washington D.C., 1995).

Lamb, Richard. *War in Italy 1943-1945: A Brutal Story,* St. Martin's Press (New York, 1993).

Langer, William L. & S. Everett Gleason. *The World Crisis and American Foreign Policy: The Undeclared War 1940-1941,* Harper & Brothers (New York, 1953).

Lapide, Pinchas E. *Three Popes and the Jews: Pope Pius XII Did Not Remain Silent,* Hawthorn Books (New York, 1967); Sands and Co. (London, 1968).

Lapomarda, Vincent A. *The Jesuits and the Third Reich,* Edwin Mellen Press (Lewiston, N.Y. 1989).

Lawson, Don. *The United States in World War II: Crusade for World Freedom,* Abelard- Schuman (San Francisco, 1963).

Leo XIII. *On Catholicism in Germany (Iampridem)* (1886).

Levai, Jenö. *Hungarian Jewry and the Papacy* (1968).

Lewy, Guenter. *The Catholic Church and Nazi Germany,* McGraw-Hill (New York, 1964).

Lindsey, Autry P. *A Little Slice of World War II* (unpublished, on file with author).

de Lubac, Henri. *Christian Resistance to Anti-Semitism: Memories from 1940-1944,* Ignatius (San Francisco, 1990).

Lukacs, John. *The Hitler of History,* A.A. Knopf (New York, 1997).

Lyons, Eugene. "Russia Postpones Utopia," *Readers Digest,* January 1936.

Maccarrone, Michele. *Il nazionalsocialismo e la Santa Sede,* Studium (Rome 1947).

Majdalany, Fred. *The Fall of Fortress Europe,* Curtis Books (New York, 1968).

Manhattan, Avro. *The Vatican in World Politics,* Gaer Associates (New York, 1949).

Marchione, Margherita. *Pope Pius XII: Architect for Peace,* Paulist Press (New York, 2000). At the time of my research this book was not yet in print. As such, reference is made to the name of the chapter rather than to a page.

———. *Yours is a Precious Witness: Memoirs of Jews and Catholics in Wartime Italy,* Paulist Press (New York, 1997).

Marrus, Michael R. & Robert O. Paxton. *Vichy France and the Jews,* Basic Books (New York, 1981).

Martin, Malachi. *The Jesuits: The Society of Jesus and the Betrayal of the Roman Catholic Church,* The Linden Press, (New York, 1987).

Matheson, Peter. *The Third Reich and the Christian Churches,* T & T Clark (Edinburgh, 1994).

Matthews, W. R. *Saint Paul's Cathedral in Wartime 1939-1945,* Hutchinson & Co. (London, 1946).

Mazgaj, Marian S. *Visiting Home in Poland After 33 Years and World War II True Stories,* McClain Printing Company (Parsons, W.Va. 1996).

Mazour, Anatole G. & John M. Peoples. *A World History,* Harcourt, Brace, Jovanovich (New York, 2d ed. 1971).

McCabeus, Jude. "Hitler: A Pioneer for the 'Politically Correct,' " *New Oxford Review,* October 1997, at 19.

McGarry, Michael B. *The Holocaust: Tragedy of Christian History, in Introduction to Jewish-Christian Relations,* Paulist Press, New York (Michael Shermis & Arthur E. Zannoni, eds. 1991).

Meltzer, Milton. *Never To Forget: The Jews of the Holocaust,* Harper & Row (New York, 1976).

Micklem, Anthaniel. *National Socialism and the Roman Catholic Church: Being an Account of the Conflict between the National Socialist Government of Germany and the Roman Catholic Church 1933-1938,* Oxford University Press (London, New York etc. 1939).

Mindszenty Report, March 1994, Cardinal Mindszenty Foundation, P.O. Box 11321, St. Louis, MO 63105.

Morison, Samuel E. *The Oxford History of the American People,* Oxford University Press (New York, 1965).

Morley, John F. *Vatican Diplomacy and the Jews during the Holocaust 1939-1943,* Ktav Pub. House (New York, 1980).

Morrow, Carol Ann. "Franciscan Maximilian Kolbe: Auschwitz Prisoner #16670," *St. Anthony Messenger,* August 1996.

Murphy, Paul I. *La Popessa,* Warner Books (New York, 1983).

Murphy, Francis X. *The Papacy Today,* Macmillan (New York, 1981).

The Nation, vol. CXLVII (September 17, 1938).

Nichols, Peter. *The Pope's Divisions: The Roman Catholic Church Today,* Faber & Faber (London, 1981).

Niezabitowska, Malgorzata. *Remnants: The Last Jews of Poland,* Friendly Press (New York 1986).

O'Carroll, Michael. *Pius XII: Greatness Dishonored,* Laetare Press (Dublin, 1980).

O'Donnell, James P. *The Bunker: The History of the Reich Chancellery Group,* Houghton Mifflin Co. (Boston, 1978).

"Of Two Popes: Jews and Yasser Arafat," *The New York Times,* Oct. 1, 1982, at A30.

Office of the United States Chief of Counsel for Prosecution of Axis Criminality, *Nazi Conspiracy and Aggression,* United States Government Printing Office (Washington D.C., 1947).

Paci, Stefano M. "Read Father Blet's book on Pius XII," *30 Days,* No. 4 - 1998, at 38.

Padellaro, Nazzareno. *Portrait of Pius XII,* J.M. Dent & Sons (London, 1956).

Palmer, Alan. *Who's Who in Modern History 1860-1980,* Holt, Rinehart, and Winston (New York, 1980).

Passelecq, Georges & Bernard Suchecky. *The Hidden Encyclical of Pius XI,* Harcourt Brace & Co. (Boston, 1997).

Payne, Robert. *The Life and Death of Adolf Hitler,* Praeger Publishers (New York, 1973).

Pepper, Curtis G. *The Pope's Back Yard,* Farrar, Straus & Giroux (New York, 1968).

Persecution of the Catholic Church in German-Occupied Poland: Reports by H.E. Cardinal Hlond, Primate of Poland, to Pope Pius XII, Vatican Broadcasts and Other Reliable Evidence, Longmans Green & Co. (New York, 1941).

Persecution of the Catholic Church in the Third Reich, Burns & Oates (London, W. Mariaux, ed. 1940).

Studio Publications, in association with Thomas Y. Crowell Co. (New York, 1955).

Pius XI, *It is Well Known to Us (Nos es muy conocido)* (1937).

———. *Of the Divine Redeemer [On Atheistic Communism] (Divini Redemptoris)* (1937).

———. *On Chastity in Marriage (Casti Connubii)* (1930).

———. *On Oppression of the Church of Spain (Dilectissima Nobis)* (1933).

———. *On Reconstruction of the Social Order (Quadragesimo Anno)* (1931).

———. *We Have No Need (Non Abbiamo Bisogno)* (1931).

———. *With Burning Anxiety (Mit brennender Sorge)* (1937).

Pius XII, *A Plea for the Care of the World's Destitute Children (Quemadmodum)* (1946).

———. *An Appeal for Prayers for Peace (Communium Interpretes Dolororum)* (1945).

——. *Condemning the Ruthless Use of Force in Hungary (Datis Nuperrime)* (1956).

——. *Darkness over the Earth (Summi Pontificatus)* (1939).

——. *Guide for Living: An Approved Selection of Letters and Addresses of His Holiness*, Evans Brothers Limited (London, Maurice Quinlan, ed. 1958).

——. *On Combating Atheistic Propaganda (Anni Sacri)* (1950).

——. *On Communism and the Church in China (Ad Apostolorum Principis)* (1958).

——. *On Consecrated Virginity (Sacra Virginitas)* (1954).

——. *On Devotion to the Sacred Heart (Haurietis Aquas)* (1956).

——. *On Evolution (Humani Generis)* (1950).

——. *On Prayers for Peace for Poland, Hungary and the Middle East (Laetamur Admodum)* (1956).

——. *On Prayers for Peace in Palestine (In Multiplicibus Curis)* (1948).

——. *On Prayers for the People of Hungary (Luctuosissimi Eventus)* (1956).

——. *On Prayers for the Persecuted Church (Meminisse Luvat)* (1958).

——. *On Promotion of Biblical Studies (Divino Afflante Spiritu)* (1943).

——. *On Promotion of Catholic Missions (Evangelii Praecones)* (1951).

——. *On Public Prayers for Peace (Optatissima Pax)* (1947).

——. *On Public Prayers for Peace (Summi Maeroris)* (1950).

——. *On Public Prayer for World Peace and Solution of the Problem of Palestine (Auspicia Quaedam)* (1948).

——. *On Sacred Music (Musicae Sacrae)* (1955).

——. *On St. Andrew Bobola (Invicti Athlaetae)* (1957).

——. *On St. Cyril, Patriarch of Alexander (Orientalis Ecclesiae)* (1944).

——. *On the Condition of the Catholic Missions (Fidei Donum)* (1957).

——. *On the Crusade of Prayer for Peace (Mirabile Illud)* (1950).

——. *On the Holy Places in Palestine (Redemptoris Nostri Cruciatus)* (1949).

——. *On the Independence of Portugal (Saeculo Exeunte Octavo)* (1940).

——. *On the Mystical Body (Mystici Corporis Christi)* (1943).

——. *On the Possibility of Defining the Assumption as a Dogma of the Church (Deiparae Virginis Mariae)* (1946).

——. *On the Reunion of the Ruthenian Church with Rome (Orientales Omnes Ecclesias)* (1945).

——. *On the Sacred Liturgy (Mediator Dei)* (1947).

——. *On the Start of the Church in the United States (Sertum Laetitiae)* (1939).

——. *On the Supranationality of the Church (Ad Sinarum Gentem)* (1954).

——. *Proclaiming a Marian Year (Fulgens Corona)* (1953).

——. *Proclaiming the Queenship of Mary (Ad Caeli Reginam)* (1954).

——. *Warning Against Materialism (Le Pèlerinage De Lourdes)* 1957.

Pius XII and the Holocaust: A Reader, Catholic League Publications (Milwaukee, 1988).

Pius XII: Selected Encyclicals and Addresses, Roman Catholic Books (Harrison, N.Y., undated).

Popes of the Twentieth Century, St. Paul Editions (Boston, 1983).

Pope Pius and Poland: A Documentary Outline of Papal Pronouncements and Relief Efforts in Behalf Of Poland, Since March, 1939, The America Press (New York, 1942).

Price, Morgan Philips. *Dispatches from the Weimar Republic: Versailles and German Fascism,* Pluto Press (London; Sterling, Virginia, 1999).

Price, Roger. *A Concise History of France,* Cambridge University Press (Cambridge; New York, 1993).

Principles for Peace: Selections from Papal Documents, Leo XIII to Pius XII, National Catholic Welfare Conference (Harry C. Koenig, ed., Washington, 1943).

Prittie, Terence. *Germany,* Life World Library (New York, 1962).

Procacci, Giuliano. *History of the Italian People,* Weidenfeld & Nicolson (London, Anthony Paul trans. 1970).

Rand McNally Encyclopedia of World War II, Rand, McNally (Chicago, John Keegan ed. 1984).

Rauschning, Hermann. *The Voice of Destruction,* G.P. Putnam's Sons (New York, 1940).

Ray, John. *Men Who Made History: Hitler and Mussolini,* Heinemann Educational Books (London, 1974).

Readers Companion to Military History, Houghton Mifflin Co. (Boston, Robert Cowley & Geoffrey Parker, eds. 1996).

Records and Documents of the Holy See Relating to the Second World War: The Holy See and the War in Europe March 1939-August 40, Corpus Books (Blet, Martini & Schneider, eds., Noel trans., Washington, 1965).

Rhodes, Anthony. *The Vatican in the Age of the Dictators: 1922-45,* Hodden and Stoughton (London, Sydney, Auckland & Toronto, 1973).

Rosenberg, Alfred. *The Myth of the Twentieth Century,* Noontide Press (Torrance, Calif. 1930).

Rousmaniere, John. *A Bridge to Dialogue: The Story of Jewish-Christian Relations,* Paulist Press (New York, 1991).

Ryan, Cornelius. *The Last Battle,* Simon and Schuster (New York, 1966).

Ryan, George E. *Figures in our Catholic History,* St. Paul Editions (Boston, 1979).

Sack, John. *An Eye for an Eye: The Untold Story of Jewish Revenge Against the Germans in 1945,* Basic Books (New York, 1993).

Sánchez, José. "The Popes and Nazi Germany: The View from Madrid," 39 *Journal of Church and State* 365 (1996).

Saperstein, Marc. *Moments of Crisis in Jewish-Christian Relations,* SCM Press/Trinity Press International (London/Philadelphia, 1989).

Savage. Katharine. *The Story of the Second World War,* Scholastic Books (New York, 1966).

Scholder, Klaus. *The Churches and the Third Reich* (Volumes I and II), Fortress Press (Philadelphia, 1988).

Scholl, Inge. *The White Rose: Munich 1942–1943,* Wesleyan University Press (Hanover, NH, A. Schultz trans. 1983).

Schom, Alan. *Napoleon Bonaparte,* Harper Perennial (New York, 1997).

Scrivener, Jane. *Inside Rome with the Germans,* The MacMillan Company (New York, 1945).

The Second Vatican Council, *Pastoral Constitution on the Church in the Modern World (Gaudium et Spes).*

Secretariat for Ecumenical and Interreligious Affairs, National Conference of Bishops, *Catholics Remember the Holocaust,* United States Catholic Conference (Washington, 1998).

Sheehan, James. "What Was in It for Them? Examining economic self-interest as the basis for Nazism's appeal," *The New York Times Book Review,* Sept. 15, 1996, at 46 (reviewing *The Logic of Evil: The Social Origins of the Nazi Party, 1925-1933,* by William Brustein).

Shiber, Etta. *Paris-Underground,* Charles Scribner's Sons (New York, 1943).

Shirer, William L. *20th Century Journey, A Memoir of a Life and the Times, Vol. II: The Nightmare Years 1930-1940,* Little, Brown & Co. (Boston, 1984).

———. *The Rise and Fall of the Third Reich: A History of Nazi Germany,* Fawcett Publications (Greenwich, 1962).

Shub, David. *Lenin,* Mentor Books (New York, 1951).

Silk, Mark. *Spiritual Politics: Religion and America Since World War II,* Simon and Schuster (New York, 1988).

Smit, Jan Olav. *Angelic Shepherd: The Life of Pope Pius XII,* Dodd, Mead (New York, Vanderveldt trans. 1950).

Snyder, Louis L. *The War: A Concise History 1939-1945,* J. Messner (New York, 1960).

Speer, Albert. *Inside the Third Reich,* Avon (New York, R. Winston & C. Winston trans., 1970).

Standard American Encyclopedia (1941).

Stehlin, Stewart A. *Weimar and the Vatican 1919 - 1933: German-Vatican Diplomatic Relations in the Interwar Years,* Princeton University Press (Princeton, N.J. 1983).

Stewart, Herbert L. "The Great Secularist Experiment," *The Hibbert Journal,* January 1944, at 107.

Stewart, Ralph. *Pope Pius XII and the Jews*, St. Martin de Porres Dominican Community & St. Joseph Canonical Foundation (New Hope, Ky. 1999).

Stille, Alexander. *Benevolence and Betrayal: Five Italian Jewish Families Under Fascism*, Summit Books (New York, 1991).

Szulc, Tad. *Pope John Paul II: The Biography*, Scribner (New York, 1995).

Tardini, Domenico. *Memories of Pius XII*, The Newman Press (Westminster, Maryland, 1961).

Taylor, A.J.P. *From Sarajevo to Potsdam*, Thames & Hudson (London, 1966).

———. *The Origins of the Second World War*, Fawcett Publications (Greenwich, 1961).

Tec, Nechama. *When Light Pierced the Darkness: Christian Rescue of Jews in Nazi Occupied Poland,* Oxford University Press (New York, 1986).

Tenen, I. *This England: Part III, Hanoverian and Modern Periods (1714-1940)*, Macmillan & Co. (London, 1952).

Terkel, Studs. *The Good War*, Ballantine Books (New York, 1984).

Thomas, Gordon & Max Morgan-Witts, *Pontiff*, Doubleday (Garden City, N.Y. 1983).

"To Adam Hochschild, a Russian Oskar Schindler," *USA Today*, March 31, 1994, at 13A.

Toland, John. *Adolf Hitler,* Ballatine (New York, 1976).

———. *Captured by History: One Man's Vision of Our Tumultuous Century*, St. Martin's Press (New York, 1997).

Toulmin, Janik & Stephen. *Wittgenstein's Vienna*, Simon & Schuster (New York, 1973).

Treece, Patricia. "Joyful Martyr," *Crisis*, July/August 1997, at 21.

Trinchese, Stefano. *La Repubblica di Weimar e la Santa Sede tra Benedetto XV e Pio XI (1919-1922)*, Edizioni Scientifiche (Naples, 1994).

Tugend, Tom. "Jewish group protests proposed Pius XII canonization," *The Jerusalem Post*, Sunday February 21, 1993.

The United States at War: The Audio Classics Series (World War II, Part II) Knowledge Products, 1990 (Nashville, Tennessee).

Van Hoek, Kees. *Pope Pius XII: Priest and Statesman*, Philosophical Library (New York, 1944).

Vida, George. *From Doom to Dawn: A Jewish Chaplain's Story of Displaced Persons*, J. David (New York, 1967).

Vatican Impressions, Sneed & Ward (New York, Francis Sweeney, S.J., ed., 1962).

Voices From America's Past: Vol. 3, The Twentieth Century, E.P. Dutton & Co. (New York, Richard B. Morris & James Woodress eds. 1963).

Walsh, Michael. *An Illustrated History of the Popes: Saint Peter to John Paul II*, St. Martin's Press (New York, 1980).

Ward, Margaret E. *Rolf Hochhuth*, Twayne Publishers (Boston, 1977).

Wartime Correspondence Between President Roosevelt and Pope Pius XII, Da Capo Press, New York (Myron C. Taylor, ed. 1975) (reprint of 1947 edition).

Waters, Harry F. "Holocaust in the Home Front," *Newsweek*, April 4, 1994, at 68.

Watson, George. "Never Blame the Left," *National Review*, Dec. 31, 1995.

Weigel, George. *Witness to Hope: The Biography of Pope John Paul II*, Cliff Street Books (New York, 1999).

Weizsäcker, Ernst, Von. *Memoirs of Ernst Von Weizsäcker*, H. Regnery Co. (Chicago, J. Andrews trans. 1951).

"Why the Churches Kept Silent," *Awake!* August 22, 1995.

"Why the Vatican Kept Silent on Nazi Atrocities," *The New York Times*, Saturday, October 7, 1989, at 1-22.

Wilhelm, Anthony. *Christ Among Us: A Modern Presentation of the Catholic Faith*, Paulist Press (New York, 1975).

Wilken, Robert L. "The Jews as the Christians Saw Them," *First Things*, May 1997, at 28.

Winowska, Maria. Winowska, *The Death Camp Proved Him Real: The Life of Father Maximilian Kolbe, Franciscan*, Prow (Kenosha, Wis. 1971).

Woestman, William H. *Allocutions to the Roman Rota 1939-1994*, St. Paul University (Ottawa 1994).

Woodward, Sir Llewellyn *British Foreign Policy in the Second World War, Vol. II,* Her Majesty's Stationary Office (London, 1971).

The World Almanac and Book of Facts (1986).

Wright, Gordon. *The Ordeal of Total War 1939-1945*, Harper Torchbooks (New York, 1968).

WWII: Time-Life Books History of the Second War (1989).

Wyman, David S. *The Abandonment of the Jews: America and the Holocaust 1941-1945*, Pantheon Books (New York, 1984).

Young, Michael. *The Trial of Adolf Hitler*, E.P. Dutton & Co. (New York, 1944).

Zolli, Eugenio. *Why I Became a Catholic,* Remnant of Israel (New Hope, KY, 1997), previously released as *Before the Dawn*, Sheed and Ward, (New York, 1954).

INDEX

Boetto, Pietro, 220
Bohemia, 43, 112
Bojanowo, 168
Bolivia, 198
Bolshevism, 14, 56, 77, 84, 119, 159, 181, 213, 234, 338
Borgia Tower, 282
Bormann, Martin, 121
Boudrillart, Cardinal, 158, 159
Boy Scouts, 67, 405
Braier, Louis, 306
Bratislava, 187, 188, 215
Braun, Eva, 11, 17, 234, 319
Braun, Sigmund von, 358
Brazil, 105, 127, 157
Breslau, 171
Brindisi, 216
British Public Records Office, 257
Brown Shirts, 46
Bruning, Heinrich, 47, 51
Brussels, 138
Buchenwald, 233
Buchkavich, Konstantin, 320
Budapest, 215, 222, 225
Buenos Aires, 75
Bukharinites, 73
Bulgaria, 188, 238
Bullitt, William C., 238
Burzio, Joseph, 215-6
Caesar, 276
Campo Verano, 194
Canada, 122
Canadian Jewish Chronicle, 109
Canadian Jewish Congress, 109
Cantoni, Raffael, 253
Capranica, 4
Carabinieri, 213
Cardinal, The (film), 346
Carmelite Order, 171
Casablanca, 182
Cassetta, Francesco Paola, 5
Cassulo, Nuncio Andrea, 2 25
Castel Gandolfo, 1, 36, 97, 105, 125, 202, 214, 246, 393
Casti Connubii, 62

Catholic Action, 22, 35, 39, 40, 63. 71, 100
Catholic Center Party, 46, 295
Catholic University of Lublin, 151
Catholic Youth League, 62
Central Conference of American Rabbis, 408
Chaillet, Pierre, 145
Chamberlain, Neville, 105, 112, 120, 268, 337
Charles-Roux, François, 60, 138, 139
Chiesa Nuova, 5
Chile, 198
China, 236
Christian Century, 241
Christian X, 137
Church of St. Mary Major, 5
Churchill, Winston, 38, 94, 159, 162, 181, 183, 198, 226, 231, 235, 237, 238
Cianfarra, Camille M., 162
Ciano, Galeazzo, 90, 117, 140, 166, 210
Cicognani, Amleto, 162
Clark, Mark, 217
Clemenceau, Georges, 318
Code of Canon Law, 297
College of Cardinals, 2
Cologne, 46
Communism, 14, 24, 79, 92, 153, 159, 226, 237, 242, 256, 307
Communium Interpretes Dolororum, 233
Confessional Church, 86, 87
Congregation for the Causes of Saints, 251
Congregation of Ecclesiastical Affairs, 292
Cornwell, John, 259, 266, 426-444
Coughlin, Charles, 295, 340
Croatia, 199, 303
Cuno, Wilhelm, 25